ROCKS, RIDDLES AND MYSTERIES

ROCKS, RIDDLES AND MYSTERIES

Folk Art, Inscriptions and Other Stories in Stone

Edward J. Lenik

American History Press
Franklin, Tennessee
(888) 521-1789

Visit us on the Internet at:
www.Americanhistorypress.com

ISBN 13: 978-0-9830827-1-2

Library of Congress Control Number: 2011901138

First Edition May 2011

Printed in the United States of America on acid-free paper.
This book meets all ANSI standards for archival quality.

To Vera

For a lifetime of patience and love
my deepest gratitude and love

CAN THE ROCKS SPEAK?

What signifies that knowledge, say some, which brings no real advantage to mankind? And what is it to anyone whether the Roman walls pass'd this way or that? Or whether such a Roman inscription is to be read this way or another? To this I would answer: there is that beauty and agreeableness in truth, even supposing it to be merely speculative, as always affords on the discovery of it real pleasure to a well-turned mind: and I will add, that it not only pleases, but enriches and cultivates it too.

- John Horsley
Britannia Romana (1732)

TABLE OF CONTENTS

PREFACE

In 1973, I set out to find and document American Indian petroglyphs (rock carvings) and pictographs (rock paintings) in the Northeast woodlands. This effort resulted in the 2002 publication of *Picture Rocks: American Indian Rock Art in the Northeast Woodlands*.[1] This new book, *Rocks, Riddles, and Mysteries: Folk Art, Inscriptions and Other Stories in Stone* is an extension of that research effort, but with a different focus. Here, I examine a variety of historic period rock art images created by Euro-American people in New England and the Mid-Atlantic areas. In using the term historic I refer to the period of time from the early European explorations and settlement of this geographic region up to the present time. The word as used here does not mean the rock images are important in history, although in some instances they might have such significance.

During my research and field work in the Northeast region, I located and recorded numerous figures, images, or symbols carved into permanent or portable stone that were clearly not of American Indian origin. Some of these images seemed to represent Indian design motifs, while others were abstract or geometric designs, human and animal figures, ships, weapons, names, dates, or initials. They truly represent a kind of Euro-American folk art either incised or carved with metal tools, or, in rare instances, painted on rock.

Many of the sites I have examined consisted of single figures or inscriptions, while others contained numerous glyphs forming a panel-like effect. Some of the glyphs were found on mountain or ridge tops, cliff faces, bedrock outcrops or boulders, billboard-like landscape features meant to be seen by those who passed by. For this book, I have selected only those glyphs or sites that had a story to tell or seemed to me to have artistic merit.

Several of the carvings or inscriptions that have been found in the Northeast region have been interpreted as ogham or runic writing and reported to be the work of Iberians, Norsemen, Phoenicians, Romans, Celts, and others. I make no such claims in this book, and leave such interpretations and speculation to others. Instead, I have tried to identify the various images, place them in historical context, and interpret their meaning based on local information, myths or legends. In some cases, I do not know what the figures represent.

It is likely that others have visited the sites and examined the figures described herein. Because little is known and understood about petroglyphs in general, many people view them with a great deal of mystery and ascribe to them a greater age than they probably warrant. Inevitably, the passage of time and the forces of nature serve to obscure the newness of many carvings and they are interpreted as old or of Indian origin, which they are not. My purpose in recording historic period rock art is to provide a permanent record of these glyphs and the stories which surround them.

Historic glyphs are like messages in a journal. They give us a small glimpse of the world in which the artists lived and worked. They are expressions of individuals whose basic message is, "I am here and I have set my mark upon the world."

- Edward J. Lenik

STORIES ON STONE

While researching Indian petroglyphs I encountered several sites that were reported to be of Indian origin but were instead Euro-American. I tell the story of such sites here, with two of these being particularly fascinating and troublesome: the Hawk Rock petroglyph site and Indian Rock in the Ramapo Mountains. Both hikers and armchair researchers claimed that these were produced by Indians, but my research showed that this is not the case. I published my findings to prevent them from being perceived as Native American, but in one case—Hawk Rock—it was a hard sell. As my investigation of these sites and others continued, I became intrigued by their individual stories, and so I relate them here.

Three types of stories emerged during my years of research. The first was the image on the stone itself: what did it represent and what did it mean? Second, who were the artists or artisans and why did they carve or paint the rock? And last the question of the site or location: why were they carved here and what clues do their environmental settings provide us in interpreting them? Not every site had a story to tell, but I present what I found in my research and what I infer based on my professional experience. Undoubtedly, some readers may know more about these sites or draw their own interpretations from what is known.

Why were the images carved or painted? Painting on a rock surface is a simple matter. In most cases, paint will stick to rock but will fade or exfoliate over time, so many painted stories that may have been present no longer exist. The carving of rock is another matter; it is extremely difficult to do well. In most cases it requires special metal tools and individual skill. In describing the images in this book I comment when they are well done, admittedly a subjective opinion. But, the question of "Why were the images made and what do they mean?" persists, and my answers range from personal opinions to empirical observations to historical accounts of events.

Stone is ubiquitous in the Northeast woodlands. It is often dramatic, as in the case of mountains and ridge tops, or mundane, as in outcrops that rise from the Earth's floor. Boulders and cobbles, transported here some 15,000 years ago by the last glacier, are present in enormous quantities over the landscape.

The Euro-American immigrants who settled the Northeast region came from stone working traditions in Europe. Stone was used by these people for many purposes: buildings, foundations, fences, cairns, paving and much more. In the eighteenth and nineteenth centuries successive generations of farmers and builders were more familiar with and closer to working with stone than people in the twentieth century. Farmers struggled to remove rock from the landscape as a new "crop" arose from the land each year. They attempted to clear fields for pasture and planting and in the process created miles of stone fences and rock mounds.

Stone was used for burial, boundary markers, monuments, and many other practical purposes. Several stories presented here illustrate these efforts. Many individuals were skilled in working stone. Artisans emerged whose work at carving stone was very skillful, resulting in a tradition of high art. However, the nature of the carvings described and illustrated in this book are in the realm of folk art. They are images made by skilled crafts persons unschooled in the artistic conventions; in other words, they were not making art as a product.

Natural formations appear on the land and in the mountains, evoking such images as human profiles, e.g., the Old Man of the Mountain in New Hampshire, or those of animals. Many were viewed as mysterious or magical and were often noted on historical maps or mentioned in local legends or accounts. These include balanced rocks, perched rocks and even aural anomalies, such as mysterious noises emanating from caves or rock crevices. These natural wonders attract the curious to this day, who attempt to explain them as being human-made.

PAINTED IMAGES

American Indian pictographs or paintings on rock surfaces are extremely rare in the northeastern United States. Only four sites have been found and documented. Two fragmentary paintings that amazingly have survived the ravages of nature are in the state of Maine, and two are in upstate New York.[1] Red ochre, composed of a mineral pigment such as hematite or limonite, was the medium used by the Indians in depicting anthropomorphic figures, thunderbirds, canoes, and geometric designs on vertical rock surfaces.

The stories surrounding two putative Indian pictograph sites that were produced by Euro-Americans are presented here. One panel was painted on a cliff face at waterside on Lake Sebago, Maine to entertain tourists and summer residents as they traveled by steamboat across the lake. Another was painted in the early 1980s by a film crew high up in the Ramapo Mountains in Orange County, New York.

A third pictograph site, which begins our story, was discovered in 1978 in the town of Peabody, Massachusetts and was allegedly associated with the Salem witchcraft trials in late seventeenth century eastern Massachusetts.

WITCHCRAFT SYMBOLS

In 1978, a cultural resources investigation was conducted in the town of Peabody, Massachusetts, in advance of a proposed expansion of State Route 128. The archaeological investigation was conducted by Dr. Richard Michael Gramly and the Institute of Conservation Archaeology, Peabody Museum of Archaeology and Ethnology, Harvard University, Cambridge, for the Department of Public Works, Office of Transportation and Construction of the Commonwealth of Massachusetts. In the course of a pedestrian reconnaissance, the survey party discovered a large outcrop of rock located just north of Route 128 that contained three pictographs.[2]

The site lay within a second growth forest within view of Route 128. The three-figure painted panel was on a vertical south-facing rock surface that measured nine feet (2.7 m) in height and ten feet (3 m) in width. The painted outcrop was among a cluster of three large rocks. A fieldstone fence was present to the east of the site, and several cart tracks leading to old dwelling sites were located nearby.

The three pictographs were described as line drawings which were executed in a freehand style with care and skill.[3] The central figure was a five-pointed star or pentacle that pointed downward and was enclosed by two slightly irregular concentric circles (Figure 1). There were four unidentified symbols situated between the concentric circles, each one located opposite a point on the star. The central figure measured forty-two inches (1.8 m) in diameter.

To the right and slightly below the pentacle was a painted cross with two horizontal bars and a horizontal figure-eight at its base. This figure was about twenty-one inches (53 cm) in height. To the left of the pentacle, and also slightly below it, was a curvilinear symbol that also measures twenty-one inches (53 cm) in height. Gramly construed the symbols to be a balanced group of three that may have held mystical and spiritual significance to the artist who painted them.[4]

Samples of paint were collected from the composition and were submitted for analysis to the Center for Conservation and Technical Studies at the Fogg Museum, Harvard University.[5] The pigment was identified as hematite; it was also reportedly present in an organic binder possibly consisting of casein (milk) or albumen (egg white). In 1978, the paintings were reported to be more than twenty years old but their exact age remains unknown.[6]

Gramly interpreted the central figure as a downward pointing pentacle that was a commonly known symbol used by followers of the occult, and often associated with witchcraft.[7] The figure to its left, he said, closely resembled the Caduceus or Staff of Mercury. In antiquity, Mercury's wand or rod was entwisted by two serpents surmounted by two wings, and was carried by Mercury, the messenger of the gods, as a symbol of his office.[8] He also described the symbol to the right of the pentacle as a common occult symbol.

Gramly speculated that the panel of symbols may have served as a type of warning against witches.[9] If the paintings dated to the late seventeenth century, during the time of the Salem witchcraft hysteria in the adjacent town, they

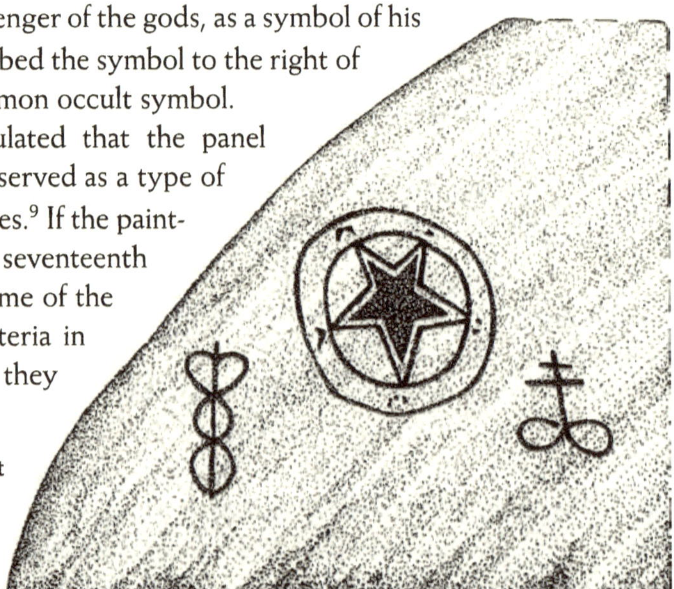

FIGURE 1. Witchcraft symbols painted on rock in Peabody, Massachusetts. ***Drawing by T. Fitzpatrick based on photo by Gramly 1981.***

would have protected nearby residents from evil, or the witches themselves. On the other hand, they may have been painted circa 1892, the bicentennial year of the Salem witchcraft frenzy, as a graphic revival of interest in witchcraft symbolism. Gramly appeared to favor the early date for their creation, and based his conclusion on their weathered condition and the type of paint used by the artist.

THE IMAGES

Sebago Lake, Maine, is located about twenty miles north of the city of Portland. The lake was once called Sebacook, apparently an Indian word that meant "Great Waters." Sebago encompasses some forty-six square miles as it extends among the surrounding forested hills; it has been referred to as the "Queen of Inland Waters."[10] In this region of Maine, a fascinating and romantic tale of adventure still survives to this day.

Raymond Neck, a five-mile-long peninsula, juts out into Sebago Lake along its easterly side. Near the end of this peninsula, on its west side, is a rock outcrop, popularly known as Fryes Leap, which rises eighty feet above the lake. Southwest of this cliff, separated by a narrow 1,500 foot (0.5 km) wide channel, is Frye Island, the largest island in Sebago Lake.

Local legends are associated with these two landscape features. The cliff and island are named for a Captain Frye, a colonial era military officer and Indian scout. In the years 1748-49 Captain Frye, with a company of soldiers, was stationed at Scarborough, Maine, which was located to the south of the lake, to protect the coastal settlements from Indian attacks.[11] The legend of Frye's Leap tells the story of Captain Frye:

> ...pursued by a band of Indians, the Captain fled to the end of the Cape coming out upon the cliff. ...He let himself drop from the top of the jagged rock into the snow which covered the frozen lake, whence he crossed to the island that bears his name. The Indians were so astonished at his daring leap when they saw his crossing thence, that they abandoned the pursuit.[12]

Another more colorful version of this story, related in an anonymous tourist booklet, indicated that the episode took place at a warmer time of year.[13] The tourist version stated that Captain Frye was being pursued by a "howling pack of painted redskins" and found himself at the edge of the cliff. "Hesitating but a moment, the gallant Captain... plunged headlong over the declivity into the waters that lap the rocks below." The Indians looked on in "speechless amazement at the audacity of the deed." When Captain Frye failed to surface from beneath the water the Indians concluded he had perished, and they left the area. However, Frye had hidden himself among some bushes, and afterwards swam to a nearby cave, where he remained until nightfall. Later, he swam to the large island that now bears his name.

A 1907 issue of *Pine Tree Magazine* contained a legend that explained the origin or formation of the cliff on the western shore of Raymond Neck (also called a cape):

> In the days when deep snow covered all the hills and ice never thawed from the streams, Manitou the Mighty One sent his son from his dwelling at the top of distant mountains, down to earth. The son's breath warmed the land and mists rose until he could no longer see his mountain home. Then all at once he felt himself falling through the air to a place beside waters of a lake. Before mists cleared sufficiently for him to see his habitat, he fell in love with the "the spirit of the lake," a beautiful girl.
>
> This emotion was against his father's wishes, and the son was changed into an unshapely mass of stone and was bound to the earth as a mass of granite, seamed in places, smooth in places, but ... the guardian of the lake from any intrusion because the rock could still hold conversation with his father, the Might Manitou, whose voice was thunder and whose weapon was lightning.[14]

From the mid to late nineteenth century, many images, or perhaps all of them, were painted on the massive vertical face of Frye's Leap by "enterprising steamboat promoters."[15] The steamboat era on Sebago Lake extended from the end of the Civil War until World War I. The steamboat operators—the "Sebago Lake, Songo River and Bay of Naples Steamboat Company"—were reportedly an early proponent of artful and dramatic advertising.[16] The images, mostly life-size, were painted in vivid colors and purport to depict Captain Frye making his famous jump off the cliff, plus other Indian scenes, animals, and legends.[17] The steamboat company hired college students to live in a tent on top of the rock. When a boatload of passengers passed near the cliff, they would don Indian costumes, perform a "whooping" Indian war dance, and fire a rifle into the air to entertain the traveling vacationers.[18]

The colorfully painted figures fascinated local residents, summer campers, and vacationers. A postcard photo dating to the early 1900s shows some of the images on the rock billboard. Clearly visible in this photo are an Indian in a canoe, Indians in the act of hunting and fishing, a bear, birds, and a steamboat near the top of the cliff. A pseudo play-Indian standing on top of the cliff is also evident (Figure 2).

Author Herbert G. Jones presented several fanciful interpretations of the figures, calling them "an Indian wigwam with a chief sitting at the doorway watching the cooking of his evening meal, a bear wounded by an Indian antagonist, an Indian war dance, and a deer bounding over the rock."[19] Jones also told the story of an "Indian girl" painted on the rock who, while being pursued by white men, jumped to her death from the cliff. The Indian girl's name was "Naragora" which translates as "gentle fawn." These scenes, if they ever even existed, are not discernible in the 1900s postcard view.

Finally, author Daphne Winslow Merrill related still another Indian legend associated with "The Images."[20] In this tale, an Indian chief once loved an Indian maiden, but his tribe barred him from marrying her. He took the maiden in his canoe and paddled to the center of the lake, where they both jumped into the water and drowned.

There are no perceptible images on the face of the Frye's Leap escarpment today.

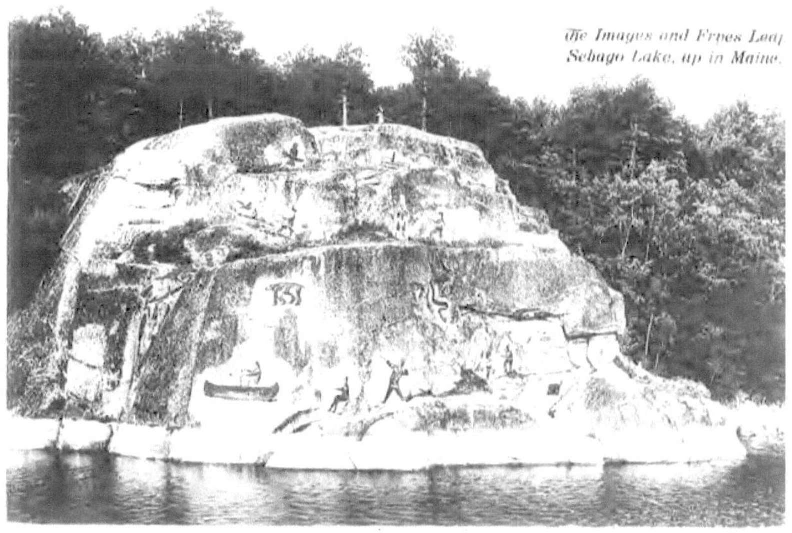

Figure 2. Postcard photo of The Images at Frye's Leap, circa 1900s. ***Courtesy of Kenneth E. Thompson, Jr.***

A LOST TRIBE OF THE RAMAPOS:
HOW INDIAN ROCK GOT THERE
A MOVIE REVIEW

Nancy L. Gibbs and Edward J. Lenik

Movie Title:	*Luggage of the Gods*
Theme:	"There were no buildings, no cities, no whipped cream ... we were a Lost Tribe. We were it."
Music:	"Build Me Up, Buttercup"
Cast:	Yuk: Mark Stolzenburg
	Hubba: Gwen Ellison
	Tull: Gabrielle Barre
Writer-Director:	David Kendall
Produced by:	General Pictures, Inc. 1984
Distributed by:	Academy Entertainment
Glossary:	Vecca – Rabbit
	Ugow – Airplane
	Bagzoa – Go, Leave

SYNOPSIS: Deep in the Ramapo Mountains, a lost tribe, apparently a mixed group of Cro-Magnon and Neanderthal types, ekes out a precarious existence. Life for this band of troglodytes centers on the procurement of food. They search for it, hunt for it, dance and beg for it. This movie shows how contact with civilization turns them into a cargo cult. Made in 1984, *Luggage of the Gods* was positioned to ride the coattails of the successful movie *The Gods Must be Crazy*, in which a South African Bushman is bopped on the head by a Coke® bottle. Our hapless hero, Yuk, a cerebral yet well-muscled man, has a similar experience. He is an artist, inventor, a thinker, and a dreamer. All in all, he is a drag on this hunting and gathering economy.

An exciting opening scene recounts a successful rabbit hunt by the tribe's two strong hunters, the Alpha males. Armed with clubs and stones, they subdue and kill a rabbit, a Vecca. Proudly, they carry their prey back to the tribe and present it to the chief for approval. The rabbit is roasted, and feasting and dancing follow. Yuk earns his roast morsel by painting a pictograph of "The Great Vecca" on a prominent standing stone near the tribe's cave.

Hubba is the love interest. Blonde and more delicate than this tribe's typical female beauty, she is courted by the heroic hunters. She, however, is drawn to the sensitive Yuk. Yuk blossoms under her adoring gaze. He demonstrates his invention, a "stoa," a spear with a projectile point and a vine to retrieve it, showing Hubba how he could catch a Vecca with just one toss. The hunters, seeing this, erupt in a fit of giggles and pantomime. Yuk's pal, Tull, sticks by him, but Yuk becomes the laughing stock of the campfire.

Meanwhile, airplanes fly over the tribe's campsite. At each sighting, the cry "Ugow!" rings out and the fierce hunters throw themselves prostrate on the ground, trembling, until the plane has passed. Only Yuk dares to lift his head and watch the plane.

One day, high overhead, in the first class cabin of a jetliner (Landum Airways), a pair of art thieves celebrate the two million dollars soon to be theirs for the exquisitely forged masterpieces they have in their crate in the cargo hold. Just then, the captain announces that all luggage is being jettisoned because the plane is low on fuel from circling.

Only Yuk sees the Ugow drop its wondrous and costly load of luggage. Instantly, the tribe is catapulted from the Stone Age into the Historic Era and the plot thickens. Exultation, exile, creative adaptive use of objects, food fights, first kisses, a gun and crate fight, and reintegration into the tribe follow. In the last scene, the three friends—Yuk, Hubba, and Tull—set off, luggage in hand, to explore the new world.

COMMENTARY: This movie was filmed at a site called Claudius Smith's Den in Harriman State Park, in the town of Tuxedo, Orange County, New York. This famous Ramapo Mountains rock shelter, once utilized by American Indians, is best known as the hiding place of notorious Tory bandit Claudius Smith. During the American Revolutionary War, Smith and his gang raided farms and homes in the adjacent Ramapo River Valley, terrorizing the populace with their killing and pillaging. Relentlessly pursued by the local militia, Claudius Smith was captured on Long Island and returned to Goshen, New York, where he was summarily hanged for his crimes. This rock shelter is well-known to present-day hikers and campers and continues to be intensively utilized. This is a popular spot for rock climbing, campfires, picnics, and general lounging about.

The filming of *Luggage of the Gods* had an intense effect on this site. From a perspective of archaeological and environmental resource preservation, the landscape surrounding the rock shelter was seriously impacted by the actors, director, support staff, equipment, and filming process. Much of the impact, however, was an exacerbation of the effects that normal activities hikers and campers have had on the location over the years. One aspect, however, has taken on a life of its own.

"Indian Rock" is a large boulder with a vertical side (face) that stands about two hundred feet from Claudius Smith's Den. Two hunters with clubs are painted on this boulder, both in pursuit of a giant black rabbit. This is Yuk's pictograph of The Great Vecca Hunt (Figure 3).

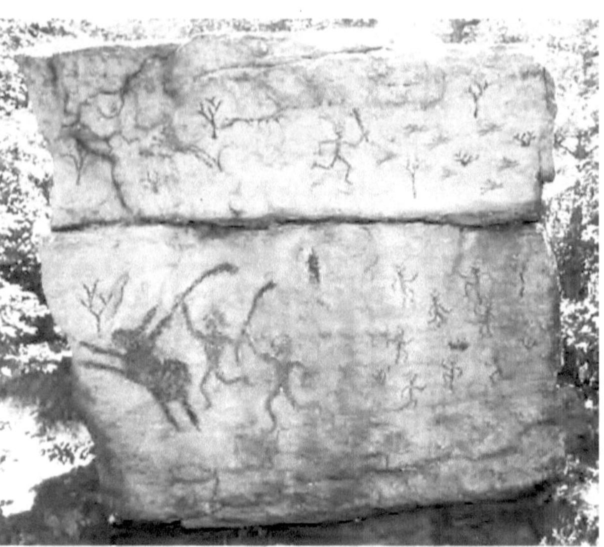

Figure 3: Pictograph of the "Great Vecca Hunt" at Claudius Smith rock shelter. ***Photo by T. Fitzpatrick 1988.***

On a recent visit to Claudius Smith's Den, the author and two of his colleagues encountered several hikers at the rock shelter. We mentioned to them that we were archaeologists studying the American Indian history of the park. At this point, one of the hikers exclaimed, "Oh, have you seen Indian Rock?" We were directed to The Great Vecca Hunt pictograph. Our explanation clarifying that this was not an Indian pictograph, but a leftover movie prop, was met with disbelief. Friends of theirs who knew about such things had told them this was a sacred Indian painting since they had seen it for themselves. We urged them to rent *Luggage of the Gods* and see for themselves how and when it was created.

The legend of Indian Rock is out there and growing. It has been reported to this author and others by excited and enthusiastic discoverers again and again. Unfortunately, as years go by, the rock paintings at Claudius Smith's Den will be seen by countless more numbers of hikers, and the Indian Rock legend will continue to spread. We have now documented the true story of Indian Rock and say, "Bagzoa!" to those who would turn this bit of twentieth century cinematic graffiti into a prehistoric masterpiece.

INDIAN LORE MOTIFS: FRAUDS AND FANCIFUL TALES

THE HAWK ROCK PETROGLYPH

Hawk Rock is a twenty-five-foot-high glacial boulder located in the town of Kent, Putnam County, New York. It stands prominently within a forested area on the west side of Horse Pound Brook south of Whangtown Road. The local name of this prominent feature is appropriate; its likeness to a perched hawk, when viewed in profile, is immediately apparent (Figure 4). This name is most likely twentieth century in origin, since it does not appear on an 1867 map of Kent by F.W. Beers on which another rock—"Horse Pound Hill & Rock"—is noted.[1]

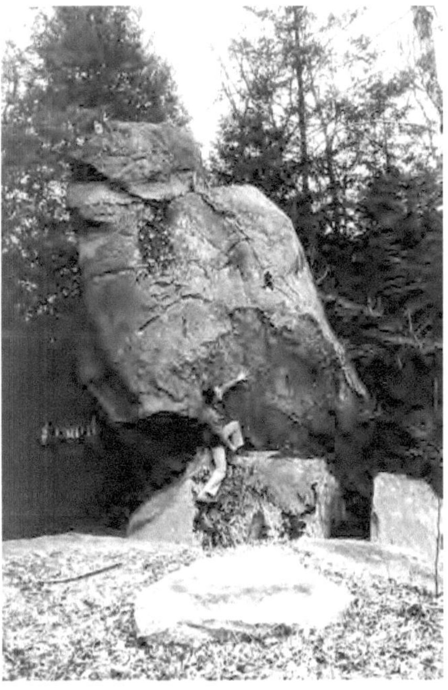

Figure 4. Hawk Rock. View of north side. ***Photo by E.J. Lenik 1987.***

Three designs are carved into the vertical north face of Hawk Rock. They are interpreted as a turtle, a beaver, and a bird. The turtle figure is 12 inches (30.5 cm) in length from head to tail, and its body is 5.75 inches (14.6 cm) in width. The figure of the beaver is 6 inches (15.3 cm) in length and 3.2 inches (8 cm) in width. The bird is 12 inches (30.5 cm) in length from its beak to its tail. A scale drawing of the figures in their exact positions on the rock is shown in Figure 5.

I examined this petroglyph in 1987 during a cultural resources investigation of the Fieldbrook Subdivision Property on which it was located.[2] All three figures were clearly produced with metal tools. The turtle is the most prominent design, and circular punch marks were visible in the grooves that form its shape or outline. There were also six punch marks or depressions in a straight line across the back of the turtle. Several punch mark holes were also visible in the grooved outline of the bird and beaver. In general, the grooves were 3 millimeters to 4 millimeters

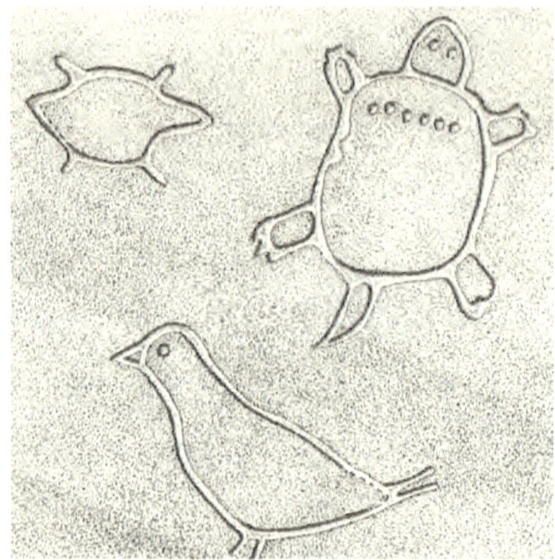

Figure 5. Detailed drawing of Hawk Rock petroglyphs. Length of bird is 31 cm. ***Drawing by T. Fitzpatrick.***

in width and 2 millimeters to 4 millimeters in depth. The turtle and bird figures were cut into the hard granite surface with some care, while the beaver was created somewhat crudely and as a result is less distinct.

Oral accounts recorded local knowledge of these carvings in the 1940s, when Myron Thompkins of Horse Pound Road recalled seeing the designs. Nick Schoumatoff, then curator of the Trailside Museum, Ward Pound Ridge Reservation, Cross River, New York, photographed and recorded the petroglyphs in 1971. He referred to the site as the "Needle" petroglyph and indicated that the area had been a Boy Scout camp. Shoumatoff[3] concluded that these carvings were twentieth century in origin and not associated with the evidence of Indian occupation recovered from a rock shelter located just north of Hawk Rock.

During my investigation in 1987, my colleague, Tom Fitzpatrick, and I concurred with Shoumatoff's conclusion. Physical evidence argued against antiquity; the designs were cut with metal tools and they lacked weathering and patination. Land use history indicated twentieth century activity at the site, and the visting of the area by Boy Scouts, an organization given to recreating Indian activities, suggested an explanation for the presence of the designs.

In 1988, Carol Reich, formerly of Kent, contacted me about the Hawk Rock petroglyph. Reich reported that her grandfather, General Leonard Smith, bought the adjoining property in 1906, and she recalled seeing the carvings at least as early as the 1930s. This information renewed my interest in the origins of the petroglyph.[4]

The following year I visited the Putnam County, New York, Hall of Records with historian Nancy L. Gibbs to read property deeds that might make reference to Hawk Rock and its carved figures. Horse Pound Brook, just east of Hawk Rock, had been used as a property boundary since colonial days. However, we found no mention of the rock and the carvings in applicable deeds. We next contacted Putnam County Historian Sallie Sypher, who had no additional knowledge of the site. Instead, she referred us to two people who were able to settle the question of the petroglyph's origin once and for all.[5]

Richard Muscarella, Kent Town Historian, wrote to us to say that he knew some old gentlemen, brothers, who resided on Horse Pound Road and had in their possession a photograph that showed a cabin located about fifty yards from Hawk Rock. According to Muscarella, the brothers told a story that as young men they had climbed a tree that had fallen against the rock and had carved their initials on it.[6] They were reticent when questioned about the animal carvings, but a friend of theirs claimed to have carved these.

More details came to light in a letter from Betty M. Light Behr, also of Horse Pound Road. Mrs. Light Behr was born and raised near the petroglyph site.[7] Her father, Frank B. Light, also native to the area, was a naturalist and photographer, and Mrs. Light Behr often accompanied him on hikes through the region. One of the early families in Kent was the Hunt family, who were related to Mrs. Light Behr. Three Hunt brothers, all in their 70s and 80s—Leroy, Harry, and Gilmore—were still living on Horse Pound Road in 1990. In 1988, Mr. and Mrs. Harry Hunt were invited to reminisce at a meeting of the Kent Historical Society. When Harry Hunt was asked what he knew about the Hawk Rock petroglyph, he related that he and his brothers and some school pals created the drawings. They placed the origin of the carvings in the late 1920s.

Mrs. Light Behr also recalled that between 1940 and 1966 "Colonel" Leonard Smith permitted use of his land near Hawk Rock by the Order of the Arrow, the most highly-ranked Boy Scouts, and those most involved in emulation of Indian-like behavior. The petroglyphs may have taken on their reputation as being of Indian origin at that time. The post-World War I youth movements from which the Boy Scouts originated in the United States drew much inspiration from a romanticized view of the American Indians. Camping, crafts, and outdoor activities were based on Indian lore, in which the native people of the North American continent were accorded a respect and admiration previously lacking in the nineteenth century. *The Book of Woodcraft* by Ernest Thompson Seton, founder and chief of the Woodcraft Indians, contains Indian signs and designs for the use of young campers.[8] Twentieth century children played "Indian" in the woods, reliving the tales and crafts of the noble savage, and sometimes leaving artifacts, such as the Hawk Rock petroglyph, which are often mistaken for the real thing.

We published a report of our findings, realizing that as years went by the Hawk Rock petroglyph would weather and develop the patina of age, which it lacked at the time of our study. Against that day, when it is newly discovered again and reported to be a real Indian carving, we documented the story of its origin, noting that it is a twentieth century tale that has its own charm and appeal.[9]

In 1997, our fear that the petroglyph would be discovered and interpreted as Indian came to pass. In his article discussing a petroglyph found near Brookfield, Connecticut, published in the *NEARA Journal*, author Iron Thunderhorse illustrated and interpreted the Hawk Rock petroglyphs as Indian, with the images representing a bird, turtle, and "dawn star motif."[10] In a letter to the editors of the *NEARA Journal*, I responded to the Iron Thunderhorse report and again stated that the figures were carved by local people in the late 1920s in a recreational context, and were not Indian.[11]

THE INDIAN ROCK PETROGLYPHS

The legend of Indian Rock, as well as its location in Orange County, New York, has been known to archaeologists, artifact collectors, historians and local residents for over seventy-five years. During that time, many individuals have hiked to the petroglyph site to gaze in wonder at the so-called Indian carvings. Every visitor to this Orange County landmark has undoubtedly heard the story that the images of "braves," horses, tepees, and other designs were the work of Indians who attempted to record an important tribal event.

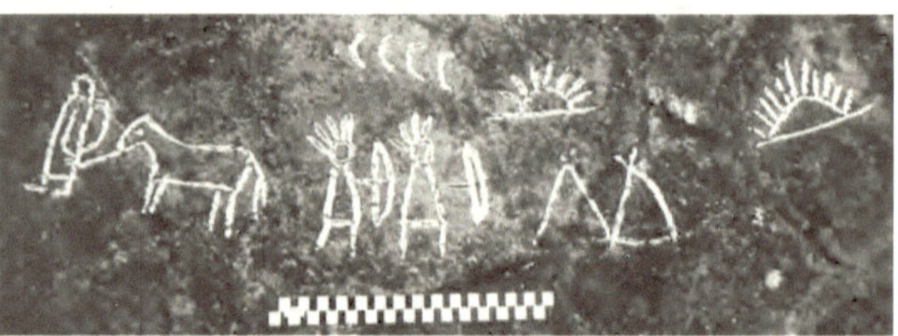

Figure 6: Indians, horse, tepees, crescent moons and suns carved on Indian Rock. ***Photo by E.J. Lenik 1974***

The Indian Rock petroglyph site is located near the village of Bloomingburg in Orange County, New York. Specifically, it lies a short distance east of Stone Schoolhouse Road, exactly three miles north of Route 17K in the town of Crawford, New York. The site was brought to my attention in the 1970s, and the exciting report of its images and legends prompted me to visit it personally to study and record the glyphs.[12]

At the time of my investigation, the petroglyph location was situated within a heavily wooded area on land with a gentle east to west slope. The remains of stone fences were visible nearby, no doubt the remnants of farm field or property lines from an earlier day. In the 1920s, the land was known as the Harris Farm.[13] A short distance below and to the west of the petroglyphs, the landscape was wet and swampy; a "bubbling mountain

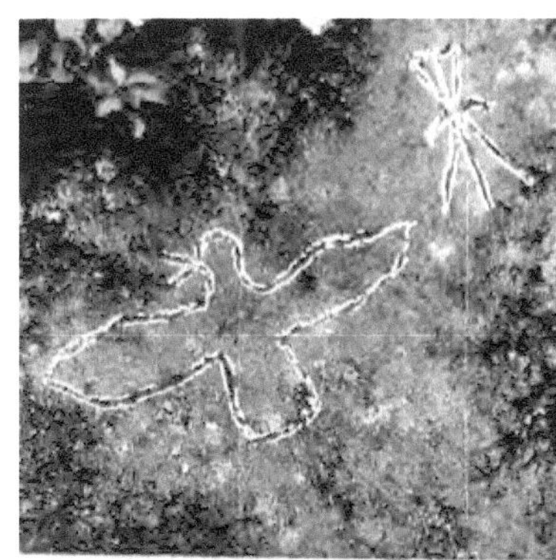

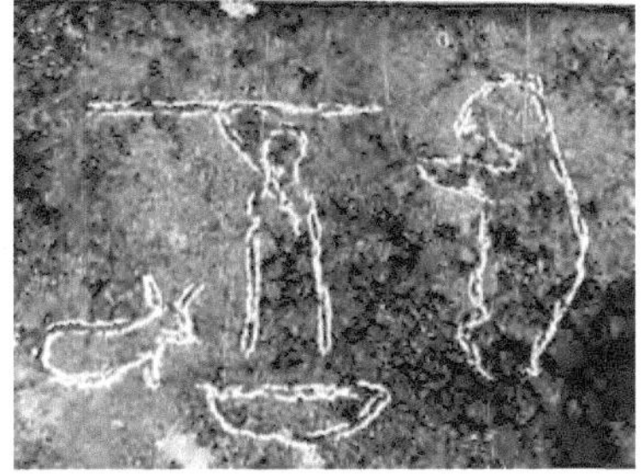

Figure 7: Thunderbird, arrows, and a hunter facing a bear carved on Indian Rock. ***Photo by E.J. Lenik 1974.***

spring" was reportedly present here in 1928 but was not evident at the time of my visit. The Shawangunk Kill (derived from a Dutch word meaning "stream" or "river") was located some eight hundred feet (235 m) to the northwest of the site.

The images were carved into a flat outcrop of granitic bedrock that measured 12 feet (3.5 m) long from north to south and 9 feet (2.65 m) wide from east to west. This naturally occurring, nearly rectangular rock "billboard" was an excellent panel for carving figures or messages. A total of twenty-eight figures were found on this granite ledge and recorded (Figures 6, 7, and 8). The images were produced in a naturalistic or realistic manner, and appeared to represent the sun, moon, tepees, horses, a thunderbird, bear and other animals. Human figures were also represented on the rock, including two Indians wearing headdresses and carrying bows and arrows, a "hunter" with a raised spear facing an upright "bear," a running figure also carrying a bow, a woman with a papoose on her back, and one other human in a frontal position with one arm holding a pipe or club. The figures were incised into the rock with metal tools and were generally well-formed on this hard artistic medium. The panel of carvings as a whole presents a triangular appearance with one figure at the top east side of the rock down to four or five figures at the bottom to the west. The reason for such an arrangement was not readily apparent.

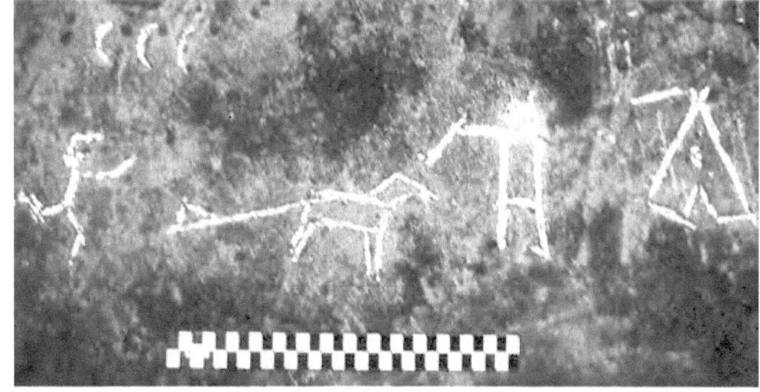

Figure 8: Running human, animal with a travois, human, tepee and crescent moons carved on Indian Rock. ***Photo by E.J. Lenik 1974.***

A short distance to the east of the petroglyph panel was a similar outcrop of flat granitic bedrock. This ledge measured 14 feet (4.15 m) long from east to west and 10 feet (3 m) wide from north to south. There were two symbols cut into this rock: the date "1928," and beneath it an arrow pointing in the direction of the Indian Rock. The figures were also cut with metal tools and their workmanship and degree of patination appeared to be similar to those on the nearby petroglyph panel.

According to a 1928 newspaper article which appeared in the *Times Herald* of Middletown, New York, the petroglyph site was first discovered in 1925 by a Charles Clapham of Bloomingburg and was then "lost."[14] It was rediscovered in 1927 by Edmund and Joseph Lloyd, also of Bloomingburg. The article reported that the area was investigated by the Lloyd brothers, Dr. E.A. Bates of Cornell University and Chief Goa-Hia-tha, also known as Jesse Lyons, of the Bear Clan of the Onondaga tribe.

The *Times Herald* article reported that both Dr. Bates and Chief Goa-Hia-tha believed that the carvings were the work of the Delaware tribe who probably carved the figures in the 1660s or 1670s. Interestingly, the article further noted that the "pictographs...aroused considerable controversy among historians and students of aboriginal America." Several unidentified "authorities" stated that the Indians of this region did not use spears or live in tepees, but these objections were rejected by Dr. Bates. Bates reportedly believed that the Indians had spears and bows, and used tepees as dwellings on hunting and fishing trips.

During his visit to the petroglyph site, Chief Goa-Hia-tha was dressed in "full regalia of his clan and rank."[15] He was very impressed with the carvings, and stood on the rock outcrop and recited a prayer in the Onondaga language to the Great Spirit. The Chief reportedly said "white man never made those signs." He interpreted the figures as representing a treaty made in 1657 between the Indians and Peter Stuyvesant, governor of New Netherland. According to the chief, the treaty was ratified in 1669 when Colonel Richard Nicolls was governor of the English colony of New York. He said the treaty stated "as long as sun shines, grass grows green, and waters flow downhill, the Indians shall have the right to hunt and fish over the territory they sold." The chief believed that the figure of an "Indian thrusting a spear at a bear" depicts their right to hunt and fish. He saw the figure of a deer killed by an arrow lying at the feet of the Indian. He interpreted the other figures as showing that the Indians may leave this area but "always" return to hunt and build tepees.

According to the *Times Herald* article, Dr. E.A. Bates interpreted "one set" of figures as representing an "attack on an Indian fort in 1663" by the Dutch. The fort was located two miles northwest of the Indian Rock site.[15] He also speculated that the figures of a horse and humans with bows drawn may indicate an Indian attack. The glyph at the top (east) end of the panel was interpreted by Bates and the chief as "three crossed arrows" which might be "a symbol for a particular union of three tribes or have some connection with the spring as a watering place for the three villages."

The 1928 newspaper account of the Bates and Chief Goa-Hia-tha investigation at Indian Rock does not mention the existence of the date "1928" and arrow on the nearby outcrop of bedrock. This suggests that these glyphs were not observed by the visiting party.

It is my opinion, the Indian Rock petroglyphs are not authentic Indian carvings. Taken as a group, the figures clearly characterize western or Plains Indians and not those groups that inhabited this region of New York. The images of tepees, full headdresses on human figures, and horses (especially the one pulling a travois) lend weight to this conclusion. In addition, there is no ethnohistoric or archaeological evidence to suggest that Indians of this region resided in tepees or utilized horses in the seventeenth century. Furthermore, the carved date of "1928" with its accompanying arrow pointing directly to the petroglyph panel strongly suggests the glyphs are of twentieth century origin. The petroglyphs are, instead, someone's fanciful representation of Indians, Indian lore and legends.

THE LENAPE STONE

In the spring of 1872, Bernard Z. Hansell, a farmer and collector of Indian relics, found a large fragment of an inscribed gorget on his father's farm located near Doylestown, Pennsylvania as he was plowing a field. He picked up the artifact from a furrow and noticed the image of "an animal like an elephant on it."[16] Nine years later, in the spring of 1881, he sold this gorget, along with other Indian artifacts, to Henry D. Paxon, another relic collector. Paxon brought his newly acquired items home and showed them to his father, who immediately recognized the elephant figure on the gorget.[17] Later that year, in October, Mr. Hansell found a smaller missing piece of the gorget near the same spot where he had found the small fragment nine years earlier.[18] The following month, Hansell gave this piece to Paxon, who then joined the two fragments together.

In 1882, Captain John S. Bailey of the Bucks County Historical Society borrowed the now-combined stone and made it the subject of a paper that he read before the society.[19] The following year Captain Bailey brought the gorget to the attention of Henry C. Mercer, a member of the Bucks County Historical Society and a well-known antiquarian. Mercer examined it and believed it to be a significant specimen that showed an encounter of an ice age mammoth and Indians. He wrote, "...it is unquestionably a picture of a combat

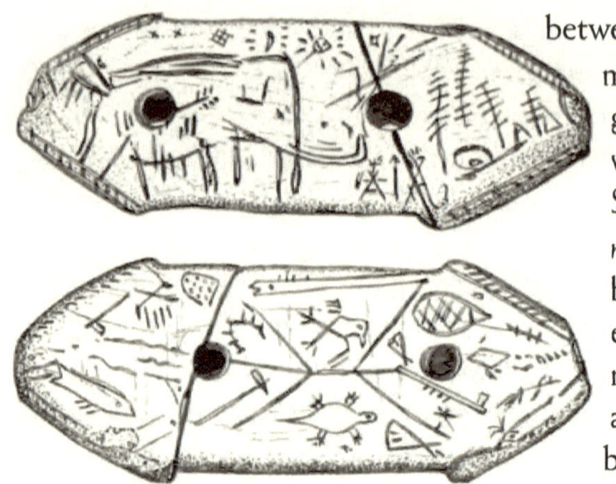

Figure 9: The Lenape Stone. Top, obverse side. Bottom, reverse side. ***Drawing by T. Fitzpatrick after Mercer 1885.***

between savages and the hairy mammoth."[20] Mercer christened the gorget the "Lenape Stone" and wrote a book titled *The Lenape Stone or The Indian and the Mammoth.*[21] Besides being intrigued by the drawing of an Indian encounter with a mammoth, he noted some twenty other images on the gorget, which he believed depicted events from the Walum Olum, or Migration Legend, of the Delaware Indians.

The obverse side of the gorget contains an incised full-body elephant-like animal facing four stick figure "Indians." One of the Indians is armed with a bow and arrow, another has a spear, a third reclines against a rock and the fourth lies "trampled" under the forefeet of the mammoth (Figure 9, top).[22] To the right side of the stone are four tree-like symbols, underneath which are two tepees. Above the mammoth's head is the symbol of a sun, a crescent moon, and what Mercer described as "forked lightning" symbols.[23] Ladder-like marks extend along the edge of the two converging ends of the stone.

The reverse side of the gorget contains twenty individual symbols that Mercer thought related to the Walum Olum. Mercer identified these figures as the outline of a fish, waving lines representing water or a river, a tobacco pipe, a turtle, a hawk, a possible wampum belt, a tomahawk, wigwams, a snowshoe, star, calumet, deer, a curved line crossed by three oblique lines, probably a war canoe, and a fish-like figure (Figure 9, bottom). He believed these symbols were the product of the Lenni Lenape Indians, whose legends or traditions told the story of their former residence in the western part of the American continent and their subsequent journey to the east.[24] Mercer strongly believed the Walum Olum to be a genuine migration story.

Several scholars believed the Lenape Stone to be a fraud, among them H.C. Lewis, Professor of Mineralogy at the Academy of Sciences, Philadelphia; anthropologist M.R. Harrington; M.E. Wadsworth of Cambridge; Joseph P. Iddings of the United States Coast Survey and Dr. D.G. Brinton of the Academy of Natural Sciences, Philadelphia.[25] A major

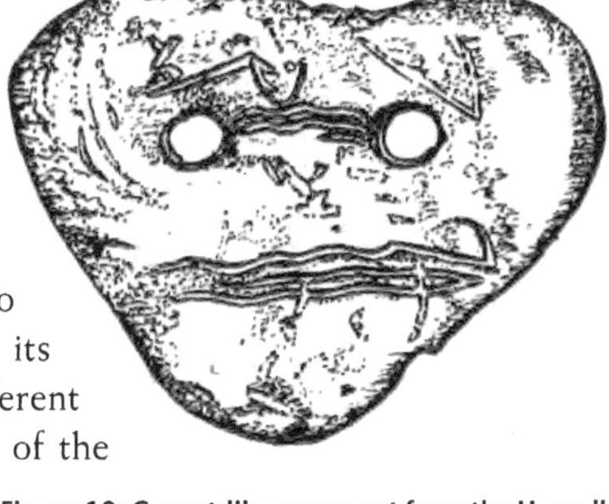

Figure 10: Gorget-like ornament from the Hansell Farm. ***Drawing by T. Fitzpatrick after Mercer 1885.***

objection to the Lenape Stone was the similarity of the mammoth figure to the engraving of a mammoth on a fragment of an ivory tusk from the cave at La Madeleine, Perigorde, France. Brinton considered the Lenape Stone to be a "modern piece of work" and its illustrations as being alien or different than those verified to be the work of the 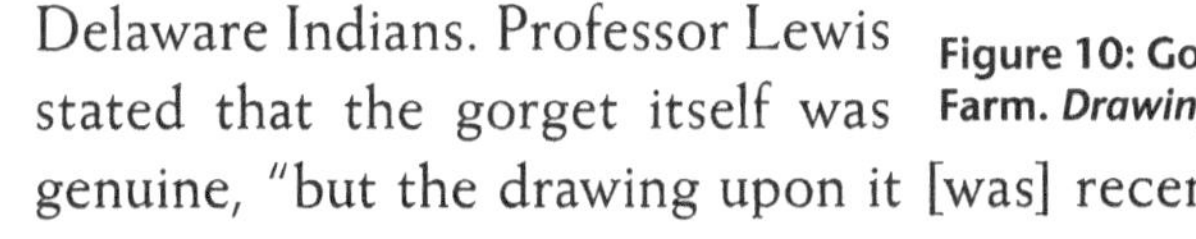 Delaware Indians. Professor Lewis stated that the gorget itself was genuine, "but the drawing upon it [was] recent"; hence he pronounced it a fraud.[26]

More recently, Professor Herbert C. Kraft of Seton Hall University cited several other objections to the authenticity of the carvings. Kraft noted that as an artifact, the gorget dates from about 1000 BC to AD 1000 in the eastern United States.[27] Furthermore, the Indian hunter depicted on the stone is shown using a bow and arrow, but archaeological evidence indicates this weapon came into use during the Middle Woodland period, circa AD 500. The bow and arrow was not used by Paleo-Indian hunters while stalking mastodons or mammoths. Tepees were not the dwellings utilized by Indians in this region, but were rather used by Native Americans of the Great Plains. Finally, the Walum Olum, a nineteenth century document claiming to tell the migration story of the Lenape, has been conclusively shown to be a hoax.[28]

The Lenape Stone was acquired by the Bucks County Historical Society in the twentieth century. It is now on exhibit in the Henry C. Mercer Museum in Doylestown, Pennsylvania.

Postscript: In the concluding pages of his book, Mercer reported that "two carved stones [were] recently discovered on the Hansell farm."[29] The first of these was a heart-shaped gorget-like ornament. His illustration of this specimen shows two incised circles, presumably intended to be drilled through to form holes. Between these two circles are two wavy lines and three additional wavy lines are present below the circles (Figure 10). The second specimen was a broken atlatl weight (also referred to as a bannerstone) containing an incised medial line with short oblique and perpendicular lines extending from it (Figure 11). Mercer states that these two finds "strongly support[ed] . . . the authenticity of the Lenape Stone and its honest discovery."[30]

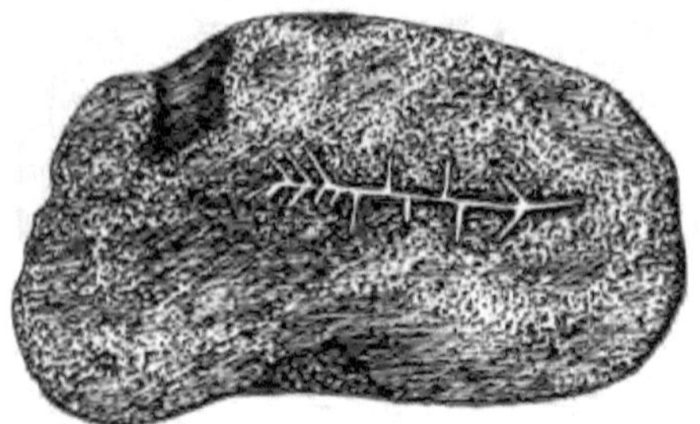

Figure 11: Broken atlatl weight from the Hansell Farm. ***Drawing by T. Fitzpatrick after Mercer 1885.***

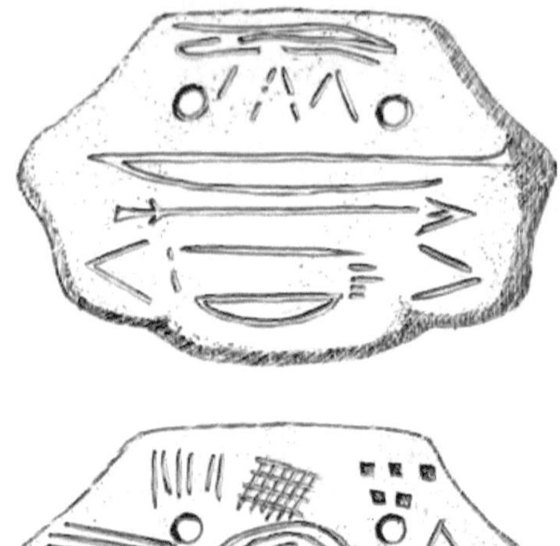

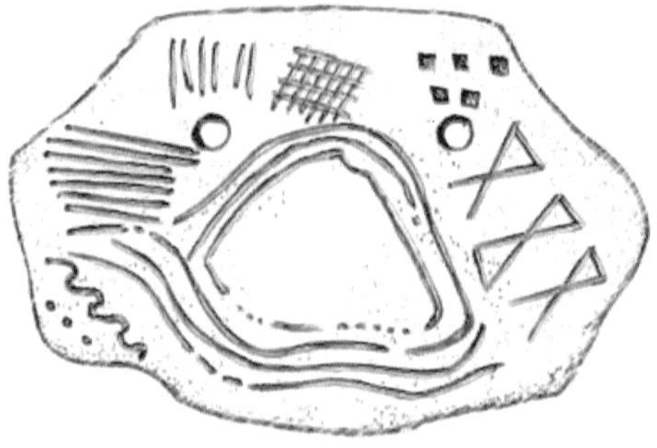

Figure 12: Engraved gorget from the Hansell Farm. Top, obverse side. Bottom, reverse side. ***Drawing by T. Fitzpatrick after Mercer 1885.***

In the last four pages of his book, Mercer reported that another carved gorget was found on the Hansell farm on January 8, 1885, just as his book was in preparation (Figure 12).[31] Once again, it was found by Bernard Hansell, the discoverer of the Lenape Stone, on a pile of unsifted soil from an excavation of a trench at the place where the heart-shaped gorget was found. An oddly-shaped specimen, it was produced from red shale and contained several incised designs. On the obverse side of this stone, Mercer characterized the designs as "three waving lines representative of water; three points between the perforations referring probably to wigwams—possibly an allusion to the triple clanship of the Lenapes and their settlement by the . . . Delaware River; a bow, arrow, and quiver." On the reverse side of the stone were "circular waving lines, representative probably of water, numerical dots and tallies, and three triangular outlines, common symbols for the human figure and again suggestive perhaps of the Wolf, Turtle, and Turkey brotherhood of the Lenapes."

Stephen Williams has suggested that Bernard Hansell perpetrated these frauds, and that the three new stones were made "by the same hand."[32]

THE KUTZTOWN GORGET

In the early twentieth century, another gorget containing incised figures was found near Kutztown, Berks County, Pennsylvania. Like the Lenape Stone and other finds on the Hansell farm, this artifact was recovered from the southeastern part of the state, which suggested to one observer that the Indians of this area "had a special type of ornament for a special purpose."[33]

F. F. Huber, the owner of the gorget, interpreted two of the markings on the artifact as an otter and a turtle, both of which represented the "totem of the Unami group of the Lenape who inhabited this part of the state" (Figure 13).[34] He noted that the symbol on the upper right corner on the obverse side of the stone was identical to one on the reverse side, but offered no explanation for this similarity. He also made no attempt to identify or interpret the geometric designs on the gorget. Huber speculated that this artifact was an ornamental piece and that the "...markings were intended to commemorate some significant event in the life of the wearer. Or...they may have belonged to some outstanding person in the tribe, such as a chief or medicine man."

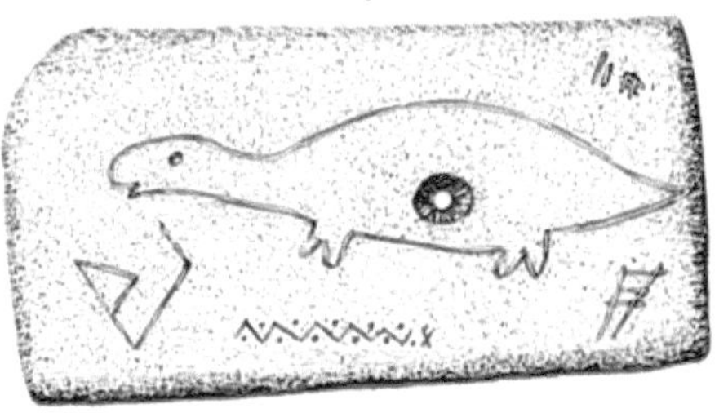

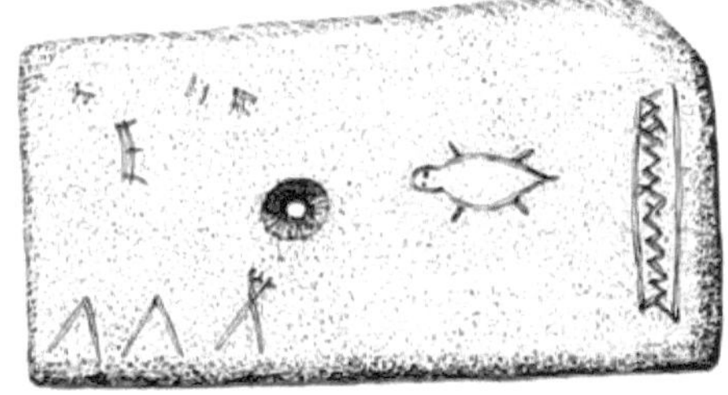

Figure 13: Gorget found near Kutztown, Pennsylvania. Top, obverse side. Bottom, reverse side. ***Drawing by T. Fitzpatrick after Huber 1935.***

New Jersey archaeologist Herbert C. Kraft suggested that the so-called otter figure "could easily be interpreted as a dinosaur."[35] Kraft apparently dismissed the authenticity of this artifact and remarked that, "like comets, many of these inscribed gorgets appeared out of nowhere, had momentary flashes, and disappeared from the archaeological record, as well they should."

THE HAMMOND TABLET

A profusely-incised stone was reportedly found on the bank of the Three Mile River near Taunton, Massachusetts in 1917.[36] Measuring 6-1/2 inches (16.5 cm) by 9-1/2 inches (24 cm), it was recovered by Frank C. Hammond, a local resident, who said it was buried a few inches deep in the soil. This discovery was described and reported by Ralph Davol in the *Boston Sunday Post* on June 26, 1921.

Edmund B. Dalabarre described the figures on the stone as "skillfully executed in the Indian manner or in evidently designed imitation of it."[37] Both sides of the stone are filled with numerous figures and symbols, many of which are similar to the Lenape Stone. The tablet itself appears to have the shape of an animal pelt (Figure 14).

The obverse side of the stone looks as if it depicts a scene of combat between a mammoth or mastodon and Indians with headdresses carrying bows. At least two of the stick figure Indians lie prostrate, presumably indicating they were killed by this great beast. Eight triangles, interpreted as representing wigwams, are situated near the Indian warriors. Three additional mammoth heads, drawn in frontal view, are illustrated above the hairy monster. Twelve vertical and parallel lines containing short oblique and perpendicular lines extend across the center of the tablet; these have been interpreted as being representative of a forest.[38] Other symbols on the stone include X's, two outlined crosses, arrows, a rising sun, and abstract designs.

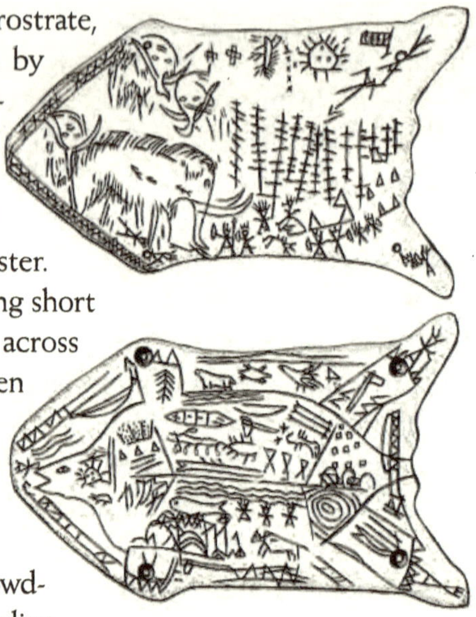

On its reverse side the stone is crowded with incised images, including stick Indian figures, a turtle, bird, fish, other animals, arrows, tomahawks, triangles, and several geometric and abstract designs. Delabarre characterized these designs as "scenes in the history of the migrations of the Lenni Lenape or Delaware Indians, as related in their historical song, the Walum Olum."[39]

Figure 14: The Hammond Tablet. Top, obverse side. Bottom, reverse side. ***Drawing by T. Fitzpatrick after Delabarre 1928.***

Several scholars have refused to accept the authenticity of this artifact and have declared it a fraud. C.C. Willoughby of the Peabody Museum of Harvard University examined the stone, and concluded that the incised motifs of the mammoth-Indian scene on the Hammond Tablet was similar to that on the Lenape Stone and "shows conclusively either that one of the pictures was copied from the other or that both were made by the same man."[40] Willoughby stated that both the Lenape Stone and Hammond Tablet were "the work of a clever maker of fraudulent antiquities." From an archaeological perspective, Professor Herbert C. Kraft of Seton Hall University also considered the Hammond Tablet to be a fraud and stated that it "has long since disappeared."[41]

THE LONG ISLAND TABLET

On October 5, 1893, Dr. Daniel D. Brinton read a paper before the Numismatic and Antiquarian Society of Philadelphia in which he reported the discovery of a small rectangular sandstone artifact that contained incised images on both sides. Prior to his presentation, Brinton had received a cast of the stone from a Professor Gifford who asked him for his opinion "as to its genuineness."

Brinton's analysis of the symbols, along with a drawing of one side of the artifact, was published the following month in a journal called The Archaeologist.[42] From the casts submitted to him, Brinton was unable to determine what was carved on the other side of the stone. He called the artifact "The Long Island Tablet."

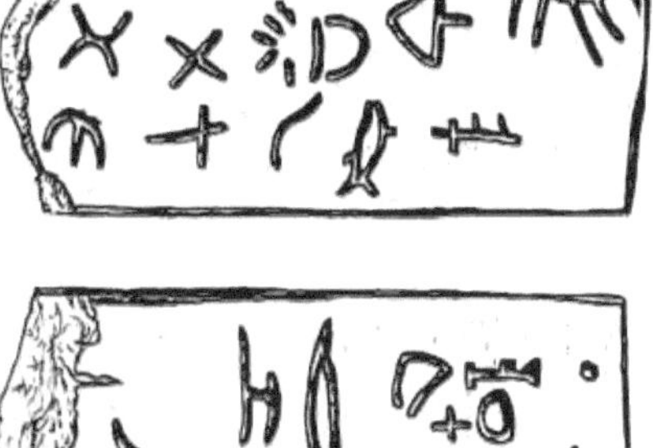

Figure 15: The Long Island Tablet. Top, obverse side. Bottom, reverse side. *Drawing by T. Fitzpatrick after Brinton 1893.*

Brinton reported that the tablet was found on an Indian site located out at the east end of Long Island, New York. Thirty-five years later, Edmund Burke Delabarre provided additional details as to its place of discovery in his 1928 book *Dighton Rock*.[43] Delabarre stated that the engraved tablet was found on a shell heap at Eagle Neck, Orient, Long Island, and that it was in the possession of the Heye Foundation at the Museum of the American Indian in New York City (now the National Museum of the American Indian). While in the possession of this museum, a careful drawing of the figures on both sides of the tablet was made by staff member Daniel A. Young (Figure 15).

The Long Island Tablet measured 7 inches (18 cm) by 4 ½ inches (11.5 cm) and was 7/8 of an inch (23 mm) thick. Brinton identified the images on the obverse side of the stone as those of a man, a canoe, a deer, a bow and arrow, the footprint of a bear, a sign of fire, a fish, an eel, a wigwam, an unknown figure and some vague lines.[44] Brinton concluded that this array of symbols seemed to be a "record of a hunting and fishing excursion of little importance which the [carver] may have amused himself in inscribing on a piece of stone simply because it was suited to the purpose; or, it may have been a mnemonic aid to retain in the memory the words of some hunting song or medicine chant, intended to propitiate the divinities who confer or deny success in fighting or the chase." He added that he saw "nothing in it to convict it as spurious."

Daniel Young's drawing of the reverse side of the table shows several incised abstract and geometric symbols. One figure, however, located at the bottom or broken end of the tablet, appears to represent a water bird.

In the 1970s, Marjorie R. King of New Hyde Park, New York, and several of her associates attempted to locate the Long Island Tablet to determine its authenticity. In a report prepared in July, 1980, King reported that the stone was missing. Attempts to locate the artifact at the Museum of the American Indian were unsuccessful. In fact, the museum reported in 1978 that they did not have either the stone or any record of it.[45] Furthermore, the plaster casts of the tablet, which Brinton stated he received from Professor Gifford of Swathmore College, could not be located. King also reported that she and her associates were unable to find any newspaper reports of the discovery of the artifact, and their consultations with museums, historical societies, and knowledgeable individuals in Suffolk County, Long Island, did not turn up any information on the tablet.[46]

King's research revealed that John Clayton Gifford, the apparent original owner of the stone, was a botany instructor at Swathmore College from 1891 to approximately 1896.[47] Born in Mays Landing, New Jersey, Gifford had an interest in American Indian artifacts and customs. He reportedly wrote several essays devoted to Indian lore and his various archaeological finds, but none of these mentioned the Long Island Tablet. Correspondence with Gifford's biographer and daughter revealed that there was no mention of such a carved stone in his private papers. Finally, a search for correspondence between Gifford and Daniel Brinton also proved to be fruitless.

King and her associates compared the drawings of figures on the obverse side of the tablet with the Hunting Scene Tablet, one of the bogus Davenport, Iowa, stones.[48] They saw a "striking resemblance" of the quadruped on the Long Island Tablet to a cow-like figure on the Davenport tablet.[49] They also observed that the rectangular shape and size of the Long Island Tablet was also similar to that of the Davenport Hunting Scene Tablet; the latter measured 12 inches (30.5 cm) by 10-1/4 inches (26 cm).[50]

The available evidence seems to suggest that the Long Island Tablet was a hoax. The figures on the stone are unlike any other petroglyphs I have examined from Long Island.[51] King and her associates concluded that the "negative evidence leans toward showing the Long Island Tablet to be another 19th century fraud—possibly a college student prank."[52]

STONE GIANT AT BALANCE ROCK STATE PARK

Balance Rock State Park is located near the northwest corner of Pontoosuc Lake, about ¼ mile west of U.S. Route 7 in the town of Lanesborough, Massachusetts. Here, a 165-ton, oblong-shaped boulder deposited by the Wisconsin glacier some 13,000 years ago is balanced precariously on one edge on top of a small rock outcrop (Figure 16). Its imposing size and prominent, curious position have attracted human interest for hundreds of years. Its surface, as well as that of other rocks nearby, is abundantly covered with graffiti, some of which is quite old and some very recent.

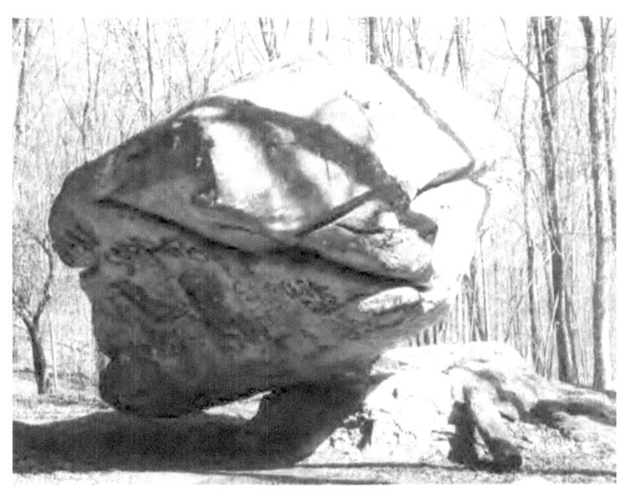

Figure 16: Balance Rock, Lanesborough, Massachusetts. ***Photo by E.J. Lenik 2003.***

An American Indian tale describes the origin of Balance Rock and associates native people and spirits with this site. Marion E. Gridley, in her 1939 book *Indian Legends of American Scenes,* relates the Indian story of an encounter with a supernatural being that placed the monolith there, and ends with a social and moral message:

> A group of Indian boys were playing games. Their games were tests of endurance, for they wished to see who was the strongest. He who won in the most events would be their leader for the year.
>
> The swimming contests had been won by Bright Star, and he had won the bow and arrow games as well. Fleet of foot, he had outdistanced all others in the races, and there now remained only the wrestling matches. Bright Star was certain of his victory, and he spoke proud words.
>
> "Hoh, there is no boy in the village that can overthrow Bright Star in wrestling. Bright Star can wrestle even the Stone Giant and win."
>
> "Those are big words, Bright Star," called a voice. "Remember,

> when you boast, you must perform the deeds of which you speak. So has the Great Spirit said."
>
> The boys were startled to see an unknown lad standing nearby. He was small and meek in appearance; his clothes tattered and torn. Jeering, the boys crowded around, Bright Star in the lead. They mocked the unknown boy, and Bright Star challenged him to try his strength against him. Unhesitatingly, the stranger accepted.
>
> Bright Star picked up a large stone and lifted it shoulder high. The boy picked up a larger stone and lifted it head high. Bright Star struggled with another boulder and lifted it over his head. The boy easily moved a still larger rock, and threw it into the air. Bright Star panted and gasped over another stone, but he was helpless to move it even a tiny bit.
>
> Now the boy picked up stones so large that none had ever thought to try to move them. With every step he grew larger until he became a giant, the Stone Giant himself! He threw rocks about as though they were pebbles. Then he placed a huge boulder on top one another one, balancing it there with his magical powers.
>
> The boys stood awestruck as Stone Giant disappeared from sight and in his place stood the meek appearing boy. They did not laugh, but hung their heads, when he said to them, "Never be uncivil to strangers, or judge by appearance alone. Never speak idle words of the great things you can accomplish, unless you can prove your words to be true. Live up to these teachings and you will be leaders among men, as well as among yourselves."
>
> When at least they raised their eyes, there was only a rabbit hopping down the trail.[53]

Folk legends about giants who were supernatural culture-heroes were common among Algonquian-speaking tribes in the northeastern United States and Canada. In southern New England, for example, there was a giant called Maushop who created many topographic features, and protected and helped the Indians.[54] In Maine and Canada, there was a giant called Gluscap who performed similar deeds.[55] The morality tale in the story cited above appears to come from this generally benevolent Algonkian tradition. However, it is interesting to note that stories of stone giants occur among the Iroquois of New York. The stone giants in Iroquois tales were monsters who frightened and often ate Indian people.[56] Historical accounts frequently mention Mohawk raids and incursions into Deerfield and Groton, Massachusetts and elsewhere in New England in the seventeenth and early eighteenth centuries during wars against the Mahicans and other Algonkian tribes.[57] It is possible that the Stone Giant story as it relates to Balance Rock may be an admixture of Iroquois and Algonkian folklore resulting from Iroquois presence and influence in the area.

Beginning in the eighteenth century and extending into the nineteenth century, Balance Rock lay within the bounds of a colonial farmstead. In 1830, the property was owned by Socrates Squire, the fourth generation of this family to occupy the site.[58] A subsequent owner of the farm, Grove Hulbert, reportedly permitted a band of gypsies to squat on his land. The gypsies then began to charge visitors ten cents to view the rock. Mr. Hulbert apparently became angry and upset at this spectacle. He tied a team of oxen to the rock in an attempt to dislodge it from its perch but this effort failed.

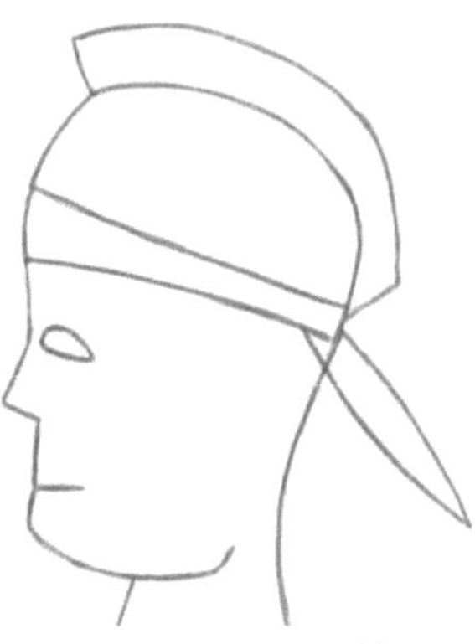

Figure 17: Carved profile of a "Mohawk Indian" at Balance Rock State Park, Lanesborough, Massachusetts. ***Drawing by T. Fitzpatrick.***

In 1911, the Balance Rock site was purchased by a group of citizens for $2,785, and the land was subsequently given to the city of Pittsfield in 1916. The property remained as open area to provide a more natural setting for the boulder, and is now part of the Massachusetts State Park system.

Balance Rock is profusely covered with graffiti, both painted and carved. Virtually every flat surface of the boulder has been painted with red, black, or white names, initials, and dates. The vandalism also includes scratches, scrapes, and carvings of inscriptions and other motifs. However, the more interesting graffiti occurs on several rock outcrops located nearby.

On top of a rock situated about one hundred feet north-northwest of Balance Rock is a carved head in profile which local people call a "Mohawk Indian" (Figure 17). The figure faces left and was cut into the rock with a metal tool as indicated by a pattern of punch marks that are present within the grooves. Its features are clearly outlined, including the shape of the head, nose, chin, and neck. On top of the head is a Mohawk-style haircut, and a headband extends across the forehead and side, dipping down at the back.

Another carved Indian head occurs about two feet away from the one described above, on the same rock outcrop. This figure also faces left and was cut into the hard surface with a metal tool. Its most prominent features are a Western Plains Indian-style headdress, a bold nose and prominent chin, and what appears to be a necklace around the neck (Figure 18).

A third Indian head is deeply carved into the slanting side of a rock outcrop located about one hundred feet to the east of Balance Rock. Metal tools were used to cut this figure as well, and it too faces to the left. The image has a distinctive Western Plains Indian-style feather headdress.

A rock outcrop contiguous to the one described immediately above also contains an image of a human head on its top surface. This figure is outlined in profile, faces left, and was boldly cut with metal tools. Its distinctive features include a flattop head, round or bulbous nose, a prominent rounded chin, a neck, and a partial chest.

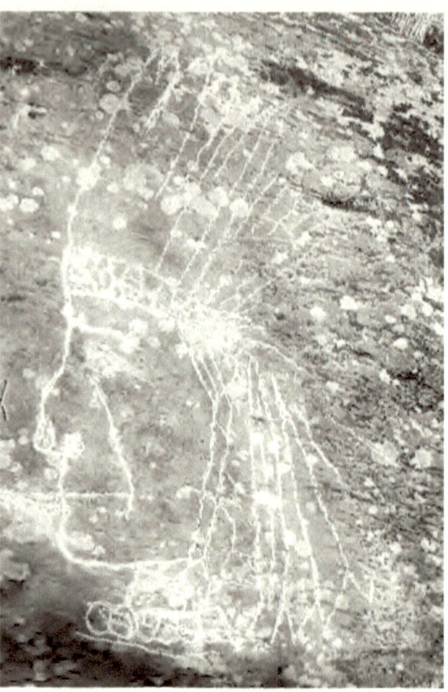

Figure 18: Carved profile of an Indian wearing a headdress and necklace at Balance Rock State Park, Lanesborough, Massachusetts. ***Photo courtesy of Matt McGurn.***

The three Indian head figures are covered with lichen and appear to be of some antiquity, possibly dating to the late nineteenth or early twentieth centuries. They may represent attempts by their artists to portray an Indian presence at the site and in the area to add credence to the legend of Balance Rock.

The fourth head more likely dates to the late twentieth century and does not represent an Indian, so its purpose remains a mystery. Furthermore, all of these rock outcrops near Balance Rock contain carved initials, names, dates, and other images as well.

I conclude that the carved "Indian Heads" are not authentic Indian carvings. I suggest they were added in the nineteenth or twentieth century by Euro-Americans in an attempt to enhance the legend of Balance Rock.

GLEN ONOKO
LEHIGH GORGE STATE PARK

The discovery of anthracite coal in the upper Lehigh River region of Pennsylvania in 1791 led to the establishment and development of mines and processing plants and the shipment of this mineral fuel to markets via barges on the Lehigh canal. By the middle of the nineteenth century, railroads became the major means of transportation, and together with coal mining, an important economic force in the region.

Steam railroads, such as the Lehigh Valley and the Central Railroad of New Jersey, along with other carriers, linked the anthracite region to markets in Philadelphia and New York. In 1855, a forty-six mile main line of the Lehigh Valley Railroad was in operation between Mauch Chunk (now the town of Jim Thorpe, Pennsylvania) and Easton on the Delaware River. By 1867, the Lehigh and Susquehanna Railroad had been completed between White Haven and Easton. In 1871, the Lehigh line was leased by the Central Railroad of New Jersey in an attempt to expand its coal distribution system to the East Coast.[59]

By the last quarter of the nineteenth century, railroads had begun to carry passengers and tourists. As a result, hotels and inns were established at Mauch Chunk (Jim Thorpe), Glen Onoko, and Summit Hill in the Lehigh Valley. A typical advertising broadside of the period described the route as "running along the charming bank of the Delaware and Lehigh Rivers and passing through the grand old mountains of Pennsylvania, affording one of the grandest panoramic views of Natural Scenery in the world."[60]

As the popularity of the scenic Lehigh Valley grew along with the ease of travel through it, the Lehigh and Central railroads sponsored a mountain resort called Glen Onoko, located near the town of Mauch Chunk. The "glen" in the name referred to a mountain stream that flowed down a steep narrow ravine with several waterfalls before entering the Lehigh River. Both the Lehigh Valley Railroad and the Central Railroad had stations near the junction of Glen Onoko and the river.

The mountain glen had been previously known as Moore's Ravine, but an enterprising tourist agent of the Lehigh Valley Railroad changed its name to Glen Onoko, a supposed Indian name.[61] To entice tourists to the area, the agent fabricated an Indian legend in which a young Indian maiden jumped off the Glen Onoko Falls to her death because she could not marry her true love. The waterfalls soon became the glen's main attraction. Thousands of people visited the Glen Onoko resort in the late nineteenth and early twentieth centuries and heard the fictitious story of the beautiful princess who tragically leaped from the upper falls to her death because of unrequited love.

The resort at Glen Onoko was built in 1885 along the mountainside near the ravine, and was called the Wahneta Hotel. The hotel contained fifty-six rooms and featured such amenities as a dance pavilion, merry-go-round, tennis courts, gardens, and stone-lined mountain trails. From the hotel, tourists hiked the mountain trails up the ravine to the waterfalls and mountain top, where they observed a "grandly picturesque" view of the Lehigh River Gorge. One observer recorded this scene in Frank Leslie's Illustrated Newspaper of July 27, 1889 as follows:

> We had been in many beautiful glens, but this was so unlike all others, so varied, grand and noble falls alternating with delightful rippling cascades, lovely moss covered grottos, marvelous combination—that we were led to exclaim 'All Hail Onoko! Queen of Glens!'

The Hotel Wahneta met a tragic end. A forest fire engulfed the hotel in 1911, inflicting heavy damage. It was never rebuilt, and it lay abandoned until 1917 when it was finally demolished.

A mountain summit called Moyer's Rock is situated on the south side of the Lehigh River opposite Glen Onoko. It too is associated with another local Indian tale. The story states that Moyer, a "famous hunter and Indian fighter," was captured by two members of a group of Indians while the others continued to hunt for game. Moyer successfully escaped by tricking his two captors. He stood at the edge of the summit and gazed intently downward at the Lehigh River. This aroused the Indians' curiosity and they moved to his side to see what he was looking at so intently. Moyer caught the two Indians off-guard, threw them off the cliff to the rocks below, and escaped.[62]

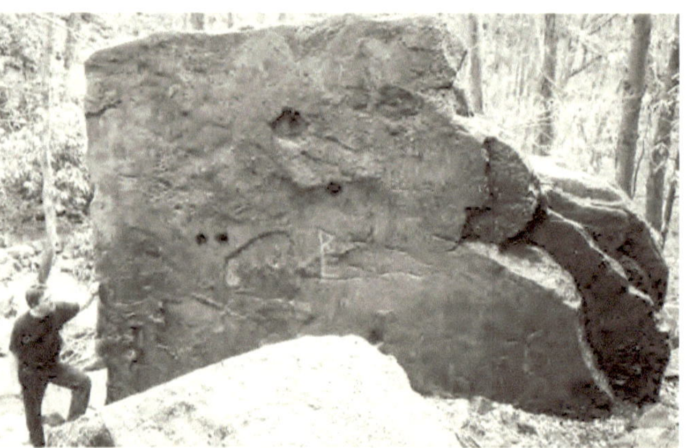

Figure 19: Pulpit or Sentimental Rock at Glen Onoko, Lehigh Gorge State Park, Pennsylvania. ***Photo by E.J. Lenik 2004.***

A short hike up the Glen Onoko ravine brings you to the lower waterfall, where there is a large standing stone on the south side of the stream. At one time, a footbridge brought visitors to the rock, which was called Pulpit or Sentimental Rock.[63] One surface of the rock is vertical and flat and provides a natural billboard on which tourists could leave their mark (Figure 19). Sentimental Rock measures 12 feet (3.6 m) in height and 15 feet (4.5 m) in width, and is now covered with graffiti.

This petroglyph panel contains numerous names, initials, dates, symbols, and figures carved by nineteenth and twentieth century tourists and hikers to the site. Some of the most prominent illustrations include a flower-like image consisting of four petals, two of which have a letter "E" and "R" respectively, a triangle with initials "GR" at its apex, a diamond symbol with an interior dot, a duck-like figure in profile, and a deeply-incised curvilinear design with cup marks.

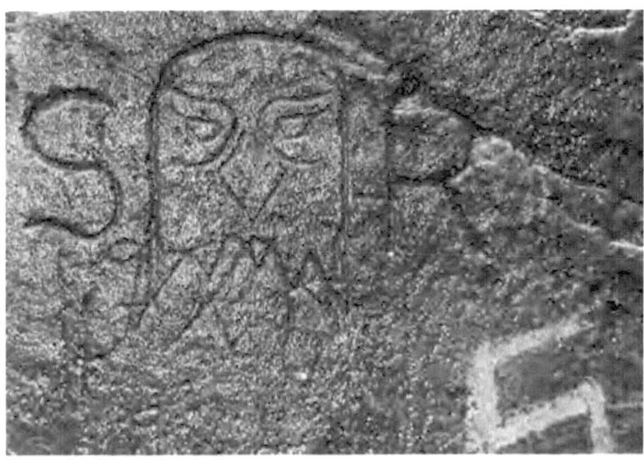

Figure 20: Incised owl-like image on Sentimenal Rock, Glen Onoko, Lehigh Gorge State Park, Pennsylvania. ***Photo by E.J. Lenik 2004.***

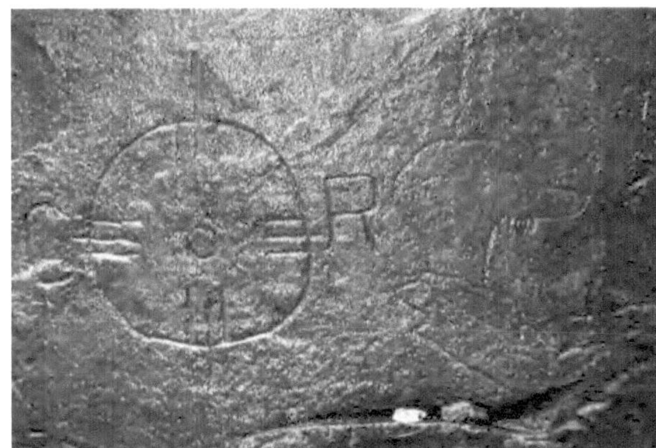

Figure 21: Possible Central Railroad symbol on Sentimenal Rock, Glen Onoko, Lehigh Gorge State Park, Pennsylvania. ***Photo by E.J. Lenik 2004.***

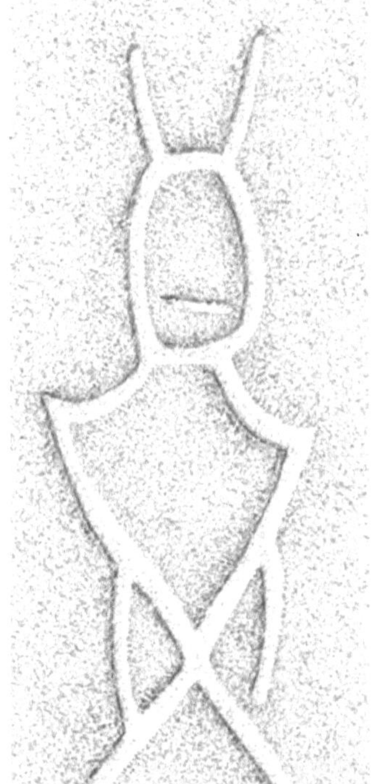

Figure 22: Incised anthropomorphic figure on Sentimenal Rock, Glen Onoko, Lehigh Gorge State Park, Pennsylvania. ***Drawing by T. Fitzpatrick.***

There is also a deeply-incised owl-like image on the rock flanked by the letters "S" and "R" (Figure 20). Another interesting design is a circle with three interior short lines at each cardinal point around a small interior circle with the letters "C" and "R" to the left and right of the outer circle (Figure 21). This latter design may refer to the Central Railroad, which had a station just below the lower falls.

There are two Indian motifs on the petroglyph panel. At the lower left side of the rock is the incised image of an anthropomorph. It consists of a diamond-shaped body, a head with two projections or horns, and arms and legs (Figure 22). This human-like figure is remarkably similar to authentic Indian glyphs found elsewhere in the Northeast. It may indeed be prehistoric in origin and may represent a shaman. At the lower right side of the panel is an incised image of an Indian "chief" complete with a Plains Indian-style headdress (Figure 23). This image is clearly a tourist's idea of what an Indian should look like.

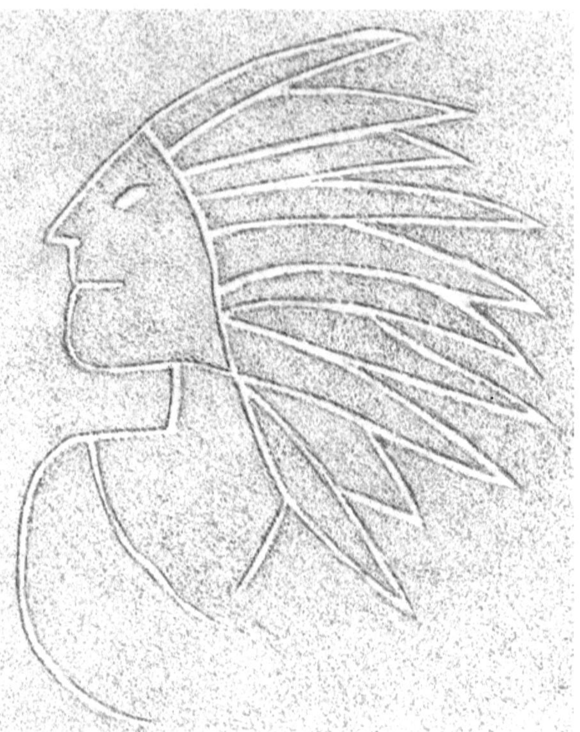

Figure 23: Image of an Indian chief with Plains style headdress on Sentimenal Rock, Glen Onoko, Lehigh Gorge State Park, Pennsylvania. ***Drawing by T. Fitzpatrick.***

The Glen Onoko area in Lehigh Gorge State Park, Pennsylvania, continues to be a popular visitation site in the twenty-first century. Unfortunately, Sentimental Rock in the glen continues to attract hikers who feel a need to place their marks on the stone.

ANTHROPOMORPHS: HUMAN FIGURES

THE WELLS BEACH PETROGLYPH

This is the story of an inscribed rock found on the rock-strewn shore of Wells, Maine. It was here that a severe hurricane lashed the area in 1953, turning over a huge boulder and bringing to light a most unusual rock carving.

In that same year Captain Austin S. Guest of Wells was wandering along the rocky beach in search of duck mussels to use as bait on his charter boat while deep sea fishing off the coast.[1] As he walked among the rocks he spotted a large granite boulder that had several symbols carved into its newly exposed upper surface. The boulder, estimated to weigh some 1,800 pounds (800 kg), had apparently been turned over by strong tides whipped up by hurricane-force winds.[2] Immediately recognizing its uniqueness, Captain Guest directed the removal of the boulder from the beach and had it placed on the front lawn of his house.

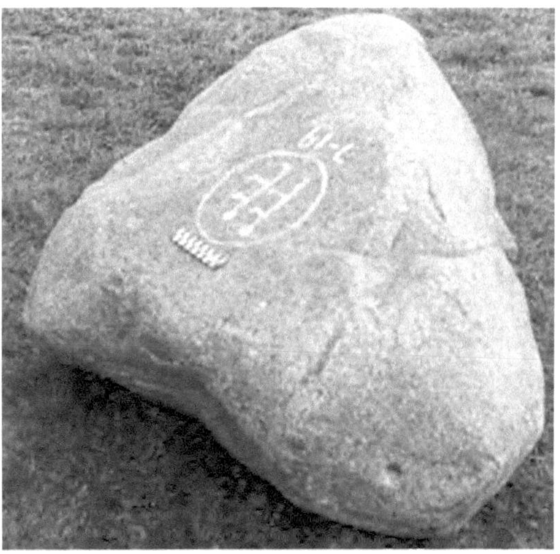

Figure 24: Wells Beach petroglyph boulder, Wells Beach, Maine. ***Photo by E.J. Lenik 1977.***

Following Captain Guest's death in 1973, the boulder was carted back to the beach. There it was placed among rocks used to shore up a retaining wall along the end of the property of the Wells Beach firehouse. Shortly thereafter, the boulder was reclaimed by Reginald Chase, Captain Guest's grandson, who had it moved to the front yard of his home. On November 20, 1977, I went to Reginald Chase's home and examined the stone and its carving (Figure 24).

The boulder was granite, a tough artistic medium, and measured 4 feet (1.2 m) long, 3 feet (90 cm) wide, and about 19 inches (50 cm) thick. The side of the boulder containing the carvings had a brown discoloration which was not in evidence on the other sides, suggesting that the images were originally face down for some length of time. Reginald Chase, its owner at the time of my visit, indicated that it was found by his grandfather near the site of the Atlantic Hotel, which was once located near the beach.[3] The hotel was "washed away" by storms around 1900, and there was some speculation that the boulder with its carved design may have been a property marker or part of the structure's foundation.

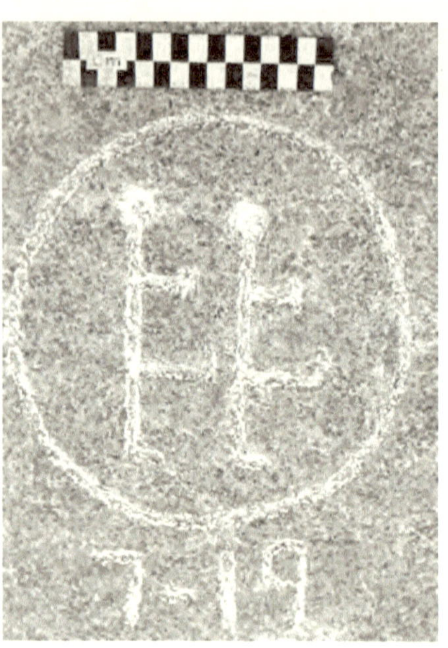

Figure 25: Detail of Wells Beach petroglyph. ***Photo by E.J. Lenik 1977.***

The Wells Beach petroglyph was carved with metal tools. The incised circle is nearly perfect and the two anthropomorphic figures within it are exactly alike (Figure 25). The grooves forming the design were shallow, but overall they were carefully planned before being cut into the rock. The "goose-stepping" figures have perfectly rounded heads, and cup-like depressions cut more deeply into the rock. The numbers "7-19" are carved into the stone underneath the encircled figures.

This petroglyph has been reported to be of American Indian origin. In 1988 Helen Butler referred to the carving as "The Heartbreak Petroglyph," and stated that the pictographic images represented a "poem" telling a "powerful" story from the past.[4] She wrote that "the minds eye can see a lone Indian sitting gazing out over the ocean to the far horizon, feeling the pain of the distance and time separating him/her from the land and the people lying somewhere beyond the horizon's rim—his/her heritage, his/her ancestors."

Butler reported that the encircled stick figures have been interpreted as follows:

> Heartbreak is the story of the desolate pain of those left behind and those taken away. It tells of the Indians who have been taken away from heart broken [sic] loved ones and transported against their will to some distant place—beyond reach and beyond help. Apparently, those separated in this traumatic way were members of a tribe, not just members of one family. There is an eloquent

> cry of pain in the loss of the comfort and protection found only in the midst of those who love and care for us—the feeling of being held. Thus speaks heartbreak.

I reject the above interpretation as fanciful. The stylistic attributes of the figures are unlike the nineteenth century Ojibway pictographs in the Great Lakes area or elsewhere in the northeastern United States and adjacent areas of Canada. I do not believe they represent Algonkian shamanistic iconography. The design elements were carved with metal tools in a precise manner as if the carver was using a template or blueprint. In addition, I do not think the boulder was once part of the foundation of the Atlantic Hotel, as there is no evidence that it was cut, dressed or mortared into such a structure. It is a historic period Euro-American carving but I can offer no further explanation of its meaning.

THE WESTFORD KNIGHT

A portrait of a knight holding a shield is painted on an exposed section of bedrock at roadside on Depot Street in the town of Westford, Massachusetts. Nearby is a commemorative marker containing a coat-of-arms and the following inscription (Figure 26):

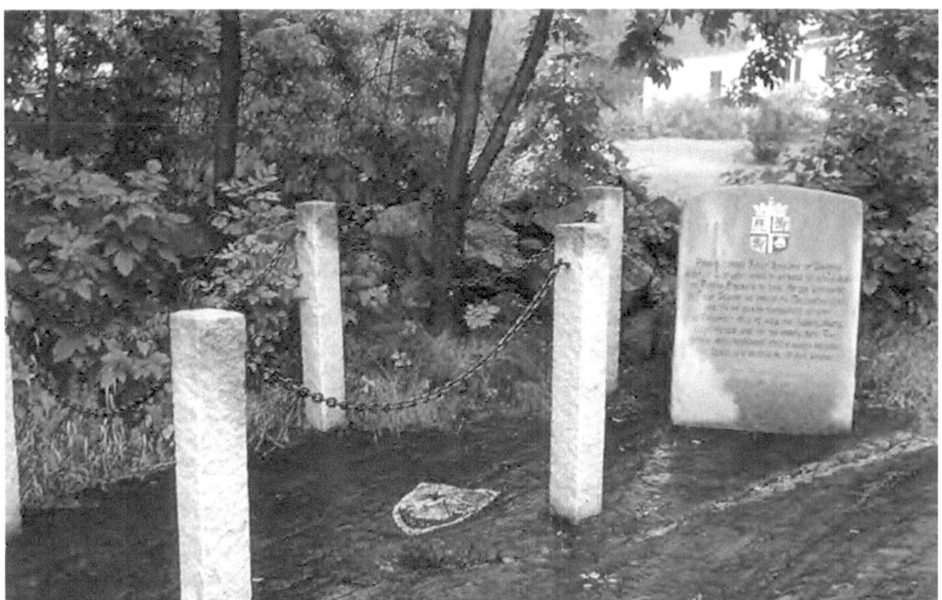

Figure 26: The Westford Knight petroglyph site and commemorative marker. ***Photo by E.J. Lenik 1979.***

> Prince Henry, First Sinclair of Orkney, born in Scotland, made a voyage of discovery to North America in 1398. After wintering in Nova Scotia he sailed to Massachusetts and, on an inland expedition in 1399 to Prospect Hill to view the surrounding countryside, one of the party died. The punch-hole armorial effigy, which adorns this ledge, is a memorial to this knight.

The Prospect Hill referred to in the inscription is a 465-foot eminence that is located about one mile south of the Westford Knight figure.

The story of Henry Sinclair's voyage has been inferred from a ship's log by Venetian Admiral Nicolo Zeno, who commanded and navigated twelve vessels with some two hundred to three hundred individuals aboard that reached North America on June 2, 1398.[5] The Zeno Narrative indicated that the admiral returned to the Orkney Islands, but Sinclair continued the journey and ultimately reached the coast of Massachusetts. While anchored off shore, the voyagers saw smoke and decided to investigate its origin. Sinclair then sent one hundred soldiers inland to explore, and in the course of their travel one of their party, Sir James Gunn, died. To mark the knight's burial site the exploring party carved his effigy on the horizontal bedrock outcrop in Westford, which is located approximately thirty miles west of Massachusetts Bay.

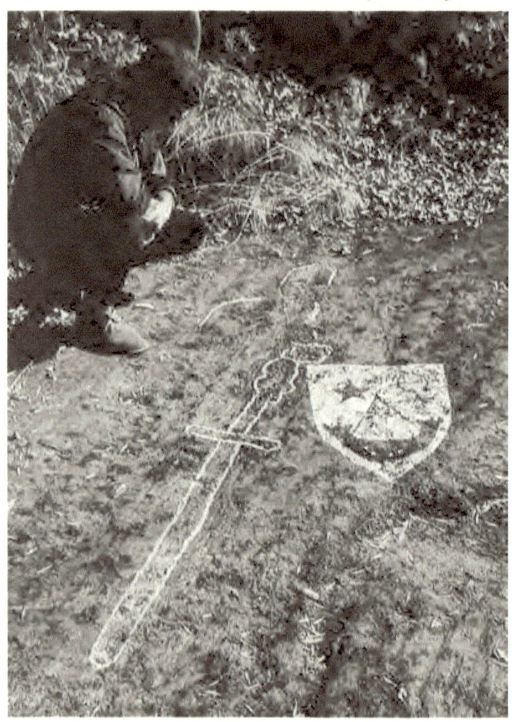

Figure 27: The Westford Knight petroglyph. ***Photo courtesy of Mead Stapler.***

The effigy purports to depict the helmet of a medieval knight, a shield containing the coat-of-arms of the Gunn family, a sword, a falcon, and a rosette (Figure 27). The sword contains a break in its blade to commemorate the death of the knight, and the rosette serves as a rest for his lance. The effigy is made up of many holes punched into the rock by a pointed metal tool. The history of the effigy figure and its interpretation as that of a knight has been a source of controversy and debate for many decades.

The Westford effigy was reportedly known to residents of Westford in the 1880s, who believed it to be an Indian carving.[6] Except for the local people, the site remained unknown for the next sixty years. In about 1945 the site was visited by Malcolm Pierson and William Goodwin, who photographed the alleged face and sword. This photo was published in Goodwin's 1946 book *The Ruins of Great Ireland in New England*.[7]

In 1954, the site came to the attention of Frank Glynn, an avocational archaeologist from Connecticut. After several years of study, Glynn concluded that the punch marks represented a "knight's face in a bassinet helmet with pendant neckmail of the kind in use in A.D. 1360-1390."[8] He also found the "handle of a knight's great sword, or shield and crest" on the rock. Glynn further reported that geological studies of the punch marks were made in 1957. One of the investigators at that time, Austin Hildreth, concluded that the "sword and profile on the rock ledge in Westford is probably five to eight hundred years old." Glynn also stated that repeated efforts were made to find the burial site of the knight but were unsuccessful.

In 1960, the Westford Knight effigy site was carefully examined by Dr. William S. Fowler of the Massachusetts Archaeological Society. Fowler discerned numerous pits on the shale outcrop which he said were the result of natural erosion.[9] He stated that "as there are no clear-cut peck marks discernible to outline the blade [of the sword], inference of its presence is untenable." However, Fowler concluded that the so-called hilt of the sword was instead the "outline of a tomahawk about 15 inches long." These markings, he said, depicted an early eighteenth century iron tomahawk that dated from between 1700 and 1750.

Do the punch marks on the rock represent the figure of a fourteenth century knight? Are they natural pits in the rock surface? One explanation may be found in the glacial striations that are evident on the rock, along with water-worn grooves and an irregularly pitted surface. I conclude that the marks are the result of natural forces such as weathering, exfoliation, abrasion and erosion.

UPPER PALEOLITHIC ART IN NEW YORK

A large boulder bearing carved images reminiscent of the famous Paleolithic cave paintings of Lascaux in the Dordogne region of France was discovered at Sneden's Landing in the hamlet of Palisades in Rockland County, New York. This boulder was found near a driveway leading to a private home on Corbett Lane, a residential area on the west side of the Hudson River in this southeastern New York community.

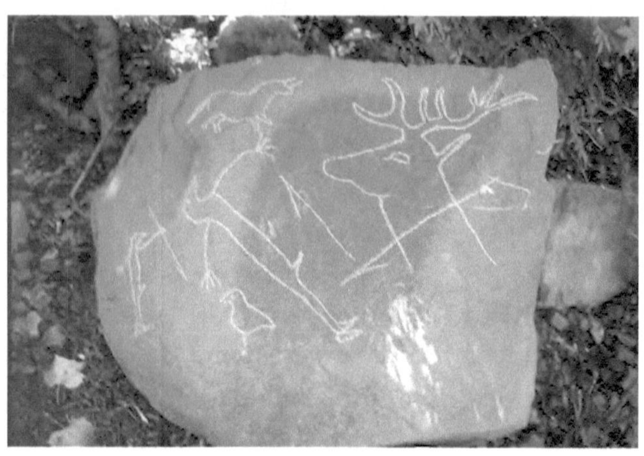

Figure 28: The Palisades, New York, petroglyph. ***Photo courtesy of Herbert C. Kraft, 1993.***

This petroglyph was examined by archaeologist Herbert C. Kraft, who described the rock type as Palisades's diabase.[10] It measured 4 feet 2 inches (127 cm) in length, 2 feet (60 cm) in thickness and 4 feet (122 cm) in height. Seven images were incised at a depth of ¼ of an inch (6 mm) into the flat surface of the stone. Kraft noted that the identification of the figures was "unmistakable."

The head and neck of a deer with antlers, facing left, are portrayed near the right edge of the rock (Figure 28). A barbed shaft of what appears to be a spear is incised across the neck of the deer. In the center of the stone is the outline of an ithyphallic man who appears to be falling backwards. The most interesting features about this man are that he has a bird's head and four-fingered, bird-like hands. In essence, he is a bird from the waist up and human from the waist down. Between the deer and the man is another spear. Above the ithyphallic man is the outlined figure of a "horse" with a pendulous belly with two horns extending forward from its head. Below the falling man is the outlined figure of a bird, facing left, which is attached to a shaft. At the left side of the rock is a standing ithyphallic man that is holding a spear in his left hand. This figure is smaller than the falling man and also has a bird-like head.

Kraft observed that the images on the stone were skillfully executed, and he identified them as reproductions of the Lascaux pictographs.[11] The figure of the horse with its two horns is virtually identical to the so-called "unicorn" painted on the wall in the Hall of the Bulls section within Lascaux. The term unicorn is, of course, inaccurate, since the animal has two horns. This part of the cave was nearest to the surface. The falling man is identical to the one in the shaft section in Lascaux and is positioned in front of the deer's head. At Lascaux, however, the falling man is in front of a bison whose head is lowered, appears to be charging, has entrails hanging from its belly, and has a spear across its body. The bird on the staff below the falling man is also similar to the one in Lascaux. David Lewis-Williams has interpreted this scene (falling man, bison, bird on shaft) at Lascaux as a "transformation by death."[12] That is, the death of the man parallels the death of the bison and as they die the man "fuses with one of his spirit helpers, a bird." Lewis-Williams concluded that these paintings in the Lascaux shaft represent the "essence of Lascaux shamanism."[13]

The panel of Paleolithic art at Sneden's Landing was most likely produced by Jane Wasey, a sculptor who once lived on Corbett Lane.[14] It was made sometime prior to 1980 by this artist, who reportedly carved other stones in the area, and was created simply to beautify the neighborhood.

ESOPUS ISLAND

In July 2003, I canoed on the Hudson River along with several colleagues and two guides to Esopus Island, located in mid-river about six miles south of Kingston, New York. The purpose of our journey was to search for carvings in stone and painted graffiti left here by many visitors to this lonely outpost. We also ventured here to search for evidence of former American Indian habitation or use of the island and to examine the mysterious remains of a stone face.

Esopus Island, which is officially part of Dutchess County, is a small and narrow strip of land in the Hudson, a rocky outcrop that is aligned north to south as it rises above the river. It is wooded, uninhabited, and is less than one-half-mile long and about 330 feet wide. The bedrock consists of Auston Glen graywacke and shale, a thin- to medium-bedded coarse dark gray sandstone.[15]

There are very few places on the island to land. We beached our canoes and kayaks in a sheltered cove on its west side and began our search. A steep cliff, which had a mysterious and dangerous appearance, rose out of the water on the east side of the island and bore evidence of painted graffiti on its vertical surface. From our landing site on the west side our guides led us to a small rock outcrop located about twenty feet from the west side of the island. The tide was low and we were able to wade out to this small ridge, much of which is normally underwater at high tide. Here, we found the beautifully carved profile of the upper part of a human figure (Figure 29). The head faced upriver and had a bulbous nose. A line extended out from the figure's mouth which suggests that the artist intended to indicate a cigar or cigarette. A straw hat covered the top of the head, and the upper torso was round and wide, suggesting a portly individual. The person appeared to be holding a newspaper under the left arm. Overall, the figure measured sixteen inches in height and thirteen and one-half inches in width at its widest point. It was cut with metal tools with great care and accuracy, and probably dated to the 1920s or 1930s. The cartoon-like figure probably represented the comedian W. C. Fields, since photographs of Fields often show him wearing a straw hat, having a bulbous nose and scowl on his face, a cigar in hand, and a well-endowed stomach, characteristics that are all present in the carving.

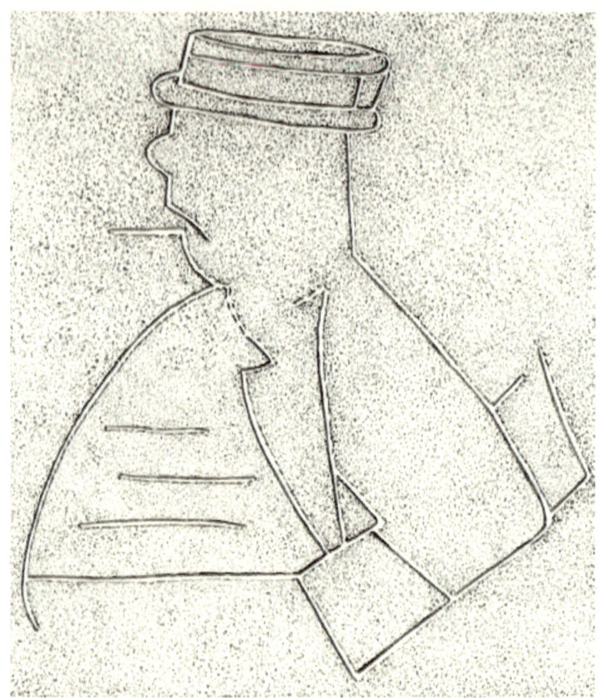

Figure 29: Incised human figure on Esopus Island, New York. ***Drawing by T. Fitzpatrick.***

Further south on the west side of the island we found a carving of a ship's steering wheel (Figure 30). The wheel had eight handles, measures thirteen inches in diameter, and was also cut with metal tools. This image may have been made to commemorate the wreck of the steamboat *Port Comfort* on a rock nearby that occurred around 1919. During World War I, the federal government ordered the removal of all navigational aids from the river as a preventative measure to thwart any enemy ships from entering and traveling upriver with ease. The steamboat was reportedly operating in a fog when its captain decided to turn to seek shelter at a Hyde Park dock on the east side of the Hudson. Unfortunately, the boat ran aground on rocks just north of Esopus Island. The wreck remained here until 1928, when it was removed from the rocks.

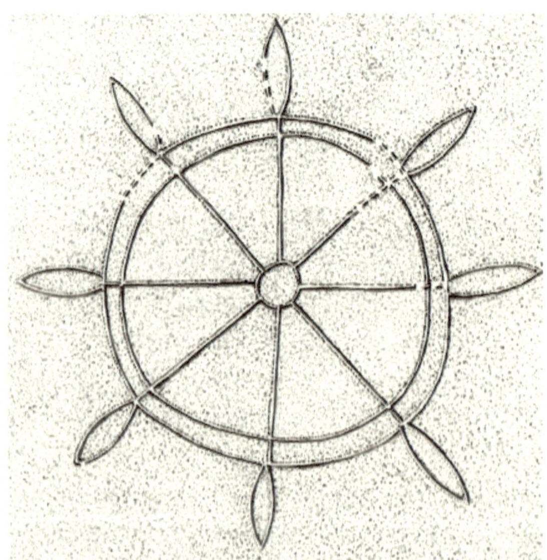

Figure 30: Carving of a ship's steering wheel on Esopus Island, New York. ***Drawing by T. Fitzpatrick.***

Numerous names, dates, and initials had been carved into the rock surfaces, particularly on the west side of the island. Many of them dated to the late nineteenth and early twentieth centuries. However, one earlier date was found: "1711" was incised into the rock at the water's edge and is covered with patina that suggests it is genuinely old and not a recent carving. The question arose as to who carved this solitary date and why.

As we explored the island, following narrow footpaths through the woods, we came upon a low stone fence. The fence ran east to west across the middle of the island. Another short segment extended north to south along a ridge that paralleled the west side. The southern half of the island appeared to have been cleared of loose surface rock. Perhaps these fences were built to delineate a property division on the island or, more likely, to serve as an enclosure for foraging animals.

The Indians were here before the white man came upon this place. We found a worked piece of black chert rock that suggests a knapper was working here making stone tools. Following the discovery of the river by Henry Hudson in 1609, Esopus Island was very likely visited by early Dutch and English settlers and later by Euro-Americans in the eighteenth, nineteenth and twentieth centuries who left their marks or imprints on the island's landscape.

ANTHROPOMORPHIC FIGURES IN FAIRFIELD, VERMONT

A human figure of large proportions is carved on a slanting section of exposed bedrock located on the town line between East Fairfield and Bakersfield in Franklin County, Vermont. The image is massive in appearance and nearly complete except for the feet, which are absent. The figure measures about 4 feet (1.2 m) in height by 5.6 feet (1.7 m) in maximum width (Figure 31). The head, shoulders, and arms of the image are cut deeply into the rock. Its arms are bent at the elbows and extend sideways from the body. Each hand has five fingers, and a lightly carved arrow extends vertically from the figure's right

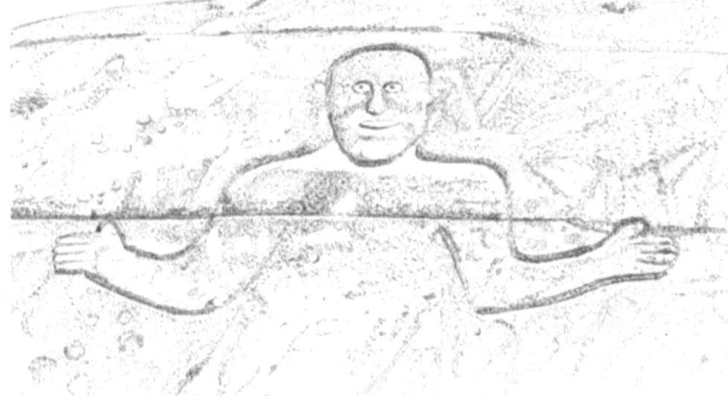

Figure 31: Carved human figure on rock ledge in East Fairfield, Vermont. ***Drawing by T. Fitzpatrick after photo by Warren Dexter.***

hand. The facial features, eyes, nose, and mouth, are also delicately carved into the rock. This petroglyph was reported to the Vermont Division for Historic Preservation (D.H.P.) in 1977. The D.H.P. report states that this fine anthropomorphic figure was carved between 1965 and 1970 by a local "power company meter reader during his lunch break and as he was so inclined."[17]

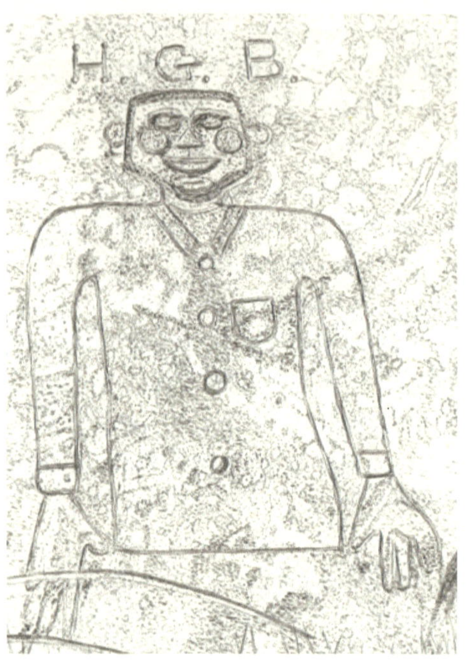

Figure 32: Carved human figure on rock outcrop in Fairfield, Vermont. ***Drawing by T. Fitzpatrick after photo by Warren Dexter.***

A second human figure is carved on a small rock outcrop located near a private home on a dead-end road in Fairfield, Franklin County, Vermont. The rock outcrop has a flat inclined surface that served as the "canvas" or panel for this carving. The head of the figure is sculpted deeply and boldly into the rock; it is somewhat rectangular and has prominent eyes, nose and mouth (Figure 32). The torso, on the other hand, consists of simple and narrow incised lines. The figure appears to be wearing a shirt or jacket, as suggested by "cuffs" on its wrists, collar, buttons, and what appears to be a pocket over its left breast. The lower part of the body is absent. According to the D.H.P. records the image was carved in 1949 by a local "boy" named Howard Bovat, whose initials are carved above the head of the figure.[18] The purpose or meaning of this carving is unknown. It is another example of a recently carved human-like figure that may someday be rediscovered and ascribed to some exotic origin, when clearly this is not the case.

THE MOUNT MINERAL MONOLITH

A human form in a squatting position, sculpted within a bell-shaped outline on a granite slab, stands along a wooded road on Mount Mineral in Shutesbury, Franklin County, Massachusetts, northeast of Springfield. This enigmatic carving was allegedly found around 1942 "partially down the hill's north side and a foot and one half deep by two men tilling the soil for a potato patch."[19] A later account of the stone's discovery stated that the "picture" of the human figure was noticed in 1950 by Henry Towne, then owner of the property, when

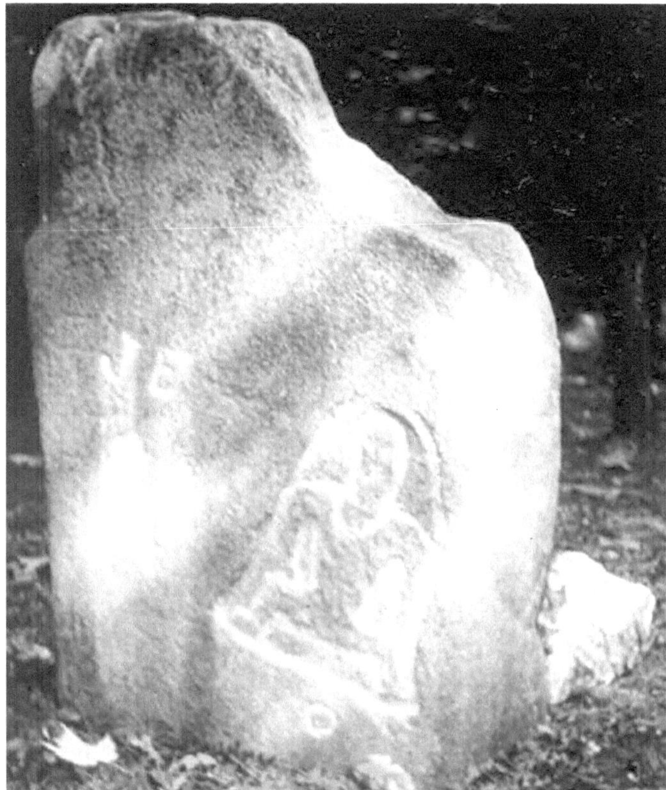

Figure 33: A human figure in a squatting position, Mount Mineral, Shutesbury, Massachusetts. *Photo by E.J. Lenik 1962.*

the rock was turned over by Towne and his assistant. It was found "buried in the earth over one of the embankments" and then brought up the hillside and placed in an upright position near the place where it was unearthed.[20]

I visited the site in 1995 to examine and assess this unusual carving and its environmental setting. The monolith stands 3 feet (90 cm) high above ground level. It is 2 feet (60 cm) wide and 7 inches (18 cm) thick. The stone is a naturally-shaped slab. There is no evidence to indicate that it was a quarried piece of stone, but a piece has been broken off its top right corner. The squatting figure is carved in bas-relief (low) on the flat surface of the rock (Figure 33). Below the human form is a small carved circle, and to the left are the initials "JE." Three lightly-incised letters are located below the first set on the stone. Although difficult to make out, they appear to represent the letters "JHT." A lightly carved arrow, pointing upward, is carved at the top left side of the stone. All of the figures are carved at an oblique angle relative to the perpendicular position of the stone. R.E. Stone indicated that the letters were carved by the potato men that found the slab, while de Lesdernier stated that the initials were those of Mr. Towne and his assistant. [21, 22]

Mount Mineral has had a long and colorful history as a health resort. Mineral springs were first discovered on the mountain in the early 1800s. The site was first known as "Horse Hill Springs," named after a horse that was lost here in the fall of one year and found in the spring of the next. The efficacy of the spring water became established when an Ephrain Pratt claimed to have been cured of cancer after drinking it. A resort hotel was built near the healthful springs in about 1840 and its business flourished for two decades. However, by the 1860s, the popularity of the resort had significantly declined.[23]

In 1865, Charles A. Perry, a retired Methodist minister, purchased the mountaintop property, renovated the existing hotel, and named the site Mount Mineral. His claims of miraculous cures caused the business to grow, but tragedy struck when the hotel was destroyed by fire in 1873. A new structure called Mount Mineral Springs House was subsequently built on the site. Reports of the curative power of the springs continued to spread, and as many as five hundred patients came here during the summer months. However, the craze for pure and healthful water soon waned and the Mount Mineral Springs Company abandoned the hotel in 1876. Empty and neglected, the hotel burned down again in 1880, and for the next sixty years the site gradually returned to its natural state and was generally forgotten.

In 1945, the Mount Mineral property was purchased by Henry Towne, who located the abandoned springs and restored them to use.[24] Towne built a house, which he called Birch Cabin, on what used to be the site of the porch of the old hotel. The place evidently continued to be used as a health resort, and by 1986 Mineral Mountain became known as Temenos, a retreat or place of seclusion for people seeking spiritual renewal. It currently serves as a conference center and retreat located on seventy-eight acres.

Over the past one hundred fifty years, numerous visitors to the health resort have left their own personal marks on the landscape. Along the woods road near the hotel site are rock outcrops that contain names, initials, and dates, all physical records of some of the past visitors to Mount Mineral. Some are carved deeply into the rock, while others are lightly incised. One inscription, in particular, contains letters and the date "1851" within a rectangular outline. The site of these inscriptions is called the "Autograph Ledges." A lye leaching stone is located at the site of the old hotel, and a carving of a horse's head and neck, along with a name, graces another rock surface nearby.

More recent artwork can be found near the hotel site. Earl Murdock, a friend of Henry Towne, carved a "horseman leading an animal" and a human figure with upraised arms on bedrock surfaces along the entrance road to the site. A third figure representing Jizo, a Buddhist saint, was beautifully carved in 1985 by Ellen Sidor on a vertical rock surface to the east of the road (Figure 34).[25]

The sculpted figure of a squatting human mentioned previously was adopted as a logo by the New England Antiquities Research Association in the 1960s. It has been suggested that this carving was produced by Irish monks in the tenth century, with the figure resembling a Celtic god, and that the carved bell shape is similar to bells used by Christian monks in Ireland.[26] I reject this interpretation. I believe the figure to be a Euro-American carving that dates to the health resort era, most likely the first half of the twentieth century. The figure, sculpted with metal tools, fits the tradition and practice of carving images and inscriptions at the site by visitors who came here to be cured of their ills.

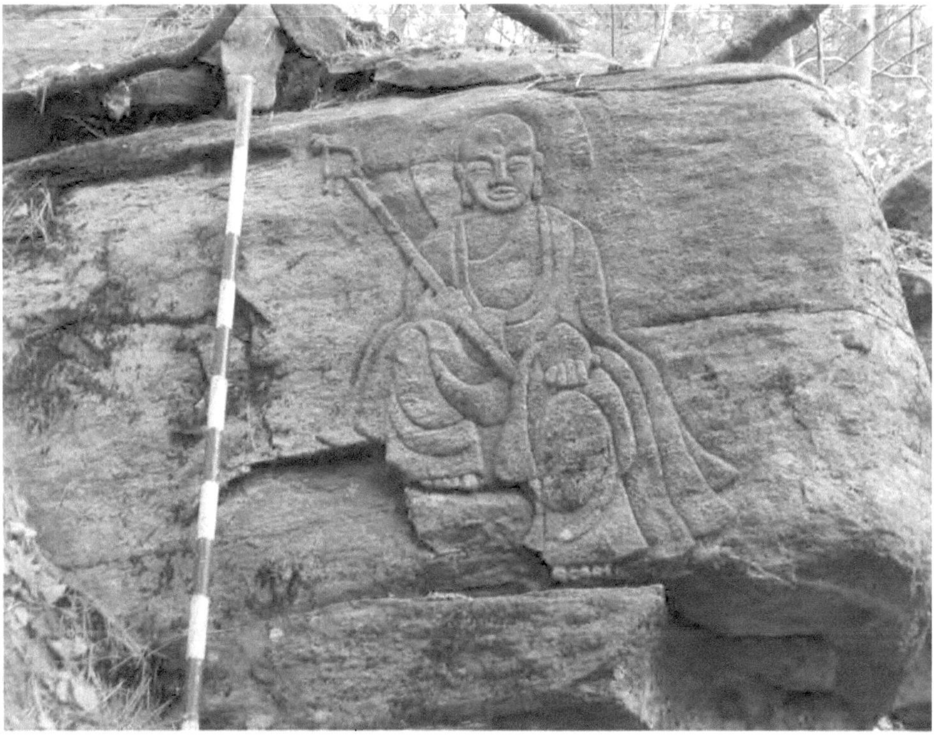

Figure 34: Sculpted figure of ZIZO, a Buddhist saint, on Mount Mineral, Shutesbury, Massachusetts. ***Photo by Colgate Gilbert, 2004.***

FACES IN STONE

One of the most impressive features of historic period rock art in New England has been the tendency of "artists" to sculpt or engrave human faces on rock. As I examined such carvings, several questions came to mind. Why were they carved on rock, which is a tough artistic medium? The obvious answer is permanency. What are the intended meanings of these images? It appears that the meaning ingrained within them is communication. The questions then become to whom would they communicate, what exactly do the faces communicate, and for what purpose? Lastly, who were the mysterious carvers? We may never know the answers to these queries, but these images are prominent indicators, and have become part of the history and culture of the Northeast region. The following are some examples of this type of rock art.

SEARSMONT, MAINE

A "massive" sculpted face, carved in "native bedrock" was found in Searsmont in Waldo County, Maine (Figure 35).[1] It clearly appears to have been chiseled from its bedrock source, as indicated by the jagged edges of the stone block. Barry Fell reported that it was part of a larger work, with the body remaining on its original site.[2] The face has sculpted eyes, a wide, flaring nose with curving nostrils, and a mouth with thick lips. The top of the head depicts what Fell describes as two "swamp-oak leaves" and an "acorn." Barry Fell has suggested that the face has "Druidic connotations and may be an example of Irish Celtic art." I discard this interpretation. There is no evidence to support such a claim. Metal tools were used to sculpt the face. Its sharp lines and bold features indicate a minimum of wear or exposure to the elements which suggest it was produced in more recent times. The carving is more likely the work of a local stone carver, quarryman, or artist who attempted to portray a classical-appearing figure.

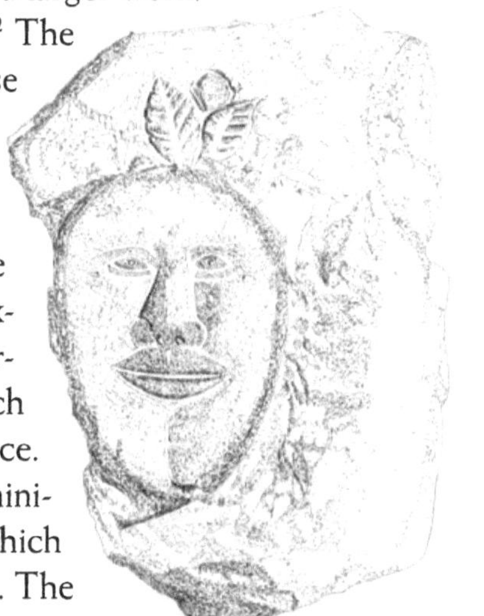

Figure 35: Sculpted face found in Searsmont, Maine. ***Drawing by T. Fitzpatrick.***

GREAT CHEBEAGUE ISLAND

Great Chebeague Island (locally pronounced Sha-big) lies two-and-one-half miles off the coast of Maine opposite the city of Yarmouth. One of the largest islands in Casco Bay, it is four-and-one-half miles long and one mile wide. The Indians who first inhabited the island gave it its name, which meant "island of many springs."

During the 1600s, several Europeans visited and explored the island, but never established a settlement here. At this time, Chebeague was considered to be a "colony of the Royal Crown of England," and its first proprietor was Sir Francis Gorges. Beginning around 1650, ownership of the island changed several times as parts of it were purchased by different individuals. The first permanent white settler on the island was Ambrose Hamilton, who built a home on its north end in 1760.[3] Soon, after other families settled on the island, most of whom were fishermen.

By 1850, a significant transportation industry had also established itself on the island. This was the rock sloop industry, which was more commonly referred to as stone slooping. A family industry, stone sloops hauled heavy loads of ballast rock to shipyards in Casco Bay, and granite blocks and other building stone from quarries on the coast of Maine to railroads in New York, Boston and other major eastern ports.

These stone sloops were unique. They were about sixty feet long and twenty feet wide, had only one sail, and were flat-bottomed, which gave them a shallow draft and thus an ability to dock close to shore. However, by the end of the nineteenth century, stone slooping had come to an end, as new and inexpensive building materials replaced the use of stone and steam power replaced the wind propulsion of sailing ships.

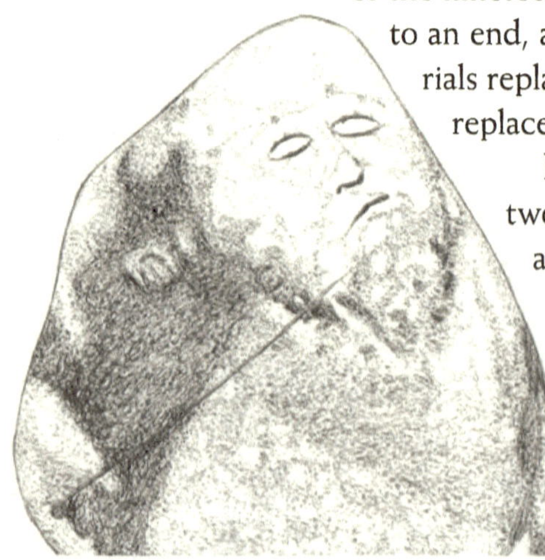

Figure 36: Carved stone face on a boulder, Great Chebeague Island, Maine. ***Drawing by T. Fitzpatrick.***

During the late nineteenth and early twentieth centuries, boarding houses and hotels were built on the island. Soon some thirty boarding houses and hotels were in operation, and the island's economy switched to tourism. Fishing and farming declined as homesteads were transformed into cottage developments as summer visitors came to the island. Later, during World War II, Chebeague Island was occupied by the U.S. Army, with as many as four hundred troops stationed here in support of the North Atlantic ship refueling station on nearby Long Island.

In 1941 two boys at play removed layers of moss from a large boulder and discovered a "life-sized" face on its top surface.[4] Apparently sculpted with considerable skill, the stone face had well defined eyes, a nose with nostrils, and a slightly downturned mouth (Figure 36). This carved stone face was reportedly known to fishermen who lived on the island in the eighteenth century but its exact location was lost until its rediscovery in 1941.

The sculpted stone face was studied by James Whittall of the Early Sites Research Society of Rowley, Massachusetts. Whittall concluded that it was carved by a "Celtic explorer sometime before 1000 A.D." He noted that "the artistic style of the carving [was] similar to that of Celtic artwork."[5] I eliminate this interpretation as being highly speculative and lacking in evidence. It was most likely carved by a Maine stonecutter-sculptor, as its features or style are not unlike others found elsewhere in New England.

CORINTH, VERMONT

A standing stone exhibiting a carved face is located in a place called Chubb Hollow near Corinth in Orange County, Vermont (Figure 37). The stone is situated in the middle of the hollow, which is approximately 50 feet (15 m) across and basically flat. A small hill lies to the east and another to the west. The land was once cleared, probably as pasturage, but is now wooded. A forest-lined road and a stone fence are located about 300 feet (90 m) south of the standing stone. According to local tradition the existence of the standing stone with its carved face has been known since the 1890s.

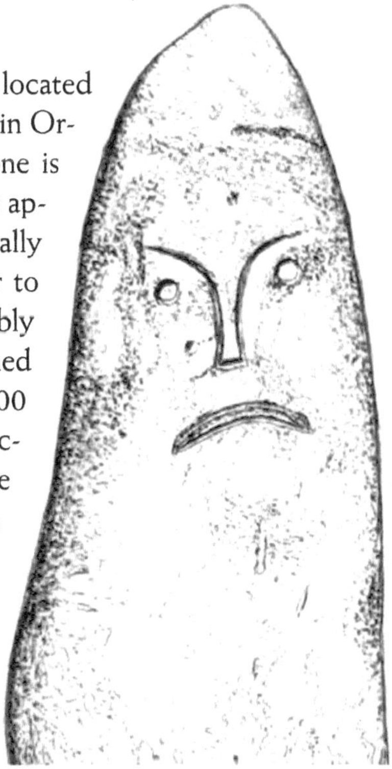

Figure 37: Standing Stone with carved face, Corinth, Vermont. ***Drawing by T. Fitzpatrick after photo by E.J. Lenik 1980.***

The standing stone consists of soft shale, and its basic shape apparently attracted the carver and ultimately influenced the design and layout of the face. The stone measures 28 inches (70 cm) in height. The nose and mouth were cut into the stone; the incised lines of the nose are 1/4 inch

(7 mm) wide. The eyes are sculpted depressions that measures ¼ inch (7 mm) in diameter. The down-turned mouth suggests a stern look or an expression of displeasure. The carved face on the stone faces south, and the features on the stone were carved with considerable skill.

The face with its sad expression probably dates to the late nineteenth century. The fact that it was carved on soft sedimentary rock, which has a tendency to erode, easily precludes any great antiquity for the carving. Perhaps it was sculpted by a hardscrabble farmer to express his difficulty in working the land.

PLAINFIELD, VERMONT

A carved stone face was found during excavations for a house foundation in Plainfield, Washington County, Vermont (Figure 38).[6] The face was carved into a rough, somewhat rectangular stone block. It is outlined by a wide and deep cut, with its features in bold relief. The eyes consisted of horizontal slits, the nose is basically triangular in shape, and the mouth was formed by a straight horizontal cut. The expression on the face suggested a sleeping or deceased person.

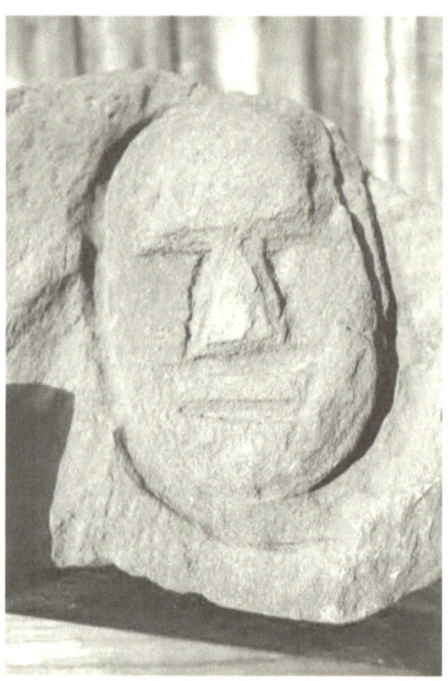

Figure 38: Carved stone face found in Plainfield, Vermont. *Photo by E.J. Lenik 1980.*

I examined this specimen in December 1980, and concluded it was sculpted with metal tools. The reverse side of the rock contains a crudely shaped spoon-like design that was cut quite deeply into the rock in some places. Punch and chisel marks are clearly evident on this figure. The face is on a quarried block of stone and is most likely the work of a local stonecutter sometime in the twentieth century.

PUTNEY, VERMONT

A round disc-like stone containing a carved face was found in 1927 in Putney in Windham County, Vermont (Figure 39).[7] The context of this find is unreported. The face has a three-dimensional quality with its sculpted eyebrows, eye sockets and nose, and a thick-lipped, open mouth which is slightly

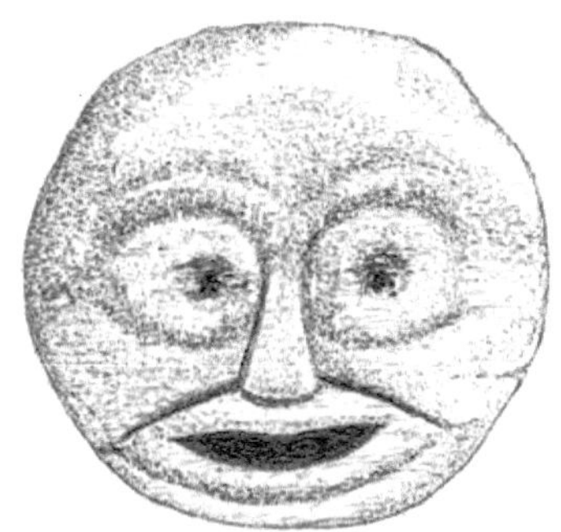

Figure 39: Disc-like stone with carved face found in Putney, Vermont. *Drawing by T. Fitzpatrick.*

upturned. At the time of its discovery, the stone was reportedly patinated, which suggested to later researchers that "it was not of recent origin."[8] The face bears a strong resemblance to classic period Maya stone and pottery faces found in Mesoamerica.[9] Perhaps this carving is an example of a Vermont Yankee's attempt at humor by creating a local oddity.

VERGENNES, VERMONT

In 1979, the Vermont Division for Historic Preservation received a report of a carved human face on a limestone ledge located in a pasture some five hundred to six hundred feet northwest of High Street in Vergennes, Vermont (Figure 40). The discovery was made by a young man who stated that the "etching was found while removing dirt and grass to look at fossils."[10] A small petroglyph and a rough sketch map showing the location of the site accompanied the report.

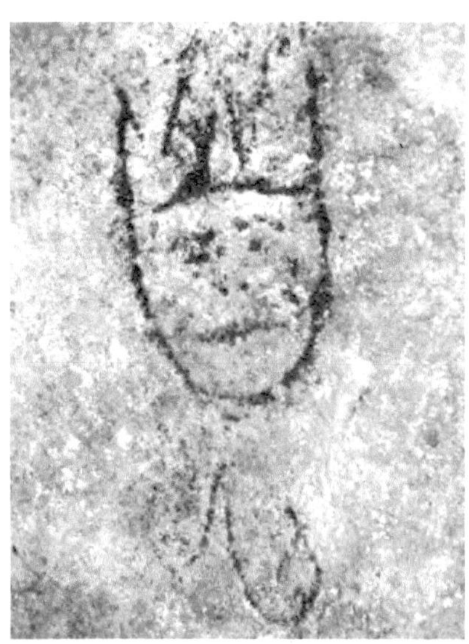

Figure 40: Carved face with spiked headdress or crown, Vergennes, Vermont. *Photo by Douglas Frink 2003.*

In the course of my search for information regarding this petroglyph, I contacted Douglas S. Frink, Principal Investigating Archaeologist with the Archaeology Consulting Team, Inc., in Essex Junction, Vermont for research assistance. In September, 2003, Frink and his associates located the Vergennes face and reported the following details:

> The [petroglyph] panel is a 20+/- foot exposed outcrop trending NE-SW, with a strike up to the south of 3% and a dip down to the west of 4-5%. The enclosed wide view of the panel (taken from the north facing south) shows only the northern half of the panel—the southern half is heavily pitted due to erosion of the surface carbonates. The northern half is surprisingly smooth for dolomite,

> although there is no indication that there was any surface preparation prior to making the glyph. Although we did not clear the entire panel, we did clear the portion that is relatively smooth and suitable for its purpose. The perimeter of the cleared panel is cracked, fissured and pitted from weathering.

This glyph is the only one we found. We cleaned the debris by hand, and then removed the fine particle soils and humus with a paint brush. We did not attempt to remove the mass growing on and into the glyph.... We avoided any rubbings or other potentially destructive documentation techniques. When done, we replaced the duff and detritus to return it to the conditions found.[11]

The glyph consists of a round face with eyes, eyebrows, two nostrils and a mouth. On top of the head is a four-spiked hat, headdress, or crown. Below the face are two opposing spirals, perhaps representing a cravat or some form of dress shirt. The figure measures approximately 6 to 7 inches (15 to 18 cm) from top to bottom. My analysis of the 1979 and 2003 photos leads me to believe the figure was carved with metal tools. Its presence on a dolomite ledge that is weathering and deteriorating precludes any great antiquity for the carving. It most likely dates to the eighteenth or nineteenth centuries.

A historic marker is present on the north side of High Street just east of a bend in the road that marks the site of the McDonough Settlement. The 1871 F. W. Beers map of the town of Vergennes identifies this location as "the oldest House in Town." The Beers map also shows the location of "The Burial Place of Donald McLintock" to the northeast of the house. This burial site is situated in the vicinity of the petroglyph site; perhaps there is some association between these two features.

BARRE, MASSACHUSETTS

Cradle Rock is located about three miles west of the center of the town of Barre in Worcester County, Massachusetts. Also known as the "Tipping Rock" and the "Rocking Stone," Cradle Rock consists of two boulders—a bottom one sitting on an outcrop of bedrock and another resting on top (Figure 41). The "Map of Barre, Mass.," published in 1835 by William F. Ainsworth, shows the location of the site and identifies it as the "Rocking Stone." The bottom stone contains a sculpted human face.

A fine example of a balanced or perched rock, this natural wonder was described and illustrated in the *Final Report on the Geology of Massachusetts,* which was published in 1841. Professor Edward Hitchcock captioned his illustration as a "Double Rocking Stone in Barre" and noted that it was "a divided block of gneiss which is nearly ten feet high and is so accurately poised upon a ledge of gneiss, that at a little distance it seems as if it could easily be thrown over; but this is no easy matter."[12] Hitchcock's report makes no mention of a carved stone face.

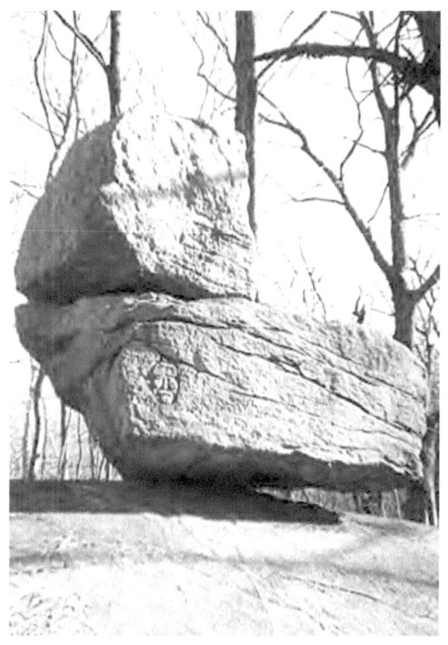

Figure 41: Cradle or Tipping Rock with sculpted human face on lower base stone, Barre, Massachusetts. ***Photo by Paul Grzybowski 2002.***

Several stories have emerged in an attempt to explain how these boulders came to be poised in their position. A WPA account in the 1930s stated that the stone could be rocked slightly by the pressure of the hand. Local Indian lore suggests that it was Manitou, their spirit that controlled the forces of nature, who placed the boulder in that position, and that it functioned as a sacred and ceremonial site. Geologists, on the other hand, state that the boulders were deposited in their positions during the melting and retreat of the last glacier, the Wisconsin, some 15,000 years ago.

In the late nineteenth century, local residents reported that the area surrounding Cradle Rock was an Indian burial ground, and that human remains and artifacts had been found nearby. These claims have not been substantiated.

In 1925, George H. Ellis, owner of the land on which the rock is situated, donated eleven acres, including Cradle Rock, to the town of Barre for a public park. Again, there was no mention of a carved face at this time. The two boulders remain on the park property today but they no longer rock. They were secured in place many years ago by a farmer to discourage trespassers from coming on his land and attempting to move the stone.

Sculpted on the lower or base stone is a human face carved in low relief (Figure 41). The face has distinct eyes, nose, a down-turned mouth, a prominent upper lip and chin, and a top-knot on its head. I suggest that these facial features closely resemble those found on Olmec culture figurines and heads found in Mesoamerica.[13] In my opinion the sculpted face dates to a time after 1925.

Several other images are present on the base rock. To the right of the face the name "SM SMITH" is cut into the rock. Around the corner of the boulder and near the top of its vertical surface is the engraved image of a wagon wheel, complete with a hole representing the hub and eight spokes. On anadjacent bedrock outcrop there is a peace symbol and an equilateral

Maltese cross that is identical to those found on Hopi pottery and rock art in northern Arizona.[14] Carved names and dates are also present on the bedrock and boulders.

TOWN OF HAVERSTRAW, ROCKLAND COUNTY, NEW YORK

In the late 1970s, Russ Smelzer, an employee of AT&T, found a granite cobble containing a carved face near a microwave tower on Jackie Jones Mountain within Harriman State Park in Haverstraw, Rockland County, New York (Figure 42). He found this cobble on a stone fence near the edge of the AT&T property on the mountaintop. It measured 11¼ inches (28.5 cm) in length, 8½ inches (21.5 cm) in width and 4½ inches (11.5 cm) in thickness. The cobble, which was partially broken, has abrasion marks on all surfaces, and in recent years had been used as a doorstop in the AT&T office.

The face on the cobble was incised into the flat surface of the rock. The face is generally round in outline or shape and contains all the usual features: two eyes, nose, mouth and two ears. The broken section of the stone, which probably contained a portion of the right ear, is missing. The face, ears, nose, and mouth are basically simple in appearance, but are made with boldly carved outlines. The eyes, however, are quite detailed, with such elements as eyebrows, eye lashes, and small holes representing the corneas. The nose contains two small holes which I interpret as nostrils. There are ten lines radiating upward from the top of the head, presumably representing hair. There is a small drilled hole 1/2 inch (13 mm) deep and 3/16 of an inch (5 mm) in diameter on the side of the cobble above the face. Close examination of the worked surface leads me to conclude the face was carved with a hammer, chisel, punch, and drill.

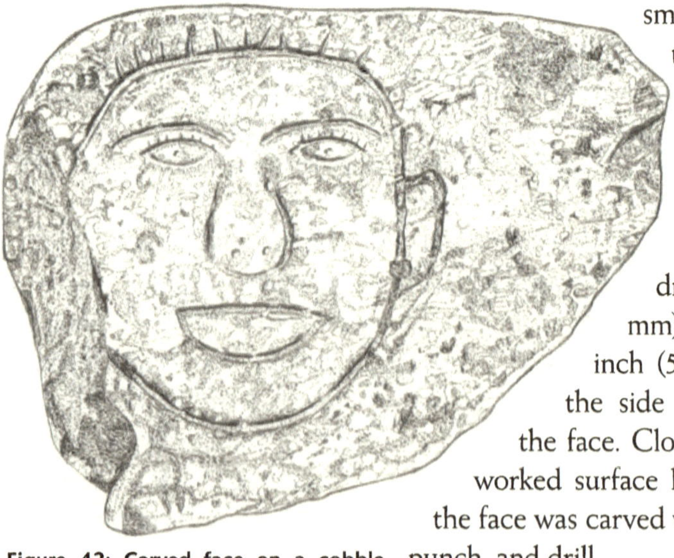

Figure 42: Carved face on a cobble stone found on Jackie Jones Mountain, Harriman State Park, New York. ***Drawing by T. Fitzpatrick.***

My analysis of the carved face also focused on the provenance of this find, i.e., the environmental setting and historic land use of the area. Jackie Jones Mountain has an elevation of 1,276 feet above mean sea level, and lies within the Hudson Highlands physiographic province. The mountaintop was scoured by the last glacier and contains bare rock surfaces and ledges, a thin mantle of soil, and numerous glacially deposited boulders and cobbles. The landscape is wooded and the area is second growth forest with a low understory.

A fire tower stands on the highest point of the mountain. This fire tower was built in 1923 and replaced an older structure on the site. The AT&T microwave tower and operations buildings are located a short distance to the northeast of the fire tower. These structures were built in 1947 during the cold war as a communication facility designed to ostensibly withstand an atomic bomb attack.15 Remnants of two dry stone walls are present immediately southeast of the AT&T structures. These stone walls indicate that an attempt was made to clear the land of boulders and cobbles and that a field was outlined for the grazing or pasturing of animals. A hiking trail extends past the fire tower and AT&T structures while a modern macadam road extends up the mountainside from Gate Hill Road to the microwave tower.

In 1923, George Briggs Buchanan, a corporate officer of the Corn Products Refining Company, which produced Karo® syrup, purchased land on the east side of Jackie Jones Mountain and built a mansion which he called Orak, which is Karo® spelled backwards.[16] The Buchanan estate was extensive and included outbuildings, gardens, and an unusual dining room that simulated a ship's cabin, complete with a rocking motion. The estate was sold to the Palisades Interstate Park Commission in 1947 and the lands were adjoined to Harriman State Park. The mansion continued to be used as a residence by park employees until 1973, at which time it was demolished.

Returning to my discussion of the carved face, I conclude that this petroglyph is a Euro-American rock carving that was probably produced at some time during the early twentieth century. The face is unlike any known American Indian carving of faces or humans that have been found in the Hudson River Valley and nearby regions. It was carved with metal tools and placed on a stone wall, probably by the unknown artist.

I offer one possible explanation for the origin of this carving. The face may have been cut into the cobble by a stonemason employed by George Buchanan in the construction of his mansion. Such a tradesperson would have had the necessary skill, tools, and time to carve the face while working in what was then a remote and sparsely settled area. However, the identity of the carver as well as the purpose of this work of art remains a mystery.

A FINAL WORD

The examples of carved faces described above indicate a tendency of some investigators to attribute several of them to exotic origins. There is no archaeological or substantive historical evidence to support such claims.

Most of the faces were found by chance, that is, in the course of such activities as construction work, hiking, field exploration, or play, as in the instance of boys clearing moss off a rock on Chebeague Island, Maine. Good provenance data are lacking in most cases.

All of the images were carved with metal tools, which suggests that they date to the period following European exploration or settlement in the region. All of them are singular images and not part of a panel of multiple glyphs.

It has been suggested that the carved faces may represent masks created by the various Indian tribes who inhabited the northeastern United States. False face harvest masks have been found in Iroquois country in New York and also in parts of New Jersey.[17] Effigy faces, consisting generally of simple eyes and a nose and/or mouth, and realistically sculpted heads, have been found at scattered sites in the Northeast region, and have been attributed to Indians. However, stone masks as such are unknown and unreported in this particular area. Also, the effigy faces and sculpted heads found on Indian sites are unlike those reported and illustrated here.

In sum, I attribute the carved faces to Euro-American artists who produced them in the nineteenth or twentieth centuries. These works of art were made to communicate some thought or idea to others. Perhaps the carvers of these faces may have attempted to represent them as powerful images in a magical or mysterious place or simply to showcase their talent or skills.

BIRD, FISH, AND ANIMAL MOTIFS

AN EGYPTIAN BIRD AT LITTLE FALLS, NEW JERSEY

A large trap rock boulder stands at the edge of a high bluff on the south side of the Passaic River overlooking the Little Falls, with the fast-flowing river below it. Dark gray to black in color, weathered and patinated, this solitary sentinel surveys this historic river valley and its early industrial remains.

The basalt boulder is 10 feet (3 m) long, more than 5 feet (1.5 m) wide and 4-1/2 feet (1.35 m) in height. To the north across the river is the Passaic Valley Water Commission pumping station and filtration plant in Totowa, New Jersey. Immediately to the south of the rock and at the same elevation is the bed of the former Morris Canal, now filled in and containing the Wanaque Aqueduct. A few feet further south and above this rock art site is Main Street in Little Falls, New Jersey.

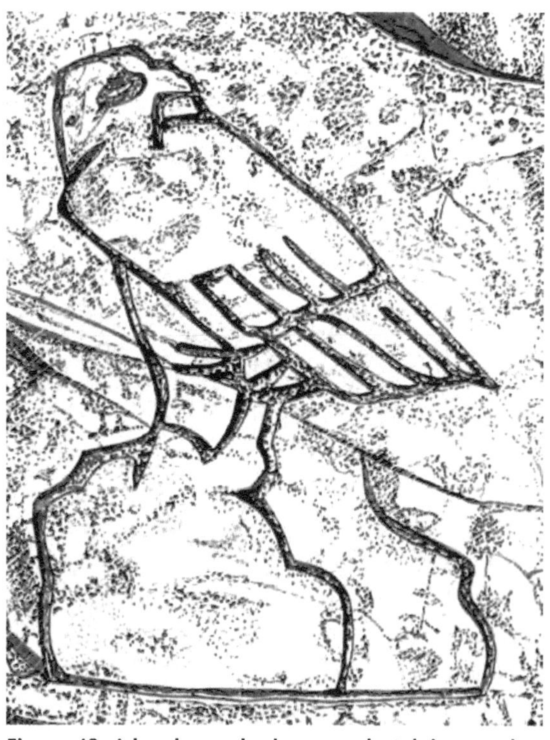

Figure 43: A hawk, perched on a pedestal, is carved on a boulder that overlooks the Passaic River and Morris Canal in Little Falls, New Jersey. ***Drawing by T. Fitzpatrick.***

A hawk is carved on the south face of the boulder (Figure 43). The bird symbol is incised on the east side and midpoint of the boulder. The hawk has been cut into the hard rock surface by a sharp metal tool. This use of metal tools dates it as a historic rather than prehistoric or Native American petroglyph. The design is well executed, and realistically captures the salient features of the bird. The presentation is formal, designed with the bird perched on a pedestal facing west. It is 8 inches (20 cm) in height and 6 inches (15 cm) in overall width. The pose with pedestal is reminiscent of Egyptian bird cartouches or hieroglyphs. Egyptology was an emerging archaeological field of study in the nineteenth century and evoked popular public interest worldwide at that time. The Little Falls hawk was clearly carved by a talented artist, but by whom, when and why?

Unfortunately, we can only speculate regarding the origin of this mysterious carving. Documentary evidence and oral history research have not provided us with any definitive answers. Its location adjacent to the Morris Canal suggests several possibilities: perhaps it was carved by a stonemason during the construction of the canal around 1829, or by a canal traveler during the period of its operation from 1829-1924. The nearby canal aqueduct which crossed the Passaic River was graced with carved stone blocks listing the canal company board members and the dimensions of the canal. These blocks with their decorative filigrees may have inspired our mysterious artist.

The site of the famous brownstone quarries of Little Falls is below the petroglyph site along both sides of the Passaic River. These quarries were in operation from earliest settlement to 1895; perhaps the bird symbol was carved by a skilled quarry worker. On the north side of the Passaic River and opposite the petroglyph site stands the last known building constructed of Little Falls Brownstone—the Passaic Valley Water Commission's 1895 pumping station and filtration plant. Just upstream are the brownstone and brick buildings of the Beattie Carpet Mill, which was in operation from 1840 until the 1970s. The river banks below the petroglyph have been the site of forges, grist mills and woolen mills during the eighteenth and nineteenth centuries. A worker with knowledge of stonework could have been associated with any of these enterprises.

It is likely that we will never know who carved the hawk or why, but we believe it was most likely carved in the nineteenth century at a time when this boulder stood amidst the industrial and commercial bustle that characterized nineteenth century Little Falls. This enigmatic symbol of strength, courage and vision is a fascinating part of Little Falls history. How long has it watched from its sentinel perch?

THE HIGH TOR EAGLE

High Tor, at an elevation of 827 feet (240 m), is a dominant promontory on the northeastern part of Hook Mountain in the town of Haverstraw, Rockland County, New York. Hook Mountain is on the west side of the Hudson River where it widens to form the Tappan Zee; it forms the backdrop to Haverstraw Bay. Named "Verdrietige Hoogte," or "tedious or troublesome point" by the Dutch, it was known to navigators of the Hudson River as a difficult area where contrary winds were often encountered. Geologically, Hook Mountain is the hook-shaped northern terminus of the Palisade ridge of intrusive igneous diabase thrust upward through the Newark sedimentary sandstone during the Triassic era of the Mesozoic age. High Tor and Hook Mountain were notable features on the landscape, landmarks in early surveys of the area, and sources of stone for the industries of the colonies and the new United States.

Henry Hudson's exploratory voyage in the *Half Moon* in 1609, up what is now called the Hudson River, produced the first historic mention of Hook Mountain and the Tappan Zee. Robert Juet, in his journal of Hudson's voyage written the same year, wrote on the fourteenth of September:

> The river is a mile broad. There is very high land on both sides. Then we went northwest a league and a half deep water. Then northeast by north five miles, then northwest by north two leagues, and anchored. The land grew very high and mountainous. The river is full of fish.

On their return voyage on October 1, 1609, at Stony Point, just to the north of Hook Mountain, Juet wrote that "The people of the mountains came aboard us...[an Indian] stole my pillow and two shirts and two bandoleers. Our master's mate shot at him and struck him in the breast, and killed him."

The *Half Moon* soon returned to England, but this incident marked the beginning of hostilities between Indians and Europeans.[1] Subsequent European settlements along the west side of the Hudson River were seriously impeded during the first half of the seventeenth century by the presence of hostile Indians.

High Tor is an evocative name. Ancient tales state that all the evils of the world are imprisoned beneath the peak, ready to spring forth should anyone dig too deeply. The Three Wise Men of biblical times visited here in the past, and ghosts of Indians, Dutch sailors, and lovelorn maidens wander its slopes.[2] High Tor was also the brand given to the first of the good Hudson

Valley wines, but it is no longer produced today. Moreover, it is the name of Maxwell Anderson's verse play *High Tor,* published in 1937, championing the cause of the wilderness conservation against those who would quarry rock away.

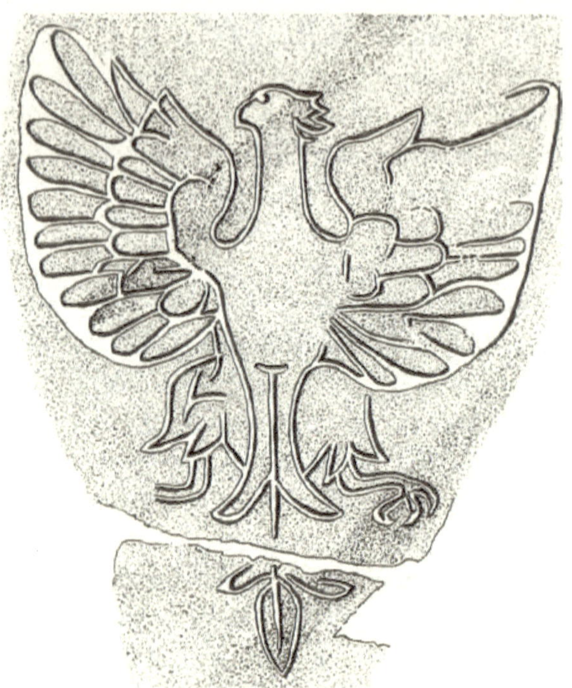

Figure 44: A carved eagle on High Tor mountain, Haverstraw, New York. ***Drawing by T. Fitzpatrick.***

The Dutch capitulation to the English in 1664 brought the land in this area under English control. In 1693, the total population of Orange and Rockland counties amounted to twenty families.[3] By the 1750s the early Dutch, German and Huguenot families at Haverstraw had been joined by a wave of second generation New Englanders.[4] High Tor and Hook Mountain were the scenes of many incidents during the Revolutionary War, when tradition holds that High Tor was both a lookout and beacon site.

Haverstraw Landing was described as having only one house in 1794, but by 1815, a brick-making industry began to thrive here. In its early days, brick-making at Haverstraw consumed many of the oaks and hickories which grew on High Tor and Hook Mountain for the production of charcoal. Afterwards, farmers on the mountainsides grazed Merino sheep on the resulting stump-strewn landscape.[5]

As shipping increased on the Hudson River and a dependable network of roads developed in the interior, more and more people were exposed to the scenic splendors of the Hudson. High Tor and Hook Mountain, as well as other promontories, were depicted in paintings and sketches. The Victorians found in the Hudson River landscape a sublime world made even more precious and romantic in their view by its association with events during the Revolutionary War.

This romantic reverence for the Hudson and its mountains developed along with increasing industrial uses of the area. These two trends clashed in the early twentieth century when the passion for preservation of the scenic splendor was at loggerheads with the rock quarrying interests. In 1900, the Palisades Interstate Park Commission was created, supported by such groups as the American Scenic and Historical Preservation Society. They were able to purchase and preserve much of the Hudson River landscape.

The High Tor promontory is now within High Tor State Park, a part of the Palisades Interstate Park system. It continues to have symbolic meaning to the broader culture and its scenic beauty continues to attract visitors to the site. The carving of an eagle is located on the edge of the mountain overlooking the village of Haverstraw to the north, and the Hudson River to the northeast and east.

The eagle was carved into the hard igneous rock with the use of metal tools. Its placement on the sloping edge of the mountain was difficult and dangerous to achieve. My own recording effort in 2002 was fraught with danger; high winds were a constant threat, and one misstep could have resulted in a fall off the mountain. The Dutch name proved to be an accurate designation.

The eagle petroglyph was beautifully crafted and is indicative of a high level of skill on the part of its maker (Figure 44). It measured 37 inches (94 cm) in length from the top of its head to the end of its tail. It maximum width was 34-1/2 inches (87.5 cm). The width and depth of the incised grooves forming the figure averaged 1/8 of an inch (3 mm). The edges of the wings were carved in low relief. At the time of my visit, the patina over the surface of the glyph had been removed, probably as a result of someone making a mold or casting of the image.

Immediately below the petroglyph were the initials and a date, "W.A. 1867." In fact, the entire top of High Tor is covered with incised, pecked or painted names, initials, and dates. The footings of a former aircraft beacon are also located here.

Who carved this bird, when and why? No information has come to light to answer these questions. We speculate, however, that the eagle's design appears to represent a Prussian/German or Eastern European heraldic figure. It may have been carved in the early decades of the twentieth century.

A WHALE AT LONG POND

Long Pond is located in southeastern Massachusetts within the town of Lakeville in Plymouth County. Together with Assawompsett Lake, Pocksha Pond, Little and Great Quitticus Ponds, it serves as the water supply for the cities of Taunton and New Bedford. These lakes drain northward through the Nemasket River into the Taunton River, which then flows southeasterly into Mount Hope Bay.[6]

In 1675, Long Pond lay within the "Sixteen Shilling Purchase" of land from the Indians.[7] A Massachusetts proprietor's record of 1694 indicates that the lake was called by the Indian name Apponaquet.[8]

Long Pond or Apponaquet is five miles (8 km) long and covers an area of 1,760 acres (704 ha). There are three small islands within the pond, and swamps are present to its south and east. To the northeast it is connected to by a small stream to Assawompset Lake, which then flows through a swampy area.[9] An Indian path previously extended northwest to southeast between the pond and lake near what is now the route of State Highway 105.

A large slab of rock lies along the shore of Long Pond near a summer cottage. This rectangular rock rests on a boulder and measures about 7 feet (2.1 m) by 5 feet (1.5 m). Its long axis is inclined toward the lake and its bottom end is broken, which gives it a wedge-shaped appearance when viewed from the side. A beautifully carved whale is located near an upper corner of the slab (Figure 45). The image is cut deeply into the rock and is patinated. It exhibits features such as a blunt head, mouth, eye and large tail, and measures 2 feet (60 cm) in length and 8 inches (21.4 cm) in height.

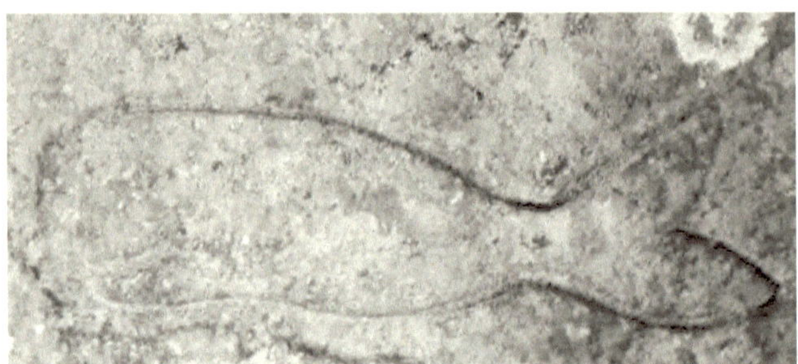

Figure 45: Carving of a whale at Long Pond, Lakeville, Massachusetts. ***Photo by E.J. Lenik.***

The system of ponds and rivers described above provided an excellent inland water route for Indian peoples in their dugout canoes. Long Pond lies some eight miles (12.8 km) north of Buzzards Bay, and is an unlikely location for a whale to be seen and recorded on stone. A local informant has indicated that the whale carving dates to around 1940.[10] The name of the carver and his or her motivation for producing it remain a mystery.

ROCK ART MYSTERIES AT MYSTERY HILL

In 1970, Mystery Hill was designated as a New Hampshire State Historic Site. Shortly thereafter, an official New Hampshire historic site marker was placed on State Route 28 in Salem, describing Mystery Hill as follows:

> Four miles east on Route 111 is a privately owned complex of strange stone structures bearing similarities to early stone work found in Western Europe. They suggest an ancient culture may have existed here more than 2,000 years ago. Sometimes called "America's Stonehenge," these intriguing chambers hold a fascinating story and could be remnants of a pre-Viking or even Phoenician civilization.

Mystery Hill, now commonly referred to as America's Stonehenge, has been the scene of historical, archaeological, and astronomical research since the early 1930s. Located in the town of North Salem, New Hampshire, America's Stonehenge consists of a one acre central complex of stone structures surrounded by woodland, stone walls, and standing stones. The site contains more than thirty-five assembled features, including such designated structures as an oracle chamber, a megaron house, a sacrificial table, watchhouse, processional path and summer solstice sunrise and sunset monoliths. Astronomical and radiocarbon data suggest that the site was constructed about 4,000 years ago.[11]

A large stone chamber, located in the main complex, is referred to as the Oracle Chamber. Inside this chamber area are a number of intriguing stone features, such as a drainage system, a speaking tube that extends outside underneath the sacrificial table, a seat, closet, fireplace flue, wall niches, and a petroglyph carving of a running deer.

The running deer carving, which has also been called an ibex, was discovered in the 1930s by Malcolm Pearson.[12] In his book *The Ruins of Great Ireland in New England* Goodwin described the glyph as an "antlered deer or elk" carved on a stone in the north wall of the chamber's east wing (Figure 46). The figure is a simple outline

Figure 46: A running deer carving inside of "Oracle Chamber" at America's Stonehenge, North Salem, New Hampshire. ***Drawing by T. Fitzpatrick after photo by E.J. Lenik 1975.***

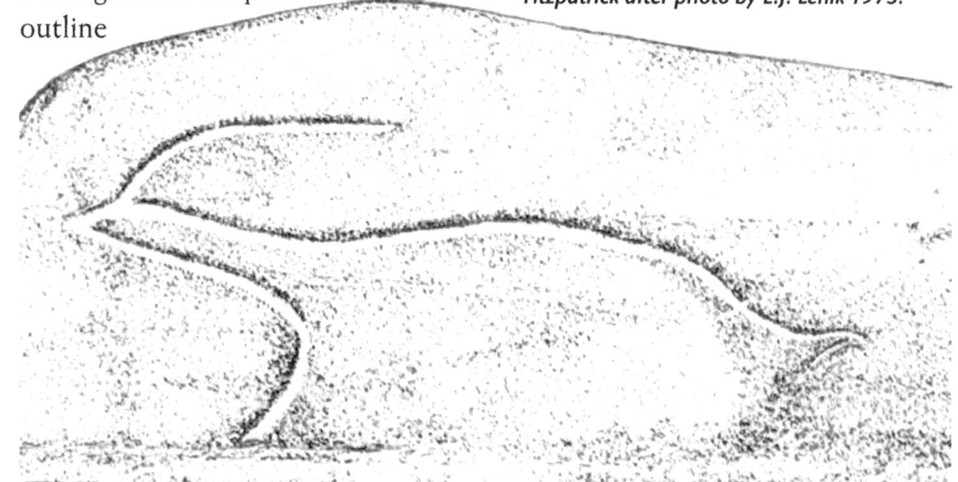

that is cut into one end of a rectangular-cut stone block within the wall. It has a slender head and neck, a single antler, a line delineating its upper body, and another line suggesting a foreleg. The animal faces left and appears to have an active posture that some viewers characterize as "running."

There are differing opinions regarding the origin and nature of the running deer petroglyph. Archaeologist Roland Wells Robbins, who conducted excavations at America's Stonehenge in the 1950s, observed that the figure "may have been inspired by carved animal figures found in northern Europe."[13] A visitor tour guide and souvenir folder characterized the animal as a "sacrificial ram."[14] A lengthy article written by historian Andrew E. Rothovius and published in *The Bulletin of the New York State Archaeological Association* described the figure as a "gazelle-like animal with swept-back horns."[15] A photo of the glyph was published in *Stone Magazine* with a caption that stated "the carving of a deer . . . resembles [a] carving found inside a cave on the island of Malta."[16] Finally, Barry Fell, in his book *America B.C.: Ancient Settlers in the New World*, stated that "it may represent a Druidic costume made from a deerskin, the tines cut away from the antlers...."[17]

Two additional petroglyphs have been found at this location. A small "arrow" is said to be located on the ceiling of the Oracle Chamber.[18] Also, an irregular slab of sandstone reportedly containing two carved figures was found in 1975 by Robert E. Stone, owner of the site, "near the main site."[19] The two figures appear to represent a "bird with [an] eye and heart clearly outlined" and an "arrow."

No one knows by whom, why, or when these petroglyphs were produced at this mysterious place.

DUTCH AND INDIANS, PIGS, AND KIEFT'S WAR

In 2001, I conducted a cultural resources sensitivity survey within the Butler Manor Watershed located in the Princess Bay section of Staten Island, New York. This investigation was in response to the New York Department of Environmental Protection's drainage management plan for the watershed, which included the construction of in-road sanitary wastewater collection lines, wetland enhancement, stream restoration and other drainage improvement features. During the course of this investigation, I discovered a large sandstone boulder lying on the beach of Raritan Bay that contained two petroglyphs and various other names, initials, and dates. Also located along the shore was a series of sculptures created out of rock, earth, driftwood, and other materials, in total numbering more than thirty individual works. These shoreline rock features were situated at the extreme eastern end of the former Mount Loretto property, which is now an undeveloped park owned by the New York State Department of Environmental Conservation.

Mount Loretto, now the property of the Mission of the Immaculate Virgin, was founded on Staten Island in 1882 by Reverend John Christopher Drumgoole, a Catholic priest, as an institution for homeless children. Fr. Drumgoole purchased a large tract of land and built a church, a five story barn, dormitories, and other structures on the property, and eventually developed it into a productive farm. Here some 2,000 children, mostly from the streets of New York City, made their own clothes and shoes, grew their own food, and raised livestock and poultry. At its peak of operation, the institution had three hundred head of cattle and many horses. The cows were sold in 1961 and were the last known remaining herd in New York City.

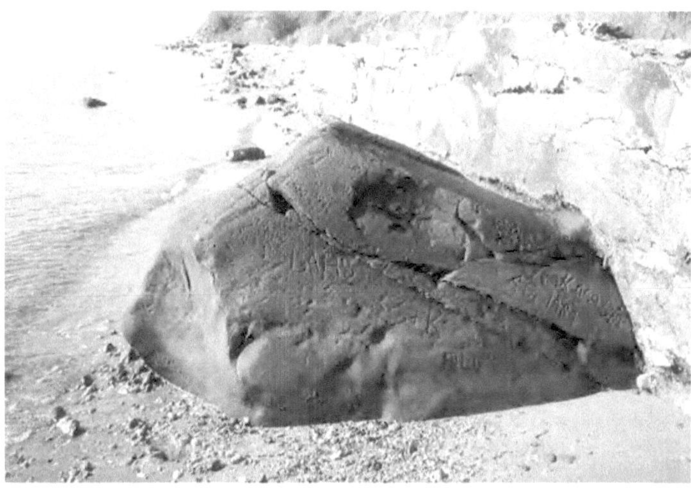

Figure 47: Sandstone rock incorporated into concrete sea wall on south shore of Staten Island, New York. Petroglyphs are situated at lower left side of rock in the photo. *Photo by E.J. Lenik 2003.*

In the year 2000, New York State acquired 194 acres of the Mount Loretto property overlooking Raritan Bay. This land, one of New York City's most spectacular open spaces, is a beautiful landscape of rolling meadows and coastal bluffs. On the red clay bluff overlooking the bay stands the nineteenth century Red Bank Lighthouse with attached keeper's house. The property is now open to the public and is administered by the New York State Department of Environmental Conservation. The former lighthouse keeper's house now serves as a residence for a park ranger.

Lying below the bluff of the former Mount Loretto property and stretching along a section of the beach are the crumbling remains of a concrete bulkhead. Here a red sandstone boulder, partially incorporated into the concrete wall, extends outward toward the water (Figure 47). The visible portion of this rock is 7-1/2 feet (2.2 m) long, 6-1/2 feet (2 m) wide and 4 feet (1.2 m)

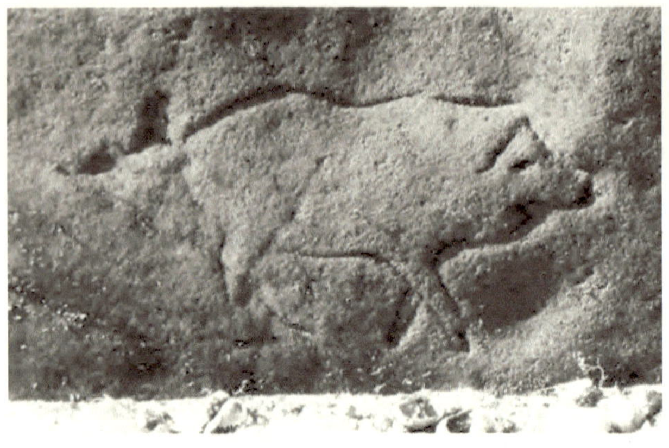

Figure 48: Incised image of a pig on sandstone boulder, Staten Island, New York. ***Photo by E.J. Lenik 2003.***

high. Located near the bottom of its northeast corner is the incised image of a pig (Figure 48). To the right of the pig are two incised lines forming an inverted "V" with the lines crossing at its apex, possibly representing an American Indian wigwam or similar structure (Figure 49).

When I first examined these glyphs in March 2001, they were situated approximately 8 inches (20 cm) above the surface of the sandy beach. At a subsequent visit to the site in October 2003, the glyphs were virtually at ground level, and at high tide most of the petroglyph rock was covered with water. The shifting sand, beach and bluff erosion were slowly encroaching upon and covering the rock and its glyphs.

How were the images of the pig and wigwam carved into the rock? I believe the boulder is in its original location; it certainly has not been moved and was incorporated into the sea wall when that structure was built in the late nineteenth century. This suggests two scenarios. First, the artist-carver was crouching or lying on the beach as he or she incised the figures into the rock. Such a posture for the carver would have been uncomfortable, at best, making the work very difficult. Alternatively, the rock may have been taller and more visible at an earlier time, which allowed the carver an opportunity to produce the images while standing, sitting or kneeling. Whatever the case, it is clear that the sand around the rock is accumulating, and that together with the sea level rise it is slowly being covered.

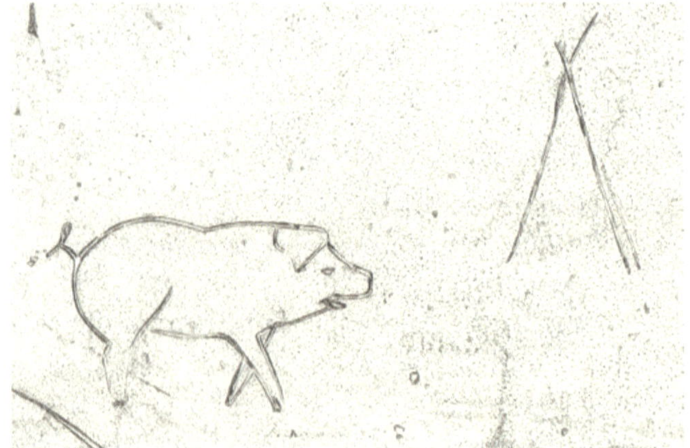

Figure 49: Pig and wigwam (?) petroglyphs on sandstone boulder, Staten Island, New York. Length of pig 7-1/2 inches (19 cm), height of wigwam 6 inches (15 cm). ***Drawing by T. Fitzpatrick.***

Who carved the pig and wigwam and when? I present the following story as a possible answer to these questions.

With the settlement of New Amsterdam by the Dutch in the early 1600s, frequent contact and trade developed between the Indians of southeastern New York, northern New Jersey and the Europeans. During the first half of the century all of Staten Island was occupied by Raritan Indians, a people affiliated with the Lenape or Delaware Indians, as they later became known. The Raritans, like their close relatives in New Jersey, Manhattan and western Long Island, practiced horticulture, hunted, fished, and lived in either single-family, bark-covered wigwams (round or oval dome-shaped structures) or multi-family bark-covered longhouses.

As the Dutch settlement of New Amsterdam grew, the pressure to acquire Indian lands also grew. In 1630, Patroon Michael Pauw, an active Indian trader, purchased part of Staten Island and an area near Hoboken, New Jersey from several Indians for "a certain quantity of merchandise."[20] His attempt to establish settlements on Staten Island failed, and in 1635 he sold his rights to the Dutch West India Company. Shortly thereafter the company sold the land rights to David Pietersz DeVries. In his journal of January 5, 1639, DeVries recorded that "I sent my people to Staten Island to begin to plant a colony there and build."[21]

Soon, farm land became economically more profitable for the Dutch than trade with the Indians, and the drive to encourage the Indian inhabitants to abandon the area increased. As the Dutch settlers bought up more and more land, tensions increased, especially since the Dutch farmers' cattle, goats and pigs wandered freely on the island and frequently trampled and consumed the Indians' gardens. The Dutch, in turn, made frequent complaints that cattle were being stolen by the Indians.[22] During this volatile time the governor of New Amsterdam was Willem Kieft, a man with a strong hatred for the Indians who considered them to be thieves in all cases.

Open warfare soon took place. In 1640, some pigs were stolen from DeVries's plantation on Staten Island by servants of the company.[23] Governor Kieft, however, believed the Raritan Indians were the perpetrators of the crime, and he subsequently sent armed men to a Raritan village to "demand satisfaction" from the Indians. The Indians denied any involvement in the theft, but the well-armed Dutch attacked and killed several of them, captured one of their chiefs, mutilated the body of another, and burned the Indians' crops.[24]

In 1641, the Raritan Indians of Staten island retaliated by killing fifteen settlers and capturing others.[25] With his attack on the Raritans, Governor Kieft began an unprovoked war against the Indians of the lower Hudson River Valley. By 1643 he broadened the war to include most Indians near Dutch settlements in the area, a war that brought devastation to both Indians and colonists for many years.

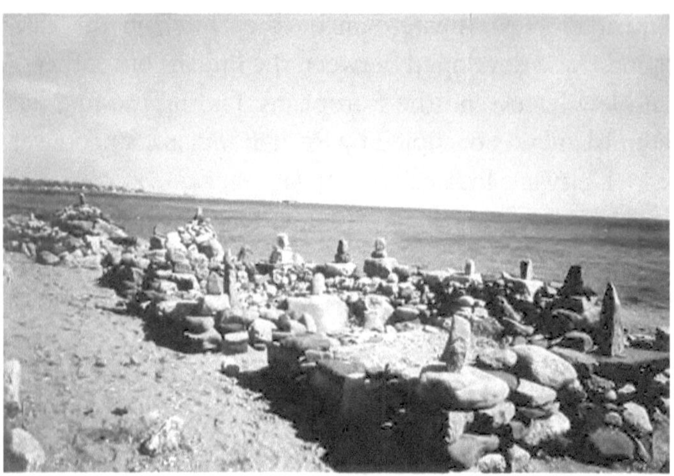

Figure 50: One of several "land art" features on the south shore of Staten Island, New York. ***Photo by E.J. Lenik 2003.***

The historical account of the "pig war" suggests to me the possibility that the pig and wigwam glyphs were carved by an Indian or European settler following the end of the Dutch-Indian wars in 1664. I believe the two realistic images are a form of biographic rock art that recorded an actual historic event. Their current placement on the boulder together with the rising sea level suggests that they are of some antiquity, possibly more than three hundred years old.

Returning now to the series of shore line sculptures, you will notice a number of rock piles and structures as you walk southerly on the beach from the Lemon Creek Park parking area. As you continue they become more frequent, and you eventually find yourself on a path winding through a maze, with some passages leading to the water and some to open air rooms. The rock piles are arranged from driftwood and debris, as well as rocks (Figure 50). Doug Schwartz, a Staten Island resident best known for his day job as the zookeeper in charge of renowned groundhog Staten Island Chuck, began this land art project in 1993.[26] Schwartz uses the flotsam that washes up on the three-mile-long south shore beach to express his environmental concerns in this massive outsider art work that responds to the water and weather, like all man-made shore structures. On any given day, you may encounter him hard at work on his next project, which is supported by grants, and is being documented as it is completed.

ZODIAC ROCK

Webster's Dictionary defines the word "zodiac" as "an imaginary belt or zone in the heavens" within which the constellations, sun, moon, and major planets move during the year. It is a confined area depicted as a circle that "was divided by the ancients into two equal portions called signs." The signs were named for the constellations that were adjacent to them.

On the north side of the York River in Maine is a large rock situated in a sloping hollow that depicts four carved images that have been characterized as zodiac signs[27] (Figure 51). The first image is that of a fish which appears to resemble a shark. Below this figure are two wavy lines. Nearby is another image that is also similar to a fish, possibly an opah. The opah (*Lampris guttatus*) is a large sea fish that is also called the kingfish, the sunfish, and the king-of-the-herrings. Both the shark and the opah are known to inhabit the ocean off the coast of Maine. The final figure is a circle that is divided internally into four equal parts with short lines extending outward from its circumference. The images were engraved into the rock with metal tools and exhibit considerable skill on the part of the artist with their realistic portrayal of fish and circle.

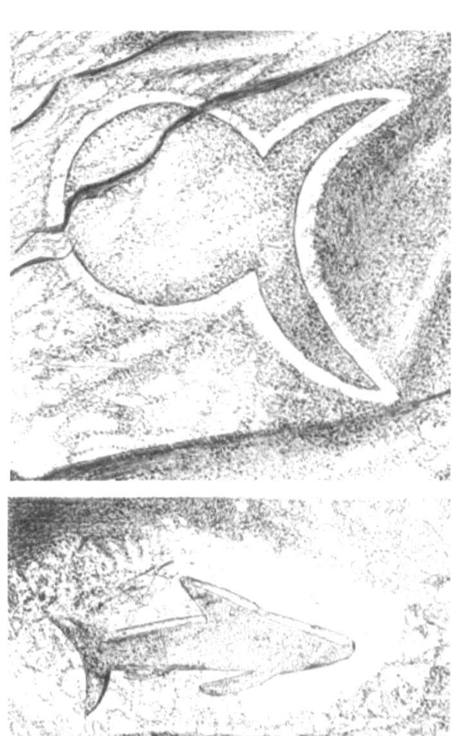

Figure 51: Images on the "Zodiac Rock," York River, Maine. *Drawing by T. Fitzpatrick after photos by G. Mellgren.*

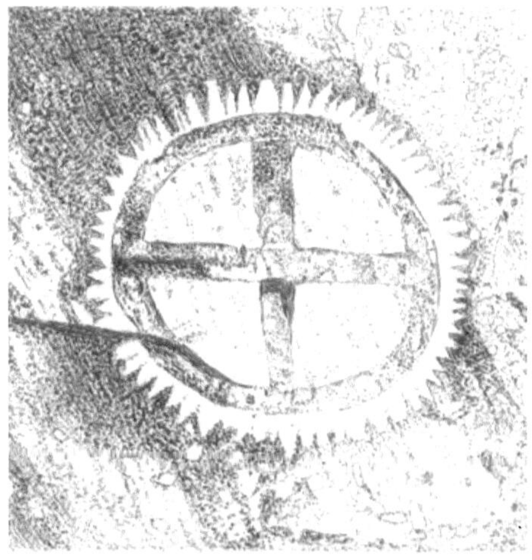

The images on the York River rock may have been intended to represent the signs of the zodiac. In ancient texts and maps the constellation Pisces is portrayed as two fishes accompanied by wavy or zig-zag lines, the latter representing water.[28] However, it is odd that the two fish illustrated on the York River rock appear to be a shark and an opah, unlike any found on typical zodiac maps. The circle or disc may be representative of the four heavenly zones or the four cardinal points of the compass. In modern astrology and astronomy the crossed circle is also used as a symbol for the planet Earth. The lines giving it a halo effect may be indicative of spiritual power or energy.

Guy Mellgren, an avocation archaeologist, examined the rock and its carvings and reported that "the work looks fresh but the location of the stone is puzzling. It looks 19th century to me."[29] Equally puzzling is the name and motivation of the artist-carver.

MORTUARY ART AND MEMORIALS

A "SOUL EFFIGY" PETROGLYPH

A single figure, characterized by its discoverers as a "circle with wings" or "winged disc" was found in 1982 on the western shore of Swanzey Lake in Cheshire County in southwestern New Hampshire.[1] This petroglyph is located within the Pilgrim Pines Bible Camp, which has been in operation at Swanzey Lake since 1957.

The design was carved into a large granite boulder that is situated at the very edge of the lake, near the top of a steeply-sloping rock surface that faces the lake. The petroglyph is about five feet above the present level of the water. It is very difficult to see it from above or from the sides of the boulder, but it can be easily viewed from a boat. The bank or lakeshore at this locus is severely eroded.

The present position of the boulder at lakeside with the petroglyph on the steep face oriented to the lake raises some questions: How was it carved? Was there once more land, since eroded away, between the lake and the boulder giving the carver a platform to work from? Was it carved from a boat? Why does it face the lake?

The petroglyph was carved into the hard granite surface. The grooves forming the design are generally uniform in depth and width. A pattern of small round pits are present within the grooves. These factors suggest that the carving was produced using a pointed metal tool, most likely when ground was present and intact on its southeasterly side.

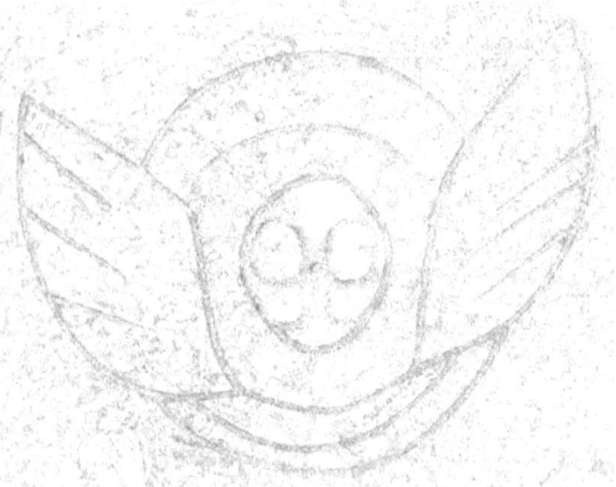

Figure 52: Soul effigy at Swanzey Lake, Cheshire County, New Hampshire. ***Drawing by T. Fitzpatrick.***

The petroglyph consists of three concentric circles with a wing on each side (Figure 52). It measures 27 inches

(70 cm) in maximum height by 31 inches (80 cm) in maximum width. The inner circle appears to represent an effigy face; it contains two small circles representing eyes and a faint outline of a nose and jowls. There is a drilled hole in the center of the face that is 3/8 inch (1 cm) wide and 5/16 inch (8 mm) deep. Each wing on the petroglyph has three oblique lines that represent feathers. The rock face is patinated, and since the petroglyph is difficult to detect, this suggests some antiquity to the carving.

Two sets of initials are carved on one side of the boulder: "RVT" and "RBB" placed one above the other. They are cut deeply into the rock, are readily visible, and appear to have been carved more recently than the winged effigy face.

This petroglyph at lakeside relates to a Euro-American tradition. It represents a soul effigy, a symbolic form of gravestone art that attests to the spiritual and religious values and beliefs of the early New England settlers. The soul effigy image first appeared on New England gravestones in the late seventeenth century and continued to be used by carvers until the end of the eighteenth century.[2] The winged anthropomorphic face represents the human soul in its heavenly ascent. This soul effigy faces the southeast, where the sun rises above the lake and announces that a new day is dawning.

The Swanzey Lake figure fits the tradition by which various master stone carvers have been identified throughout New England by their styles and by historic accounts. An important feature about this petroglyph is its context. It is not on a traditional gravestone; it is placed on a boulder facing east to the sunrise at the edge of the lake. It is also considerably larger than the typical grave marker carving.

Is it a practice carving by a gravestone carver? Does it mark a grave? Is it possibly an example of American Indian post-contact adaption of a Euro-American motif? I have no firm evidence to address these and the other questions that were raised earlier.

My analysis of the Swanzey Lake petroglyph indicates it is most likely of Euro-American origin and dates to the eighteenth century, based on its design motif, patination, and geographical context. It is situated in a region that has several old burial grounds, e.g., Keene, Jeffrey Center, Hinsdale, Chesterfield, and Peterborough, New Hampshire, where the soul effigy style is in evidence. An old hotel was once located along a former country road near the west side of the lake, and a two-story frame Bible Camp structure is now located here. Near the entrance to the camp building lies a large boulder that contained many heavily patinated and worn carvings, including names, a rectangular frame-like design and other symbols that are now virtually indistinguishable. It appears that an attempt was made to obliterate some of these figures. Thus, the hotel-religious retreat site appears to have a long tradition of visitors carving their personal marks on rocks in the area.

THE BOGTOWN PETROGLYPHS

In 1886, Westchester County, New York historian J. Thomas Scharf noted that Bogtown was located in an area once known as Yerkes's Corners.[3] Here there was a large grain distillery that "received and purchased...rye and wheat from the inhabitants residing in a circuit of twenty-five miles around." At Bogtown, Scharf wrote, there was also "a nail factory which employed some twenty or thirty hands constantly in the manufacture of nails. These industries have, however, entirely disappeared and nothing but the traces of the old dams or foundations of the buildings can be discovered."

Today, the area once known as Bogtown is part of the town of North Salem in upper Westchester County, New York. The name Yerkes's Corners has not disappeared, as stated by Scharf; it is still noted on the Hagstrom Company maps of the county. Yerkes's Corners is at the intersection of Yerkes Road, Cat Ridge Road and Bogtown Road. The origin of the name Bogtown is reminiscent of a very swampy area located west of the corners; the swamp was made into a lake in the twentieth century.[4]

The Bogtown petroglyphs consist of a large panel of mortuary art located on the southwest side of Bogtown Road (Figure 53). The site was investigated and recorded in the 1970s by Nicholas Shoumatoff, then curator of the Trailside

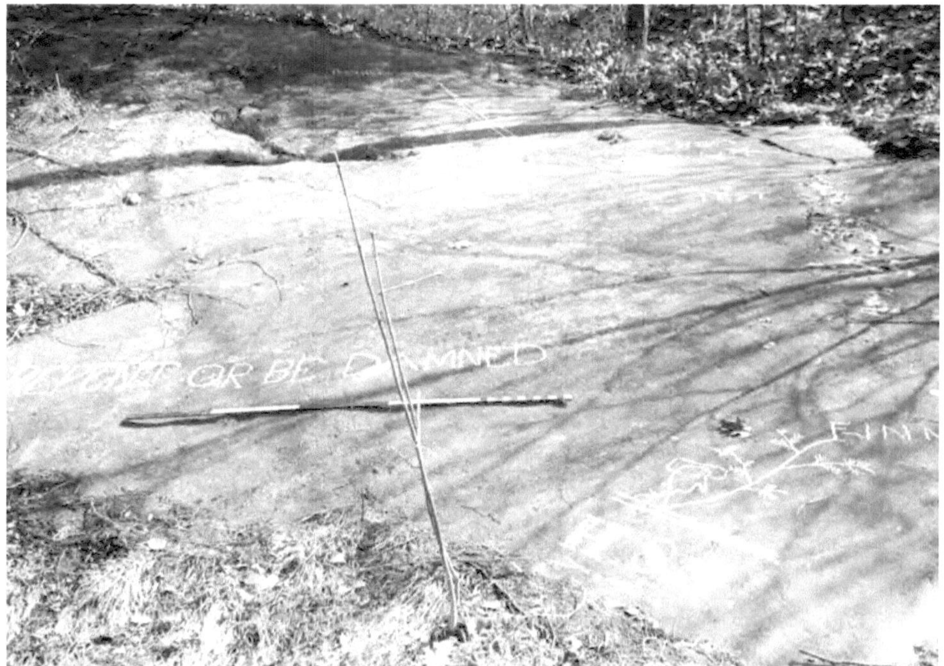

Figure 53: The Bogtown petroglyph site, North Salem, New York. ***Photo by E.J. Lenik 1975.***

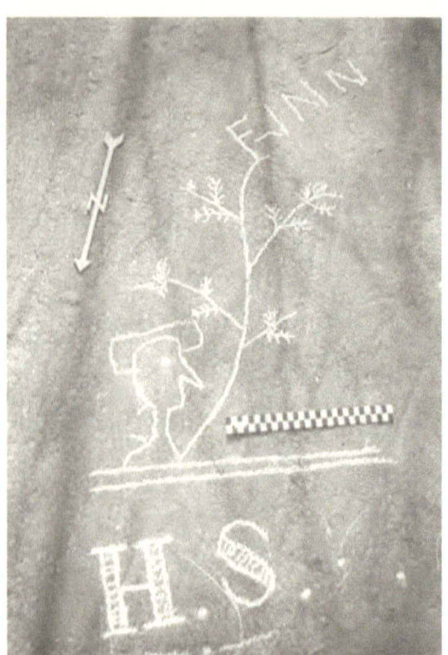

Figure 54: Human head, tree, and name of FINN at Bogtown Petroglyph site, North Salem, New York. *Photo by E.J. Lenik 1975.*

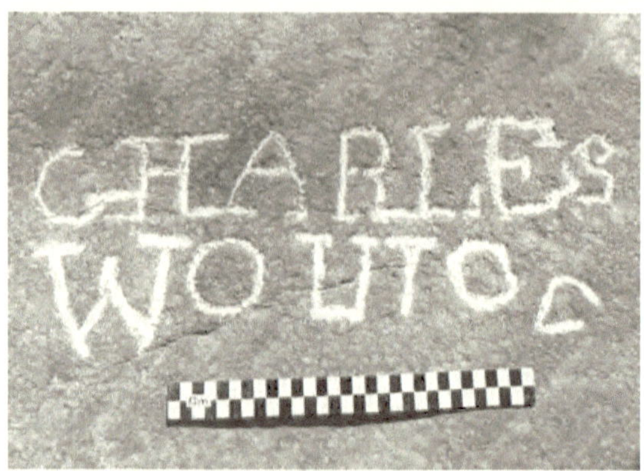

Figure 55: Carved name of CHARLES WOUTOC at Bogtown Petroglyph site, North Salem, New York. *Photo by E.J. Lenik 1975.*

Museum of Ward Pound Ridge Reservation in Cross River, New York. Shoumatoff brought the site to my attention and I subsequently conducted my own examination of it.

An outcrop of flat, gently sloping granite gneiss bedrock situated at roadside is the medium on which the petroglyphs have been carved. The rock outcrop contains fifteen petroglyphs, nearly all of which appear to represent gravestones or religious motifs. They were carved within an area of approximately 135 square feet (12.5 m2) with most of them placed near the periphery of the panel. The petroglyphs have been carved with the use of metal tools, since punch marks are in evidence within the grooves, which vary in depth and width. Components of the design motifs include the following:

Dates: 1850, 1851 (2), 1897
Initials: A.B.O., H.S., IVS, EQ
Names: FINN, CHARLES WOUTOC (Figure 54, 55)
Human heads (2) carved in profile (Figure 56)
Trees (2) (Figure 57)
Willow urn (Figure 58)
Christian cross
Religious statements: HOLYNESS TO THE LORD: REPENT OR BE DAMNED, GET THY (Figure 59)
Star-like symbol Abstract Designs (3)

The overall quality of the carvings is variable, which suggests that different individuals with various skill levels produced the images. Some of the letter petroglyphs are well-made, indicating that the carvers had good manual

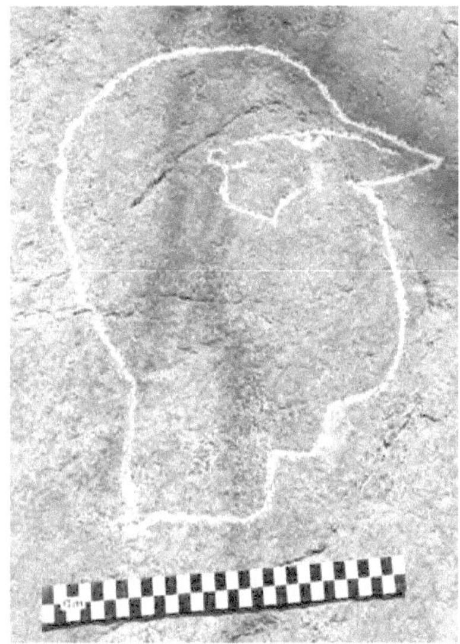

Figure 56: Human head in profile at Bogtown Petroglyph site, North Salem, New York. *Photo by E.J. Lenik 1975.*

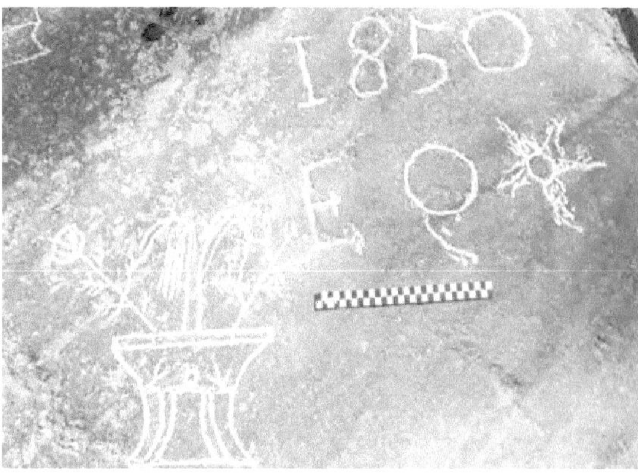

Figure 58: Willow urn, date, letters and star-like symbol. Bogtown Petroglyph site, North Salem, New York. *Photo by E.J. Lenik 1975.*

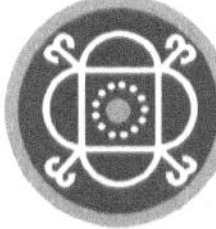

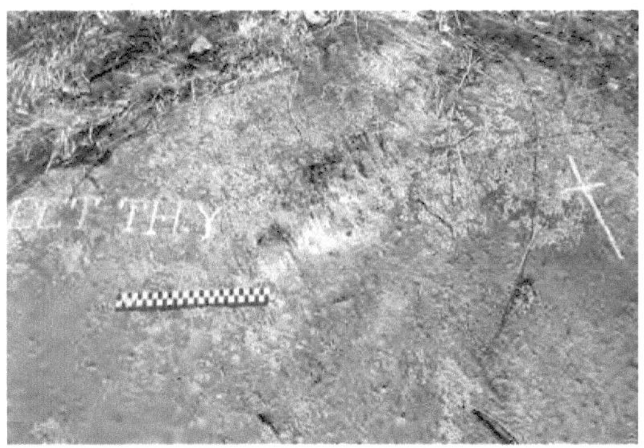

Figure 59: Religious statement and Christian cross at Bogtown Petroglyph site, North Salem, New York. *Photo by E.J. Lenik 1975.*

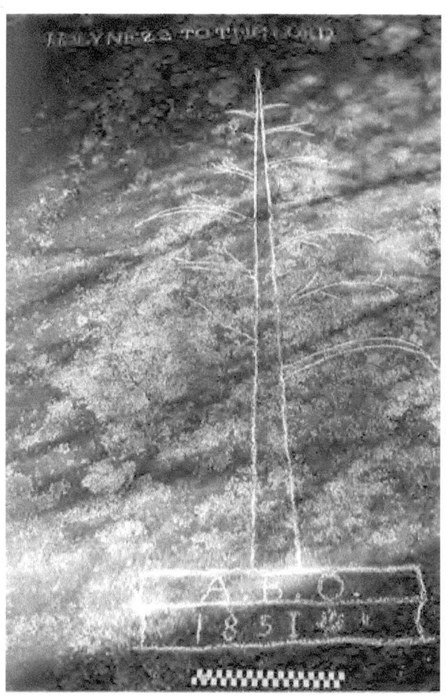

Figure 57: Tree on base with initials and date. Bogtown Petroglyph site, North Salem, New York. *Photo by E.J. Lenik 1975.*

control and skill. These include the initials "H.S." and the three religious statements. In particular, note that the two "S" letters in the word "HOLYNESS" have been carved backward. Other lettering, dates, and images are not as well-executed, and the two human heads are crudely carved.

The Bogtown petroglyphs were produced during the last half of the nineteenth century on a convenient rock billboard at roadside near the town center. It appears that these glyphs were meant to be seen by travelers passing by.

In the nineteenth century, death was ever present and often occurred at home. Some of the petroglyphs were meant to commemorate the death of individuals who lived nearby while others conveyed a religious message to those who stopped here. The floral motifs and urn were viewed as symbols or metaphors for mourning, death or mortality. Some of the petroglyphs may have been produced by apprentice stone carvers who were practicing their art, and by local individuals. Unfortunately, the identity of the various artists remains unknown.

A TOMBSTONE MYSTERY

Angela Leach, nee Sprague (1861-1926), was a Nipmuc Indian who was orphaned at an early age. She was raised by the Bemis family in Brimfield, Massachusetts and spent her childhood as a servant with this white family, a common practice with orphaned or bound-out children during the nineteenth century.[5]

Angela Sprague's lifeways, work and appearance were similar to those of her white neighbors. She married Philip Arnold Leach, a white man, was an active member of the Baptist Church in East Brimfield, and was a well-known personage in the area. Despite her white family upbringing and lifestyle she was acutely aware of her Indian identity and continued to express her native customs and knowledge throughout her entire life.

In 1914, Angela was interviewed by a reporter from the *Boston Sunday Herald*. His subsequent account of Angela's life was published in an article titled "Last Survivor of the Nipmucs Tells of Her Tribe's History." In the interview Angela reportedly stated that "My people were Webster or Dudley tribe of Nipmucs." The Nipmucs, an Algonquian-speaking people, consisted of several communities or villages whose homeland extended throughout central Massachusetts and northeastern Connecticut during the early European settlement of the region. In the seventeenth century an Indian reservation or "Praying Indian" town was established by the Massachusetts Bay Colony in what is now Webster, Massachusetts. The title of the *Boston Sunday Herald* article was erroneous and misleading because Angela was not the last of her people, since at the time she had fifteen Indian cousins and numerous extended relatives.

The Leachs' tombstone is located in the Oakridge Cemetery in Southbridge, Worcester County, Massachusetts (Figure 60). It displays the carved names of both husband and wife: on the left side it reads "PHILIP A. 1870-1933" and on the right "ANGELA M. 1861-1926." Below Angela's name and dates are three curiously engraved figures. A large letter "N" is cut into the stone. On each side of the letter N is an image that appears to resemble pre-

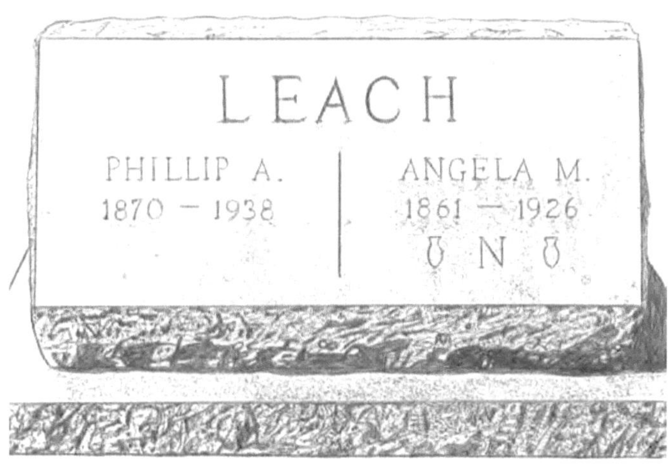

Figure 60: Tombstone of Phillip and Angela Leach in Oakridge Cemetery, Southbridge, Massachusetts. Note letter "N" flanked by two Indian pots below name of Angela. ***Drawing by T. Fitzpatrick.***

colonial style Indian pots. We can only speculate as to the meaning of the symbols. It can be argued that they represent or refer to her Indian heritage. The letter "N" may refer to her ethnic background, the Nipmuc tribe, and the two pots may be metaphors for Indian womanhood.

TATSON: A MOHEGAN INDIAN

East Haddam, Connecticut is situated on the east bank of the Connecticut River about fifteen miles north of its mouth. Founded in about 1668, the town was named after the English town of Great Hadam in Hertfordshire. In 1754 Haddam was divided into two towns, each separated by the river.[6]

The original settlers of East Haddam laid out thc town into nine sections, each three-fourths of a mile square. Several turnpike or post-roads eventually ran though the town.

The Native Indians name for East Haddam was Morehemoodus, or place of noises. Earth noises, a peculiar type of earthquake rumbling, apparently had been occurring in that region for years, even prior to the advent of Europeans. In fact, the most severe earthquake in Connecticut's history occurred at East Haddam on May 16, 1791, and was felt as far away as New York City.[7]

An observer said, "It began at 8 o'clock p.m., with two very heavy shocks in quick succession. The first was the most powerful; the earth appeared to undergo very violent convulsions. The stone walls were thrown down, chimneys were untopped, doors which were latched were thrown open, and a fissure in the ground of several rods in extent was afterwards discovered. Thirty lighter ones followed in a short time, and upward of one hundred were counted in the course of the night.

The shock was felt at a great distance. It was so severe at Clinton, about 12 miles south, that a Capt. Benedict, walking the deck of his vessel, then lying in the harbor at that place, observed the fish to leap out of the water in every direction as far as his eyes could reach."[7]

Prior to 1650, this area was inhabited by at least three tribes of Native Americans: the Wangunks in the north, the Mohegans in the east, and the Nehantics in the south. Mt. Tom was the dwelling place of Hobbamock, a spirit deity, and was called "Machimodus," or "the place of noises".[8]

Three Bridges Cemetery lies at the terminus of a dead end road, partially occupying an open field. The earliest recorded burial is that of Betsey Hamlin Baker, wife of Nathaniel, who died June 10, 1768 at ninety-one years old. The majority of burials cluster around the period between 1795 and 1830. The most recent is Nancy Griffin, wife of Samuel B., who died June 20, 1879 at age eighty-nine. In 1935, L. Hayden Pratt and G. C. Johnson recorded inscriptions from fifty-seven stones in the cemetery. They also found about twenty plain field stones. In 2003, when I visited this cemetery, there were fewer than twenty-five stones with legible inscriptions.

The stone of interest to this study is inscribed "IN MEMORY OF WARREN TATSON SON OF TOM AND BETTY 1796-1870 MOHEGANS." The stone has an image of an Indian in profile carved above the inscription (Figure 61).

The Tatson tombstone is relatively late in the history of the cemetery. The impulse to carve the profile on the stone may have been inspired from observation of the winged angel or death heads carved on many of the surrounding stones dating between 1797 and 1815. Both head and footstones with winged heads on them can be found in the cemetery. This early work is consistent and stylistically appears to be the work of one carver. The heads are simple and efficient in form and carving, which lends them a primitive effect. I have not found any documentation that might identify the carver, who would have been deceased long before the Tatson burial.

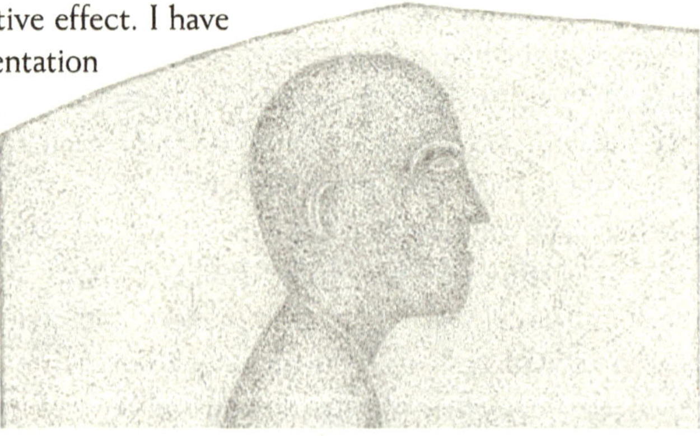

Figure 61: Image of an Indian in profile on the tombstone of Warren Tatson, a Mohegan. ***Drawing by T. Fitzpatrick.***

The cemetery is poorly tended and many of the sandstone tombstones are flaking and splitting apart. The Tatson stone is very weathered and the profile is difficult to discern.

It is interesting to note that Devil's Hopyard State Park and Hobbamock's Cave are located nearby.

The origin of the name Devil's Hopyard is wrapped in mystery. One story refers to cylindrical potholes located near a waterfall within the park. Early settlers apparently associated them with the supernatural: "They thought that the Devil had passed by the falls, accidentally getting his tail wet. This made him so mad he burned holes in the stones with his hooves as he bounded away."[9] The name may also have been derived from Indian legends or myths. The waterfall with its tumbling, roaring water and deep potholes would have had a visual and emotional impact upon the Indians who frequented this site, since their basic cosmology consisted of several levels above and below the earth. These levels were connected by holes through which the souls of the dead passed from one world to another.[10]

Hobbamock was an Indian deity who was associated with death, the deceased, the cold northeast wind and the color black. He was often seen by the Indians in forests and swamps, and a large cave or cavern near Mount Tom was thought to be his dwelling place.[11] Historian John DeForest recorded that Hobbamock was considered to be "the spirit of evil, the author of all human plagues and calamities."[12] He was feared by the Indians, but they also greatly revered him because of his vast power.

THE CAPTIVITY OF MRS. JOHNSON

Two carved slate "Indian Stones," each representing grave markers, stand by the side of a road near the town of Reading, Vermont (Figures 62, 63). One stone marks the spot where the Indians camped after capturing Mrs. Susanna Johnson and her family from Charlestown, New Hampshire, in 1754. The second stone indicates where she gave birth to her daughter Elizabeth Captive Johnson about 1/2 mile away.[13] The story of Mrs. Johnson's captivity was recorded in a diary written twenty-five years after her capture. In it she describes the suffering she and her family endured as they were carried off to Canada. The following details of Mrs. Johnson's capture and ordeal are abstracted from Mary M. Billings French's 1926 book, *A New England Pioneer.* French was the great, great-granddaughter of Mrs. Johnson.

On August 29, 1754, Indians surprised the occupants of the Johnson home, which was located near Fort Number Four in Charlestown, New Hampshire. They seized Mrs. Johnson, her husband James, her three children—Sylvanus, six years old, Susanna, age four, Polly, age two—as well as Ebenezer

Farnsworth and a friend of the family named Labaree. After plundering the house, the Indians ordered the captives to march, and they began traveling north along the east side of the Connecticut River. In her diary, Mrs. Johnson described her ordeal: "Two savages laid hold of each of my arms, and hurried me through thorny thickets in a most unmerciful manner. I lost a shoe and suffered exceedingly." They traveled about three miles when, "by this time my legs and feet were covered with blood and the Indians gave me a pair of Moggasons [sic]."

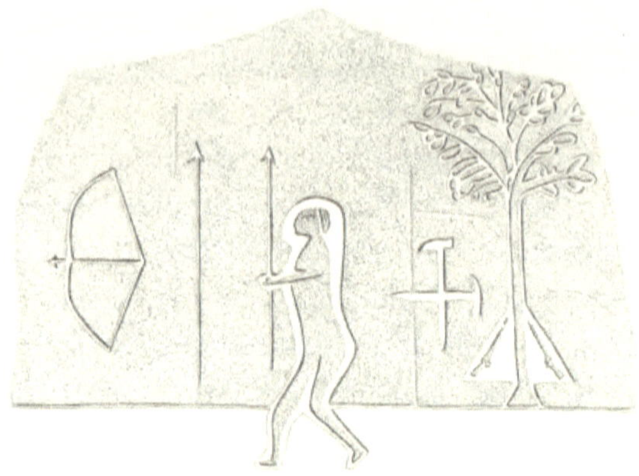

Figure 62: Carved stone depicting the captivity of Mrs. Johnson near Reading, VT. ***Drawing by T. Fitzpatrick.***

Soon they crossed to the opposite side of the Connecticut River into what is now Vermont. Here, beside a stony brook, she gave birth to her daughter. Hunger stalked both Indians and captives. On the fifth day of their journey the Indians went hunting for game, but were unsuccessful in their quest. Instead, the Indians captured a horse, shot it, cooked the meat and ate it.

By the sixth day, their march was continuing on a northwesterly course. Two days later, a severe storm arose at night, which Mrs. Johnson described as "terrible with thunder, lightning, and rain; the cold earth to lie on and no cover over our heads." Finally, on the ninth day, they reached East Bay on Lake Champlain.

The party crossed the lake and entered Fort St. Frederick at Crown Point, New York. Here the prisoners were taken to the French commander, where they were treated with kindness and allowed to rest for three days. Then the entire group traveled north by boat up the lake. After three days, they arrived at St. Johns, Quebec, where the prisoners were taken to the St. Francis Indian village. Mrs. Johnson and her baby lived in captivity with an Indian family for over sixty days, and were then taken to Montreal, where Mrs. Johnson was reunited with her husband James.

In Montreal, the Johnsons stayed with a French family named DuQuesne. Mr. Johnson was paroled and allowed to return to New England to raise money to redeem his family. An anticipated invasion by the French delayed his return to Canada. Six months later Mr. Johnson finally did return to Montreal, but was summarily thrown in jail because his captors said he had violated his parole by remaining in New England too long. Mr. and Mrs. Johnson and their two youngest daughters were then taken to Quebec City, where they all languished in jail for an additional five months.

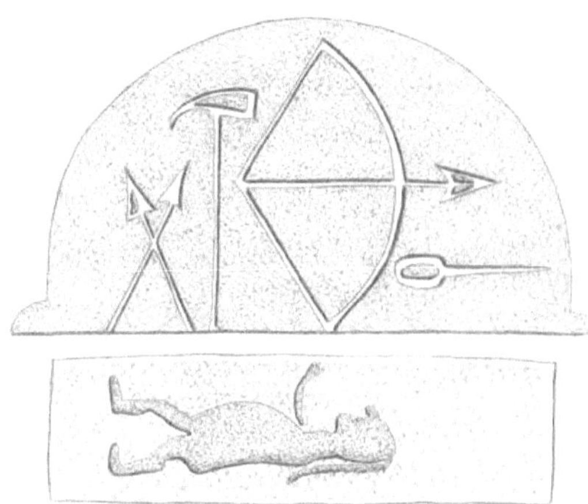

Figure 63: Carved stone indicating the location where Mrs. Johnson gave birth to a daughter, Reading, VT. ***Drawing by T. Fitzpatrick.***

On July 20, 1757, nearly three years after their capture, Mrs. Johnson, her sister, and two of her daughters were released from the prison and allowed to sail for England. One month later, they arrived in Plymouth, where they stayed for several days before moving on to Portsmouth. At Portsmouth they boarded a ship bound for America. On December 11, 1757 they landed in New York, where they stayed for ten days. From New York, Mrs. Johnson and her party continued by boat to New Haven, Connecticut.

In the meantime, James Johnson was released from prison in Quebec, and his son Sylvanus was redeemed from the Indians. Mr. Johnson first traveled to Boston, and then Springfield, Massachusetts, where he was reunited with Mrs. Johnson on January 1, 1758. A few days later, Mr. Johnson traveled to New York to settle his Canadian accounts. While on this journey he accepted a captain's commission from Governor Thomas Pownall of Massachusetts to join forces bound for Fort Ticonderoga, New York. On July 8, 1758, James Johnson was killed in battle.

In October, 1759, Mrs. Johnson returned to Charlestown, New Hampshire, where she had inherited a house from her mother. There she and her brother operated a small store. In 1762, at the age of 32, Mrs. Johnson married John Hastings, by whom she had seven additional children. In November, 1810, Mrs. Johnson died at the age of 81. Shortly before her death, she had completed writing a manuscript of a book which she called *The Captivity of Mrs. Johnson*.

The two Indian stones, mentioned at the beginning of this story, were erected by Mrs. Johnson in about 1762.[14] The larger of the two stones has carved images at the top, including a bow and arrow in a drawn position, a spear, an Indian holding a spear, two tomahawks, a tree, and two muskets within a triangle. The text below reads in part:

> This is near the spot
> that the Indians encampd the
> Night after they took Mrs. Johnson &
> Family, Mr. Labaree & Farnsworth
> August 30 1754 And Mrs.
> Johnson was delivered of her child
> Half a mile up this brook.

At the top of the other smaller stone are two crossed spears, a possible axe, a bow and arrow in a drawn position, and a war club. The text below reads as follows:

> On the 31st of
> August 1754
> Capt. James
> Johnson had a Daughter born
> on this spot of
> Ground being
> Captivated with
> his whole Family
> by the Indians.

Following the text is a recumbent figure presumably representing Mrs. Johnson in childbirth.

The two old stones are now encased in granite to preserve them. Mrs. Johnson's last visit to these monuments was made in 1808.

HANDWRITING AND INSCRIPTIONS

THOMAS KING

In March, 1605, Captain George Waymouth, in command of the ship *Archangel*, sailed from England on an exploratory expedition to the American coast.[1] Waymouth's planned sailing route was toward the southwest but prevailing southerly winds forced him northward. On May 13, the *Archangel* was off the coast of Nantucket Island in southern New England, but the winds continued to drive the vessel northward. Some four to five days later the ship was anchored off the Coast of Monhegan Island, Maine. With a party of twelve, Waymouth rowed to the shore of the island in order to obtain a fresh supply of water and wood for his ship. While at Monhegan, Waymouth and his crew spotted other islands, in addition to the mainland coast to the west.

After a brief stay at Monhegan, Waymouth weighed anchor and sailed his ship northward, where he ultimately anchored in St. George Harbor, which is closer to the mainland. Following a few days of rest, Waymouth headed toward the mainland to explore the area, discover its resources, and determine its suitability for future colonization. On June 11, 1605, he sailed his vessel into the mouth of the St. George River and proceeded inland where he observed a beautiful landscape and numerous coves that appeared to be excellent for ship moorages. He reportedly anchored the *Archangel* near the present site of Fort St. George on the east bank of the river, and on the following day continued up the river, pausing near what is now Thomaston, Maine. He landed there with an exploratory party of ten men and proceeded to explore the area for a distance of approximately twenty miles. After a few days, they returned to their ship, and sailed back down the river. At the harbor, Waymouth and his crew took on a fresh supply of water, and on June 16, 1605, the *Archangel* set sail for a return passage to England.

In 1978, Dr. Robert L. Bradley of the Maine Historic Preservation Commission reported the discovery of an inscription located near the Meduncook River in Cushing, Maine. Carved into an outcrop of bedrock was a cross, below which was the date "1605" and below that the name "Th. King" (Figure 64). As previously discussed, Captain George Waymouth explored the St. George River located just east of the Medun-cook in 1605. There was a boatswain named Thomas King on Waymouth's ship, the *Archangel*. Dr. Bradley stated that the location of the inscription was "logical," "much eroded," and the signature "a bit garbled."[2] It certainly had the appearance of great antiquity. Bradley believed the inscription was authentic and represented the first "physical evidence of Captain George Waymouth's voyage of exploration to the Maine coast."

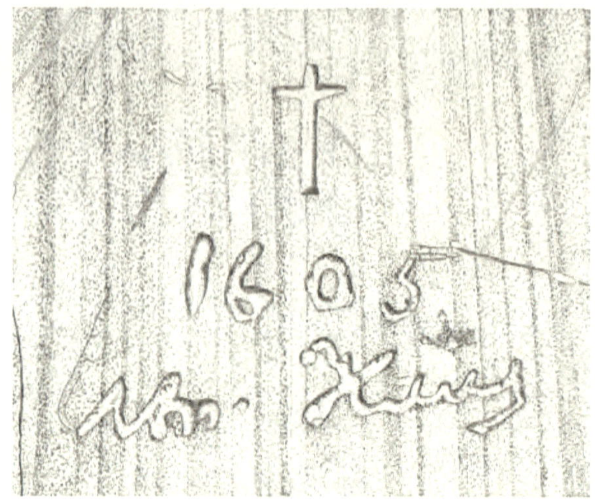

Figure 64: Signature and date of explorer Thomas King on bedrock outcrop in Cushing, Maine. ***Drawing by T. Fitzpatrick after photo by R. Bradley.***

THE HEBREW INSCRIPTION

The study of inscriptions requires a considerable amount of time researching the historical documents that concern a specific site and its related area. In all cases, the primary sources—diaries, letters, journals, maps, and similar items—must be examined for their accuracy concerning their factual and interpretive information. Did the writer-reporter really see an inscription on a rock? Or, were the strange carvings the result of some natural phenomenon or a vivid imagination? Could the writer accurately report what he saw without introducing some cultural, historic, religious or other ethnocentric bias? These and other related questions were vital during my search for genuine inscriptions and petroglyph sites.

The chance purchase of an out-of-print book titled *Travels Through the Northern Parts of the United States in the Years 1807-8* by Edward Augustus Kendall provided the initial stimulus for my search for two inscription sites in western Connecticut. In his book, Kendall stated that a "Hebrew Inscription" recorded by Dr. Ezra Stiles was carved into rock located on the "Hebrew Pinnacle," a hill or mountain near New Preston, Connecticut.[3] This chronicle set in motion a swarm of activity involving documentary research and field reconnaissance, all culminating in the rediscovery of the Hebrew inscription, as well as another site called Molly Fisher Rock.[4]

The usual procedure in any historical research project is to consult the original sources of information, and such was the case with respect to the Hebrew inscription. In the manuscript collection of Yale University's Beinecke Library are six volumes of the *Itineraries and Memoirs of Ezra Stiles* (1727-1795) who was president of Yale College from 1778 to 1795. Dr. Stiles extensively studied and recorded the Hebrew inscription site, and his original manuscript notes provided me with the needed clues to locate it.

Stiles's first entry in his diary regarding the Hebrew inscription is dated September 14, 1789, when he recorded that three Yale students brought him a drawing of the carvings. The Stiles manuscript located the inscription at a place called "The Pinnacle" near New Preston. Stiles noted that the Hebrew carving was on "Pinnacle Mountain" which adjoins the "E. end of Raumang Pond."[5] The pond referred to is present day Lake Waramaug. Stiles noted that the inscription was engraved "on the horizontal summit" of the mountain.

Dr. Stiles transcribed the Hebrew inscription on October 8, 1789, and his notes and observations are extensive. His manuscript contains a sketch map of the location of the site, and he indicated that there were four words in Hebrew that had been "well engraved" into the rock. The characters apparently had been inscribed by an iron chisel. Stiles made extensive measurements of the inscriptions, noting such details as the height of the letters, the distances between the words and their orientation. His manuscript contains three separate sketches of them.

On December 11, 1976, this author and two colleagues climbed up The Pinnacle near New Preston, Connecticut and located the Hebrew inscription site on the extreme northwest corner of the summit of the mountain. As Stiles had done nearly two hundred years before us, we carefully recorded and photographed the inscriptions.

The location for carving the letters was apparently very carefully selected. Whereas most of the mountaintop was rough, irregular and pockmarked disintegrating mica schist, the place where the inscriptions were cut was smooth. There are four separate inscriptions or words, each enclosed in a semi-circle which was carefully cut into the rock. The words are grouped into two pairs with the each pairs located 210 centimeters apart. The open end of each word enclosure faces northwest toward Lake Waramaug. At the time of our survey, we observed that some vandalism of the inscriptions had previously taken place (Figure 65).

Two of the word groups had initials cut over the top of the original Hebrew inscriptions. There were also other nineteenth and twentieth century dates, plus initials and rectangles cut into the rock surface near the inscriptions.

The inscriptions do indeed represent Hebrew writing. Based on Stiles's drawing, the northerly pair of words translates to "Abram," i.e., Abraham, and "Isaac," respectively, and the southern pair reads "Sarah" and "Adam."

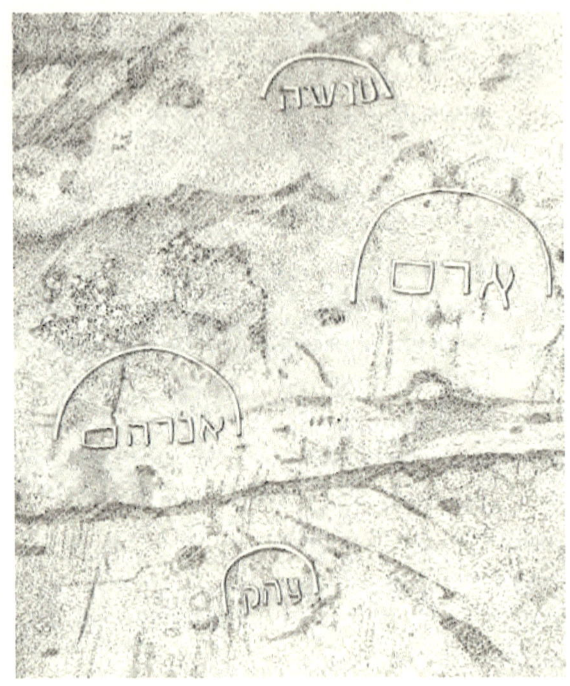

Figure 65: Hebrew inscription on Pinnacle Mountain, New Preston, Connecticut. ***Drawing by T. Fitzpatrick.***

Stiles's initial transliteration of the carvings stated that "two contain[ed] the names Adam and Abraham" and "the other two [were] unintelligible."[6] Later, in a diary entry dated October 8, 1789, Stiles stated, "The Characters are good Hebrew well engraved and I believe by some Jews who have been visiting the Kent & New Milford Mountains for Gold Mines for 30 y. past."[7] Stiles sketched the "letters" in the same diary entry and rendered the names as "Adam," "Terasha & Isaac" and "Abraham." Rabbi Arthur A. Chiel has suggested that the name Terasha may have been incorrectly transliterated by Stiles, and instead may possibly be the Hebrew word "Teresh" which means "rugged, stony ground," certainly an accurate description of the area's landscape.[8]

The question that now remains is who carved the Hebrew inscription, when and why? In another manuscript entry of October 8, 1789, Stiles wrote that the inscriptions were "said to be engraved by the French army in 1781." It was asserted that a party of French officers visited Pinnacle Mountain "on a party of pleasure" and produced the carvings.[9] However, this explanation was unlikely, as the French Army marched from Providence, Rhode Island to Dobb's Ferry, New York in a forced march covering 220 miles in eleven days (June 26 - July 6, 1781) and came no closer than twenty miles south of New Preston. This schedule hardly allowed time for the officers to wander two days' march off the route to climb a remote mountain and take the time to carve Hebrew names on the rock. Stiles believed the inscriptions to be "very new in 1780," and maintained that they were not engraved by the French.[10]

Other potential carvers are a possibility. Stiles stated that two or three Jews owned and operated a mine at New Milford, Connecticut. He proposed that a "Jew, Mr. Moses, might have engraved this inscription; as he resided in Cornwall, adjoining it, half a year, between 1766 and 1770, and spent his time in examining and searching for mines in Cornwall, Kent, and New Milford. He professed the art of refining metals. I thus have no doubt that this inscription is to be ascribed to some of these Jews and that it was probably made since the year 1760."[11]

After much speculation what appears to be an answer to the question of who carved these inscriptions was found in at the Gunn Historical Museum in Washington, Connecticut in an early ledger kept for the general store in New Preston. Tucked into the ledger on a scrap of rag paper was a note written by John Buckingham of Marble Dale. He spoke specifically of "the characters engraved on the Pinnacle rock that have been the subject of much wonder. Many learned men have examined them, but they remain a mystery... The truth has been given me by a grandson of the individual who engraved them...Ebenezer Beeman, an eccentric who made pretensions to great learning and had in his possession a Hebrew and Greek dictionary, went to the top of the rock in 1774, taking with him some books and tools. He attempted to engrave the names of Issac, Moses, Adam, and Abraham. The last name was unfinished on account of a heavy thunder shower...This, I am told, may be relied on as a true account of those Mysterious Characters."[12]

THE SCATICOOK OR MOLLY FISHER ROCK

On November 18, 1789, Ezra Stiles recorded in his *Itineraries and Memoirs* that he "found a rock in Kent [Connecticut] on Housatunnuck River near Scattikuk, charged with unknown characters. The manner of inscription, by Picking with an iron tool, not by chiszel [sic] or engraving."[13] In another manuscript entry he wrote that "Mark't on Scaticook" were the initials "BH," pecked into the rock. He notes that "NB Barnabas Hatch Father of Nath Hatch settled at Kent in 1741 and lived within 100 rods of this rock." This entry was accompanied by a very simple sketch map that indicated the location of the rock.

In a letter to James Bowdoin, President of the Academy of Arts & Sciences, Stiles wrote a more detailed description of the Scaticook Rock:

> Upon the Summit of Cobble Hill, which commands a View into Scatticook WigWams, stands the rock charged with Characters, the Rock being to this day inveloped & concealed in a Forest... This Rock is along by itself, and not a portion of a Mountain; it is of white Flint. It ranges N&S & is about twelve to 14 feet long; eight to ten feet wide at the base & on the top; six feet high at the N. End, & five feet high at the S. End, of an uneven & rather globular than angular surface...On the Top I did not perceive any Character. But the sides all around appear to be irregularly charged with unknown Characters, made not indeed with the incisions of a Chiszel, yet most certainly with an Iron Tool, and that by Pecks or picking after the manner of the Dighton Rock. The lacunae or Excavations are from a quarter of an inch to an inch broad, but generally from half to three quarters of an inch wide & from one to two tenths of an inch deep...after a little familiarizing the mode of inscription or engraving, one may clearly & satisfactorily perceive real artificial letters & Marks...And, after a more attentive examination & inspection the sides of this rock all around appeared to be pretty fully charged with character. The engraving did not appear to be recent or new, but very old. [14]

In this 1790 report to the American Academy, Stiles indicated that this rock with its inscription was unknown to the Euro-American inhabitants of Kent or the nearby Indians in their wigwams on the west side of the Housatonic River. The Indian settlement was called Scaticook. Stiles recorded the inscription by placing a sheet of paper on the rock and with his fingers and the blunt end of a pencil he depressed it into the "Lacunae or excavations." He rubbed it vigorously to make an impression and then traced the lines with the pencil while the paper was still over the characters. It is clear that Stiles made a careful and detailed study of the Scaticook Rock; included in his report to the academy were his drawings of the inscription and a more detailed map showing the location of the rock.

Kendall, in his book *Travels Through the Northern Parts of the United States in the Years 1807-8*, confused the Scaticook Rock with the Hebrew inscription site.[15] He wrote that in about 1760 the symbols on the rock were thought to relate to buried treasure, and it was said that up to the year 1774 several efforts had been made to dig up and find the valuable cache. Furthermore, Kendall stated that pieces of rock were said to have been broken away and sent to New York in an attempt to "decipher" the inscription.

On December 11, 1976, I visited a site near Kent, Connecticut called Spooner Hill, where local legends indicated there was a rock bearing an inscription somewhere nearby. Together with two colleagues, I was led to a large glacial boulder located about one-half mile north of Spooner Hill Road by Irving Conboy, the owner of the property. Mr. Conboy called this boulder Molly Fisher Rock, based on an old legend of this person and the surrounding area, and he showed us a 1930 photograph of the rock and its inscription.[16]

Molly Fisher Rock appeared to have a human-made inscription on it. The rock was a metasedimentary (sandstone) boulder that measured 13 feet, 6 inches (4 m) long by 10 feet (3 m) wide and averaged 5 feet (1.5 m) in height. About 1 inch (30 cm) down from its top was a vein of quartz 7 to 10 centimeters in thickness that completely encircled the boulder. The symbols were cut or incised with a metal tool on the vertical northeastern face of the rock just above the quartz vein.

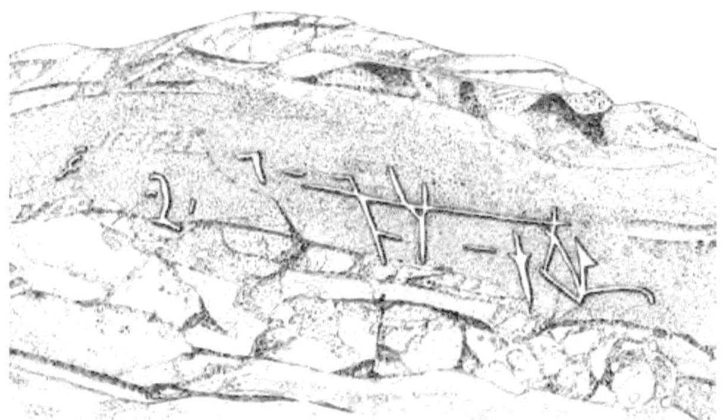

Figure 66: Inscription on Scaticook or Molly Fisher Rock, Kent, Connecticut. ***Drawing by T. Fitzpatrick after photo by E.J. Lenik 1976.***

The symbols formed a linear pattern with the incised lines or grooves measuring 1 cm to 1.5 cm in width, and ranging in depth from 2 mm to 8 mm. There seemed to be nine or ten distinct symbols or clusters of symbols and a long horizontal line, giving it the appearance of some type of writing (Figure 66). The meaning of this so-called inscription is unknown.

Three additional incised symbols were located below the main linear pattern, but these were clearly of different workmanship. These three symbols were lightly incised narrow grooves, with two vertical lines that resembled a "leg," and a "penis." They were lightly covered with lichen at the time of our visit and were not visible in the 1930 photograph.

My study of the inscription and its surroundings raised several questions. We judged that the inscription was carved in a poor location on the boulder. The top of the rock, as well as other areas around the stone, were smoother and presumably would have been better suited for carving. Another mystery is the reason why this particular rock was selected for carving the inscription, since there are many glacial boulders located throughout the area. This carved boulder appeared to have no discernible relationship to the surrounding land scape. However, it was located just west of an old abandoned woods road. We also observed that some recent digging had taken place around the boulder.

An account of the Molly Fisher Rock and legend was published in 1930. It states that "about 100 years ago a party of professors and students came here just to see this rock and to study the writing on it, but they could make nothing of it."[17] Is this a reference to Stiles's visit in 1789? The published account of the legend also relates a story of buried treasure, the source of which may have been the same one recorded by Kendall in his 1809 journal.

The Stiles 1789 and 1790 descriptions of the rock as Scaticook, vis-à-vis the Molly Fisher Rock, do not agree. Although Stiles drew a map showing the location of an inscribed stone in this area, he wrote that the hill on which it stood was called "Cobble Hill." Furthermore, Molly Fisher Rock is not the block of white flint as described by Stiles. The inscription on Molly Fisher Rock is incised, whereas Stiles noted that he saw "pecked" characters. Stiles also said that the characters on the Scaticook Rock were ¼ inch to 1 inch wide and located all around the rock, whereas the symbols on Molly Fisher Rock are located in one area only. Finally, he recorded in his manuscript and letter that the Scaticook Rock contained the initials "BH," but we found no evidence of this on Molly Fisher Rock.

The apparent discrepancies or differences between Stiles's account of the rock and my own would seem to suggest that Stiles was talking about a different site, and not Molly Fisher Rock. However, some of the discrepancies can be explained, so I believe that Molly Fisher Rock is the one visited and recorded by Stiles in 1789. His 1790 map shows its location in Kent relative to the Housatonic River, the Indian land and wigwams on the east side of the river, and its placement on what was then called Cobble Hill (but now Spooner Hill). His description of the rock as "white flint" was a commonly used term for quartz in the eighteenth century. Finally, his drawing "No II" is very similar to the one I produced in 1976. In his drawing "No IV" Stiles saw the letters BH, but as I noted earlier we found no evidence of this. Perhaps the letters had either been removed or had eroded away in the intervening 187 years.

Stiles believed the symbols were similar to those on Dighton Rock and shared the same Phoenician origin. My own examination indicates they may be nothing more than irregular and weathered natural cracks and veins. If the grooves are truly human-made, then I would attribute them to Euro-Americans. Among the most likely suspects are the Hatch family, who lived nearby in the 1740s, or the Moravian missionaries who lived among the Scaticook Indians from 1750 to 1770.

STONE CUTTERS' ART AT BEATTIE'S QUARRIES

Beattie's Quarries were located in the Leete's Island District of Guilford, Connecticut. Established in 1870 by Scotsman John Beattie, this granite quarry was one of the largest industries bordering Long Island Sound in Connecticut during the late nineteenth and early twentieth centuries. The quarries produced granite blocks for railroad bridges, breakwaters, lighthouses, and hotel plazas.[18] Rock from this quarry forms the pedestal of the Statue of Liberty in New York Harbor, the abutments for the Brooklyn Bridge, and part of the North Lighthouse on Block Island, Rhode Island. Following the end of World War I, rising production costs and changes in construction materials caused the quarry to cease operations.

At the peak of its production, Beattie's Quarries extended over 350 acres (140+ ha) of land on Hoadley's Neck. The quarry area came to be known as "the Patch," and employed five hundred people.[19] Its workforce consisted of immigrants who came to the United States in the late nineteenth century, among them Scots, Finns, Swedes, Italians, and Hungarians. These employees lived in shacks, shanties, and boarding houses scattered throughout the area, while superintendents and schooner captains, whose ships transported the stone blocks, lived in Victorian houses on Old Quarry Road.

Patch Road (unmarked) extends south from Leete's Island Road (Connecticut Route 146) toward Hoadley Neck, and ends at a driveway leading to a private home. A short hike along this stretch of road brings you to a vertical rock outcrop on the east side that contains numerous pits or cupules similar to those found at Hanna's Quarry, as described elsewhere in this volume. At the end of the road, on its west side, is a low slanting outcrop of bedrock that is covered with inscriptions made by workers from Beattie's Quarries. The slanting face of the ledge contains names, initials, unidentified words, messages, and Christian motifs.

One carefully incised message reads "CASTLE GARDEN / NEW YRK BAY / EMIGRANTS ON / BOARD EUROPEAN / STEAMER." The letter "N" in this message has been cut backwards. Another message appears to say "LETTES ISLAND / ATJGRANITHA." Perhaps it originally read "LEETES ISLAND GRANITE" but initials were added later to the beginning and end of the word "granite". A third readable inscription states "HOTEVE HAOSY / rESTAUrENT." Other recognizable names and initials include "W.E.," "Besse Brigham," "K.B.," "RATS," "William Nelsfan" in script, "DT," and a number of illegible inscriptions.

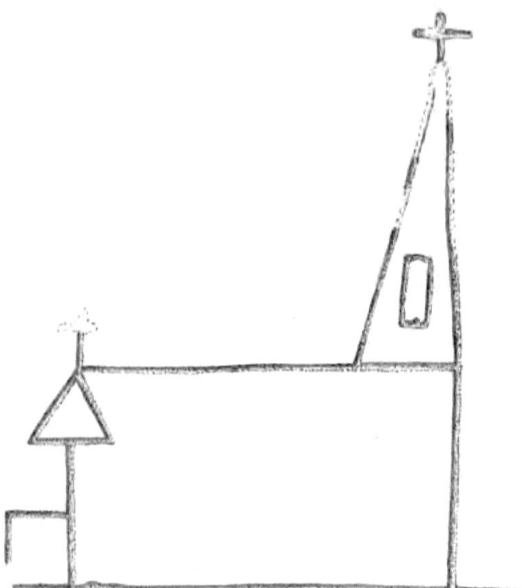

Figure 67: Incised profile of a church, Beattie's Quarry, Guilford, Connecticut. *Drawing by T. Fitzpatrick.*

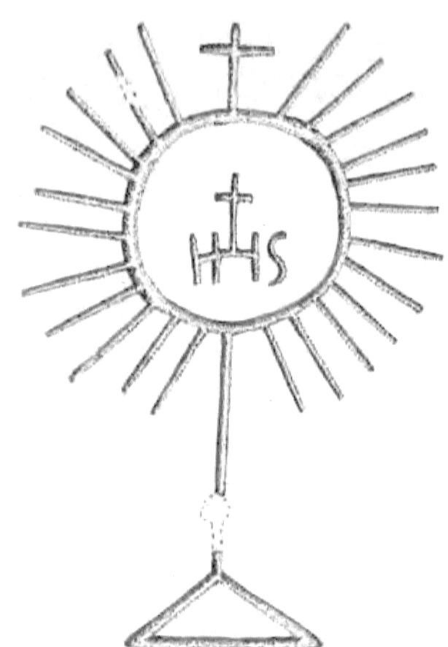

Figure 68: Incised Roman Catholic monstrance near profile image of church, Beattie's Quarry, Guilford, Connecticut. *Drawing by T. Fitzpatrick.*

There are four Christian motifs on the rock. On the far right end of the outcrop is the incised figure of a church with a steeple surmounted by a cross (Figure 67). An entryway and window appear to be portrayed on this structure. To the left of this church is an incised monstrance on a stand with a cross at its top, spires around its circumference and a cross with letters inside the circle (Figure 68). In the Roman Catholic Church, the monstrance is a shrine in which a consecrated host is presented for the adoration of the people either while being carried in a procession or when raised by a priest at the altar as part of the Catholic liturgical ritual.

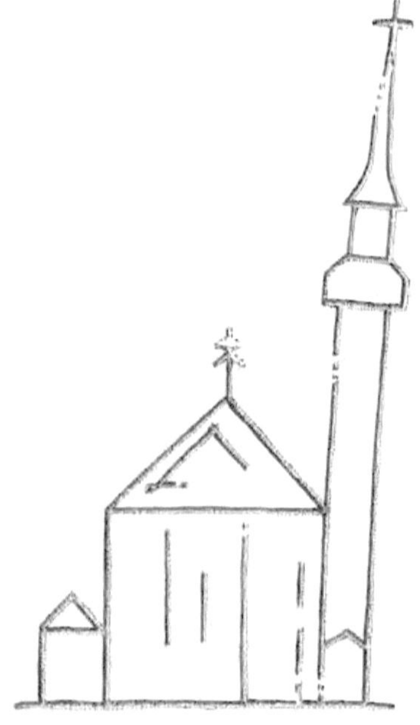

Figure 69: Incised image of church with high steeple, Beattie's Quarry, Guilford, Connecticut. *Drawing by T. Fitzpatrick.*

Another figure of a church was incised into the left side of the rock. This structural figure has a gabled roof with a cross on top, an entryway on its left side, and a high steeple with a cross on its right (Figure 69). Above the church and slightly to its right is another incised monstrance on a stand that contains a cross on its top, spikes around its circumference, and a cross with letters inside a circle (Figure 70).

According to Guilford historian Joel E. Helander the inscriptions and Christian motifs on Old Patch Road were carved by Hungarian quarry workers. This site was a "rock altar" at which religious services were held.[20]

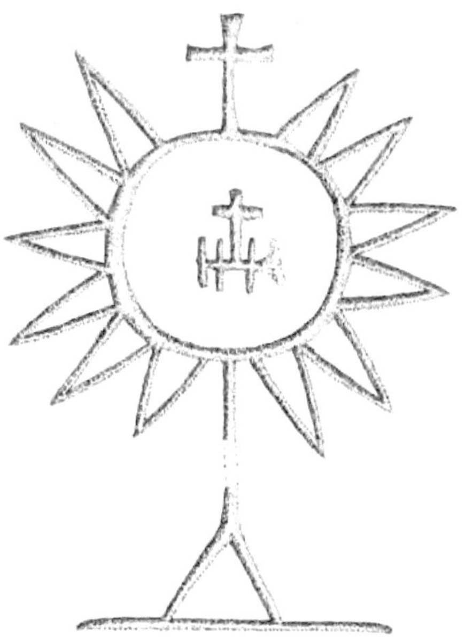

Figure 70: Incised Roman Catholic monstrance above church steeple, Beattie's Quarry, Guilford, Connecticut. ***Drawing by T. Fitzpatrick***

ENDICOTT ROCK

In May 1652, the General Court of the Massachusetts Bay Colony reviewed its royal charter and concluded that the northern boundary of its colony was a straight line that extended east and west from a point located three miles north of "the northermost [sic] part of the Merimacke" River in present day New Hampshire.[21] If this was indeed the case, then the Bay Colony could annex additional land and its residents, particularly that portion along the coast of Maine.

In order to clearly establish this northern boundary, the colonial government appointed Captain Simon Willard of Concord and Captain Edward Johnson of Woburn as commissioners to explore the Merrimack River, determine its beginning or source, and thus the northern extent of their territory. In addition to the two commissioners, the exploration party included surveyors John Sherman of Watertown, Jonathan Ince of Boston, and two Indian guides who were reportedly familiar with the Merrimack River Valley and its source—a "great lake."[22]

In the summer of 1652, the survey party proceeded up the Merrimack River, exploring the land along the way. In time, they reached the juncture of the Pemigewasset and Winnipesaukee Rivers, which joined to form the Merrimack in what is now Franklin, New Hampshire. The Indians indicated that the Winnipesaukee was the Merrimack and so the party followed this river through a chain of small ponds until they reached the shore of the "great lake." The Indians called the lake Winnepesaukee and the locale Aquedahtan, which is now known as "The Weirs," since the Indians had fished there for many years.[23]

Here were the headwaters of the Merrimack, and this indicated the northern boundary of Massachusetts that would extend east-west from a point three miles north of this location.

At the outlet of the lake in the middle of the river was a large boulder that extended above the surface of the water (Figure 71). On the oblong top surface of this rock one of the members of the survey party, thought to be Jonathan Ince, cut the following inscription:

EI SW
WP IOHN
ENDICVT
GOV
IS II

The 1652 inscription has been interpreted as follows: The initials "EI" are those of Commissioner Edward Johnson (the capital I can also be read as a capital J and was much easier to carve into the rock). The initials "SW" are those of Commissioner Simon Willard. "WP" is thought to be an abbreviation of the word "Worshipful." The letters "IOHN ENDICUT GOV" refer to John Endicott, then governor of Massachusetts. The initials "IS" are those of John Sherman, and "II" are those of Jonathan Ince, the presumed engraver.[24]

Returning from their journey, the commissioners reported to the General Court that they were treated "kindly" by the Indians they encountered along their route.[25] The court later established the northeastern corner of the colony's boundary on the shore of Casco Bay in Maine.

In the eighteenth century the boulder with its inscription disappeared under the rising waters of the lake and river. In about 1833 the rock was rediscovered during construction of a dam across the head of The Weirs during the excavation and clearing of the river channel.[26] Since that time the rock with its inscription has been called Endicott

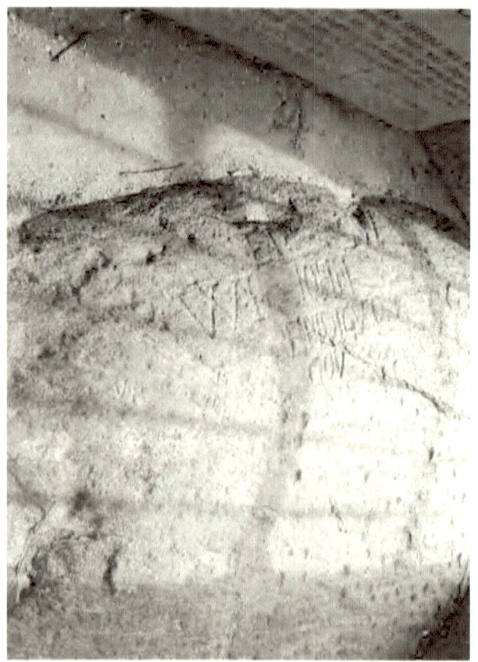

Figure 71: Inscribed name of "John Endicot Gov" on boulder, The Weirs, Lake Winnipesauke, New Hampshire. **Photo courtesy of D. Leary 2003.**

Rock. Today it is enclosed within a granite structure located on the shore of Lake Winnipesaukee, erected in 1892 by the state of New Hampshire to provide cover and protection for the rock. It can be viewed through an iron protective gate on one side of the enclosure.

THE POOLE-WHITTIER INSCRIPTION

Between the eighteenth and twentieth centuries, historians, archaeologists, scholars and antiquarians have speculated about the existence and location of Norse or Viking landings and settlements in North America. Numerous alleged sites have been identified along the coast, from the Arctic to New Jersey, as well as in the interior of the continent, based on literary sources, relic finds, and especially stones inscribed with runic letters. Various sources have attempted to establish the fact that the Norse visited North America some five hundred years before Columbus.[27]

In an account published in *The New England Historical and Genealogical Register* in 1854, George I. Poole described and illustrated an inscription on a rock outcrop located in West Newbury, Massachusetts.[28] His report took the form of a letter to a "Mr. Drake" and reads as follows:

> Dear Sir, —At different periods discoveries have been made in our country, which indicate plainly the existence, at some past time, of a race of people considerably advanced in many arts, and evidently very much superior to the Indian tribes. Knowing the interest you take in these matters, I have taken the liberty...to address you on this subject. During the past summer I was visiting the town of West Newbury, Massachusetts, and while on a shooting expedition, in company with Mr. Silas Pillsbury, a worthy and veracious farmer of that place, he informed me that a rock situated in a pasture belonging to Mr. Farmer had an inscription upon it supposed to have been written by the Indians. I desired him to lead me to it, which he did. Guiding me to the foot of a small precipice about twelve or fifteen feet in height, formed by the cropping out of a granite ledge, of the common coarse hard granite; the precipice overhanging considerably has protected the inscription in a measure. This inscription, which is on the east side of the rock, is deeply graven with some instrument as it appears of a triangular shape, as the grooves are all of that form. The inscription comprises two lines, although part of the lower line has been effaced by the action of the elements. In the centre of the lower line there the figure of a man, which appears to

> be armed with a spear. I send you a hasty copy of a sketch I made upon the spot, a profile of the rock, and a copy as perfect as I could make of the inscription. ...I have a poor copy of the Dighton rock inscription, and by comparing them I think I discover a similarity in some of the figures. ...The rock is situated about two miles from the river Merrimack, and about a quarter of a mile from the road between West Newbury and Georgetown.

George Poole's drawing of the inscription depicts two lines of symbols in slanting rows from left to right (Figure 72). The top row consists of geometric images, including vertical and slanting lines, curvilinear lines and dots. The bottom row contains an arrow-like symbol at the left end with the artist's scrawl marks at the end of the shaft. Next is a trapezoid with two internal horizontal lines, and two curvilinear figures. The central figure appears to represent an anthropomorph consisting of a round head, two eyes, nostrils, mouth, zig-zag lines representing its body, and an adjacent "spear." Again, there appears to be the artist's scrawl mark extending downward from the side of the head and across the spear. To the right of the anthropomorphic figure is a diamond-like symbol followed by three vertical rows of scrawl marks. The scrawl marks are most likely Poole's attempt to illustrate exfoliated areas on the rock.

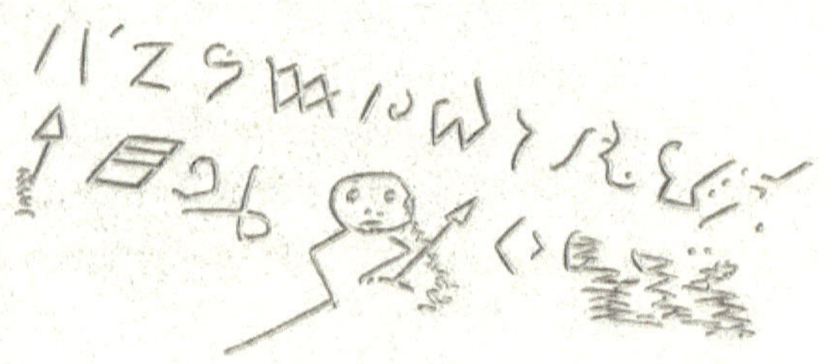

Figure 72: Poole-Whittier inscription, West Newberry, Massachusetts. ***Drawing by T. Fitzpatrick after Poole 1854.***

During the last half of the nineteenth century, the location of the so-called inscription was known to area residents and the site became somewhat of an attraction for visitors. However, as time passed, interest in the inscription waned and the location of the site was lost to memory.

In 1928, Edmund Burke Delabarre, in his book *Dighton Rock*, discussed the inscription in a chapter titled "Frauds, Rumors and Mistaken Reports." Delabarre reported that he found no evidence of its authenticity and concluded it was a "mistaken report."[29] He stated that the site was investigated by antiquarians George Francis Dow and a local man by the name of William Merrill. Dow, in a letter to Delabarre, stated that the inscriptions were "only natural cracks in the rocks" with no sign of human or "artificial" marks on the surface. Dow's letter also stated that a "Mr.

Follansbee" told Merrill that he, Follansbee, had accompanied George Poole to the rock ledge and that Poole was "much intoxicated."[30]

In 1948, Olaf Strandwold published his interpretation of the Poole-Whittier inscription in his book *Norse Inscriptions on American Stones.* Strandwold referred to the site as "The Shipwreck or Poole-Whittier Inscription," the latter name referring to poet John Greenleaf Whittier.[31] Whittier was reported to have submitted the original drawing to *The New England Historical and Genealogical Register.* Whittier's home was in Haverhill, Massachusetts, a short distance to the west of West Newbury, and he evidently visited the site. In a poem titled, "The Double-Headed Snake of Newbury," Whittier referred to the site as a "Northman's Written Rock."[32]

Strandwold stated that it was "one of the most remarkable of all runic inscriptions."[33] He described the top line of the inscription as "Christian" and the bottom line as "heathen." He said the message recorded a "tragic saga of the sea" in which thirty-four men were helplessly stranded on an island in winter. His translation of the top line of the inscription was, "On the ice are 34 men, on an island. God, on dry land is Yule-Tide." He speculated that the shipwreck was perhaps the same one referred to in an old Indian tale. The bottom line, he said, was an appeal to the god Thor "to use the great magic power of the runic alphabet to save the men from a weird, cruel fate."

The exact location of the inscription site was lost for many years. Then, in 1976, it was rediscovered by Milo M. Williams, a retired professor of archaeology, and his wife Laurie Williams. By this time, the site was known by some people as "Old Hang Rock," although the origin or meaning of this designation is not known.[34] Williams reportedly found only one identifiable portion of the inscription on the rock ledge—the anthropomorphic figure seemingly holding a spear as illustrated in Poole's drawing.

On August 6, 1976 I visited the Poole-Whittier inscription site recently rediscovered by the Williamses. My own examination of the vertical rock surface revealed only natural cracks. I saw no evidence of human-produced symbols or figures. Furthermore, I believe that Poole mistook the cracks for carvings by humans when he produced his drawing in 1854. In my opinion the drawing does not represent an inscription; therefore, Standwold's interpretation of the marks as runic writing was in error.

HOSPITAL ROCK

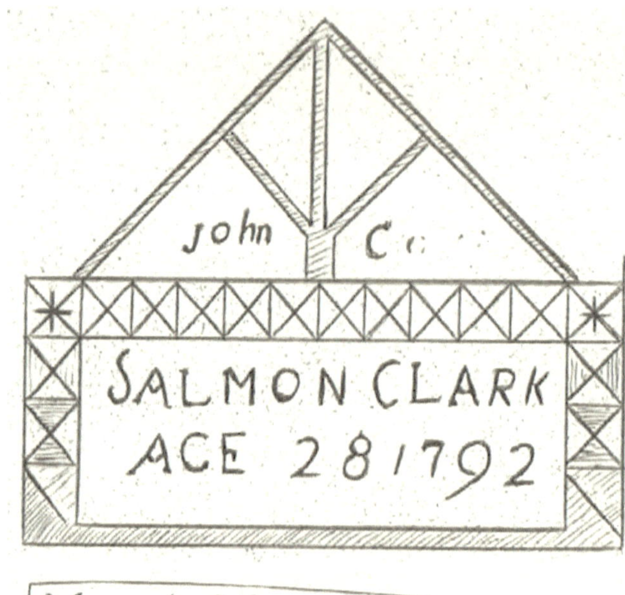

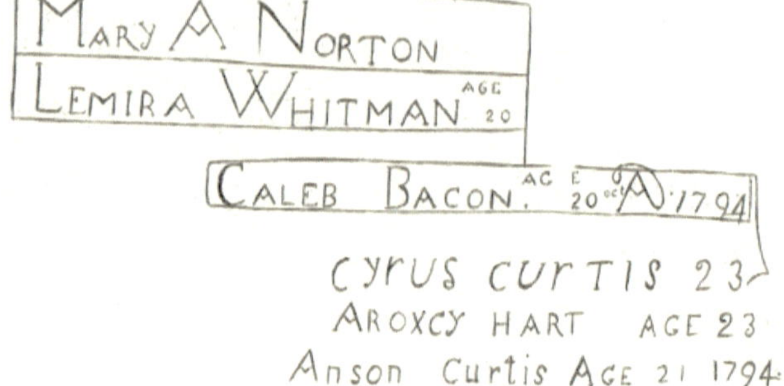

Figure 73: Inscriptions on Hospital Rock in Farmington, Connecticut. *Drawing by T. Fitzpatrick after 1895 illustrations by J. Shepard.*

On December 12, 1791, Doctors Eli Todd and Theodore Wadsworth received approval from the town of Farmington, Connecticut to establish a hospital for the purpose of inoculating people against smallpox, a deadly and highly contagious disease at the time. The hospital was subsequently built in an isolated and remote area on Rattlesnake Mountain, located southeast of the town. The Todd-Wadsworth Smallpox Hospital was in operation at this location from 1792 to 1794; for unknown reasons it later moved several times to other locations.[35]

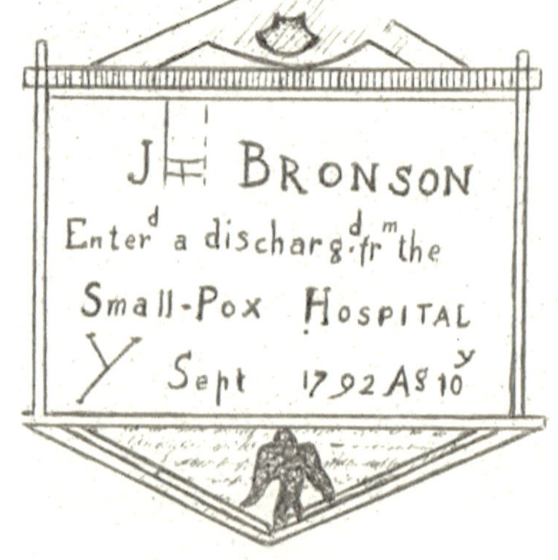

Near the site of the smallpox hospital is an exposed outcrop of basalt that contains the names of more than one hundred individuals who were either patients quarantined at the facility or other persons associated with them or the hospital.[36] The bedrock extends over an area that measures 25 feet (7.2 m) by 30 feet (8.4 m) and is known as Hospital Rock. In an 1895 article in the *Connecticut*

Quarterly, James Shepard recorded many of the names, initials, ages, and dates on the rock of a number of people who came to the hospital to be deliberately infected with smallpox in order to acquire immunity from this disease. This rocky slab was a meeting place of hospital attendants and messengers and a drop-off area for food, clothing, and messages from patients' families during the quarantine period.[37]

According to Shepard, the inscriptions were carved with hammer and chisel by persons who were skilled in the use of these tools (Figure 73). Shepard recorded the names of sixty-six individuals, including any ages and dates associated with them that were visible and legible in 1895. One name also included a town address as well as the person's age, i.e., "Luther Seymour, of Hartford, CT. 22." The oldest date is October, 1794; this suggests that the hospital was in operation nearby during this span of time. In his article, Shepard illustrated a group of six names, a structure that possibly represented the hospital, and the phrase "J. Bronson Enterd & dischargd frm the Small-Pox Hospital Y Sept 1792 Ag 10y" within an elaborate frame. He also noted that there were "various figures, borders, and embellishments… and the numerals 1 to 35 inclusive [were] strung in a continuous row across the rock…."[38]

The inscriptions on Hospital Rock are a historical testament in the battle to conquer the smallpox disease by individuals in the late eighteenth century. They undoubtedly wanted to be remembered by having their names carved into the rock. Among the many inscriptions still visible are "T. Cowles, 1794," "Anson Curtis, age 2, 1794," "William Hooker 1792," "Amos Hull 23, 1793," "Peter Hull, age 18, 1794," "Anna Mix 1794," "Nathan North, 15, 1794," "Abigail Scott, age 26, 1794," and that of "J. Bronson" described above. Unfortunately, other names and graffiti have been carved into the rock by more recent visitors to the site. Hospital Rock is a unique historical document, and it has been included in Connecticut's historic resources inventory.

A Latin Inscription at York Harbor, Maine

The rocky and rugged coast of southern Maine exhibits a superb scenic beauty. Here one can view jagged blocks of stone, large and small, covering a bedrock surface that is washed by the rise and fall of ocean tides. At York Harbor, in the midst of just such a setting, is a rock outcrop on Western Point that bears a most unusual Latin inscription.

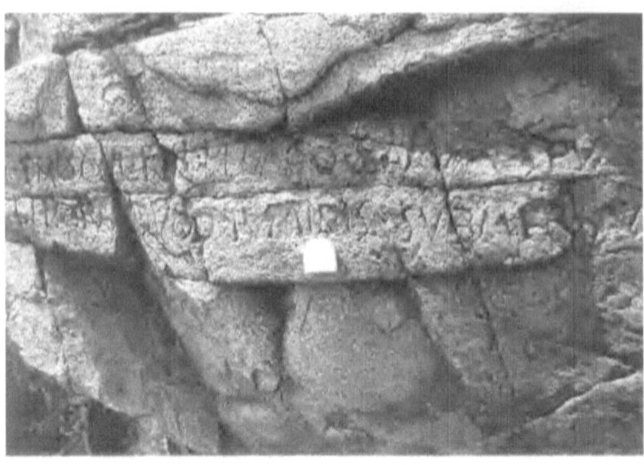
Figure 74: Latin inscription at York Harbor, Maine. *Photo by E.J. Lenik 1974.*

The Latin inscription consists of two lines of letters, sixty-four and forty-four inches long respectively.[39] The letters are about two inches high and are organized into ten words with a dot between each word. The inscription was cut with precision and care into the rock surface by metal tools. It faces the ocean and is high above normal tide level (Figure 74). According to historian W. Mead Stapler, who visited the site in 1969, the inscription has been known by local residents for at least fifty years.[40]

Chris Ritter, a local artist who first reported the site, transcribed the inscription as follows:

EST . PROCVL . IN . PELAGO . SAXVM . SPVMANTIA . CONTRA .
LITORA . QVOD . TVMIDIS . SVBMERSUM

The Latin words appear to be a quotation from Book V, line 24 of Virgil's Aeneid, which reads:

it is…far off…open sea…large rock…foam
shore…low…submerge.

An interpretation of these words by New Hampshire history buff Andrew Rothovius reads as follows:

There is, afar off in the open sea
And facing a storm beaten shoreline
A reef often wholly submerged, and
Pounded by towering breakers when the
Northerly winds of the winter have
Hidden the stars in the heavens.[41]

Rothovius stated that the passage "refers to the boat race held by Aeneas and his Trojan crew of Sicily on their way to Rome, for which race the reef was a turn-around marker." He speculated that the description in the passage may refer to Boon Island, which is visible from the beach, and was a method for warning ancient voyagers that upon reaching this point they should turn around and go back.

A large "pointer rock" is located about one hundred feet shoreward from the Latin inscription.[42] It points across the bay, but not towards Boon Island. Its relationship to the inscription, if any, is unknown.

It has been suggested that the inscription was the work of Romans who "were no strangers along the New England coast," and that the script dates to the fourth or fifth century AD.[43] Chris Ritter also speculated that it might be of Roman origin. He considered the possibility of a modern origin of the carving but rejected this idea based on "the apparent age of the rock and the corresponding wear on the letters."[44] I reject these interpretations and offer instead the following scenario.

Boon Island Ledge is a boulder-strewn humpback rock outcrop that is located some six miles east of York Harbor, Maine. At high tide and during stormy seas it is covered by waves and foam, which make it barely visible to people living along the coast of southern Maine or to ships at sea. Today, a lighthouse rises from the rock and warns coastal shipping of this navigational hazard.

In the winter of 1710, the English ship Nottingham was sailing southerly along the coast during a fierce storm; at this time there was no lighthouse on the ledge.[45] Helpless among the darkness, blowing snow, freezing cold, and poor visibility, the ill fated ship struck the ledge and sank with loss of life. Perhaps the Latin inscription was carved on the shore at York Harbor by a survivor of this tragedy, or alternatively by a local person to commemorate this event.

Whatever its origin, the inscription is an intriguing feature on the coast of Maine.

MYSTERIOUS INSCRIPTIONS AT WESTON MILLS

Enigmatic symbols, dates, and images of skulls and crossbones are carved into reddish brown sandstone ledges that extend along both banks of Lawrence Brook in New Brunswick, Middlesex County, New Jersey. The brook, a ten-mile tributary of the Raritan River, extends through several ponds, crosses through the Rutgers University campus, and is tidal below the Weston Mills dam. There is physical evidence that the rock ledges in this area have been quarried.

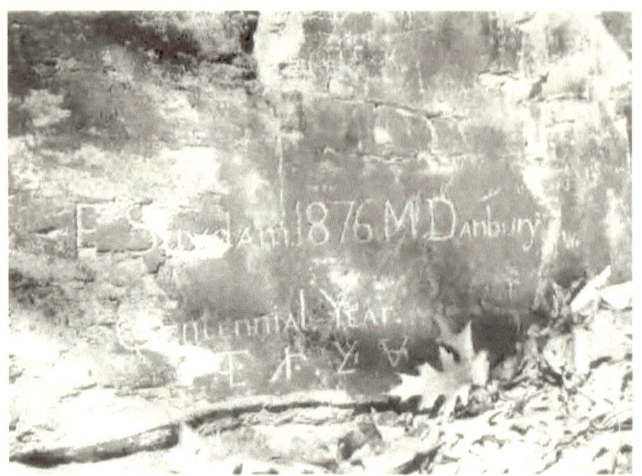

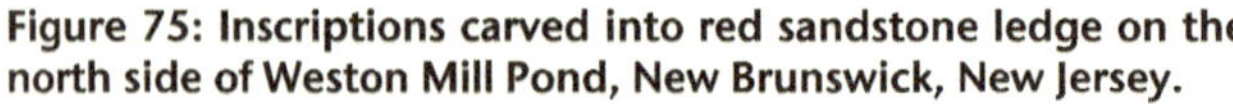
Figure 75: Inscriptions carved into red sandstone ledge on the north side of Weston Mill Pond, New Brunswick, New Jersey.

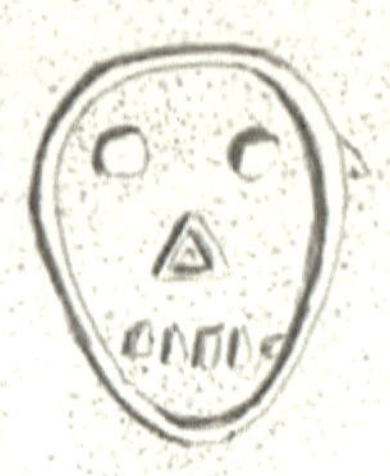
Figure 76: Carved image of a skull on petroglyph panel located on the north side of Weston Mill Pond, New Brunswick, NJ. *Drawing by T. Fitzpatrick.*

Three panels of petroglyphs can be found in the area known as Weston Mills, formerly a thriving nineteenth century community that included a snuff mill, stores, and homes. Today it is a modern urban community consisting of high-rise commercial buildings, parking garages, gas stations, and upscale homes, all surrounded by multi-lane highways.

One panel of petroglyphs is situated on the north bank of Weston Mill Pond in the municipality of New Brunswick. Carved deeply and with considerable skill into this rock billboard is the following inscription: "E. Suydam. 1876 M. Danbury," below which are the words "Centennial Year." Below that are some symbols or letters (Figure 75), and below and to the

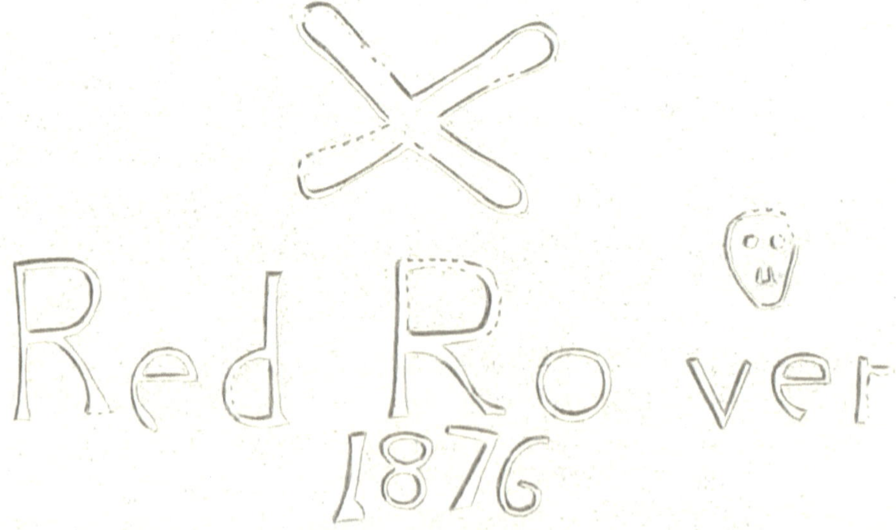

Figure 77: Skull and crossbones, "Red Rover," and "1876" carved on red sandstone ledge on the north side of Lawrence Brook, New Brunswick, NJ. *Drawing by T. Fitzpatrick.*

right of this group is a carved image of a skull (Figure 76).

Further down the Lawrence Brook and below the Weston Mills Dam in New Brunswick is another panel of petroglyphs carved into the same reddish brown sandstone ledge. Depicted here on a vertical surface are the words "Red Rover," below which is the date "1876." Above this inscription is a skull and crossbones (Figure 77). There is also additional graffiti on this petroglyph panel.

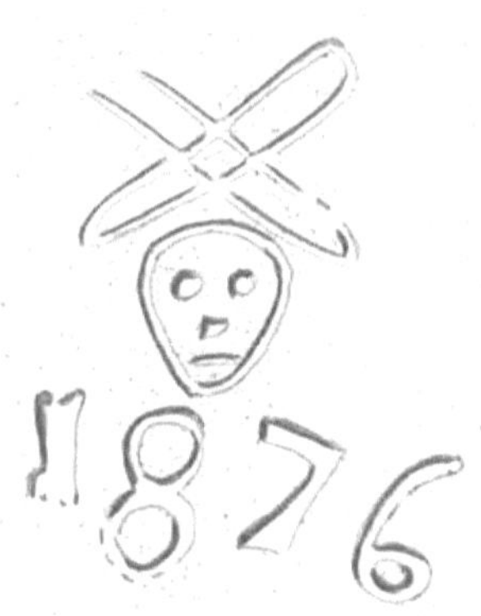

Figure 78: Skull and crossbones and date "1876" carved on red sandstone ledge on south side of Lawrence Brook, East Brunswick, NJ. ***Drawing by T. Fitzpatrick.***

A third panel of petroglyphs is located on the south side of Lawrence Brook, directly across from the panel described above, in the municipality of East Brunswick. Here, on what appears to be a quarried vertical ledge of reddish brown sandstone, are carved and punched-in initials, again with the name "E. Suydam" and the date "1876." Also present on this panel is another carved skull and crossbones image below which is the date "1876" (Figure 78). According to Mark Nonestied of the Middlesex County, New Jersey Cultural and Heritage Commission, the East Brunswick Bicentennial Commission added their "insignia" to the panel in 1976.[46]

Who carved these inscriptions, why were they made, and what do they mean? The names carved into the rock were those of New Brunswick residents whose names appear on old maps and in census records. The mysterious letters or symbols that occur on the panel above Weston Mill Pond remain a puzzle. Perhaps they were the work of an individual from nearby Rutgers University and represent fraternity or sorority symbols.

The words "Red Rover" are the title of a pirate novel written in 1827 by James Fenimore Cooper. Cooper was born in Burlington, New Jersey, lived at various locations in New York, and served in the United States Navy from 1806 to 1811. His experiences aboard sailing ships apparently inspired him to write sea stories. *The Red Rover* is a story of adventure and romance about pirates, ships, and a hero that takes place in the late eighteenth century, just prior to and after America's War for Independence: "The tale recounts the exploits of a noble outcast and visionary who foresees America's destiny as a sovereign nation. Forced into a life of piracy, the Rover conducts his private war of independence in a story that equates the free and daring life of the sea with the American dream of self-reliance and liberty from British rule."[47]

Cooper's novel was still very popular in 1876, the centennial year of American independence. In his story, a sea captain describes the ship's "bunting," or flag, as a "deep, blood-red field without relief or ornament."[48] Red, the captain said, is "the color of a rover" that was "better than your gloomy fields of black with death's heads and other childish scarecrows." It is apparent, therefore, that the Red Rover and skull and crossbones petroglyphs carved on the reddish-brown sandstone ledges along Lawrence Brook were inspired by Cooper's story in commemoration of America's one hundredth anniversary of its independence.

IMAGES OF TRANSPORTATION AND INDUSTRY

THE SKOWHEGAN STONE

In 1978, in company with historians John W. Briggs and White Nichols, I traveled to central Maine to examine a petroglyph boulder reported to have ancient carvings on its flat surface. We found the rock in the town of Skowhegan, and undertook an examination of its unusual and intriguing figures.

A gray quartzite boulder containing carved designs lay in an open field located along State Route 104, also known as Middle Road. This boulder measured 4 feet (1.2 m) in length, 3 feet (90 cm) in width and was partially broken. The carved boulder was not in its original location, since it was found in the late 1930s by Elmer and Sidney Johnson in a hayfield on the opposite side of the road and moved to its present location a short distance to the north of the Johnson farmhouse. The boulder was fractured by attempts to break it up in order to remove it to clear the field.

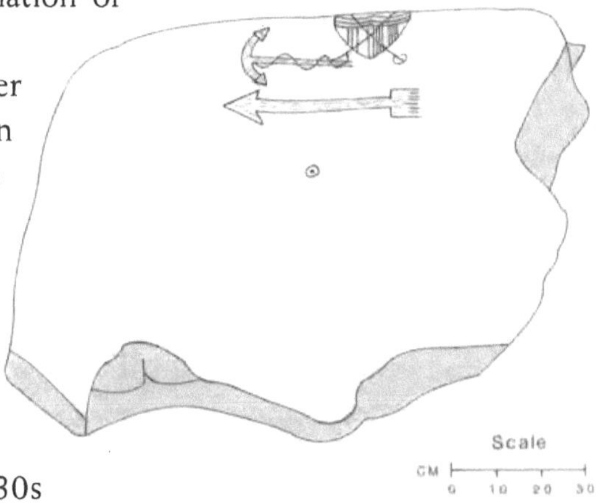

Figure 79: Field sketch of the Skowhegan, Maine, marker stone ***by E.J. Lenik and F. Dulfer.***

The Skowhegan Stone contained four incised designs (Figure 79). The designs were cut with sharp metal tools into this tough artistic medium. The lines forming the designs were thin and shallow, and the entire surface of the stone was covered with lichen. These factors made the designs difficult to see. The four designs were interpreted as:

1. A coat of arms or shield with two crossed swords. The shield measured 6-1/2 inches (16.5 cm) across and 5-1/8 inches (13 cm) from top to bottom.
2. An anchor with a rope (?) around its straight member.
3. An arrow consisting of a triangular point, shaft, and fletching.

4. A circular depression below the arrow with a punch mark in its center. This concavity measured 1 inch (2.5 cm) in diameter and had a maximum depth of 1/4 inch (7 mm).

There were several other small punch marks scattered over the flat surface of the rock, most likely the result of the attempt to split the boulder. The shield/coat of arms, anchor, and arrow were neat and well formed which suggests that some degree of care, time and effort was expended in cutting them.

Who carved the designs on the Skowhegan stone, when, and why? What was their meaning or purpose? Unfortunately, I can only speculate on these matters. No documentary record, tradition, or oral account with respect to this stone has come to light at this point in time. However, I would like to suggest one possible explanation of their meaning.

The designs on the boulder may be related in some way to the "Arnold Trail." In the fall of 1775, Colonel Benedict Arnold and a force of 1,100 soldiers attempted to cross through six hundred miles of wilderness between Maine and Canada in order to storm the British stronghold at Quebec. The route of this attacking force was up the Kennebec River by boat, passing through the town of Skowhegan on its tortuous journey. Although the Skowhegan stone was located some distance from the river, perhaps it was incised by a local resident or one of Arnold's men to commemorate the route and event. Again, this is purely a hypothetical construct.

My analysis of the carvings indicates that the designs were produced by a Euro-American using metal tools. I believe that the stone may have been carved in the late eighteenth or nineteenth centuries because the designs were covered with a heavy growth of lichen. I recognize the difficulty in using lichenometry to date rock art because of the sensitivity of lichens to variations in micro-environmental conditions. When a design is carved into rock the freshly exposed surface is subject to new lichen growth. The rate at which lichens recolonize this surface can be used as a measurement of age. The growth rate is highly variable, depending on the species of lichen, rock type, and such environmental variables as water, temperature, and light. The Skowhegan stone's location in a farmer's field indicates it was exposed to normal rainfall, sunlight, and temperature in the Skowhegan area. In general, lichen growth is quite slow, and under these conditions I conclude the carvings are of some antiquity.

MEDIEVAL SHIP FIGURE

A granite boulder with intriguing images carved on its surface is located in the Westford, Massachusetts Public Library. Nearly square in shape, it measures about 20 inches (50 cm) across its flat surface and contains three figures—a ship, an arrow, and the number "184" (Figure 80).

The figures were produced with metal tools; the ship is outlined by punch marks, and similar marks also make up the arrow and numbers. The ship figure contains a single mast with square sails topped by what appears to be a pennant or banner. A line of eight punch marks or pits extend horizontally along the ship's hull just below its railing. The arrow figure to the right of the ship points downward. Four chevron-like designs are at the upper end of the arrow shaft that presumably represent feathers. Below the hull of the ship are the numbers "184"; the middle number is incomplete at the top but has been interpreted as an eight.

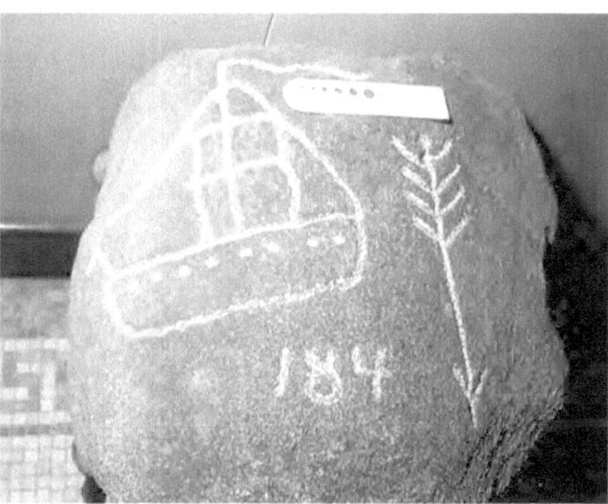

Figure 80: A granite boulder with a carved "Medieval" ship in Westford, Massachusetts. ***Photo courtesy of M. Stapler 1978.***

According to archaeologist Frank Glynn, the boulder was formerly located about 2.5 miles (4 km) northwest of Prospect Hill at the juncture of two roads that were once Indian trails.[1] It was removed from its original location in 1932 during road widening work and stored in William Wyman's barn. The stone was eventually obtained from Wyman and donated to the Westford Public Library in 1963.

The ship has been interpreted as a fourteenth century knarr (Viking trading ship) with eight oar ports. Its long bowsprit suggested that it dated to the period 1350 to 1400 AD.[2]

The purpose or meaning of the carved figures has been intensively investigated. Frank Glynn reported that English archaeologist T.C. Lethbridge of the University Museum of Cambridge was contacted regarding the figures on the rock. Lethbridge replied that "the thing is obviously a message. 184 paces from the track on which that stone was placed you will find a snug little corner where [Prince Henry] Sinclair's bothy, hut, tent was set up…if you take a circle with a radius of 184 paces from the spot where the stone was found, the old H.Q. lies somewhere on it."[3]

From 1963 to 1966 a search was made along the circles suggested by Lethbridge in an attempt to find the Westford Knight campsite. At a place called Wyman's Corner on State Route 40 in Graniteville, some two and one-half miles north of Westford, Glynn found a stone enclosure that measured 40 feet (12 m) by 32 feet (9.6 m) and was about 3 feet (0.9 m) in height. A spring was situated within the southeastern corner of the enclosure and an entrance was at the northwest corner. Inside the enclosure, along its west wall, was a "collapsed small stone structure."[4] The distance from the entrance to the road juncture where the stone was found measured 187 paces.

STAGECOACH ROCK

Following the Revolutionary War, the American countryside was rapidly transformed from a vast wilderness into burgeoning cities, towns, villages, and farms, as land-hungry settlers sought a better life for themselves and their families. Emigration into open interior land from coastal areas was swift, and as a consequence there was an enormous demand for new roads. Old Indian trails and pathways were transformed into turnpikes, plank roads or corduroy (log) roads. In the early days the road conditions were very primitive; however, as soon as wagon roads were broken through the countryside the stagecoach made its appearance. Rain or shine, stagecoaches carried passengers, mail, and freight, and this method of travel by horse drawn coach extended for over one hundred years. The stagecoach was a unique vehicle in the history of American overland transportation.

During the last half of the nineteenth century, the Adirondack Mountains in upstate New York began to attract many visitors seeking relief from the heat and stifling condition in cities such as New York, Boston, and Philadelphia. A vast, unsettled, and untamed area of dense forest, rugged landscape, pristine lakes and fast flowing rivers and streams, the Adirondacks beckoned to hunters, fishers, and others seeking a return to nature and the great outdoors. Year after year, an increasing flow of visitors came to seek solace, escape and recreation in the mountains and lakes of the region.

To fill the need for accommodations, grand hotels, great camps and cottages were built along the banks of various lakes in the area. Villages sprang up in the region and developed into transportation hubs for those entering the wilderness. At Blue Mountain Lake, for example, three grand hotels were built in the late nineteenth century: Holland's Blue Mountain Lake Hotel, Potter's Hotel, and Merwin's Blue Mountain House. These hotels attracted so many visitors that two competing lines of stagecoaches went into service in 1878 to bring passengers from the village of North Creek to the lake.[5] Crowds flocked to these grand hotels and camps—naturalists, climbers, fishers, artists and dreamers, and others—seeking private communion with nature, and from 1855 through the early twentieth century the stagecoach was their principal means of travel through the Adirondack Mountains.

Stagecoach travel along rough roads was not without its difficulties. On August 14, 1901, a stagecoach driven by four horses was on its way from the village of North Creek to Blue Mountain Lake when it was held up by two masked highwaymen.[6] The stagecoach contained seven passengers—four men and three women. The highwaymen appeared out of the forest and ordered the driver to stop, but he refused, so they shot the two lead horses. According to an associated article in *The New York Times*, "three of the male passengers jumped off and took to the woods. The fourth male passenger had his wife with him, and he likewise would have sought shelter had it not been that his wife grabbed his coattails and delayed his progress." The robbers relieved

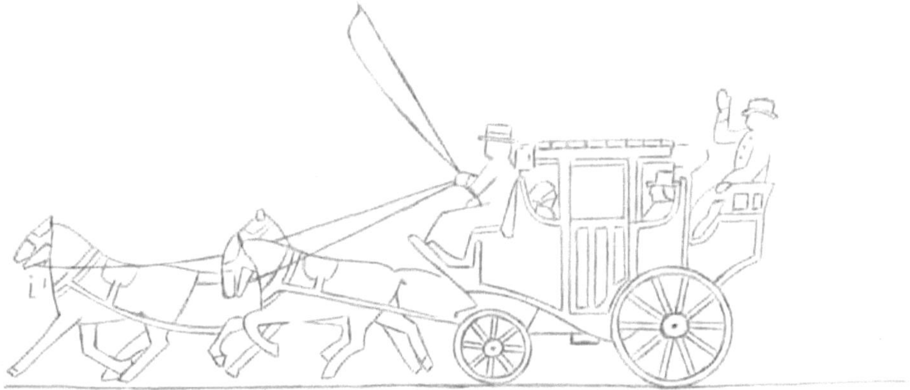

Figure 81: Carving of a stagecoach in motion with driver and passengers in Keene, New York. ***Drawing by T. Fitzpatrick after photo by R. Grubsmith 2003.***

the passengers of their valuables, ransacked the mail sacks and packages and then fled into the woods. A handbill of the *Utica Saturday Globe* described the scene as "A regular Wild West Hold-Up in the Peaceful Adirondacks that netted the thieves 1000 dollars."[7]

Southeast of Lake Placid, on State Route 73 in the town of Keene, New York, is a large boulder at roadside that contains an incised carving of a stagecoach pulled by four horses (Figure 81). The coach has a straight top and sides, a side door, small front wheels and larger rear wheels. The design characteristics as portrayed suggest that the stagecoach is an Eastern or Light Concord Coach.[8] A driver with a long whip in one hand and reins in the other is in the front boot and driver's seat. He appears to be wearing a long coat and has a hat on his head. On the rear boot and seat is another person with a hat on his head and upraised arm, apparently waving. Inside the coach are three seats, a person (possibly a woman) is seated on the front seat facing the rear of the coach, and a man wearing a hat is on the rear seat facing forward. Harnesses are indicated on the horses. The image is about 18 inches (45.5 cm) long.

According to the Essex County Historical Society, Stage Coach Rock was carved by the Carnes Granite Company of Au Sable Forks, New York, in the 1930s on a boulder that slid off the mountain.[9] At that time, the company was working on the stone base for the John Brown statue at the John Brown Farm near Lake Placid. The artist who produced the beautiful image was Wilfred Carnes, who used "sand blasting equipment" to do so. The rendering of the old stagecoach was said to commemorate the old stage lines that once carried thousands of visitors to Adirondack resorts.

PRATT'S ROCK: A BIOGRAPHY IN STONE

Petroglyphs dating to the historic period are numerous in the Catskill Mountains of southeastern New York. One of the most unusual of this genre is a site called Pratt's Rock located near the village of Prattsville in Greene County.

Zadock Pratt (1790-1871) was the founder of the tanning industry in the Catskills.[10] In 1824 he purchased a large tract of land located near the juncture of Batavia Creek and Schoharie Creek. A picturesque and sparsely settled valley, the region contained abundant hemlock trees, which were used in the tanning process. By June, 1825, Pratt had completed construction of a tannery that was 170 feet (50 m) long by 43 (10.6 m) feet wide. Shortly thereafter, the tannery was enlarged to 550 (153 m) feet by 43 (10.6 m) feet, which made it the largest of its kind at that time.

By 1829, Pratt had established a small village, later to bear his name, adjacent to Schoharie Creek. Here he laid out the village's streets, built over one hundred houses (many in the Greek Revival style), founded churches, a town academy, and planted trees along the streets. Together with other investors, he established numerous industries in the area, including a saw mill, grist mill, a cabinet shop, machine shop, match factory, glove factory, oilcloth factory, chair factory, and an iron foundry. Zadock also established the village newspaper and built a covered bridge across Schoharie Creek.

Over time, Pratt's village grew to include stores, saddle and harness makers, wagon shops, turning shops, tailors and seamstresses, shoemakers, a cooperage, two churches, a dentist, doctors and lawyers. The village with its supporting industries was truly a planned community dominated by Zadock Pratt. On March 8, 1833, the township of Prattsville was officially recognized by the New York State Legislature.

Zadock Pratt was elected to Congress, serving two terms (from 1837-1839 and 1843-1845). In 1843 he established the Prattsville Bank, and even printed his own money. By 1846, his Prattsville tannery, so dependent upon the bark of the hemlock trees, had closed its doors because all of the trees had been cut down. In 1852, the bank was also closed.

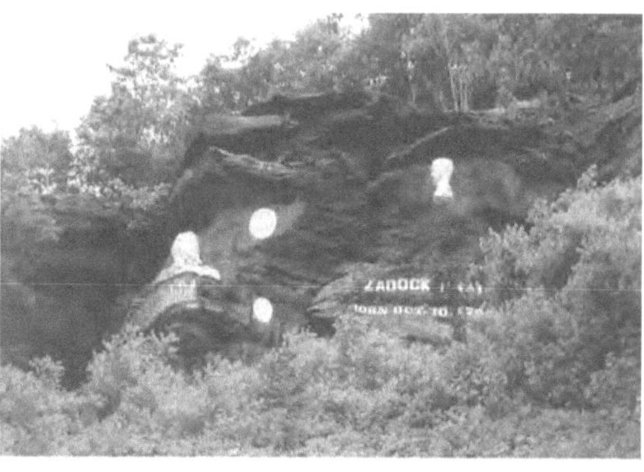

Figure 82: Pratt Rock Park on State Route 23, Prattsville, New York. ***Photo by E.J. Lenik 1996.***

In sum, Pratt was a village planner, wealthy landowner, entrepreneur, legislator, tanner and banker, besides being a colonel in the New York State Militia. His influence and personality dominated the village.

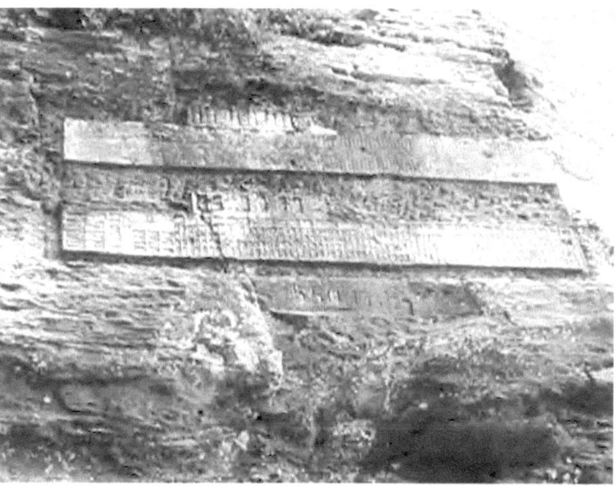

Figure 83: Bas relief of tannery building with legend indicating it was 550 feet long. Plan view of lower level (top) and second story (bottom). Pratt Rock Park, Prattsville, New York. ***Photo by Mountain Top Historical Society 2001 as posted on <http://mths.org/hikes/tannery.jpg> Nov. 2003.***

Local folklore states that an itinerant and penniless sculptor came to Prattsville in 1843 and solicited money from Zadock, the village's foremost citizen. Pratt reportedly gave him fifty cents, and in return asked the sculptor to carve a profile of him on a cliff high above the village. Pratt was so pleased by his likeness that he commissioned the sculptor to carve other images depicting his life in the rock ledge surrounding his profile. These images are now within Pratt Rock Park, which is located along State Route 23 and open to the public. Pratt's Rock is an exciting and fascinating visual record-in-stone of Zadock Pratt's life, as well as an example of the stonecutter/sculptor's art (Figure 82).

The bas-relief of the tannery building, showing two stories in plan view, was carved here, along with the legend "ONE MILLION SIDES OF SOLE LEATHER TANNED WITH HEMLOCK BARK, IN TWENTY YEARS BY Z. PRATT." This shoe leather was produced for the New York City market (Figure 83).

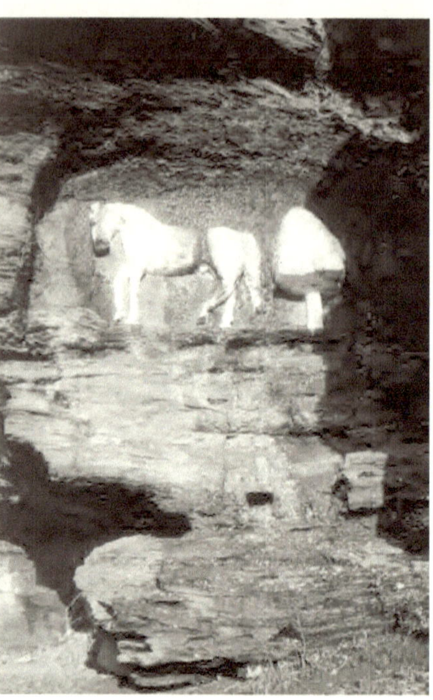
Figure 84: Sculpted horse and conventionalized hemlock tree at Pratt Rock Park, Prattsville, New York. *Photo by E.J. Lenik 1996.*

A horse and stylized hemlock tree, which were important natural resources in the leather tanning business, were also carved in bold relief (Figure 84). This panel pays tribute to the horses who hauled the hemlock bark, represented by the tree, to the Pratt tannery.

The vertical cliff face contains the Pratt coat of arms with the motto "DO WELL AND DOUBT NOT." There is also a wreath that includes the names of his children George W. and Julia H.

Under the profile of Zadock Pratt is the legend, "ZADOCK PRATT / BORN OCT. 30, 1790" (Figure 85). A large bust of his son George was carved to the left of Zadock's, with the following legend: "HON. G.W. PRATT, Ph.D. / COL XX Regt., N.Y.S.M., ULSTER Co., BORN APRIL 18 1830 / WOUNDED AUG. 30, IN THE 2nd BATTLE OF / MANASSAS, VA. DIED AT ALBANY, N.Y. Sep. 11th / GOOD BRAVE HONORABLE 1862." George's vital statistics were carved into the rock along with a right hand. To the right of this image is a right arm with rolled up shirt sleeve and raised hand holding a hammer (Figure 86). This latter figure may represent the sculptor's tribute to himself.

There are other carvings in Pratt Rock State Park. A steep path ascends the hillside to the base of the cliff containing the Pratt carvings.

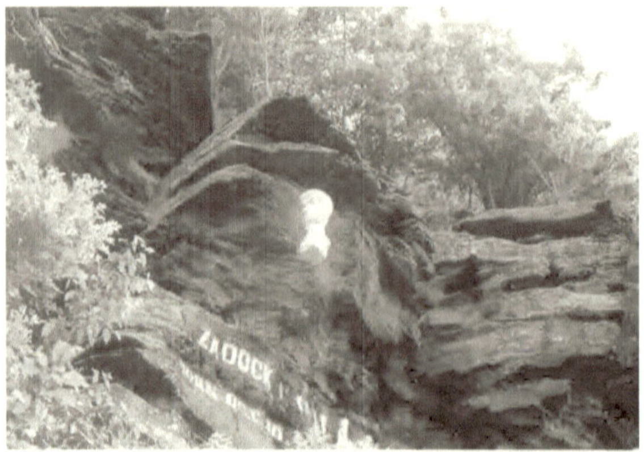

Figure 85: Profile of Zaddock Pratt at Pratt Rock Park, Prattsville, New York. *Photo by E.J. Lenik 1996.*

Along the way, the sculptor carved chairs and benches with hemlock trees. Several of the stone benches are decorated with finely carved concentric circles and oblique lines. At the bottom of the cliff is a rectangular, vertical recessed chamber that was reportedly carved as a tomb for Zadock Pratt, but due to leakage during storms he was not buried there. Instead, he was buried in a nearby cemetery.

There is a stone wall with large flat capstones along the road at Pratt Rock Park. Several incised figures are carved into the capstones on top of the wall, including initials, dates, a hand, a house, and a pennant. There is also an elephant carved in low relief, probably to commemorate a circus that passed through the village. The style and method of execution of these figures are unlike the sculptures on the cliff above and were undoubtedly carved by village residents and other visitors or passers-by to the site.

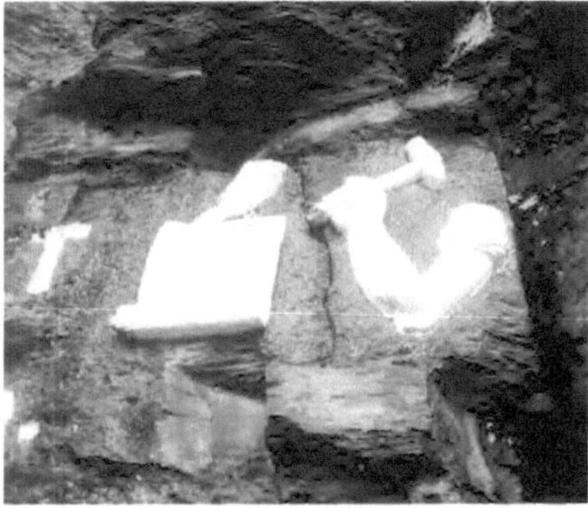

Figure 86: A hand holding a scroll and an arm holding a hammer at Pratt Rock Park, Prattsville, New York. ***Photo by E.J. Lenik 1996.***

A TRAIN PETROGLYPH ON HOG MOUNTAIN

In 1899, the Jersey City Water Supply Company began construction of a water supply reservoir in the town of Boonton and Township of Parsippany-Troy Hills in Morris County, New Jersey. The Boonton Reservoir, as it is called locally, consists of nine hundred acres of surface area extending across the two municipalities. The reservoir impounds the water of the Rockaway River just after it passes through Boonton. Construction extended until 1904 when work was completed and the gates of a new dam were closed. When finished, the reservoir had a storage capacity of nine billion gallons and provided potable water for public consumption in the city of Jersey City, New Jersey.

The reservoir project included the construction of a dam 3,200 feet (960 m) long consisting of 220 feet (660 m) of solid masonry with 500 feet (150 m) of concrete, with earthen dikes at each end. In 1903, the Newark Sunday News described the reservoir dam as "one of the three wonders of the world in structures of this character." The newspaper further characterized its construction as "cyclopean in the size of the granite blocks used."[11]

In order to procure stone fill for the construction of the dam, the contractors purchased Hog Mountain, located in Montville Township, about four miles northwest of the dam site.[12] A railroad was built from the quarry to the dam to carry large blacks of granite and crushed stone used in its construction.

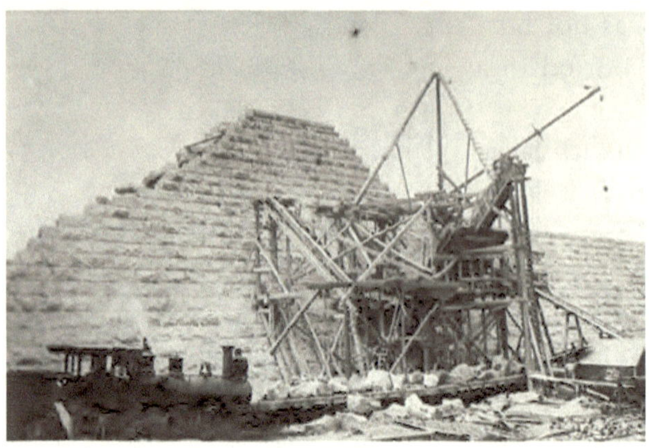

Figure 87: Circa 1900 photograph of the Boonton, New Jersey, reservoir dam under construction. Note locomotive at left bringing stone blocks. ***Photo courtesy of R.C. Stevralia.***

The railroad was incorporated under the name of the Rockaway River and Montville Railroad Company. The railroad's operating stock consisted of "four full-sized six-driving wheel locomotives," and "several trains of flat, gondola and gravel" dump cars (Figure 87).

According to several newspaper reports, employment at the Hog Mountain quarry ranged from about two hundred men in 1899 to four hundred men in 1901. Stone cutters and "blasters" remained busy removing the rock, dressing granite blocks, crushing the stone for use in concrete, and loading the railroad cars.[13]At various times thirty derricks and a stone crusher were in operation at the quarry. The workers were primarily Italian stone cutters and laborers, and their work was extremely hard and dangerous. The *Boonton Times* reported that four Italian workers were killed, three seriously injured, and one contracted after contracting small pox between 1899 and 1904. In another incident a railroad car became loose at the quarry and ran down the track at "terrific" speed to the new dam, where it jumped off the track and was badly damaged.

In 1973 Russell C. Stevralia, a resident and neighbor of the Hog Mountain quarry site in Montville, discovered a carving of a locomotive on the ridge top above the now abandoned quarry (Figure 88). In 1983 he contacted this author to report his find, and we subsequently hiked to the site to examine this image.[14] The glyph is that of a steam locomotive that was chiseled into an exposed surface of bedrock at the very top edge of the quarry. The image measured 21-1/2 inches (54.5 cm) in length and 13-1/2 inches (35 cm) in maximum height, and was produced by hammering the outline with a metal chisel or drill. The quarryman's

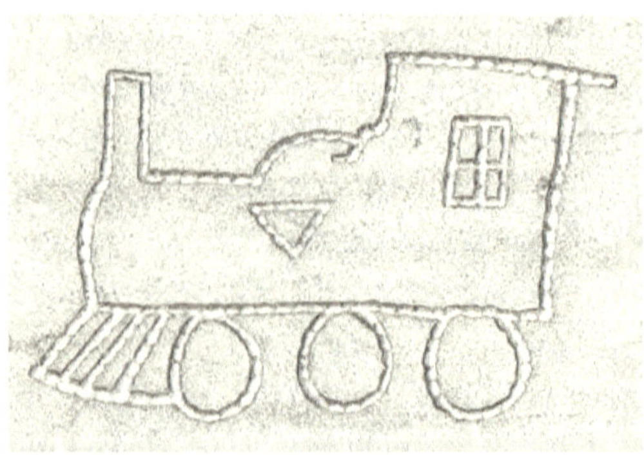

Figure 88: Image of a steam locomotive chiseled into bedrock at Hog Mountain quarry, Montville, New Jersey. ***Drawing by T. Fitzpatrick.***

rendering of the steam locomotive, with its drive wheels, cab, and smokestack, is very similar to those locomotives used to haul stones from the quarry to the reservoir dam. It is highly probable that the locomotive petroglyph was made by one of the Italian stonecutters who worked in the quarry during the period from 1899 to 1905.

I can visualize a quarryman sitting at the edge of the quarry chiseling the familiar figure of the steam locomotive as it traveled back and forth through the bottom of the quarry. Why would this Italian stonecutter resort to such doodling on the hard rock after a day or week of hard, backbreaking work? Perhaps he was simply practicing his artistic skill, or wanted to pass away the time. We will never know his true motivation.

A "VIKING" SHIP CARVING

In 1972, I traveled to Medomak in the town of Bremen, Lincoln County, Maine, to investigate a reported carving of a Viking ship on a slab of rock located on private property. The village of Medomak is situated on Keene Neck, a peninsula that extends southerly toward Muscongus Bay. On the west side of the peninsula is Greenland Cove, and to the east is Hockomock Channel. The Viking ship carving was first reported to the New England Antiquities Research Association in 1962.[15]

The carved rock was a quarried piece of granite, rough in appearance, which stood 5 feet (1.5 m) high, 3-1/2 feet (1 m) wide, and 1 foot (30 cm) in thickness. The rock slab was in an upright position and rested on a stone base. A large realistic-looking sail was sculpted with considerable skill into one side of the rock with a pennant flying from the top of the mast (Figure 89). The figure was cut with metal tools with much of the sail appearing in low relief.

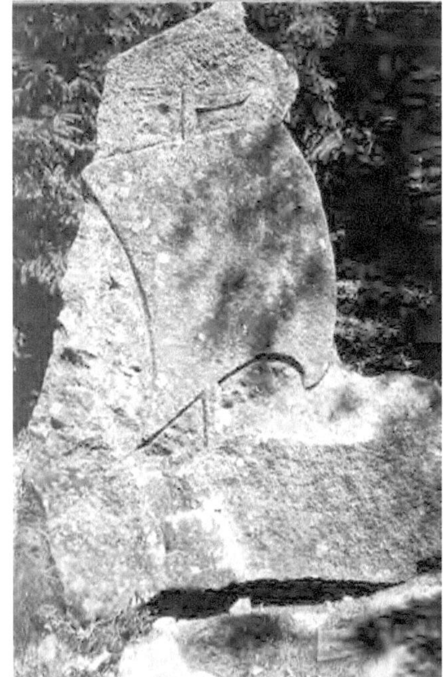

Figure 89: Sculpted image of a sail, Medomak, Maine. ***Photo by E.J. Lenik 1972.***

The carving was examined by members of the New England Antiquities Research Association in 1963. A photograph of the image was taken with an accompanying sketch that labeled it a "Viking Ship Carving."[16] I can only speculate as to the origin of the name. Perhaps it was labeled as a Viking ship based on the shape of the sail, although the ship itself was not carved into the rock. The location of the carving on a peninsula near the ocean, together with Greenland Cove on one side and Hockamock Channel on the other, may have influenced the choice of the name. The name Hockamock may be a corruption of the name Hobbamock, a spiritual deity of the Algonkian Indians who once inhabited this area of Maine. The Vikings are known to have encountered Indians, whom they referred to as *scraelings*, during their explorations along the North American coast. A subsequent report mentioned that some type of inscription was present on the rock, but I found no evidence of this during my visit in 1972.

Further research, however, has solved the mystery surrounding the nature of the sail carving. In October 1972, William H. Brooks, Jr., Town Clerk of Waldoboro, Maine, wrote a letter to the newsletter editor of the New England Antiquities Research Association regarding the Viking ship carving. In his letter Brooks revealed when the stone was carved, why the sail motif was selected, and the name of the artist:

> There used to be a granite quarry in Waldoboro on Depot Street, near the railroad tracks, which was owned and operated by William Grant. I used to spend quite a bit of time there back in the 1920s watching them drill, blow out huge chunks of granite and then fashion it into paving blocks....
>
> I used to spend summers at Medomak at the cottage of Dr. and Mrs. A.R. Benedict...Mrs. Benedict used a little ship as a sort of trademark....
>
> One day rather a large piece of granite was blown out which could not be used for paving blocks...and it attracted me, due to the outline of it. The Benedicts were interested in it too, and with the permission of Mr. Grant it was hauled down to Medomak. John Watts of North Waldoboro, whose profession was lettering grave stones, was engaged to fashion the sail, mast, and flag. It was then placed on the ledge where it now stands...the handiwork of John Watts was well known in this section. [17]

STEAMBOAT IN VERMONT

The ruins of two historic period structures stand silently and mysteriously on private land a short distance off Morgan Road in South Woodstock, Windsor County, Vermont. These features, once part of a colonial-era farm and mill complex, have evoked questions about their age, purpose, and cultural origin for many years.

The first of these structures is a stone chamber, also referred to as a beehive or root cellar. In the late twentieth century, the chamber was examined and excavated to some extent by Barry Fell, a retired marine biologist from Harvard University, and his associates. Fell reported finding a bird-like "painted" figure with "arms [spread] like wings" on the ceiling of the chamber, which he identified as "Tanith," a Phoenician Mother Goddess. This ceiling was constructed of large stone slabs. On the outside entrance of the chamber, Fell's excavations uncovered a stone bearing the inscribed name "B-Ya-N or Byanu," which Fell claimed was written in Ogam, a language that lacked vowels.[18]

The so-called Mother Earth figure on the ceiling was described by two subsequent investigators of the chamber, who seem to have subscribed to Fell's interpretation of the various markings. The figure on the chamber's ceiling was accepted as representing Mother Earth, with "her robe flairs out to form a triangle below her head. Her winged arms stretched out to either side."[19]

The so-called Tanith Chamber was investigated by archaeologist Giovanna Neudorfer in the 1970s, along with more than fifty other such structures throughout the state of Vermont. She described the chamber as "incorporated into a hillside" and "attached to a foundation wall of a defunct cider mill."[20] Her investigation revealed that the property on which the chamber is situated was settled circa 1784. The chamber was built prior to 1855 and was located 125 feet (38 m) from a second house built on the same site. A well and outbuilding were also present nearby. Neudorfer concluded that there was "no evidence of ancient European settlement in Vermont."[21]

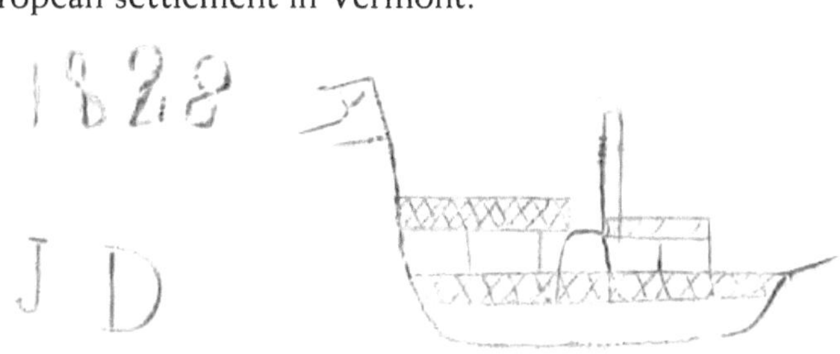

Figure 90: Incised image of a steamboat in South Woodstock, VT. ***Drawing by T. Fitzpatrick.***

The foundation of the cider mill is located about 200 feet (60 m) from the road. It is constructed of large rectangular-cut stone blocks and thin slabs of limestone and schist. At one corner of the structure is a large rectangular-cut stone block that contains an incised image of a steamboat.[22] The steamboat figure appears to have a side paddle wheel, a funnel at midpoint, and a flag or pennant on a mast at the stern of the vessel. To the left of the boat is a carved date "1828" below which are the initials "JD." The date is crudely carved, but the initials are well formed and appear to be contemporary with the boat. They may be those of the carver-artist (Figure 90).

As European settlers moved into the upper Connecticut River Valley in the eighteenth century, towns were established along its banks. In time, agriculture became an important part of life in the river valley. Simultaneously, small water-powered mills, such as grist, saw, and cider mills, were built along the tributaries of the Connecticut River. Agricultural and forest products were shipped down the river to Hartford, Connecticut, and the river became "an artery of commerce, the region's economic link to the world."[23] Canals were built at several locations in order to facilitate transportation along the river, and steamboats plied the river in the period from the late 1820s to the early 1840s.

The purpose or meaning of the steamboat carving on a cornerstone of a cider mill in South Woodstock is unknown. Perhaps the artist once saw such a vessel on the Connecticut River, which is located about twenty miles to the east of the site, and carved its image to record this event.

WEAPONS

A PETROGLYPH ON ARROW HILL

A bow and arrow petroglyph in association with abstract rectilinear drawings is carved into an outcrop of granite located on the summit of Arrow Hill in the town of Surry in southwestern New Hampshire. Are these symbols the work of Indians, as some people believe, or the work of a Euro-American settler? Local residents, both past and present, seem to believe the site was of Indian origin, and as a result the petroglyph is referred to as the "Indian Bow and Arrow Carving."[1] Published historical accounts, on the other hand, offer several explanations for its origin.

In 1925, an article appeared in the local *Repertory* magazine titled "An Enigma in Stone" that described the site, presented several theories about its origin, and included a photograph of the bow and arrow petroglyph. The anonymous author reported that "this rock carving was the work of an eccentric inhabitant of the locality who is known to have made somewhat similar sculptures on rock in the vicinity" in apparent imitation of ancient ones.[2] In this article, the writer stated that he was informed "several years ago" by a Dr. William R. Duncan that "the petroglyph was of supposed aboriginal origin and was known to the earliest settlers...." The writer went on to say that the site was also investigated by Dr. Josiah L. Seward, who ascribed its authorship to the St. Francis (Abenaki) Indians. Finally, Charles M. Scovell, a long-time resident, told the writer that "his father knew of its existence in 1845."

A 1920 *Map of the Town of Surry, New Hampshire* by Frank B. Kingsbury marked the location of the petroglyph site on Arrow Hill with a symbol of a bow and arrow. Kingsbury, a local historian, reported that the petroglyph was carved around 1860 by William P. Mason.[3] Mason, a local "eccentric," allegedly carved several other bow and arrow petroglyphs on top of the same hill and on boulders on his brother's farm nearby.[4]

A third account of the petroglyph site was published in 1932 in a book titled *Historical Notes of Keene and Roxbury, New Hampshire*. Author Samuel Wadsworth reiterated the previous reports cited above regarding the origin and age of the carvings, but added some additional details, stating that William P. Mason "cut" the petroglyphs with a "sharp tool" which produced v-shaped grooves.[5]

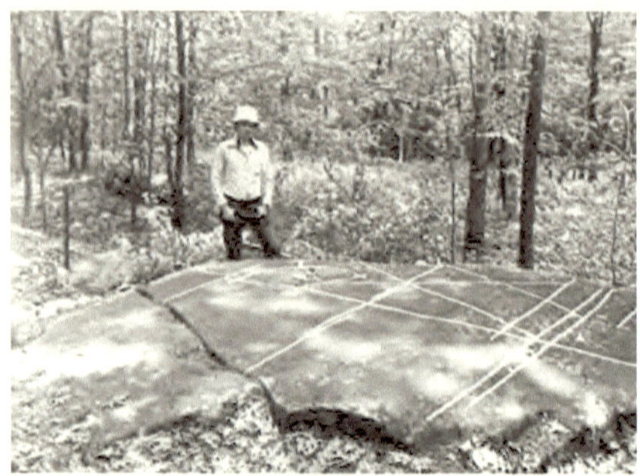

Figure 91: Arrow Hill petroglyph, Surrey, New Hampshire. ***Photo by E.J. Lenik 1983.***

I hiked to the top of Arrow Hill in 1983 with two colleagues to examine and record the bow and arrow carving. The hill, at an elevation of 1,280 feet (384 m), afforded a commanding view of the surrounding area. The Ashuelot River is located about 2-1/2 miles (4 km) to the east of Arrow Hill, and Mount Monadnock lies some distance to the south.

The bow and arrow petroglyph was carved into an isolated outcrop of granite situated on the southeastern top of the hill, its highest elevation (Figure 91). The rock outcrop was nearly flat and had a table-like appearance; it measured 20 feet (6 m) in maximum length and 8-1/4 feet (2.5 m) in width. The bow and arrow figure was found on the southeast side of the rock outcrop.

The petroglyph was cut into the hard rock with metal tools which formed u-shaped grooves, not v-shaped as reported by Wadsworth in 1932. The arrow pointed in a southeasterly direction. Wadsworth noted that it pointed toward the city of Keene and Mount Monadnock, and "nearly in the direction of the old Indian village just south of the covered highway bridge at Sawyer's Crossing and on the east side of the Ashuelot River."[6]

The bow and draw string is in an active or drawn position with the arrow set to be released (Figure 92). The length of the bow was 3 feet, 2-1/2 inches (100 cm) and the length of the arrow was 13-3/4 inches (35 cm). A portion of the arrow shaft and its feathered end was cracked and broken into several pieces, the result of frost action or perhaps vandalism. The width of the grooves ranged from 3/4 of an inch to 1-3/16 inches (2 to 3 cm), and the depth averaged 5/16 of an inch (8.5 mm). The incised figure was conspicuous in appearance and well made.

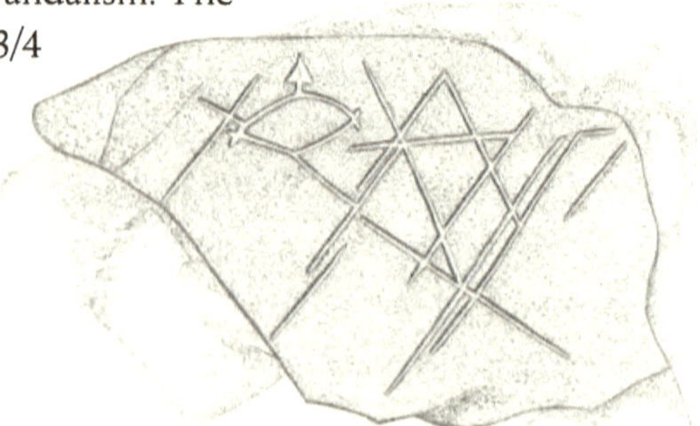

Figure 92: ***Measured drawing of the Arrow Hill petroglyph in Surrey, New Hampshire, by T. Fitzpatrick.***

A series of straight lines are incised into the rock immediately to the west and east of the bow and arrow, and seven parallel lines extend north-south on the west side of it. Another line is perpendicular to and crosses the seven parallel lines, essentially forming a right angle. Two additional lines extend obliquely (northwest to southeast) across five of the parallel lines, while another extends roughly east to west. There were also two crossed lines on the east side of the bow. Overall, these lines form triangles, parallelograms and trapezoids. It has been suggested that these lines may represent a map, "possibly of trails."[7] I discard this speculation; there is no evidence to support such conjecture. The lines were incised to depths ranging from 1/8 of an inch (3 mm) to 3/8 of an inch (9 mm) and were 3/8 of an inch (1 cm) wide; they were v-shaped in plan view. These abstract rectilinear drawings are unlike the representational bow and arrow glyph, and were most likely produced by a different person.

The Arrow Hill petroglyph site was intensively investigated by Colgate Gilbert and a team of researchers representing the New England Antiquities Research Association in the 1980s. In a published report, Gilbert tentatively concluded that the petroglyph was carved at some time following the early Euro-American exploration and settlement of this region, i.e., the early eighteenth century.[8] In an unpublished "updated" report of his research, Gilbert suggested that the petroglyphs were carved some time between 1735 and 1840 and implied that they were made by Euro-Americans. He further noted that "the question of why these carvings were made...still eludes us."[9]

My reading of the historical reports leads me to the conclusion that the bow and arrow petroglyph was most likely carved in the early nineteenth century by the so-called "eccentric" local resident William P. Mason. The lines or rectilinear drawings were added to the rock by a different person at another time. The meaning or purpose of these figures remains an enigma in stone.

MORE BOWS AND ARROWS ON SURRY MOUNTAIN

Surry Mountain, situated on the east side of the Ashuelot River, rises steeply to an elevation of 1,100 feet (330 m) above the river's flood plain below. It is located about three miles due east of the Arrow Hill petroglyph site in the town of Surry, Cheshire County, New Hampshire. Here, scattered around the southern end of the mountain, are a number of petroglyphs carved on boulders and rock outcrops. The most common design element is a bow and arrow—seven in number—but other figures are also present, including three muskets, a tomahawk, a crescent moon and star, isolated grooves, and initials. For the most part, the petroglyphs occur as single figures on boulders or rock ledges.

In 1994, I joined a survey team from the New England Antiquities Research Association in conducting an in-depth study, recording and photographing this intriguing collection of petroglyphs on the mountaintop. My record of the several images follows.

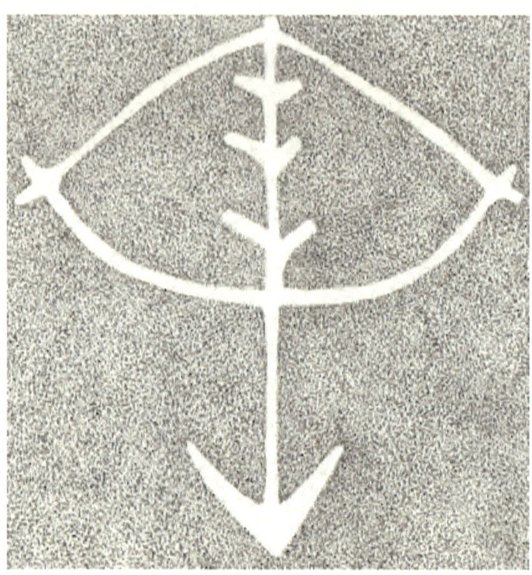

Figure 93: Bow and arrow in active or drawn position on Surrey Mountain, New Hampshire. *Drawing by T. Fitzpatrick.*

Petroglyph #1 was a deeply incised bow and arrow on the west facing and slanting surface of a large boulder located at the southern end of the mountain (Figure 93). The bow and its draw string are depicted in an active position with the arrow set to be released. The arrow points downward and three chevron-like cuts resembling fletching (presumably feathers) are illustrated along the shaft. The point of the arrow is barb-like. A deeply cut v-shaped notch was present at the edge of the rock above the drawstring. The boulder measured 13 feet 2 inches (4 m) in height and the petroglyph was carved near the top of the rock. It is likely that the carver-artist needed a ladder or other device for elevation to execute this figure (Figure 94).

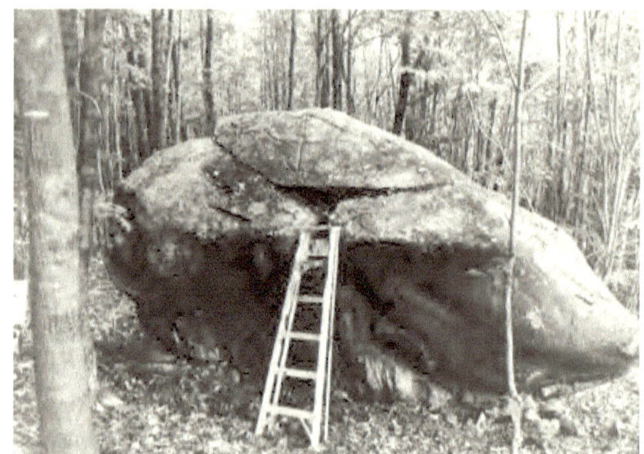

Figure 94: Bow and arrow pointing downward (see Figure 93) carved near op of large boulder on Surrey Mountain, New Hampshire. Photo by E.J. Lenik 1994.

Petroglyph Panel #2 consisted of four deeply incised designs on an area of exposed granite bedrock located 30 feet (90 m) from the southern edge of the cliff. The exposed rock surface was flat, inclined, and measured 9 feet 2 inches (2.8 m) by 5 feet 7 inches (1.7 m). This panel contained a crescent moon (?), a star, a musket (?), and a bow and arrow. The bow and its drawstring are in an at-rest position (Figure 95). The rock surface has been excised to form the bow and arrow figure. The arrow points in an easterly direction and has a barbed tip. All of the figures on this panel were heavily patinated and covered with lichen.

Petroglyph #3 was a deeply incised bow and arrow design located on the vertical face of an outcrop of bedrock near the southeastern edge of the site (Figure 96). The rock surface on which the figure was cut was a ventral or quarried surface; the section of rock that was split off from the parent outcrop lay nearby, along with other pieces of quarried rock. The bow and its drawstring were in an active position and the arrow pointed down toward the ground. The overall quality of workmanship or appearance of this carving was cruder than most of the others at the site; the grooves were wider, had flaked edges, and the arrow shaft was positioned off center. There was a v-shaped groove at the top edge of the rock that was smooth, suggesting it may have been used to sharpen the edges of metal tools. The rock was lightly covered with lichen.

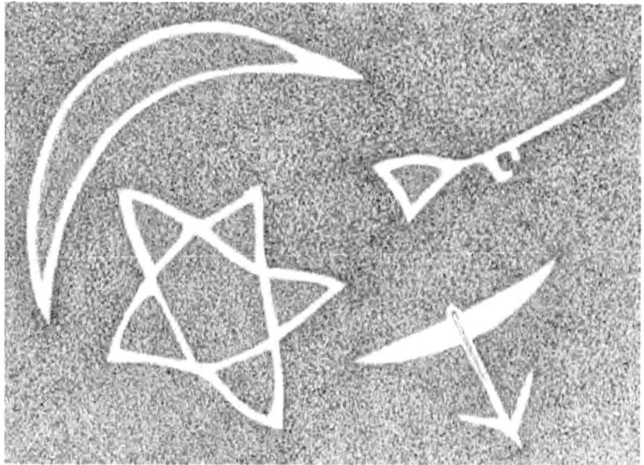

Figure 95: Detail drawing of panel of images on petroglyph panel #2. ***Drawing by T. Fitzpatrick.***

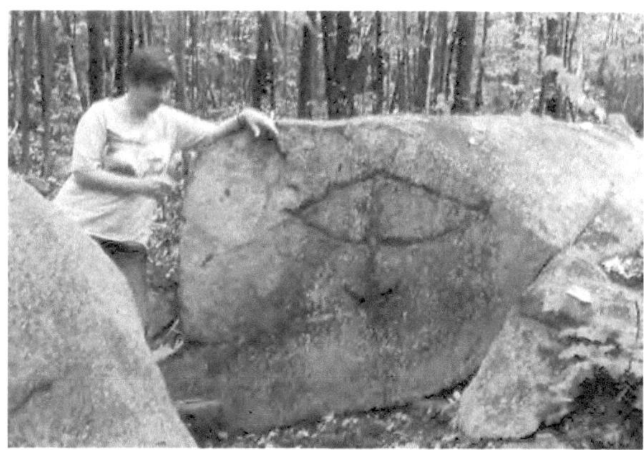

Figure 96: Incised bow and arrow on ventral surface of rock outcrop on Surrey Mountain, New Hampshire. ***Photo by E.J. Lenik 1994.***

Petroglyph #4 (Figure 97) was another incised bow and arrow figure located on a large boulder that was situated at the southeastern end of the mountain. The surface of the rock was covered

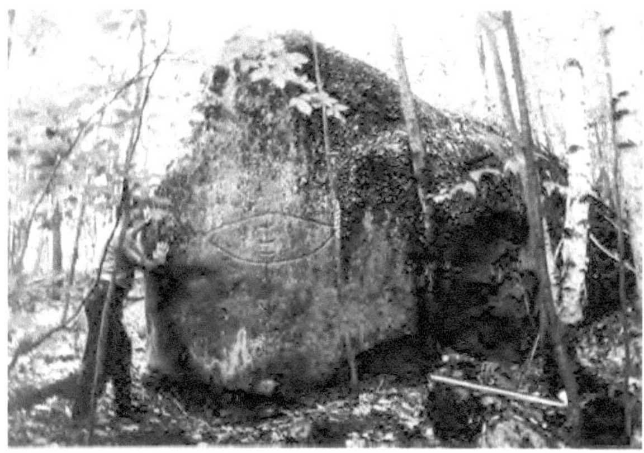

Figure 97: Bow and arrow petroglyph carved in center of large boulder on Surrey Mountain, New Hampshire. ***Photo by E.J. Lenik 1994.***

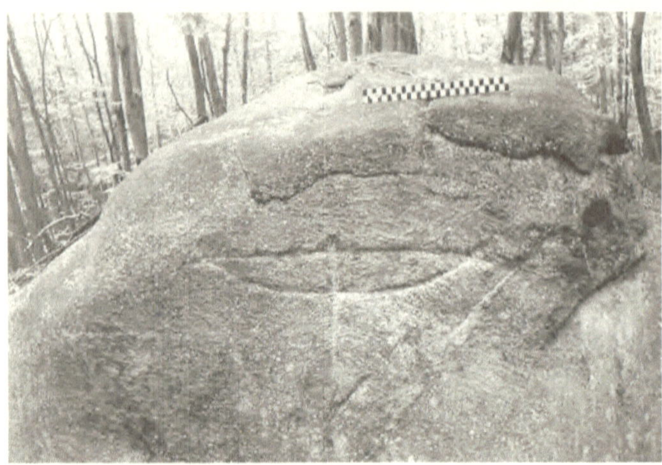

Figure 98: Bow and arrow petroglyph on granite boulder on Surrey Mountain, New Hampshire. ***Photo by E.J. Lenik 1994.***

with lichen and rock tripe (a lichen of the genus *Umbilicaria*). The bow and its draw string were in an active position with the barb tipped arrow pointing down toward the ground. There were three somewhat horizontal cut marks across the arrow shaft, presumably representing feathers. A deep groove was present to the left of the arrowhead below the bow; it had a smooth interior surface.

Petroglyph #5 was also a bow and arrow figure incised into a flat vertical surface on the southwest side of a granite boulder (Figure 98). This boulder was located at the north side of the petroglyph complex. This rock showed evidence of exfoliation on the carved surface that was likely caused by the act of carving the design. The bow and drawstring were in an at-rest position with the barbed arrow pointing downward.

Petroglyph #6 was still another bow and arrow figure that was carved on the top flat surface of a glacial erratic situated at the edge of the ridge. This boulder measured 10 feet 11 inches (3.3 m) in length 6 feet 7 inches (2 m) in width and 4 feet 3 inches (1.3 m) in height. The bow and drawstring were in an active position with the arrow about to be released (Figure 99). The barbed arrow extended in an easterly direction and down the slope. The arrow shaft had three horizontal chevron-like cuts, seemingly intended to represent feathers. The figure was boldly incised into the rock as the depths of the grooves ranged from 7/16 of an inch to 5/8 of an inch (11 mm to 15 mm) There was a deep v-shaped notch cut into the top edge of the rock on its west side.

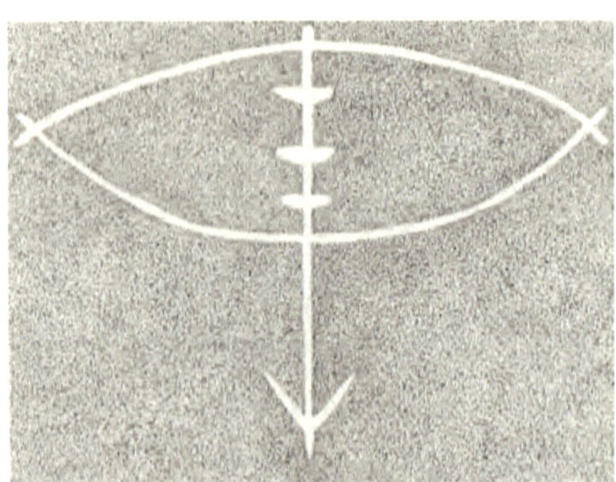

Figure 99: Detail drawing of bow and arrow in active position on top of a glacial erratic, Surrey Mountain, New Hampshire. ***Drawing by T. Fitzpatrick.***

Petroglyph #7 was a bow and arrow petroglyph incised into a flat surface of a boulder that was once situated on the brow of the ridge on the northwest side of the petroglyph complex. The boulder had been moved off the ridge top; it tumbled down the hillside for a short distance, where its movement was stopped by other rocks on the slope. The rock's surface was covered with rock tripe. The bow and draw string were in an active position with the barbed arrow about to be released. Four chevron-like cuts were present across the proximal end of the shaft, again apparently representing feathers (Figure 100). The grooves of the bow and arrow were deep and wide. The carved surface was probably the top of the rock when it was in its original position.

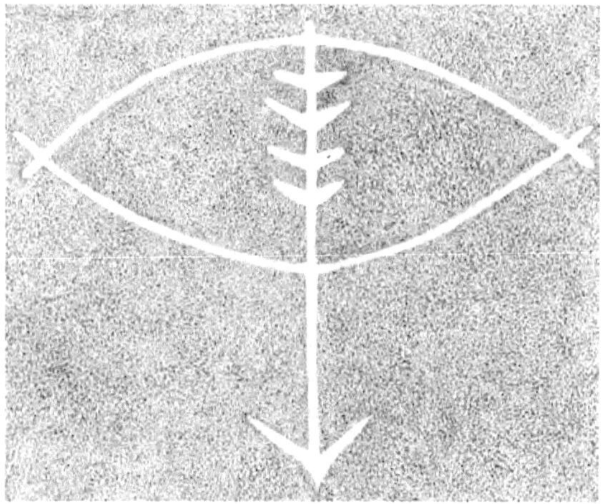

Figure 100: Detail drawing of bow and arrow in active position with barb-tipped arrow with four feathers. ***Drawing by T. Fitzpatrick.***

The seven panels of incised figures described above generally form a circular pattern at the southern end of the mountain. In addition to these loci, two other carved boulders were present within this complex. The first was a single v-shaped notch cut into the edge of a glacial erratic at the north end of the pattern of carved rocks. The second was the initial "W" incised into the vertical face of a ledge at the extreme south end of the site. This initial may be the mark of Samuel Wadsworth, who surveyed this area in the early twentieth century.

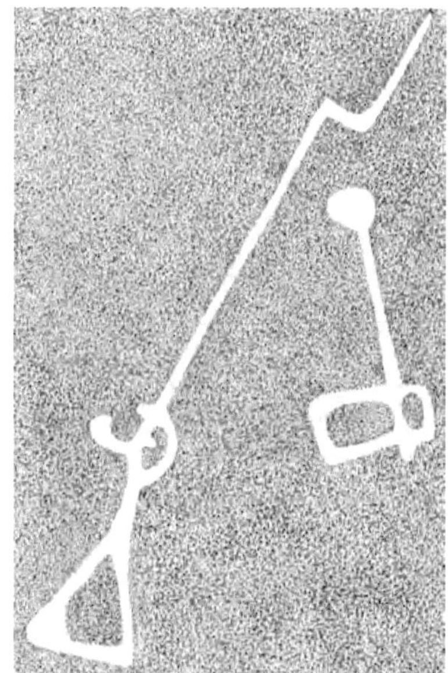

Figure 101: Incised musket and tomahawk on top surface of granite outcrop. Surrey Mountain, New Hampshire. ***Drawing by T. Fitzpatrick.***

Petroglyph #8 was located about 1/2 mile (0.8 km) north of the group described above on the same mountaintop (Figure 101). Two figures were incised into the top surface of a large outcrop of granite located on a steeply sloping gully. These figures appear to represent a musket with a bayonet attached, and a tomahawk. The petroglyphs were well made and deeply cut to 1/2 inch (11 mm) into the rock.

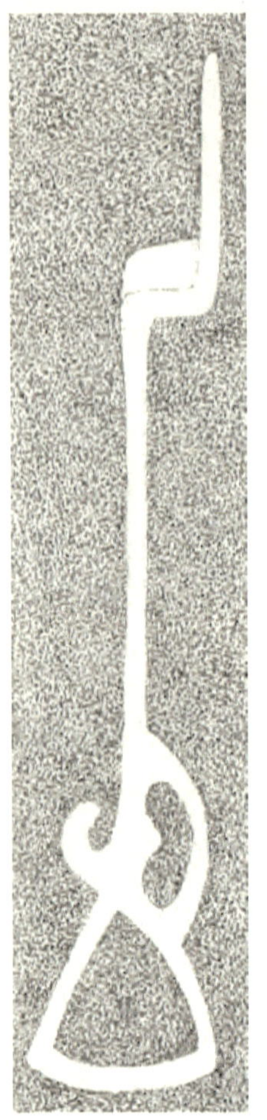

Figure 102: Incised musket carved in vertical position on the northwest face of a large boulder. Surrey Mountain, New Hampshire. ***Drawing by T. Fitzpatrick.***

Petroglyph #9 was the figure of a musket with bayonet that was incised into the northwest face of a large boulder located near petroglyph #8 (Figure 102). The musket was carved in a vertical position with its barrel and bayonet pointing upward. The grooves of the figure were u-shaped, ¼ inch (6 mm) deep and 3/4 inch (2 cm) wide.

Who carved this complex of figures, when and why? Why were so many bow and arrow figures illustrated here along with three muskets and a tomahawk? Were these figures made to commemorate a battle? Why were so many arrow shafts pointing downward; perhaps to convey some special meaning? The arrows were unusual in their portrayal with barbed points and several of them with three and four areas of fletching. We may never completely answer these questions, but several factors are clear.

It is evident that a great deal of time, effort, and skill were involved in their creation. Undoubtedly metal tools were used in the process, and at least in one instance a ladder or similar device. The presences of v-shaped grooves on several of the rocks along with indications of quarrying activity support these conclusions.

Most of the petroglyphs consist of the bow and arrow motif, and the technique and manner of rendering suggests that a work plan was being followed by one or more persons.

In 1925 local historian Samuel Wadsworth produced a drawing of the Arrow Hill petroglyph and hypothesized about its possible origin. He also delineated the 1920 map of the town of Surry showing the location of the Bow and Arrow petroglyph on Arrow Hill, yet failed to show or mention the petroglyphs on Surry Mountain.[10] Perhaps this site was also the nineteenth century work of William P. Mason, since he reportedly made the Arrow Hill petroglyph and carved several other boulders nearby.

"PEACE FOREVER" ROCK

The year 1984 saw the discovery of yet another unusual inscribed rock in Vermont. A large boulder composed of Waits River limestone was rediscovered in the town of Woodstock near the driveway of a private home. This rock, which measures 8 feet (2.3 m) long, 5 feet (1.5 m) wide, and 3 feet (0.9 meters) high contains several realistically carved images that portray a war and peace motif.[11] The rock has two flat surfaces, each rising from the ground at an acute angle to a peak, forming a triangular-shaped boulder when viewed from its side. The rock is not in its original location. It was formerly situated in a wooded area just beyond an open pasture but was "skidded down by a logger" employed by the landowner so that it would be closer to his home and more easily shown to visitors (Figure 103).[12]

There are seven images carved into one flat inclined surface of the rock near its apex: a pistol, a drawn bow and arrow, a tomahawk or hatchet, a smoking pipe, a bow at rest, an arrow, and a knife. Below these images are the words "PEACE FOREVER" carved in a semicircular pattern with an unidentified symbol to the left of the letter P. In the center of the rock is an anchor with a rope attached to it (Figure 103). These images, which are shallow, were formed by cutting through a dark reddish brown patina on the surface of the rock down to a lighter colored material underneath.[13]

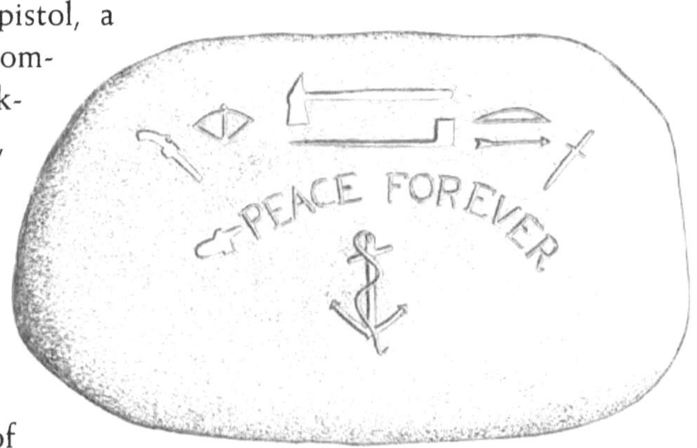

Figure 103: Detail drawing of "Peace Forever" rock images ***by T. Fitzpatrick after B. Sager 1984.***

In 1984, Barbara Sager, the New England Antiquities Research Association (NEARA) Vermont chapter coordinator, reported that the rock "has been known by the previous landowners for the last 100 years."[14] During an investigative trip to the site, Neal Sager observed that the pistol portrayed on the rock appeared to be of "Civil War vintage."[15] Perhaps this message of peace was carved by an unknown veteran of that brutal conflict.

ABSTRACT AND GEOMETRICAL MYSTERIES

THE ARNOLD'S POINT PIT AND GROOVE STONE

A sandstone boulder containing six deep holes connected by shallow grooves lies on the eastern shore of Narragansett Bay near Portsmouth, Newport County, Rhode Island (Figure 104). The boulder is situated at the edge of the beach and is covered and uncovered daily by the tidal action of the bay. This marked stone was first reported in 1910 and has been a source of speculation ever since. Is it a typical Indian cup stone, such as those found in abundance out west, or a European product? What do the pits and grooves represent?

The Arnold Point Cup Stone, as it became known, was investigated in the early part of the twentieth century by Edmund B. Delabarre, a professor of psychology at Brown University. Delabarre measured the stone and its pits and grooves, described its geographic setting and character, and speculated about its origin.[1] The stone measured 4-1/2 feet (1.35 m) in length by 3 feet (0.9 meters) in width and ranged in thickness from 16 inches (40 cm) to 22 inches (53 cm). The six holes are round with surface diameters of 1-5/8 inches (42 mm) to 1-3/4 inches (45 cm). They vary in depth from 2-1/2 inches (64 mm) to 3-1/4 inches (83 mm). Delabarre noted that the holes "appear to have been drilled, and are not circular, but more like triangles with rounded angles."[2] This

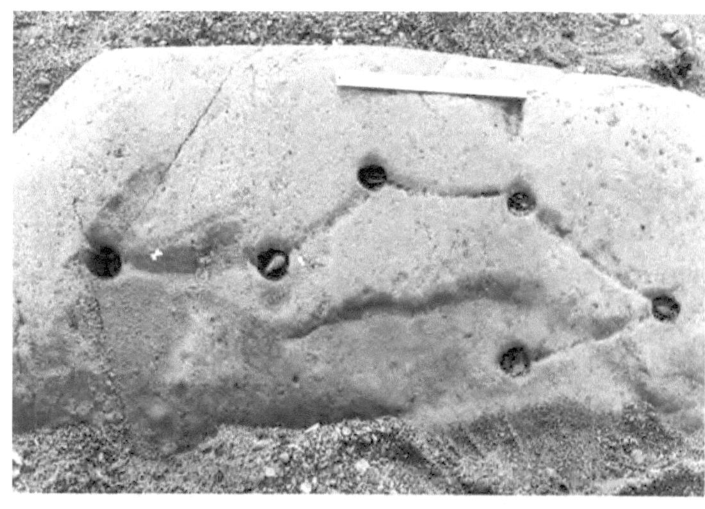

Figure 104: The Arnold's Point, Rhode Island, cup stone. ***Photo courtesy of C. Devine 1979.***

condition, he said, would be expected if the holes had been made with a straight edge steel drill. The grooves connecting the holes were irregular in width and depth and were produced by pecking into the rock.

On September 9, 1979, I visited the site to examine the stone and gain my own impressions of the holes and grooves. The first thing I noticed was the change in position of the boulder in relation to the edge of the beach. Delabarre's photograph of the rock shows it positioned at an oblique angle to the shore, but I found it parallel to the shore and partially buried by sand; obviously it had been moved and covered by storms and tidal action. In my examination of the holes, I found them to be rough at the surface, not angular as Delabarre reported. I was unable to measure the depth of the holes or examine their interior surface because they were filled with sand that had solidified. The grooves were pecked into the rock and ranged in width from 3/8 inches (10 mm) to ¾ inches (20 mm) and in depth from 3/16 inches (5 mm) to ½ inch (13 mm).

Delabarre reported that the Arnold's Point Cup Stone was lying near the shore of the bay and was near "one of the Portsmouth coal mines" which was located inland to the east of the rock.[3] He noted that coal mines operated intermittently in the area from 1808 to 1883. In his analysis of the pits, he considered three hypotheses to account for their origin. First, that it was an Indian cup stone. Secondly, that they were made by "miners in idle moments," or by their "children at play." Lastly, that the holes were originally typical Indian cup marks that were deepened with drills by the miners or their children.[4] Delabarre concluded that we can never "be sure which of the three hypotheses is the true one" since each presents plausible arguments for their origin.[5]

It was suggested that the arrangement of the holes and grooves on the flat rock surface may represent the celestial star formation known as "The Big Dipper" but this explanation was rejected since the "seventh star was missing."[6] I reject this interpretation as well, on similar grounds. I believe that the pits and grooves were the work of Euro-Americans, most likely miners working in the area with easy access to drills and hammers. The seventy-five year history of coal mining near the site of the rock lends weight to this conclusion. The holes were drilled deeply and are unlike Indian cup marks. Their rounded shape is similar to numerous mooring holes found in rocks throughout southern New England, but their number, pattern and placement on the rock eludes a logical explanation. Finally, I believe the pecked grooves could easily have been made with the same steel drill used to produce the holes.

GEOMETRIC ENIGMAS IN MAINE

In the course of my research and field work in Maine, I have come across several petroglyph sites that are not of Indian origin. In my judgment they were produced by Euro-Americans. In recent years, many carvings and so-called inscriptions have been found and often reported to be the work of Norsemen, Phoenicians, Romans, Iberian Celts and similar groups of people. I make no such claims for the glyphs described here, and leave such speculation and interpretation to others. Instead, my purpose in recording these glyphs is to make a permanent record of these enigmatic carvings and to point out that they are not of great antiquity. Because so little is known about petroglyphs in the Northeast in general, many people are inclined to view them with a great deal of mystery and ascribe to them a greater age than they warrant. It is my hope that this account will stimulate serious scholarly research into such carvings.

THE MONMOUTH STONE was found in 1976 about 1.8 miles due east from the junction of State Routes 132 and 135 in the village of Monmouth, Kennebec County, Maine (Figure 105). It was originally located on top of a ridge overlooking Lake Annabesacook and Lake Cobbosseecontee.[7] However, the stone has since been removed from this site and placed in front of the Monmouth Museum on Main Street.

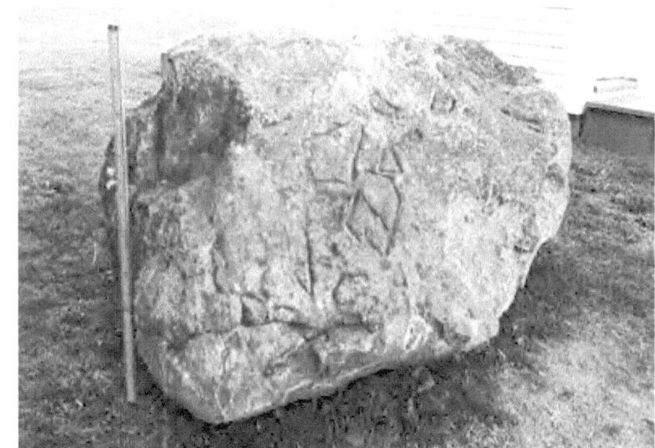

Figure 105: The Monmouth, Maine, stone. ***Photo by E.J. Lenik 1976.***

In August 1976, I examined the stone at its new location. The Monmouth Stone was a quartzite sandstone boulder that was light in color and had a fine grained texture. The boulder measured 6 feet 3 inches (1.9 m) in length, 4 feet 3 inches (1.3 m) in width, and 3 feet 3 inches (1 m) in height. Fungus and lichen covered some parts of the stone, and there was evidence of disintegration fractures caused by weathering.

The designs or symbols appear on a flat sloping surface of the rock. They were cut clearly and boldly into the rock with metal tools. The grooves were deep, in some cases as much as 5/8 of an inch (17 mm). There was some indication that an attempt was made to smooth and polish the grooves. Despite this, some punch marks were clearly visible in several of them.

The interpretation of this curvilinear design on this stone remains speculative. The most common thought, among local observers, was that it represents a map that depicts such features as islands, coves, and shoreline. Alternative interpretations are indeed possible but its original intent remains unknown.

The **DEVIL'S HEAD** petroglyph (Figure 106) is located on top of a mountain called Devil's Head in the town of Harmony, Somerset County, Maine. This mountain has an elevation of 860 feet (260 m) from which an observer may enjoy an excellent view of Great Moose Lake to the south. The area is remote and wooded, and is visited only by an occasional hunter or rock art enthusiast.

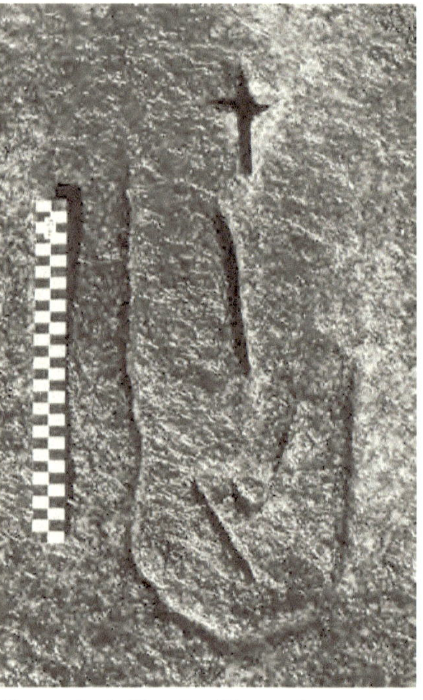

Figure 106: The Devil's Head Mountain petroglyph in Harmony, Maine. ***Photo by E.J. Lenik 1977.***

The petroglyph consists of three symbols which are enclosed by a U-shaped open-end loop. The figures were carved into a vertical granite surface located very close to the edge of the cliff. The designs were deeply incised into the rock and were protected to some extent from the weather by an overhanging granite boulder.

The Devil's Head petroglyph was executed with metal tools. I interpret the upper figure as a "cross" which was cut into the rock to a depth of 1-3/4 inches (45 mm). Below the cross is a vertical line, cut somewhat obliquely to a depth of 1 9/16 inches (40 mm). The third symbol can be described as a "double comma" cut to a depth of 3/16 of an inch (4-5 mm). The open ended loop was cut to a depth of 3/16 of an inch (3 mm). The petroglyph faces south in the direction of Great Moose Lake.

I examined this petroglyph in 1977, at which time there was considerable evidence of former granite quarrying on top of Devil's Head Mountain. Local tradition indicates that this granite quarry was in operation from around 1870 to 1900, and numerous cut stone blocks with drill marks can still be found throughout the area.[8]

We can only speculate regarding the meaning or purpose of these symbols. Perhaps they were carved by a lone quarry worker for some personal or superstitious reason. The difficulties involved in the carving of the petroglyphs into the hard granite at the edge of the cliff seem to suggest a strong desire by someone to leave a permanent and personal mark here.

The MAP STONE petroglyph was located off Freeman Street in York Beach, York County, Maine, on a rocky stretch between the rear of a cottage and the ocean (Figure 107). The existence of this petroglyph had been known for quite some time and was first reported to the New England Antiquities Research Association in the 1960s. It was named the "Map Stone" petroglyph because most viewers believed it resembled such an item.

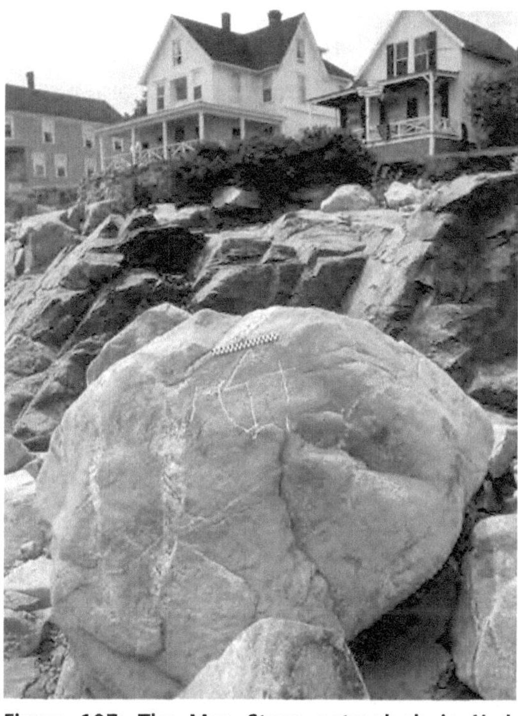

Figure 107: The Map Stone petroglyph in York Beach, Maine. ***Photo by E.J. Lenik 1977.***

I investigated this petroglyph site in 1977.[9] The designs were carved on the east face of a free standing granite boulder that was 16 feet 5 inches (5 m) high. This boulder revealed white quartz veins and was different in composition from the nearby granite ledges. The designs were cut into the vertical surface of the rock with metal tools. The angular central figure and the cross on the right were probably executed with the aid of a straight edge. A conical punched hole measuring 3/8 of an inch (10 mm) in diameter and 5/32 of an inch (3.5 mm) was present at the top end of the central design. The curvilinear designs to the left and below the central one appear to have been executed in a haphazard or free-style manner.

The meaning or purpose of this carving is unknown.

PETROGLYPHS ON DAMARISCOVE ISLAND

Damariscove Island is located in the Gulf of Maine about five miles south of Booth Bay Harbor. The island, one of Maine's earliest permanent settlement sites, is on the National Register of Historic Places. Presently a nature preserve, it is largely uninhabited, except for a few fishermen who reside here during warm months, and the summer residents of a former, and now privately owned, Coast Guard station.

Except for what is left of the Coast Guard station and several stone foundations and fences, there is little evidence of the community that once flourished here.

Damariscove Island was settled in 1622 by English fishermen employed by Sir Ferdinando Gorges, who established a fortified year-round cod fishing community on the island.[10] At this time, Gorges owned the island and the majority of what is now the state of Maine. The island settlement prospered as a fishing station for most of the seventeenth century. By 1671, however, the Puritans of Massachusetts had claimed the island and subsequently established government control and a military presence there.

In August of 1676, the Indian revolt against the English, known as King Philip's War, spread to Maine. Some three hundred persons were driven from their homes along the coast of Maine, seeking refuge from the Indians on Damariscove Island. In late August, a band of eighty Indians attacked the island and burned houses, killed cattle, captured a sloop and killed one resident. The island was evacuated for brief periods during the war but by 1689 its fishery was active and flourishing once again. Skirmishes between the Indians and settlers continued sporadically, resulting in loss of life on both sides, but by 1725 the Indian hostilities had ended.

During the eighteenth century, farming and sheep farming became important to Damariscove's economy, in addition to fishing. By the end of the nineteenth century, the island's fishing and sheep farming industries were greatly diminished because of their low profitability. In 1882, a dairy industry was established here, with the milk being sold to residents of summer cottages and hotels on nearby Squirrel Island. Some granite quarrying was carried out on the island for a period of about one hundred years, with the stone blocks being used in the construction of a stone wharf and house foundations.

In 1896, a life saving station was erected at the southern end of the island, followed by an attempt to establish a resort industry in hopes of luring tourists. A few cottages were built but this effort was largely unsuccessful. Farming and fishing continued to be the principal economic activity until the middle of the twentieth century. In 1966, the island was finally donated to The Nature Conservancy of Maine.

Maine historian Rufus King Sewall reported the presence of "antiquities" on Damariscove Island in 1859 consisting of an ancient fortification, an earthwork, and petroglyphs. In his book *Ancient Dominions of Maine* he wrote the following:

> On the south-eastern slope...lifting the covering of the shallow soil, a smooth rock appears, whereon the washing of the sea has laid bare numerous inscriptions, in writing apparently cut by hu-

> man art in characters from one to four inches long, one-eighth of an inch deep, and covering a surface of ten feet. The locality of the inscriptions is assigned to the summit of the cliff, on the right of the harbor, as it is entered....[11]

Sewall published a second account of the inscription together with a drawing of the symbols in 1895. In this report, Sewall noted that the "Damariscove characters are like tracings. Impression much abraded and weatherworn and fragmentary. Intervening and connecting parts are gone" (Figure 108). [12]

In 1903, C.A. Fernald visited Damariscove Island and also produced a drawing of the alleged inscriptions. Fernald's drawing, as published in E.B. Delabarre's book about Dighton Rock, is identical to Sewall's except for the short markings on the right of Sewall's drawing.[13] Fernald wrote that the rock contained inscriptions by "Marcus Agrippa (29 BC), by his son Graecianus, by Christ (15 AD) and by Fnr Chia and Fna Bahman (222 AD)."[14]

On August 19, 1977, Maine historians White Nichols, John W. Briggs, and Harold Brown visited the island to study the inscriptions. In a letter to this author, Brown reported that the inscriptions were "located on the east shore of the island directly east of what was called the East Watch Tower, a part of the former Coast Guard Station. They are...on a horizontal shelf....Three of the figures...are quite apparent but appear to be somewhat eroded. The pictograms are not carved or pecked but seem to have [been] created by rubbing with an abrasive tool. They are not more than 1/16 inch in depth and cover an area of about four feet square."[15] Photographs, "rubbings," and measurements of the inscription were taken and a drawing was later produced from a tracing. In White Nichols's notes on the "Rock Art of Maine's Early People" is a tracing of Sewall's drawing, below which is the notation "Coast tradition says that this writing is old Indian."[16]

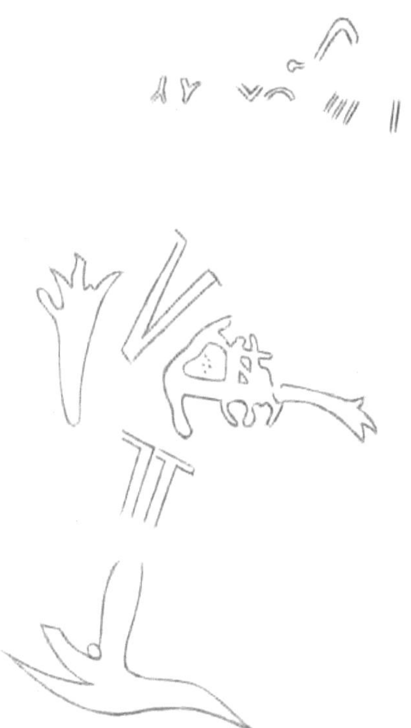

Figure 108: The alleged Damariscove Island, Maine, inscription. ***Drawing by T. Fitzpatrick after Sewall 1895.***

Barry Fell studied the sketches of the Damariscove inscriptions and identified them as ancient North African or Phoenician script. There were two messages on the rocks, one which read "Dama is waterless" and the other in Libyan script read "Dama lacks water, the spring is blocked."[17]

On August 8, 1978, I sailed to Damariscove Island with White Nichols and John W. Briggs to examine the alleged inscription. The figures or symbols, as previously reported, were on a horizontal metamorphic sandstone ledge. The rock was cracked and very weathered. The symbols were shallow and ranged in depth from 1/32 inch (1 mm) to 3/32 inch (2.5 mm), and were discernible against a background of reddish brown iron oxide stain. The symbols appeared to be abraded into the rock, exposing a gray undersurface.

While pre-European contact Abenaki Indians are known to have visited the island, the images on the rock are unlike any of their petroglyphs and pictographs found in Maine, the Canadian Maritimes, and elsewhere in New England. They were also not the product of European visitors or settlers to the site. I concluded that the alleged inscriptions were not produced by human hands. They are natural impressions in the rock, produced by the movement of plant roots abrading the surface of the rock, in addition to rain, sea water, and erosion.

MEREDITH MYSTERY STONE

In 1872, an extraordinary stone was dug up near the shore of Lake Winnipesaukee in Meredith, Belknap County, New Hampshire. A full account of its discovery, including descriptions of its design element, and four drawings of the stone with images, was published in the *Manchester Union* newspaper of May 15, 1895.[18] Portions of this accurate and colorful story are presented here:

A MYSTERIOUS STONE
INTERESTED THE CURIOUS AND PUZZLED SCIENTISTS
INCIDENTS IN CONNECTION WITH THE FINDING AND PRESERVATION

> MEREDITH, May 11. – Early in the summer of 1872, while a trench was being dug near the lake and not far from where Hodgson's Mill used to stand, a stone was discovered that has ever since interested the curious and puzzled the scientist.
>
> The ditch where the strange stone was found was perhaps three feet deep, and the earth was the ordinary clay soil peculiar to the vicinity. One day while the digging was in progress Seneca A. Ladd, at that time cashier of the bank, happened to be standing near; a workman threw out on his shovel an odd-looking bit of earth that attracted Mr. Ladd's attention. The cashier had for a number of

years devoted considerable time to the study and collection of Indian relics, and his intelligently directed research had resulted in a large show-case full of valuable articles which he took pleasure in showing to those who came to see them at the reception room of the bank. The mass, when Mr. Ladd picked it up was, as he once described it to the writer, an irregular ovoid of about eight inches in length. A considerable amount of the outside surface came off when rapped with a stick, but a harder incrustation remained clinging to some queer object which the solid coating enclosed. The enthusiastic possessor of the unearthed treasure went directly home, and began to wash it in the sink, when, to his intense delight, the clay shell softened and washed away, leaving the mysterious rock clean and bare; and exposed again after nobody knows how many hundreds of years of concealment, the picture-writing carved with startling skill and accuracy upon the surface of the egg-shaped stone.

The mystery begins with the fact that the stone—a fine siliceous sandstone, harder than granite, is unlike any stone to be found in the vicinity. Its shape is a perfect ovoid, corresponding to the finest geometrical measurements. Although not turned on a lathe, it deviates but slightly from a solid revolution. This strange egg-shaped rock is exactly 3-3/4 inches long, while at the thickest part it measures 2-5/8 inches. Its weight is 18 ounces.... A conical hole 5/8 inch at the base, and 1/8 inch at the summit, passes along the axis, but lacks nearly 1/8 inch of being concentric with the base and less at the summit [Figure 109]. Ten figures, some in low relief but sunk below the surface, are cut with workmanship far superior to any ever found on Indian relics on this continent.

Although the face, oval in form, is executed with less precision and skill than the rest of the carving, it is the most unaccountable of all because of the strange ethnological combination. It will be seen, by reference to the picture, that the forehead is that of an Indian, while the lower portion of the face is that of the Eskimo...[Figure 110].

The geometrical figures are wonderfully accurate. The inscribed circle is as perfect as if struck by a compass or cut by a skilled engraver [Figure 111]. The variable spiral is likewise perfect. On the base the eight-pointed star is symmetrical...[Figure 112]. On the ear of corn there are seventeen kernels in a row, and four of the rows are clearly visible, with two more partially in sight [Figure 113]. In a circle, near the broad end, is what appears to be the scalp of an animal with large ears; also there is a deer's leg and a three-pointed cap. On another side is an Indian lodge, with four poles visible above where they

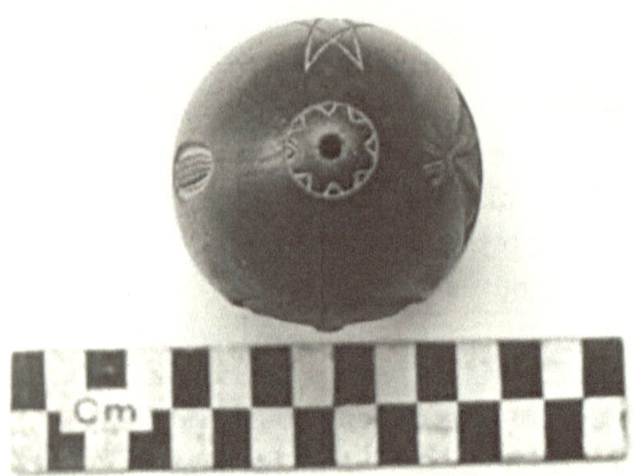

Figure 109: Top view of Meredith, New Hampshire, Mystery Stone with drilled hole surrounded by circular sun-burst design. *Photo by E.J. Lenik 1978.*

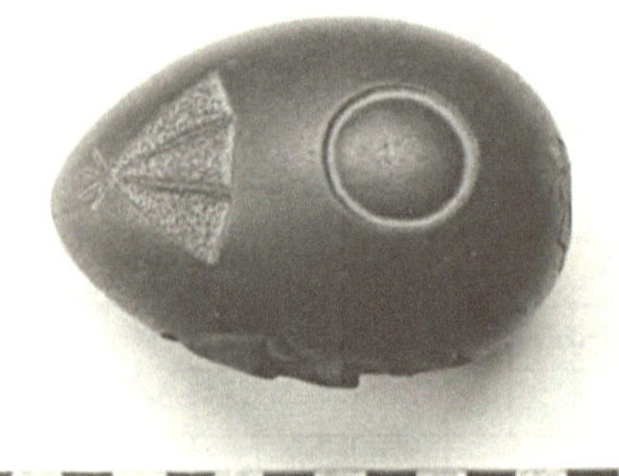

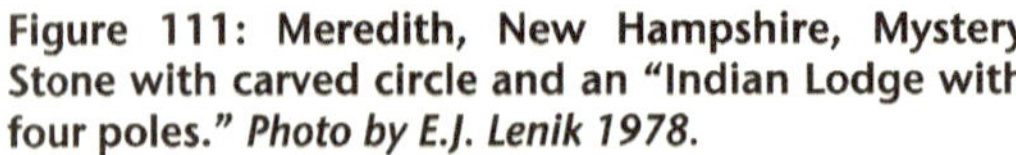

Figure 111: Meredith, New Hampshire, Mystery Stone with carved circle and an "Indian Lodge with four poles." *Photo by E.J. Lenik 1978.*

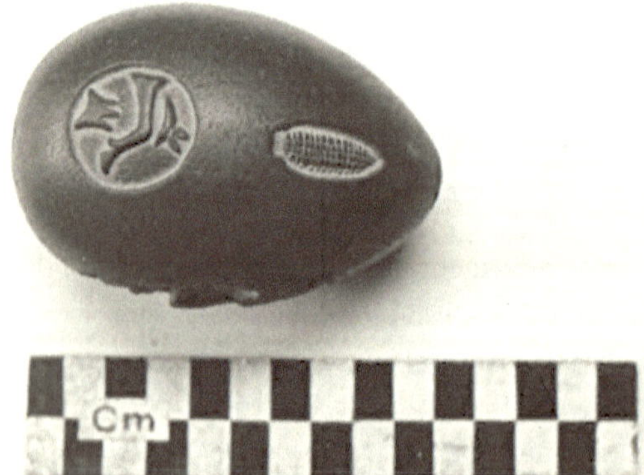

Figure 113: Side view of Meredith, New Hampshire, Mystery Stone with carved ear of corn at top and sculpted "animal with large ears . . . a deer's leg, and a three-pointed cap." *Photo by E.J. Lenik 1978.*

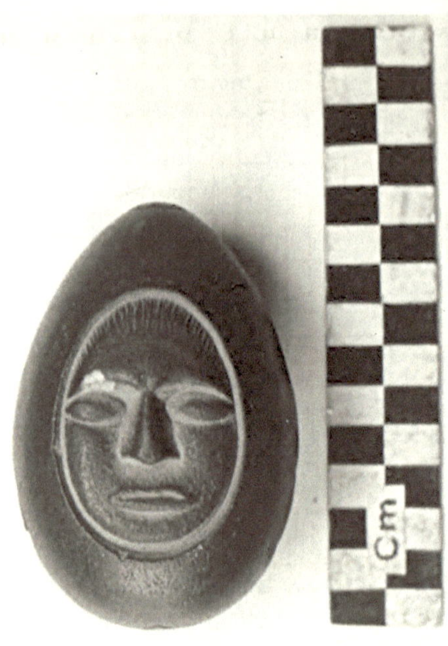

Figure 110: Meredith, New Hampshire, Mystery Stone with sculpted face. *Photo by E.J. Lenik 1978.*

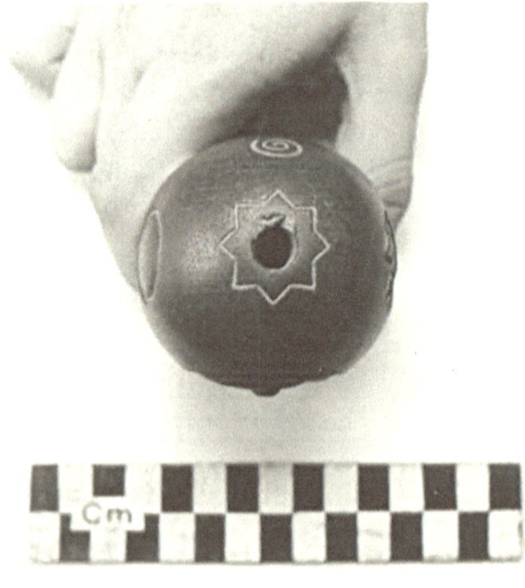

Figure 112: Base of Meredith, new Hampshire, Mystery Stone with drilled hole surrounded by eight-pointed star. *Photo by E.J. Lenik 1978.*

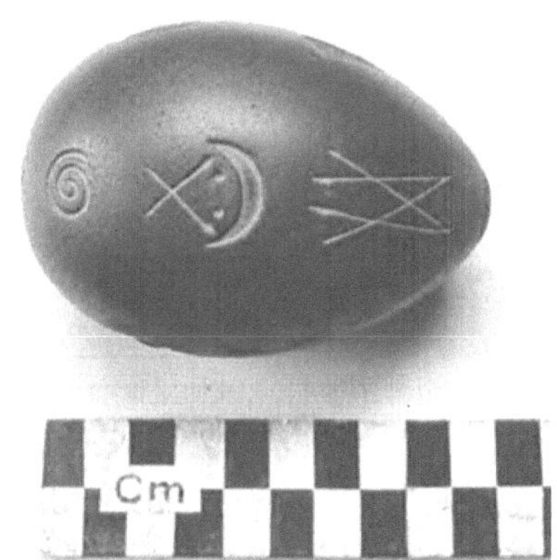

Figure 114: Side view of Meredith, New Hampshire, Mystery Stone with four carved spears (?), a crescent and two "maces." ***Photo by E.J. Lenik 1978.***

> cross at the top; the three breadths of curtains are roughened to give the appearance of hide. Following in what appears to be order are four spears or paddles crossed in the form of a letter M, with a dot between the heads. There is also a crescent, and under it two maces crossed in the form of St. Andew's cross [Figure 114].
>
> The color of the stone is dark brown, with a slightly yellowish tinge on one side. The whole surface surrounding the carving is lightly polished, and smooth to the touch. It will be observed that the oval face corresponds very nearly with the ovoid form of the stone....
>
> The strange relic has attracted much attention. The Smithsonian Institute in Washington, and the Essex Institute in Salem, MA, were at one time greatly interested in it.... The strange carving and its mysterious symbols have been the theme of scientific writing and the subject of learned lectures, as well as the study and puzzle of theorists. Where lived the wise prophet, priest and artist who wrote the riddle of life—for that is presumably what it is – "on the stone, and lost it under the mountain by the margin of the lake...." [signed] STRANGER

The Meredith Mystery Stone is now in the possession of the New Hampshire Historical Society in Concord. It is truly a remarkable artifact. Who carved it, when was it produced, and what was its purpose or function remain a source of speculation. The stone was supposedly studied by experts from the Smithsonian Institute, who determined that it was not of American Indian origin.

The stone is polished, brownish gray in color, and has the appearance of having been turned on a lathe. A conical hole extends through its length with geometric, somewhat star-like carvings around each hole; the stone can stand on its large end. The longitudinal hole suggests it may have functioned as a pendant. The face, carved in relief, has been characterized as part Indian and part Eskimo. I reject this highly speculative and subjective interpretation. To me it represents a mask-like figure. The so-called "spears" that form the letter "M," upon close examination, are simply incised lines without any distinguishing characteristics. The two "maces" described in the 1895 article are more likely crossing spears or arrows.

What do all the figures mean? Here is my admittedly highly speculative interpretation for some of them. The stone is clearly shaped like an egg, which generally implies creation or re-birth. At the bottom, or large end of the stone, is an eight-pointed star which represents human regeneration.[19] At the top, surrounding the small hole, is a gear-like symbol with eight projections within a circle which may represent creation. The crescent moon frequently appears on shields in old English churches. The circle may stand for the universe or imply eternity. All of these design features seem to suggest church symbolism.

The rest of the symbols on the stone seem to suggest an American Indian influence. Spiral motifs, for example, have been found on several petroglyph sites throughout the United States. Spirals are a basic element in Indian ideography and may represent wind, water, serpents, snails, or the journey of people to a center place.[20] Human faces are a common design motif on portable petroglyphs found in the northeastern United States, and generally have a spiritual connotation. Spears or arrows, animal figures, teepees or wigwams are also common design elements on American Indian and historic-era petroglyph sites as described elsewhere in this book. Corn, or corn plants, are rarely found at petroglyph sites or on artifacts, but are mentioned in Indian myths and legends, and are used during festivals.[21]

In sum, I conclude that the Meredith Mystery Stone contains typical Christian and Indian design motifs. The artifact may have been created as part of some fraternal organization's belief system or rituals. It most likely dates to the nineteenth century.

A GAME BOARD CARVED IN ROCK

The Dyckman House Museum, a late-eighteenth-century farmhouse, is located at 4881 Broadway in Upper Manhattan, New York City. During the entire American Revolution, from 1776 to 1783, the Dyckman farm was the site of an extensive military encampment.[22]

In 1662, Jan Dyckman emigrated to New York from Westphalia (Germany) and built a house on the bank of the Harlem River at what is now 210th Street in Upper Manhattan. Here he cleared the land, planted fruit trees, and established a family homestead and farm that survived until the mid-nineteenth century.

At the start of the American Revolution, William Dyckman, Jan's grandson, fled from the homestead with his family upon the arrival of British forces in New York City. The family farm was then occupied by British and Hessian troops who built a military camp on the land which consisted of officers' and enlisted mens' huts, a series of fortifications, and a parade ground.[23]

In 1784, following the end of the Revolutionary War, the Dyckman family returned to Manhattan Island. The original family homestead on the Harlem River had been destroyed by the British when they evacuated New York City, so the Dyckmans built the present house at Broadway and 204th Street in the Flemish Colonial style on top of a rock outcrop.[24] The house is a stone and clapboard structure with a gambrel roof, double doors and a small gabled wing.

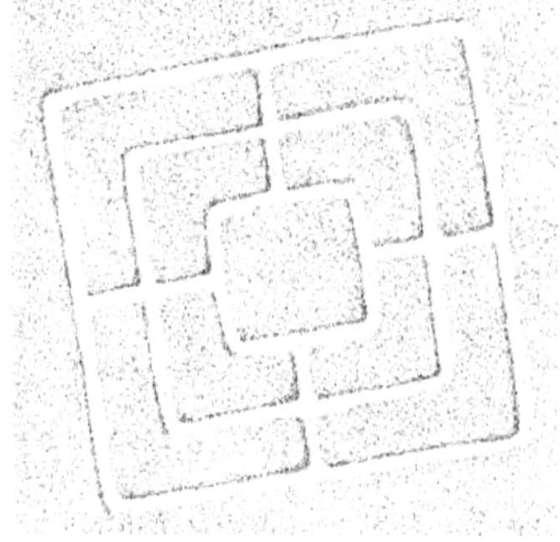

Figure 115: Grid pattern cut into bedrock in the Dykman House, New York City. ***Drawing by T. Fitzpatrick.***

Jacobus Dyckman, William's son, and his other sons Isaac and Michael purchased additional contiguous land, eventually enlarging the farmstead to four-hundred-fifty acres, which made it one of the largest estates on Manhattan Island. Fruit and vegetable crops were produced on the farm, and cattle were grazed and pastured around the house. By 1850, the development of upper Manhattan was approaching the farmstead, and Isaac and Michael Dyckman moved out of the house. Following Isaac's death in 1871 it was sold, and soon fell into disrepair. By the early twentieth century the house and its immediate surroundings were threatened by developers. It was purchased in 1915 by two direct descendants of Jan Dyckman, who restored and furnished the house in order to preserve it. They then gave it to the city of New York in 1916.

In 1914, archaeological excavations were conducted in the area of the house by William L. Calver and Reginald P. Bolton, both members of the Field Exploration Committee of the New York Historical Society. They discovered and excavated a British officers' hut on the former Dyckman farm and recovered numerous artifacts from the military encampment. A replica of a Revolutionary War hut was subsequently constructed in the garden behind the house.

Located in the cellar of the Dyckman house is a mysterious grid carved into the outcrop of granite on which the house was built. The grid pattern consists of a square within a square within another square (Figure 115). Overall, the carving measures one foot by one foot. The pattern of squares was cut into the rock and its condition and patination suggests that it is quite old. The grid reportedly represents a playing board for a colonial game variously called Nine Man Morris, Nine Penny Morris, Mill or Morelles.[25] This ancient game originated in northern Europe and has been played by children and adults for at least a thousand years. It was very popular in Scandinavia and Great Britain.

The game is played by two persons each using nine checker-like pieces on the grid. According to David Dunlap, "each player gets nine pieces and places them around the twenty-four points formed by the grid's corners and intersections. The game proceeds by turns. A piece may be moved but only to the next unoccupied spot. The player who gets three pieces in a row may remove one of the opponent's pieces, unless that piece is already part of another row. The player reduced to two pieces on the board is the loser."[26]

Who carved the Morris board and when? Was it the work of British or Hessian troops who were camped on the site before the present Dyckman house was built? Or, was it inscribed by the Dyckman family as a form of amusement to be played in the comfort of the warm cellar during the winter months? The answers to these questions continue to elude modern day visitors to the house. However, the carving presents a small glimpse of late eighteenth or early nineteenth century life in this colonial homestead.

SYMBOL ROCK

The Yawgoog Boy Scout Reservation in Rockville, Washington County, Rhode Island is situated in the southwestern part of the state near its border with Connecticut. Camp Yawgoog, a summer camp on Yawgoog Pond, was established in 1916 in what was once a rural, forested area. The first known settler in the area was Joel Maxon, whose house and farm once occupied land off of the northeast corner of the pond.[27]

The reservation contains three ponds. Yawgoog, which is 3/4 mile long and 1/2 mile wide, and Wincheck, a former cedar swamp, are located to the southeast. These ponds were named after two local Indians, Chief Yagoog and his son Wincheck.[28] The third pond, Hidden Lake, lies to the north of Yawgoog. The reservation encompasses about 1,500 acres, including thick woods, granite outcrops and glacially-deposited boulders. In the eighteenth century mills were built along the outlet streams; the remains of one can still be seen between Yawgoog Pond and Hidden Lake to the north. There are many rock piles in the forest that indicate the land was cleared for settlement and agricultural pursuits. South of Yawgoog Pond, in what is now forest, are the remains of charcoal burners' huts.[29]

Symbol Rock, a name given to it by the Boy Scouts, is a gneissic boulder partially covered by lichen that is situated on the side of a hill just south of Yawgoog Pond. It stands approximately 7 feet (2 m) high and is about 8 feet (2.4 m) in diameter at its base.[30] Four abstract designs are "pecked" into the boulder (Figure 116). Three of the designs consist of curved channels or grooves that are 3/4 inch (2 cm) wide and 3/16 to 5/16 inch (5 mm to 7.5 mm) deep. The fourth design appears to represent a trident with its tines in an upright position. The main stem and curved tines were reported as "pecked out" with grooves that measured 3/16 inch (5 mm) wide; the short center line or tine measured 1/16 inch (2 mm) wide.[31] The overall length of the figure is 8 inches (20 cm). A description of the designs on the rock follows:

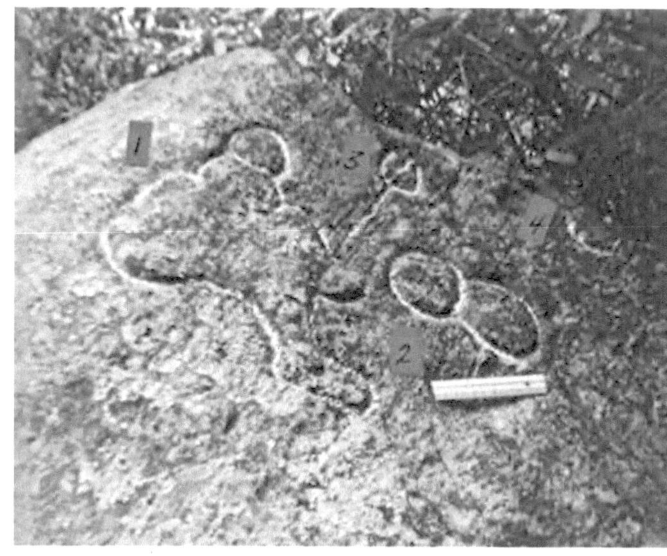

Figure 116: Symbol Rock in Yawgoog Boy Scout Reservation, Rockville, Rhode Island. ***Photo courtesy of B. Corcoran 1989.***

Design No. 1 is a non-representational symbol with bold curving lines. At its top is an oval, below which is a wide curving shape that terminates in an appendage.

Design No. 2 consists of two contiguous circles and is positioned in such a manner that it resembles a "figure 8" on its side.

Design No. 3 appears to represent a trident, but this is clearly a subjective opinion. The surface of the rock in this area has striations that extend in the same direction as the main stem of the trident.[32] However, the curves comprising the shoulders of the fork cut across the striations on both sides and form a graceful shape. Although not visible in the photograph, the central tine extends to and joins the main stem.

Design No. 4 is a U-shaped symbol that is located above the "figure 8" symbol near the top edge of the rock.

Camp historian H. Harold Williams reported that "a cache of Indian arrowheads and artifacts" was discovered by Boy Scouts in the 1920s in a "hollow" located to the north of Yawgoog Pond.[33] The scouts named the spot "Indian Caves," terms that most likely refer to overhanging ledges. Williams stated that he had found six arrowheads himself during low water levels of the pond. At some unreported time, the scouts investigated "two triangular-shaped rocks" in the woods to the east of the pond that were "believed to mark the graves of Chief Yawgoog and his son Wincheck."[34] Excavations were conducted at this supposed burial site but no evidence of either of the deceased was found.

In May 1930, a forest fire engulfed Yawgoog Pond and the surrounding woodlands, destroying some cottages, tent platforms, docks, and all but fifty acres of forest.[35] The land, now cleared of trees and brush, revealed Symbol Rock for the first time. Former camp chief J. Harold Williams stated that he believed the designs on Symbol Rock were made by Indians, and represented a "tomahawk and arrowhead which served as a guide for a cache of Indian weapons." Once again, excavations were conducted at the site that "revealed nothing."[36]

Archaeologists and rock art experts have inspected the images on Symbol Rock, but opinions vary regarding their origin. In 1981, Dr. James L. Swauger of the Carnegie Museum of Natural History in Pittsburgh visited Yawgoog Reservation and examined the designs on the rock. Swauger, in a letter to several individuals, reported that "the designs were foreign to anything else" he had encountered in his twenty-five years of petroglyph studies. At first, Swauger believed them to be of Native American origin, but by 1985 he revised his opinion and thought the designs were "probably a natural occurrence."[37] In 1983 Dr. William Turnbaugh noted that "at least" some of the designs seemed to be "manmade and possibly of some age" but he had not determined their origin.[38] In a 1989 letter to this author, Archaeologist Barbara Corcoran indicated that the designs were pecked into the rock and thus were produced by human hands.

To date, the origin of the designs on Symbol Rock remains a mystery. Were they produced by Indians, settlers, colliers or charcoal burners, woodcutters or mill workers, or are they simply natural grooves created by differential weathering of the rock surface?

CUPMARKED BOULDERS

Cup marks on rocks, more commonly called *cupules* in rock art and archaeological reports, were produced in abundance by Indians throughout North America. Carefully made, they were generally pecked into rock surface with stone picks or hammer stones. Their diagnostic characteristics include a circular form in plain view, and a rounded or basin-like profile. Occasionally, they were produced by grinding and are semi-conical in shape. In general, they range in diameter from 3/4 inch (2 cm) to 3 inches (7.5 cm) and in depth from 6/16 inch (5 mm) to 1-1/2 inches (4 cm). Occasionally, a secondary and smaller, deeper cupule may be present within them. Cupules may occur singularly, in groups, or arranged in rows. They are sometimes encircled by rings, attached to linear grooves, or exist as part of multiple image panels. They have been found in a variety of environmental settings, such as vertical ledges, horizontal rock outcrops, boulders, and in the interior of rock shelters.

Cup-marked stones are found throughout the world and are one of the oldest rock art motifs.[39] In North America, they are particularly abundant in California.[40] In the Great Basin area of western Nevada and eastern California, they are believed to be five to seven thousand years old.[41]

In the northeastern United States the presence of Indian-made cup marks is rare, but this may be due to the fact that they are unrecognized as cultural features by archaeologists working in this region. In 1878, a lone granite boulder containing six cup marks was found in Niantic, New London County, Connecticut, overlooking Long Island Sound.[42] My recent study of this rock suggests that they were produced by Indians.[43] A boulder containing "at least" two cupules made by "people," presumably Indians, has also been reported and documented in Stamford, Connecticut.[44] In New Jersey, cup marks were found on the Jennings petroglyph, a large sandstone block recovered from the east bank of the Delaware River in Walpack Township, Sussex County. Archaeologist Herbert C. Kraft reported the presence of twenty-one designs on the rock, including human figures, mammals, a bird track, face, and nine cup marks or pits.[45] Much earlier, Charles Conrad Abbott described a pitted stone slab about 9-3/4 inches (25 cm) long of unknown provenance that contained five pecked cupules of variable size; its function was unknown.[46] A more recent find was the discovery of two cup-marked boulders in Mahwah, Bergen County, New Jersey.

Deep within the Ramapo Mountains of West Mahwah, New Jersey, is a narrow and picturesque hollow known locally as Green Mountain Valley. This isolated gap, once a travel route through the mountains and home to Indian bands, is quiet and serene, and is seldom visited except by occasional hikers. In the nineteenth and early twentieth centuries, Green Mountain Valley was home to the Ramapo Mountain People, descendants of the Indians who occupied this region for 10,000 years.[47] Historical records indicate that the Ramapo Mountain People established a settlement here in about 1825. The settlement grew and prospered within its isolated and rocky hollow until the 1940s or 1950s, at which time it was completely abandoned.

The Green Mountain Valley settlement, also known as Havermeyer Hollow and Halifax, began when James DeGrote and Robert Lowder purchased ten acres of land in the valley.[48] By 1830, there were nine families living there with a total population of fifty-five persons. The valley settlers were employed at nearby farms and estates along the Ramapo River.

In 1857, a Methodist chapel was established by the inhabitants near the entrance to the Green Mountain Valley, but later the meetings were moved into the valley itself.[49] Historical accounts indicate that in 1876 the local preacher was Elliot Mann, and that William Mann was the licensed exhorter, both of whom were Ramapo Mountain People.[50] In 1877, church meetings were held at the log cabin of Johnnie Degroat, and the Reverend Mr. Jackson came from Paterson, New Jersey each Sunday morning to preach.[51] These accounts seem to indicate that there was no church building within the valley as of 1877.

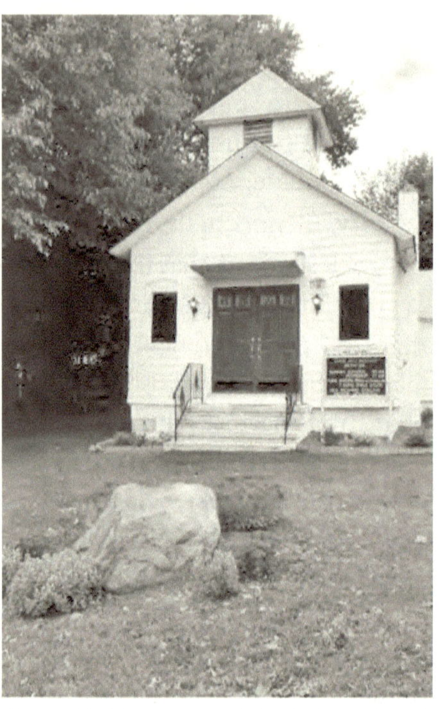

Figure 117: Re-erected A.M.E. Zion Church on Grove Street, Mahwah, New Jersey. Note the presence of a large boulder in front. A boulder was adjacent to the stone foundation of the church when it was located in Green Mountain Valley, Mahwah, New Jersey. *Photo by E.J. Lenik 2001.*

In 1892, a one-room school house was donated to the Ramapo Mountain People by H.O. Havermeyer, owner of an adjacent estate located on Ramapo Valley Road in Mahwah. The mountain people moved the wooden school into Green Mountain Valley, refurbished it, and used it as their church.[52]

During the 1870s, Theodore A. Havermeyer bought up several local farms and named his resulting estate Mountainside Farm. It totaled about 3,200 acres, and included Green Mountain Valley. Many of the mountain people continued to work on the Havermeyer farm, while others worked on the A.B. Darling estate located adjacent to and south of the Havermeyer property.

The early 1900s brought radical changes to the area. In 1904, the church congregation withdrew from the Union of Methodist Churches and joined the African Methodist Episcopal Zion Conference. By 1912, the Havermeyer family began to sell off portions of their estate. Two years later, H.O. Havermeyer requested the valley inhabitants to move out. In 1915, the A.M.E. Zion Church building was dismantled, moved out of Green Mountain Valley, and re-erected on Grove Street in Mahwah (Figure 117). During the 1920s, the valley residents continued to relocate and settle elsewhere. By the 1950s Green Mountain Valley had been completely abandoned.

Over many years, I have conducted several field investigations of the Green Mountain Valley site in an attempt to document the remains of this abandoned community. During field reconnaissance, my archaeological team located stone foundations, walls, privies, wells, and enclosures. These features were photographed, and a rough map showing the overall layout of the community was made. No archaeological excavations have been undertaken at the site. For many years it was threatened by encroaching residential development, but fortunately the land has been acquired for public use and is now part of the Ramapo Valley County (Bergen) Reservation.

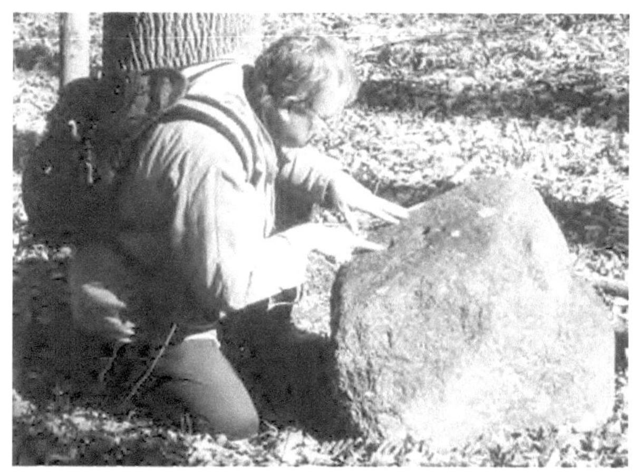

Figure 118: The author examining cup marked boulder at site of A.M.E. church in Green Mountain Valley, Mahwah, New Jersey. ***Photo by T. Fitzpatrick 2001.***

During my field investigations, particular attention was given to two locations within the abandoned community: a stone foundation of the one-room Methodist Chapel and a stone foundation that was allegedly the site of Samuel Jennings cabin, an early settler in the valley. These foundations were measured and described, and field sketch maps were produced.

In March 2001, I visited the site once again, accompanied by two colleagues, in a continuing effort to investigate and document it. Upon entering the settlement area we stopped to re-examine the stone foundation on which the Methodist Chapel once sat. There, immediately adjacent to the south side of the foundation, I observed a solitary upright boulder. I examined this rock and found two pecked cup marks on its top surface (Figure 118).

The cup-marked boulder is granite and was deposited here by the last glacier, more than 12,000 years ago. The rock is ovoid in plan view and measures 3 feet (90.15 cm) in maximum length, 19-11/16 inches (50.1 cm) in width, and 2 feet 4 inches (70 cm) in maximum height. The long axis of the stone is oriented north-south. The top surface of the boulder is flat, slants downward, and contains two cup marks. The upper or higher cup mark is bowl-shaped, patinated, and measures 1.5 inches (3.8 cm) in diameter across its top. Inside this cupule is a secondary pit of smaller diameter. The total depth of this cup mark is 1-1/16 inches (2.7 cm). The rough interior of this cupule suggests it was pecked into the rock. The second cup mark is situated 2-5/32 inches (5.5 cm) below the first on the slanting rock surface. It is also bowl-shaped, and measures 1-9/16 inches (4 cm) in diameter and 7/16 inch (1.1 cm) in depth and has a rough interior surface. No indication of the use of a metal drill was found within or adjacent to the two cup marks. Except for these cupules, the boulder has not been altered in any way. Therefore, I infer that the cup marks were produced by pecking into the granite surface.

A second cup-marked boulder was found in July, 2001. This one is located 50 feet (15 m) north of the northeast corner of the chapel foundation. It is an ovoid-shaped, free-standing glacial erratic situated on a low flat terrace. It is the only boulder on this small terrace. The rock measured 3 feet 10 inches (1.15 m) long, 3 feet (90.15 cm) wide and 2 feet (61 cm) in height. It contains one cupule on its top east-slanting surface. The cupule is perfectly rounded, conical in shape, and measures 7/8 inch (22 mm) in diameter at the surface and 13/16 inch (21 mm) in depth. The interior of the surface is smooth. We found no evidence of metal tool marks, such as nicks, cuts, or scratches, within the hole or elsewhere on the granite boulder.

The foundation of the Methodist Chapel was constructed out of the large cobbles and small boulders that are abundant in the region. Although some of the foundation stones are cut or broken, I found no evidence of tool marks on them. The foundation stones have not been quarried from bedrock sources nor have they been dressed. My colleagues and I intensively examined other stone foundations located nearby and have found no evidence of metal drill use on any stones used in their construction. We also examined boulders close to these other sites and found no additional cupules.

Who produced the cup marks on the two boulders, when were they made, and what do they represent or mean? Which came first at the site, the cupules or the chapel? The spatial association of the cupule boulders with the chapel foundation seems to suggest there could be a temporal association, but this may not be the case.

Archaeological research in the region indicates that Indian peoples were present in the area from the Paleo-Indian period (ca. 10,500 BC) to the Historic Contact period (ca. 1750 AD) and beyond.[53] They occupied open-air campsites and rock shelters in a variety of environmental settings. For example, there were several Historic Contact period sites located along the Ramapo River near the entrance to Green Mountain Valley. These include a village on the Havermeyer estate, a campsite at the eighteenth century Hopper-Van Horn House, the Stag Run campsite and an Indian trading post established here around 1700.[54] Three rock shelters are located a short distance to the northwest of the Green Mountain Valley that were occupied during the Archaic period (ca. 6000 BC - 1000 BC) and also the early Historic Contact period. These data suggest that Indians could have made the cup marks.

As previously discussed, Green Mountain Valley was occupied by Ramapo Mountain People from 1825 until at least 1940. A legend of these people, related by Otto Mann, states that there was a "dance rock . . . a flat ledge," a place where Indians danced, that was located along the road that extended from Bear Swamp on the northwest through Green Mountain Valley to Havermeyer's on the Ramapo River.[55] Ethno-historic accounts of the Lenape (Delaware) Indians clearly indicate that dancing was an important and commonplace activity of native life. Dances were performed for various reasons or occasions, such as to please or seek help from spiritual forces during ceremonies in times of war and peace, or simply as social events.[56]

When were the cup marks made? We have no direct empirical evidence to indicate the period in which they were produced. The two cup-marked boulders appear to be in their original location where they were deposited by the glacier. They were not moved to clear the way for building the foundation of the chapel. The boulders and their cup marks are uniformly patinated. There are no scratches or scars on the boulders, nor evidence of metal tool use.

What do the cup marks represent? Their small size indicates that they could not have functioned as grinding mortars for processing food or raw materials. They were not used for grinding down the ends of stone pestles because the pits are small, and in two instances the depressions are rough, not smooth. Also, they are not nutting pits; the lack of scars and scratches and their placement on slanting surfaces are factors that lend weight to this conclusion.

The cup-marked boulders themselves do not have any unusual features; they are not different from many other rocks in the valley. Their location on the west side of the valley floor at the bottom of a hill does not appear to be unusual. These boulders lie along a former trail, now an unimproved road that extended from the Ramapo River through the valley and deep into the mountains. On their travels through the valley, the Indians may have perceived these rocks to be spiritually charged. The historic Lenape, for example, believed that some rocks had spiritual power and referred to them as "our grandfathers."[57]

Ethno-historic data pertaining to the meaning of cupules are lacking for this geographic region. However, several possible interpretations regarding these simple, easily-produced cup marks come to mind when considering their context. For example, they may have been made by Indians for ritual purposes during vision quest activity. Perhaps the Indians believed that by pecking holes into the rock surface they were gaining access to supernatural power. The rhythmic, sound-producing hammering action may have led to a trance state, which is an important aspect of ritual behavior. The rock dust produced during pecking or grinding may have been ingested by men to gain spiritual power, or by women who decorated their bodies with the dust in order to increase their fertility.[58]

Alternatively, perhaps the cup marks were produced during the time the Methodist chapel was an active religious institution—1892 to 1915—for the community. They may have been associated with fertility enhancement rituals, or created during puberty initiations, or to symbolically mark or represent a new birth or death within the community.

In summary, I present the following hypothesis to account for the juxtaposition of the cup-marked boulders and the chapel foundation. I suggest that the nineteenth century valley dwellers saw the cup-marked stones and recognized their spiritual value and power. When the chapel, a structure of a new religious faith, was moved into Green Mountain Valley in 1892 it was placed at a site already occupied by spirits and sacred to Indian people.

The question of when the cupules were produced remains unanswered. They may be ancient or they may be contemporaneous with the settlement of the valley by the Ramapo Mountain People. Their placement near the entrance of the valley and near the site of an Indian village is also worthy of note. Was this valley a special place in need of protection from the Euro-Americans who took possession of the Ramapo River Valley?

SCULPTURES IN GRANITE

Strange stone carvings created by stone cutters in the distant past are located in the Westwoods section of Cockaponsett State Forest, about two miles southwest of the town of Guilford, New Haven County, Connecticut. They are curious rock sculptures situated within what was once Hanna's Quarry, which operated there in the last half of the nineteenth century.

The remains of Hanna's Quarry can be accessed by way of a hiking trail that extends west and then turns northwest from a small parking area located at the intersection of Connecticut Route 146 and Sam Hill Road in Guilford. A short hike of about 1/2 mile (0.8 km) along a white circular-blazed

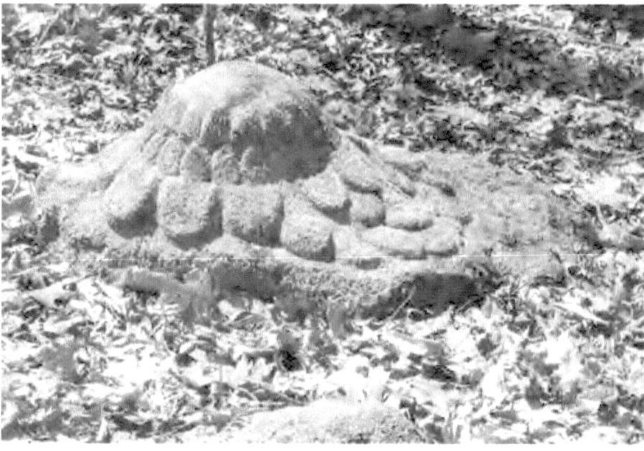

Figure 119: Sculpted stone with petal-like design in Hanna's Quarry, Guilford, Connecticut. ***Photo by E.J. Lenik 1982.***

trail will bring rock art enthusiasts to the rock sculptures site.

As you proceed along the trail, which parallels the Amtrak rail corridor, you will come across the remains of the quarry, the most prominent feature of which is an immense block of cut granite perched precariously on a high rock outcrop. Continue along the White Circle Trail past the intersection of an orange-blazed trail, and two white square loop trails, one to the left and the other to the right, until you reach the bottom of a small rise. Turn left (west) and follow another White Square loop trail uphill to where it overlooks Lost Lake. A hiking map of the Westwoods trail can be obtained at several commercial outlets and the town hall in Guilford.

The carvings are on the top of the small wooded hill that rises above a cove of Lost Lake, a now land-locked harbor inlet from Long Island Sound. There are eight carvings randomly scattered along both sides of the trail within an area that measures 150 feet (44 m) from north to south and 100 feet (30 m) from east to west.

The first carving to be encountered is on the brow of the hill facing the cove. Here on an outcrop of rock is a carved granite seat with a back. The word "seat" is somewhat misleading because an average person would not be able to sit comfortably within this feature; it is very small and measures 12 inches (30 cm) square and is cut 4 inches (10 cm) deep into the rock.

Twenty feet (5.5 m) east-northeast of the stone seat is a round pyramid-like rock that is completely decorated with rings of sculpted "scallops" or petals that overlap each other (Figure 119). This feature stands about 18 inches (45 cm) in height. A short distance to the northeast is a small flat outcrop that contains a carved flower with four petals (Figure 120).

Further along to the northeast, on top of a wide outcrop of bedrock, is a sculpted oval-shaped bowl that measures 18 inches (45 cm) by 15 inches (38 cm). There are several drilled holes along the outer edge of the bowl. Ten feet (3 meters) north-northwest of the bowl feature is an incised inscription, but its lines are barely visible and cannot be identified.

The most visible carving is at the southeast corner of a large outcrop of rock to the west of the trail that is about 7 feet (2 m) in height. Cut into the corner of the rock are a series of semicircular grooves surmounted by seven horizontal ridges that resemble a classical architectural column (Figure 121). About a quarter of the column appears to be emerging from the rock and at its top is a flat carved out area that contains thirteen drilled holes. On the vertical face of the rock, to the left of the column, are thirty drilled holes in an irregular pattern.

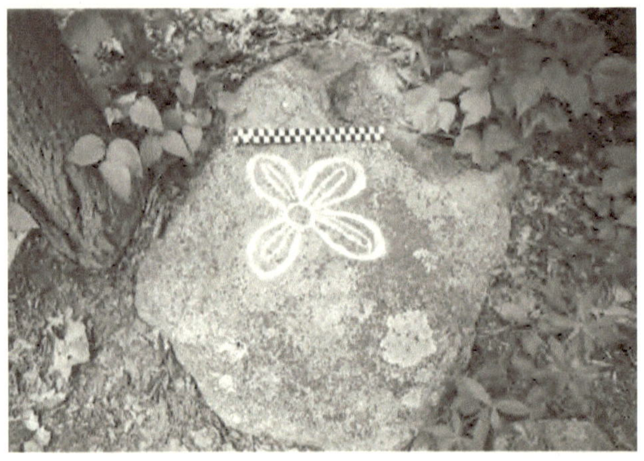
Figure 120: Flat rock with carved flower in Hanna's Quarry, Guilford, Connecticut. ***Photo by E.J. Lenik 1980.***

Two carved basins, each resembling water troughs, are also present on this hilltop site. The first lies 60 feet (17.5 m) northeast of the oval-shaped bowl described above. It is cut into a small outcrop of bedrock and measured 5 inches (12.7 cm) by 4 inches (10.2 cm) by 3 inches (7.5 cm) deep. There are three parallel lines cut into the rock that measured 5 inches (12.7 cm), 4 inches (10.2 cm), and 2 inches (5 cm) respectively. The second rock basin is located at the north end of the site. This carved trough measured 22 inches (56 cm) by 15 inches (38 cm).

According to Guilford historian Joel E. Helander, the sculpted rocks were discovered by hunters around 1930, and archaeologists and historians have been arguing over their origins ever since. One of the first to offer an explanation of the carvings was Charles M. Boland in his 1961 book *They All Discovered America*. Boland suggested that the carvings were the work of Phoenicians who were at the site at some time between 480 BC and 146 BC.[59] He envisioned their ship anchoring off of Leete's Island to make repairs while a party of artisans went ashore and chiseled the figures into the rock.

Other investigators and interpretations followed. In 1980, John P. Gallagher and Frederick J. Pohl attributed the carvings to Christian monks who escaped religious persecution in Morocco, North Africa by sailing west across the Atlantic to America in 480 AD.[60] Gallagher and Pohl believed that the drilled holes located near the carved classical column represented Greek letters and symbols relating to Christianity. To illustrate this point, they arbitrarily connected several of the pits with imaginary lines, which produced the outline of a "fish" which was a sign for Jesus Christ, and the letters "I" and "C," which were abbreviations for fish or Christ. By connecting other holes with imaginary lines they reported seeing the letters "I S Ch S Y Th S" which meant "Iesous Christos Yious Theou Soter" or "Jesus Christ Son of God Savior."

Gallagher and Pohl identified the sculpted oval-shaped bowl with its drill marks as a "libation bowl used for baptism."[61] They described the drilled holes as receptacles for a "candelabrum." They also believed that the rectangular trough at the north end of the site was another baptismal vessel. The flower with its four petals, they said, may represent "Hyssop," a plant that was native to the Mediterranean region and associated with biblical purification rites. In sum, Gallagher and Pohl believed "the site must have been a church" occupied by "orthodox Christians...using Byzantine symbols and rituals."[62]

Most scholars reject the claims that Phoenicians or early Christians produced the carvings. Other alternative interpretations have been proffered. For example, when the carvings were examined by C.C. Willoughby of the Peabody Museum in Cambridge, Massachusetts, on July 11, 1931, he described them as "the work of a white man, probably one of the workmen at a nearby quarry for his own amusement or because he was mentally unbalanced."[63] He also reported that there were two sculpted heads at the site, but these items have been removed by anonymous persons and their current whereabouts are unknown.

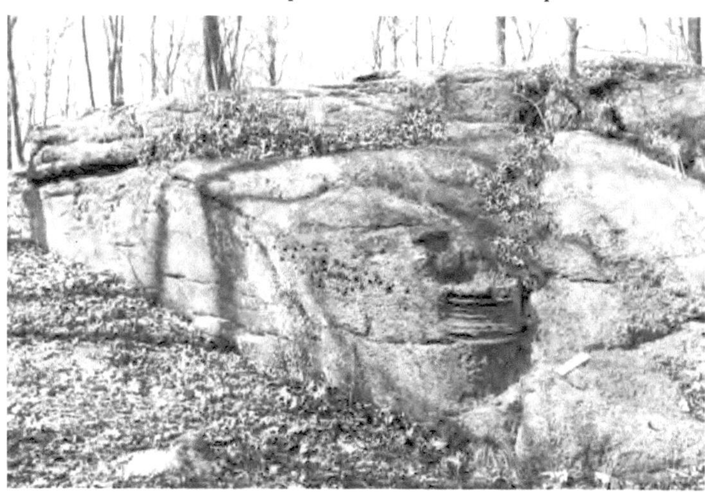

Figure 121: Sculpted edge of bedrock (center) resembling a classical architectural column. Note presence of many drilled holes to the left of the column. ***Photo by E.J. Lenik 1982.***

The most plausible theory is that the carvings were made by nineteenth century quarrymen, since this land was the site of Hanna's Quarry, which operated here from around 1888 to 1908.[64] The quarry was established by John Hanna, an immigrant from Ireland who purchased 38 acres (15.2 ha) of land next to the old Shore Line Railroad. Hanna was a sculptor, monumental architect, contractor and builder. Located near the carvings are quarry pits, numerous cut stone blocks with drill marks and holes, iron tie rods, several foundations and a stone-lined well. These remains of a once-flourishing stone quarry operation now lie hidden in this forested area.

THE SEBEC STONE

One of the most puzzling of Maine's inscribed stones was found at Greeley's Landing on Sebec Lake in Piscataquis County (Figure 122). A deeply-incised stone block, it was discovered by Andrew McSorley in 1938 on the south shore of the lake about 26 feet (8 m) from the shoreline. The stone is granite, roughly rectangular in shape, and measures 18 inches (49 cm) long, 16-1/2 inches (42 cm) wide, and varies in thickness from 6 inches (15 cm) to 8 inches (20 cm). McSorley found the stone lying among similar sized stones with its incised design face down.[65] A sawmill reportedly stood in the area where the stone was found, and indeed McSorley stated that saw dust and wood chip piles were present in the area when he discovered the stone.

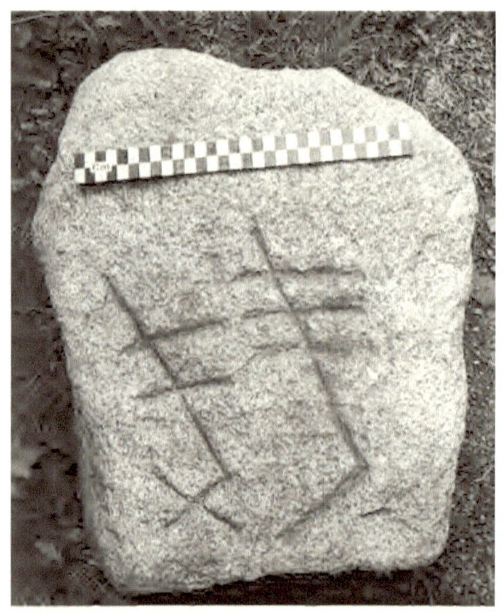

Figure 122: The Sebec Stone, Greeleys Landing, Maine. ***Photo by E.J. Lenik 1978.***

The geometric designs on the rock consist of clear, sharp, incised straight lines. The grooves measure 3/16 inch (5 mm) in depth and range in width from 3/16 inch (5 mm) to 3/8 inch (10 mm) in depth. The two designs are well made and were produced with some degree of skill and effort on this tough artistic medium. It has been suggested that the incised lines were a quarryman's marks made with metal tools. However, I found no evidence that this stone was quarried and incised with metal tools when I examined it in the 1970s; there was no sign of hammer, punch, drill, or chisel marks on the rock. The rock was not a quarried block of stone but rather a natural boulder. Which tool was used to produce the incised lines remains an open question.

A photograph of the Sebec Stone, along with an interpretation of its markings, was published in 1948 in a booklet titled *Norse Inscriptions On American Stones*. Its author, Olaf Strandwold, stated that the two sets of symbols represented runic writing. The top line represented the Norse word "AUTHR" or "AUDR," which he said means "luck, ease, plenty," while the bottom set of runes represented the word "REKA," which means "to drift along."[66] He reported that the inscription was "perhaps an ancient sign to direct fishermen." I do not accept his interpretation, as the markings do not represent runic writing. In fact, Strandwold enhanced the symbols on his published photograph and added two lines on the bottom set that are not on the stone itself.

An alternative explanation to be considered is that the symbols might be of Indian origin. The symbols may possibly represent a form of sign language, indicating direction of travel, and a time marker on a Sebec Lake canoe route. Garrick Mallery, in his book *Picture Writing of the American Indians*, reported that Abenaki Indians used a stick stuck into the ground diagonally, pointing in the direction of travel, with a number of other sticks set vertically across the diagonal one to indicate the number of days journey.[67] Perhaps the same method was employed on the Sebec Stone to guide travelers.

Mallery further notes that nineteenth century Abenaki produced pictographs and geometric marks on pieces of birch bark as a way of informing other persons of their departure, direction of travel, and purpose of the trip. This method of communication was called "wikhegan," a Passamaquoddy word that means a "message" or "letter."[68] A similar method, also called wikhegan, was used by the Penobscot Indians of Oldtown, Penobscot County, Maine, in the late nineteenth century. They incised symbols on birch bark to indicate where they were going, and the direction and purpose of the trip.[69]

From earliest times to well into the nineteenth century, travel by birch bark canoe was the simplest and perhaps only way to go. One major east-west canoe route to Moosehead Lake began at Howland, Maine. It ran down the Penobscot River and then along the Sebec River to Sebec Lake, then northwesterly via Onawa Lake and Wilson Ponds, with several portages, to Moosehead Lake.[70] In 1761 Colonel John Montressor traveled by canoe from Quebec to the Penobscot River and observed that "The Abenaquis, jealous of the knowledge of their country, took care to leave but few vestiges of their route. Even here we found but few knotches [sic] on the trees, commonly called blazes, the savages' constant guide in the woods...."[71] Archaeologists David Cook and Arthur Spiess have indicated that Sebec Lake has many Indian occupation sites near its east end outlet, and also near Wilson Stream in the northwest corner of the lake. Cook and Spiess suggest that the lake had a "resident band" of Indian people, and was not just a place to stop while traveling.[72] Artifacts collected from the lakeside indicate occupation during the Moorehead

Phase Late Archaic period, ca. 5000 B.P. ("Before Present") to 4500 B.P., the Susquehanna Tradition ca. 3700 B.P. to 3600 B.P., and during the Ceramic period ca. 3000 B.P. to 400 B.P.

I examined, photographed, sketched and measured the Sebec Stone in 1978 but was unable to reach any conclusions regarding the origin and meaning of the carvings. Following my visit, I consulted with several archaeologists, rock art experts, local residents, and documentary sources regarding the symbols on the rock. However, a definitive explanation continues to elude me.

ENDING OBSERVATIONS

The historic period rock art documented here is in essence the egocentric effort of individuals, and is not a widespread cultural or ethnic practice. The content of the rock art is extremely varied. The carving of inscriptions, including such features as names, initials, dates, religious and secular statements, and other related images, is the most common and widespread practice in the Northeast region. Clearly, human beings have a propensity to record their presence or their feelings or beliefs on rock surfaces. Such carvings are not hidden but are placed on billboard-like rocks and are meant to be seen. This act of carving names, initials, and dates continues in many forms or mediums to this day.

In most instances, the identity of individuals creating the inscriptions is unknown or of little historic importance, except of course to the individuals themselves. There are exceptions to this general pattern, such as Endicott Rock in New Hampshire and the Thomas King carving in Maine, which record events and facts of history and are important contributions to our knowledge.

Abstract and geometric designs are commonly portrayed, but are virtually impossible to interpret. These designs occur as individual images or in groups, and include such symbols as X's, crosses, V-shaped grooves, circles, straight, curved, oblique or perpendicular lines, rectilinear shapes, and pits or cup marks. What did these symbols mean to those who produced them? Do they mark a significant place at a particular time? To the modern viewer they appear to be nothing more than gibberish or graffiti.

The carvings of human figures and body parts are, in most cases, realistically illustrated and usually easy to identify. The types of figures range from full-bodied individuals, upper body, heads and faces to legs, arms, or male genitalia. Several Indian heads, often with headdresses, have been portrayed that may reflect the rock artist's romantic images of Native Americans in a natural or woodland setting.

There is a tendency on the part of some viewers and researchers to immediately interpret these images as being ancient, which they are not. Some carved heads and faces have been identified as representing exotic peoples, such as Irish Celts, but such speculation is without any factual foundation. One carving purports to show a fourteenth century Scottish knight with sword and shield, a highly fanciful interpretation by those who believe that

North America was visited by many European and Asian people long before Columbus's voyages. Such interpretations are an effort by individuals and groups to promote their diffusionist theories, which lack solid evidence at this point in time.

Some petroglyphs are a valuable part of the historic record of the Northeast region, and it is important that a graphic and written account be made of them. They tell us about people and events in the past. A prime example is the story of the captivity of Mrs. Johnson and her family by the Indians in the eighteenth century, and their ensuing journey from New Hampshire to Canada. The carved profiles of W.C. Fields, the famous early twentieth century comedian, emblazoned on a rock at Esopus Island in the Hudson River, is another. A third illustration is the carving of a ship's steering wheel, perhaps commemorating the tragic 1919 sinking of a steamboat near the island.

In the Adirondack Mountains of New York there is a beautifully carved stagecoach, complete with horses, driver and passengers. The stagecoach was a major mode of transportation and communication for tourists and residents in this remote region for nearly one hundred years. The carving of a steamboat in South Woodstock, Vermont, recalls a by-gone era of transportation and commerce on the nearby Connecticut River. At the Hog Mountain quarry in Montville, New Jersey, an Italian stonemason carved the likeness of a steam locomotive that hauled rock from the quarry to build a dam around 1900.

What was important to the quarry men who carved their names and several images in Guilford, Connecticut? At Beattie's Quarries religion was an essential element in the lives of eastern European immigrants who worked here. At Hanna's Quarry beauty was apparently important to those Italian stonecutters who sculpted a pyramid of petals, a Doric column, and a carved flower with four petals. All of these artists exhibited their skills and left tangible evidence of having worked there.

Biographic rock art in naturalistic form is represented at two sites. On Staten Island, New York, we have a carved image of a pig and wigwam which is most likely a record of the war between the Dutch settlers and Indians in the seventeenth century. And, in the Village of Prattsville, New York, there is an entire cliff face carved with images of Zadock Pratt, the founder of the community and its tanning industry in the nineteenth century. These carvings and sculptures are detailed and readily identifiable, each telling a story of actual events important in the lives of people in these areas.

Numerous artifacts are illustrated, usually as part of rock art compositions. These include pipes, spears, arrows, canoes, tomahawks, and other items. Some, however, appear singularly, such as the bows and arrows and musket and bayonet on a mountaintop in Keene, New Hampshire. Mammals and birds are also depicted, including horses, bears, deer, a pig, whale, beaver, rabbit, hawk and eagle. The motive behind the carving of single faunal creatures is baffling.

My experience of traveling to the sites of permanent rock carvings and examining portable specimens has been a voyage of discovery, since each revealed some aspect of history or artistic endeavor. I marvel at the creativity and productivity of the human spirit that each site reveals.

The permanent rock art sites mark places in the landscape, but they are fast disappearing. The passage of time and the natural processes of weathering and erosion will ultimately erase many of them. Some will be destroyed by construction activity, such as residential and commercial developments, roads, and various other elements of the human infrastructure. Others, unfortunately, will be destroyed by visitors to the sites, who feel compelled to place their own marks on the rocks. It is, therefore, essential that a record be made of them. This book has been my attempt to do so.

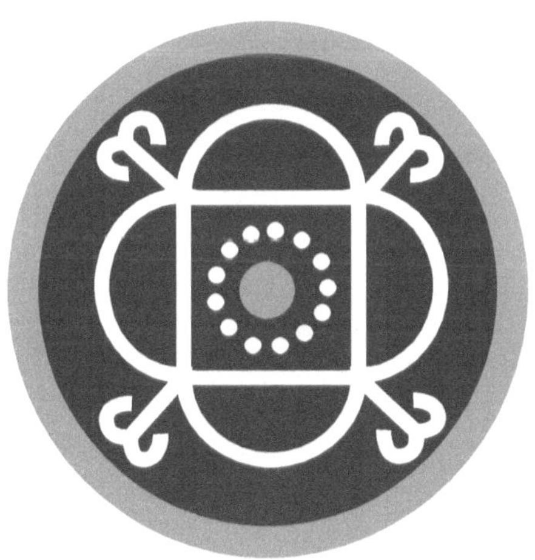

GLOSSARY OF ROCK ART TERMS AND FEATURES

Rock art research, as with other types of archaeological studies, has its own particular language and terminology. To aid in understanding the petroglyph sites, here are some definitions of figures, terms, methods, and techniques used to describe and interpret them.

Abrading. Rubbing or scraping the surface of a rock with a hard stone in order to create a smooth surface.

Abstract. Figures that are unrecognizable or nonrepresentational.

Algonkian. Relating to a tribe or family group of Indians and their culture.

Algonquian. Relating to the language of the Algonkian Indians.

Artifact. Any object or material produced or modified by human beings.

Bedrock. A solid rock formation lying at and below the surface of the ground.

Chert. A compact, opaque to slightly translucent micro-crystalline silica rock.

Cobble. A rock bigger that a pebble and smaller than a boulder.

Cupules. Shallow, circular pit pecked in a rock surface. Also referred to as cup marks.

Diffusionism. A theory that cultural and technological innovation in general has spread outward from a small number of sources.

Drilling. Rotating a stone or metal tool to produce small, round, and sometimes deep holes in a rock surface.

Element. A single figure or design within a site.

Erratic. A boulder transported from its place of origin by a glacier and deposited when the ice melted.

Ethnohistoric. The study of native or non-western people from a combined historical and anthropological viewpoint using written documents, oral accounts, material culture and ethnographic data.

Excising. Gouging out stone material with a chisel or a chisel and hammer stone.

Exfoliation. The natural flaking and spilling away of the surface of a rock.

Flint knapping. Stone tool making consisting of a process of reduction in which the knapper (toolmaker) removes flakes from a stone in a prescribed manner to shape a tool.

Geometric. Designs or shapes including diamond-like figures, rectangles, spirals, wavy lines, zigzag lines, straight lines, concentric circles, dots, cup marks, crosshatched patterns, grids and crosses.

Glyphs. Designs carved or painted; often part of a writing system.

Gorget. An ornament with two holes that is worn suspended from the neck.

Groove. A linear indentation in the surface of a rock created by incising or rubbing.

Hammer stone. A hard, usually round or ovoid stone showing worn or pitted surface areas from use as a percussion tool

Historic Contact Period. The period of time extending from the first documented contacts between Indians and Europeans to the end of the eighteenth century.

Historic Period. The period of time following the European settlement of an area.

Ideograms. Mnemonic symbols.

Incising. Carving lines with a sharp object such as a stone flake or metal tools. Also called scratching.

Intaglio. A recessed figure made by gouging and scraping away the rock.

Ithyphallic. A human figure with an erect penis.

Lichenometry. A dating technique involving measurements of the area of petroglyphs covered by lichen along with a time estimate for the rate at which specific lichen grows at the sites being studied.

Lye stone. Usually a large, flat stone with a circular groove used for leaching lye from wood ashes through a drip groove into a container. Also called a lye leaching stone or a potash stone.

Motif. A specific, distinctive symbol or image such as the hand design, thunderbird, or effigy face.

Naturalistic. A figure made in a realistic way; it resembles a real-life object.

Ogham/Ogam. An unusual type of writing consisting primarily of vertical or oblique straight lines placed over or under a main horizontal line; used by ancient Irish or Celtic people.

Nutting stone. A flat stone with deep, rounded and smooth multiple concavities thought by some archaeologists to have been used to crush nuts.

Paleo-Indian. A cultural period extending from ca. 12,500 B.P. - 10,000 B.P. (B.P. means Before Present).

Petroglyphs. Figures, images, symbols that have been carved into non-portable stone.

Pictograph. A painting on non-portable stone.

Portable petroglyphs. Pecked, sculpted or incised figures, images, or symbols on stone artifacts such as pebbles, pendants, pipes, axes, gorgets, and atlatl weights.

Prehistoric. The period in which archaeological evidence or oral accounts are the only known record of Native American peoples.

Quadruped. Four-legged animal. Often used to describe an unidentified animal.

Radiocarbon dating. A method used to date organic material based on the measured decay of radioactive carbon in an organism. Also known as C-14 dating.

Rectilinear. Straight lines forming rectangular symbols.

Red ochre. A natural material used as a pigment in painting glyphs. Also called red hematite.

Shaman. A person with the "power" to communicate with spirits and humans. He/she may conduct ceremonies to exorcise evil spirits, appeal for the protection of good spirits, attempt to heal the sick, and control the weather.

Shamanism. Defined as an "archaic technique of ecstasy."

Site. A location that was occupied or used by humans and where archaeological remains are present.

Style. The particular way in which a glyph is made, including method of manufacture, subject matter, attributes, location, theme, or relationship to other glyphs. Styles are often specific to a period of time and region.

Stylized. An identifiable figure made in an elemental form such as a stick figure.

Superimposing. The placing of one figure or image on top of another.

Symbolism. An element or figure that carries a particular meaning to individuals of a social/cultural group.

Therianthrope. A combination being, part human and part animal.

Weathering. The physical and or chemical decomposition of rock at or near the exposed surfaces.

SEE FOR YOURSELF

A number of the rock art sites discussed in this book are on public land or in private facilities that are open to the public. Listed here by state/town are sites you can visit. These properties and website addresses were accessible at the time of publication of this book.

CONNECTICUT

East Haddam: Three Bridges Cemetery. Tombstone of Warren Tatson with carved Indian in profile. On Three Bridges Road.

Farmington: Hospital Rock. Hospital Rock is within the Hartford Watershed land in Farmington. It is off the Metacomet Trail, but its exact location is undisclosed to protect the site. Check for guided hikes into this state archaeological preserve.

Guilford Westwoods, Leetes Island & Hannah's Quarry. Stone cutter's art and granite sculptures on land owned by the Guilford Land Conservation Trust and land within Cockaponsett State Forest. Some carved pieces are found along the White Square Trail. See trail description at: <http://guilfordlandtrust.org/wordpress/2010/02/westwoods-warrior-loop-1>

New Preston: The Pinnacle. Hebrew Inscriptions on the summit of this mountain east of Lake Waramaug—not to be confused with Pinnacle Rock near Plainsville. The Pinnacle is a hill just southeast of Lake Waramaug.

MAINE

Wells Beach: Wells Public Library, 1434 Post Road. Wells Beach Petroglyph boulder is reportedly now outside the public library.

Darmariscove Island, Darmariscove Inscriptions. The Island is owned by the Boothbay Region Land Trust, which maintains two moorings for visitors. See: <http://www.bbrlt.org/bbrlt_islands.html>

Monmouth, Monmouth Museum, Main Street at Flanders Drive. The Monmouth Stone is on the Museum grounds near the small white building.

MASSACHUSETTS

Barre: Rocking Stone Park, on Dana Road. Cradle Rock has an Olmec-like face carved on it as well as other designs.

Lanesborough: Balance Rock State Park. Indian heads and figures are carved on the balanced rock and surrounding rocks.

Shutesbury: Temenos (Private) A squatting figure and ZIZO, a Buddhist Saint, are carved on rocks at the site of old Mount Mineral Springs House hotel, now a retreat center. Contact retreat office for information on visiting center. See: <http://www.massretreats.com/temenos.html>

Southbridge: Oakridge Cemetery. Angela Leach tombstone with two carved Indian pots. On Main Street, access is from Oak Ridge Street and Cohasse Street. This historic (1810) cemetery is managed by the Town of Southbridge.

Westford: Depot Street. The Westford Knight is painted on bedrock. Look for a roadside marker.

Westford: J. V. Fletcher Library, 50 Main Street. Medieval ship carving known as the "Westford Boat Stone" is housed here.

NEW HAMPSHIRE

Concord: New Hampshire Historical Society Museum, 30 Park Street. The "Meredith Mystery Stone" is on display here.

Salem: Mystery Hill (Private) Running deer petroglyph and others are found in the "Oracle Chamber." See: <http://www.stonehengeusa.com/>

Swanzey: Pilgrim Pines Conference Center (Private), 22 West Shore Road. Soul effigy carved on rock at water's edge on Swanzey Lake. Conference center is owned by the Evangelical Covenant Church. Contact for access: (http://www.pilgrimpines.org/index.php)

Weirs Beach: Endicott Rock Park. Look for carvings on Endicott Rock itself.

NEW JERSEY

Little Falls: Morris Canal Preserve. Main Street, between Union and Stevens Avenues. Look for Egyptian bird carved on a boulder just off path at canal level between the bed of the canal and the Passaic River below.

Mahwah: Ramapo Valley County Reservation. This Bergen County Park is located on Route 202 south of Ramapo College. Green Mountain Valley, also known as Halifax can be reached by taking the Green Trail (Halifax Trail). The former church site where the two cup-marked boulders are found is at the junction of this trail and the old Halifax Road, along which the trail runs after descending from Hawk Rock.

New Brunswick: Weston Mill Pond and Lawrence Brook. Inscriptions, skull and cross bones "Red Rover" and other carvings can be found along the pond and on riverside cliffs.

NEW YORK

Keene: Stagecoach Rock. This large boulder with a carving of a stagecoach is found along Route 73 between Keene and Lake Placid. The rock is protected by a metal railing and a small parking area was created here when the highway was recently repaired.

Kent, Putnam County: Hawk Rock. Carvings on hawk-shaped boulder. Watershed Access Permit needed. See: (http://www.nyc.gov/html/dep/html/watershed_protection/access.shtml)

Manhattan: Dyckman Farmhouse Museum, 4881 Broadway at 204th Street. See gameboard carved in a boulder in the cellar kitchen of Manhattan's last colonial farmhouse, built in 1784.

New City: High Tor State Park. Eagle petroglyph is found on summit near the Long Path Trail. This portion of the trail involves scrambling over rocks and boulders. Caution: the carving on the mountain slope overlooking Haverstraw is difficult and dangerous to access and view.

North Salem: Roadside carved ledge on Bogtown Road. Mortuary art and practice along a long rock ledge on west side of road between intersections with Yerkes Road and Wheeler Road.

Prattsville: Pratt's Rock Park and Zadock Pratt Museum. Sculpted figures of Zadock Pratt, hemlock trees, tannery building, horse, scroll, etc. along with stone sofas to rest on as you climb trail to carvings. Zadock Pratt Museum next door provides history.

Staasburg: Esopus Island, Norrie State Park. Esopus Island is accessible by water to the public from the marina. Site of human figure and steering wheel petroglyphs.

Staten Island: Lemon Creek Park. Pig and Wigwam petroglyphs and the curious stone structures built by Doug Schwartz, who is also the zoo keeper for the groundhog known as "Staten Island Chuck." Entrance to pier and beach area is at intersection of Sharrot Avenue and Hylan Boulevard. Petroglyphs and stone structures are found south of the pier.

Tuxedo: Harriman State Park. Pictograph of the Giant Vecca (rabbit) from "Luggage of the Gods" is near Claudius Smith's Den just off the Tuxedo-Mount Ivy Trail.

PENNSYLVANIA

Jim Thorpe: Leigh Gorge State Park, Glen Onoko section. Pulpit or Sentimental Rock near the lower waterfall near the start of the Glen Onoko Falls trail has a petroglyph panel including animal figures, Indians and carved initials.

Doylestown: Mercer Museum, 84 South Pine Street. The Lenape Stone is on exhibit here.

RHODE ISLAND

Rockville: Yawgoog Boy Scout Camp. Symbol Rock is located at the end of the Symbol Rock Trail, a side trail on the Green Trail. See: <http://www.mdc.net/~dbrier/yawgoog/trails/green.html> Please obtain hiking permission from the camp. See: <http://www.yawgoog.com/>

VERMONT

Reading: Indian Stones at Roadside on Route 106. Carved stone markers depicting the captivity of Mrs. Johnson by the Abnaki Indians in 1754. Look for Vermont Historic Roadside Marker.

NOTES

PREFACE (Pages i-ii)

1. Lenik 2002

PAINTED IMAGES (Pages 3-10)

1. Lenik 2002: 64-67; 195-198
2. Gramly 1978
3. Gramly 1978: 108-2:11
4. Gramly 1978: 108-2:12
5. Gramly 1981:113
6. Gramly 1978:108-2:12
7. Gramly 1981:116
8. Webster 1940:239
9. Gramly 1981:116
10. Merrill 1973:118
11. Knight 1996:6
12. Thompson 1981:56
13. Briggs 2000, personal communication
14. Merrill 1973:122
15. Thompson 1981:56
16. Knight 1996:7
17. Merrill 1973:121
18. Knight 1996:7
19. Jones 1949:13-15
20. Merrill 1973:121

INDIAN LORE MOTIFS: FRAUDS AND FANCIFUL TALES (Pages 11-32)

1. Beers 1867
2. Lenik and Crichton 1988
3. Shoumatoff 1971
4. Reich 1988, personal communication
5. Sypher 1990, personal communication
6. Muscarella 1990, personal communication
7. Light Behr 1990, personal communication. Ms. Behr was the Associate Historian for the Town of Kent, New York.

8. Seton 1921
9. Lenik, Ftizpatrick and Gibbs 1993:3-5
10. Thunderhorse 1997
11. Lenik 1997:58
12. Lenik 1976:1-2
13. Weisshaar 1928
14. Weisshaar 1928
15. Weisshaar 1928
16. Mercer 1885:61-62
17. Mercer 1885:65
18. Mercer 1885:2
19. Mercer 1885:2, 65
20. Mercer 1885:5
21. Mercer 1885:
22. Mercer 1885:6
23. Mercer 1885:6
24. Mercer 1885:39-45
25. Mercer 1885:77-78
26. Mercer 1885:70
27. Kraft 1996:7, 9
28. Oestreicher 1994, 1995, 1996
29. Mercer 1885::83
30. Mercer 1885::83
31. Mercer 1885:92-95
32. Williams 1991:119
33. Huber 1935:42
34. Huber 1935:42-43
35. Kraft 1996:7
36. Delabarre 1928:275
37. Delabarre 1928:275
38. Kraft 1996:6
39. Delabarre 1928:278
40. Letter quoted in Delabarre 1928:278
41. Kraft 1996:7-9
42. Brinton 1893:201-203
43. Delabarre 1928:259-260
44. Brinton 1893:203
45. King 1980:2
46. King 1980:4
47. King 1980:5

48. See McKusick 1970:124
49. King 1980:2
50. McKusick 1970:99
51. See for example Lenik 2002:182-188
52. King 1980:6
53. Gridley 1939:50-51. An earlier, somewhat similar version of the stone giant story can be found in Graylock 1879:82-83.
54. See Simmons 1986:172-234
55. Leland 1884:15-139
56. Smith 1883:16-18; Converse 1908:135; Bruchac 1985:161-168
57. Fenton and Tooker 1978:471; Snow 1996:82, 114; Day 1998:206
58. Anonymous 2003 <http://members.aol.com/MAspeleo/balancesp.html> [no longer valid]
59. Eckhart 1996:217
60. Eckhart 1996:404
61. Eckhart 1996:413
62. Eckhart 1996:413
63. Eckhart 1996:414

ANTHROPOMORPHS (Pages 33-46)

1. Butler 1988:3
2. Chase 1977, personal communication
3. Chase 1977, personal communication
4. Butler 1988:3-5
5. Isa 2002
6. Westknight 2002 http://www.orkneyjar.com/history/historical figures/henrysinclair/westknight.htm [no longer valid]
7. Goodwin 1946
8. Glynn 1967:14
9. Fowler 1960:21-22
10. Kraft 1994:38-42
11. Kraft 1994:39-40
12. Lewis-Williams 2002:265
13. Lewis-Williams 2002:266
14. Kraft 1994:41
15. Anonymous 1985:31; Rogers et al. 1990
16. See Lenik 2002:168-169
17. Vermont Division for Historic Preservation 1997
18. Vermont Division for Historic Preservation 1997
19. Stone 1967:35

20. deLesdernier 1976:5-6
21. Stone 1967:35
22. deLesdernier 1976:5
23. deLesdernier 1976:2-5
24. deLesdernier 1976:8-9
25. deLesdernier 1976:9
26. deLesdernier 1976:6

FACES IN STONE (Pages 47-56)

1. Fell 1980:203
2. Fell 1982:97
3. Anonymous 2003 <http://www.cascobay.com/educ/spie/chebehst.html> [no longer valid]
4. Cahill 1993:12, 20
5. Cahill 1993:12
6. Cook 1978: figure 15
7. Cook 1978: figure 22
8. Dexter and Martin 1995:166
9. See for example Weaver 1972: 240; Thompson 1975: plates 16 a, d, 28b, 29, 32
10. Colomb 1979
11. Frink 2003, personal communication
12. Hitchcock 1841: 376
13. See Weaver 1972: 46, 47, 49
14. Patterson 1992:77
15. Miles 1992:142
16. Miles 1992:142
17. See for example Lenik 2002:82, 180, 187, 200, 233-23519.

BIRD, FISH, AND ANIMAL MOTIFS (Pages 57-70)

1. Norman 1968:260-268
2. Crosby 1973: 35
3. Green 1886
4. O'Brien 1981:60
5. O'Brien 1981: 93-95
6. Robbins 1980:1
7. Robbins 1973
8. Robbins 1980:1
9. Robbins 1980:2-3

10. Duprey, personal communication 1993
11. Feldman 1977; Goudsward and Stone 2003
12. Goodwin 1946:59
13. Robbins and Jones 1959:137
14. Anonymous 1962
15. Rothovius 1963:7
16. Anonymous 1964
17. Fell 1976:201
18. Feldman 1977:99
19. Feldman 1977:35
20. Kraft 2001:412
21. Jameson 1909:202
22. Ruttenber 1872:101; Kraft 2001:413
23. Ruttenber 1872:101
24. O'Callahan 1855:226-227; Ruttenber 1872:101
25. Venables 1989:6
26. Schwartz, personal communication 2003
27. Mellgren, personal communication 1976
28. Krupp 1978:216
29. Mellgren, pesonal communication 1976

MORTUARY ART (Pages 71-82)

1. Gilbert 1996, personal communication; Leary 1997, personal communication
2. Duval and Rigby 1978
3. Scharf 1886: II: 533
4. Lederer 1978:41
5. Information abstracted from the exhibit "The Enduring people. Native American Life in Central Massachusetts," at Old Sturbridge Vilage, Sturbridge, MA April 27, 2002-January 4, 2004.
6. Simon Pure History of East Haddam 2003
7. United States Geological Survey website 2003
8. Helfferich 2003
9. Connecticut Department of Environmental Protection 2003
10. See for example Lenik 2002:87-103
11. Simmons 1986:39
12. DeForest 1851:24
13. Mussey 1947:16-17
14. Anonymous 1970:63

HANDWRITING AND INSCRIPTIONS (Pages 83-104)

1. Historical background abstracted from Burrage 1914:37-51
2. Bradley 1978, personal communication
3. Kendall 1809 I:242-246
4. See Lenik 1978:5-13
5. Stiles 1789:333
6. Kendall 1809:244
7. Quotations in Chiel 1981:75
8. Chiel 1981:76
9. Kendall 1809:245-246
10. Kendall 1809:245
11. Quotation in Kendall 1809:246
12. Stiles 1789:333
13. Stiles 1790:3
14. Kendall 1809:243-244
15. Spooner 1930
16. Spooner 1930:5
17. Helander 2000:33
18. Helander 2000:34
19. Helander 2000:34
20. Mayo 1936:223
21. Hurd 1885:141; Mayo 1936:223
22. Mayo 1936:223
23. Hurd 1885:141; Mayo 1936:224
24. Hurd 1885: 141
25. Mayo 1936:225
26. For examples see Strandwold 1948, Enterline 1972, Pohl 1972, Fell 1980.
27. Poole 1854(VIII):185
28. Delabarre 1928:280
29. Delabarre 1928:27
30. Strandwold 1948:27
31. Delabarre 1928:279
32. Strandwold 1948:27-29
33. Rowell 1976
34. Shepard 1895:50, 54
35. Mayo 2001
36. Shepard 1895:54
37. Shepard 1895:52-53
38. Ritter 1968
39. Stapler 1969

40. Rothovius 1967:46
41. Stapler 1969
42. Fell 1980: 131, 137
43. Ritter 1967:17
44. Roberts 1956
45. Nonestied 2004 personal communication
46. Quotation from the dust jacket notes written by Kay Seymour House and Thomas L. Philbrook on the 1991 edition of J.F. Cooper's book Sea Tales.
47. Cooper 1827 (1991 edition):509.

IMAGES OF TRANSPORTATION AND INDUSTRY (Pages 105-118)

1. Glynn 1967:14
2. Glynn 1967:14
3. Glynn 1967:14
4. Glynn 1967:14
5. Hochschild 1962:10
6. Hochschild 1962:14
7. Hochschild 1962:20
8. See for example Eggenhoffer 1961:165
9. Essex County (NY) Historical Society 2003
10. This historical background was abstracted from Evers 1962 and the Pratt Museum website 2002
11. Newark Sunday News 1903
12. Newark Sunday News 1903
13. Anonymous 1895-1905
14. Stevralia 1983, personal communication
15. Stone 1969
16. Stone 1962
17. Brooks, Jr. 1972
18. Fell 1976: 236, 238
19. Dexter and Martin 1995:124
20. Neudorfer 1980: 13, 70, note 68
21. Neudorfer 1980: 61, 99
22. Martin 2004, personal communication
23. Carnahan 1983

WEAPONS (Pages 119-128)

1. Gilbert 1988:1
2. Anonymous 1925:316-318
3. Kingsbury 1925:10

4. Kingsbury 1925:767-768
5. Wadsworth 1932, n.p.
6. Wadsworth 1932, n.p.
7. Gilbert 1988:3
8. Gilbert 1988:1
9. Gilbert 1994
10. Wadsworth 1932, n.p.
11. Sager 1984a:38
12. Sager 1984b, personal communication
13. Sager 1984b, personal communication
14. Sager 1984a:38
15. Sager 1984b, personal communication

ABSTRACT AND GEOMETRIC MYSTERIES

(Pages 129-156)

1. Delabarre 1928:216-220
2. Delabarre 1928:216
3. Delabarre 1928:216; Figure 55
4. Delabarre 1928:219
5. Delabarre 1928:220
6. Delabarre 1928:217
7. Nichols 1976, personal communication
8. Briggs 1977, personal communication
9. Lenik 1978:11
10. The history of Damariscove Island is abstracted from "Damariscove: History and Traditions" written by Alaric Faulkner in Griffin and Faulkner 1980:10-33
11. Sewall 1859:106
12. Sewall 1859: 8, 10
13. Delabarre 1928:283
14. Delabarre 1928:327, notes 201-202
15. Brown 1977, personal communication
16. Copy of page 1-73 of White Nichols' notes in possession of this author
17. Cahill 1993:11
18. Anonymous 1895, photocopy in possession of this author
19. Webber 1927:26
20. Young 1988:136
21. See Smith 1883:82-83; Bierhorst 1995:91; Lenik 1999:74-77
22. Calver and Bolton 1950:11-18
23. Calver and Bolton 1950:11-15

24. Morrison 1952:131
25. Dunlap 1989: B-4
26. Dunlap 1989: B-4
27. Williams 1985:2
28. Williams 1985:2
29. Williams 1985:2
30. Corcoran 1989, personal communication
31. Corcoran 1989, personal communication
32. Corcoran 1989, personal communication
33. Williams 1965:1
34. Williams 1965:2
35. Williams 1965:15-16
36. Williams 1965:26
37. Swauger 1985
38. Turnbaugh 1983, personal communication
39. Mallery 1893:189-200
40. For example, see Parkman 1995
41. Heizer and Baumhoff 1962
42. Rau 1882
43. Lenik 2002:159-160
44. Loubser 2000
45. Kraft 1965; see also lenik 2002:219-220
46. Abbott 181
47. Lenik 1999
48. Cohen 1974:45-46
49. Cohen 1974:63, 114; Bischoff and Kahn 1976:98
50. Cohen 1974:111; Bischoff and Kahn 1976:98, 110
51. Bischoff and Kahn 1976:209-210
52. Bischoff and Kahn 1976:210
53. See Lenik 1999
54. Lenik 1999:45-46
55. Tholl 1975:49
56. Kraft 1986:165-169, 175; Loskiel 1794:104-106
57. Tantaquidgeon 1972;23
58. Parkman 1995:8; Hedges 1983:10-11; Nissen and Ritter 1986:66
59. Boland 1961:33
60. Gallagher and Pohl 1908:49-53
61. Gallagher and Pohl 1908:52
62. Gallagher and Pohl 1908:53
63. Willoughby 1931

64. Helander 2000:41
65. McSorley 1978, personal communication
66. Strandwold 1948:45
67. Mallery 1893:334
68. Mallery 1893:330, 331, 339
69. Mallery 1893:338
70. Cook and Spiess 1981:31-32
71. Cook and Spiess 1981:30
72. Cook and Spiess 1981:36

BIBLIOGRAPHY

Abbott, Charles C.
1881 *Primitive Industry*. Salem, MA: George A. Bates.

Alducin, Ediciones
1986 *Yucatan and the Mayas. Merida - Luxmal - Chichen Itza - Palenque*. Updated edition. Self-published mar Tirreno 96 Col. Popótla 11400 Mexica, D.F.

Anonymous
1895 "A Mysterious Stone. Interested the Curious and Puzzled Scientists. Incidents in Connection With the Finding and Preservation." *Manchester Union*, May 15. New Hampshire.

1899-1905 "Hog Mountain Quarry Remembered." Extracts of articles from the *Boonton Times* newspaper. Copy on file at the Montville Township Historical Commission, Montville, NJ.

1925 "An Enigma In Stone." The Reportory 1(7):314-318 Keene, NH: Repertory Publishing Company.

1962 *Mystery Hill Caves*. Tour Guide and Souvenir Folder.

1964 "No One Knows by Whom or Why or How or When Stone Structures in North Salem Were Built." *Stone Magazine*, June.

1970 "The Johnson Petroglyphs at Reading, Vermont." *NEARA Newsletter* 5(3):63-64. Published by the New England Antiquities Research Association, Milford, NH.

1985 *Dutchess County, New York Natural Resources*. Prepared by the Dutchess County Department of Planning and the Dutchess County Environmental Management Council.

2003 http://members.aol.com/MAspeleo/balancesp.html [no longer valid]

2003 <http://www.cascobay.com/educ/spie/chebehst.html> [no longer valid]

Behr, Betty M. Light
1990 Letter of October 3, to Nancy L. Gibbs, Sheffield Archaeological Consultants, Butler, NJ.

Beers, F.W.
1867 "Map of the Town of Kent." *Atlas of New York and Vicinity*. New York: Beers, Ellis & Soule.

Bierhorst, John
1995 *Mythology of the Lenape: Guide and Texts*. Guide and Text. Tuscon: The University of Arizona Press.

Bischoff, H. and M. Kahn
1976 *From Pioneer Settlement to Suburb: A History of Mahwah, New Jersey, 1700 - 1976*. So. Brunswick, NJ: A.S. Barnes & Co.

Boland, Charles M.
1961 *They All Discovered America*. Garden City, NY: Doubleday & Co., Inc.

Bradley, Robert L.
1978 Letter of October 31 to the author. Augusta, ME: Maine Historic Preservation Commission.

Briggs, John W.
1977 Personal communication with the author. Augusta, ME. Mr. Briggs is a historian and natural philosopher.

2000 Page from an unidentified tourist booklet sent to the author. It describes Fryes Leap on Sebago Lake, ME.

Brinton, Daniel G.
1893 "On An Inscribed Tablet from Long Island." *The Archaeologist* 1(11):201-203.

Brooks, William H., Jr.
1972 Letter of October 16 to Andrew E. Rothovius, Editor of the NEARA Newsletter. Mr. Brooks was Town Clerk of the Town of Waldoboro, ME. Copy of letter on file with author.

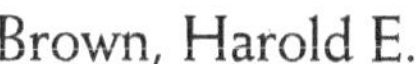

Brown, Harold E.
1977 Letter of September 7 to the author from Bath, Maine. Mr. Brown was an avocational archaeologist and historian.

Bruchac, Joseph
1985 *Iroquois Stories. Heroes and Heroines, Monsters and Magic*. Freedom, CA: The Crossing Press.

Burrage, Henry S.
1914 *Beginning of Colonial Maine*. Augusta, ME: Printed for the state by Marks Printing House.

Butler, Helen
1988 "The Heartbreak Petroglyphs of Wells, Maine. The Discovery and Rescue of an Archaeological Treasure." *Coast Pilot*, Week of July 13, pp. 1-5.

Cahill, Robert Ellis
1993 *New England's Ancient Mysteries*. Salem, MA: Old Saltbox Publishing House.

Calver, William L. and Reginald P. Bolton
1950 *History Written with Pick and Shovel*. New York: The New York Historical Society.

Carnahan, Paul A.
1983 "The River & The Valley." Historical brochure accompanying an exhibit of the history of human relationship to the Connecticut River from Deerfield, Massachusetts to Bellows Falls, Vermont, at the Brattleboro Museum & Art Center, April 29 through July 31.

Chase, Reginald
1977 Personal communication with the author at Wells, ME.

Chiel, Rabbi Arthur A.
1981 "The Hebrew Inscription At Pinnacle Mountain." *Bulletin of the Archaeological Society of Connecticut, Inc.* 44:74-77.

Cohen, David S.
1974 *The Ramapo Mountain People*. New Brunswick, NJ: Rutgers University Press.

Colomb, R.
1979 Letter of August 22, photograph and sketch map sent to Vermont Division for Historic Preservation, Montpelier, VT.

Connecticut Department of Environmental Protection
2003 < http://www.ct.gov/dep/site/default.asp >

Converse, Harriet M.
[1908] *Myths and Legends of the New York State Iroquois*. Edited and annotated by Arthur C. Parker. Museum Bulletin 125, Reprint 1981, New York State Museum and Science Service, Albany.

Cook, David and Arthur Spiess
1981 "Archaeology of the Piscataquis Ahwangan: Preliminary Results." *Maine Archaeological Society, Inc.*, Bulletin 21(1):29-38.

Cooper, James Fenimore
1827 *Sea Tales. The Pilot. The Red Rover.* The Library of America. 1991 edition published by the State University of New York Press.

Corcoran, Barbara
1989 Letter of May 22 to the author.

Crosby, Everett S.
1973 *The Vintage Years*. New York: Harper and Row.

Day, Gordon M.
1998 *In Search of New England's Native Past*. Selected Essays by Gordon M. Day. Edited by Michael K. Foster and William Cowan. Amherst, MA: University of Massachusetts Press.

DeForest, John W.
1851 *History of the Indians of Connecticut from the Earliest Known Period to 1850*. Hartford: Wm. Jas. Hammersley.

Delabarre, Edmund B.
1928 *Dighton Rock. A Study of the Written Rocks of New England*. New York: Walter Neale.

de Lesdernier, Suzanne
1976 *A Bit of History – Horse Hill – Mt. Mineral – Temenos*. Pamphlet privately printed. Revised in 1986 by Teresina Havens.

Dexter, Warren W. and Donna Martin
1995 *America's Ancient Stone Relics*. Rutland, VT: Academy Books.

Dunlap, David W.
1989 "Out of the Faint Past, a Trace of Fun." *The New York Times*, February 23, pp. B1, B4.

Duprey, Diane
1993 Personal communication with the author in Lakeville, MA.

Duval, Frances Y. and Ivan B. Rigby
1978 *Early American Gravestone Art in Pictures*. New York: Dover Publications, Inc.

Eckhart, Thomas D.
1996 *The History of Carbon County, Volume II*. Walnutport, PA: Thomas D. Eckhart.

Eggenhoffer, Nick
1961 *Wagons, Mules, and Men. How the Frontier Moved West*. New York: Hastings House Publishers.

Enterline, James R.
1972 *Viking America. The Norse Crossings and Their Legacy*. Garden City, NY: Doubleday & Co. Inc.

Essex County (NY) Historical Society
2003 Personal communication with R.A. Grubsmith.

Evers, Alf
1982 *The Catskills. From Wilderness to Woodstock*. Woodstock, NY: The Overlook Press.

Feldman, Mark
1977 *The Mystery Hill Story*. North Salem, NH: Mystery Hill Press.

Fell, Barry
1976 *American B.C.: Ancient Settlers in the New World*. New York: Pocket Books.

1980 *Saga America*. New York: Times Books.

Fenton, William M. and Elizabeth Tooker
1978 "Mohawk." In *Handbook of North American Indians* 15:466-480 Washington, D.C.: Smithsonian Institution.

Fowler, William S.
1960 "The Westford Indian Rock." *Bulletin of the Massachusetts Archaeological Society, Inc.* 21(2):21-22.

French, Mary M. Billings
1926 *A New England Pioneer: The Captivity of Mrs. Johnson*. Woodstock, VT: Elm Tree Press.

Frink, Douglas S,
2003 Letter of September 30, with photographs, to the author.

Gallagher, John P. and Frederick J. Pohl
1980 "1000 Years Before Columbus There Were Catholics in Connecticut." *Catholic Digest* 44(10):49-53.

Gilbert, Colgate
1988 "Bow and Arrow Petroglyphs of Chesire County." *NEARA Journal* 23(1&2):1-12. New England Antiquities Research Association.

1994 "Bow and Arrow Petroglyphs of Chesire County: An Update." Unpublished manuscript. Copy in possession of the author.

1996 "Coordinator's Report: New Hampshire." *NEARA Transit* 8(1):2. Edgecomb, ME: New England Antiquities Research Association.

Gillon, Edmund V., Jr.
[1966] *Early New England Gravestone Rubbings*. Second edition, 1981. New York: Dover Publications, Inc.

Glynn, Frank
1967 "A Second Mediaeval Marker at Westford, Massachusetts." *Eastern States Archaeological Federation Bulletin* 26:14.

Goodwin, William B.
1946 *The Ruins of Great Ireland in America*. Boston: Meador Publishing Co.

Goudsward, David and Robert E. Stone
2003 *America's Stonehenge. The Mystery Hill Story*. Wellesley, MA: Brandon Books.

Gramly, Richard Michael
1978 "Phase I Step 2 Archaeological Investigation For Peabody Task A, Peabody, Massachusetts." Cambridge, MA: Institute for Conservation Archaeology, Harvard University.

1981 "Witchcraft Pictographs from Near Salem, Massachusetts." *Historical Archaeology* 15(1)113-116.

Graylock, Godfrey
1879 *Taghconic: The Romance and Beauty of the Hills*. Boston: Lea and Shepard, Publishers.

Green, Frank B.
1886 *The History of Rockland County. New York*. A.S. Barnes & Co.

Griffin, Carl R. III, and Alaric Faulkner
1982 *Coming of Age on Damariscove Island, Maine*. Orono, ME: Northeast Folklore Society.

Hedges, Ken
1983 "A Re-examination of Pomo Baby Rocks." *American Indian Rock Art*, pp. 10-21. El Toro, CA: American Rock Art Research Association.

Heizer, R.F. and M.A. Baumhoff
1962 *Prehistoric Rock Art of Nevada and Eastern California*. Berkeley, CA: University of California Press.

Helander, Joel E.
2000 "Hanna's Quarry" and "Beattie's Quarries." In *Flesh and Stone. Stony Creek and the Age of Granite*. Edited by Deborah DeFord. Published by Stony Creek Workers Celebration in association with Leete's Island Books, Stony Creek, CT.

Helfferich, Carla
2003 "Things That Go Book in the Night. Article #896."
<http://www.gi.alaska.edu/scienceforum/ASF8/896.html.> [accessed 25 September]

Hitchcock, Edward
1841 *Final Report of the Geology of Massachusetts*. Amherst, Northhampton, MA: J.S. & C. Adams, J.H. Butler, Publisher.

Hochschild, Harold K.
1962 *An Adirondack Resort in the Nineteenth Century. Blue Mountain Lake. 1870-1900. Stagecoaches and Luxury Hotels*. Blue Mountain Lake, NY: Adirondack Museum.

Huber, F.F.
1935 "Pictographic Gorgets." *Pennsylvania Archaeologist* 5(2): 42-43.

Hurd, D. Hamilton
1885 *History of Hillsborough County, New Hampshire*. Philadelphia: J.W. Lewis & Co.

Isa, Mistress
2002 <http://www.renaissancemagazine.com/backissues/sinclair.html> [accessed 16 September]

Jameson, J. Franklin, editor
1909 *Narratives of New Netherland 1609-1664*. New York: Barnes & Noble, Inc.

Jones, Herbert G.
1949 "Sebago Lake Land". In *History, Legend, & Romance*. Portland, ME: The Bowker Press.

Juet, Robert
1609 (1959) *Juet's Journal. The Voyage of the Half Moon from 4 April to 7 November 1609*. Edited by Robert M. Lunny for the New Jersey Historical Society, Newark, NJ.

Kendall, Edward Augustus
1809 *Travels through the Northern Parts of the United States in the Years 1807-1809*. Volume 1. New York: I. Riley.

King, Marjorie R.
1980 "A Summary of the Search for the Long Island Tablet and its Authenticity." Copy of unpublished typescript in the possession of the author.

Kingsbury, Frank B.
1920 "Map of the Town of Surry New Hampshire with Data Relating to its Settlement and History."

1925 *History of Surry, New Hampshire 1769-1922*. Concord, NH: Concord Press.

Knight, Ernest H.
1996 *Historical Gems of Raymond and Casco.* Raymond-Casco, ME: Raymond-Casco Historical Society.

Kraft, Herbert C.
1965 "The First Petroglyph Found in New Jersey." *Pennsylvania Archaeologist* 35(2): 93-100.

1986 *The Lenape. Archaeology, History and Ethnography*. Newark, NJ: New Jersey Historical Society.

1994 "Was Cro-Magnon Man in the Palisades." *The Bulletin Journal of the New York State Archaeological Association* 107:38-42.

1996 "Mammoth Frauds in Archaeology." *Bulletin of the Archaeological Society of New Jersey* 51:1-11.

2001 *The Lenape-Delware Indian Heritage 10,000 B.C. to A.D. 2000*. Elizabeth, NJ: Lenape Books.

Krupp, E.C., editor
1978 *In Search of Ancient Astronomies*. Garden City, NY: Doubleday & Co., Inc.

Leary, Dan
1997 Letter of August 11 from Pembroke, N.H. to the author.

Lenik, Edward J.
1976 "The Indian Rock Petroglyphs: Fact or Forgery." *The Bulletin*, New York State Archaeological Association 66:1-2.

1978 "Ancient Inscriptions in Western Connecticut." *Bulletin of the Archaeological Society of Connecticut, Inc.* 41:5-13.

1978 "Riddles On Rock: Non-Aboriginal Petroglyphs in Maine." *Bulletin of the Maine Archaeological Society* 18(2):4-13.

1997 Letter to the Editor. *NEARA Journal* 31(2): 58. The New England Antiquities Research Association.

1999 *Indians in the Ramapos. Survival, Persistence and Presence*. Ringwood, NJ: The North Jersey Highlands Historical Society.

2002 *Picture Rocks. American Indian Rock Art in the Northeast Woodlands*. Hanover, NH: The University Press of New England.

Lenik, Edward J. and Deborah J. Crichton
1988 *Cultural Resources Reconnaissance Survey of the Fieldbrook Subdivision Property, Town of Kent, Putnam County, New York*. Sheffield Archaeological Consultants, Wayne, NJ.

Lenik, Edward J., Thomas Fitzpatrick, and Nancy L. Gibbs
1993 "A Twentieth Century Petroglyph on Horse Pound Brook." *The Bulletin, New York State Archaeological Association* 105:3-5.

Lewis-Williams, David
2002 *The Mind in the Cave. Consciousness and the Origins of Art*. London: Thames & Hudson.

Leyland, Charles G.
[1884] *Algonquin Legends*. Reprinted 1992. New York: Dover Publications, Inc.

Loskiel, George H.
1794 *History of the Mission of the United Brethren Among the Indians in North America. Part I*. Printed for the Brethren's Society For the Furtherance of the Gospel, London.

Loubser, Johannes H.N.
2000 "Investigation of Depressions on the Surface of Boulders in Rosa Hartman Park, Stamford, Connecticut." Letter to Dr. Nicholas Bellantoni, University of Connecticut, Storrs, CT

Mallery, Garrick
[1893] *Picture Writing of the American Indians*. Reprinted 1972. New York: Dover Publications, Inc.

Martin, Donna
2004 Letter of January 19th from Chittenden, Vermont, including photocopies of cider mill ruins and steamboat carving.

Mayo, Lawrence S.
1936 *John Endicott. A Biography*. Cambridge, MA: Harvard University Press.

McKusick, Marshall
1970 *The Davenport Conspiracy*. Iowa City, IA: A Report from the Office of the State Archaeologist.

McSorley, Andrew
1978 Personal communication with the author at Greeley's Landing, Maine, on August 9.

Mellgren, Guy
1976 Letter of February 3rd from Centerville, MA to the author.

Mercer, Henry C.
1885 *The Lenape Stone or the Indian and the Mammoth*. New York: G.P. Putnam & Sons.

Merrill, Daphne W.
1973 *The Lakes of Maine. A Compilation of Fact and Legend*. Rockland, ME: Printed by Courier-Gazette Inc.

Miller, Donald L., and Richard E. Sharpless
1998 *The Kingdom of Coal: Work, Enterprise and Ethnic Communities in the Mine Fields*. Easton, PA: Canal History and Technology Press.

Morrison, Hugh
1952 *Early American Architecture from the First Colonial Settlements to the National Period*. New York: Oxford University Press.

Moy, Kimberly W.
2001 "Hospital Rock Recalls Fight Against Smallpox. History Buffs Hope to Protect Remote Site in Farmington from Vandals and Development." *Hartford Courant*, p. A1, Monday, December 10.

Muscarella, Richard
1990 Letter of October 5 to the author. Mr. Muscarella was the Town of Kent, NY historian.

Mussey, Barrows
1947 *Vermont Heritage: A Picture Story*. New York: A.A. Wyn, Inc.

Myles, William J.
1992 *Harriman Trails. A Guide and History*. New York: The New York-New Jersey Trail Conference.

Neudorfer, Giovanna
1980 *Vermont's Stone Chambers: An Inquiry Into Their Past*. Montpelier, VT: Vermont Historical Society. Newark Sunday News

1903 "Jersey City's New Water Plant at Boonton." October 30th. Newark, NJ.

Nichols, White.
1976 Personal communication with the author, Wiscasset, ME.

Nissen, Karen M. and Eric W. Ritter
1986 "Cupped Rock Art in North Central California: Hypothesis Regarding Age and Social/Ecological Context." *American Indian Rock Art* pp. 59-76. El Toro, CA: American Rock Art Research Association.

O'Brien, Raymond J.
1981 *American Sublime*. New York: Columbia University Press.

O'Callaghan, Edmund B.
1855 *History of New Netherland. Vol. I*. New York: D. Appleton & Co.

Oestreicher, David M.
1994 "Unmasking the Walum Olum, a 19th Century Hoax." *Bulletin of the Archaeological Society of New Jersey* 49:1-44.

1995 "Text Out of Context: The Arguments That Created and Sustained the Walum Olum." *Bulletin of the Archaeological Society of New Jersey* 50:31-52.

1996 "Unraveling the Walum Olum." *Natural History* 105:14-21.
Parkman, E.B.

1995 "California Dreamin: Cupule Petroglyph Occurrences in the American West." In *Rock Art Studies in the Americas*, edited by Jack Steinbring, pp. 1-12. Oxbow Monograph 45. Oxbow, England: Oxbow Books.

Patterson, Alex
1992 *A Field Guide to Rock Art Symbols of the Greater Southwest*. Boulder, CO: Johnson Books.

Pohl, Frederick J.
1972 *The Viking Settlements of North America*. New York: Clarkson N. Potter, Inc.

Poole, George I.
1854 "An Antiquity Discovered in the Valley of the Merrimack." *The New England Historical and Genealogical Register* VIII:185.

Pratt, L. Hayden and G.C. Johnson
1935 "Three Bridges Cemetery (1769) East Haddam, Middlessex County, Connecticut." Tombstone data copied on January 2. Copy of listing in The Hale Collection, Connecticut State Library, Hartford, CT.

Rau, Charles
1882 "Observations on Cup-Shaped and Other Lapidarian Sculptures in the Old World and in America." In *Contributions to North American Ethnology. Vol. 5*, edited by J.W. Powell. Washington, D.C.: Department of the Interior, U.S. Geographical and Geological Survey of the Rocky Mountain region.

Reich, Carol
1988 Personal communication with the author. Ms. Reich was a former resident of Kent, NY.

Ritter, Chris
1967 "Did The Romans Visit Maine?" *NEARA Newsletter* 2(2):16-18. Published by the New England Antiquities Research Association.

1968 Transcription of an article from *The York County Coast Star* of February 28th in the "Roman Inscription" file of W. Mead Stapler, Wantage, NJ.

Robbins, Maurice
1973 Middle Purchases. A map, copy on file with the author.

1980 *Wapanucket. An Archaeological Report*. Attleboro, MA: The Massachusetts Archaeological Society, Inc.

Robbins, Roland Wells and Evan Jones
1959 *Hidden America*. New York: Alfred A. Knopf.

Roberts, Kenneth
1956 *Boon Island*. Garden City, New York: Doubleday & Co., Inc.

Rogers, William B., Yngar W. Isachsen, T. D. Mock and R.E. Nyahay
1990 New York State Geological Highway Map. The University of the State of New York, The State Education Department, New York State Geological Survey, New York State Museum Cultural Education Center, Albany, NY.

Rothovius, Andrew E.
1963 "A Possible Megalithic Settlement Complex at North Salem, New Hampshire and Apparently Related Structures Elsewhere in New England." *The Bulletin*, New York State Archaeological Association 27:2-12.

1967 "A Footnote To Did The Romans Visit Maine." *NEARA Newsletter* 2(3):46. Published by the New England Antiquities Research Association.

Rowell, Barbara
1976 "Couple Finds Landmark." *The Haverhill Gazette*, Haverhill, MA, Wednesday, July 28.

Ruttenber, E.M.
1872 *History of the Indian Tribes of Hudson's River*. 1992 facsimile reprint of the original book. Saugerties, NY: Hope Farm Press.

Sager, Barbara
1984a "NEARA Chapter News: Vermont." *NEARA Journal* 19(1&2): 38. New England Antiquities Research Association, Paxton, MA.

1984b Letter of October 17th to the author from Wolcott, VT.

Schwartz, Douglas
2003 Personal communication with E.J. Lenik, N.L. Gibbs, and T. Fitzpatrick on the south shore beach, Staten Island, NY.

Seton, Ernest Thompson
1921 *The Book of Woodcraft*. Garden City, NY: Garden City Publishing Co., Inc.

Sewall, Rufus King
1859 *Ancient Dominions of Maine*. Bath, ME: Elisha Clark & Co.

1895 *Ancient Voyages to the Western Continent*. New York: The Knickerbocker Press, G.P. Putnam's Sons.

Shephard, James
1895 "The Small-Pox Hospital Rock." *Connecticut Quarterly* 1:50-55.

Shoumatoff, Nicholas
1971 *Balgooyen Needle Field Notes*. On file, Delaware Indian Resource Center, Ward Pound Ridge Reservation, Cross River, NY.

Simmons, William S.
1986 *Spirit of the New England Tribes. Indian History and Folklore, 1620-1984*. Hanover & London: University Press of New England.

Simon Pure
2003 "History of East Haddam." Taken from East Haddam Swing Bridge Official Program of the Formal Opening, Flag Day, June 14, 1913: <http://www.simonpure.com/bridge/htm> [no longer valid]

Smith, Erminnie A.
[1883] *Myths of the Iroquois*. Washington, D.C.: Smithsonian Institution Bureau of Ethnology, 2nd Annual Report 1880-81. Reprinted in 1994. Ontario, Canada: Iroquois Publishing and Craft Supplies, Inc.

Snow, Dean R.
1996 *The Iroquois*. Cambridge, MA: Blackwell Publishers, Inc.

Spooner, Clifford C.
1930 *The Story of Molly Fisher and the Molly Fisher Rock.* A Legend of Old Kent, Connecticut. Copy of booklet in the possession of this author.

Stapler, W. Mead
1969 NEARA (New England Antiquities Research Association) Site Report Sheet. On file, Exeter, N.H. Library.

Stevralia, Russell C.
1983 Letter of July 2 to the author.

Stiles, Ezra
n.d. *Literary Diary*. Unpublished manuscript in Beinecke Rare Book and Manuscript Library, Yale University, New Haven, CT.

1789 *Itineraries and Memoirs*. Manuscript in Beinecke Rare Book and Manuscript Library, Yale University, New Haven, CT.

1790 "An Account of Two Inscriptions upon Rocks in Kent and Washington in the Northern Part of the State of Connecticut taken off 1789 by Ezra Stiles, and by him communicated to the Head of Arts and Sciences." Manuscript on file at the American Academy of Arts and Sciences, Boston, MA.

Stone, Robert E.
1962 Sketch labeled "Viking Ship Carving, Medomek Maine near Damariscotta." Oct. 11. Copy on file with this author.

1967 *NEARA Newsletter* 2(3):35. Published by the New England Antiquities Research Association, North Salem, NH.

1969 NEARA Site Report Sheet with photograph and sketch of the Viking Ship carving. Copy on file with the author.

Strandwold, Olaf
1948 *Norse Inscriptions on American Stones*. Weehauken, NJ: Magnus Bjorndal, publisher.

Swauger, James L.
1985 Letter of January 30 to Ed Kanze, Ward Pound Ridge Reservation, Dr. William Turnbaugh, University of Rhode Island, and Al Gunther, Yagoog Scout Reservation. Copy on file at Yagoog Scout Reservation, Rockville, RI.

Sypher, Sally
1990 Personal communication with the author, Mahopac Falls, NY. Ms. Sypher was the Putnam County, NY Historian.

Tholl, Clair K.
1975 "The Original Inhabitants of Bergen County and the Ramapo Mountain People." *Bergen County History. 1975 Annual Report*. River Edge, NJ: Bergen County Historical Society.Thompson, J. Eric
1975 *The Rise and Fall of Maya Civilization*. Fifth printing. Norman, OK: University of Oklahoma Press.

Thompson, Kenneth E., Jr.
1981 "Major General Joseph Frye of Maine. The Life and Times of a Colonial Officer." A thesis submitted in partial fulfillment of the requirements for the degree of Master of Science in Education, University of Southern Maine.

2003 Letter of June 19th to the author from Portland, ME.

Thunderhorse, Iron
1997 "The Dawn Star Carved in Stone." *NEARA Journal* 31(1): 48-50. Edgecomb, ME: The New England Antiquities Research Association.

Turnbaugh, William
1983 Letter of July 11 to the author with a rough field sketch of Symbol Rock. Kingston, RI.

United States Geological Survey
2003 "Earthquake History of Connecticut." Website on earthquake hazards: <http://neic.usgs.gov/neis/states/connecticut/connecticuthistory.html>. [accessed 25 September]

Venables, Robert W.
1989 "A Historical Overview of Staten Island's Trade Networks." Proceedings. Staten Island Institute of Arts and Sciences 34(1):1-24.
Vermont Division for Historic Preservation
1977 Photographs with accompanying notes pertaining to two anthropomorphic figures in Fairfield, VT, May 13. On file in Montpelier, VT.

Wadsworth, Samuel
1932 *Historical Notes of Keene and Roxbury, New Hampshire*. Keene, NH: Sentinel Printing Co.

Weaver, Muriel Porter
1972 *The Aztecs, Maya, and Their Predecessors*. New York: Seminar Press.

Webber, F.R.
1927 *Church Symbolism. An Explanation of the More Important Symbols of the Old and New Testament., the Primitive, the Mediaeval, and the Modern Church*. Cleveland, OH: J.H. Jansen, Publisher.

Webster, Noah
1940 *Webster's Twentieth Century Dictionary of the English Language*. New York: Publishers Guild, Inc.

Weisshaar, Paul
1928 Transcript of untitled article in *Times-Herald*, Middletown, NY dated April 20. Copy on file with the author.

Westknight
2002 <http://www.orkneyjar.com/history/historicalfigures/henrysinclair/westknight.htm> Accessed September 16.

Williams, J. Harold
1985 *The Yawgoog Story. A Half Century of Scout Camping in Rhode Island*. Providence, RI: Narragansett Council, Boy Scouts of America.

Williams, Stephen
1991 *Fantastic Archaeology: The Wild Side of North American Prehistory*. Philadelphia: University of Pennsylvania Press.

Young, M. Jane
1988 *Signs from the Ancestors. Zuni Cultural Symbolism and Perceptions of Rock Art*. Albuquerque, NM: University of New Mexico Press.

Zadock Pratt Museum
2002 <http://www.prattmuseum.com> [accessed 25 September]

ACKNOWLEDGMENTS

Many people have generously assisted me over the years in providing me with information regarding the location of petroglyph sites, artifact collections, and historical background material. Those who gave me valuable and indispensable help include Edward Bell, Robert Bradley, John W. Briggs, Nicholas Bellantoni, Harold Brown, Mary Brown, Reginald Chase, Barbara Corcoran, Charles Devine, Michael D. Giacomo, Diane Duprey, Cathy Fisher, Jack Focht, Douglas Frink, Wayne Gilcrest, Robert Grubsmith, Paul Grzybowski, Herbert C. Kraft, Dan Leary, Donna Martin, Matt McGurn, Guy Mellgren, Elford Messer, Richard Muscarella, White Nichols, Mark Nonestied, Giovanna Peebles, Carol Reich, Maurice Robbins, Nick Shoumatoff, Paul Stephenson, Russell C. Stevralia, Robert Stone, Roslyn Strong, Arthur E. Speiss, Sally Sypher, Kenneth E. Thompson, Jr., Barbara Sager. I am truly grateful to all of them.

I am especially grateful to my friend, artist and colleague Tom Fitzpatrick. Tom accompanied me on many field trips to study rock art and produced many of the splendid illustrations in this book. I have enjoyed many illuminating conversations with Tom who also read a draft manuscript of my book and deserves a great deal of credit for this book.

My work in rock art research was aided immensely by the research assistance provided by Nancy L. Gibbs. Nancy also read a draft of this book and offered many helpful suggestions and insights. In large measure this book is a product of her many hours of assistance.

Special thanks goes to Jean E. LeBlanc, a teacher of English and friend who edited and typed several drafts of this book. I also thank several museums and archives and their staffs for access to petroglyph material. These include the Massachusetts Historical Commission, New Hampshire Historical Society, Maine Historic Preservation Commission, Vermont Division for Historic Preservation, and the Peabody Museum, Cambridge, Massachusetts.

INDEX

ABOUT THE AUTHOR

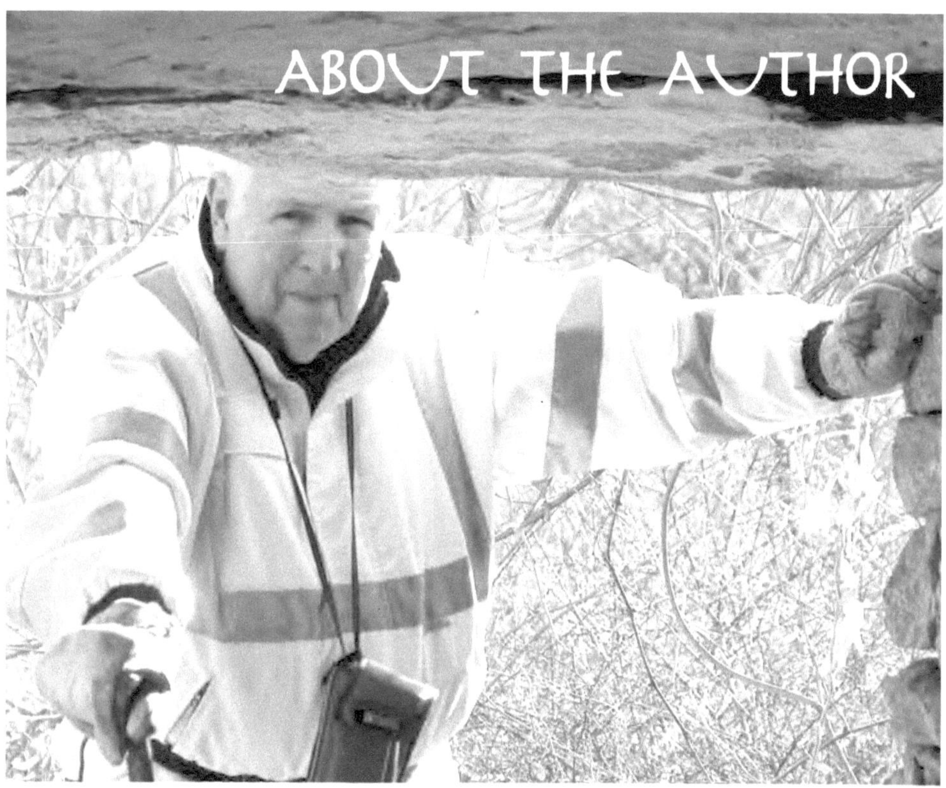

Ed Lenik is one of New Jersey's best known archaeologists. His research interests include early American Ironworks, military sites archaeology and American Indian history and rock art. He is a fellow of the Archaeological Society of New Jersey and the New York State Archaeological Association.

His major excavations include work at Forts Montgomery and Clinton in Bear Mountain State Park, New York, work at Spirit Pond, Maine, the Spring House Rockshelter, New York and the Monksville Reservoir, New Jersey.

Ed is an avid historical hiker, a well-received lecturer and the author of many books. He has published two volumes on American Indian rock art in the northeast, PICTURE ROCKS and MAKING PICTURES IN STONE. In addition, his hiking guide, IRON MINE TRAILS, can be found in many backpacks.

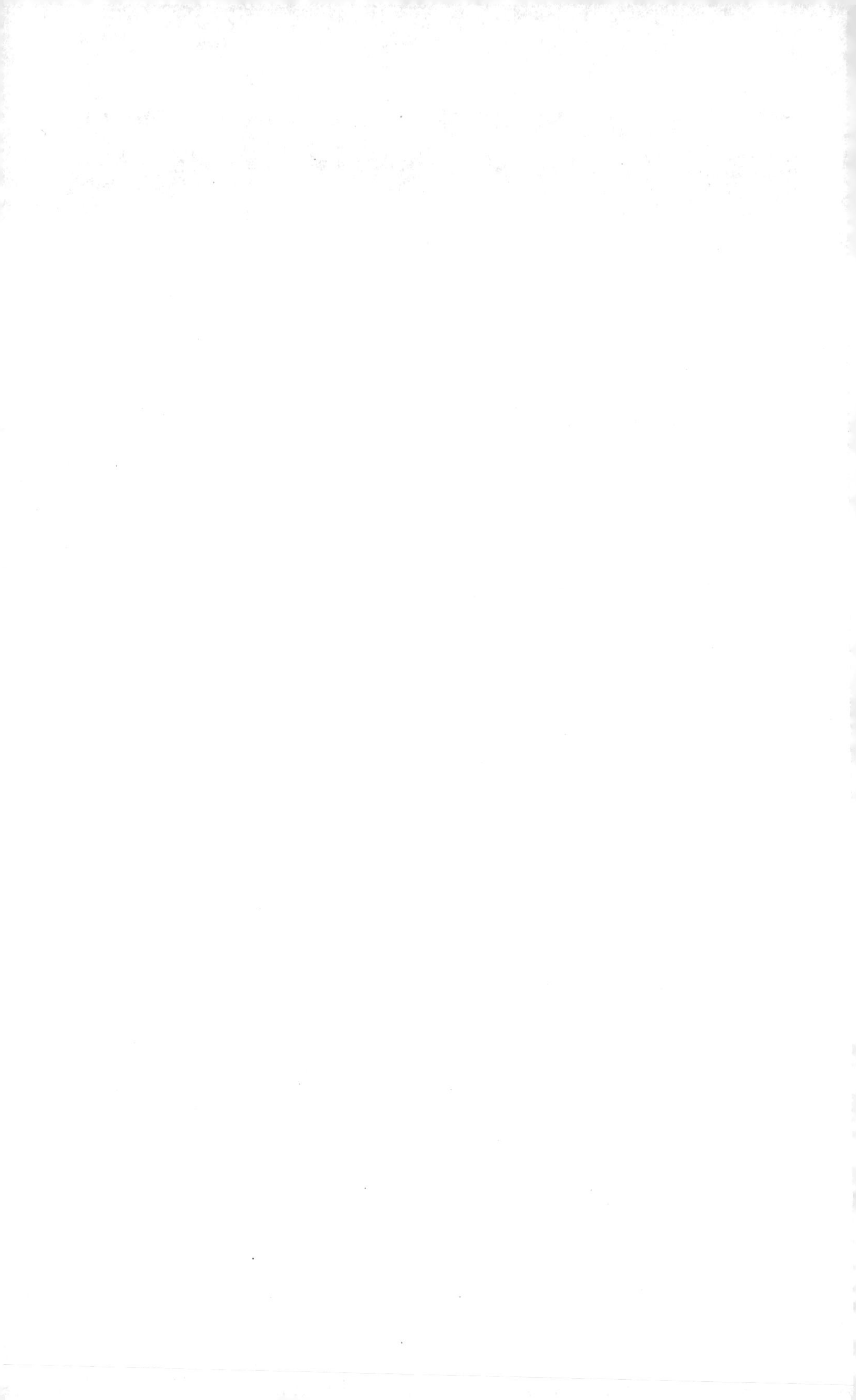

www.ingramcontent.com/pod-product-compliance
Lightning Source LLC
LaVergne TN
LVHW090936080826
845145LV00003B/765

humanities. Alma was perfectly hair-sprayed curls, and Grace was baseball caps. Alma was dark lipstick, and Grace was medical-grade lip balm. None of that mattered, though. Despite all their differences they still fit together. Their mutual love of reality television and margaritas, constant wisecracks and dancing until dawn had been enough to draw them together, enough to create a bond that went beyond celebrity gossip and binge-watching *The Great British Bake Off.* Almost from the moment Grace walked into her freshman dorm room and saw the girl sprawled across a tiny dorm bed with cucumbers over her eyes, she had a sense she'd found a kindred spirit. It led to them telling each other everything, supporting each other at all times. It led them to something that would last a lifetime.

"How are *you* today?" Grace asked, very aware that the past several months had been completely one-sided in terms of their friendship, all about her problems and heartbreak and agony. Alma had been a great confidante, had barely said a single word about herself the whole time. She'd been so caring and selfless, but Grace felt like she barely knew what was happening in Alma's life anymore. She'd hardly even asked.

"Honestly, I spend most of my time worrying about you." Alma glanced over with a small smile. "Work is the same."

"Oh so the genetic sequences for the DNA genome biology haven't changed at all?" Grace asked, pleased with the note of teasing in her voice. It was nice to tease Alma again, to make fun of herself for something as simple as never having the tiniest clue about Alma's research.

Alma grinned and shook her head. Grace knew enough to know Alma did some kind of fancy biological research about cell proteins and genomes, or something like that. Grace could never keep up, and Alma was so steeped in the science, so brilliant, that her explanations sounded more like lectures for Biology PhD students than fifth grade science books, which meant they left Grace completely baffled. "Exactly correct," Alma affirmed.

"Tell me about Obinna, then," Grace said, slapping a hand against her suitcase. She knew Alma had stopped talking about him on purpose. Their relationship was still so fresh and exciting, only six months in, and Alma was head over heels, but she'd been keeping it to herself lately, trying not to rub it in after everything with Grace and Derek had imploded.

Alma opened her mouth to speak, but then she paused. "We don't have to talk about it," she said at last.

Grace reached out a hand and squeezed her best friend's arm. "I'm happy for you. It's wonderful. You don't have to hide it from me."

Grace could see Alma considering how to proceed, the way she pursed her lips and furrowed her brow, but still Alma's eyes twinkled like they just couldn't help themselves. "He's unlike anyone I've ever been with, Gracie."

"So not a total dirtbag who treats you like crap?"

"Not at all," Alma replied, not even slightly offended by her best friend's assessment of her past liaisons. "He's so sweet and romantic. He takes me out on picnics! And he puts his arm around me as we stroll through the park, and he tells me I'm beautiful."

"He's not lying."

Alma waved a hand. "But then at night he's so...masculine."

"Masculine?" Grace raised a brow.

"*Sexy*. There's something about his thighs. I don't know how they're so firm." She started fanning herself with one hand, while the other hand gripped the steering wheel.

Grace laughed and clung to her suitcase as they bounced over a rough spot in the road. "I'd like one of those for myself."

Alma nodded. "We'll find you one, *mi media naranja*. Now you are single, and all the boys will go crazy for you."

"Doubtful."

"Just wait," Alma said.

They were nearing the heart of the city, streets and buildings inching closer to each other as they drove. With every turn down a new, narrow street, Grace's eyes went wider. The cobblestone roads, the blend of Moorish, Renaissance, Gothic, and Baroque architecture. Beautiful stone structures towered over them, as if they were perfectly normal scenery at a stoplight. It was absolutely breathtaking. It didn't seem possible that Grace could live in it.

"Thank you, Alma," Grace said suddenly. "Truly."

"I've told you to stop thanking me. I get to live with you again. I never thought this would happen."

Grace pressed her face to the window as she noticed the huge bunches of colorful flowers hanging from streetlamps that lined the road. "I just don't know how I would have survived all of this without you. I don't think I could have."

Grace really couldn't believe it, actually, the way Alma had been there for her. She'd called every day, texted constantly. She'd planned to hop on a plane and show up in Chicago, but Grace finally managed to convince her that she just needed to deal with a few remaining details before moving to Spain, and Alma shouldn't upend her life. It had been nice to know she would have, though. She would have dropped everything, and that meant the world.

Alma shook her head. "You're tougher than you think, Gracie. I keep telling you."

"Yes, you keep telling me, but I don't know why you think that. It's not true."

Alma didn't reply, just smoothed a hand over her hair.

Grace stared at the Spanish shop names and the window displays, impressed by everything. There were palm trees here, which gave her yet another reason to feel like she was on vacation, that it was all just a break from reality and not her real life. Real life was the ice-covered streets of Chicago, gusts of wind slamming against her back on Armitage Avenue. It was the boxes on the side of the road while she waited for the moving truck, tears running down her face. It was loneliness and an aching in her chest that never went away. Real life couldn't include palm trees.

"Almost there," Alma said. "We'll see if my brother is actually going to be a gentleman and come help with your bags like I told him to."

Grace startled. "Your brother?"

"Yes?" Alma's tone was filled with sarcasm. "You remember I have a brother, right?"

The brilliant and beautiful Alma Ferrer-Martín had only one flaw, and it was one she couldn't help. It was the fact that she was related to Rafael Ferrer-Martín.

"Of course I remember you have a brother. I just thought he was still in the States."

Alma shook her head. "He's been back a few months now. He started his own little company here."

Grace rolled that over in her mind for a moment. She couldn't be too surprised about missing out on that tidbit of information. It was yet another thing she'd failed to ask about, too distracted by her own series of crises. Grace just hadn't realized quite how much Alma had skirted around the details of her daily existence. To not even mention her brother...

Not that it would have changed anything. Grace would still have moved across the ocean even if she'd known Rafael would be there. She didn't really have a choice, but she could have prepared herself, as least, with the knowledge that her new life in Spain would also include run-ins with Alma's super-jerk sibling.

"Are you happy to have him around?" Grace asked. Alma and Rafael had always weirdly seemed to get along, despite their differences.

Alma considered the question. "Yes, it's nice that he's nearby. It's good for us, I think."

Grace felt a scoff rising to her lips, but she smothered the sound. It was possible that Rafael had changed, of course. She should give him the benefit of the doubt. They met only once, during that summer in college. He'd been living with friends in Barcelona for the summer, so they all had spent a lot of the visit together. He'd been gracious enough to give the grand tour to his little sister and her friend, and it had clearly been a burden to him, but Grace thought he could have at least pretended to have fun. Instead, he'd been stern all week long. He hadn't laughed at a single joke she made, and she'd made a lot, from stupid puns to humor about the phallic shapes of certain architecture. She'd even tried slapstick (unintentionally) when they'd visited a giant garden, and a bird pooped in her hair. It was disgusting, of course, but Grace and Alma were in stitches, doubled over and almost crying.

Rafael never even cracked a smile. He was always so disapproving, like he thought they were utterly immature, like his three additional years of life had provided him with experience and insight that far surpassed theirs. He couldn't handle their fifty cent tequila shots or their embarrassing dance moves, their uninhibited laughter or dirty jokes.

He'd been insufferable.

Alma didn't seem to mind it. She'd just rolled her eyes and shrugged it off. But for Grace, it felt personal. It was her first time meeting her best friend's family, and she'd wanted to make a good impression. She'd asked him lots of questions about himself or about whatever piece of Barcelona history he was explaining, trying to take an interest, to get on his good side. But even if he was just a stick in the mud, it felt very much like he didn't like *her*, as if she was the real burden who was killing his grown-up vibes.

That was, until he'd tried to kiss her.

"Grace?"

Alma had been talking about something, and yet again, Grace was being a terrible friend, lost in her own head and picking at memories that would be better left alone in the dark recesses of her subconscious. She snapped out of her reverie and looked back at the driver's seat.

"What? Sorry."

"I was just thinking about ordering in tonight for dinner. I thought you would be tired."

"Yes, that sounds great."

She was coming up on thirteen hours since she'd left Chicago on her overnight flight, and she was looking forward to falling into a bed. She knew Alma would want to show her around her hometown, and Grace was excited to see it, but she was also drained from traveling, from uprooting whatever semblance of a life she had left and flying across the world.

"Here we are," Alma announced.

They pulled up to Alma's apartment building, which was smaller than Grace had expected, only a few stories. There were little balconies over the street. Pedestrians sauntered down the sidewalk speaking rapid Spanish. Grace noticed a Domino's Pizza down the block, and she breathed a sigh of relief, as if somehow Domino's could save her.

Alma whipped into a parking garage, hopped out of the car, and signaled for Grace to follow.

"Leave the suitcases for now," she said. "We'll see if Rafael's able to help."

Grace bit her lip and sauntered through the garage, around the corner, and up the stairs of the residential complex all the way to the third floor, where Alma unlocked the door to the last apartment at the end of the hall.

"Ah," she said, as she walked inside. *"Estas aqui mi hermano. Que lindo."*

Alma opened the door wide to allow Grace to walk in behind her, and there was Rafael, perched on the arm of a little sofa, staring at his cell phone. Apparently, he had a key to the place, which wasn't entirely surprising. Whatever his faults, Grace knew Alma trusted her brother with her life.

It made sense, of course, that if Alma was the most beautiful woman Grace had ever seen in real life, then Rafael was the most attractive man. It was one of the reasons she'd been so disappointed he didn't like her when they first met, if she was being honest. It also made the almost-kiss even more confusing, because, God, to kiss a man that gorgeous, what must that have been like? Her body—her lips—had wanted to do it. But after the way he'd behaved that whole trip, she just couldn't. She still didn't know what in the world he'd been thinking. The whole incident was completely out of character, and they'd both pretended it never happened. Grace could almost convince herself she'd imagined it, but the look in his eyes...

Was best forgotten, she reminded herself again.

When Rafael finally glanced up from his phone and turned to reply to Alma, those eyes scanned over to Grace. Something warm rushed through her body in an instant, which was annoying. She didn't even like this guy. It was unfair that just because he was hot her body couldn't help reacting.

He didn't speak. Alma noticed this, too, and switched to English for Grace's benefit. "Aren't you going to say hello, Rafa? You remember Grace, right?"

Grace shuffled uncomfortably as he glared at her. She felt like she was on display, an old relic from the past laid out in a glass case at a museum.

"Yes," Rafael said without smiling, his dark eyes focused on her face. "Hello."

CHAPTER TWO

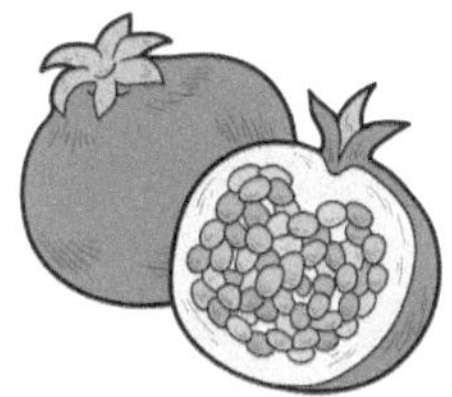

RAFAEL HAD KNOWN plenty of American women, and as a twenty-something student in New York, he'd been fairly certain they were all the same. He'd taken the opportunity to sleep with quite a few of them, and it had been nice. Perfectly pleasant, really, but that was all. They were frivolous and self-absorbed and shallow. He wasn't sure they could ever be serious about anything, and that suited Rafael just fine, since he wasn't ever interested in spending more than a few nights with them. He couldn't complain, honestly. He'd had a great time.

When he first met Grace, he'd assumed Alma's little American friend would be just like all those other women he had judged so decidedly, and he felt validated by his initial opinion. He tried to talk about the mastery of the Torre Agbar in Barcelona, and the two of them just kept chortling about how it looked like a giant penis. Grace had been studying art history, for God's sake, so he thought she might have a little appreciation for the great postmodern icon, but she had just laughed along with his sister, completely ignoring his explanations of how it was inspired by Monserrat, the mountain near the city, and it was supposed to be representative of a geyser rising into the air.

"Sure," Grace had joked, "a geyser. Better watch out or it might spurt all over the tech district."

He'd almost smiled at that. Almost.

It was the first thing Rafael had thought of when Alma told him her depressed best friend was coming to live with her in Granada—how he'd judged her and been so sure he was correct in his opinions. If not giggle fits and dumb jokes, then what else would he have expected from a twenty-year-old American college student, especially one who was so close with his silly sister? But there were moments when she'd managed to break through the haze of his superiority, even then.

Grace.

Her captivating blue eyes had always stared right into his when she wanted his attention, and she'd smirked like they had a secret between them. Or maybe like she was laughing at him; he was never sure.

The second thing he'd thought of was how he'd tried to kiss her.

That had obviously been a stupid mistake, and considering the fact that it was almost ten years ago, he didn't even feel the need to be embarrassed about it anymore. There was no doubt he'd been a complete idiot in his youth, and if he bothered to spend too much time dwelling on that, he'd waste much of his adulthood as well.

But when Grace walked into Alma's apartment for the first time—her long, dirty blonde hair a rat's nest from the convertible, her blue t-shirt wrinkled and worn—she looked at him in just the same way she had back then, as if she was studying him, or maybe, as if she didn't need to study him. As if she *knew* him already. Somehow, she'd figured out everything she needed to understand about Alma's older brother, and there was no need to pass a second judgement.

He didn't blame her. It may have taken a while, but obviously he'd come to realize what a giant asshole he'd been during those years after college, how he'd never actually gotten to know any of the American women he took to his bed, never even tried to open up or form a real connection with them. He also realized how much he'd been influenced by his father when he was yet to completely comprehend that his father was a total *cabrón* and not someone to emulate. Rafael had probably been at his very worst during that summer in Barcelona when he met

Grace, and he didn't need to read minds to know what she thought of him.

"Hi," she said in response to his greeting. "Thanks for coming to help."

"No problem," he said, pocketing his phone. "Good trip?"

She nodded but clearly didn't feel the need to say anything more about it. "How are you?" she asked without smiling.

He nodded, too, mirroring her movement, but nothing came out of his mouth.

She looked almost the same as she had ten years ago, except for the dark circles under her eyes. She was still beautiful. Her lips still puckered in that same inviting way that had gotten him into trouble in the first place, but he could already tell she didn't have that same lightness about her, that she was no longer floating through life without a care in the world. He'd thought it shallow and superficial at the time, her innate *happiness*, but now she seemed like a complete stranger.

If he'd imagined her greeting him at all, he would have expected her to throw her arms around him with abandon and squeeze him too tightly, loudly declaring how thrilled she was to see him again. She would have grinned up at him like they were old friends, rather than forced acquaintances. Maybe she would have even teased him about his fancy gold watch or his loafers. That's how she'd been ten years ago, without a worry to spare about what he or anyone else thought of her.

Now, she carried herself like her limbs were too heavy for her, like the sound of a twig snapping would frighten her. Cautious and uneasy, where before she'd been all carefree glee. She *was* a stranger.

"Keys?" he asked his sister. "I'll get the bags."

"I can help you," Grace said. "There are a lot of them."

"That's okay," he said. "I can handle it."

He quickly discovered he couldn't handle it, at least not all at once. Four large bags and three flights of stairs was impossible, so he took two trips, and he was sweating through his Sea Island cotton shirt by the end of it.

When he finally finished, he was annoyed to be sweating and annoyed that Grace would see him sweating, even though she didn't look like the picture of perfection herself, and he didn't know why he cared in the first place. He slid the bags into the apartment but straightened when he heard the sound of her voice.

"He's so gorgeous," she said. "Was he a model at some point?"

Alma poured another splash of wine into Grace's glass as they huddled in the corner of the small kitchen. Rafael wasn't remotely surprised to hear them chatting about Alma's boyfriend, since Alma talked about him constantly.

"You'll meet him tomorrow," Alma answered. "Just wait until you see him in person. And I told you, Gracie, he's *kind*. That's the thing that blows my mind."

Obinna was kind, and on the several occasions that Rafael had spent any time with him, he'd actually enjoyed his company, which wasn't something he could say about any other man that had captured his sister's attention. He still didn't understand why she felt the need to go on and on about him like she did. No one was *that* great.

Alma teased Rafael about going on and on about his work, though, so he supposed they were even. "So busy and important, aren't you, Rafa?" Alma would say, and even though she was poking fun at him, Rafael couldn't help but agree.

He was busy. New company, new client, new important project. There was nothing wrong with that. He approached the counter where Alma was taking a long drink of wine, and Grace's head cocked toward the side as she looked at him.

"Thank you for taking time out of your day to help," Grace said. "I honestly think we could have managed, so I'm not sure why Alma made you do this."

"Well, now that he's here, he can stay for dinner," Alma offered.

Rafael stiffened. Sitting around in his sweaty clothes watching sad Grace eat take-out paella did not sound appealing at all. Grace's face seemed to reveal that she didn't think so either.

"No." He brushed his palm against the back of his head and glanced toward the door, eyeballing the distance to the exit. "I'll let you two catch up."

"I want to hear about your new project," Alma complained. "And you know that's not something I say very often, so you should probably take advantage of my interest."

Rafael blew out a breath. "Can't even tell you about it. It's top secret." He glanced at Grace, who seemed lost in thought.

"Come on, *Raf*," Alma scolded, emphasizing his Americanized nickname. "You know you can't resist talking about yourself for an hour, and you know you want to impress Grace with all your 'ultimate luxury escapades' shit."

At the sound of her name, Grace's head jerked up, and their eyes met. He couldn't believe it for a moment, how he was filled with the same feeling he'd had the first time he met her, that she could *see* him somehow.

"What is it that you do?" Grace asked politely.

Alma was correct that he was great at talking about himself, at spouting whatever bullshit sounded good, whatever made him look impressive. But he didn't think he could do that now, for some reason. Not with Grace looking at him like that.

He cleared his throat. "I'm building a company that—uh—helps clients to cultivate curated cultural experiences." He didn't feel the need to mention his miserable finance job in the States or his father's disappointment when he decided to leave it for something "frivolous." No, disappointment wasn't the word, actually. More like, *wrath*. Rafael needed to focus on the future, though. He needed to focus on what he was building, not the thing he'd finally worked up the courage to abandon. "It's for elite events and exhibitions throughout the region."

Grace smiled. It was the first time he'd seen her smile in this new life—the life where they were both adults, and they both lived in Spain. "I don't think I know what that means," she admitted.

"It means he makes a lot of money helping rich people throw fancy parties for other rich people," Alma said with a wink in Grace's direction.

"Not parties," Rafael objected.

Grace stared at him.

"Well sometimes parties," he conceded.

She nodded and looked as if she might say something, but she didn't.

"What's the latest bourgeoisie extravaganza?" Alma asked.

Rafael didn't want to tell her. He realized the irony here, that he'd always thought his sister was a ridiculous party girl with no ambition, and now she was a biologist developing some DNA sequence something—he could never understand the details—and he was...planning parties. It was not how he imagined things would turn out, and he didn't like talking about it in front of Alma, who seemed to think it was all some hilarious joke. Even more, he didn't want to talk about it in front of her friend, who was still staring at him with those big, sad blue eyes, waiting for him to explain this thing that had somehow become his life's work.

At least his new project was impressive, there was no denying that. He wasn't sure how to handle it yet. He hadn't quite figured out the details, but it was cultured and sophisticated and everything he'd always valued so much since his pig-headed elitist father had expected it of him.

"Well, it's top secret, like I said, but it's not a party. It's more of an event space for upscale exhibitions."

"Huh?" Alma said. "What kind of exhibitions? You're saying the vaguest words possible."

Rafael's eyes darted between them, and he realized both women were frowning at him with the same wrinkled up foreheads. He found himself lowering his voice to an almost hushed tone and felt like an idiot. This is what he did, after all. Sell the experience, make it sound special and appealing and confidential. He didn't know why he was doing it with his sister and her friend. "We have a new client that has one of the largest personal collections of Picassos in the world. He wants to find a way to share them, but without selling them to a museum or just letting people into his home. Essentially, we're trying to create a space for them where he can invite guests or other people could host certain events in this miniature underground museum that will house his collection."

He saw Grace scrunch up her nose and had no clue what it meant, so he kept explaining.

"It would be a secret, though, something special. Invitation only. People lucky enough to get asked to these events would have a chance to see the artwork, but the public wouldn't even know about it. It offers the intimacy of being invited into his private collection without him having to do the hosting."

Again, Grace looked annoyed, like she wanted to say something, but she didn't speak.

"That sounds kind of cool," Alma said, but Rafael couldn't help thinking she looked unimpressed.

"We still have a lot of details to figure out, but I think it could be amazing."

"The Nahmads?" Grace asked at last.

"Pardon?"

"The Nahmads own the largest private collection of Picasso's work. They're billionaire art collectors, and sometimes they put on their own exhibitions."

"Oh," Rafael said. He supposed it was within her field of study, so it probably made sense for her to be aware of that kind of thing. "Um, no, not them."

"That gives me an idea," Alma said. "It's Picasso stuff?"

"The client has a lot of influential twentieth century artwork."

"Perfect!" Alma exclaimed, raising her wine glass in the air so the dark liquid almost splashed over the rim.

Rafael and Grace both turned toward her, giving her their full attention as Alma continued. "Grace should work with you to curate the exhibit. You could hire her part-time as your assistant or something. You don't know anything about Picasso or paintings, Rafa, and she knows *everything* about it. She literally wrote articles about twentieth century art."

"Oh," Rafael said again, sure he was starting to come off like a buffoon, not the cultured sophisticate he was supposed to be. He didn't know what to say, though. He didn't want to work with Grace, and he certainly didn't need her help. She would just get in the way, a total distraction hanging around and mooning over the artwork instead of getting any work done.

"I don't think so, Alma." Grace pushed some hair behind her ear, and something about the movement made Rafael stare in wonder. "I still need to settle into the new teaching gig and make sure I have all my lesson plans ready. I know it's just a few classes, but I want to do a great job."

Alma made an indelicate sound with her mouth that rained spittle over her kitchen counter. "You'll be fine, Gracie. You don't even need to prepare. You could teach that class in your sleep."

Rafael decided to jump in. "I don't need an assistant, though. This is my job, and I know what I'm doing." That wasn't entirely true, but confidence was key.

"What do you know about Picasso?" Alma asked accusingly.

Rafael opened his mouth and then shut it. What *did* he know about Picasso? He knew about architecture, sure. He was a master of the Gothic, the Baroque, Romanesque, and Art Deco. That's what he'd been more interested in in school. But he didn't know about painting.

"You heard him, Alma." Grace chimed in. "He doesn't need me, and I just moved to a new country to start a new job at a campus I've never seen in my life. I should probably worry about that for now."

Alma's voice softened as she spoke to her friend. She was so tender toward Grace in a way that made Rafael feel like he was intruding. "But it might help to have another project to work on to help take your mind off everything..."

Everything, everything. Rafael couldn't quite remember what everything was. She'd lost her job, that much was clear. But there was also something about a boyfriend. And a grandmother?

"I'll be okay." Grace insisted. "You've already done so much for me; you don't need to force your brother into helping me out too. Except for bringing up the luggage, I guess. And even that was unnecessary."

"Well," Rafael said. He was starting to get the feeling that Grace didn't want him here. She could have brought up the luggage on her own, and if she had no interest in his silly underground art exhibit, that was just fine. He suddenly wanted to be out of his sister's apartment. He had work to do.

"I'll let you enjoy your evening." He excused himself, giving them a curt nod.

"Sure you don't want to eat with us?" Alma asked.

He couldn't help glancing at Grace again, to see how she would react to that. Did she want him to stay?

But her face was neutral, and he wasn't even sure what he was looking for. This woman didn't like him. She'd made that clear ten years ago when she backed away from his lips like they were poisoned, and she'd made it clear tonight when she kept her distance from him. She might look impartial now, but he was sure she did not want him to stay for dinner.

He wouldn't bother getting upset. He didn't like her either. He hadn't liked her at twenty-years-old when she was young and frivolous, and he didn't like her now, when she was...whatever this was.

"Some other time," he said. "Adios."

Why did he look over at her again before he walked out the door? It was like he expected her to do something, though he didn't know what. Instead, she just gave him a little wave and a sad smile.

Words jumbled against his tongue, but instead of letting any of them out, he gave her a last perfunctory nod and left.

He sighed with relief when he was on the other side of the door, finally out from under her gaze.

CHAPTER THREE

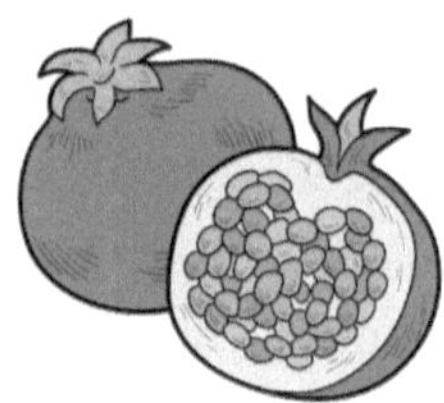

"SORRY ABOUT MY BROTHER," Alma said when Raf was gone.

"What do you mean?" Grace asked. Sure, she had her own silly historical beef with him, and he didn't seem far off from the snooty, pretentious boy in her memory, but she wasn't sure why Alma was apologizing for him.

"I swear he's the best brother in the world, but I'm not blind to his shortcomings. This is one of those situations where he despises my father and so desperately tries to be nothing like him, but it seems he just can't help himself sometimes. He can be so cold and serious."

"I remember," Grace murmured.

Every time Grace had met Alma's father when he visited America, he'd seemed perfectly charming. He was always taking them out to dinner and buying Alma presents, doting on her and spoiling her. But Grace still knew what Alma was referring to. She'd heard plenty about how cold the patriarch of the Ferrer-Martín family could be, how demanding, especially with Rafael. There was something intimidating about him, even when he was being jovial, like maybe he was only ever pretending. He was a rich and successful man with expensive tastes and certain expectations for his son. He wanted Raf to be rich and powerful in his own right, to be elite in every way possible. In Grace's estimation, Rafael was succeeding.

Not only was Rafael starting up some extravagant underground art exhibit, but there was also something about the way he kept glaring at her. She knew she didn't look her best right now, but that's because she wasn't at her best. Not at all. He didn't need to keep gawking at her and making her feel like such a mess under his scrutiny.

Grace looked around the room and decided to change the subject. "Your apartment, Alma. It's amazing."

She'd seen the place in videos, of course, or online when Alma was chatting with her by the window that looked out over the street, but it was even better in person. Small, but well organized and tidy. It reminded Grace of one of those little Ikea displays of what you could do with a small space, but it had more color and personality—bright, beautiful throw pillows and tasseled blankets, potted plants and shelves of science books. Even if Alma's relationship with her father wasn't as complicated as Rafael's, Grace knew how important it had been for Alma to have a place of her own, something she had earned without the help of her rich family.

"Your apartment now, too," Alma said. "We're living together again, so feel free to make it your own. And don't worry, I won't complain as long as there's a path through all of your clothes on the floor."

Grace rolled her eyes. "I'm going to try very hard to be neat. You know I will. I managed last time we were roommates. Mostly."

Alma smiled and walked over, wrapping her arms around Grace as soon as she could reach her. "A proper hug at last."

Grace let herself lean against her friend, comforted by her warmth. When was the last time she'd even hugged someone? Her grandmother, over a month ago? She'd needed a hug so badly, and finally, *finally,* she had someone to care for her, someone who knew her life was a disaster and would love her anyway, someone who would call in so many favors to get her a job, who would offer her a home and whole new life at a moment's notice. Alma was the best part of her life now. She was the only thing worth holding onto from the old one, and she was truly Grace's savior.

Even when Grace was panicking about work permits and visas and starting to worry that moving to another country was just another giant burden on her to-do list, Alma had helped with all of it. Luckily, getting a visa as a lecturer at a university was quicker than a lot of other work permits, and they were somehow able to get her on track for the start of the next series of courses at the end of September.

"Let me show you your room," Alma said, releasing Grace from the hug and linking their arms together before leading her over the fluffy Turkish rug.

She gave Grace the grand tour: the tiny hallway, the two bedrooms, the one little bathroom where Alma had already cleared a space for Grace's toothbrush and face creams. Alma's bedroom was much like the living area, tidy with touches of bright colors. One of the walls was papered with a plant print, and a stack of books was on the bedside table.

Grace's new room was sparse—a bed, a nightstand, a big, opened window. It was ready and waiting for her to turn it into something of her own. "What was this room for before?" she asked.

"Oh, it was just an office, but I barely used it." Alma waved a hand. "Let's get your stuff."

They slid the luggage into the room and stacked it in the corner, waiting to be unpacked and sorted. Then they ordered food and ate on the sofa. The TV was on in the background, but Grace didn't understand a word of it, despite three years of high school Spanish and one conversational class in grad school. Instead, they talked and talked like they hadn't in ages—not just about Grace and her string of disasters, but about Alma's annoying colleague and her vacation in Portugal and even more about her boyfriend, Obinna, the agricultural engineer extraordinaire.

As the room grew darker, Grace's eyelids started to feel heavy. The day—or days, really—of traveling was catching up to her at last, despite the adrenaline from being in the middle of Granada, from being reunited with Alma.

"Time for bed?" Alma whispered, and Grace nodded against her shoulder.

She barely managed to change into her pajamas and brush her teeth before she collapsed onto the little bed in her room, exhausted. There was an up-side to exhaustion, though. Maybe, just maybe, she was tired enough to trick her body into sleeping. For the past month she'd spent every night just hoping to fall into oblivion, and every night her brain had refused, whirring wildly in the darkness, rehashing all the memories Grace was trying to ignore.

She hoped Spain would be different. She hoped, at the very least, hours of standing in security lines, in-flight movies, and rolling her carry-on through multiple airports would be enough to settle her mind for one night. Grace was drifting off before she could comprehend that it had actually worked. It was the best sleep she'd had in ages.

In the days that followed, Grace set out to carve a new life for herself in southern Spain. Of course, Alma had a job. Alma had a life full of responsibilities, and she couldn't wander around the middle of Granada during the day to help Grace get settled in, as much as she might want to spend every moment helping her best friend. It meant Grace would be largely on her own until her classes began. Alma did show her around the neighborhood, pointing in the direction of the university and the Alhambra. She took her to the grocery store and her favorite coffee shop. But otherwise, Grace was wandering, untethered, muddling through with her broken Spanish and trying not to get lost.

In the middle of the week, she had an appointment with the art department at the university, an orientation of sorts. Her classes would be taught in English, obviously, especially because there would be a large number of international students enrolled in them. It was thrilling and terrifying to think of teaching students from all over the world, but Grace felt up for it. Sharing her passion for modern art was the easy part.

The university was like something from a fairy tale, a far cry from the concrete towers in Chicago where she'd studied and taught before. It was a large and diverse campus, and some of the structures looked more like castles than anything else. She'd wandered through buildings with painted ceilings and marble statues, through grottos of greenery and stucco arches. It was impressive, to say the least. Intimidating, too.

Her new colleagues were welcoming, though, and even if Grace felt like a fish out of water, she could imagine herself putting roots here, growing into this place and finding a steady rhythm, something that would help her to get a grip again, to discover if she was still the same person as before, somewhere deep inside. It was something she'd been mourning with everything else—a lost part of herself that didn't exist any longer. To some degree, she didn't even feel like she had a personality anymore; she was just a walking ball of grief instead of a person, too sad and boring to have much to offer anyone.

She was forever changed, no doubt about that, but seeing the campus offered some kind of hope. Maybe she could fit there. Maybe someday the old Grace would peek out at the spiraling staircase in the middle of the university *biblioteca* in a vast hall surrounded by books and remember what it was like to feel joy.

"We're lucky, honestly, that you were able to join us," Professor Medina offered at the end of Grace's first faculty meeting. "One of our instructors decided to run off to Greece at the end of last term, and so many of the candidates for the position had very little teaching experience. This is a rigorous group of students. They need someone with your expertise."

Grace was grateful for the man's comment, especially since she felt guilty about the strange kind of favoritism that had gotten her the job. Alma's mother knew the vice provost who had a background in art, and she'd revealed they were in urgent need of a new instructor. It wasn't often that anyone was in urgent need of an art history instructor, hence why Grace's old department had been completely dissolved. Despite all the other turmoil she'd suffered, getting the job was a strange kind of magic, even if it was a position for which she was well qualified.

She continued to aimlessly roam the campus and then branched out to aimlessly roaming the city, trying to picture what life would be like.

You don't need to picture it anymore, she told herself. *You're already here.*

But she still felt outside of it all—an interloper, an onlooker. She wasn't completely certain whether her move to Spain had just been running away from grief and pain or if she was running toward something exciting and new. Okay, actually, she was certain. It was definitely the former, but now that she'd done it, she wanted to make life in Spain something worth running toward.

One night, Alma took Grace to dinner with Obinna, so she was finally able to meet the man who'd stolen her best friend's heart. He was even more attractive in person, incredibly tall with one of the brightest smiles she'd ever seen, instantly disarming even though they'd never spoken a single time.

"I've heard a lot about you," he said, and Grace swallowed, guilt rising in her throat. She hadn't heard nearly enough about him, but she decided to rectify that as quickly as possible. If he'd managed to get Alma to commit for more than a couple of months, then he must be worth knowing, and Grace wanted to learn all about him.

They talked about his engineering job, which Grace understood only slightly more than she understood Alma's research, and they talked about food and music and Granada. Obinna was exceedingly fond of his home in Spain, but he talked about his childhood as well.

"You grew up in Nigeria?" Grace asked him from across the table.

He nodded and glanced at Alma. "She's not going to ask if I'm a prince, right?" he joked. Then he looked back at Grace, eyes gleaming. "That's always what Americans ask right away."

"I'm not going to ask if you're a prince." Grace laughed, embarrassed. "I was just going to ask when you moved here."

"I was just a boy, only eight-years old. My father had studied here when he was young, and he always wanted to return. It took a long time, but eventually he decided we would live in Granada."

"He went to the university?"

"Yes," Obinna said. "And eventually he taught there as well, like you. He just retired a couple of years ago. He was a businessman, but he really enjoyed teaching."

Grace took a sip from her sangria and leaned back into her chair, surprised at the feeling of contentment that washed over her. How many nights had she played third wheel on Alma's dates with handsome men? Admittedly, though, a lot of those guys had barely been able to carry on a conversation. "And how did you meet Alma?"

"She didn't tell you the story?" Obinna asked. He turned to Alma and shook his head in a playful scold.

"She did, but I want to hear it from your perspective. I always like a romance where you get both sides of it."

Obinna chuckled at that, and Alma grinned up at him, clearly enamored. He was such a warm person, and Grace felt a swell of happiness for her best friend. She didn't know how Alma had ended up with him, honestly. It was such a departure from her usual type in the best way possible. But Grace had always believed there was something about timing that was mixed up in the important elements of a relationship. It wasn't just the attraction or the fact that Obinna was a nice, intelligent guy, it was that Alma was ready to fall for him—to open herself up to a real commitment. Her longest relationship before this had lasted a month at best, but when an interest in exploring something serious started to creep into Alma's consciousness, she found Obinna at the right moment. Or maybe he found her.

Thank goodness she hadn't met him in college when she was doing body shots off random men at the bars. She would have run in the other direction.

"It's not really the most thrilling tale when you think about it," Obinna said. "There's a little—um—what would you call it?"

"A courtyard?" Alma offered.

"A courtyard, yes, that's a good word. It's in between our buildings where we work. The first time I saw Alma she was out there pacing and talking to herself, clearly worked up and full of passion, and I was intrigued."

"I was trying to work out why we hadn't been able to repeat the results of the Salas experiment."

"Of course," Grace said with no idea what she was talking about.

Obinna fixed his eyes on Alma. "You can imagine, I was afraid to talk to her then. I didn't want to interrupt her thoughts, but I started spending more time out in the courtyard. The next time I saw her I said hello."

"And begged me to go out with you," Alma added.

"*Beg* is a strong word."

"I seem to recall you taking my hand and saying 'please, please, please."

"Maybe I begged a little." Obinna shrugged.

"And you kissed my hand!" Alma clapped a palm over her mouth, as if she'd given away a secret.

Obinna's eyes shined. "I did do that."

Grace watched them in wonder. In all the years she'd known Alma, she had never seen her best friend like this before. Acting *cute*. Finishing her boyfriend's sentences and looking at him with untamed adoration. Seriously, even Grace and Derek had never acted this smitten in their three years together. Derek was a great listener who was very supportive, but they were never this mad about each other, never gripping each other's thighs under the table when they just couldn't help themselves, never telling the story of how they met with such joy.

Grace was happy for her best friend, if also a little taken aback. It was hard to imagine Alma settled. She was the kind of woman who never waited around for a phone call or text message, who never made any of her plans based on a man. She was fiercely caring, and everything she'd done for Grace the past few months only proved that, but she'd never directed any of that nurturing or protectiveness toward a guy she was dating.

"I'm happy you're here, Grace. Alma talks about you so much," Obinna said.

Grace winced. "Only because I'm a mess."

"No. You're so brave and so strong. I want you to say that to yourself in the mirror every morning until you believe it like I do." Alma gave her a little wink. They'd always encouraged each other with silly affirmations, but Grace couldn't help but feel like there was something more to this one.

Grace pushed some hair from her face and tried to smile. It was hard to imagine doing much of anything when she was trying so hard just to stay afloat. At least Alma was there, full of hope for the future, full of memories of who she once was. At least someone seemed to know her, even if she couldn't remember herself.

Grace was startled a couple of nights later when there was a knock on Alma's door—on *her* door, she supposed. Alma was still at the lab, which was unusual at the late hour, but apparently there was some kind of science experiment emergency that Grace could only barely try to comprehend. She was content to be alone, planning her upcoming courses and attempting not to wallow in her own self-pity.

Okay, maybe there was a little wallowing. A teeny tiny, barely worth commenting on amount of wallowing with a dash of checking her rapidly depleting bank account and Derek's social media.

She expected to find Obinna at the door, there to meet Alma, or maybe Alma herself with her hands full of books or food. Instead, Grace's mouth fell open as she stared up into chocolatey brown eyes and pouting lips, thick brows that were drawn into a frown, and—she couldn't help notice—a muscled arm that was raised against the door frame.

Rafael.

Grace tried to find her voice, but he beat her to it.

"I'm on duty, it seems." His exasperation was as thick as his accent.

"On duty?"

"Yes, Alma said she's stuck at the lab, so I'm required to check in and care for you."

Grace regained her composure quickly, reminding herself not to be distracted by Raf's pretty face or impressive physique. "You are *not* required to check in and care for me," she said.

He raised his hands. "I'm only following instructions."

"Well then, thanks for stopping by. As you can see, I'm perfectly fine, so you may go."

"You know how Alma is."

"Yes?"

Raf shook his head. "She'll kill me if I don't entertain you."

Grace huffed a mirthless laugh. "You don't need to entertain me, I promise."

"That's what I told her, but as *you* can see, I lost that battle."

Grace turned away without replying—because what could she even say to that?—and allowed Rafael to enter the apartment. Here he was, forced to spend time with her *again.* She hadn't come to Spain for pity hangouts and overwrought sympathy, but she could admit she didn't want to be alone all the time. She hadn't been close with her co-workers in Chicago, at least not close enough to hang out when they weren't co-workers any longer. Derek had been her closest friend, and obviously, that was no longer the case. And then there was her grandmother… Grace didn't even want to think about it. Yes, sure, she could admit it. She'd been sad and lonely and pathetic, but that didn't mean she needed this buzzkill showing up to spend time with her out of obligation. She had been managing just fine without him.

"Have you eaten?" Rafael asked.

Grace thought for a moment, trying to remember her last meal. Finally, she shook her head.

"Well." Raf slid his sunglasses back on top of his scalp, and Grace watched their path as they made little waves through his hair. "Let's go then."

"We don't have to do that."

"You have something to eat here?"

Grace glanced toward the kitchen. She had…a jar of Nutella.

"Come on then." Raf waved a hand toward the door. "I haven't eaten anything either. *Vamos*."

Grace pursed her lips. "I don't need you to come check on me and make sure I eat. You can tell Alma that was very thoughtful of her, but I don't need a babysitter."

"Graciela," Raf said sternly.

A shiver went down her spine. No one had ever called her that before, and there was something about it, something undeniably hot. His accent was already delicious, but to hear him use it like that…those soft a's and rolling r's… For a moment, she was caught so off guard that she forgot to be stubborn, and Rafael was able to push her out the door and down the stairs before she could give it any more thought.

Graciela. An image flashed in her head of Raf in bed, calling her that name, a flick of his tongue as he was licking her earlobe, then pressing his lips to the side of her neck. No, no. That wasn't right. She was not going to start having fantasies of Rafael Ferrer-Martín, even if he was stupidly good looking. Grace had never been shallow, or she would have kissed him ten years ago. It was *personality* that mattered. Intelligence and kindness and a sense of humor for goodness' sake. She knew Raf didn't have that last one. He was stone-faced and unshakeable. Don't bother telling him an ancient statue looked like Keanu Reeves on a motorcycle. Definitely don't bother trying to give the statue a lap dance. Even when she and Alma tried to get Rafael in on their inside jokes, he remained willfully *outside*.

So, no, she would not be developing an attraction for Rafael. At least, not a real one. Physically, he was an absolute feast for the eyes, but it wasn't enough to merit bedroom fantasies.

The sun had already set, but there was still a lingering remnant of deep purple on the horizon. Grace took a moment to appreciate it, to catalog that color as one of the things she could be grateful for, something she would always want to remember about living in Spain. She and Raf didn't talk as they walked, but before she knew it, they'd ducked into a small, hole-in-the-wall place, not the kind of establishment where she'd pictured Rafael. She eyed him curiously, and he shrugged before pulling out a chair for her.

"Thanks," she said.

"Share some tapas? They have really good *patatas bravas*. Always delicious."

She did a double take, checking if he was serious. It wasn't that unbelievable that he would want to share a meal with her, but he was being a little too nice.

"Sure." She dragged out the word, filling it with her skepticism.

"Come on, Grace. You might as well enjoy some good food."

She nodded and added a glass of sangria to her order as well. She felt like she deserved it for some reason. What a toil it was to wander around Spain all day and then have dinner with a hot Andalusian man. Definitely something to be rewarded with alcohol.

Rafael was quiet for a long time, and Grace didn't try to break the silence. Rather, she opted to fidget with her fingers in her lap before gulping her sangria so quickly that her cheeks flushed.

"It's been a long time since I've seen you," Raf said at last.

Grace raised her gaze to him, surprised he would bring up their odd history, though she supposed they had nothing else to talk about other than their uncomfortable past. "It has," she agreed, not sure what else to add.

"You're different," he said, matter-of-factly. Apparently in the brief amount of time it had taken to carry up her luggage and in the fifteen minutes since he'd forced her to join him for dinner, he'd been able to make a full assessment. It was like one of those side-by-side pictures. *How are they alike? How are they different?* Raf had cracked the code, solved the puzzle in record time.

"I guess so." She raised a shoulder.

He took a long swig of his own drink. "So what brings you to Granada?"

Grace narrowed her eyes at him. Surely, Alma would have told him something about her situation. "A run of bad luck."

Rafael waited, taking another sip.

She sighed. "I lost my job. My boyfriend broke up with me, and I had to move out of his apartment. And my grandma passed away."

Rafael's face softened, and he leaned forward, ever-so-slightly. "Sorry about your grandmother," he said. "Sorry about all of it."

Grace blinked rapidly. "She—she was sick for a long time, but she didn't tell me. I wasn't around enough to notice, or I would have figured it out sooner. I should have been there. When I moved in with her, I realized how frail she was, and she finally told me the truth. I guess that's the good thing about Derek breaking up with me. I got to live with her again in those final months."

"You'd lived with her before?" Raf's gaze was concentrated on her face, so serious, as it usually was, but there was something else too. Something kind, maybe? Concerned?

"She raised me. My parents... Well, they had me when they were very young, and they never really got their shit together. I don't have much of a relationship with them. Gram was my family."

Rafael twisted his mouth like he was mulling over the words. "I'm sorry that you lost her," he said again. "That's terrible."

Grace shifted uncomfortably in her chair as the waiter approached with their order. She hadn't planned to open up to Raf like this. She hadn't even been planning to eat in front of him, but here they were. The *patatas bravas* were delicious. The sangria was perfect. And Rafael, it turned out, was kind of a good listener.

"Thank you for saying that." Grace picked up on their conversation after swallowing a large bite of potato. "Alma is the reason I survived, of course. She was there for me through all of it, and even though my grandma left me the house, I just couldn't be there alone." Her voice broke, and she paused, regaining her composure. "I'd be lost without Alma."

"And she'd be lost without you, I think. You two have always been there for each other."

They were quiet again for a moment, chewing slowly. Additional tapas had appeared after Rafael spoke rapid (or possibly perfectly normal) Spanish to the waiter, and each dish was amazing, even though Grace couldn't have named them. There was some kind of beef and what she thought was possibly octopus? It didn't matter. She kept eating.

"So, are you not a fan of Picasso?" Rafael asked suddenly.

Grace cocked her head. "What?"

"The other day when I was talking about my project, you made a face."

"What kind of face?"

Raf shook his head. "I don't know what kind of face, that's why I'm asking."

"I'm not sure what you mean." Her leg was bouncing under the table.

"I think you know exactly what I mean."

Grace glanced away for a moment, hesitating. She'd been honest with him so far. Why stop now? "I just—" she started, then cleared her throat. "Picasso was obviously talented and prolific and hugely influential, but as a person he was..." She trailed off, unsure of how to put it.

"Yes?" Rafael prompted.

"A misogynist. Who preyed on women and young girls. He was also known for being quite volatile and manipulative."

Rafael was silent for a moment, considering all of this. "I don't know much about his art or the man himself, if I'm honest. You don't think we should display his work?"

"I didn't say that. It's just...complicated. I don't have a solution, but if you're going to consider the kind of man he was, then full-on emulation seems like a bit much, especially when you're creating an entire exhibit full of his art without any context."

Rafael frowned. "It's not all about Picasso. And it doesn't have to be without any context. My client is a big collector. He has work from many different artists. He wants to fill it with a lot of his favorite pieces."

"Well, that's another problem I have with the idea."

"What is?" Rafael asked, and Grace was surprised at how eager he was to hear her opinion.

"I think an art museum should be accessible to everyone who would like to see it, not just hidden away in some secret hideout for rich people."

"Ah, there it is," Rafael said, pointing a finger at her, his voice changing. "I got ya. There was quite a lot going on in that face you made when I was talking about the gallery. I knew it."

"You sound very American sometimes," Grace commented.

He leaned forward in his chair. "I lived in America for many years, Grace. But tell me this, if it's not exclusive, then what's the draw? People want to experience something special. Something that makes *them* feel special."

Grace sighed. "The draw is the art, isn't it?"

"Really?"

"Yes." Grace almost laughed. "Aren't people going to art museums for the art all the time?"

"But what about the excitement? The mystery? There's something about how secretive it will be."

Grace studied his face. There was honestly something kind of cute about his excitement, even if she didn't agree with anything he was saying. "You think the work of Picasso and whoever else your client is collecting is something that only a select few people who are invited should be able to experience just so they can feel special?"

"Look, that's not what I'm saying, but there are other museums. The purpose of this exhibit is to create a cultured space where my client's guests and whoever might use the venue can have an exclusive experience. He owns the art, after all. He can invite whoever he wants to see it."

Grace shook her head absently. *This* was the Rafael she was familiar with. He always assumed exclusivity and quality went hand in hand, and he must already think she was as silly as she was at twenty. Silly for thinking that art could be something for everyone, something to bring together an entire community. For him, it was a commodity, and that was all. For a second, she thought maybe he'd changed. He hadn't seemed quite so unfeeling as the last time she'd met him, and he was a bit more open, willing to engage with her even as she railed against his ideas. But he was the man she remembered after all, a man who valued money and status over everything else.

"People will pay a lot for a VIP experience," he said. "It could be almost anything in the room, as long as it's private."

"Maybe that's part of the issue," Grace said in a clipped tone.

"What issue?" Rafael asked.

They went on like that, eating and arguing for almost an hour, and despite the fact that he was incredibly frustrating and she took issue with almost every word that came out of his mouth, Grace had to admit it helped to take her mind off of things. It was nice to talk about something else. Something other than her losses and how she was coping. When she was talking with Alma, or friends back home, or even with Rafael at the outset of dinner, the conversation was always about her messy life. But as she and Raf settled into the evening and into their arguments, it was nice to have a conversation with someone who didn't care enough to treat her like a crystal trinket, too breakable to handle. Even if Rafael was a total snob, at least he offered a nice distraction.

And, well, his face was also a nice distraction, even if she would never admit that to him in a million years.

CHAPTER FOUR

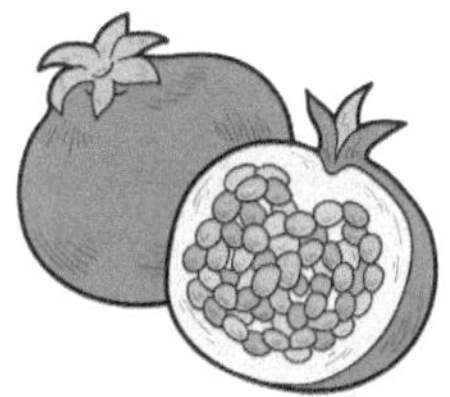

CHRISTIAN OCANDO'S appearance didn't quite match Rafael's expectations. Before this moment, Rafael had been imagining someone in a dark suit with sleek graying hair and a fancy watch, tall and fit and stern. Rafael supposed he'd really been imagining his father. Christian was clearly wealthy, but his wealth was understated. Though they'd communicated via email and phone call, this was their first official meeting, and Christian's clothing was casual but crisp and clean in a way that alluded to affluence. He wore beige slacks rolled at the ankles and a blue collared shirt, and his hair was a mess of curls on his head. He had a round belly and a big laugh, and he welcomed Rafael into his beautiful minimalist home with a pat on the back.

"Rafael," Christian said warmly, "so happy you could make it. We'll go to the gallery, but a lot of the pieces are in storage."

The man spoke impeccable Spanish, but Rafael detected an accent. Something he couldn't place.

"How did you end up with so many Picassos?" Rafael asked.

"I've always been a collector. A collector of many artists, really. Gris, Matisse, Blanchard, Braque, Dali, Gilot. Picasso is of monumental cultural significance, of course, but also...I don't know. Something about his particular aesthetic appeals to me."

Rafael patted himself on the back for recognizing a few of the names Christian listed, but he also couldn't help thinking of his conversation with Grace a few nights before, about the impossibility of separating art and artist and her qualms about complete admiration of the man without regard to who he was as a person. He'd never given any of it much consideration, but he was interested in listening to what she had to say, even if she thought he was nothing but a dilettante.

Christian offered a big smile and opened the door to the gallery. The space was small but miraculous, home to the kind of pieces one would imagine in the Prado or the Louvre, not a person's home. Thirty or so paintings lined the walls and sculptures in the middle of the long aisle. Everything was well lit and well placed, and while Rafael couldn't have named the artist for a single painting, they all seemed to fit in the room together.

Christian walked alongside him, offering anecdotes about the acquisition of each of the pieces, though he clearly expected that Rafael had some basic knowledge, like the era or style of each work. He didn't though. Rafael would have loved to claim some kind of expertise in this world and its history, but he'd never taken much of an interest in it before, and he was at a loss. He nodded and smiled, trying to appear as if all of this wasn't going right over his head when he had no clue what Christian was talking about. This *had* to go well, after all. Christian was a big client, not only one of his earliest, but the wealthiest as well. This was Rafael's chance to prove that leaving his job in finance, refusing to work for his father, putting everything at risk to start his company, it was all worth it.

"This is one of my favorites," Christian said as they stopped before an abstract portrait of a man. It was a cubist piece, maybe? Rafael thought that seemed correct, but he still didn't dare to say it aloud. What a mediocre assessment it would be even if he was correct. He was knowledgeable enough to understand that the painting was indeed something of consequence. The way the artist used shape and color, the man's face was distorted but it still shone with personality. He was holding something, but Rafael couldn't tell what it was. The painting almost seemed to move somehow, like it was rippling from within. He stared and stared until he finally realized that Christian was waiting for him to speak.

"I'm speechless," Rafael said finally, since that really was the truth, regardless of the reason.

Christian's eyes lit with enthusiasm. "Ah, I'm not surprised," he said. "This is one of the great works of the movement." He moved forward and waved a hand to present the next piece. Rafael was fairly certain the previous one hadn't been a Picasso, but perhaps he was safe to assume the next one was? He kept his mouth shut all the same and pursed his lips when it crossed his mind that Grace would have known everything about this work. She could have probably talked about it for hours on end. He had a feeling he'd only barely scratched the surface of her thoughts on the exhibition, but, even so, she would have been astounded by this place. He was certain of it.

"Here we are," Christian announced. "Picasso was only twenty-four when he painted this one. It was his Rose Period, of course."

Rafael was astounded again. How the work of one man could be so vastly different was beyond him. He never would have guessed the painting was a Picasso as it didn't match any of the kinds of images he had in his head. It was quite realistic actually, depicting a boy in front of a flowered background, and again, he was holding something that Rafael couldn't identify. Rafael couldn't stop looking at the boy's one visible ear, which seemed out of proportion despite the painting's realism. The boy's eyes were dark, and he looked somber. But that ear...why was that ear so haunting?

He was increasingly aware that his cursory research before this meeting had not been enough.

"I paid too much for it, if I'm honest," Christian said with a laugh. "But I suppose there are worse vices!"

Rafael nodded absently.

"Now, of course, I have a great many ideas, but I've been told you have a knack for designing an enriching space. I'm hoping we can do that for the exhibit and really curate the paintings in a way that will do them justice."

Rafael tried not to startle. He wasn't one for modesty. He *did* have a knack for designing enticing spaces. Every event he'd worked on thus far had been a product of his vision, of the way people would move through the room, where they would sit, how every piece of furniture and every flower would add to the whole experience. He knew how to make everything just right. But when it came to curating artwork, well, Rafael would have no idea what in the hell he was doing.

"Perhaps we might bring on a team as well for curation and any restoration that's needed," he suggested.

Christian let out a hardy laugh. "Restoration, sure. Some of them need new frames, but I don't need a stuffy curator telling me what to do with *my* paintings," Christian said. "You and I will handle it."

Rafael didn't know where Christian's misplaced confidence in him was coming from, but he was positive he would have absolutely no idea what to do with the collection. And while Christian certainly seemed to know what he was talking about, Rafael couldn't help the itch in the back of his mind that told him they needed someone who knew a bit more about all of this. Someone to provide the context.

Not that he would admit it, of course. He returned Christian's smile. "It's going to be spectacular," he confirmed, but his eyes wandered back to the boy in the painting before them. He still couldn't stop staring at that damned ear.

The next day, Christian and Rafael embarked on a journey through Granada to find the perfect location for the elite underground exhibit. Rafael had researched a long list of possible locations and set up viewings, but Christian eliminated several of them before they even began.

When they arrived at the first spot and started down the stairs into the door of the venue, Rafael looked over at his wealthy companion and put on a charming smile. "You know, just because you're thinking of this as an 'underground' museum doesn't mean that it literally needs to be located underground." Rafael had received an email from Christian that morning, and every street-level location had been crossed off the list.

Christian barked out a laugh. "You would get along with my wife," he said. "She thinks I'm a silly old man, but I want it to feel hidden and secret.

Like a speakeasy through a hidden passage. Then, boom, some of the most spectacular art you've ever seen by some of the most famous painters in a place you would never expect."

"Ah," was the only response Rafael could muster as they walked into the building, and he was distracted by the disaster before them. The problem with an underground venue was that underground was often a dirty former dive-bar that had been abandoned years ago, and was now just full of slabs of wood, old buckets, and loose drywall. It looked far worse than the pictures Rafael had seen, and he wondered just how many years ago those photos had been taken. It was like they were meeting an online date whose profile picture was from when they were in secondary school.

"I didn't expect this," Rafael said, embarrassed that he'd even brought Christian here to begin with. It was a complete waste of time.

"It certainly could use some work." Christian spun in a circle and shook his head. The place looked like a dungeon.

"Maybe I should check out some of these places first to make sure they're up to our standards," Rafael said. "Then you can look at those that might be a fit for you."

Christian waved a hand. "This is half the fun. I'm not afraid of getting a little dirty."

Despite Christian's enthusiasm, the next five locations were a mix of old wine cellars, parking garages, and one utility closet that was barely large enough for them to walk around inside of it, especially because it still housed quite a few utilities. The most promising option they saw was an underground tunnel that the realtor claimed could connect all the way to secret tunnels under the Alhambra, even though Rafael had his doubts about the claim. It was too narrow, though. They needed something small enough to feel intimate and large enough to fit a large number of people inside.

By the end of the day, Rafael was discouraged and embarrassed, though trying not to show it, but Christian was still flitting about the city happily, as if they hadn't just spent the day in unkempt underground hell mouths.

"There's always tomorrow," Christian said, giving Rafael another pat on the back.

He couldn't help but relax a little bit at the man's jovial attitude. At least someone was having fun. They walked back to where Christian's car was parked at the last place, just as the sun was setting. It was one of those days that forced Rafael to take the time to notice how beautiful it was, a rose gold sky shimmering over the dark outlines of the Granada skyline, the Alhambra on a hilltop in the distance, and faint music playing from one of the windows down the road wrapping them in an atmosphere of calm.

"Why'd you choose Granada?" Rafael asked. "For this underground exhibit?"

Christian looked surprised he would even ask. "Barcelona has a Picasso Museum already, and there's the Prado in Madrid. In Malaga, where Picasso was born, they have the Museo Picasso. Of course, there's plenty of art to see here as well, but it would be something different and special to have the exhibition in Granada." Christian chuckled to himself. "And my wife was born here, so that might be the real answer to your question. This is my home."

"I see." Rafael swallowed. He did understand it. He'd just returned to Spain, and he knew what it meant to be drawn to the idea of home.

Christian barked his big laugh again, and Rafael couldn't help but smile. "Well," Rafael sighed, "tomorrow we go to Sacromonte."

Christian clapped his hands. "Don't despair, my friend. Sacromonte may be just what we're looking for."

Sacromonte was just what *Christian* was looking for, but Rafael couldn't see it. Usually, these things appeared in his brain as fully formed visions—the layout, the table settings, all the details that made his events truly unparalleled. But when they walked into the cave house in Sacromonte, Rafael had no idea how it would be done.

Christian was like a schoolboy, running around and clapping with gleeful squeaks as they toured the property. Of course, the older man would be delighted by the culture and history of the place. Rafael barely knew him, but he could already tell this was just the kind of thing he would go for.

The cave houses in Sacromonte had a rich history indeed. They'd been around since the 16th century when they were literally carved out of the hillside. Historically, Romani families had lived there, and people still referred to it as the "Gypsy Neighborhood" for that very reason. The cave houses provided shelter from persecution and were often a haven for groups that had been cast out from the city. An intriguing history, and there was already a historic museum in the caves to tell it, but Rafael could see that Christian was thrilled with the prospect of the cave houses hosting his little artistic endeavor as well. It was still home to a vibrant community that embraced art and the Flamenco.

It was off the beaten path, certainly, since you had to climb a hill or drive up a cliff to get there, and the potential site of Christian's museum was tucked into the side of the white-washed hill, with a little door in the rocky cave that almost seemed to appear out of nowhere.

But that was just the thing. How were you supposed to hang paintings on the rocky curved walls of a cave?

Christian didn't seem to think this was a problem, and after half an hour of bouncing around the rooms of the cave house, he returned to Rafael's side and clapped his hands together, the sound echoing from the arched walls. "This is it!"

"Some of the paintings are quite large, though, aren't they? I don't understand how we'll display them." Admittedly, the space was larger than Rafael had expected, but he still wasn't sure how it would work. He knew plenty of people lived in these houses, and there were Airbnb rentals available for curious tourists. There *was* a sense of coziness, a homey feel that was unique for the type of exhibit they were trying to create. It was interesting, to say the least. However, filling it with priceless art was another matter.

"You'll figure out something." Christian clapped him on the back with enthusiasm. "I've been to one of your events. I know your work. I'm sure you can make this happen, and just look at this place. It's secluded and different, tucked away into a cave. I don't think there could be anything better."

Rafael nodded as he looked around the space again. Was it a cool setting? Sure, it was all the things Christian said, but for an art exhibit? Even for a party? It would certainly have to be small and intimate. And Rafael didn't know anything about art, much less how to curate a museum's worth of paintings and hang them on a cave wall. He was in over his head, and there was no way around it. But for his reputation, for his career, for his own sense of pride that wouldn't allow him to go to Christian with his tail between his legs to admit there was no way in hell he could make this work, he needed to figure something out quickly. Christian was already talking about a moving truck to get the paintings here as soon as humanly possible, but thankfully Rafael knew it would take some time. The paintings had to be carefully packed in specially designed boxes filled with foam and packing materials, and even if Christian was eager to get things going, Rafael knew he wouldn't risk rushing the process.

An unbidden image of Grace materialized in his brain. He wasn't sure why he had the vague notion that Grace would know just what to do. She would know the paintings, she would know where to put them, she would be able to make this work somehow, if only she didn't despise the entire idea to begin with.

"Come, Rafael," Christian called, and he realized he'd been standing as still as a statue for several minutes. "Let's go see the view."

CHAPTER FIVE

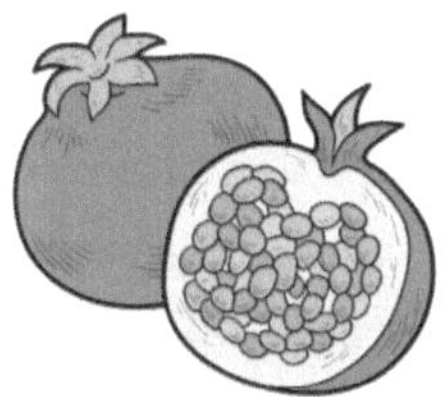

GRACE WAS TRYING REALLY HARD NOT to puke. Obviously, she was used to the feeling. She'd had many first-day-of-class days in many had-no-idea-where-she-was-going places, but no matter what, she always wanted to puke. Especially now that she was going to be teaching students from all over the world. Cosmopolitan students who spoke several languages and probably grew up with baby books full of post-impressionist artwork. They'd analyzed Gauguin and Carr while they sucked on their pacifiers. They probably had rattles printed with Munch paintings.

Okay, maybe that was unlikely, but it didn't lessen the need to hurl.

Grace had been so confident while she'd planned her lectures, so sure that even if she had used Alma's connections to get the job, she was qualified. Professor Medina had even confirmed she was the best candidate. She'd already taught loads of classes on twentieth century art and female artists. She'd done plenty of surveys in art history, from the renaissance to modernity. It was what she loved to do. However, first day jitters were real, and it appeared that first day jitters in a new country where you barely spoke the language were very real indeed.

Wasn't it strange that the very things that were often best when they were solitary—studying artwork or painting or writing—often required encounters with the public? How odd that those members of the community who were wrapped up in their own thoughts and ideas and would be content studying and researching in isolation were required to go out to the masses and make themselves known if they wanted to make a living. And a modest living at that.

Not that Grace didn't enjoy talking with her students about art. She loved sharing her passion with them, watching their faces the first time she showed them *The Large Bathers* or *From the Lake*. She loved to observe them as looks of admiration and appreciation and awe settled in, and she loved to talk about their questions and interests.

It was just that all of this involved standing in front of a big group of people and commanding their attention, when Grace would have liked to fade into the background. It required a place in the front and center, when Grace would have preferred to be a shadow on the wall that no one gave much thought, even though it completed the picture and gave the work a new dimension.

Even though some of the buildings on campus were intimidating Renaissance church-like structures, Grace was pleased to find that her classroom looked similar to almost every small, wood-paneled auditorium that was designed in the 1970s. That was comforting, at least. The projector and the little podium and the weird lighting. Those were the things that made her feel a sense of familiarity that might allow her to keep her breakfast down.

She cleared her throat as she watched the clock. Students drifted in and took their seats, and she smiled at them when she made eye contact, but she tried to busy herself with her notes, shuffling her stack of syllabi just to pretend she had a reason not to look up.

But eventually, she had to look up. Class was meant to begin. She was meant to teach it if she could figure out how to speak.

"Good morning, everyone," she said too softly. She cleared her throat, pushed her shoulders back, and tried to project. "I'm supposed to remind you that this course will be taught in English, though you may have guessed that immediately."

There were a few smiles throughout the room. "The first thing I like to do," Grace continued, "is to have everyone introduce themselves, so we can start to get acquainted and feel comfortable with each other. And then we can start talking about art."

The students were actually eager to introduce themselves, and they already showed way more confidence than Grace, unafraid to ensure that she understood why they took the class—because they needed a cultural studies credit or because they had to fulfill something in fine arts or because this was their major, and maybe they had no idea what they would ever do with it, but they loved art, just like she did, and they wanted her to know that.

Grace listened and nodded, making notes on her attendance sheet about preferred names and tricks to try to remember all of them. *Armand* with the big glasses and *Zhou Xi* with the pink lip gloss. *Elyse* with dark, haunting eyes and *Marco* with the bleach blonde hair.

She started going through the syllabus, talking about assignments and the different units and time periods they would cover. Before she was even five minutes in, one of the students raised a hand.

"Umm, yes?" She glanced at her notes. Very Blonde. "Marco?"

"What's your favorite painting?" he asked in enthusiastic, heavily accented English.

"My favorite?" She cocked her head to the side, as if the question was confounding. Of course she'd been asked her about her favorite painting before. It was a common question for an art history professor, but that was also part of the reason she couldn't really choose. It was like asking someone to choose a favorite song or a favorite child.

The truth was that she couldn't possibly have a favorite painting. There were too many brilliant works to choose from, too many different styles that evoked different emotions and reminded her of different moments from her life. Many were moments she'd shared with her grandmother at the Art Institute of Chicago, where they'd spent weekend mornings when Grace was a kid. She remembered her grandma staring at Georgia O'Keefe's *Sky Above Clouds IV* for so long that Grace worried something bad had happened, but she did the same thing at *Water Lilies* and *Inventions of the Monsters*, until Grace understood that this was the kind of dedication and time that art required—to stare and stare and take it all in, every drop and detail, to find a way inside the piece and to feel it as if it were a part of you. And perhaps, on some rare occasions, it really would become a part of you forever.

Grace's grandma liked the beautiful stuff, the impressionists and the landscapes and the bright colors and people dancing in summer. But as she got older, Grace wandered off on her own to explore the weirder stuff, the stuff that seemed to appeal to her more and more. She couldn't stop thinking about Francis Bacon's *Figure with Meat.* For all of the complicated feelings about Picasso she'd discussed with Rafael, *The Old Guitarist* haunted her dreams. And that was before she started to really study art, to actually learn about the techniques and the context. With all of that, how could she possibly choose a favorite?

"What's *your* favorite painting?" she asked Marco, because that's what teachers did. They just asked the tough questions back to the class, especially when they didn't have the answer.

Marco scrunched up his face, clearly giving it some thought. "My mother painted a vase of flowers that she hung up in our house," he said. "It's very nice."

Grace smiled. "That's lovely. Maybe as we start to talk, you can learn about some of her influences."

"I think she was just influenced by our garden," Marco said.

"How was it?" Alma asked the second Grace walked through their door. Alma was sprawled across the couch with a magazine and a glass of wine, but she sat up as if she'd been waiting all day to talk to her best friend.

Grace smiled before she could find any words. "Terrifying," she said at last. "And wonderful."

"You liked your students?"

"They were kind and enthusiastic and patient with me when I couldn't work the projector. It was better than I could have imagined. Usually there are a few in the class that don't care much, and I'm sure that will be the case, but they were engaged today."

"Oh Gracie, that's amazing. See? You made the right decision coming here."

Grace nodded. "Time will tell, I suppose, but Alma—"

"No, don't you dare. If you thank me one more time, I'm kicking you out of the apartment."

"I wasn't going to say thank you."

"You weren't? What were you going to say?"

"I was going to say I'm so *grateful* to you."

Alma shook her head. "Get out of here. Actually, yes, do get out. We should go somewhere and celebrate your first day."

Grace leaned against the counter and hung her head. "I'm tired."

"Come on, we have to do something. A drink? *Helado*?"

Grace knew it would be suspicious to say no to ice cream. She never said no to ice cream, but she felt worn out. She'd felt worn out for the past three months or more, and even with the excitement of a new class, a new city, a new country, she couldn't help wishing that she could feel like herself again. It seemed impossible when she'd lost her entire life and imagined future. Her career. Her partner. Her family. How could she ever be the same?

Alma's face fell, and Grace hated to disappoint her. She hated that she couldn't be the girl who talked about hand-jobs on the college quad and loaded up on soft-serve with sprinkles for dinner, the girl that danced until her legs were literally aching and stayed out until four o'clock in the morning just because her best friend wasn't quite ready to go to bed. They'd met the sunrise on several occasions, just because they couldn't stop talking to each other about anything and everything.

That seemed like another life, a life that required more energy than Grace could muster. "I think I might just start planning for my next class," she said guiltily.

Alma nodded.

"Sorry."

"Don't apologize, Gracie. I understand."

Grace sighed. "Yes, but you probably weren't prepared to have a mopey weirdo living with you and killing your vibes. Especially when you've been so happy with Obinna."

"You're *my* mopey weirdo, and I want you here, no matter what."

Alma's phone rang, and she went to pick it up. "Hola?"

Grace sat on the sofa, curling her knees to her chest. Maybe Alma was right that she needed to do something, to get out of her comfort zone and live a little. She'd moved across the world, which seemed like a good step, but after a bit of exploring, she'd been doing the same thing she'd been doing in Chicago, tucking herself away in her room and trying to avoid the world. As much as she could logically tell herself she needed to get out, however, her grief didn't want to listen. It wanted a bed and darkness and reality TV show repeats. She wanted to feel numb, but the pain was always there, right under the surface. Even in the moments when she managed to forget, just for a moment, the ache was there waiting to surge up again.

Alma walked back toward Grace and held out her cell phone. "For you," she said casually, as if Grace would be expecting a random phone call in Spain.

Grace scrunched up her face, but Alma gestured again, waiting for Grace to take the phone.

"Hello?"

"Graciela." The voice on the other end of the line was deep and stern, and Grace's skin felt instantly warm.

"Rafael." She glanced at Alma, confused. Alma just shrugged and picked up her magazine.

"I need your help with something." His voice made it sound like this was more of a command, rather than a request, but she supposed Rafael was used to commanding.

"You need my help?" Grace's voice was incredulous and a bit sharp.

Rafael's tone softened a bit. "Yes, can you meet? I'd like to talk about it with you in person. Tomorrow?"

On what planet could Rafael possibly need her help with something? She wouldn't have even been able to imagine him *asking* for her help, except that he'd just done it. "I have a class in the morning."

"After your class then."

She hesitated.

"I promise it's not a strange request, Grace. Just meet me tomorrow after your class."

"Where?" she asked, trying to ignore the disappointment that he hadn't called her "Graciela" again.

"You said you've never been to the Alhambra, correct? Let's meet there. Kill two birds with one stone, as they say."

The Alhambra? Her brain wasn't functioning properly, and she couldn't seem to comprehend anything he was saying. Was this some kind of tourism outing? What in the world did he want?

"Fine," she said at last. "I'll get your number from Alma."

"Good." Rafael released a soft breath that seemed to take over the line. "Tomorrow."

"Yes," Grace replied, unsure why something seemed to be crawling down and settling in her stomach, dread or excitement or desire, she wasn't sure. "Tomorrow."

CHAPTER SIX

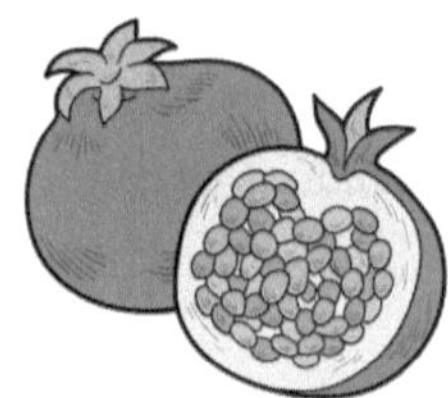

RAFAEL PACED OUTSIDE the main entrance to the Alhambra, though he wasn't sure why he was nervous. Maybe it was because everything was happening so quickly. Christian had already made an offer to purchase the cave dwelling in Sacromonte, and by all accounts, the paperwork to turn it into an exhibit was simpler than expected. It wasn't lost on Rafael that things went faster and smoother when you had millions of dollars to throw at every potential problem. Christian was eager to reserve moving vans and hire art handlers to transport some of the paintings to the cave, but Rafael was still at a loss. How to hang the paintings, how to organize them and light them, how to make sure the air had the correct humidity and temperature, how to get the art to look impressive and imposing in the little rooms of a cave. He couldn't envision it, and that had never happened to him before.

He continued to trace an erratic path on the ground until his eyes spotted a familiar figure in the distance. His breath caught as Grace approached him, which was odd. She was beautiful, certainly, but so were a lot of the women he knew. Her skin seemed to glow from within, and there was something so enticing about the soft pink color of her cheeks and the rosy tinge on the tip of her nose…

She didn't smile when she noticed him but instead seemed to take a breath and steel herself, as if she needed to find the strength for whatever was to come. Rafael didn't know why that bothered him, why he would have expected her to greet him warmly or feel at ease around him, but he realized he felt somewhat sore about it.

"You made it," he said, inadvertently closing the final bit of distance between them with a long stride.

She nodded and squinted up at him. It was a sunny, perfect day, and Rafael knew the bright light would be gleaming off the colorful tiles of the palace behind him. The Alhambra was going to look its best, and that's what he wanted to show Grace, that there was a certain kind of magic in this city. If nothing else, he hoped to put her in a good mood, soften her up a bit so, just maybe, he could convince her to use her expertise to get him out of his mess.

She raised her hands in front of her, palms up, as if presenting herself. Rafael was surprised to find that he wanted to reach out and touch her. He couldn't make sense of it. It was the same as it had been ten years ago when he'd wanted to be around her for no discernable reason. Then, she'd been so full of life, and now she was so somber, but the feeling still held, something strong and inexplicable.

She stared up into his eyes, unblinking. Waiting. He cleared his throat. "What do you think?"

"Just wondering why I'm here."

Rafael frowned and tilted his head. "I meant what do you think of the Alhambra? You don't want to enjoy this spectacular Nasrid creation from the thirteenth century?"

She glanced at the giant structure looming over them. "It's obviously impressive, and I want to see every inch of it, but—"

"But you'd rather not see it with me?"

"It's not that."

"You're concerned about what I could possibly want from you? I told you, it's nothing major or dangerous. There's no reason to be so skeptical."

She shrugged. "You didn't give me much to go on, Raf."

Rafael's mouth hung slightly ajar. She'd given him a nickname. It was something Alma called him sometimes as kind of a joke since people had often shortened his name that way in America. He'd never cared for it much, but the way Grace said it—with some level of familiarity and intimacy, like she'd been calling him that for ages—was something he found himself liking very much.

He didn't want to lay out his plan and the entirety of his request for her right away, though. After all, they'd both already resisted the idea of working together when Alma brought it up. He wanted to give her some time to mull it over. If she was walking the halls of one of the most extraordinary buildings in the region, then perhaps it would only whet her appetite for more. More of the culture—the caves, the paintings, the views of Granada. One taste of the Alhambra, and she would be hooked.

"Let's go inside," he said, placing a hand on the small of her back and then quickly drawing it away again. "I have all afternoon. Plenty of time to discuss the details."

She sighed. "I kind of feel like I'm being kidnapped and held hostage in a gorgeous castle."

"I'll remind you that you came here freely."

"I'll remind you that I still don't know what you want from me."

Rafael huffed. He hadn't expected her to be quite so difficult. It was rather uncommon for a woman to *not* want to spend time with him. He needed to turn up the charm a bit.

"It was good of you to take the time out of your day to meet with me," he said, lowering his voice ever so slightly. "I'm sure an intelligent art professor such as yourself is very busy, but it's nice to have you here."

Grace frowned and turned away from him, but Rafael thought he caught her rolling her eyes. She started marching toward the Alhambra as if to say "let's get this over with."

Rafael followed, trying to work out his next move. Maybe this was going to be much harder than he'd anticipated.

Luckily, even if Grace wasn't entirely impressed with him, she was awestruck by the palace. After they'd gotten inside, she spun around while staring up at the ceiling, mouth agape, fingertips gliding against the cool mosaic tiles. It was a busy day but not horribly crowded, and they had plenty of room to wander down the long hallways and gaze out at the view of the whole city.

She tried to be aloof, but Grace was enamored with all of it, just as he knew she would be. By the time they reached the giant reflecting pool and the gardens, Rafael thought she may have forgotten that he'd had to coerce her into this.

"You know," Rafael said, hoping that offering even more knowledge about the place would only improve his position, "many of the walls have inscriptions. Quotes and poems from the Qur'an. They praise and glorify God but offer blessings as well."

"It's lovely." She'd been taking pictures of everything while they walked through the palace, but eventually she leaned against one of the columns and turned her phone camera toward him. He pretended not to notice, pushing his sunglasses onto his face and sliding his hands in his pockets, trying to be nonchalant. He leaned against the column next to hers.

Finally, he looked over and shook his head, lifting a hand to try to guard himself like he was a celebrity caught by the paparazzi.

"Come on. Don't waste your camera space on me."

"But I can't leave out the coolest guy at the Alhambra. I don't think I've ever seen you look so relaxed."

"Then you better not show anyone the photo. For the sake of my reputation."

She paused. "You like to be unapproachable then?"

"Unapproachable? That's what you think?" A little uptight, sure, but he never thought he was downright unapproachable. There was the charm, after all. He was sure he made people feel like they could talk to him.

Grace stared at him, as if considering.

"Have you ever had any problem approaching me?" he asked, and he leaned toward her, just a little, without thinking about it.

Grace opened her mouth and then shut it before she finally said, "I can't even get you to tell me what I'm doing here, Raf."

"Right. Worth the trip though?"

"I'm inclined to think so, granted you won't be trying to harvest my organs or anything like that."

Rafael smirked. "All kidneys will remain intact."

Grace didn't smile, but there was a hint of something in her eyes. Call it a sparkle, perhaps. Rafael would take that as a win. But then she looked at him again with that way she had, full on eye contact, and he forgot how to be charming.

He started fidgeting and cracking his knuckles, a habit that had always driven his father mad. Confident, sophisticated people didn't fidget, apparently, according to the lord of the manor.

"So..." Grace said, prompting him again to explain why he'd dragged her out to this historic monument in the middle of the week.

"Well," Rafael started. He could do this. This was his livelihood. When he'd worked in finance and even with his new company, he'd always had a vision and a plan, and he was able to sell that plan to other people to make them see it too. Only now his only vision involved one thing: get Grace to come up with a plan. He didn't know why he was so sure that she would be able to figure it out, to make something of the little art gallery he couldn't even imagine. Alma's first suggestion that Grace could help him out had been totally casual, but for some reason, Rafael could feel it. Grace was the person to make this happen, the person to be his partner. He didn't believe in fate or destiny. He would never in a million years say that Grace had moved to Spain because she was meant to curate an art exhibit for him, obviously, but now she was here, and she might just be the perfect person for the job.

"Remember that client I told you about? The one with all the Picassos?"

Obviously, she remembered. They'd had like two conversations, and one of them had been about art.

Grace nodded, a loose strand of hair hanging in her face. "That wasn't very long ago, Raf."

She wasn't looking at him, and he had no way of reading her expression. He didn't want to just launch right into talking about the favor, so he tried another tactic. "Did you really write articles about Picasso?'

That got her to turn toward him. "Not about him exactly. Some of his contemporaries and influences," she said. "It was a chapter of my dissertation."

"A dissertation, wow. That sounds very official." What was he saying? *Ay Dios mio*, he was trying to be flattering, but he knew he sounded like an idiot, and Grace was staring at him like she thought so too.

"I thought maybe you could put some of that knowledge to good use." Was that condescending? Like she wasn't already putting that knowledge to good use? Like that knowledge was actually *useless*?

This was a disaster, seriously. He was asking for a very simple favor, just the tiniest bit of guidance, but he'd never wanted to bite his tongue so hard in his life, and she was just frowning at him. Then, she crossed her arms across her chest, and he knew he was losing her. It was so rare for him to have trouble convincing anyone of anything, except for maybe his father. Otherwise, it was easy—catering menus and invitations and monetary donations and *sign on the dotted line*. People were easy. They did what he wanted if they felt like they were getting something out of it too. Maybe that's what he was missing. What would Grace be getting out of this?

"Is there something else you wanted to say?" Grace asked, clearly ready to dismiss him and be on her way if he'd ever get to the point. "Or is that it?"

Rafael nodded. "Right, yes. I was just thinking. I met with Christian the other day. The client. And he's a little...unusual. I mean, not in a bad way. He knows what he wants, and he's very determined, but we have some differences of opinion. He wants to do this underground art exhibit in a place that's partially underground. In a cave, actually. Over in Sacromonte. You've heard of it?"

"I haven't."

"There are these cave houses over there that are very cool and historic, and he was mentioning that his wife might actually be a descendent of the community that lives there. Her ancestors were in Sacromonte." *What the hell was he talking about?*

Grace raised an eyebrow, but other than the confusion on her face, Rafael couldn't get a sense of what she might be thinking. He was rambling. He shut his mouth and paused, trying to make sense of his thoughts.

Grace bit her lip, and he watched as her tooth rubbed the pink flesh there. "Sorry," she said. "I think I might have lost you. This is about a cave?"

"This is about Picasso." *It's a sales pitch, Rafael. Start with what she knows. Dangle the carrot.* "And other artists, too. A whole collection." If only he could remember the other names Christian had listed, but *c'est la vie*. "At least one hundred paintings, Grace. They're going to be delivered to a cave to create a fantastic exhibit and event experience, but I don't know art like you do, and I'd like to bring you on board. To curate the exhibition, essentially."

Grace was quiet again. For a long time, she was quiet, and in the interim between him finishing his sentence and her finally saying something, she studied his face. He'd done his job, at last. She was intrigued. She was tempted. She might even be excited.

"I don't think so," she said without an ounce of feeling.

She was indifferent.

He could fix it. He tried to start again. "You don't want to have access to one hundred paintings by wildly famous artists? To examine them? To show them off however you please, within the confines of a cave, of course. You don't have any desire to spend your days surrounded by the work of one of the greatest painters that ever lived?"

Now he was getting into the swing of things and feeling like himself. That's what was in it for her, after all. Even if she didn't like the *man*, he could offer the art of Picasso and...other people. She loved these old artists, he just knew it, and Rafael could share them with her.

"I—" she started, seeming to turn this over in her mind.

Rafael flashed her a bright smile. This had to work.

"I don't think I can really work in another position." Grace looked off into the distance, to the gardens, as if eager to make a run for it. "My visa, you know?"

Rafael nodded. He hadn't really thought of that, but it was something they could overcome. "I'm sure my company can work something out," he said. "Or if you just come to the site once, maybe twice, I can take it from there, and then I'll give you whatever you want. Any favor you need or anything I can help with. Anything."

Lord, did this sound completely desperate? He knew it did. *Anything.* What did that even mean? What could he possibly do for her?

"Don't you think it would be strange, working with your sister's best friend and roommate?" Grace asked.

She was grasping at straws now. What did he care if she was Alma's friend? It made little difference to him. He just needed someone who knew Picasso. Someone who could possibly imagine how to cram these paintings into a cave without ruining them or making them look like shit. "Not a problem for me," he answered.

"It's not that I don't want to help you," she continued, pushing some hair behind her ear. His eyes followed her fingers as they slid down the silky locks toward the base of her throat. He swallowed.

"What is it then?" He tore his gaze from her collarbone and forced it back to her serious face.

"Rafael, there are way more qualified people than me that could do this. I've never curated anything before. And Picasso? I seriously don't know what to do with him. I'm sure you could find someone who would have a better idea."

Rafael exhaled. "Look, Christian doesn't want any kind of fancy museum curator or someone who's done this hundreds of times. He wants to do it all on his own, really, but I know we need help. You know about Picasso. You can offer some kind of balance, right? You said full-on emulation didn't seem appropriate, but what if that's exactly how Christian decides to present his art to the world? We need another perspective."

Grace tugged at the sleeve of her sweater. "I just don't really want to be a part of any of it, honestly. A secret exhibit only for rich people? A significant part of culture and history that only elite socialites get to see? The whole thing is a gatekeeping fantasy, and yes, art is a business and loads of money is exchanged, but that's not what I'm interested in. How could I work on a project that no one I know would even be allowed to visit? It's a project you barely told your sister about because it's top secret, and that's not really my thing."

Rafael pressed his lips together. She didn't want access to hundreds of Picasso paintings because this whole endeavor was too exclusive? Usually, people begged him for just a taste of one of these events, pleading for one invitation, one chance to get in, but she was getting all high and mighty about art being for rich people?

"Come on, Graciela. Even the artists knew their work was a commodity. Do you think they weren't in it for the money and fame?"

Admittedly, Rafael should have prepared a response to this particular concern, especially since they'd already had a similar argument over dinner. While he was prepared to tell her they would work really well together or that this was a once-in-a-lifetime opportunity, he didn't know how to alleviate her fears that this was just some over-the-top exhibit for a fancy man to show off his money to his fancy friends. Even if Christian was a nicer fancy man than most—far more palatable than Rafael's father, certainly—he was still just another billionaire with too much time on his hands, and Rafael had no way to deny it. Was this some kind of pretentious vanity endeavor? Sure, but it could still be *cool*.

"To have this kind of recognition, to bring people from all over the world? That's good for Granada, right?" It was the best he could come up with off the top of his head.

Grace cocked her head to the side. "I'm sure you'll figure this out. It sounds like you're really good at what you do, and I don't even think you need me. I'm sure it will work out for you, Raf."

He tried to keep his face neutral, but she was calling him by that nickname again, like they were casual and close. Rafael didn't know why it made his pulse race a bit faster, but he calmed down enough to remain still, determined not to give himself away.

"I think you're making a mistake, Graciela. How could you pass up this chance? Imagine going to your class and sharing all this first-hand knowledge with your students. You're not just walking through a museum here. You're up close and personal. You're creating it."

"Isn't the whole point that I wouldn't be able to tell my students about any of it?"

Rafael rolled his eyes. "Yeah, okay, maybe not all the details, but you could talk to them about it in general terms."

Grace shook her head, glancing into the distance. "Are you going to let me walk around the gardens?"

"I'm not holding you captive here. I'm just shocked that you won't even entertain the idea of it. I thought it would be a dream come true."

Grace narrowed her eyes at him. "There's an appeal to it, but I just don't think I'm the right fit. I mean it. I have no idea what your client might want."

"You don't have to worry about that part. I can handle him. I just need you to tell me about the paintings."

Grace bit her lip, and Rafael waited. Then, he found himself staring at her mouth, which clearly wasn't his fault, because she was the one drawing attention to it.

"I'm sorry, Raf. I don't think I'm going to change my mind."

Rafael sighed. Maybe she was right. Maybe he didn't really need her. He just needed to get back to the cave and figure things out for himself. Just because he didn't see it immediately didn't mean he couldn't accomplish this with a little hard work, a little trial and error, a little more research so he could at least remember the names of the artists.

"Right," he conceded. "Okay."

Grace yawned. "I'm tired anyway. I've already grown accustomed to my siesta nap."

He couldn't help smiling. She said it so seriously, her eyelids fluttering closed. "Well then, let's see the gardens and get you home for your beauty sleep, *princesa*."

She frowned again and slipped away from him, wandering ahead onto the path. He took long strides to catch up to her, realizing that even though he was frustrated by her refusal to assist him, he wanted to be beside her, to talk to her about anything. It was an inclination he still couldn't understand, and when she turned her head and started asking him questions about the castle in a fiery tone like she was angry even to be curious, he answered. He told her everything she wanted to know.

CHAPTER SEVEN

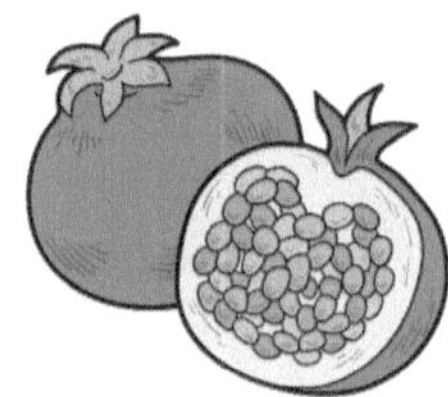

THE PUKE-BEFORE-CLASS FEELING SUBSIDED QUICKLY. In fact, Grace started to look forward to her classes more than she ever had before. Her students were actually engaged with the material. They got so excited about surrealism, they started talking loudly over each other. Sometimes they went on sudden rants in their first language, and since many of them had different first languages, the class became a beautiful cacophony of impassioned arguments. She'd never had to calm an art class down or ask her students to take a breath. She'd never had to let them know class time was over, and they would need to continue the discussion next time.

Class, teaching, *art.* Grace threw herself into them, the simple things she could control. No, she could not bring her grandmother back. She couldn't even find a way to cope with the grief, guilt, and constant ache. She also couldn't force herself to find a new forever with a different man now that the one she'd been counting on had ended. It turned out forever was far shorter than expected, and starting at square one didn't appeal to her at all.

But the paintings, the sculptures, the twentieth century masterpieces. She could escape into another world if she concentrated hard enough.

"Excuse me, Profesora Cameron?"

Professors weren't supposed to pick favorites, and she never would have admitted it, but Marco was quickly becoming Grace's favorite student. He wasn't afraid to ask questions and speak up in class, and he always seemed entirely comfortable with himself. His roots were showing in his bleach blonde faux-hawk, but it looked better that way somehow, like he styled it like that on purpose, and maybe he did.

"Like I said, you can all call me Grace."

"Yes, pardon. Grace." His voice echoed through the auditorium as the other students shuffled out of the room. "I brought the picture of my mother's painting. I asked her about her influences, and she stared at me like I had three heads, but I thought you might like to see it?"

Grace smiled and leaned toward his phone. "Of course." The photo was bright on the screen, and just as Marco had described, it showed a vase of colorful flowers done in oil, reminiscent of any number of flower vase still lifes and well done too. It was clear that the artist had experience and had perfected her craft. "It's beautiful," Grace said. "Your mother is quite talented."

"You think so? She saw me taking the picture and couldn't imagine what I was doing with it. I think she was embarrassed when I told her I wanted to show it to you, but I insisted you wouldn't judge."

Grace couldn't seem to stop staring at the phone. A vase of flowers. It wasn't exactly an unexpected subject, but there was something about this painting, the way it played with light and had a real background full of other significant objects. There were little details there Grace hadn't noticed at first—a dirty dish, a baby bottle, a wet sponge. The flowers were beautiful; they were the focal point, but there was something more there. There was life. This was Marco's mother's vase of flowers from her garden in her very real and slightly messy kitchen. Grace loved it instantly.

"Profesora Cameron?" Marco must have been talking, but Grace could tune out anything when she was staring at a work like this, even if she didn't mean to.

"Yes, sorry. I—" *Words, words.* "I really like this, Marco."

"See, this is what I keep telling *mi mamá.* This is something, correct? But she doesn't want to hear it." He eagerly searched Grace's face, so thrilled to have a second opinion. Maybe her view didn't mean very much, but it meant something to him, her young, optimistic student who adored his mamá.

"Yes," Grace breathed, still strangely dazed. "This is something."

She walked home with a head full of flowers. She appreciated a good distraction these days. Even Rafael's little pitch for her to curate the art exhibit offered an escape from her usual loop of thoughts—the conversations she played in her head again and again. The day her grandmother had finally confessed that she was dying was like a broken record in Grace's brain. She'd played the memory so many times that it was almost distorted, and she couldn't quite make sense of it all—why Gram hadn't told her from the day she was diagnosed, why she would keep something like that a secret. The guilt of not knowing, of not being there from the start, had weighed on her, and she didn't know how to get out from under it.

For that reason, Grace rather liked being able to focus on Rafael's persuasion tactics—his bright grin and his passionate appeal to her love of twentieth century art, even though he clearly couldn't remember everything Christian had in the collection. She'd almost laughed at how much Raf tried to sell it to her, and she had to admit, if anyone could sell something with charm and good looks alone, it was him. He'd even smiled at her and told jokes. Kind of.

Obviously, the idea of hundreds of paintings in an actual historic cave was enticing, but she wasn't kidding about the visa problem and her concerns about the exclusivity. Shouldn't the people of Granada get to see their own museum? And Picasso, ugh. Some of the biggest museums in the world weren't quite sure how to present him, to reconcile the genius of his art and the reality of who he was. Grace certainly didn't have any clue how she would handle him. In class, she just did her best to tell the truth, to present all the information and let her students decide for themselves what to make of it. They looked at one of his paintings of Françoise Gilot, and they talked about an excerpt from her memoir, about Picasso holding a cigarette to her cheek, watching it burn her. He was It wasn't like there was a dearth of artists who were terrible people; it was something they came up against quite regularly, and Grace included it in the discussion of their work.

She also had to admit, even if she refused to ever say it aloud, there was also an inkling of fear about working that closely to Rafael, though she couldn't pinpoint its source. Was she afraid he would be too bossy or get angry with her about the placement of some painting, that he would be utterly disappointed by her efforts, or was she afraid of something else? No reason to examine that too closely or tease it out.

Marco's mother's painting, though, that gave Grace *feelings.* Her grandmother would have loved it, how it was so beautiful and honest at the same time, a kitchen she would have recognized. Grace perceived the comfort of it as well, and she wished she could live in that painting like it was her home…a home that no longer existed for her.

Sometimes when Grace thought of her grandmother, she thought of Mary Cassatt's *In the Loge,* not only because Gram loved that piece, but also because there was a quiet power in the woman in the painting. She was bold and present and active, but still, she had her limitations. Grace thought her grandmother had felt a twinge of familiarity when she saw the woman. It was the kind of thing that spoke to you, even when you weren't sure why. The coffee table book where they'd look at Cassatt's work was in storage with most of her grandmother's things, but Grace took out her phone and pulled up an image.

Memories stirred to the surface. *"Looking at the Cassatt again, Gram? I'm going to get you a poster print of it for the ceiling over your bed."*

Grace wished she could call Gram and tell her about the flower vase. She wished she could call Gram and tell her anything.

She was so lost in the thought of it, she didn't notice the people rushing through her apartment building or the frantic conversations of neighbors in the hallway. She marched up the stairs in a daze, ready to lie down in her bed for the only good sleep she ever got. Night was for insomnia and sorrow, but there was something about the light through her window in the late afternoon, something that allowed her to nap and feel safe.

It was on the second floor of the building that she realized the floor was wet, but it didn't fully register in her brain. Grace kept walking through the water as if it was just a figment of her imagination, as if the mess would simply disappear at any moment.

It didn't disappear, though. In fact, it seemed to get worse, and Grace found herself swiveling back and forth, staring at the slick floor in silence, trying to understand. After a moment, she held her breath and opened the apartment door, only to discover that the flood was in the apartment as well. She scanned the ground, frantically trying to locate the source, to make sense of the damp living room, but the pieces weren't arranging themselves into an understandable pattern in her mind. "Shit," she whispered, still baffled about what was happening but sure it was awful as she pulled out her phone and started to call Alma.

Apparently, water heaters burst. Like, literally, they could explode and flood an entire nearby apartment, soaking the floors and carpet and furniture. Wet rugs did not smell great. Shop vacs and open windows to let things air out only did so much. Oh, and according to the landlord, parts of the floor really needed to be pulled up and replaced in such a situation.

Grace paced back and forth on a limited path next to the dining table in Obinna's studio apartment, trying to figure out a plan. She'd only been in Spain for a month, and here was yet another disaster to contend with. Somehow, it barely registered anymore, even though she didn't have a place to live. Disasters were a dime a dozen these days. Alma stared up at her from the couch, tossing out ideas for a temporary place to stay.

"You can't be that far away, Grace," she said. "It's madness."

Alma's landlord had been kind enough to offer one of his empty apartments for their use while the contractors were working on the place, and it was only a fifty-minute bus ride away even if it was in a sketchy rundown building. Alma had immediately declined the offer, but Grace supposed she would at least have to take a look, because what other options did she have? Sure, Obinna had already proposed that Alma and Grace could stay with him. In his studio apartment. Alma could share his bed, and Grace could...sleep on an air mattress in the middle of the room indefinitely? One night had been enough.

She would pass on that offer, which meant she was off to check out the rundown place in the middle of nowhere. Maybe it wouldn't be so bad, and plenty of people commuted fifty minutes. Most importantly, it was temporary.

Alma volunteered her brother as the perfect helper to escort Grace to view the apartment. "He can drive you!" she'd announced, as if Raf didn't have a job to worry about, and the matter was already settled. Alma needed to be in the lab, but Rafael was flexible. He could make himself available in a crisis, especially since he didn't have client meetings or vendor research on the calendar. Alma had strong-armed him into being Grace's chauffeur for the day before Grace could offer a single protest.

"I know it might be awkward, but I really wish you'd just stay with Obinna and me. It will be cramped, but we could manage. It will be like a —um—what do you call it?"

"An orgy?"

"A slumber party! But I'm glad to see you still have jokes."

Grace glanced at the deflated mattress slumped against the wall. "Obinna is so kind to offer, but I'm sure he doesn't want his girlfriend's best friend sleeping in the same room."

"What about my parents? They have plenty of room. It's still a bit far out. You couldn't walk to the campus anymore, but I could go with you. We could both stay there."

Grace crossed her arms. "I know you don't want to stay with your parents, Alma. You would fight with your mother constantly. Seriously, this isn't a problem you have to solve for me, and you have to take the opportunity to spend extra time with Obinna. This will be fun for the two of you, and I'll be fine on my own."

"Rafael?" Alma tried another possibility as if Grace hadn't even spoken. "He has an extra room."

"You're kidding."

"What? That could work. I just feel terrible for putting you through this. I was supposed to protect you. All I have to offer is some shitty rental insurance that barely covers anything. Or Obinna, my parents, or Rafael."

"This isn't your fault, babe." Grace said. "And I'll figure something out without you bending over backwards to fix it. End of discussion. Go to the lab already. I'll be fine."

Alma puckered her perfect lips in a pout, but she still accepted her defeat. She crossed the small room and gave Grace a quick cheek-kiss, before doing as she was told and going to the lab.

"Tough week?" Rafael asked as Grace climbed into the car. He was wearing a white shirt with a button undone and damn it if she didn't stare at the triangle of bare chest peeking out, just for a moment.

"You could say that." She flipped her hair out of the way and put on the seatbelt, and when she glanced up to find Raf's eyes on her, he simply gave her a lopsided grin and turned back to the steering wheel.

"Ready?" he asked.

Grace nodded, but since he wasn't looking at her anymore, she took a breath and coughed out, "yes."

There was something about the small space of the car that made her feel a little claustrophobic. Rafael's arms were right there, almost brushing against hers, and his scent filled the entire vehicle. She *smelled* him even though she didn't mean to, and he smelled like warm laundry right out of the dryer. "Thank you," she said, "for driving me. I know you probably had other plans today, so I really appreciate you taking time—"

"Alma was right." He cut in with a sigh.

"What?"

"She said you would ramble on and on about how grateful you are to me just for giving you a lift. It's nice that you're so appreciative, Graciela, but you don't have to thank me. If the situation were reversed, I know you'd do the same for me."

"I don't have a car."

Raf let out a little laugh. "Fair point."

Grace leaned back in the seat trying to relax, but without her overwrought outpouring of gratitude, she wasn't sure what else to talk about, and the silence hovered over them.

"Are you feeling homesick for America?" Rafael asked.

Grace glanced at him, surprised he'd made the effort to start a conversation. She wasn't really homesick for *America.* She was homesick for the things that weren't there anymore, things that no longer existed anywhere. Not that she was going to start wading into her emotional turmoil with Alma's older brother…again. "Mostly, I could just go for a good hot dog," she said.

She swallowed as a lump formed in her throat. Beer and hot dogs, that was how she and Derek celebrated everything. The end of the semester? Derek's big raise? Anniversaries? They marked every occasion with beer and hot dogs. It had been a long time since Grace felt like celebrating, though.

Rafael was aghast. "A hot dog? No."

She shrugged. "Something from Portillo's. That's all I want."

"A hot dog, Graciela?" Raf shook his head in disgust, just as she suspected he would.

She exhaled a little laugh, inordinately pleased to have irked him. "Is there something in particular you miss from your time in America?"

He pressed his lips together, thinking. "As far as American cuisine goes, there is not much to miss. Certainly not hot dogs."

Grace rolled her eyes.

"But there was a pizza place in New York City. Scarr's. I get a craving for that on occasion."

"You like pizza, Raf?"

He frowned. "Is that so hard to believe?"

Grace smiled and shook her head. She definitely wouldn't have pegged him as a "craving a slice" kind of guy. "And that's it? Nothing else you miss about America?"

He seemed to be thinking very seriously about the question. "New York was too loud and crowded and over-the-top for me. I liked the M&M store in Time's Square though." He smirked but didn't look at her.

Grace's mouth dropped. "Did you just make a joke, Rafael?"

His smirk suddenly turned into a laugh. "Why are you so surprised?"

Grace was somewhat hopeful as they neared the landlord's building with an empty unit. Yes, this was the middle of nowhere. They passed the bus stop where Grace would catch the bus every day, and it was so dead, Grace wouldn't be surprised to see a tumbleweed rolling by. If they had tumbleweeds in Spain. But the drive hadn't been terrible, and a quiet little area certainly wasn't the worst thing in the world.

Some of the houses they passed appeared nice and well maintained, and even though Grace really was not looking forward to almost two hours of bussing every single day, she wanted this to work out. If she could get her shit together enough so she could avoid begging Alma for more help, she would consider it a win. It was temporary, after all. Her grandma always said you could do anything for two weeks. There had been no promises about how long it would take to get back into Alma's apartment, but it couldn't be too long, right?

Then they pulled up to the building, and Grace's grand ideas for making this work started to wane. But she could handle chipped paint. She could handle broken gutters. She could maybe handle rickety stairs. She had to.

Rafael scanned the scene and made a noise.

"What?"

He turned and raised an eyebrow as if to say *what do you think?*

"It has some cosmetic issues, but it's not terrible."

"It looks like your apartment here is ten times more likely to flood than the last one."

Grace bit her lip. Raf followed her up the stairs, and when Grace got to the open unit, she put the key from the landlord in the lock and turned. It seemed to work easily, but when she tried the door, it wouldn't budge.

"Allow me," Rafael said. He turned the knob. He jiggled the handle. The lock wasn't the problem, it was more like the entire door just didn't want to move. Raf shoved a shoulder into it and then gave it a kick. Finally, it busted open.

Grace didn't need to look over at him to know the face he was making, but still, she tried to tell herself that she could do this. She wasn't a *princesa*. She didn't need perfect conditions. She just needed a place to stay for a little while.

They walked through the musty unit and uttered not a single word until she reached the bedroom. Then, she spotted the cockroach in the corner and backed up so quickly she fell right into Rafael. He caught her easily, his arms pressed against hers, his breath on her neck.

"What is it?" He followed her gaze to the massive bug and nodded without letting go of her. "Ah. Let's go outside and discuss."

"Okay," Grace said, trying to keep her voice steady. "Just a minute."

She walked into the dingy bathroom with chipped tile and stared at the ceiling, trying to prevent tears from escaping down her face. She did not want to cry in front of Rafael. She didn't want to cry at all anymore. She was so sick of it. She pressed her fingers under her eyes as if she could squeeze her tear ducts shut and took a few deep breaths until she felt composed again. She remembered looking at apartments when she and Derek had decided to move in together, how everything had felt so fresh and exciting, like a whole new life was waiting for them. This experience was…the opposite. She splashed some cold water on her face and inhaled a deep breath through her nose. She couldn't fall apart again, not now. She refused to let one crappy apartment get the best of her. She exhaled through her mouth and fixed her hair. Then she walked back into the empty living room to join Rafael.

"Everything okay?" he asked.

She nodded. "Ready."

"Good." He ushered her toward the front door. "Let's get out of here."

It took a while to get the door back into place well enough to lock it, but they managed eventually, and then Rafael stood on the sidewalk by his car with his hands on his hips. "You cannot live there," he said, as if he'd just been waiting for the appropriate moment to make this announcement. "You won't even be able to get the door open in the first place."

Grace stared at the building. She knew he was right, but what choice did she have? There was no other viable option, and she would rather punch through her door each night than sleep at the foot of Alma and Obinna's bed. "It's not so bad. It could be much worse." She could fear the tears welling up again and tried to turn her face from Raf's line of sight.

"It could be worse, certainly, but there's no reason to live here, Graciela. You don't need to be out in the middle of nowhere all alone."

"What would you suggest I do then?" she asked, a spark of anger flaring inside of her. Water was rushing over her cheeks, and she tried to wipe it away discreetly.

"Well." Rafael paused, running a hand through his hair. "It's just for a little while." He cleared his throat. "Come live with me."

She couldn't help turning back toward him then to gauge if he was serious, but when she did his expression changed, his eyes filling with concern. "Grace," he whispered, reaching out a hand.

She didn't stop him as he pressed the pad of his thumb to one of her tears. Then he let out breathy laugh. "I didn't realize just the idea of living with me would make you cry. I promise it wouldn't be that terrible."

She laughed in spite of everything and shook her head. The idea of living with him was completely ridiculous, but she appreciated his generosity. She never would have expected him to be so soft and comforting.

"Come on, *princesa,*" he continued. "What do you say?"

CHAPTER EIGHT

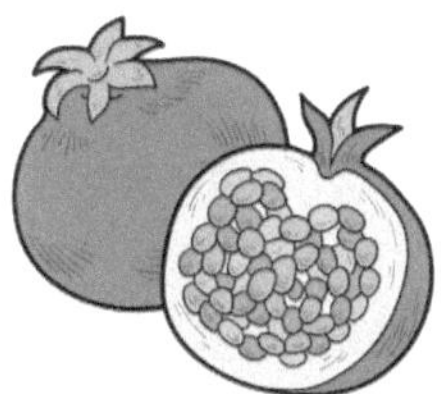

"NO." Rafael watched as Grace pressed her lips into a line and clenched her hands into fists. She was as stubborn as a mule even in these terrible circumstances. "I don't want to put you out like that, Raf," she said, "and we—we don't even know each other."

She was right, of course. They didn't know each other, but since when was that a requirement for sharing an apartment? "Look, there is no way I'm letting you stay here, so either you bunk up with Alma and Obinna in his tiny apartment, or you come to stay with me. I have an extra room. It's not big, by any means, but I'm sure we can fit your bed in there. I don't know about the table or desk, but you'd have your own room and a safe place to sleep. And it won't be for very long, right? You'll be back to your place in no time. It's no inconvenience."

Grace started to pace on the sidewalk, and Rafael could tell she was considering it. It really wasn't a big deal to him; they would probably hardly see each other, and it was just a temporary fix.

Grace paused. "I hope it will be quick, but the landlord didn't give us a timeline. They have to replace the whole floor, so I'm not sure—"

Rafael waved a hand. "Doesn't matter. As long as you need."

She resumed pacing for a moment before pausing again. "I could pay you rent, of course. This isn't just, like, a favor. I can give you something."

Rafael considered this. His chivalry refused to allow her to pay, but he knew she wanted to offer some kind of contribution. She would never agree if she saw it as anything less than a fair deal.

Suddenly, an idea lit inside him like a match. "No money," he asserted, and when Grace started to protest immediately, he kept talking. "But you could just take a glance at some pictures of Christian's collection. Give me your opinion, a little insight, any ideas you have. That's it."

Grace froze with her mouth hanging open. Then she narrowed her eyes at him. "Was this your plan all along? Bring me out to the middle of nowhere so I'm stranded and desperate and you can convince me to work on your art project?"

Rafael raised his hands and backed away. "Not at all. I just had the idea, and it's a *good* idea. You'll be able to live in a safe environment without feeling like you owe me anything. And the art thing isn't a job. I swear I won't make you lift a finger. I just want to see what you think."

"You think we can be roommates?"

Rafael put his hands in his pockets and leaned against the car. "Why not?"

"We don't exactly get along."

"We get along fine, Grace. I don't think we need to be *friends*."

"But if you drive me nuts, it might upset Alma. I won't even be able to complain to her about you because you're her brother."

"Why would *I* be the one driving *you* nuts? Maybe you'll drive me nuts." There was some precedent for that after all. "And I'm sure Alma would love to hear you complain about me. She'll even go first."

Something happened then that Rafael wasn't expecting. Grace laughed. A real, honest-to-goodness laugh that rushed out of her mouth and sailed through the air around him. He remembered that laugh. He'd heard it so many times ten years ago—loud and bold and carefree—but it had been lost somewhere before she returned to Spain. He couldn't help the stupid grin that spread across his face at the sound of it.

"Why am I considering this?" Grace put a hand to her forehead. "This is a terrible idea, Raf."

His smile widened. "Honestly, what could go wrong? Your apartment will be ready before you know it, and you'll barely remember that I ever had to beg you not to live in this creepy cockroach building. And you can do anything for two weeks, right?"

Rafael was so close, he could taste it. With her help, maybe this underground exhibition thing could turn into a success after all. With her help, maybe he could stay in the good graces of his company's largest client and start making some real profits. And Christian would tell his rich friends about the whole thing, too, of course. Christian would brag to anyone who would listen, and Rafael would be the person who made it all happen.

She eyed him warily. "Did I say that?"

"Say what?"

"The comment about how you can do anything for two weeks?"

"Oh, um, I don't think so? I was just guessing how long it might take."

She was quiet for a long moment, and then she started pacing again. He wished he could hear the back-and-forth conversation that must be happening in her brain, but it didn't matter. She was going to say yes. He could feel it.

Finally, she halted on the sidewalk in front of him and stuck out her hand. "Alright," she said. "You've got a deal." He took her hand in his, ignoring the soft curve of her fingers and the way his palm was so much bigger it swallowed hers whole. This was a business transaction like any other. Handshakes were not sexy. The press of her thumb on the back of his hand was *not* sexy. The determined look in her eyes as she stared at him was *not* sexy.

It was then that Rafael started to worry Grace might be right about one thing. Perhaps living with her really was a terrible idea after all.

Despite his earlier confidence, Rafael wasn't really sure Grace's bed would fit in the tiny room in his apartment until the moment they managed to get it in there. It was crowded, but at least she had a place to sleep, and she had a closet and a window and a door that would close and open, all the way, without any force.

When he'd offered her the room, he hadn't bothered to picture the actual living-together part of the equation. But when she arrived in his apartment with most of the items she'd brought to Spain, he started to consider what being roommates might look like. Would she just stay shut up in her tiny room with her laptop and a stack of art history textbooks? Would they eat dinner together? Would they sit side-by-side on the couch in silence while he typed up emails to various potential clients, and she read through a list of American novels?

It was night one, and his palms were sweaty.

The last time he'd lived with someone was in college, but Rafael had never lived with a woman, and certainly not a woman he was attracted to. He kept telling himself it didn't matter. It was temporary. She was Alma's best friend, and he was relatively sure Grace didn't even like him. They would keep their distance and act casual and limit their topics of conversation to Pablo Picasso, and she would probably get so annoyed about his ignorance on the subject she wouldn't bother even trying to speak to him anymore.

"What is this?" Grace asked, pointing at a bowl of fruit on the counter. "You planning to paint a still life?"

"No," Rafael replied. "I'm planning to eat fruit."

Grace leaned over the bowl, inspecting its contents. "What are they? Some kind of weird apple?"

Rafael walked toward her and rested an arm on the counter. "You've never had a..." Rafael paused, trying to think of the word in English. "A pomegranate?"

Grace shook her head. "Never had the pleasure. I think I've tasted pomegranate juice. Does that count?"

"No." Rafael fought off an image of the juice running over her lips. "Especially if you don't even remember it. Want to try one?"

She wrinkled her nose. "Um, maybe another time. I'm not really hungry."

"Another time then. You don't want to miss out, especially because it's the fruit of our province."

Grace rested her chin in her hand, as if settling in. "What do you mean?"

Rafael held up one of the round fruits. "Granada. It got its name from this. There's even a picture of one on the Spanish flag."

Rafael couldn't help but notice Grace leaning in even closer to him. "Do you all grow a lot of them here or something? Where did that come from?"

"There are different stories. Some say that it was a symbol of the Catholics—Ferdinand and Isabella using it to mark their victory over the Moors. Some say the name was given by the Romans because there was a fortress where a pomegranate tree grew. There's also a legend that someone saw a sunset over the city that looked like an open pomegranate."

"Okay, now that you mention it, I think I have seen these on signs around the city. I didn't realize that's what they were."

"Yes, it's an important symbol for us."

Grace picked up one of the fruits and held it in her hand, her fingers curling around it as if memorizing its shape. "Now I'm going to see them everywhere. It's like when you're pregnant and you see pregnant ladies everywhere."

Rafael's eyes went wide. "You've been pregnant?" he blurted out before realizing what he was saying. "I mean, sorry. I didn't mean to—"

Grace smiled. "No, that's just a thing they say. I guess when you are pregnant, you're more aware of other pregnant people in everyday life. You notice them more because it's on your mind."

"Ah." Rafael nudged her shoulder with his and relaxed again. "And now that you are a pomegranate, you will notice more pomegranates. Makes sense."

Grace laughed again, just as she had outside the shitty apartment. The sound echoed through his bones. "Yes, I will be one with the pomegranate and find all the other pomegranates all over this town. I know you said you plan to eat them, but these do really look like they're begging to be painted."

"I don't know if you should paint them. They're already a nice color, don't you think?" His mouth lifted at the corner.

"No I meant—" Grace started, but then she noticed his smirk and her gaze locked with his. "Did you just make two jokes in a row? Who are you?"

Rafael scoffed. "What do you mean? I make jokes."

"*Now* you do, I guess."

"When didn't I make jokes? I can be funny."

Grace kept staring at him, as if trying to determine if this was some kind of trick. "You… never mind."

Rafael leaned even further toward her. "You have to tell me what you're thinking now. There's no turning back."

Grace placed the fruit back in the bowl and shrugged. "I just don't remember you ever making a joke before. I don't even remember you laughing."

"Before?"

"You know, forever ago when we met. In Barcelona."

"Oh." Rafael's palms were sweating again. He thought they'd both been avoiding the topic of *before*. He didn't want Grace to think about that. He didn't want her to remember the almost-kiss or how she'd turned away at the last second. In fact, he was still hoping she'd forgotten it altogether. "I wasn't very funny then," he admitted. "I took myself too seriously, and I expected the same from everyone else."

"And you're different now?" Grace asked, giving him that look she had, the one that saw him so clearly. He didn't know how they'd gotten to this point. Less than an hour ago he'd determined they would only discuss safe topics. Picasso. Pomegranates were probably harmless, too. But talking about their past and how he'd changed was too personal, too intimate. Who knew where that would lead?

That didn't stop the next words from coming out of his mouth with a gravelly rasp that scraped over his question. "Am I different now?"

Their faces were so near to each other, as if they'd been moving fractions of centimeters closer without either of them noticing. Rafael could hear his own ragged breath. How had they ended up like this? Why hadn't she backed away? Why hadn't he?

He knew one thing for certain. He was not going to try to kiss her again. She was his roommate now and his sister's best friend. Her life was in complete disarray, which was the reason she was here in the first place —in Spain and in his apartment. And, even if he was starting to think maybe she didn't completely dislike him, that didn't mean she actively *liked* him either.

Finally, she eased her body away from the counter, away from him. Her only response to his question was a small shrug. "It's been a long day," she said. "I should probably get some rest."

"Of course. I hope everything's okay for you in the room. Is there anything else you need?"

She shook her head. "It's perfect actually. I love the little window and the view. You're lucky you're up on a hill and not just staring at the building across the street. You can see trees and rooftops. Maybe I'll even look out and see if I can find a pomegranate on the side of a building somewhere."

Rafael smiled. "I'm glad it's working out."

Grace pushed some of her dirty blonde hair behind her ear. "Let me know when you have those pictures from Christian's collection."

"Of course. Don't worry, I'm holding you to our deal. I just thought I would let you get settled first."

"Good." She bobbed her head. "Okay then. Goodnight."

"Goodnight, Graciela," Rafael said. She turned away, and he watched her move through the apartment, her steps careful as she maneuvered the coffee table and the sofa. When she reached the bedroom, Rafael thought she may have hesitated, but she didn't look back. At last, she walked into her new space and closed the door.

She would be right there all night, just across the hall from him, lying on a bed, sleeping, *breathing*. Something about it sent a shiver up the back of his neck.

He let out a loud exhale. If he was going to get through this, he needed to hold firm to his boundaries. No more talking about the past or his hopefully improved personality. No more deep dives into her personal life, even if he hated to think of everything she'd been going through the last several months. No more staring deeply into each other's eyes for no reason. Pomegranates and Picasso. Those were the safe topics, and that's what they would be sticking to from now on.

Grace preferred tea in the mornings, but she sometimes switched to coffee for the caffeine boost since she'd been sleeping so terribly. She listened to podcasts too loudly in her headphones, so loud Rafael could hear the American accents when she walked by him. She liked beer, but she was a slow drinker, usually unable to get through more than one without feeling bloated. She liked cheese, but she ate it far too quickly. Rafael had to make his own bowl of queso if he wanted a chance to enjoy a bite of it.

He didn't mean to learn these things, especially not in such a short amount of time. Again and again, he reminded himself of the boundaries. Pomegranates and Picasso, he repeated like a mantra, as if he could create a wall in his mind to keep her out, as if he could prevent any more knowledge from getting past that very specific barrier. It was a flawed system, though. He didn't mean to pay any attention, but it seemed impossible to ignore the little details of Grace's existence as he shared his space with her. She left her hairbrush on the counter, which was disgusting. She walked around the apartment while brushing her teeth. She left socks on the floor in the living room, but they always seemed to disappear before he could comment on their presence.

He couldn't help talking to her, as well. She asked him an endless series of questions whenever they were in the same room. Why did he live in the US? Why did he come back? How did he get his company started? What was his favorite project? She was happiest after her siesta, and she would watch cooking shows on her laptop even though she hated to cook. Then she would work on her lectures, scouring the internet for pictures of famous paintings for her presentations.

"How'd you get into this stuff?" he'd asked her once when he saw a collage of abstract art on her laptop screen.

She turned to look at him, as if just noticing he was in the room. "Into what?"

"I don't know." He shrugged, then pointed a finger at the screen. "Whatever this is."

Grace smiled as she studied the images. "It started with Gram," she said. "She didn't study it or anything. She worked in a cafeteria, but she always loved art and traveling. Curated cultural experiences, I guess," she joked, mimicking his words to describe his company. "She took me to museums as early as I can remember."

Rafael nodded. "She liked this, too? This weird stuff?"

Grace let out a little laugh. "No, actually. When I started getting into abstract art as a teenager, she didn't understand it. Thought it was just a phase of my rebellious youth."

Rafael leaned in closer, squinting his eyes at the screen. "I don't blame her," he teased.

"It grows on you," Grace said, a hint of a smile still lingering on her lips. "Just wait. After you work on the exhibition some more, the art might surprise you." He hadn't wanted to push her too hard to help with the exhibition, but they'd started to discuss it more and more. He still had time before the paintings were ready to be moved, and he wanted to give her some space to get settled, but they'd started to talk about some of the details, little by little. Still, he didn't mean for those conversations to get so wrapped up in their personal lives as well.

All of it was accidental. Talking with her about everything, getting to know her. Rafael especially didn't plan to let her get to know him. He still felt safe, though. Even if he was attracted to her, they hadn't crossed any lines. All of it was perfectly friendly.

"What about you?" Grace had asked. "How'd you learn about architecture?"

Rafael thought for a moment. He certainly hadn't studied architecture, even if he would have liked to, but he couldn't help being fascinated by different spaces, how they were designed, how they were used, practical function and impractical beauty. "I don't know," he said. "It definitely wasn't something anyone encouraged."

Grace cocked her head at him. "Really? Well, let me be the first to encourage you. Your knowledge of the Alhambra was astounding."

Rafael grinned. "And here I was thinking you were there against your will the whole time."

Grace had thrown her head back in a silent laugh, and Rafael felt his heart speed up. In a perfectly *friendly* way, of course.

Maybe they'd gotten to know each other and spent more time together than he'd anticipated, but this was a good stopping point. Attraction was easy to come by. A nice chat wasn't so unusual. He and Grace would be friends, which was more than he expected, but that was all. It was nothing out of the ordinary.

"Well, I have to be nicer to you now that you've let me live with you," she'd said.

He tried not to notice the way her cheeks turned pink when she laughed. He tried not to notice the way her lips gleamed after a fresh coat of balm. He tried not to notice the glimmer in her eyes when she teased him. All of that could be overcome. They could just be *nice,* and that was enough.

CHAPTER NINE

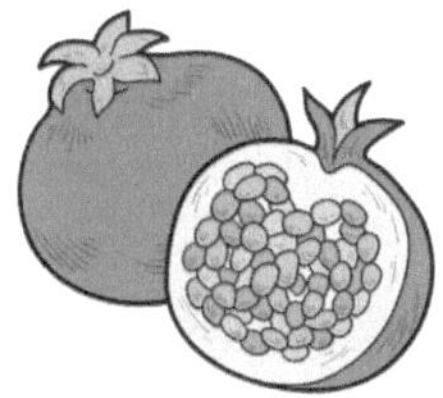

"SHE DIDN'T BELIEVE ME," Marco complained as he perched on the edge of the huge metal desk after class.

"Didn't believe what?" Grace tugged on the sleeve of her cardigan and scratched her arm. She liked dressing like a professor, and she liked how the cardigan looked, but she was also hot and itchy from standing in the front of the room, pacing around and lecturing her students about Futurism.

"That you liked her painting. I explained how I just wanted to show you, and she said you only told me you liked it to be nice. I think she's self-conscious about it, but it's hanging in our entryway! And it's beautiful!"

Grace grinned at his enthusiasm. "It *is* beautiful. And I would be happy to tell her that in person and to see more of her work. I mean, I'm not an artist or an art critic. I have no connections, Marco. I'm just a fan, and I have no reason to pretend to think her painting is brilliant."

Marco swung his legs back and forth. "But this is your *thing*. You know this stuff better than anybody else in my life."

Grace tried to reply, but she wasn't sure what to say. She wasn't sure she'd ever been admired by someone for her knowledge of art history. Most people seemed rather indifferent about it.

Marco jumped off the desk, oblivious to Grace's inner struggle. "You should meet her," he continued. "Could you come over to dinner? Or is that not allowed?"

"Well, I don't think there are explicit rules against that, but—"

Marco smacked his forehead. "Sorry, that was a weird thing to ask, huh? Felipe told me not to ask."

"Who's Felipe?" Grace swiped a hand across her forehead.

"My boyfriend. He explicitly told me not to be a creep about it. What if we met at a restaurant or something and you didn't have to come to my house?" Marco turned his whole body toward her, tense with anticipation.

"I think that could work. Maybe we could do some kind of field trip. Invite the whole class. But does your mother even want to meet me? It sounds like she might not be very enthusiastic about the whole idea."

Marco's shoulders relaxed. "She will be. I know she will. Actually, I'm not entirely sure, because she doesn't talk about her painting very much, and I kind of have to pry it out of her, but I can tell it's something important. It means a lot."

Grace tried not to show her skepticism. She wanted to meet Marco's mom and get the full picture for herself. Pun intended. "Well then, we should plan something she will enjoy. I really would like to see her work in-person."

"Yes!" Marco rushed forward and wrapped Grace in a tight hug before remembering himself and releasing her. "Sorry, I'm just too excited. Her work is amazing, and I just want her to be appreciated by someone other than me. Someone who knows about this stuff."

Grace grabbed her bag and threw it over her shoulder. She couldn't believe how easily Marco made her smile, and she was happy to return the favor whenever she could. "I'm excited, too. I would love to see more of her paintings."

"It's not so bad, is it?" Alma asked, her eyes darting around Grace's little room.

Grace sat on her bed and stared out the small window. She loved the view. She'd been looking out the window a lot since she moved in. "It's not so bad."

"You're comfortable? I feel terrible that you just moved across the world only to be displaced almost immediately."

Alma dove onto the bed and began to analyze her best friend's face in much the same way she had been eyeing the bedroom. Grace trained her expression into a smile, though she didn't have to pretend too much. Everything was going as well as it could be, given the circumstances.

"And I know Rafa can be a pain in the butt. I hope he's not giving you a hard time."

Grace shook her head. When she'd imagined what it would be like to live with Rafael as they stood on that sidewalk in front of the nearly dilapidated building, she'd imagined distance. Silence. Separation. He'd made a point of letting her know she would have a room with a door, and she kind of thought he expected her to stay there, relegated to her own little corner of the apartment, not bothering him.

In reality, their experience as roommates for the past several days had greatly deviated from her expectations. She and Rafael talked on occasion. They shared *buñuelos de bacalao* at the kitchen counter and drank beers on the couch. The other night, she'd sat with her legs tucked up under her and a can of Estrella Galicia in her hand and told him about Marco and his mother's painting. He'd told her how he didn't know how in the world they would pull off this cave business, how it was the only project that had ever given him this much grief. He'd worked on some impressive stuff—fundraising galas, celebrity birthday parties, and staging the VIP area at music festivals. Usually, he was able to work it all out, even the major kinks and problems. People respected him, and he could get his way when he needed to.

But not this time.

Grace couldn't help feeling a little sorry for him as she'd watched his throat work to swallow another gulp of beer. He really cared about pulling off the cave exhibit and making a good impression, and the complexities of the whole thing was stressing him out.

"I'll see what I can do, Raf," she'd told him. "But I don't know if I'm going to have any solutions for you." She certainly didn't want to get his hopes up. It wasn't like she had any experience with curating exhibits or appeasing billionaires or…caves.

"I have a good feeling about this, Grace Cameron." He'd still been smiling, but there was something still and serious in his eyes. "I think you're just the person for the job."

Grace didn't know why he was so confident about it. Maybe he was in so far over his head, he would have taken help from anyone. She'd taken another sip from her can, tasting the bitter hops on her tongue and trying not to think about the way he looked at her sometimes, as if she would somehow have all the answers. She wasn't sure why she was so loath to disappoint him.

Grace pulled herself from the memory and turned toward Alma on the little bed before resting her head on her arm. "Rafael's been fine. I can handle him."

"Thank goodness for that. If it were anyone else, I'd be worried, though I don't know whether I would be more concerned about him driving you mad or trying to hook up with you. Admittedly, he's known for his powers of seduction. But if there's anyone that's immune to his charms, it's you, Gracie."

Grace stared down at her finger as she traced shapes on the bedspread. She must be blushing, but she would do her best to hide it from Alma. If there was anyone who was immune to Rafael's charms, maybe it *was* Grace. She'd resisted him once, after all. Just barely. And it wasn't like he was currently trying to seduce her. He'd done nothing to indicate he had any interest in her beyond her art brain and knowledge of Pablo Picasso. He'd been a perfect gentleman, in fact.

He'd even been funny, too, just a little. Grace still couldn't quite wrap her head around it, this new, mature version of him who made jokes, who still took himself too seriously but had managed to loosen up—just a smidge—this version who actually laughed on occasion. He had a nice laugh as well, especially when he was teasing her about her dirty hairbrush or the way she licked the cheese bowl.

"What are you smiling at?" Alma asked.

Grace froze. "Sorry, I just randomly thought of something one of my students said in class."

Alma twisted her lips and squinted at Grace with suspicion. "It's not because of Rafa? You will be careful, right, Gracie? I'm telling you. He's never been interested in a relationship, but he knows how to get women in bed. It happened to another friend of mine."

That got Grace's attention. "Really?"

"Of course. I wasn't super close with her, thank the Lord, because she became so obsessed with him it was unbearable."

Grace tried not to react to this information. She supposed she shouldn't be surprised Raf had gone after *another* one of Alma's friends. Grace had never told Alma about the almost-kiss in Barcelona. At the time, it seemed too embarrassing. How could Grace have even let him get close to letting his lips touch hers after he'd acted like such a pretentious dickhead that whole week? She may have been a little embarrassed on Raf's behalf, too, since Alma would never let him hear the end of it if she knew he'd made such an attempt. Also, the whole event happened in a matter of ten seconds, so it didn't bear mentioning.

"What happened after that?" Grace asked.

Alma clicked her tongue. "Oh, he wouldn't even answer her calls, so she just came to me over and over, asking what was going on and if I would speak to him for her. She was pining and heartbroken, and Rafael was completely disinterested. She didn't want to talk to me after that."

Grace swallowed, secretly grateful she hadn't let Raf kiss her, even if she'd imagined the experience once or twice since.

"Honestly, it's been this way since we were teenagers," Alma continued. "The girls were always chasing after him, and he was completely immovable. I imagine he thought it would impress our father—to show no emotion, to avoid any point of vulnerability. He's always been good to me. He's the only person I could ever talk to after having a blowout with my mother, but the walls he puts up with everyone else are so high."

Grace frowned. She hated to think of Rafael that way, fighting so hard not to let anyone in. "You don't have to worry about anything like that, Alma. And you know I'm not looking for a relationship anyway. Look how the last one turned out."

"Exactly," Alma said firmly. "You will not get hurt again. I won't let it happen."

But maybe since Grace was absolutely not interested in a relationship—maybe a night spent across the hall in the bedroom of the most gorgeous man she'd ever seen wouldn't be the worst thing in the world...

No. Nope. No way. *Bad idea, Grace.*

She would take heed of Alma's warning; she would tuck it away in the back of her mind just in case. Rafael was her temporary roommate. He was her best friend's brother. He was still a little stuck-up. And there was no way she would get involved with him.

A few days later, when Grace emerged from her bedroom after a surprisingly restful siesta, Raf was sitting at the kitchen counter with his laptop open in front of him and his head in his hands.

She padded over to him, trying to figure out what he was doing. "You okay?"

"Uggghhhhh."

"Doesn't sound good."

"Trying to learn about art so I can put it up on the textured walls of a dark little cave." He lifted his head and looked over at her hopefully. "You here to save me?"

She pursed her lips together, trying to seem annoyed, but he looked kind of cute when he was flustered. He was always so confident and in control, but Grace could appreciate his grumpy, floundering, vulnerable side.

"Let me see what you're working with."

Raf opened a file on his computer, and a gallery of pictures of some of Christian's paintings appeared on the screen. The first one he clicked on was a self-portrait of Picasso.

"Christian owns all of these?"

Rafael's mouth quirked up to the side. "I knew it."

"What?"

"I knew you'd be impressed. I knew you couldn't resist having access to history like this. Don't deny it."

Grace rolled her eyes. "Yes, I'm impressed. You caught me."

"And you're dying to help me out?"

"I didn't say that."

Raf clicked the mouse, and another painting lit up on his laptop screen. "Christian says this is by Maruja Mallo. Ever heard of her?"

Grace smiled. "I've heard of her."

"And she was a...cubist?"

"She was a surrealist. This is so vibrant, isn't it?" She was staring at the wild colors, completely transfixed.

When she remembered Rafael was still there and glanced over, he was grinning at her like a kid who knew he was about to get his way after throwing a tantrum. He knew exactly what he was doing—making the catch, reeling her in—and Grace knew it, too.

Besides the mention of Picasso, Grace had been unaware of what else Christian's collection had to offer. But a Mallo? Grace clicked the mouse and saw the next photograph. A new pallet of colors spilled across the screen. It was a piece by Maria Blanchard. The opportunity to see these paintings in person, to get to study them up close for herself without anyone else there, to bask in their presence...Rafael was right. It would be a dream come true for her.

Perhaps Grace had judged Christian too quickly for his obsession with Picasso. There was more to his collection than she'd ever anticipated. Maybe she still wouldn't have any clue what to do with it, and maybe she was still just an amateur who'd be playing at curator despite a complete lack of experience, but Rafael was spiraling, and he was only asking for her ideas and input. It wasn't like she'd committed to anything more than that.

"I think I'd like to see the venue," she announced with a small nod, trying to infuse her voice with a certainty she didn't quite feel.

Rafael jerked his head up; his eyes went wide. "Seriously? That would be amazing, Graciela. Thank you."

She hesitated, surprised again by his enthusiasm for her help. "I'm still not making any promises. I might take one look at the place and have nothing to offer."

"I completely understand. No pressure." He was excited, though. She could see it in his eyes. He touched her hand, and Grace's face went blank from shock. The air almost crackled with energy all around them.

Rafael seemed to remember himself, and he turned back to the computer, fingertips hovering over the keys instead of against her skin.

Ding!

Grace startled as Rafael's ridiculously high-volume phone chime echoed through the room. "That's quite a notification," she commented when her heart rate slowed again.

"Don't want to miss any important business." He glanced at the screen and gave it a few quick taps before releasing a heavy sigh.

"Everything okay?"

"It's nothing," Raf said. "Just an email from my father."

"He emails you?"

"It's the method of correspondence that works best for us. It's always the same thing, 'stop messing around with your life, and come work at this big, important job instead.'"

Grace grimaced. She could relate to part of this. Her mother only communicated in sporadic text messages, and usually only when she wanted something. An update on any items of interest in Gram's will, for instance. That was expected. However, it would have been the shock of Grace's life if her mother reached out to pester her about career opportunities. Becky Cameron couldn't very well try to push Grace into pursuing bigger goals when she was hardly doing anything herself.

"Don't you own your own company?" Grace asked. "It's not like you're an embarrassment to your family.

Rafael shrugged, but the vulnerability that flashed across his face carved out a little tender spot in Grace's heart before she could think better of it.

"I am an embarrassment to my family, actually. There's no living up to Simón's expectations," he explained. "All you can do is come to terms with it."

"Have you?" Grace chewed on the nail of her pinky finger and studied him more closely. "Come to terms with it?'

Rafael turned back toward his computer again, focusing on the screen with a quiet determination. "Let's see what else Christian owns that might interest you, shall we?"

. . .

The drive to Sacromonte only took about thirty minutes, but Grace felt like they were traveling through time. There was a narrow road that skirted the edge of a cliff, and she was clinging to the side of Rafael's car with white knuckles even while she was gasping at the gorgeous views. The houses, the hills, the bright whitewashed buildings—all of it was like something from a story book, so beautiful and unique she could hardly believe it was real. Every time they rounded a corner there was a new landscape to behold. The greenest trees sprouted from the hillside, flashes of the whole city visible from way up there, as if they were on the edge of the world looking over everything.

Rafael kept glancing over to gauge her reactions, which she found flattering and frustrating at the same time.

"Keep your eyes on the road!" she yelled when he took a corner too quickly for her liking.

"Oh, you want to drive next time?" he asked with a grin.

"Not even a little." She could see how this place held a great appeal for Rafael's client. Besides how beautiful and extraordinary it all was, it also felt tucked away and hard to get to. Something special. Something secret. Just what he was looking for.

"Look at that!" Grace called, pointing.

Rafael jerked the wheel in alarm before straightening it out and following her gaze. "You know what that is, Graciela?" he asked, tilting his chin toward her and trying to hide his smile.

"A pomegranate tree," she said, laughter bubbling out of her at the sight of the big, beautiful plant. It had become a scavenger hunt to her now, and she'd spotted several carvings and plaques with pomegranates, but this was the first time she'd noticed a whole, real-life tree.

"It takes one to know one, Little Pomegranate," Raf said, his accent even thicker than usual as he enunciated the English words. The sweetness and familiarity of it seemed to seep into her skin. It was hard to believe he'd practically had to force her to come here, to this magical place of caves and pomegranate trees. She was in love with it already, and she hadn't even set foot inside the exhibit space.

The truth was Grace was having fun. She was having fun riding along in the car while enjoying the views. She was having fun finding pomegranates everywhere as if this was her new mission in life. She was having fun with Rafael, and it surprised her as soon as she recognized the feeling. It had been a long time since she'd truly enjoyed herself, but she wasn't sure quite what to make of the revelation.

"I don't think anyone's here right now," Rafael said as they pulled up to a small building at the end of a road that looked similar to the others—which meant stark white and curving into the side of a cliff with little windows surrounding a peach-colored door. It was difficult to determine how large the place was since it was built on the side of a hill. *How deep underground did this thing go?* she wondered, staring with her mouth agape. "We can take a look around so you can get a feel for the place, and then a van is coming with some of the art later on."

Grace shuddered at the thought of a big van on the narrow roads. She wondered how many trips it would take to get all the paintings to the cave.

She followed Raf as he unlocked the narrow doors that led inside. Grace instinctively ducked her head as she walked down into the first room, but it was larger than she'd expected. For all that Rafael had complained about how they were going to make this space work, she'd been expecting some kind of a Hobbit hole. But the ceilings left plenty of room for her to stand and walk around comfortably, and the first room was actually quite large compared to the image she'd conjured in her head. While you could tell you were in a cave, the bright white walls and natural light from carved windows were enough to make it feel open and comfortable. Grace suddenly thought of the neighbors who were living in similar houses nearby and wondered how they'd decorated and designed their homes.

Rafael typed in a code on a small keypad near the door. Of course they'd already installed some kind of security system and some fancy temperature and humidity control unit prior to transporting hundreds of priceless pieces to the venue. The panel beeped, and then Rafael flipped a switch, further illuminating the room with an overhead light.

Grace reviewed the scene before her again, taking in the oval shape of the entryway and the large arches that led to other rooms. One obstacle—one that Rafael had been sure to mention several times—was the texture of the walls. They were very rough, walls of rock rather than smooth drywall, and it was difficult to imagine hanging anything on them, much less finding a way to hang the work of some of the most famous artists of all time. This wasn't her area of expertise by any means, but Grace was already making calculations in her head. This wall might hold a larger painting, but could they smooth it out somehow or frame in in a way that would let it hang evenly against the wall? Where might they put smaller works side by side? Would this little alcove work for a larger piece? Perhaps one of great significance? At least they didn't have to worry about fitting *Guernica* or *Les Demoiselles d'Avignon* anywhere in the small space.

Just as he had on the road, Rafael watched for her reactions as he guided her through the place that would become Christian's own underground art gallery. Raf seemed to be waiting for her to say something, to let him know if there was any way they could make this work.

"What do you think?" he asked at last, clearly unable to hold himself back any longer.

Grace gave him an encouraging smile. "It's hard to know without seeing the art in person," she started.

"Of course, but if you just imagine..."

"It seems possible," Grace said, putting him out of his misery. "I don't have it all worked out exactly, but it's larger than I was expecting. I think we could make something work."

"But will it actually look good?" Rafael pressed anxiously. "Or will it just look like too many paintings shoved in a little cave house? It has to be a whole experience."

Grace couldn't help letting out a little snort. She didn't mean to. She knew how much this meant to him, how much he worried, but the way he was freaking out about designing a private art exhibition was kind of adorable. "So you've told me. A cultural phenomenon, I believe you said."

Rafael frowned at her.

She patted his arm and tried her encouraging smile one more time. "I think you can make it beautiful, Raf. I really do."

They walked around the cave house several more times as Rafael wrote notes she couldn't read in a tiny journal. She took pictures and videos on her phone to remember every detail—the alcove off the largest room, the long hallway that spread out and ended in a large, strange cavern that looked like a mushroom. Everything was white. The front rooms glowed with some natural light, while the other rooms were dim—something they would have to consider for the placement of each piece of art. Grace couldn't help wondering about whoever had come up with the idea to create this place, to carve out a cozy little dwelling from the rock on the side of a cliff. It did inspire her, though. She was already imagining where they might add lighting and how they would try to direct the flow of traffic, that is, if Christian's guests actually cared to look at the art during his fancy parties.

As if she had summoned him with her thoughts, the man she assumed was Christian appeared with his arms outstretched and sporting a giant grin. His white teeth shined, seeming to reflect the walls of the cave, and just a sliver of his round belly was visible under his shirt. When he dropped his arms, the sliver disappeared.

Grace had been picturing someone more glamorous, someone who wore clothes that looked too nice to touch, but Christian was clearly prepared to work. His linen pants were well made, but they looked comfortable. No suit and tie. No fancy watch. Nothing to get caught on his precious paintings as he helped to haul them from the truck. The fact that Christian planned to help with the hauling at all showed just how precious they were to him.

"Who do we have here?" he asked in Spanish, his eyes fixed on Grace.

She tried to smooth her loose braid and thin sweater and waited for Rafael to introduce her.

"This is Grace Cameron," Rafael said in English, for her benefit. "She's a professor at the international university and an expert on modern art. I thought she might be able to offer a few insights to help us get started."

"*Si, si,* the American art instructor," Christian said, switching to English as well. "You mentioned you were bringing someone, but I didn't expect her to be so lovely, Rafael. I should have known you would find the most beautiful expert possible to help with your work."

Rafael averted his gaze from Grace and cleared his throat. He clearly wasn't going to be agreeing with that sentiment.

Christian patted his arm and murmured something else to Rafael in Spanish before moving forward to shake Grace's hand. Raf's eyes went wide at whatever Christian had told him, but he didn't respond as Christian switched back to English. "Nice to have you here, Senorita Cameron. I'm excited to show you the work and see what you think."

Grace shifted on her feet. "It's nice to meet you, but I'm just here to see if I can help a bit. This isn't really what I do."

"Yes, you are a teacher, and that's even more important. But if you have any ideas at all to help with our little project, we'll be very grateful to you."

Christian swept past her and started to wander around the building as if refreshing his memory. His shiny shoes squeaked across the brushed concrete floor, before he popped up on his tiptoes and peered out one of the little carved windows. The bright sun lit up his face, and he nodded happily as he moved on to the next room, clearly reassured that he'd chosen the perfect venue.

When Grace found Rafael's eyes, they were already trained on her.

"What?" she asked, smoothing a hand down her braid again.

Rafael opened his mouth and then closed it without speaking.

"What is it?" Grace pressed.

He cleared his throat and turned away. "Come back to the kitchen area again," he said. "I don't know how we're going to cater anything here."

"You're such a pessimist, Raf," she scolded. She couldn't help but feel like he had something else on his mind, but obviously it wasn't something he planned to share with her. She glanced around the front room another time, imagining how it might look when it was no longer bare, when priceless works of art were spread out all over the cave walls, and then she followed Rafael to the little kitchen.

CHAPTER TEN

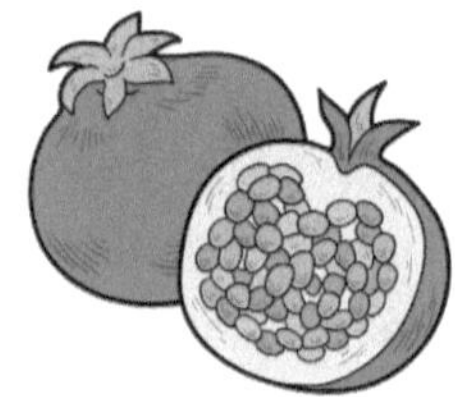

OH, *I already see how you look at her. Can't get that past an old man.*

Rafael was lucky Grace's Spanish was terrible. Thankfully, she seemed to have no clue that Christian had already remarked on Rafael's attraction. Rafael wasn't sure how he'd been looking at her, exactly, but he didn't find it hard to believe that he'd been staring. The way her hair fell over her shoulder, little wisps escaping her braid and framing her face. The way she pursed her lips at him when she was annoyed, which was often, even if her grimaces were starting to turn into smiles far more than before. The way she rested her body against the cave wall, clearly lost in thought, her blue eyes gleaming when she had another idea. The way she hovered over him while he was writing in his notebook even though she couldn't read a word of it. He could smell her lavender soap. He could feel her breath on his neck.

He'd always been attracted to her. The first time he'd met her, and then the first time he saw her in Alma's apartment so many years later. It wasn't exactly newsworthy. He supposed the intensity of his attraction had crept up a few notches since she moved in, but he was spending so much more time with her, it was expected that his level of interest would increase, too.

He ran the water at the faucet in the little kitchen and washed his hands before splashing some of the cool water against his face. Clearly, things were getting worse. When she'd first arrived, he'd thought about her on occasion. She was an attractive woman, but she was living with his sister, and she clearly wasn't his biggest fan. Then, she moved in with him, and she didn't seem to hate him as much anymore. Actually, it almost seemed like she enjoyed talking to him, at least a small amount. Sometimes he made her laugh, and *Ay Dios mio,* if that wasn't the greatest sound he'd ever heard. It was a stupid thought. Absolutely idiotic. But she'd been so sad lately, and to hear her laugh at something he'd said—it felt like the instant warmth from a shot of tequila but without the burn. It felt like the sun.

What a ridiculous load of sentimental bullshit. One pretty girl smiled at him and suddenly he was a completely different person full of nonsense and bad poetry? He groaned inwardly and took a sip from his bottle of water. Grace had followed him into the room, and now she was waiting for him to do something—like his job, perhaps? He was supposed to be working, not thinking about how the smell of his temporary roommate seemed to waft through the entire apartment after she stepped out of the shower.

Christian only made it worse by commenting on it. Rafael had assumed that all the heat inside of him was his alone, safe inside his body for no one else to ever know. Did his face look different somehow when she was around? Was it that evident to everyone? To her?

"Is everything okay?" Grace asked. "I know the kitchen's small, but I'm sure you'll be able to figure something out."

"Yes." Rafael swallowed and started fidgeting before quickly stopping himself. "I think we can manage something. There's enough room for a large refrigerator, and while the oven is small, it should be enough for reheating food. Counter space might be the big concern, really, and then we need somewhere for the food to go. Maybe we could fit a large table in that side room? Tapas would be fine, but if someone were to host a full dinner, it might get tricky. I'll have to take some more measurements."

He was rambling. And sweating. *Estupido.*

Grace was patient, waiting for him to finish his thoughts, even though he'd lost track of them himself. He wasn't entirely sure what was happening to him, but between trying to figure out what to do with this exhibition and spending so much time with Grace, he didn't feel quite like himself. He was flustered and insecure, two things that could rarely have been used to describe him in his entire life. He wasn't sure how to overcome it, but he was sure that he would. His confidence in that fact remained. He would figure his shit out and get back on track.

It turned out the van with the paintings was delayed. Christian had forgotten to mention that upon his arrival. With no artwork, Rafael decided there was no reason to keep Grace hanging around the cave for the rest of the day. They chatted with Christian for a while and then said their farewells. Grace was calm and kind, even though Rafael knew she probably had some choice words for Christian in her head—her criticisms of the whole endeavor, the limited audience, the exclusivity of it all. He could tell her smile was tighter than usual, her face a mask of indifference.

The drive back to the apartment was quieter than it had been on the way to the cave house, perhaps because Rafael's head was busy analyzing every look he'd given Grace, the tone of his every phrase, the way he'd taken her hand after opening the car door for her or placed his palm on the small of her back to make sure she was safely inside. What was she thinking over there in the passenger seat as she twisted the tail of her braid around her finger?

Finally, it came to him: the logical explanation. Rafael knew what this was, and it wasn't some weird crush or overpowering magnetism between them. Now that he realized what was going on, it all made sense. *This* was way more in line with his personality.

Grace was forbidden. Not in the *Romeo and Juliet* kind of way, but he couldn't have her, not even for one night. It would make everything far too complicated. She was his sister's best friend in the entire world, and now she was living in his home and helping him with his work, and she was in an extremely vulnerable place, and all of that added up to one thing. He could not sleep with her.

That was exactly the problem. It was in his nature to want the very thing he couldn't have. It wasn't like they shared some special connection or some particularly meaningful bond. She was hot. She was off limits. And therefore, the more time he spent with her, the more he wanted to put his hands on her. That was the simple truth of it. Mystery solved. If he could have just slept with her one time and gotten it all out of his system, he could have forgotten her immediately and gone on with his life, but as it was, he just needed to recognize his area of weakness, accept his ill-timed attraction, and move on with his life.

Rafael exhaled, and then he felt Grace glance over at him. He was relieved to have figured this out. He could handle it. He simply needed to name the issue and address it in his mind, and it would lose its power over him.

"I'm starving," Grace said, and Rafael immediately conjured an image of the two of them out for a meal at his favorite restaurant. Dim lighting and her wine-stained lips. Her leg brushing his underneath the table.

Where was this coming from? They'd talked about work and Picasso. They'd barely even flirted, and yet a couple hours in a historic cave had him fighting his attraction? He almost banged his head against the steering wheel. "Me too, yes. We should eat something."

"You're sure everything's alright? You're acting kind of weird."

"I'm not."

"You are. You're all jumpy and tense. Did something happen with Christian?"

He hesitated. *Oh, I already see how you look at her.* "No."

"Why do I not find that convincing?"

There she was again, pestering him. He worked hard to see it in a negative light, as if she was annoying rather than endearing, as if everything else was just a silly infatuation.

Rafael adjusted his facial expression, trying to present a mask of calm. "Leave it alone, Grace," he said, and she did.

She was craving pizza, so they stopped at a simple pizza counter in the city center with bright lights and checkered tablecloths. There was no wine and no touching, and as Rafael gnawed on the crust of his final slice, he started to feel like himself again. "What do you think of the venue?" he asked.

Grace smiled with her mouth closed, cheeks full of mozzarella. She chewed and chewed until she was finally able to swallow and answer the question. "I know you're frustrated that he chose this place, and I can see why. It will be difficult for large paintings, but also…it's amazing. I've never seen anything like that before in my life. It has so much character, and I know you said you don't have quite the vision for what to do yet, but I am positive you'll make something beautiful."

Rafael's hands fidgeted in his lap again. At least someone believed he could pull this off. "And what do you think about where to put the paintings?"

"It's hard to know without having seen the collection yet." She took a sip of her water. "I think there's more wall space than you realize, though, and it's not all curved. There are several long walls with plenty of space. I was also thinking, maybe in that large room, we could add something. Like, maybe build a free-standing wall in the center that would split the room and allow you to hang several large pieces there as a focal point?"

Rafael could see it immediately. They didn't have enough wall space, but they had enough room to build their own wall—something large and perfectly straight that wasn't made of rock. That seemed to unlock something in his brain. He could see the wall they would build—stark white, of course—and he could see how that would change the space. In the next room, they could have benches. The food would all be done via caterers with trays to save space, unless someone wanted to use the venue for a full dinner, but they could likely set up their guests in different areas, spread throughout the exhibit instead of at one big table. Then they'd break everything down, so the guests could mingle and look at the artwork.

"You're brilliant," Rafael said. "See, I knew you would have some ideas, and as you said, you haven't even seen the paintings, yet. I can only imagine what you'll come up with then."

Grace stared down at her pizza. It almost looked like she was blushing, but Rafael couldn't tell if it was the color of her cheeks or just a trick of the light.

"I don't know if this is really good or if I was just craving it so badly that anything would hit the spot."

Rafael grinned. "I don't think this is really good."

Grace frowned at him. "Well, it's not Scarr's, obviously, but it's not bad. I'm not sure I trust your pizza judgment anyway."

Rafael gave a mock-offended gasp. Inwardly, he noted that Grace remembered what he'd said about his favorite NYC pizza place. "Why wouldn't you trust my pizza judgement? I lived in New York for years. I've dined at the finest Italian restaurants in Sicily, places where they practically invented pizza."

Grace was biting back a smile. Clearly, she loved getting a rise out of him. "But how much pizza did you really eat? Have you ever even tried a Chicago deep dish? I feel like we're only scratching the surface here."

Rafael shrugged and watched her devour another bite. "I don't know if I told you how grateful I am that you came today," he said. "It was nice having you there."

Grace narrowed her eyes at him. "Are you about to ask me for another favor?"

"Not at all."

She pressed her lips together, and Rafael couldn't help staring at them. "I'm not used to being the one who's getting thanked," she said. "Usually, I'm the grateful one."

"I'm aware of that. I've been bombarded with your gratitude. It's very annoying."

Grace nodded. "I'm trying to cut back," she said, as if she was talking about an unsavory addiction. "It's just that when you've been sinking into a dark hole for so long, it's hard not to be wildly enthusiastic when someone reaches out a hand."

Why did it hurt him so much to think about how miserable she'd been? He barely even knew her, but he hated it just the same. It wasn't like that usually. Empathy wasn't really one of his strong points, but for her he could feel the ache right in the middle of his chest. "I'm sorry," he said, almost in a whisper. "About your dark hole."

Grace surprised him by laughing. "You did not just say that."

"What?" Rafael smiled, catching on. "My English is bad. You were the one who brought up your dark hole."

"God, stop saying *hole* already."

He shook his head, eyes gleaming. "Hhhh—" he started.

She held up a hand, as if that would be enough to stop the word from escaping his lips. "Nope, your English is perfect, and I think you know exactly what you said."

"It's not my fault you have a dirty mind. It was an accident."

"Sure, Raf," she said as she shoved another bite of crust in her mouth and moaned. The hairs on Rafael's arms stood on end.

"What happened?" he asked suddenly. "With you and your ex-boyfriend? Sorry, if that's overstepping."

Grace shook her head. "No, I think you've seen me miserable enough that it would be hard not to be curious." She sighed and chewed a slow bite of pizza. "I don't really know, exactly," she said. "That was the worst part. We had so much in common. We barely fought. Everything was simple and easy, and it all made sense." She licked a spot of sauce from her thumb and continued. "We met at a bar we both liked to go to for the happy hour specials. We both liked museums and hockey and indie rock. We had so much in common, but then... Maybe he just decided that wasn't enough. Maybe it wasn't. Looking back on it, I think we were kind of boring. I don't know if something brought that to light for him, or if he'd been bored of me for a long time."

Rafael stared at her, unsure of how to respond even though he felt some kind of nonsensical rage toward this man he'd never met. "How could anyone ever think you're boring? You make everything more interesting. Every moment. That's just—" He cut himself off, not sure what he was saying or if he should be saying it.

Grace's mouth twitched. "Thank you," she said. "For not thinking I'm boring." She dropped her crust onto her plate and dusted off her hands.

"Finished?" Rafael asked, imagining it was best to retreat from wherever this conversation was going, best to ignore all the ways he found her the opposite of boring.

Grace nodded and swept up the trash.

"Good. Let's go home."

That night, sleep evaded him. He felt like he'd been lying in bed for hours, tossing and turning, straining his ears for any signs of Grace's movement. She'd mentioned that she didn't sleep much at night, though she did enjoy her "siesta naps," as she called them, and he couldn't help wondering if she was lying there awake, too, tossing and turning in her bed and thinking about the exhibit, about the cave, about him. Small exchanges from the day crept into his mind like little ninjas—her rolling her eyes at him when he tried to brag about anything, the feeling of her finger poking him in the ribs when he'd tried to suggest that some of Picasso's art was mediocre. He shouldn't have been so thrilled at the feeling of one fucking fingertip against his shirt.

He sighed.

For a long time, everything was quiet. Rafael was exhausted, but he also felt like his whole body was on-call, ready to jump out of bed at the slightest indication that Grace was awake. He wanted to see her. He wanted to talk to her again. They'd spent the whole day together, and somehow it wasn't quite enough.

But as much as he strained, he didn't hear a thing.

He foolishly considered getting out of bed. He didn't need anything, and wandering around his room would only make things worse. He rubbed a hand over his face. Usually, he slept like a baby. Usually, he didn't have some strange electric current that seemed to run right through him and into the hallway, tethering him to the bedroom right next to his own.

He picked up his phone and scrolled mindlessly. Alma would have scolded him and railed about the science of phone screens' impact on sleep, but maybe it would draw his mind elsewhere, if only he could think about anything but the woman sleeping in his apartment.

He filled his head with futbol scores and meeting schedules and dinner menus. It was still a long time before he was able to calm the stirring thoughts in his head. He took slow deep breaths and tried to clear his mind, and after what felt like forever, his eyes drifted closed. Perhaps it wasn't a deep sleep, not yet. Perhaps it wasn't total oblivion, but he was calm enough that there was the hope of sleep, and for the moment, that was enough.

CHAPTER ELEVEN

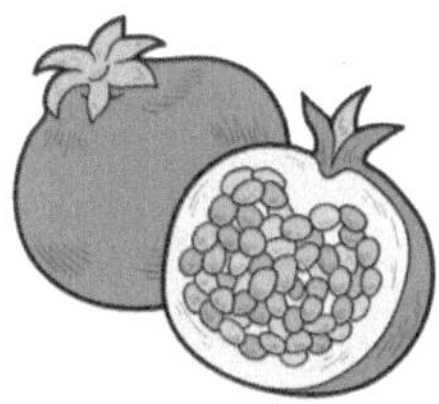

"SORRY, Gracie. The landlord said he's been having a hard time getting the contractors in to finish the apartment. They're so booked up."

Grace sat cross-legged on Obinna's loveseat as Alma handed her a mug of tea. "It's okay. It's just taking longer than I expected." She didn't think Rafael would mind her staying with him for a while longer, but she also didn't want to get in the way. Just because he hadn't tried to kick her out yet didn't mean he would want her to stay indefinitely.

"I know. I can't believe we can't move back into our place yet. Although, I will say it's been fun living here with Obinna. It's like a sleepover every night, and we have so much fun talking. We're both exhausted from staying up too late, but I like imagining this is for real. Like, this is what it might be for us to share a life."

Grace puffed out her cheeks, shocked and elated. Alma had never said something like that in her life. "Who the hell are you?" she teased.

Alma shrugged, as if she was also struggling to make sense of it. "We were forced into this whole situation, but it's kind of working out, and maybe someday we'll choose this, you know? Not because of an accident, but because we want to."

Grace leaned back and fell into the cushion behind her as if she was fainting. "Seriously, what is happening right now? Where is the girl who said she'd never settle down with one person because there are far too many to choose from?"

Alma laughed. "I don't think that girl was wrong. There are so many people to choose from. It's just that Obinna is maybe the best one that I've ever met, and I feel like I could be ready, you know?"

"That's big, Alma. I mean, it's big in a good way."

"Don't worry. That's a way-in-the-future thing. I'm not going to abandon you when I just convinced you to move to Spain in the first place."

"You don't have to worry about that."

"Yes, I do." She gave Grace a look of exasperation. "I hate to break it to you, *mejor amiga,* but you've basically been the most important person in my life for the past ten years. We'll be back together in our apartment soon, and I'm going to continue to support you even when you're whining about it. You know, in usual circumstances this is when I would use one of my favorite American phrases, but you've been through a lot, so I'll be nice."

Grace smiled, already guessing the phrase Alma was referring to. "Suck it up, buttercup?"

"Suck it up, buttercup!" Alma echoed even more enthusiastically. "But I'm not saying that. I'm sympathizing. I know it sucks that you're stuck with Rafa even longer."

Grace turned Alma's words over in her mind. *Stuck with Rafa.* She didn't feel so stuck. They'd fallen into some kind of routine—coffee and tea at the counter in the morning, drinks after her siesta nap. Sometimes they had dinner together and went for a walk through the city. It had only been a couple of weeks, but Grace felt so comfortable with him, more at ease than she ever could have imagined. They might even be friends.

Which was silly, honestly. They'd been forced into this whole thing, and they were making the best of it. He was probably just being nice because she was such a sad, giant mess. He'd called her idea to add their own wall to the middle of the cave "brilliant." Clearly, he was humoring her. It wasn't a bad idea, and she thought it could work, but it wasn't brilliant. It was just a wall. He was trying to build her up and make her feel better, though Grace wasn't sure why. Maybe he thought she would do more work for him on the exhibit? She'd already been planning to do some more research about the caves and see if she could come up with other ideas to help him. Maybe he was just trying to keep their roommate experience as civil as possible?

It was maybe a little too civil though. If Rafael was kind and friendly while also continuing to be the hottest guy she'd ever seen, then Grace was in trouble.

Of course, she couldn't mention this to Alma. He was her *brother.* You couldn't indulge in sexual fantasies about your best friend's brother, even if he had eyes that seemed to draw you in further with every look. Alma had already warned her about this once.

Even though Raf was being super nice, it didn't feel like he was trying to make a move on her, as Alma had feared. Grace couldn't help feeling slightly disappointed. The heat she was experiencing during their interactions was so one-sided, it seemed more likely that she would end up seducing herself on his behalf just by imagining the way his lips curled up when she called him a snob.

"I'll survive another week or two with Rafael," Grace said, taking a sip from her mug and offering Alma an encouraging smile.

She *would* survive. Though the fact that every time she used her vibrator, she was afraid Raf would hear it wasn't exactly helping the situation. And the fact that her vibrator and Rafael were now tied together in her mind since she always worried about him whenever she thought of using it wasn't great either. It had the potential to become a Pavlovian situation. But she wouldn't be ashamed. It was nothing she couldn't handle. She'd been through so much already. Indulging in fantasies of her best friend's brother that involved sex toys—while he was right across the hall—was nothing.

Rafael was still awake when she returned from visiting Alma. He sprawled lazily across the couch with his laptop, feet on the table, one hand in his hair. He straightened a bit as she approached and lifted his hand in a little salute.

"Hey," she said.

There was something comforting about returning home to him, about saying goodnight before tucking herself into bed after another long day. Maybe she was just grasping at straws to fill the void of Derek, or maybe she was just so fucking lonely that even a polite nod from Raf was enough to make her desperate for some human connection.

Back in Chicago, her ex-boyfriend had ripped away the entire idea of her future, of sharing her life with him, of relying on him. Relying on someone was a big deal for Grace since she'd had so few people in her life to fill that role. Her grandmother, Alma, Derek. That was it. That was the list. There'd never really been anyone else she could count on, and so the fact that two of the pillars of her life weren't there anymore was all the more devastating.

It was, perhaps, too much pressure for Alma, but the thing Alma always seemed to forget was that Grace could rely on herself as well. She was used to that. Her mother and father had barely been in the picture, and as much as she'd been loved by Gram, Grace had realized how important it was that she was independent from a young age. Though she had to admit, sometimes she wasn't as tough as she would have liked. It was a work in progress.

Maybe all of her history, all of her damage and baggage, was wrapped up in the reason Rafael's lazy smile had suddenly become such a consolation to her. She refused to imagine any other explanation.

"You okay?" Raf asked.

She must have been drifting off into space. She removed her shoes and put them on the rack by the door. "Yeah, just too many thoughts."

"Any you feel like sharing?"

Grace shrugged. "I was with your sister."

"Oh yeah? How is Alma? Struggling to find enough closet space at Obinna's apartment?"

"Yes, actually, but she doesn't seem to mind it."

Rafael typed something on his keyboard and then set the laptop aside. "How are you?" he asked. He'd started asking her every day, as if this were a perfectly normal and regular kind of question and not one that should make her consider straddling his lap.

"I'm good," she said with another shrug.

"Yeah?"

"Yeah."

"Did you eat something?" He analyzed her face, as if he might be able to decipher the answer if he looked hard enough.

It was another question she wanted to read into as some kind of evidence he might care about her, but it was so perfectly innocuous. "I did. I think I'm just going to head to bed."

"Even though you can't sleep?" He was frowning at her, but there seemed to be the barest hint of a smile working at the edge of his lips.

"You never know if you don't try." She gave him a little wave and retreated to her room, annoyed that her heart rate was faster than it should have been.

She did sleep at night, sometimes. She often dreamt of her grandmother, and sometimes they were nice dreams. Art museums and champagne at breakfast. "A mimosa without the orange juice," Gram would say. Sometimes Grace was a girl again, and her grandma was scolding her for letting a boy at school make her feel bad about herself. "I know it hurts, Gracie, but you have to be strong. You'll meet so many stupid men in your life, you might as well prepare for it now." She'd gotten her sense of humor from her grandmother—and her sense of adventure. Gram would have loved that Grace moved to Spain, even if she thought it was for the wrong reasons.

Sometimes the dreams were more nightmarish. The final days. Hospice and beeping machines and grasping onto a too-thin hand. That's what she was dreaming about after she returned from Obinna's place—her grandmother's pale face, eyes closed, her veiny, weathered skin and hollowed cheeks. The shaky sounds of agony when she tried to speak. Grace, at her bedside, trying so hard not to sob.

She was sobbing in her dream, and it must have carried over into real life, too, because before she knew it, she was awake in her bed with tears streaming down her face and a lump in her throat. She gasped for breath, waiting to remember where she was, *when* she was, trying to shake the images of Gram she hated to remember.

There was a knock at her door, and she wondered if that's what had broken her out of the nightmare in the first place. "Grace?" She heard Rafael's voice, soft and worried, on the other side of it. She wasn't sure how long he'd been standing there, but she was too dazed to be embarrassed.

"Yeah?" she croaked. "Sorry, you can come in."

Rafael eased open the door and peeked into her room, searching her face to try to puzzle out what was happening. He must have heard her crying. She felt like a child who'd been bawling in her sleep, and even though she suddenly felt very awake, she couldn't seem to stop. Her shoulders were shaking, and tears were still streaming down her cheeks.

Rafael took all of it in and moved toward her, hesitating for only a moment before sitting on the bed and wrapping her in his arms. "Are you okay?" he whispered into her hair. "What's going on?"

Grace let herself sink into him, taking another breath to gain her composure only to find herself inhaling the scent of his skin, the expensive sandalwood soap and a hint of lemon. It took a moment before Grace managed to find any words and a moment more before she could actually get them out. "Bad dream." She coughed. "I'm okay. Sorry for waking you up."

"Stop apologizing, Graciela," he said. "What did you dream?"

"My grandma. It was the last time I saw her. The last day…" The tears picked up again, and Grace couldn't seem to finish the sentence.

Rafael held her and stroked her hair. She cried into him, and even though she expected to feel mortified and burdensome, she mostly just felt a sense of calm washing over her. She was safe, and some part of that was because of him. Because he was holding her, because he didn't let go. Because, somehow, they'd been drawn together in this little city, and he wasn't the person she'd expected—at least not anymore.

They stayed like that for a long time, until her breath evened out and the tears slowed. "Can I get you something?" Rafael asked. "A glass of water?"

The truth was she didn't want him to let go. If he could have just stayed there all night, holding her…

"No," she rasped, remaining still in the hopes that he might not move away. "I'm better now. I would thank you, but I know how you feel about that."

"Good." Rafael loosened his grip on her, and she tried very hard not to cling to him too tightly. "Don't thank me. Just think of me as a hand in your dark hole."

"Rafael," she scolded.

"What?"

"I know it was on purpose that time."

His mouth twitched. "I'm not sure what you mean."

She pressed her forehead against his chest again to hide her smile. Grace was shocked to find herself smiling after she'd been falling apart at the seams just minutes before. She was even more surprised that the person making her smile was *him.* Mr. Serious. The man who never laughed. Except, apparently, that wasn't exactly true.

"You're not allowed to use the word *hole* anymore," she whispered into his shirt. "It's forbidden."

"Come on, Graciela," he teased. "You like it."

Grace was suddenly extremely conscious of her breasts pressing into his torso every time she took a breath, his fingers against her neck, and his nose in her hair. She'd wanted him to hold onto her for comfort, but she was starting to understand that there was more to it than that. His touch wasn't just comforting, it was...alluring. She eased back and looked up at him and knew instantly it was a mistake, because he was so beautiful, and his eyes were so dark as they locked on hers with a force she'd never seen in a gaze.

"Are you sure I can't get you anything?" he asked. It was barely a whisper, but she could feel the breath of each word brushing against her skin.

She nodded slowly, still staring at him.

Her heart sped up again, and she parted her lips. His mouth was so perfect, so close, inches away from her own. She tilted her head ever-so-slightly and leaned toward him without meaning to, the tiniest little bit. Then her eyelids fluttered as if ready to close the moment his lips touched hers. As if in slow motion, she could feel the minimal distance between them closing. Closer and closer, his nose almost nudging hers, his breath ragged in the dark.

"I should let you get some sleep," he said, pulling away.

Grace tensed. *How fucking mortifying.* She cleared her throat. "Yes, you too. I mean, you should get some sleep."

He nodded and untangled himself from her before rising from the bed. He shuffled backwards but stopped in the doorway and made eye contact with her again. Grace was grateful for the darkness, which she hoped would hide her flushed, tear-stained cheeks and swollen eyes. If she was really lucky, it might also hide her accidental desire and complete embarrassment. She had a faded birthmark on her forehead that only seemed to show itself when she was angry or devastated, but she imagined her flaws were safe in the shadows, hidden from his gaze.

"I—uh," Rafael started.

Grace held her breath. What was he going to say? *I would absolutely never kiss you? I hope you didn't get the wrong idea, I'm just nice to sobbing women on occasion? I certainly pity you, but I'm not attracted to you?*

The silence stretched across the room, filling the space between them. Grace refused to break it; she didn't know if she could find words. Maybe he hadn't noticed how primed she was for him to go to town on her mouth. Maybe he didn't realize anything weird had happened at all.

She would go with that. Nothing weird to see here, just a sad girl losing her shit in her dreams, only to get all horny the second a hot dude lays a hand on her. No worries.

"Goodnight," Rafael said at last. It felt like ten minutes had gone by, even if it had only been a matter of seconds. Her face felt so hot, and she actually could have gone for that glass of water; she was probably dehydrated, but she would have to deal with it on her own when he was gone—when he wasn't just standing there, unmoving, his gorgeous figure hovering in the doorway in a way that was totally going to haunt her sexual fantasies. Except in her fantasies, he wouldn't have pulled away.

"Goodnight. Thanks for—" She wasn't sure how to finish that sentence. Thanks for waking me up from a terrible nightmare and pressing me into your body? She shrugged. "You know. Goodnight."

He gave an almost imperceptible nod and backed out of the room, closing the door behind him, and Grace fell back against her pillow with a sigh. *Shit.* That hadn't been her best moment, but she was still holding onto the hope he hadn't noticed. Maybe that was naïve, but a girl could pretend, and if they never spoke of it again, she would go right on pretending. She resolved not to make a fool of herself again…at least for a few days. She was going to do some research about Sacromonte and its history, and she was going to come up with brilliant ideas to help him. She would impress him for real, not just with one stupid wall in the middle of the room, but with a whole host of knowledge and ideas for the underground exhibit. And she would keep it so professional, it would be clear she wasn't thinking about kissing him. This was a business relationship. And maybe a weird roommate situation. And maybe also some kind of friendship. But it was not romantic.

She just needed to keep repeating that to herself over and over again.

CHAPTER TWELVE

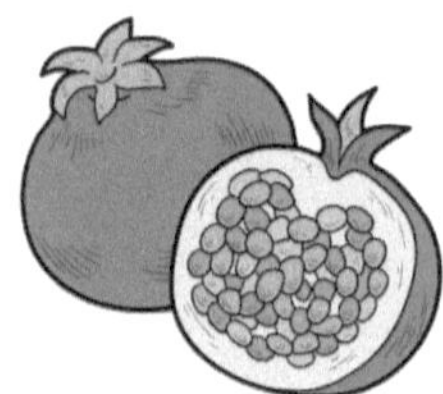

HAD she wanted him to kiss her? Rafael stood over his bed, unable to lie down. It seemed possible she was expecting a kiss, but he couldn't be sure. It had been too dark to fully comprehend her facial expressions, but hopefully that meant it was also too dark for her to see his erection, and he'd tried very hard to hide that merciless betrayal of a bulge as he backed out of the room. Grace was upset, and it obviously wasn't the time for that kind of thing, but for a moment there it had seemed like that kind of thing wouldn't be entirely unwelcome.

Rafael put both hands on his head. He couldn't help it if this whole forbidden attraction scenario got him going. It would have been so easy to give into it, to lean in and let his lips touch hers, to find some quick relief for his wanting.

But *no.* He'd made a promise to himself not to try to kiss her again. He could just see it now—an exact repeat of what happened last time—her shock and hesitation, her confusion, the way she jerked away as if he was trying to bite her. Well, okay, he wanted to bite her. But in a *nice* way.

Once again, he imagined how easy this would be if she was just a random woman off the street. One night together, and he would be cured. This whole thing would be over and done with and he could get back to work without thinking of the way she twisted the little end of her braid between her fingers and without staring at her like a ravenous fool every time she walked into the room. He pressed his hand against the tent of his sweatpants and rolled his eyes. All she'd done was *look* at him, and his cock was acting like she'd been whispering filthy nothings in his ear. How had it all escalated so quickly?

He blew out a breath. He needed to get a handle on himself. Actually, handling himself sounded like the best possible solution for the moment, so he would indulge that instinct. He'd let himself think about her while he did it. But tomorrow was another day, and tomorrow, he was going to stop lusting after Grace Cameron.

The next day, Christian's mood was buoyant from the moment Rafael strolled into the cave at Sacromonte. "Look around, my friend! We're in business!"

If business meant that the cave was littered with tons of paintings, many of them still safely tucked into special boxes filled with foam and packing materials, then yes, they were in business.

"That was fast."

"Wee hours of the morning," Christian explained in Spanish. "Trying to avoid any traffic or prying eyes on the road. We'll have another shipment in a couple of days, and the art handlers will work to get them into position when they're all acclimated and ready to hang."

Rafael almost laughed remembering when Christian had said the two of them could handle most of the exhibit, and now there were art handlers in white gloves rushing around in a frenzy. He was happy to have them there, though. Seeing the large crates everywhere didn't exactly bring Rafael any comfort since he had no idea what the hell to do with them, but he was relieved he'd missed out on helping to haul them in. His certainty that he would trip over a stone and send a priceless Picasso tumbling down the side of the cliff made him a bit paranoid.

"Speaking of prying eyes," Christian began, and Rafael froze. He'd been dreading this—a private conversation where Christian would tease him about this thing with Grace. It was embarrassing enough that a client had witnessed his ridiculous infatuation, even worse would be to mull it over with them afterward. But Christian surprised him. "There's a travel journalist that's been sniffing around, asking questions about what we're doing here. She says she loves this area and heard that we were up to something, and she might be interested in writing a piece about it. I'm counting on you to nip that in the bud."

"You don't want her to write about the exhibition?"

"And spoil all my secrets? Of course not! I told her you would meet with her, tell her about some of your other projects. I was hoping you might be able to distract her with some other exciting public event, and we can keep her from digging around here."

Rafael thought for a moment. He supposed he could come up with something to talk about. Something that might make a good post on a travel blog.

"Do you want me to reach out to her?"

"No need. You're having dinner with her tonight. She might bring her fiancé."

Rafael's mouth fell open. He was a bit surprised Christian would take such a liberty in making plans for him, but he halted his protest when he realized it wasn't a bad idea. It would be good to have plans outside the apartment, to give Grace a bit of distance for the evening.

"You should take your girlfriend," Christian said.

Rafael raised an eyebrow. "My girlfriend?"

"Yes, Senorita Cameron? The travel writer is American, too. Perhaps they'll get along well. Just make sure there's no mention of my secret underground exhibition."

"Grace isn't—we're not—"

Christian laughed. "I didn't think you'd get flustered so easily! I don't care what she is to you, just ask her to the dinner. Show the writer and her fiancé a good time. Give her a story. I know you're the best in the business, so it won't be a problem, correct?"

Rafael stood very still, taking in everything Christian was telling him. "Correct," he said slowly. In an instant, Rafael completely changed his mind about how it would be nice to get some distance from Grace for the evening. In fact, taking Grace out to meet new people and chat with a fellow American might not be the worst thing in the world. She could use a night on the town to distract her from everything else she'd been going through. Something casual and normal and fun. He could make that happen for her. It wouldn't be just the two of them, and it would still be a work event, all of it very platonic.

"I guess it's settled then," Rafael said.

"Good man."

Rafael was used to this—giving the client what they wanted, going out of his way to please them. He'd learned it well from trying so hard to please his father for his entire life. In one area, at least, he'd been successful. With his father, not so much.

"Oh," Christian called over his shoulder as he examined a painting. "Her name is Nora, by the way. She's expecting a message from you to confirm the time."

Rafael nodded distractedly. He would message Grace first, make sure she'd be able to go with him. Then he could confirm with the travel writer.

But when Grace's reply came, he wasn't sure how much to read into it. "I guess so," was all she said. It didn't seem to hold much enthusiasm, but Rafael would take it. Another night with Grace. Another night to prove to himself he had it all under control.

Raphael was humming as he rushed up the steps to his apartment, taking some of them two at a time. Perhaps he should have been concerned about how much he was looking forward to seeing her, to taking her out for the night, even if it was just a matter of business. But he didn't even consider it. He wasn't sure why he felt quite so buoyant, and he didn't bother to question it. He paused before he opened the door, though, remembering everything from the night before, how Grace pressed against him, his fingertips on her skin, her wet eyes fixed on his face.

She'd already been gone that morning when he finally rolled out of bed and made his way to the kitchen. They had a little morning routine, but it wasn't set in stone. Sometimes she left early to get a jumpstart on grading papers or planning her lectures. He'd tried to brush off the disappointment he felt when she'd already been gone, but a strange wistfulness had haunted his morning anyway.

With a hand on the door to his apartment, he took a breath, steeling himself for something, even if he wasn't sure what it was. It was unusual for him to feel nervous. Restless, maybe. Fidgety. But not nervous.

He opened the door and scanned the room for Grace, finding her almost immediately where she was sitting in the middle of the sofa in her pajamas—those ridiculous flannel ones with the little hamsters all over them—a book opened on her lap. He put down his bag and made his way toward her, as casual as could be.

She didn't look up at first, so he just stood there watching her, waiting. He imagined she was engrossed by whatever she was reading, and any moment she would turn to him with a smile. Except that wasn't happening. She was still just reading her book, not looking at him, and even though something prickled all over his skin, a feeling that something was wrong, he didn't know for sure if he was correct.

He waited. He put down his keys and removed his jacket and waited some more. Still, she didn't move. She didn't acknowledge his presence. He also noted that she didn't turn a page. She certainly didn't look like she was prepared to go out to their dinner, even though she'd agreed to it earlier.

What was this? Was she so embarrassed by their late-night encounter that she wouldn't look at him? Had he done something wrong?

Finally, he moved toward her, his heartbeat picking up as he grew more concerned. "Graciela?"

She exhaled. Slowly, she turned her head in his direction, but she stared off into the distance over his shoulder instead of looking him in the eye.

"How are you?" he ventured. His brain started whirring, scanning for any mistakes he had made, any other reason she might be upset with him. It had only been a few minutes, but he already hated the feeling of this distance she was creating between them. He held his breath as he waited for her to finally reply.

"I've been researching Sacramonte," she said, her voice laced with something sharp.

Rafael's brain scrambled to keep up. "Okay," he said slowly, because he had no clue where this was going and couldn't seem to land on an idea of the potential problem.

"You mentioned something about the history there, but I didn't realize..."

"Yes?" he prompted when she trailed off.

"It's been the home of a large community of Roma people for so long." Suddenly, it spilled out of her, everything she was thinking, which was somehow all tangled up with how angry she was at him. "Since the 15th century when they felt like outcasts and made a home on the outskirts of the city."

"Right," Rafael said. "I don't know much about the history—"

"But you should," she insisted as he zoned in on her clenched fists. "Sometimes they were allowed to live in peace, and other times they were persecuted. At times, they were forbidden from wearing traditional clothing or speaking the language of their people."

"Yes," he said again, almost breathless. He thought he was beginning to understand. He *knew* he was.

"You want to create a little playground for millionaires in a place that was sustained by the *gitanos*? An exhibition they won't even be allowed to visit if they aren't of a certain class?"

Rafael shook his head. She was getting it all wrong. It was a celebration of the area and its people. "I also mentioned that Christian's wife is a descendent of *gitanos* who live in that area. That was part of his interest."

Grace scoffed. "Come on, Rafael. You really think that makes it okay? Christian's wife has a connection, so he can do whatever he wants?"

"Yes. I mean, no. Christian's also planning to put up a plaque to commemorate the history of the cave houses."

"A plaque?" She stood, finally looking him right in the eyes, instead of avoiding his gaze.

"Yes, a plaque. What's wrong with that?" Rafael took a step toward the sofa without breaking eye contact.

Grace turned away, gathering her book and her notepad, as if preparing to storm off. "No one is going to pay attention to a plaque.

That's nothing." She took another breath. "People live in these houses, Rafael. People you've barely bothered to consider."

Rafael swallowed. Perhaps he was an awful person since he hadn't thought all that much about the history of Sacromonte. The implications had faded into the background the second Christian made up his mind, and Rafael failed to consider that this wasn't just some place they could move in and take over without considering its past. He hadn't even thought of the neighbors who lived in the nearby cave houses, of whether they had any say in the development of Christian's exhibit. He'd been brought into Christian's view of things—the view that you could do whatever you wanted if you paid enough, and so far it had proven true, even if that didn't mean it was right.

"What would you have me do, Grace? You remember I didn't want the exhibit there in the first place? I've been against it from the beginning."

He moved toward her, and she clung to her book, as if using it as a shield. It was ridiculous how much he wanted to wrap his arms around her, to hold her again and make all this animosity melt away, to try whatever he could to get her anger to evaporate.

"You've been against it because it's impractical, not because it's abhorrent. And that was never enough for you to stand up to Christian. Maybe that's what I would have you do. Stand up to him and tell him the truth. You could start by allowing the people who live here to enter the premises in the first place. Maybe by acknowledging their existence? It sounds to me like the area has always been a home to people who were overlooked. Don't perpetuate that, please. If you insist on commandeering a cave, then you could at least invite the community to be part of it. You could incorporate the history of the place, rather than trying to brush it away."

"There *is* a cave museum, Graciela. A museum that already exists and showcases the history there, the people and how they lived, the *gitano* culture."

Grace studied him for a moment. "That's good," she said. "I'm glad there is a place to represent the history of the area, but that doesn't mean you can get away with ignoring it, Raf. It doesn't mean you can exclude the people who live there now."

Rafael nodded, scanning the ideas in his head, trying to think of a solution. He could figure out a way to make this work. He always figured out a way. There was a solution to keep everyone happy, and he would conjure it. He snapped his fingers. "We could set up some kind of fund. Something to give back to the community."

Grace rolled her eyes. "Sure," she said. "I mean, yes, you should, but you're still just throwing money at it. It's not really a meaningful gesture."

Rafael took another step toward her. Perhaps he was a little too eager. "I *will* talk to Christian," he insisted. "We can discuss it. I can have you present some ideas to him as well, if there's something you want to suggest to him. I know he won't move the event; he thinks the setting is perfect, but there has to be something, and I'll make sure he listens to any ideas we have. I will stand up to him, Grace."

Grace stared, her expression full of skepticism. "Really? You aren't worried about pissing off your rich boss?"

"Well, it's not like you're saying anything unreasonable. It's an excellent point, and it's something Christian and I both should have given more thought. We've been remiss, obviously, and you're right. We should find a solution."

After all, he agreed with her now that the issue had been brought to his attention, and Rafael was sure they could convince Christian to take action. Christian wasn't a bad man, if a little self-centered and shortsighted. Perhaps those adjectives could describe Rafael as well. But Christian would understand, and if nothing else, he would be concerned with optics. He didn't want to look like an insensitive billionaire who was taking advantage of a marginalized community. He wanted to be a kind, sensitive billionaire. A billionaire of the people.

"Well..." Grace tugged on a button on the front of her pajamas. "That's good."

"That's good?" Rafael said, trying to hold himself still. If he took another step toward her, he would be close enough to touch her, and if he was close enough to touch her, he wasn't sure he would be able to stop himself from reaching out and doing it.

Grace bit her lip, and they were quiet for a long moment. "I'm not going to let it go or forget about this, Raf. The community in Sacromonte needs to be part of this."

"I know." He clenched his hands into fists, as if it would imbue additional strength into his words. "I agree with you."

"You do?" She studied him with that way she had—the way that made him feel utterly exposed—as if wary of how much she could believe him. He hoped she could see he was in earnest.

"I mean it, Graciela. This is why I needed your help in the first place. I knew I was in over my head, but you can make this work."

"I don't know," she said. "I'm not the expert here. Even if I can figure out a way to handle Picasso, there are so many things to consider."

"You know enough to berate me when I'm an idiot."

Her smile was a small one, but Raf clung to it like a life raft. She was warming up to him again. "Will you still come to dinner with me tonight?" he asked at last. He didn't know why it mattered so much to him that she did, why he was so desperate for her forgiveness and approval just because he was attracted to her. It didn't quite add up, but he didn't plan to consider it any further.

"Yes." She let out a breath and finally relaxed her shoulders, loosening the grip on her book. Perhaps he hadn't disappointed her too much.

He gave a curt nod, attempting not to show her the full force of his relief.

"I'll have to get changed, obviously." A spark of something shined in her eyes, mischief or joy, he didn't know, but Rafael tried not to think about how much it thrilled him to see that spark.

"You could wear your hamster pajamas. I wouldn't judge you."

Grace shook her head. "I know you, and I think you would."

Rafael grasped his chest with a dramatic flair. "What must you think of me, Graciela? I love hamster pajamas."

"Oh really? Even for fancy dinners with travel writers?"

He grinned at her. "You'd still look beautiful."

Grace's smile faltered, and Rafael wanted to kick himself. *Shit.* Why would he say that? He was going to freak her out. She was going to run for the hills.

"I'll be right back," she said, and she rushed for the door to her bedroom, leaving him alone to scold himself. She was beautiful, but that didn't mean he should say it out loud. It was too dangerous. He needed to get ahold of himself.

She wasn't making it easy for him, though. When she emerged from her room just a short time later, Rafael glanced up to find her in a silky blue dress that clung to her curves like plastic wrap. Her cheeks and lips were tinted pink, and everything about her seemed so inviting, it seemed a crime that he couldn't casually touch her—sweeping loose strands of hair from her face or curling his arm around her waist.

"Rafael?" she asked, and he realized he'd been staring, though he couldn't be sure how much time had passed. "Ready to go?"

He shook himself and tried to offer her a casual smile. "Yes," he coughed out. "*Vamos.*"

The travel writer was already seated at the table with her fiancé when Grace and Rafael arrived. They were pressed up against each other on the same side of the table, and Rafael realized for the first time how awkward the whole situation could be. This happy couple would be sitting there touching each other while he tried not to think about Grace's lips, about the way she might have leaned toward him the night before, about how she'd run off as fast as she could the moment he'd said the word *beautiful.*

The couple stood up as he and Grace approached and greeted them warmly. "You must be Rafael." The writer's smile was wide and bright. "I'm Nora, and this is Julian, my fiancé."

Rafael held out a hand. "A pleasure to meet you both. This is Grace, my —um—"

Nora waited, her eyes going back and forth between them.

"It's complicated," Grace jumped in. "We kind of live together, and we kind of work together, but not really. And he's my best friend's brother."

Rafael narrowed his eyes. He didn't know why Grace felt the need to offer that much information to strangers.

"Oh," Nora said, clearly confused.

Julian was grinning beside her, as if this explanation made perfect sense to him. They all took their seats, and Julian leaned over to Nora. "I remember when I didn't know how I should introduce you to people," he mumbled, and Nora's expression suddenly changed to one of understanding. She looked back to Grace and Rafael with even more interest.

Great, she definitely assumed they were sleeping together.

"You're American, Grace?" Nora asked. "Where are you from?"

A soft pink blush spread across Grace's face, as if she was embarrassed by the attention. "I am American," she said. "I think that's mostly why I'm here, so that I could meet a fellow countrywoman. I'm from Chicago."

Nora raised a hand. "New York. Upstate, though. Not the city."

"Oh, I've never been there before." Grace seemed to relax slightly, warming to the conversation. "I'm more of a city person, but I could be convinced to check it out."

Nora grinned. "You should definitely visit the area sometime. It's wonderful." She nudged the man beside her. "Right, Julian?"

"Of course," he agreed, leaning in toward his fiancée. "One of my favorite places to visit."

"And where are you from, Julian?" Rafael asked, jumping into the conversation rather than continuing to gape at the couple's easy affection. This felt so much like a double date, and Rafael needed a drink. Why had Christian wanted him to bring Grace along? Why had Rafael agreed to it?

"The UK," he said with a smile. "London, specifically. I've lived there my whole life."

"I've never been there either!" Grace chirped. "Always wanted to, though. How did you two meet, then?"

Nora and Julian glanced at each other with knowing expressions. "I was on an assignment," Nora started. "My first real assignment, and it was kind of a shitshow. I needed a cute British man to help me out."

Julian rolled his eyes. "Not true. I did absolutely nothing to help. And you're leaving out the part where I already knew you. And you waltzed back into my life ready to turn everything upside down."

They didn't break eye contact, and Rafael didn't know where to look. He'd never been bothered by observing people in relationships before. He'd never even thought about it. They could behave however they wanted, and it didn't make a difference to him in the least. But with Grace sitting there next to him—suddenly it felt strange to witness their intimacy. Something about the way Nora and Julian were looking at each other—their private jokes and heated glances—made him all too aware of Grace's presence at his side, of the hair spilling over her shoulder, the scent of it drifting into his face, her warm thigh so near to his, her fingers almost brushing his leg under the table.

Finally, Nora turned back toward him. "So tell me, Rafael, do you really have events and stories interesting enough to make me forget all about whatever is happening in Sacromonte? I've been told I'm not allowed to ask questions about all the recent activity in that area."

Rafael could feel Grace's attention on him, but he tried to ignore it as he slipped into the charming, placating character he played so well for his business. "I think I do," he said with a wave of his hand. "No need to worry about Sacromonte. I've got plenty that might interest you."

"Is that so?" Nora asked, taking out her pen with a dramatic flair. Julian was still grinning beside her.

Rafael racked his brain. He'd been so distracted by Grace and their earlier argument he'd forgotten to come up with intriguing stories for this writer, but he knew he could manage something. That was his job, after all.

CHAPTER THIRTEEN

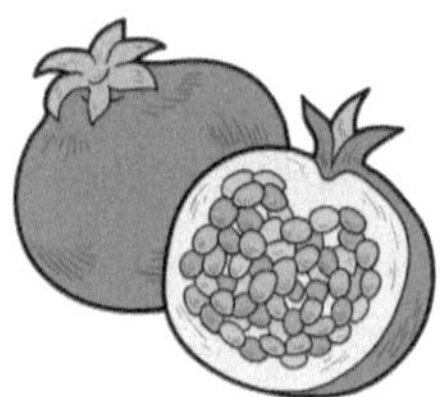

GRACE SPOKE LITTLE AT DINNER, instead opting to listen intently to every word that came out of Rafael's mouth. He had a way about him, this *charm,* and she couldn't help but be washed away with his words, caught up in his tales of celebrity clients and extravagant fundraising events. He talked about the city, too, and his descriptions were so full of excitement and affection that Grace wanted to go exploring even more. She remembered this side of him from when he'd answered all of her questions about the Alhambra or even when he'd suggested tapas at a restaurant. He had this confidence and this knowledge that made you want to hang on his every word.

Unfortunately, Grace was so focused on Rafael's words that when Nora or Julian started contributing to the conversation, she was lost in another world, still thinking about *him.* Honestly, for all Alma had warned her about him, Grace was still waiting for Rafael to turn the full force of his charm in her direction—to make any kind of move on her at all. He'd called her beautiful back at the apartment, of course. The word had sparked through her like she'd stuck her pinky finger in an electric socket. For a brief moment she wondered if it might be the start of something, some kind of foray into seduction, Rafael dipping in a toe to test the waters.

But once they'd started walking to the restaurant, he was all business. He kept his distance and barely even glanced in her direction. Even in the moments when she expected Rafael to charm her pants off a little more, he was restrained. He was thoughtful and honest in their conversation about the caves, for example. He'd even seemed a little flustered, no hint of the smooth talker that was now regaling Nora and Julian of tales of La Chica De Ayer and late-night extravaganzas at La Quaracha, of designing the spaces and the place-settings, curating menus and choosing invitations, taking charge of every fantastic evening from start to finish.

As he settled further into the dinner conversation, clearly more comfortable by the minute, his second glass of wine swirling in his right hand, Rafael eased back and rested his arm on the back of her chair. It wasn't on *her* exactly, but she could feel the warmth of his bicep against her shoulder, and even though it was the lightest of touches, the heat started to build and spread everywhere, in her belly and her toes, in her core.

Grace tried not to think about it. She tried not to *feel* it the way she did, the heat from his skin radiating through her entire body. She'd already taken too much notice of the way he'd removed his jacket and rolled his shirtsleeves up his forearms. She'd already clocked the dark little hairs that coated those forearms when he'd hung his jacket over his chair. She didn't know why she couldn't seem to focus on anything else.

Grace took a sip of water and forced herself to remember his less attractive qualities. He was so infuriating sometimes. How could he not consider the entire complex history of the place where they'd decided to stage their little exhibition? It was like the past oppression of marginalized people had never even crossed his mind. But then he listened to her when she brought it up. *Really* listened and seemed to want to change their strategy, like he was taking what she said to heart and hated that he'd upset her. He truly appeared shaken by the revelation, in a way she hadn't expected. She'd thought he would just brush it off without taking her seriously for even a moment.

Not for the first time, she was remembering that this Rafael was a different man than the one she'd known ten years ago. Maybe her first impression had been completely off, or maybe Rafael really had changed.

He'd grown into this intelligent, impressive person who laughed at her jokes, who held her in the night when she was devastated, who respected her and wanted to hear her opinions. He definitely had not cared for her opinion ten years ago when she was making a bunch of dick jokes, but now it seemed like her ideas mattered to him, and she liked it. As much as she didn't want to admit it—not even to herself—she liked *him*.

"You'll have to see that, Grace, I don't think you've been there yet," Rafael said, and Grace realized she was still completely tuned out of the conversation.

She nodded absently. "Of course. I want to see it all." Her voice sounded more wistful and longing than she would have liked.

He removed his arm from her chair, and she mourned the loss of the minimal contact, but then he placed a hand on her thigh instead. "You okay?" he asked.

Grace swallowed. She wanted to rub her face against the nape of his neck. She wanted to put her hand over his on her thigh and guide it up to just the right spot. She wanted to bite his bottom lip until he made sounds she could only imagine. Probably none of that was okay to be thinking about, and she wasn't sure where the hell it was coming from. Suddenly, it was like the person she thought of as Alma's older brother, and the person she thought of as Rafael, *her* Rafael, were entirely different people, and one of them was entirely too appealing.

"Yes, sorry, I just totally zoned out for a minute."

Nora grinned and put a hand to her chest. "A woman after my own heart. I'm a total zoner-outer."

Grace gave her a grateful smile. "I honestly don't know how to stop it from happening."

She tried not to visibly react when Rafael removed his hand from her thigh. "Your brain is too busy," he said, turning toward his dinner.

She hoped he had no idea what was going on in her busy brain. She was relieved to have a break from the constant swirl of thoughts that usually consumed her—death and loss and loneliness—but the ferocity with which her mind had latched on to this attraction to the man beside her was concerning.

From then on, Grace was determined to stay focused. She jumped into the conversation with both feet, asking all kinds of questions about Nora's job and the places she'd been. Grace could act normal, as if she couldn't feel the occasional brush of Raf's thigh against her own. All she had to do was ignore it.

She liked Nora and Julian and was glad to have met them, even if she wasn't entirely certain of her purpose at this dinner. It seemed like Nora had gotten what she came for, though, and they'd all enjoyed each other's company. Nora even mentioned she would be in Spain for a while, and they exchanged numbers. It was nice to have a new friend, someone who could relate to the fish-out-of-water feeling that crept over Grace on the days when she was lost on the edge of town, trying to remember which street led toward Raf's apartment. It was clear the evening was winding down, and it felt precarious, somehow. Grace got the sense that she was about to say or do something entirely foolish, that being left alone with Rafael after spending so much time focused on his mouth at dinner was a very dangerous thing.

It was serendipitous when the live band started to play after their meal. Everyone seemed eager to linger then, as if unwilling to miss out on hearing the beat of the music as it pumped through the restaurant. Soon, other patrons were rising from their tables and rushing to the dance floor by the little stage. Julian stuck out a hand to Nora, inviting her to dance as well.

Nora grinned up at him, full of delight. "We'll be right back," she said, and Grace continued watching them as they started to dance, ignoring the sudden realization that she was alone at the table with Rafael. She was alone with him all the time. She lived with him. She didn't know why it should be any different while they were at some kind of work-related dinner, but it was. She was aware of his every movement, every time his fingers twitched, every time his thigh shifted.

He took a sip of water and looked over at her. Her instinct was to avert her eyes, to hide, but she didn't. She swayed a bit with the music, and he bit his lip, and they were still just staring at each other.

"Do you—uh." He cleared his throat and gestured toward Nora and Julian. "Do you want to dance?"

Grace glanced back at the dance floor, how the couples were twisting around, spinning and then pressing their bodies together, intertwining their fingers. Dancing required a lot of touching. She wanted to, and she also didn't. "Sure," she said, before she'd even decided to say it. It was as if her mouth had made up her mind without consulting her brain.

Rafael raised an eyebrow as if he didn't quite believe her. "We don't have to."

She looked down at her hands and tried to collect her thoughts. It was just a dance. At a work dinner. "No, we should. I like the music."

He took her hand, and she trailed after him until they joined the other couples. Nora gave her a little nod and another knowing glance, and Grace shrugged as if to say *he's too hot to resist.* She knew Alma would have disapproved of the whole thing—the dinner and the dancing, the moment when Rafael had placed a hand on her thigh, but Grace forgot all about her promise to heed Alma's warning when Raf's palm warmed her hip, when he clutched her fingers and spun her in a circle, when he pressed her back against his front and swayed to the beat.

Was Rafael simply so good at seducing women that you didn't even realize it was happening until it was too late? Or was he just being polite, asking her to dance because everyone else was doing it, and he was a well-bred gentleman?

He spun her around again and clasped both of her hands in his. Their eyes met, and Grace swallowed, hoping her face wasn't giving her away. If he tried to kiss her right now, she couldn't resist. If he tried to kiss her ever again... Well, she probably didn't need to worry about that anyway. This was all completely platonic, and Raf could have any woman he wanted. Why would he ever get involved in a messy situation with his sister's mopey best friend?

The song ended too soon, but Rafael didn't let go of her. He smelled like white wine and lemon. His fingers intertwined with hers. His thumbs pressed against the back of her hands. They continued to look into each other's eyes, still swaying slightly, while he drew her even closer, inch by inch. He wet his lips, and Grace could hear his ragged breath, could feel his heartbeat. She couldn't help but wonder if it meant something after all—the way he gripped her hands, the way he stared. The way they lingered like that far longer than was appropriate for "colleagues," until Nora and

Julian approached, both of them smiling widely. Rafael finally released her and turned to face them, but it was too late for her. Something had changed, even if she didn't know what. Something had shifted, the world tilting further on its axis, the moon tugging harder at the tides.

"That was a fantastic band," Nora said. Her cheeks were glowing slightly, and there was a gleam of sweat on her forehead. Grace couldn't help wondering if she was flushed herself from the dancing like Nora or if her face was hot from something else. Either way, she couldn't imagine sweating as beautifully as Nora.

"I'm glad you enjoyed it." Rafael shook himself, as if trying to reclaim his businesslike persona. "A hint of the magic of Granada."

"More than a hint," Julian added, and he kissed Nora's hand before they went to gather their things.

"It was so nice meeting you both," Nora said as they stood outside the restaurant. "And I want to see you again, Grace. I feel so adrift sometimes when I'm traveling, especially when Julian's back in London. It would be nice to have a friend."

"Definitely," Grace replied, trying to sound nonchalant, like there wasn't a storm of wanting thrashing around inside of her. Julian laced his fingers with Nora's. It seemed like they were politely including Grace and Raf in conversation, even though they simultaneously had their own little world. She'd never had that with Derek—that level of connection. She'd never even known she was missing it.

"Ready to go?" Rafael asked as they waved a final goodbye to the happy couple.

Grace pursed her lips and tried to curve them into a smile. Rafael set his hand on her lower back to guide her, and she wanted to lean into it—to lean against him.

Instead, Grace reminded herself of his faults. How could he just cater to Christian's whims without even considering their impact? How could he forget to include the people who were from the area as part of their project? How could he jerk away from her when she'd leaned toward him in her bedroom? How could his gentle hand on her back, touching her through layers of clothing, make her feel like her whole body was about to burst into flames?

He was maddening, and she didn't know how to handle it any longer. Obviously, he wasn't perfect, but she was all too familiar with her own imperfections. How could she judge him so harshly when she knew she could be selfish and shortsighted and oblivious? But she wanted to be a thoughtful person and a good friend. She was *trying*. And she could tell Rafael was trying too.

"That was surprisingly enjoyable," he said.

"Yeah." She worked so hard to sound normal. "I liked them."

"Thanks for coming with me. It just felt more natural to have you there, like it was a casual dinner among friends rather than some uncomfortable work thing. I think you prevented them from interrogating me about the exhibition."

Grace nodded absently. "You—uh—you were great."

They walked in silence for a while, Grace chewing on her lower lip, desperate to return home and run to her room and close the door. Tomorrow, in the light of day, everything would be clear again. She'd be able to look at him without feeling it in her knees.

When they got to the front door of the apartment, Raf finally broke their silent spell. "Is everything good? I know it may have been weird to go to dinner and pretend like nothing was wrong—"

"Wrong?" Grace's gaze shot in his direction.

"From our argument earlier. We can talk more about it. I just hope that didn't ruin your evening."

"No." She tried to reply casually, but it came out like a breathless whisper. Why wasn't he unlocking the door so she could make a run for it? Why were they lingering in the hallway, too close...

"Graciela?" Raf leaned in and she could feel his breath.

Open the door. Open the door.

"Hmm?"

He was so close to her, and aside from turning and bolting down the hall, Grace wasn't sure what she could possibly do. Maybe he wanted to kiss her after all? A flash of the night at the club in Barcelona filled her mind. He had the same look on his face now, the same liquid eyes.

Who was she kidding, there was no way she was going to stop him if he tried to kiss her again. She was dying for it, every hair on her body standing on end.

"I want to know what you're thinking. You were so quiet on the way home. If it wasn't the argument, then what's going on? Are you still upset about the dream from last night?"

Her tongue felt heavy. She didn't know what to say to him. She didn't want to admit the truth. "No, it's nothing. Don't worry about it."

He exhaled, and somehow he was still leaning closer. "You can tell me, truly. If it's something I can help—"

"It's not," Grace interrupted. She looked toward their apartment door, as if it could save her. "It's too embarrassing." She thought of the way he had touched her at dinner, his hand on her thigh, however briefly, his arms around her when they danced. She couldn't admit the effect it had on her, how it had consumed her so quickly.

"I doubt that," he said, reaching out and lifting her chin. "Especially if you knew what's been going through my mind."

Grace's breath hitched, and she blinked up at him, every nerve ending in her entire body suddenly on high alert. She tried to restrain herself, as desperate as she was to know what he meant. "What?" Her voice came out in a husky whisper.

Rafael paused for a moment, eyeing her warily, as if trying to decide if he should answer. "I was thinking about that crease on your forehead whenever you're scolding me." He lifted a hand, and his thumb traced a spot between her eyebrows. "And about how you bite your lip when you're nervous. I can't stop thinking about your lips, actually, and wondering if you might have been wanting to kiss me last night." His thumb trailed down her face until it brushed her bottom lip so lightly, she wasn't sure he was really touching her. "Or maybe that's totally inappropriate, and I shouldn't even be bringing it up."

Grace's throat seemed to constrict, and her breath became shallow. She couldn't move for a moment. Elation and terror shot through her, but she already knew she was done for. She didn't even think about what would happen next. She slid her hands up against Rafael's chest and then behind his neck and pressed forward on her toes. She moved up in one quick rush until her mouth was on his at last, and the delicious thrill of it filled her. It was better than she'd ever imagined, how he hungrily deepened the kiss and wrapped her in his arms, pressing her entire body flush against his own. He spun her until her back was pinned against their front door and anchored himself even harder against her until she could feel every part of him—his firm chest rising to meet her breasts, his tongue searching her mouth, his thigh pressing between her legs as she involuntarily thrust her hips to feel the friction between them.

Rafael let out a satisfied groan, and Grace was lost to the world. She didn't even know where she was anymore. It was as if she'd entered another plane entirely, a place she'd never been before. If she would have known ten years ago when he'd tried to kiss her that it would be like this, she would have just let him, all her pride and his surliness be damned.

His mouth moved to her neck, and she gasped. Her hands went into his hair, while his fingers started to roam her body. First, they glided up her spine, then back down to her ass. Then he clutched at the neckline of her shirt and tugged down as his lips made his way down her to the base of her throat. His kisses covered her clavicle and her chest, and Grace's head fell back against the door with a thud.

"Should we go inside?" Raf asked.

"Yes," she whispered, though. her brain was screaming. *Yes. Yes. Yes.*

He unlocked the door at last, and they fell into the apartment, eagerly reaching for each other as soon as they could. He tugged her shirt over her head and wrapped his arms around her as she slid her hands under his clothing, elated to be tracing the hard muscles of his abdomen.

God, he was so hot. Honestly, how could a woman resist him? Sorry, Alma, it just wasn't possible. She'd tried to heed the warning, but how could she stop herself when he felt like *this?!*

"Grace," he moaned into her mouth. "I haven't been able to stop thinking about you." He hitched her up against him, and she immediately tightened her legs around his middle.

"Really?" she breathed, and he replied by letting out a string of whispered words in Spanish.

"I don't know what you just said."

He nuzzled into her neck. "That's probably for the best, because it was filthy."

"Oh." He scraped her bottom lip with his teeth, and all the fantasies Grace had been holding back started to play out in her mind. Rafael moving over her, his bare skin gleaming in the dim light, his hands all over her body, and then his mouth...

Suddenly, a loud buzzing echoed through the entryway, and they both froze. It took a moment for Grace to realize the sound was coming from her bag, which had been abandoned on the floor the second she'd stepped through the threshold of the apartment.

They remained completely still until the vibration stopped, and then they looked at each other, each waiting to see what the other would do.

Rafael's breath was heavy. "Grace," he said, taking a moment to catch his breath.

"You can call me Graciela." She smirked, bolder now after everything he'd admitted to her.

His lips twitched into a smile. "Graciela," he said, and the sound made her tighten her legs around him. He groaned then and nuzzled into her hair. "Should we talk about this?"

Should they talk about this? Yes, probably. As much as she wished they could just plow forward, full steam ahead, Grace didn't want to think anymore. She didn't want to consider the consequences, no matter how complicated they could be. Of course, Alma had warned her that this would happen, that Rafael was used to getting his way with women, and it was never anything more than sex. But the idea of "just sex" kind of appealed to Grace. She'd just gotten out of a three-year relationship and moved to a new country. It wasn't like her life screamed ready-for-a-serious-thing. "Just sex" could be simple and fun.

If only it wasn't Rafael. All their little ties to each other, not to mention the fact that they were living together for who knows how long since the contractors were in no rush to work on her apartment, added a level of intensity to the whole endeavor.

She released her grip on him, and he let her down slowly, waiting for her to say something.

Before Grace could answer his question, her phone started vibrating again. Somehow, it sounded louder and angrier if that was possible. She reluctantly turned away from Raf and grabbed her bag from the floor. She already knew who it would be, the one person who would call her more than once, the whole reason she was here to begin with, the person who had given her the possibility of a new life.

"It's Alma," she said, holding up the cell for him to see. Alma had been expecting her to call hours ago, but with all the distractions of the cave research, and dinner, and Rafael... Her throat constricted at the thought of what her best friend would say about all of this.

"Go ahead." Rafael gave her a sad smile, acknowledging that the fire between them was extinguished, the moment of recklessness at an end.

Grace nodded and tried to gather her wits. Half of her brain was still clinging to bedroom fantasies of Rafael, wishing she could forget everything else in the world. She didn't know how to answer Alma's call while still sounding like her usual self, but if she didn't pick up, Alma would only call again, worried about why she'd never checked in. Grace put the phone to her ear, and made her best effort.

"Hi," she choked out, trying to steady her voice. "What's up?"

"Where have you been?" Alma's voice was high-pitched through the phone speaker. "You said you would call me earlier! Is everything okay?"

Grace nodded even though Alma couldn't see her, guilt washing over her. "I know. I was just so busy with grading papers and planning and everything."

That was partly true. Before Raf had arrived home, she'd spent hours working on her classes.

"Well, tell me about all of it! Have you met Marco's mom yet? What's going on with that?"

Alma seemed prepared to settle in for a long conversation, and Grace didn't know what to do. How could she say, "actually, I'll have to let you go so I can keep making out with your brother even though you told me not to?"

She couldn't.

Instead, she looked toward Rafael as she started to answer Alma's questions. She tried to convey everything she was feeling with a look—her apology for letting their evening end like this, her longing. Perhaps her uncertainty was written there as well. Rafael kept his distance, nodding solemnly before gesturing toward his bedroom. He was giving her privacy. He was relinquishing his hold on her for the evening. He wasn't going to touch her anymore, even if she would have killed for a hand pressed into her back or a kiss on the forehead before he left.

It would be better this way, to quit while they were ahead, before things got messier than they already were. Maybe they would laugh about that time they kissed and shake their heads, thinking of how foolish they'd been. It was the right call. Better to forget about all of it. Better to play it safe and protect herself.

CHAPTER FOURTEEN

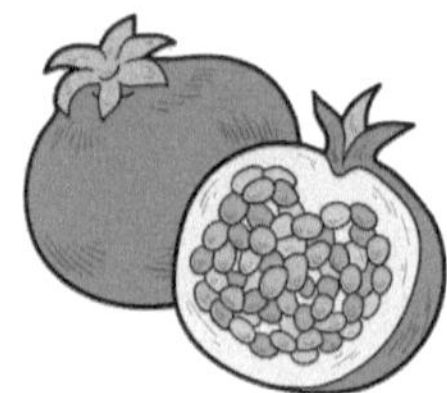

THINGS WERE WORSE. So much worse.

Rafael had been relatively sure he could get Grace out of his system if they had a night together, but to leave things hanging like that, right in the middle of it? To be tortured by the taste of her tongue, the way she squeezed her legs around him and stroked her fingers through his hair? He was going to lose it. Instead of getting it out of his system, she'd hijacked the system. She'd infiltrated him with her satisfied little moans and the eager *yes* she'd breathed into his ear. It didn't help that she'd also been so adorable and charming at dinner, chatting with the travel writer about America and leaning into the arm he draped over her chair, looking at him with big eyes and glowing cheeks, as if she was happy to be there beside him. As if it was the most natural thing in the world.

And then she'd danced with him…

He sat at the kitchen counter the next morning slicing a pomegranate, drinking his coffee, and waiting for Grace to emerge from her bedroom. She'd been on the phone with Alma forever, and Rafael hadn't even tried to approach her after that, but if she joined him in the kitchen soon, they would have time—time to feed the hunger that was expanding in his belly. Time to explore what was happening between them and to kiss and to finish what they started. He didn't know what would happen after that, and he was barely able to consider it. He was consumed only by what would take place in the minutes after she opened that door. It was as far into the future as he could imagine, because it was all he could think about.

Finally, Grace emerged, fully clothed, which was disappointing but not impossible to overcome. Her hair was in a loose braid over her shoulder, and she was wearing one of those professor ensembles, a creamy blouse tucked into a colorful skirt, exactly the kind you might imagine an art history instructor to wear. He couldn't remember if he'd ever found it sexy before, but now his head was filled with pornographic images that revolved around that bohemian skirt.

He was still lost in dirty thoughts when he realized Grace was already across the room, standing right on the other side of the counter with a sheepish smile, fiddling with the end of her braid.

"I've still never eaten one of those," she said, nodding toward the pomegranate.

He remembered this was one of his safe areas of conversation, and perhaps he should have taken it as a sign to retreat back to normalcy, to pretend nothing happened. But his body was screaming to move toward her, to caress her, and he gave in easily, dropping the knife and moving around the counter until he was standing before her and ready to take her into his arms again.

She chewed her lip and gazed up at him, and just as he went to put a hand to her face, she said, "I was thinking..."

That could be okay. He loved when she was thinking. He loved watching her concentrate, the little faded birthmark that darkened on her forehead as she tried to solve a problem. He loved when she was lecturing him about Picasso or income equality or Sacromonte. It was thrilling to watch her mind work.

"Si.¿En qué estabas pensando?" His voice was deeper than he'd intended. What was the word? *Husky. Gruff.*

He stared as she inhaled the air in the space between them. "I—uh—well maybe Alma interrupting was a good thing. We don't want to make this too weird, right? You're one of the only people I know in the entire country of Spain, and I like you. I like spending time with you, I mean. I don't want it to get all wonky."

"What's *wonky?*" The things she said sometimes. Who talked like this? Maybe if he could focus on the strange words, he could forget about their meaning.

"You know, like, all out of whack? Messed up?"

He nodded, but he was staring at her lips again. "Right."

"You agree with me, then?"

No, I want to splay you across this counter and taste every inch of you. Rafael took a breath, trying to build something inside of himself brick by brick, something that wouldn't topple over with the slightest look from her. "It makes sense. It would be complicated."

"Exactly." Grace looked relieved, happy they were on the same page. "It would probably be weird for Alma, and she's my closest friend."

Rafael nodded, hoping his disappointment wasn't visible. It all made perfect sense. It was the reason he hadn't made a move before last night. He just wasn't sure he wanted to hear it out loud. He didn't want her to make the case against something happening between them. "Of course."

Grace's smile was perfectly friendly. "Okay, good."

Neither of them moved for a moment. They just stood and stared at each other.

"You want to have a pomegranate?" he asked, backing into familiar, innocent territory.

"I do, but maybe later? I have to get to class."

"Later then."

"Great." She hesitated for the first time, as if the planned part of her speech had come to an end, and she was wading into unfamiliar waters. "Um, yes, okay."

Rafael put his hands in his pockets, a pretense of nonchalance. "I'll see you tonight." Tonight, when he wouldn't be able to put his hands on her again. Tonight, when he would just have to lie there alone in his bed, even though she was so close, even though he knew the sounds she made when he pressed his mouth to hers. What sounds might she make if he pressed his mouth to other places? He wouldn't be finding out, apparently.

She finally turned and walked out the front door with a little wave.

Rafael raised a hand before rubbing it over his face when she was gone. He let out a dramatic sigh. *Santo cielo.* Everything was so much worse.

They kept their distance for a couple of days, as much as was possible in a small apartment. Grace seemed to spend longer days at the university and meet up with Alma more frequently after classes. Rafael threw himself into his work and courting other clients, but one fact remained: the cave was littered with crates of priceless Picasso paintings, and Rafael had no idea what to do with them. As much as he was dreading the long drive and the unavoidable proximity of his small vehicle, as much as he couldn't imagine being tucked into a dark curve of the cave wall with Grace so near to him, he couldn't put it off any longer. He needed her help. And as uncomfortable as it might have been when he brought it up to her, she agreed easily enough.

It was awkward on the way there with nothing to focus on but the road and the tension between them. Rafael could barely think of a word to say to her after he'd explained the disastrous state of the exhibition.

Grace nodded along, but she looked distracted too, like she couldn't quite concentrate on what he was saying. She was wearing a silky purple scarf, and Rafael wanted to slide the material between his fingers, to tug at the fabric until it unraveled from her neck, coming undone. He wanted to make Grace come undone.

It was fine. Maybe he would go out with some friends that evening to take his mind off it. He could chat with another pretty girl at the bar, and all would be right with the world. It would settle back to the way it had always been. No more longing or aching or whatever the hell this was. It didn't suit him. He was a man of action, a man who made detailed plans and executed them with precision. He didn't need to sit around *pining.* It was childish and ridiculous. It was beneath him.

Grace pointed at a sign that displayed a giant pomegranate, her face lit up with delight, and Rafael felt his chest tighten. Okay, so his aching hadn't subsided quite yet, but it would. He just needed to get through this one difficult day, and then he wouldn't be required to spend time with her anymore.

It was easier in Sacromonte when they had something to talk about. They had quite a lot to talk about, actually, considering the utter disaster hiding out inside the walls of the cave. There were packaged precious paintings everywhere, each one accompanied by pictures, notes, and measurements, and while Christian had been a stickler about temperature settings and humidity and special gloves, without anywhere for them to *go*, the pieces were just waiting for the meticulous art handlers to get them perfectly placed on the walls of the venue. Christian was in a rush to get it all in order before something got damaged.

They'd also upgraded the security system in the cave, and Rafael gave a small nod to acknowledge the man in the suit near the front door. He was included in the package Christian had purchased, apparently, or he was on a roster of bodyguards Christian seemed to have handy whenever he needed to protect something precious. Grace barely seemed to notice the guard, sliding right past him and into the first room where priceless works of art rested in their expensive crates, waiting for examination.

"Holy shit," Grace said, her mouth open with awe. She looked at him, as if for confirmation all of this was real. A flurry of art handlers rushed around, ensuring that each box was appropriately labeled and ready to be opened.

Rafael shrugged, but he couldn't stop from grinning, pleased with how impressed she was. Grace crouched down by the nearest crate and picked up the packet of literature from the side pocket. She got to work in an instant, already spouting off knowledge about "periods," early work, color, and brushstrokes.

Then Grace pointed at the painting that an art handler was unboxing with white gloves, an excited gasp escaping her lips. "Just look at this, Raf. Have you seen this?"

He was happy she was still using the nickname and their level of familiarity hadn't completely fallen to pieces because of one perfect kiss.

"I've seen it at Christian's estate, but I don't know what I'm looking at." Grace cocked her head at him, and he felt obligated to continue.

"Well, obviously it's a woman." He was aware he sounded like an idiot, but of course, he had no better analysis to offer. He was convinced the art handler snickered.

"Yes," Grace deadpanned, but she didn't bother teasing him. Instead, she went back to staring at the painting, and Rafael let out a sigh of relief to be free from her scrutiny.

"And?" he prompted, surprised by his curiosity about the work.

"Picasso painted a lot of portraits of her. This was one of his lovers. Dora Maar."

The air seemed to thicken, and Rafael very deliberately kept his eyes on the painting. "Interesting way to portray your lover," he said. Though the bright colors could have been called appealing, the subject of the piece was quite...abstract. He couldn't help but think if he could paint, he would paint Grace a bit more proportionally. Not that *she* was his lover.

Grace shook her head. "But look at how he captures different aspects of who she is. She looks thoughtful and serious, but the background is bright and bold. She had a fiery side to her. And her eyes really feel like they're looking at you, don't they?"

Rafael coughed. "Almost too much." The eyes were also uneven on the face, which made them even more unsettling.

Grace inched closer, and the art handler flinched, so she took a step back again. "I won't touch it, I promise," Grace said, and Rafael hid a smile.

"They had an intense relationship," Grace continued. "I feel like you can see it in the way he paints her. I've never seen one of his portraits of her in real life like this. They were partners. They challenged each other intellectually. They had a passionate affair, but he was with other women at the time, too."

Rafael's eyes went wide. "What a guy."

Grace was still staring at the work of art. "I told you," she said. "His personal life..." She finally looked back at Rafael and shrugged. "There's a reason I don't know what to do with him. The way he saw these women in real life bleeds into his art. He also painted Dora Maar as his weeping woman, turning her into nothing more than an image of the suffering that he had caused. But she was a great artist and photographer herself."

"You always have a way of making this stuff very interesting."

She gave him a sad smile. "I don't have to make it interesting. I mean, the man was so volatile, there's no way it could be boring. Even if it's also hard to swallow."

"Yes," Rafael said, "but the art. I couldn't even pretend to care about it, but with you explaining, it seems to organize itself into some kind of sense. You see so much when you look at a painting, so much I've never even bothered to notice. I can see why your students adore you."

"Huh." Grace let out a breath. "Who said they adore me?"

"Alma."

"Alma just says that because *she* adores me, but it's really only her."

"It's not only her." The words were out before he could stop them, and he didn't know whether to wish he could take them back. She was facing the painting, only her profile in view, so he couldn't make out her expression. Slowly, she turned, and somehow, she looked more beautiful in that moment, surprise and confusion and maybe a little pleasure written across her face, as she stood in front of that strange, colorful portrait. He could see her chest moving up and down with each breath. Suddenly, he found himself closer to her, like his body had carried him a few centimeters forward without bothering to mention it to his brain.

The art handler glanced at both of them before carrying Dora Marr's portrait to an art rack to conduct a thorough inspection.

Grace slipped away into the nearby alcove, her lips parted as she watched him, alert and wary, and eager, too, if he wasn't imagining it. "Raf," she breathed.

"Mmm," he hummed, trying to stop himself, even though he couldn't help moving with her, matching her step for step. There was still a rush of activity throughout the cave, but in this spot they were out of view, as if no one else existed.

"We agreed…"

"We did." He refused to move any closer. Clearly, he wanted her. If she reciprocated, then she would just have to make a move. She was the one who'd called it off, and she would have to call it back on. He would just stand there hoping to God that she would.

She lunged for him, then, and her mouth was on his before he knew what was happening, but he caught up quickly, wrapping his arms around her, pressing them closer together, his fingers in her hair, then a hand on her hip. She moaned into his mouth again, just as she had a few nights earlier. It was a sound he'd been hearing in his dreams, a sound that made him hard in an instant. He backed her into the wall of the big alcove, to ensure they wouldn't be seen unless someone walked right over to them. He felt the rough texture of the cave wall against the smoothness of her skin, and he traced his hand against her cheek, cradling her head so it wouldn't hit the wall.

She pulled away almost as quickly as she'd kissed him, but her hair was mussed, and her lips were pink and swollen, proof that it had really happened.

Rafael forced himself to take a step backward, giving her space so she would know she was the one in control of the situation.

"Sorry." She tried to cover her face with her hands, but he pulled them back down to see her expression. "That was unintentional."

"You're completely forgiven," he said, swallowing hard, burying the tiny hope that had bloomed inside him. "Don't worry."

Grace exhaled in frustration and shook her head. "What are we doing?"

She was always asking him questions he wasn't prepared for. Normally, he liked every angle mapped out, every talking point ready to go to make a sale, to impress a client, to win over a vendor. But with her, he was always at a loss, always trying to catch up and find the right thing to say.

"I don't know." It wasn't very elegant, but it was honest. It was all he had at the moment.

"Me neither," she said. She put her hands to her cheeks again and sighed. "I think, maybe, until we have a handle on what this is, we probably shouldn't..." She trailed off, absently touching a fingertip to her lips.

Rafael didn't know if he would ever have a handle on what this was when it was so unlike any situation he'd been in before. He supposed that meant it was never going to happen, because he would never be able to puzzle it out. He wanted to sleep with her, certainly, but he was starting to worry there was more to it than that. Even in the past few days when she'd been distant, he'd thought about her too often, missed her too much. Her laugh, hearing about her students, watching her wrinkle her nose as she studied a book, planning her next class. But what did that mean? Did he want to have a relationship with Grace Cameron? It seemed impossible to even think such a thing, but here he was, imagining what it might be like. He could picture it so easily—lazy Sundays in bed, cocktails before dinner, holding hands in the park. Suddenly his fantasies had morphed from fevered kisses to long, intimate conversations with her, which only made him more concerned he was losing his mind.

"Sure," Rafael said, making every effort not to sound like his brain was spinning in circles.

Grace's face was tinged pink. "Okay. Sorry, again. I know that was my fault."

Rafael trained his face into an easy smile despite the feeling that something was ripping open inside of him. "Nothing to worry about."

CHAPTER FIFTEEN

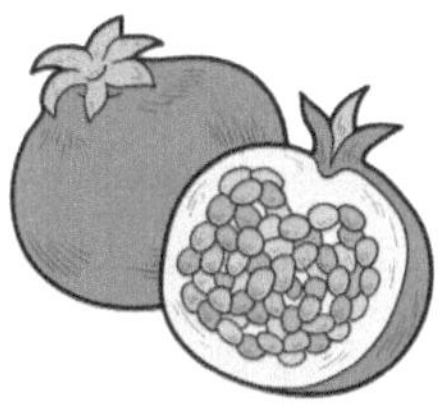

GRACE WAS grateful for a distraction the next day, after she'd spent hours replaying that moment in the cave, reliving every second when Rafael's lips had been on hers, every smile and lingering glance. As desperate as she was for things to go back to normal between them—for Alma's sake, for her own—she hadn't been able to resist him when they were in such close proximity, talking of lovers and art. She needed to get it out of her head. Thankfully, she'd invited all her students for a little field trip to an artsy café in the city center where she'd be able to concentrate on something else for a few hours. It wasn't a mandatory event, and except for Marco and his mother, she was unsure how many would show up, but when she arrived on Thursday evening, she was surprised to find that eleven other students had come, which she considered a miraculous turnout. The café walls were covered in pieces from local artists with no consistent theme or style. There were landscapes and portraits and fantastical images of angels and demons. It was a lot to take in, but her students seemed excited to wander around and view all of it while they chatted.

"I honestly never cared that much about art," her student, Elyse, said as Grace joined the class at a counter-height table. "But now I'm intrigued. I know there's still so much I don't know, but I like to look at it, at least."

Grace smiled. "That's really the only qualification you need. An appreciation for the work."

Grace chewed the tip of her thumbnail and looked up at the small sketch she'd been admiring on the wall. It was a little drawing of the Alhambra in pencil. She tried not to think of the day she'd spent there with Rafael. *No, she was not supposed to be thinking of him.* She'd basically attacked him with her mouth after saying they should just be friends, and everything was too confusing. She'd already had her heart broken once this year. She needed to keep her mind on the art.

"Hola, Profesora," Marco chirped cheekily from where he stood on the other side of the table, bouncing on the balls of his feet. "This is my mother, Lucia."

Grace stuck out a hand to the woman hiding behind Marco. She was petite and shy, her big eyes peeking out from behind shaggy dark bangs. Her resemblance to Marco was entirely evident in the shape of her face and her button nose. He even had her little chin dimple. "*Encantada,* Lucia," Grace said.

Lucia simply nodded, her lips pressed together.

"I made her bring pictures of other paintings," Marco said, rocking on his feet. "There were some I'd never even seen before, and they're so good. At least, I think they are."

"Oh, I would love to see them," Grace gushed, trying to sound as friendly as possible. She could tell Lucia was uncomfortable.

Marco whipped out a tablet from his bag to pull up the images, and Grace gave Lucia another reassuring smile. Of course, it must be terrifying to share your work with a stranger, especially when it seemed that Lucia didn't really share her work with anyone anymore.

"This was a long time ago," Lucia said slowly.

When Marco handed Grace the tablet with the first painting pulled up on the screen, Grace let out a breath. "Wow." The word hung in the air as Grace stared at the photo. The painting was similar in color to the other one Grace had seen, but this time it was a half-eaten loaf of bread on the kitchen table. Once again, the focus of the piece was done beautifully, but it was the background that captured Grace's attention. There were blocks and other toys on the table, a chair with a sweater flung over it. There were dirty dishes that looked like they'd been left after someone had finished eating and a highchair covered in bits of food. Lucia's soft brushstrokes made every object seem like it was almost glowing from within. For a moment, Grace forgot where she was. She felt like she was in this room. In this kitchen, at this little table. She could almost hear it—the clinking of silverware as someone came around to clear the remaining dishes, the water running in the faucet and the happy screams of a child playing in the next room. It felt warm and real and alive.

Despite the realism, though, there was something that seemed almost like magic, something that turned a dirty dish into a relic of comfort and peace. It was the color, maybe, or the texture of the dish. It was the way the painting captured the angle of the sunlight and made every object look like you could reach out and touch it.

Before she was ready for him to move on, Marco reached out a finger and swiped the screen to show the next picture. It was another still life, but it hinted so much at the motion of life, at the frantic morning that had led to this scene. There was a pitcher of juice on the counter in the foreground and a glass with lingering pulp pressed against one side. In the background was a stack of dirty dishes and crumpled cloth napkins. On the other side was a pile of papers that looked like mail that was somewhat covered by a burnt oven mitt. It was all so beautiful, Grace couldn't tear her eyes away. It transported her back to her childhood and life with her grandmother, to the days when Grace would be begging to go somewhere or for Gram to play cards, but she would be stuck at the sink washing dishes before sorting through the mail and folding the laundry. "I'm so bored," Grace would complain, not considering that Gram was doing everything—taking care of all the chores so that life would run smoothly, so she could eat and do her schoolwork without worrying about anything else.

Grace chipped in when she got older, of course, but even then it took her a long time to appreciate everything Gram had done to make her comfortable, to be her parent. Grace's mom was living with her boyfriend, dropping by every couple of weeks to kiss her daughter on the head and tell her she was pretty. Grace's dad was MIA most of the time, off on another bender. But Gram had stepped up and loved her so well. She'd been there for her until the last moment, and even when she was sick in bed, it was Grace who Gram had worried about. Alma and Raf might have teased her about saying *thank you* too much, but with Gram, she'd never said it enough.

She could feel the tears welling in her eyes. She started coughing just to excuse herself from Marco and Lucia for a moment and took a long drink of water while she wiped her face. She'd been doing better lately. She hadn't cried nearly as much, but grief was a funny, never-ending thing. It was always there, sometimes dormant, but it could flare up in an instant.

"Sorry about that," she said, returning to Marco and his mother. "These are amazing, Lucia. I absolutely love them, and I'm not just saying that because you're Marco's mom. Do you still paint?"

Lucia shook her head. "I took a lot of classes when I was young, and I loved it, but it was a long time ago. It's easy for life to get in the way of this kind of thing."

"I keep telling her she should take it up again," Marco said, nudging his mother in the arm.

Lucia glanced over at him, her eyes full of adoration. "Ever since he started this class," she said haltingly, considering each English word, "he's obsessed with the idea."

"Well." Grace took the tablet in her hands again and stared at the pitcher. "I have to say, I'm inclined to agree with him."

The rest of the evening was lovely. Grace talked with her students about art, of course, and about their classes, but also about their lives—where they were from and their families and their plans. They asked her questions about Chicago, too, about what made her want to come to Spain, and if she did any kind of painting herself.

"I've tried," she said, huffing a laugh. "It did not go well. I'm more of an observer."

As things were winding down and students said their goodbyes, Marco approached her again. His mother had left early, claiming she wanted to let her son have a good time with his friends and his boyfriend, who had joined them toward the end of the night.

"Thank you for that," Marco said. He chewed on his pinky nail as if he was nervous.

"For what?"

"For, I don't know. Agreeing with me? Encouraging my mamá? Since my dad passed, I think she cut herself off from a lot of things that brought her joy, opting to wallow in her misery instead. She's getting better now, I'm sure. It's been hard for all of us, but she hasn't picked up the things she once enjoyed. She's been too busy taking care of our family—my grandparents and my aunt. She doesn't do anything for herself."

Grace knew what he meant so keenly. She knew what it was like to try to return the favor to someone who'd given you everything, how it could never be enough. And she knew what it must be like for Lucia, too, trying to find herself and her passions again after her world had been shaken to its core.

"I hope she will take up painting again," Grace said quietly. "I'm glad you're encouraging her, and I'll help however I can. Truly, her paintings are fantastic."

"I thought she was good, but I'm glad you do too. She's an artist. I can't believe I didn't even realize it about her until now."

Grace stared into the distance. "It's funny sometimes—the things we miss about the people we love. She's lucky to have you," she said.

Marco shrugged. "I'm lucky to have her."

"Yeah." Grace smiled. She was happy for Marco in a way that swelled up in her chest until it hurt. "You're both lucky, I think."

Grace walked home at a leisurely pace, enjoying the sounds and smells of Granada at night. The scent of roasted chestnuts from a place down the road wafted through the air. Ever since the weather had turned and they'd started selling them at that stall, Grace insisted on making the chestnuts part of her weekly schedule. She'd developed a routine the last couple of weeks that didn't involve hiding in her bed and sulking. She had favorite places—

Carmen de los Martires Park and the specialty coffee place a few streets from the apartment. She'd even started spending time with some of her colleagues outside of mandatory faculty meetings—taking walks around campus and chatting about their research. She was building a life for herself here.

Of course, parts of her routine were spent with Rafael—breakfast at the counter in the mornings, evening strolls, relaxing on the couch after dinner. She didn't want to screw those parts up by complicating their relationship.

When she walked into the apartment, Rafael was lounging on the sofa with a thick book in his hands. She tried to act normal, like it was any other night after she returned home from work, and it seemed like he was willing to follow her lead.

He sat up while she unwrapped the scarf from her neck. "How did it go?" he asked.

"Great. Twelve students."

"Twelve? For a non-mandatory school event? They really do adore you."

Grace blushed thinking of the last time they'd had this conversation, right before she'd kissed him, but she shrugged and tried to play it cool. "What can I say? Art is fun."

"Did you meet Marco's mother?"

Grace grinned, pleased he'd remembered that part of the plan. "I did, and she was lovely. Marco showed me more of her work. You wouldn't believe how brilliant it is, Raf. I honestly think she might be my favorite artist now."

Rafael smirked up at her. "You'd throw over Picasso that quickly?"

She laughed. "You know I'd throw him over in a heartbeat. Though it was exciting to see his work in real life like that in the cave."

Grace tried to keep herself from turning a deeper shade of red. *The cave.* Where they'd made out, surrounded by priceless pieces of artwork. Good gracious, she wanted to do it again. And sometimes she wondered why she didn't. Yes, she wanted to heed Alma's warning, and she was sure Alma was right, that Rafael was only interested in one thing, but, honestly, who cared if it was just one single night? She would take it. She was sure it would be worth it.

Though there was a significant part of her that worried even one night would change things between them, that it would change things with Alma, too. She worried that Raf wouldn't talk to her like this anymore, that he wouldn't lecture her about Spanish architecture or the history of Granada any longer. Most of all, she worried that she liked him far too much. She wanted to spend more time with him, even if it was a terrible idea. There was still a lot to do in the museum, and after seeing all the artwork there, she was starting to believe Rafael's confidence in her wasn't entirely misplaced.

"I was thinking," Grace started, hesitating a moment to find the right words. She'd been loath to be involved with Christian's exhibit, and now she was completely shifting her position. "I know I've technically completed my end of the bargain. We've been to Sacromonte twice, but there is still so much I wasn't able to see or organize yet. Maybe we could go again, so I could see things coming together a bit more. And it would give me a chance to speak with Christian to try to convince him to do something more for the region."

Rafael looked up at her, some measure of surprise written across his face. "Actually, I did bring that up with him, and he wants to hear more about your ideas. We'd love for you to be more involved."

"Really?"

"Of course. Christian was impressed with you, and he respects your opinions."

"Well, maybe I could come with you then, next time you go out there."

"That sounds reasonable," Rafael said. "Tomorrow?"

Was she imagining it or did he sound eager? Maybe he was picturing a repeat of the last time they'd been there alone together, even if he seemed perfectly fine with keeping his distance lately. He was probably sick of the back and forth of it all, anyway. Why waste his time with Grace, when he could easily find a sure thing? He must have just been relieved to have more help when he had no clue where to put all those Picassos, but Grace found herself wishing it was something else, something that had little to do with a nineteenth-century painter or an underground museum.

"Tomorrow works."

. . .

The drive to Sacromonte already felt so familiar. Riding in Raf's passenger seat felt familiar too, even if the proximity of his fingers to her thigh made her breath hitch. He wasn't even doing anything, just resting a hand on the center console, but she could feel it there during every mile, like it was radiating pulsing waves.

"Christian will be there today, so it's the perfect time to make your pitch."

"Great," Grace said, but she could hear the tone in her voice, and it didn't sound convincing.

"Don't be nervous. He's a reasonable man."

Grace looked down to see her fingers fidgeting in her lap. She wasn't nervous about that. She could handle Christian, but she didn't want to explain the true cause of her nerves, especially when she was trying so hard to stop thinking about it.

When they arrived, Raf dashed off to the biggest room to speak with some of the contractors about the walls they'd built and to ensure they had the correct hardware to hang the paintings, leaving her to talk to Christian. Christian was jovial, as always, and so she tried to keep her tone light, like this was just a fun random idea she had about how they could make the event more community-friendly. It didn't take long to make her case for opening the exhibition to locals in addition to the plaque about the history of the caves and the fund to support the community and restore some of the other caves. She suggested making a donation to the historical museum in Sacromonte as well, a place that focused solely on the history of the caves and people who'd lived there for centuries.

Christian readily agreed to anything that involved writing a check. He clearly wasn't worried about that part of the equation since it was an easy solution for him. It was opening the underground exhibit up to the community that was a sticking point, but he said he would think more about it, at least.

He scratched the top of his head and eyed her curiously. "Surely, Rafael has mentioned that part of the appeal of this place is the secrecy. It's not to be advertised or featured in magazines. I don't want the word to spread too far."

"Rafael explained that," Grace said, trying to keep her fingers still. "But it wouldn't have to be all the time," Grace said. "Perhaps on special occasions? That might offer some level of legitimacy."

"Hmmm," Christian stared off into the distance, considering. "I will keep thinking about it, as I said. That's all I'll promise for now, but it might be a good idea. You know, I might even like to look at some of the local artists to display. Maybe have a small showcase of some work coming from this area."

Grace nodded, surprised to hear him suggest such an idea. It was more than she'd hoped for when trying to come up with ways to incorporate the local community. Whatever else he was—hideously rich, entirely used to getting his own way—Grace couldn't deny that Christian loved the art. Picasso and Matisse, sure, but it didn't seem to be all in the name for Christian. He could appreciate good work, no matter the painter, and he clearly enjoyed sharing it with others.

"Anyway, Senorita," Christian said, obviously changing the subject. "How are your classes? Do you enjoy teaching at the university?"

Grace paused, considering her answer. Though he'd been nothing but warm toward her, Grace still felt uncomfortable chatting with a billionaire, especially when she knew how easily he got whatever he wanted, as if he could hold the world in his hand and shape it to his will. She knew how Rafael worked to please him, how hard he worked to make sure Christian got his way. She also found it hard to believe Christian was all that interested as she rambled on about her students and their interests, about how she'd taken the job with a sense of desperation. *Did Christian know what it was like to lose everything, to log into a checking account with an impending sense of doom? Could he imagine starting over in a new place, just hoping for a chance to find a new life?* Grace had been so unlucky and then so lucky in a way that didn't quite balance out exactly, but it still counted for something. She loved the university. And she loved Granada. "Very much, actually," she said finally. "I couldn't have wished for a better position."

"And what about Rafael?" Christian asked. He'd surprised her again by listening with some level of sympathy and interest. "He's treating you right?"

"Oh—um—yes." Grace looked down and rubbed her palms against her slacks. "I mean, we're just temporary roommates. I'll move out soon. And we're friends."

"I didn't realize you were living together," Christian commented, rubbing the scruff of his beard. "How interesting."

Grace coughed and avoided his gaze, ignoring his implications. "Oh, we're not really living together. It's just a short-term arrangement."

Christian gave her a knowing smile. "Ah, I see. Well, I hope he's a good friend to you then. He seems like he's been very happy to have you around."

Grace cleared her throat. "Well, yes. I'm sure it's helpful to have someone who specializes in this particular period since you have such a large collection. I better get to work, actually. There's still a lot I haven't sorted."

"Of course," Christian said. "I do appreciate all of your help. I told Rafael we could handle it on our own, but I admit it's been nice to have your input." He offered her another grin and promised again to thoroughly consider her suggestions.

The rest of the day went smoothly, Grace and Rafael both too focused on the exhibit to talk about anything else. Grace talked about the artists and different movements and time periods, and Raf took copious notes on everything she said. Then they wandered back and forth through the cave taking measurements and imagining where each piece would fit. Grace was exhausted by the time they got through the rest of them, and she slumped on the floor with her back against the cool cave wall as Rafael stuck post-its with their ideas on the walls.

Her mouth was dry from talking so much, but she couldn't seem to stop. Obviously, she was telling Rafael all about the paintings so he could try to piece together a museum, but she couldn't help telling him stories, too. She was full of fun facts and historical tidbits that were probably completely useless to him, but she couldn't seem to stop herself from letting it spill out, offering the details of every piece of information that popped into her brain. Perhaps, she was just trying to keep herself from mentioning the other things that kept surfacing in her mind, the things she shouldn't be allowing herself to dwell on any longer.

"Did you know that Picasso was accused of stealing the *Mona Lisa?*" she asked from her position on the floor. She was trying to keep herself from reflecting on the feeling of his tongue on her earlobe.

"Really?!" He turned away from his notes, shocked.

She nodded. "It was 1911. Picasso had this friend, Guillarme Apollinaire, and Guillarme's secretary had stolen Iberian sculptures from the Louvre a few years earlier. The guy had just put them under his coat and walked right out of the Louvre with them. Can you imagine?"

"Not remotely," Rafael said, a hint of a smile playing on his lips. "That's wild."

"I know. So unbelievable." Grace continued. "Anyway, Picasso had bought these stolen sculptures from the secretary and had them in his studio. When he heard about the *Mona Lisa* disappearing, he panicked, afraid they would suspect he was connected to the crime since he had other stolen art from the Louvre. He even tried to get rid of the sculptures —he planned to toss them in the Seine, but he couldn't do it. Someone must have ratted him out, though, and the police picked him up. He was freaking out."

"It's hard to imagine such a legendary figure acting that way." Raf said, leaning toward her with rapt attention. "Did he have anything to do with it?"

"No, the police figured out he was innocent, but they really spooked him."

"And what happened to *Mona Lisa?* Clearly, they found her."

"They did. A couple of years later they arrested a guy who'd been a carpenter and worked at the Louvre. He said he stole it so he could return it to Italy."

"You're just full of interesting information, aren't you?" Raf asked, a smile tugging at the corner of his mouth.

"It's interesting to me, at least." Grace shrugged, the picture of nonchalance, even as she felt like she was blushing at his level of focus on her.

He picked up some of his notes again, putting pen to paper. "What else?" he asked.

Grace broke out into a wide smile then, trying to decide what to tell him next.

She had to admit she was filled with some sense of contentment while she watched him work, pacing back and forth and talking to himself, his investment and enthusiasm apparent the whole time. He pushed his hands through his hair as he chewed the end of a pen, staring at a blank wall. She wished she could get in his head and see what he was seeing. She knew it had clicked for him at some point, and now he had some vision he was holding in his brain, something only he could see until he brought it to life.

He wrote another note in his book before turning to her, letting out a long breath. "Okay, I think I'm done for now. Should we go?"

Grace let her gaze drift back to the Françoise Gilot painting right in front of her on the specially built art table. It had been a long day, but a day filled with things she loved. She'd never had trouble staring at artwork for hours on end. "I don't mind staying a while. You look like you're inspired."

Rafael nodded. "I was inspired, but I think I've figured it out, thanks to you."

"I didn't do anything but ramble at you for hours."

Rafael's lips quirked up. "It was just the rambling I needed."

Christian asked for a word with Raf as they were heading out, and Grace waited in the car with her eyes closed. She was exhausted, but in the best way, in the way that tells you it's all been worth it, that you've put in the work and accomplished a goal. She didn't hear Rafael coming out until he opened the door and hopped into the seat beside her.

"What was that about?" she asked.

Raf gave her a teasing grin. "I bet you'd like to know."

She sat up straighter. "What? Tell me."

"I thought I was the one with the gift of persuasion, but apparently, you have it as well. Christian said he wants to let anyone from the local community come to the exhibition for free."

Grace gasped.

"Hold on, let me tell you the stipulations. Just one or two days a month. Consistent days and limited hours. No ads, no website. All just word of mouth in the community, but if people come, he'll let them in."

"Well, that's still something," said Grace, delighted to have a small win for the people who lived in the area.

"Yes, he thinks if it's limited and word-of-mouth, it will still be mysterious and special."

Grace nodded, taking in the idea. "Sure, I can see that. I'll take what I can get."

Rafael leaned an elbow on the center console of the car. "Here's the best part. He also wants to have a night to host a party. Just for you and your students."

"For my students? Are you serious?" Grace sat up straighter in her seat, turning toward Raf and pressing a hand against his shoulder.

"Of course. This place wouldn't exist without you."

"That's amazing! Oh, maybe Lucia can come, too. I hope everyone will be able to attend." She paused, releasing his arm, her eyes narrowing. "How did he get that idea, Raf? He just randomly decided he wanted to have a party for my classes?"

Rafael grinned, clearly pleased with himself. "I might have mentioned it would be a nice way to work out any kinks before he starts hosting other events, and you deserve it after all your help. He loved the idea. He was very enthusiastic." He paused. "What? Why are you staring at me like that?"

Grace almost couldn't breathe. Rafael suggested a night just for her students. She could bring them to the exhibition and show them what she'd been working on—this thing no one was supposed to know, and they would get to experience first-hand, to see all of these masterpieces. "I can't believe you did that."

Rafael frowned at her before he started the car's engine and headed down the road. "I'm slightly offended you're so surprised, Graciela."

It had been days since he'd called her that, but now Grace could feel the word in her bones. She shouldn't be surprised. Rafael had given her a place to live. He'd helped her move, he'd held her when she'd cried from a bad dream. He was not the stern boy who'd been annoyed by her in Barcelona. He was a kind, beautiful, man who'd found a sense of humor somewhere along the way, who'd stopped trying to please his father and started living his own life.

Shit. She was really in trouble if just because he'd done something nice for her and her students, she was dying to jump out of her seat and slip into his lap. She wouldn't do that, though, for safety reasons, but when they got home…she wasn't sure she could be responsible any longer. She was sick of trying. In their three-year relationship, Derek had been perfectly nice. He'd washed dishes and asked about her day and bought her presents on her birthday. But never once had he done something so thoughtful, so tapped into exactly what would make her happy. To share this amazing art with her students was a gift, and Rafael had not only recognized that, he'd gone out of his way to make it happen. She wanted to show him what this meant to her. She wanted to let herself feel all the things she'd been feeling and show him that too, the attraction and desire, all of it.

She clenched her hands into fists at her sides, willing herself not to touch him. She kept them like that for the whole drive, the whole walk to the apartment from the car, the whole time he was unlocking the door. She was tense and quiet, contemplating what she was about to do like she was analyzing a painting by Lee Krasner. She couldn't see any way around it. She couldn't convince herself to walk away. The moment they stepped inside, she unclenched her hands and reached for his shirt instead. She made fists again, but this time they were full of soft cotton as she yanked him toward her.

"Grace?" He arched an eyebrow at her, dropping his bag on the floor.

"Yes," she said, hoping she understood the question he'd asked with her name, because, if so, the answer was definitely yes.

Rafael stayed perfectly still, like he was waiting to understand what she was doing. He probably expected her to panic and push him away again, to change her mind after one kiss. "You said we needed to figure out what this was," he whispered.

Grace pulled him closer, nuzzling into his neck and inhaling his scent. "I did say that, but I don't care anymore."

"I'm sure you were right though." Rafael's voice caught. "This is complicated."

She pressed her lips together for a moment, gathering her courage. Then she looked him in the eyes. Defiant. Certain. "It is complicated, but I know what I want."

He started to ease into her, his hands moving against her back. "What do you want?" he breathed into her ear, his voice suddenly deeper and sexier than anything she'd ever heard in her life.

Grace swallowed, goosebumps cascading down her arms. "You. Tonight. That's all I need to know for now."

He leaned toward her, his nose tracing her jawline. "Maybe it's a bad idea, Graciela, but I can't think about that now. I can't think of anything but touching you."

"Yes," she said again. She'd say it many more times that night, she was sure. She hoped she would scream it from his bed.

He exhaled a thick breath then, as if taking a moment to prepare himself, and then he put his hands against her face and kissed her.

It started slow at first. A soft, delicious kiss, tender and sweet, but when Grace moaned, he pushed harder against her, sucking her bottom lip between his teeth. He wrapped an arm around her back to anchor her against him and pressed another hand to the back of her neck to hold her firmly in place so he could keep kissing her. She could barely breathe, but she didn't care. She wanted more and more and more.

She leaned against him, easing her whole torso into the firm shape of his body and sighing. This ache had been building inside of her for days, and finally she was getting some relief, finally she was able to touch him again—to put her fingers in his hair, to slide her hands under his shirt to feel his smooth skin and the muscles of his abdomen.

He felt exactly as she'd imagined, firm and perfect and warm. She wanted to explore him. She wanted to see all of him, every inch of his incredible form, so ridiculously proportionate and beautiful, so unlike a Picasso painting, but a work of art, nonetheless.

She tugged his shirt until he yanked it off the rest of the way. Her eyes moved down his body, drinking in the sight of him before she spread her fingers over his chest and then gripped his arms. *His arms, holy moly.*

When she felt his eagerness pressing between her thighs, her whole body seemed to hum with anticipation. She was going to have sex with Rafael Ferrer-Martín. She'd fantasized about it. She'd imagined it many, many times, but she never really believed it would happen. And in that moment, she didn't care if it was only one time. It didn't matter if she was just a conquest, like Alma suggested. She was willing to be conquered, a notch on his bedpost, whatever it took. It would be worth it. And he would be a notch on her bedpost, too. It would be a point of pride that she'd landed someone who looked like him, even if she never told a soul.

Raf herded her toward his bedroom with his body, pushing her backward until her back was against the door. He found the knob, and they stumbled to the bed while he unbuttoned her shirt, whispering Spanish phrases as he revealed more of her skin, inch by inch. When her shirt was on the floor, he paused and took her in, his eyes landing on the swell of her small breasts compressed against the cups of her bra.

"Dios mio, Graciela. You're so fucking beautiful." He lowered himself over her on the mattress, his hands working her bra hooks, and then he let out another string of Spanish that she could only assume was absolutely filthy.

"I was thinking the same thing about you."

He laughed and nuzzled into her neck again before raising up enough to reach the button of her pants. She wriggled around desperately, helping him to strip them off. Then she started in on him, tugging at his slacks until he leaned back and pulled them off the rest of the way.

Soon, they were both left in only their underwear, and Grace marveled at the body before her, a sculpted figure in boxer briefs.

Raf let out a grunt and pressed his fingers between her legs. He kissed her wildly. First her lips, then her neck. Then he left a trail of kisses between her breasts and down her belly until his hot breath joined his hand.

Grace writhed beneath his touch, too eager for him to keep going.

"You want this, Graciela?" His voice was laced with barely restrained need.

"Yes," Grace said in a whimper, just as she'd known she would. *Yes. Yes.*

He put his mouth against the fabric between her legs and sucked before teasing her with his teeth on the cotton. She responded by arching her hips toward him and sliding her fingers through his hair. He rubbed his thumb against the edge of her panty line, teasing her.

"Raf," she said, breathless.

"Mmm?"

"I'm ready." She wiggled on the bed, desperate for more contact.

He looked up and locked eyes with her with a smirk. "I can tell."

She exhaled, letting her head fall back on his pillow. "Then get going already. You're killing me."

"So impatient, Graciela. I've been waiting a long time for this. I'm not going to rush through it now." She groaned as he moved up her body, pressing his fingers between her legs again.

Finally, she managed to tug at the waistband of his briefs until they were around his thighs. He ripped them off, then he lifted her ankles in the air and slid her cotton underwear down her legs. He pressed kisses to her hips and licked her inner thigh while grabbing onto her ass. She twisted to take his bare erection in her hand and stroked it, trying to drive him as wild as she was so he would move faster.

"Ahh," he said. "Alright. Slow down or this will all be over too quickly."

"What?" she asked innocently, batting her eyelashes. She did slow down, but she tightened her grip.

He gasped. "Fuck, Graciela."

She got her way at last, and he moved over her again, positioning himself at her center and spreading her legs wider. She helped to guide him where she wanted him and then pushed her hands against the back of his neck, bringing his lips back to hers so she could kiss him.

"Do you have...?" For some reason she couldn't say the words, but of course he knew what she meant and leaned toward the nightstand. Grace tried not to think about the other girls who had been in this bed making use of this same box of condoms. She wasn't supposed to care about that. She didn't. All she needed was this one, perfect night and nothing else.

Raf rolled back toward her as slid on the unwrapped condom. She watched him with bated breath until he turned and focused his attention on her once again, kissing her fiercely until he was positioned over her again, his erection between her legs.

"Oh, wowza," she said as he finally pushed himself inside her. Grace clapped a hand over her mouth and then froze, horrified she'd ruined the hottest moment of her entire life.

Rafael laughed, seemingly thrilled by her ridiculous reaction. "That's a good sign, right?"

She nodded. It didn't take long until they were both slick from sweat, Rafael's damp forehead crushed to hers, his gasps of pleasure matching her own. His hand slid back down her belly and he pressed it between them until she could move against it at the perfect angle.

"Yes, Raf. Right there." She kissed him forcefully, biting at his lower lip.

"I've thought about this so much," he admitted. "You are terribly distracting."

"Really?" Obviously, Grace could tell he was attracted to her, but it was hard to believe she could have overwhelmed his thoughts in the same way he'd overwhelmed hers.

His response wasn't English.

More and more and more. The friction between them grew as they started to move faster, setting pace with a wild rhythm.

"Graciela," he groaned. "I'm almost..."

The pleasure built inside of her until it hit its peak, and waves of satisfaction thrashed from her core to her limbs to her toes. Rafael let out another groan, reaching his climax and falling against her, his breath warm against her breasts. She relished the feeling of his weight on her—heavy and limp and glorious.

They were both still for a moment, panting. Grace felt a smile spread across her face. She absently rubbed her thumb against the back of his neck. She could hear both of their hearts beating, both pounding until she couldn't tell them apart anymore, and whether it was his heart racing double-time or if it was her own no longer seemed to matter.

Raf glanced up at her with a gleam in his eyes. "Oh, wowza," he said in an American accent. He looked utterly thrilled with himself and full of mischief. He gave her a lazy grin, his fingers digging into her side.

She shook her head as a blush colored her cheeks and flicked him lightly on the back. "Hey," she teased. "It just slipped out. Don't mock me."

He kissed her neck reverently, again and again and again. "Oh, trust me, I'm not mocking you. It seems like the perfect reaction in this situation. I mean it."

Grace rolled toward him, burying her face against his chest with a laugh. "It was good then?" she asked playfully, though she was anxious to hear his response.

He tilted her chin up and held her gaze, but he was no longer smiling. "Fuck yes, Graciela. Without a doubt."

CHAPTER SIXTEEN

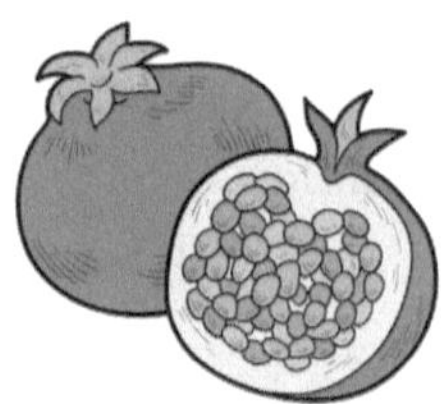

AT LAST. *Madre mía, it happened at last.* Grace slept in his arms, and he stroked her hair. Perhaps it was entirely misguided, but he'd been holding out hope that their night together would cure him somehow, that all the desperation and yearning and desire that had been haunting his nights would disappear in an instant, suddenly satisfied. He knew it was too much to wish for, but still, he'd wished. He should be quite content, after all. Under normal circumstances this one night with Grace would be enough.

And yet…

He already knew he'd miscalculated. Maybe one evening of passion would have fulfilled him at any other time, but he already knew he wasn't satisfied. The entire night with Grace was exactly what he'd been hoping for, but it was also insufficient. He was dying to wake her up and start all over again, to spend Saturday in bed with this woman, to try and try to get his fill, even though it seemed impossible he ever would.

She'd been correct before when she said they should figure it all out before sleeping together, but they'd both neglected that sound reasoning, and here they were, tangled up in each other, connected without a clue as to what it might mean and how to move forward. Normally, none of this mattered. Normally, there was no moving forward, but she was living in his apartment. He saw her every single day, and perhaps the scarier part was that he didn't want it to stop.

But he had no idea what Grace wanted. She'd said this was a bad idea multiple times, but was it just because of Alma or because she'd just gotten out of a long relationship? Or because she was in a vulnerable place? Or because she had no choice but to live with him? There were a lot of reasons this was a bad idea, it turned out.

Grace shifted in his arms, and he hoped she wasn't waking up. If they could stay like this for a while longer... Well, it wouldn't solve anything, but he wanted to delay the talking part as long as possible. He could happily remain like this, watching her sleep, remembering all the details about the night before, for a very long time.

"Hi," Grace said, and Rafael realized her eyes were open and trained on his face.

"Hi."

She batted her lashes at him. "You look...concerned."

"Do I?" He tightened his arm around her slightly. "Probably just tired."

"Mmm." Grace leaned into him. She seemed perfectly at ease. "I'm starving. We didn't eat anything last night."

Rafael continued to play the events of last night in his head and agreed that none of them had involved dinner. "I guess you're right."

"I need food," she grumbled like a zombie.

Rafael swallowed and nodded. He wasn't sure how to act. He was just going through the motions, trying to remain calm until he could figure out what came next.

Grace lifted her head and looked at him. "You're quiet," she said. "I'm going to find some breakfast. That's the first order of business. You can come or you can stay here, or you know. Whatever."

She was acting so casual, almost as if they hadn't just entirely changed the course of their relationship, potentially making a total mess of everything. She didn't seem concerned about it at all, and if she was totally fine with the whole situation, then he would be too. They didn't need to talk about everything or make any decision right away. They could just eat some food. One thing at a time.

He cleared his throat. "I would like to join you."

"You want to go out somewhere?" The sheet slipped away from her body as she left the bed, and Rafael couldn't help watching her, her skin still bare, illuminated by the soft morning light.

He continued to linger with his head propped on one arm, drinking in the sight of her. "Yes."

"Okay then," she said with a grin. She covered herself with her previously discarded shirt, hastily plucked from the floor. "Let's do it."

They didn't spend the day *in bed* together, but they did spend the day together. Breakfast first, just as Grace had commanded. They started at the Stories café, because Rafael was already becoming familiar with Grace's tastes, and he knew she would fawn all over the avocado salmon toast. He was right, of course. She went nuts over it, and then she went nuts over the croissants as well. Rafael enjoyed watching her eat, the pure joy on her face when she took another bite and moaned, not too far off from the moaning she'd been doing the night before, but he managed to put that from his mind.

It reminded him of the Grace from ten years ago. Grace, who was fearless and carefree and silly. Grace who loved to try new things and start up a conversation with anyone—the waiter, the tourists at the next table, the couple outside with the dog. It had driven him crazy when he'd first met her, and now he couldn't understand why. It must have been because he was craving her attention, because when she was making jokes and twirling down the street and chatting with strangers, she wasn't focused on him in the slightest. Back then, he'd been so insecure and so stupid. When she'd joked about something, he'd felt like she was laughing at him because he was too uptight to laugh at himself. It was like any bit of fun had been a personal affront to him, even if that was so far removed from the actual intention of her comments. Now, he could see how wrong he'd been about all of it, and he couldn't take his eyes off her.

Rafael was relieved this version of Grace was still inside her somewhere, and he couldn't help hoping that maybe he had something to do with her lively demeanor. Was she happy because of him? Because they'd finally spent the night together? Or was it just that the avocado salmon toast really was that good?

"Should we go back?" she asked at the end of the meal. "What are you doing today?"

He pressed a napkin to his mouth. He didn't want to go back. He wanted to spend the day with her like they were back in Barcelona, ten years younger. He wanted to gallivant around the city, but instead of being a sour killjoy, he would embrace every second and enjoy it. He would laugh and make jokes. He might even try to hold her hand, which seemed simultaneously outrageous and exactly right.

"I have some ideas." He raised his eyebrows, gauging her interest.

"Ideas? Ideas about what?"

"About what we should do today. Have you been to Monasterio de la cartuja?"

Grace frowned at him, but the edges of her lips started to curve into a smile. "*Monasterio*? You want to take me to a monastery?"

"It's beautiful. Many of the cathedrals are as well."

She bit her lip. "Is this some kind of repentance for last night? We spend the day in churches?"

It was the first time either of them had fully acknowledged the events of last night. Grace sounded relaxed, but he could see a pink flush on her cheeks, and he wanted to kiss her everywhere.

Rafael shook his head and locked eyes with her. "No, I have nothing to repent for. But you'll appreciate the history. And the design."

Grace shifted in her seat and picked up her glass of juice. "Oh, it's an excuse to teach me about architecture."

Rafael smirked. "It's only fair, after everything you've taught me about paintings."

"Only twentieth century art, Rafael. We've barely scratched the surface."

"Well, this is just a few cathedrals." He smiled conspiratorially, leaning toward her. "What do they call it? Crash course."

They started at the monastery, though Rafael wasn't entirely sure why he picked the place beyond the fact that it was beautiful. He just had a feeling Grace would enjoy it—the history and the design, the breathtaking artwork inside. He would have taken her anywhere, done anything, but he was pleased to see her gazing up at arched ceilings, taking it all in like it was something precious. Their quiet words echoed through the long hallways as they wandered, as he whispered about Carthusian monks and Baroque architecture.

The rest of the day passed in a beautiful blur. Grace was impressed by the cathedrals as well, just as he knew she would be. She ambled through each of them with her head thrown back and her mouth open, eyes so fixed to the ceiling that he'd had to stop her from walking into a stranger on more than one occasion. For that very reason, it was easier just to hold her hand when she wasn't paying attention to where she was going, and that's what he did, surprised at the surge of excitement that shot through him when his fingers brushed hers.

He was nervous the first time, slipping his hand into hers, intertwining their fingers. It was easier since she was so focused on the murals on the ceiling and wasn't even looking at him, but he still experienced a moment of panic, worried she might pull away.

She didn't though. She kept her eyes on the art, and she didn't say a word, but she held onto him. He could feel the pressure from the swirls of her fingerprints grazing the back of his hand. Rafael couldn't remember the last time he done something like that—just held someone's fucking hand. Clearly, he had intimacy issues and father issues, and probably a whole host of other issues, but at least, for one single day (if that was as long as this thing lasted), he could walk through the streets of Granada with a beautiful, funny woman, and he could hold onto her as if they really belonged to each other.

"Isn't it strange to think about how many hundreds of years old this is? It blows my mind." Grace finally lowered her gaze to focus on him, but she still didn't let go of his hand.

"It's hard to imagine."

Grace brushed some loose hair behind her ear with her free hand. "It is. It makes me feel so small."

Rafael tried not to stare at her. He tried not to wonder what would happen after this, after their whirlwind adventures at cathedrals and monasteries. Maybe they would eat and drink wine. Maybe they would kiss again. Maybe they would return home and stumble back to his bedroom...

"What?" Grace asked.

"What?" he repeated, feigning innocence.

"Stop staring at me," she said, leaning over and nudging her shoulder against his.

The side of his mouth hitched. "Why? I like looking at you."

She rolled her eyes. "Such a charmer," she said.

He was a charmer when he wanted to be. He prided himself on it, in fact. But this felt different somehow. It felt real.

"Do you come here often?" Grace asked. "That's not a line," she clarified.

"What's a line?" Rafael asked, pretending to be oblivious.

Grace cleared her throat. "You know, like a come on."

He shook his head, trying not to smile.

"I mean, I'm not just flirting." A blush crept into her cheeks again before she caught his eye and realized he was teasing her. "Just answer the question."

He smiled and leaned toward her, almost whispering. "No," he said. "I do not come here often. I might like you to think I hang out at beautiful, historic cathedrals on a regular basis, but it's a special occasion."

"What's the occasion?" Grace asked, a hint of flirtation creeping into her voice.

He didn't answer, choosing instead to distract her with the glimmering sacristy at the head of the building. "Would you believe I've never paid much attention to any of this. It almost seems like it should be a crime."

"What? Gilding a chubby angel in that much gold?"

"Not appreciating something so spectacular when it's right in front of you." He squeezed her hand, and Grace rolled her eyes, but she was still smiling.

She turned away from him toward the figures at the front of the building, everything golden or brightly colored, everything breathtaking. The beauty of it all made Rafael feel like he was almost outside of himself, a separation of soul and body that wasn't religious or spiritual, despite the setting. It was unlike anything he'd ever imagined before. It was like he was floating.

Grace stifled a yawn with her sleeve then glanced at him sheepishly.

"Are you bored with all of this art, Graciela?" Rafael joked.

"Of course not. I just didn't get a lot of sleep last night." She looked down, trying to hide her small smile from view.

"Very true." That reminder sent a thrill through him. "And it's been a long day," he added. He couldn't wait to touch her again, more than just her hand. "Should we go home?" How did that feel so natural? The two of them together, comfortable and happy, heading *home.*

Grace nodded and bit her lip.

"Now *you're* being quiet. And there weren't nearly as many penis jokes as I remember from the last time I was your tour guide through a Spanish city."

The tension in her eyes seemed to ease. "Oh, I had a few of them, but I kept them to myself. I know how you feel about that kind of humor."

Rafael put his palm to his chest. "I'm a changed man, aren't I? I can take a good dick joke. I want to hear them all. Don't hold back."

A surprised laugh slipped out as Grace shook her head. "You're ridiculous."

"I can be, if given the chance. Sometimes I'm even a little funny."

She eased back, as if assessing him, trying to take in the full picture. "I guess we'll see about that," she replied.

"I don't know what that means. Are you keeping a record of my jokes?"

She laughed, and the couple walking nearby glanced in their direction. He wanted to wrap an arm around her, to claim her as if to say, "I made that happen. That laugh belongs to me."

"I don't know either." Grace shrugged. "I'm too tired to know what I'm talking about."

"I'm sorry someone wore you out so much," he teased.

Grace pressed her lips together, clearly trying hard to hide her satisfied smile.

. . .

The air in the apartment seemed charged when they arrived, and Rafael allowed the flashes of memory to play through his mind—Grace pressed between him and the wall, her legs wrapped around his middle, the way she'd hurried him along, so eager and ready, as if she'd been waiting for it too.

Now that they were back to the apartment in the light of day, however, neither of them seemed sure of what to do next. They no longer had fifteenth century architecture or fat gilded angels to distract them. Rafael wasn't sure how to behave.

Grace hung her jacket on a hook, and then looked around the room, searching for something. Then she went to the kitchen and started washing a few dishes that were in the sink.

He stood behind the counter, trying to lean against it with an air of nonchalance, but in reality, he wasn't sure what to do with himself. They'd had a beautiful day together, but something felt off. Rafael took a breath and decided to address it. "Um, are you okay?" he asked.

She glanced over her shoulder at him with a tight smile. "Of course. What do you mean?"

He stood up straighter, trying to parse out her expression and body language, nervous there was something she wasn't telling him. "Just making sure. I—um—had a good time today."

She put the last dish in the drying rack and turned around, her shoulders relaxing. "So did I."

He was frozen, unsure if he should go toward her, unsure what this thing was between them and how to navigate it. His fingers twitched at his sides. "We haven't—" he started.

"I was thinking—" she said at the same time.

They both paused. Even when they'd first started living together, they hadn't been quite like this, so unsure of each other, so hesitant. Rafael started to move slowly around the counter, wanting to be nearer to her without putting too much pressure on the situation. Grace dried her hands on a dish towel, studying him. Surely, she could see how anxious he was, how unlike his usual self.

"We can talk about everything, and I just want to make sure—"

Grace tossed the towel aside, then pushed herself up so she was sitting on top of the counter. "Maybe we should just kiss."

Rafael's body went rigid. "Hmm? I know we live together right now, and I don't want you to be uncomfortable or feel like—"

"Come here," she ordered, and he obeyed. He wasn't used to her being so commanding, but he didn't mind in the least.

She lifted a hand and ran it through his hair, and he closed his eyes, memorizing her touch. He'd craved this all day, but he still felt nervous. He was so aware that they'd still never had a discussion about what all of this meant, and even if he tried to play it cool, he was dying to know what she was thinking. He *cared* what this meant, but he didn't want to ruin the moment. He never wanted her to stop.

"There's too much tension," she explained, and Rafael finally opened his eyes. "I think if we can just get this part out of the way, it won't be so awkward."

She bit her lip, and for a brief moment he could see the hesitation in her eyes. He could tell she was pretending to be surer and more confident than she was, telling him what she wanted even if she might have been afraid to say it out loud. He leaned in and pressed his body against hers until her thighs were spread, and she was straddling him from the counter. Rafael let himself feel the warmth of her every curve, the soft breath on his cheek as she exhaled with relief and excitement.

"Please, Raf," she whispered into his ear. "Kiss me."

He nuzzled into her neck, then grazed his nose along her jaw, anticipation building as he made his way toward her mouth. When he finally pressed his lips to hers, she let out a satisfied breath, encouraging him further. His hands went under her shirt. His erection strained against his pants already, aching.

She moved to his neck, sucking his skin between her teeth. Her hand slid down to where their bodies were pressed together, and she reached for the buttons of his pants.

"Graciela," he hissed.

She gasped and moved back toward his lips, still fumbling with his buttons. The top one sprang open. What a terrible pair of pants. No one needed this many buttons along the ridge of their crotch. He couldn't wait to be free. Button number two came undone while his fingers worked that back of her bra, and all the while they were still kissing—hungry, excited kisses.

Suddenly, a loud banging echoed through the room. Rafael and Grace jerked apart, both searching for the source of the noise before staring at the front door.

"Hello?" a voice said, and the pounding started again.

Grace glanced at him. "Alma?" she whispered. She slid from the counter and started across the room in a panic.

"Shit," Rafael said, looking down at his pants, hurriedly trying to button himself back together and hide his bulge. He stepped behind the counter, hoping he could perch there until he'd calmed himself a bit.

Grace glanced at him before she opened the door, and he gave a quick nod.

Alma burst into the room in a frenzy, marching right past Grace and unwinding her scarf, obviously clueless about what she was interrupting. His sister apparently had a knack for cock-blocking his passionate encounters with her best friend, even if she was completely oblivious each time.

"What's going on?" Grace asked, shutting the door and trailing behind his sister.

Alma started pacing a route through the living room. She eyed Rafael wearily and then whipped back around toward Grace.

"Obinna and I are done," she said, her voice full of an emotion he'd never heard from her before. "And I don't know what to do."

CHAPTER SEVENTEEN

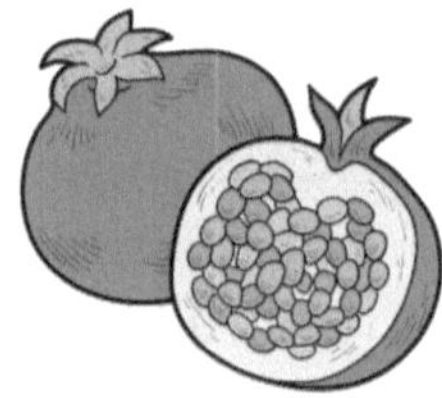

"WHAT?" Grace tried to regain her composure and focus on what Alma was saying, but she was still breathing a little harder than usual, and her bra hung limply under her shirt. Maybe she should have tried to hook it back into place before opening the door. She snuck a glance over to Raf, who was tucked behind the counter, leaning with his forearms pressed to the shiny black surface. God, he was gorgeous, and there was still an almost painful warmth spreading between her thighs, but she wasn't supposed to be thinking about that. She needed to reset her brain and listen to her best friend. There was no way Alma and Obinna could be done.

Alma resumed her pacing, and words fell out of her mouth, English mixed with Spanish, so Grace was only catching pieces of the rant. "Too much pressure," she was saying, and "of course I've thought about it, but just not to that extent."

Rafael, who must have had a better grasp of what was happening, spoke up then. "It's all new for you, *mi hermana*. Obinna must understand that. Have a seat, and I'll make you something to drink."

"I'm too furious," Alma said, pressing her hands to her cheeks. She didn't look furious, though, more like she was on the edge of crumbling, just barely holding herself together. It was a side of Alma that Grace had never known before.

Grace stroked Alma's arm and led her toward the sofa. "Sorry," she said. "I don't think I'm quite understanding."

Despite her frantic energy, Alma did manage to relax into the couch with Grace by her side. She took a breath and started up again but stuck to English. "He started talking about marriage and children. And I was open to having that discussion, I really was, but then he got so upset that I hadn't given it much thought, as if that meant I'm not committed to our life together. I mean, we've barely said we love each other, you know? I'm not one to get ahead of myself, and I still don't know if I want to get married or any of that. Not because of him, but just because..."

Grace nodded, and suddenly Rafael's earlier response made perfect sense. All of this was very new to Alma. She'd never had such a serious relationship in her life, and it wasn't surprising that she was hesitant and unsure.

"Anyway, it turned into something much larger than I was anticipating. About how I don't feel the same way he does, and if I'm not certain of us then something must be wrong with our relationship. He said if we don't want the same things, then it's better to know that now, and if I'm not serious enough about us..." She hung her head, covering her face with her hands.

"Oh, Alma," Grace cooed. In ten years of friendship, it was rare that Grace was the one doing the comforting. She wasn't sure where to begin.

Rafael handed over the drink before settling himself into the chair across from them.

"It sounds like tensions were high, and you just need to have another conversation when you've both calmed down," Grace said.

Alma shook her head. "He was so upset with me, Gracie. So hurt. He said maybe we should take some time away from each other, but I don't think he'll even want to speak to me again."

"I'm sure that's not true," Raf said.

"I just walked out. I didn't know what to say anymore. I felt like he wanted me to decide our whole future right away, like I should just *know.*

I'm sorry to barge in like this. I meant to call on my way, but I was too overwhelmed. I didn't mean to ruin your plans for the night."

Grace and Rafael shared a glance, and Grace used all her might to keep her face neutral. She couldn't imagine offering up the news that she'd started boning Alma's brother in the midst of everything else. "It's totally fine. I was just doing some dishes."

Alma glanced over at Rafael. "I'm surprised you're not out for a wild night on the town charming some beautiful women."

Grace started coughing uncontrollably. Even before anything had happened between the two of them, Grace had never known Rafael to do such a thing. She'd never even seen him with another woman, but maybe he just refrained from bringing women home while she lived there.

"I don't do that," Raf said, frowning. He jumped up and grabbed Grace a glass of water.

Alma squinted her eyes at him. "Um, yes, you do. I also thought you'd both be trying to get out of the apartment and as far away from each other as possible, but I'm glad you're both here." She took a sip of the concoction Raf had created for her. "Can I stay with you?"

"Stay?" Rafael repeated.

Grace finally stopped coughing and nodded instead. This was probably a sign. She shouldn't be having sex with Rafael, and here was her reminder, waltzing in and throwing a blanket over the fire, making sure Grace didn't make any further mistakes.

"I could sleep with you, Gracie?"

Grace didn't hesitate. "Of course." She thought she might have seen Rafael flinch out of the corner of her eye. "Whatever you need."

That night after they'd tucked themselves into Grace's bedroom, Alma told her even more about the fight, and Grace listened with rapt attention, sure her friend had never been so vulnerable in her life. Perhaps the closest Alma had come was after a fight with her mother, but even that didn't seem to compare to this argument with Obinna. "I think I'm just not cut out for this, Gracie, this relationship thing," Alma explained. "You were so good at it."

Grace snorted. "I thought so, too, and look where that got me."

They were side by side in Grace's tiny bed, whispering in the dark just as they had for so many nights throughout their entire friendship.

"It takes some adjustments," Grace said. "But that doesn't mean you're bad at relationships or this isn't meant to be. You and Obinna love each other. You just have to figure out the best way to fight and work through this stuff."

"I don't know how to fight when he can't even look at me. And I was so angry."

"I'm sorry, Alma. I know it's hard, but it doesn't mean you can't handle it. Sometimes you'll get angry. Sometimes you might want to scream, but it doesn't mean it's over."

Alma's eyes softened. "I'm so glad you're here, Gracie. This is exactly the situation where I need my best friend in the same city. I wish we were living together right now, but I'll take what I can get."

Grace reached out and put a hand on her best friend's arm. "I'm glad I can be here for you, too." She meant it with every fiber of her being. When Derek had ended things with Grace, Alma had called every day and listened to Grace cry. Alma had never needed this kind of support before; she'd always been so tough and independent, but now that she was in crisis, Grace wanted to return the favor, to be the friend Alma deserved. "We'll figure this out."

Alma blew out a thick breath. "I don't know. We've had fights before, but not like this. This felt like too much."

"Too much because you don't want to deal with it? Or too much because of how much you care?"

Alma groaned. "The second one. That's the scary part."

"We'll get through this, Alma. I promise, and you know I wouldn't promise that if I didn't mean it." After all, Grace was still standing after everything had happened, and she was sure Alma was a stronger woman than she was.

Alma squeezed her eyes shut, as if trying to hold back tears. "I don't know how to fix it, though."

"Maybe you both need a little time before you talk it out. Maybe you need time to consider all the marriage and kids stuff. That's not unreasonable." Grace shifted on the bed, turning further toward her best friend.

"He thinks I already should have been considering it." Alma opened her eyes and frowned.

"That sounds like it's just coming from a place of insecurity. He's worried about how you really feel."

Alma sighed, adjusting her position so she could lean her head on Grace's shoulder. "I love him, Gracie. You know I do, but that's a lot to consider."

"It is. And he should understand that."

"I'm so glad you're my best friend," Alma said, and Grace felt a new sense of guilt bubbling under the surface of her skin.

"Me too," she whispered.

Despite how keyed up Alma had been when she arrived, she fell asleep next to Grace quickly, her breath heavy and her knees digging into Grace's side. It was Grace who was too agitated to sleep, too wrapped up in her own thoughts, consumed by daydreams of slipping out of bed and into Rafael's room to pick up where they'd left off.

She knew that made her a terrible person. After everything Alma had done for her—beautiful, fierce, heartbroken Alma—Grace was just flagrantly ignoring all of her advice and good judgment and obsessing over Rafael anyway. But the way his skin felt against hers made her feel like she was about to burst into flames. She hadn't even known that was possible. And the way he looked at her... Who could resist that? Why would you ever want to?

Because most likely she would end up with a broken heart all over again. And then she would still have to see him and be civil for the rest of their lives. It would make things awkward for Alma, and at the moment, Grace was still living with the guy. She could get kicked out on the street again, just like with Derek. What would happen when he woke up one morning, ready to move on with someone else, and Grace was still just there in his apartment, pining for him? That was pathetic. She was pathetic, and painfully aware of it.

Grace's phone vibrated with a text alert on the nightstand, and she snatched it up, knowing it could only be one person, the person she most wanted to talk to.

Rafael: "How quickly do you think we can get them back together?"

Grace smiled to herself and started typing. She was going to let him destroy her, wasn't she? She'd already been through hell. She could take it. She might as well just enjoy it and then start bracing for the aftermath.

Grace: "Should we invite Obinna for breakfast? At dawn?"

Rafael: "That's still too long to wait. I want you now."

Ugh, how could her nipples get hard from a single text message? And the way her body was thrumming, she couldn't possibly sleep. Not that she was a great sleeper anyway, but there was no longer any hope.

"What would you do?" she asked, sending the message before she could think twice.

The three dots to indicate that Raf was typing were torture. Alma let out a loud snore beside her, and Grace jumped, then covered her mouth to hold in a laugh.

Rafael: "What if you came in here and found out?"

Grace felt the flush spreading down her face and neck. If she had a single ounce of will power left in her body, she couldn't find it. She *needed* him. It was as simple as that. She glanced at Alma and released a long breath. Then she stretched her legs over the side of the bed, easing them down as carefully as possible until her feet were on the floor. As lightly as she possibly could, she padded out of the room, closing the door behind her.

She felt more confident than she had all afternoon. Her desperation had hit its peak, and there was no turning back, no stopping herself. For some reason, he wanted her, and she couldn't walk away from that so easily.

"*Gracias a Dios,*" Raf huffed when Grace slipped into the room. It sent a thrill through her, the way his eyes eagerly took her in, even though she was dressed in her stupid hamster pajamas and her hair was a mess. None of that mattered to him.

She locked his door, then stood with her back up against it, breathing heavily as if she'd traveled miles to get to his room instead of mere feet.

There was no hesitation then. No awkwardness like when they returned from the cathedrals and didn't know where to start. They'd been hungry for each other for hours, and there was no time for gentle kisses or cheek caressing. Rafael got to his knees on the bed in anticipation, and as soon as Grace was within reach, he kissed her fiercely, his hands already tugging at her shirt, his firm length already pressed against her middle.

He spun her around and threw her on the bed, and she let out a little squeal.

"Shhhh," he scolded. "You'll have to be quiet this time. Think you can do that?"

Grace smirked up at him. "I'll try."

"I've been wasting away over here," he said as he leaned over her, pressing a trail of kisses down her neck and her chest before he continued down and down and down. He tugged at the waistband of her hamster pajamas. "I wasn't expecting to be so turned on by these."

Grace writhed against his touch, but before she could reply, the pajamas were around her knees, and then her ankles, and Rafael was making himself right at home between her thighs.

"Hnmm," he said, and she fell against the pillows on his bed with her palm covering her mouth. Yes, it was settled then. She was definitely going to let him destroy her.

Grace woke up to the sound of Alma crying. She'd slipped back into her own bed the night before, even though she'd so desperately wanted to sleep next to Rafael, to feel him curved against her body all night long. Instead, she was hanging halfway off the tiny mattress in her room, and she glanced up to find Alma standing near the door, phone clutched in hand, tears streaming down her cheeks.

"What's going on?" Grace asked. "Are you okay?"

Alma pouted. "He hasn't called or texted or anything, Gracie. He really must not want to speak to me again."

Grace glanced at her own phone. "It's 6:00 in the morning." She'd been joking about inviting Obinna over at dawn, but maybe that wouldn't have been a bad idea.

"I know he's awake. I know his routine."

Grace got out of bed and shuffled toward Alma, then pulled her into a hug. "I don't think I've ever seen you cry before. I'm not sure what to do."

"I know," Alma said. "I don't like this. I should have known falling in love was a terrible idea."

"There's no way that man doesn't want to talk to you. It sounds like his whole problem is that he thinks he loves you more."

Alma groaned. "I know you were with Derek way longer, but now I can understand a little bit of what you were going through after your breakup. I feel like my heart has burst, and now all of the juices are leaking out of it until I die."

"That's quite an image."

"I'm just at a loss."

"I know." Grace rubbed her friend's back and held her close. Alma had been there for her through everything, when she lost her job and Derek and Gram. Alma had helped move her across the world, given her a home, a life. And here was ungrateful, idiotic Grace, sneaking out of the room to fool around with Alma's big brother. Clearly, she was an asshole. But she was going to be better in the future. She was going to take care of Alma. And even though she was sure Alma and Obinna would work this out, she was going to pull out all the stops. Ice cream and rom coms and painting toenails on the couch while listening to Celine Dion and drinking sangria. She was going to be the most amazing friend on the planet.

"What do you want to do today?" she asked. "Anything at all."

"I don't know. Sit in your bed and cry?" Alma sighed. "I've never felt like this in my life. I don't know how to handle it. What's happened to me?"

"It's not a bad thing to care so much for someone, Alma."

"Then why does it hurt like this?"

A familiar pain rose to the surface in Grace's chest. She knew exactly what Alma was feeling—the loss and the grief and the fear that the person you spent every day with was suddenly no longer there. When Derek broke up with her, she was lost in the same way and so confused. She couldn't understand how he would upend their lives like that. What could she have possibly done wrong to make him blow up their relationship?

But months of distance and the move to another country was starting to make her think he'd done the right thing. Life with Derek had been... fine. It was comfortable and easy, for the most part. They rarely argued. They rarely did much of anything. Derek never even seemed that interested in listening to her, not in the way Rafael did—sitting with his chin in his hands, drinking in every word she spoke, like all of it was important and monumental. Like she mattered. Not in a million years would she have expected Raf to be the person to make her feel that way. She'd never come alive when Derek put a hand on her thigh. She'd never longed for him, desperate to get home and feel his fingers in her hair. She'd never felt an electric spark that sizzled right under her skin. She'd never known what she was missing.

She bit her lip and tried to stifle the sudden feeling that bubbled up in her belly, forcing herself to ignore it.

Alma and Obinna weren't Grace and Derek, and Grace was sure this wasn't the end of their story. She just needed to figure out how to get Alma to feel her feelings, to let Obinna know what she really wanted, to be vulnerable for the first time in her entire life.

"I need a drink," Alma said.

Grace pulled back and examined her friend's face to see if she was serious. "It's Sunday. And the sun isn't even up."

Alma scoffed. "When would it be appropriate to drink then, Gracie? I thought we could do whatever I wanted."

Grace scrunched up her face. "Mimosas?"

Alma smiled, a hint of her usual self peeking out. "Now you're talking."

CHAPTER EIGHTEEN

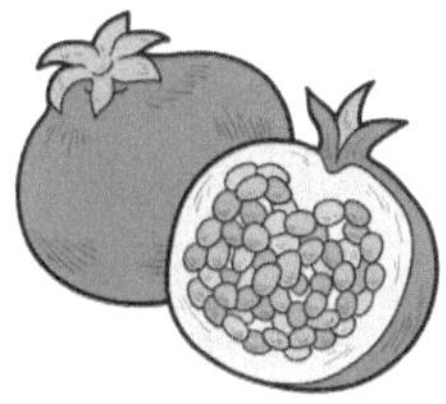

RAFAEL DRESSED to the sound of giggling outside his door. He supposed that was a good sign. At least Alma wasn't crying again. He shivered. He'd never seen his sister cry before, and he didn't want to repeat the experience. Of course, if anyone in the world could get Alma to giggle when she was at her worst, it was Graciela.

Vaya, why did something swell inside of him at the thought of Grace? She was so funny and smart and passionate. It had taken everything out of him to watch her leave his room in the middle of the night when all he wanted was to hold her and smell her hair. Apparently, both Ferrer-Martín siblings were starting to experience emotions they'd never had before.

Rafael was afraid to leave his room, afraid that he would take one look at his sister's best friend, and everything would be written all over his face. Alma would know it in an instant. He was *pining*. Even if it was a completely new look for him, his sister would be able to spot it. He didn't know how to act like a regular person when this feeling was churning inside of him—this thing he'd never quite experienced in his life. He didn't know how to name it, but he was giddy. He was gleeful. Alma was going to think he was a total idiot.

He took a deep breath, trying to keep his face neutral, and exited the bedroom.

There was a contained bit of chaos in his kitchen. Both women were seated at the counter with a mess of glasses and bottles littered before them, Grace with her head on the granite and Alma cackling. Grace lifted her head slightly at the sound of his bedroom door creaking, and he saw the blush creeping up her cheeks. Then Alma knocked a shoulder into her, and they both nearly tumbled from their stools.

"Are you two drunk?" He checked his watch.

That set Alma off on another fit of laughter. "Gracie's cheering me up," she said.

"I can see that." Except Grace hadn't looked at him again. She was clearly avoiding eye contact.

"And we were reminiscing about old times. Like the time—"

"Alma!" Grace jumped in, trying to cut her off.

But Alma persevered. "Grace made out with a guy dressed like the Grinch at a Christmas party, and she had green paint smudged all over her face and neck and arms." She let out another laugh. "At least, that was the paint I could *see*. Might have been somewhere else, too."

Grace dropped her head into her hands, her groan muffled by her palms, and Rafael laughed softly. "Did he taste weird from all that paint?"

Alma took a large gulp from her drink and put a hand on Grace's shoulder. "That gives me a good idea!"

Rafael stepped closer, watching the pair of them with amusement.

"You want to dress up like the Grinch? It's not even Christmas yet," Grace said.

"No, you know what always cheers me up and brings me so much joy? Watching your escapades with random men. And I haven't gotten to see that for a *long* time. I'm not really up for any escapades myself, but going out and seeing you hook up with someone..."

Grace looked anywhere in the room but at Rafael, and he knew it well, since he hadn't managed to take his eyes off her. The thought of her with someone else blazed in his mind, and he rubbed a hand against the back of his head, trying to stay calm.

Was this jealousy? Because of someone who didn't even exist? Jealousy at just the thought of her kissing someone else? Or looking at someone else the way she looked at him? Not that she looked at him like that anymore, apparently, since she was so clearly avoiding his gaze.

Would she want that—to be with some other guy? To have an escapade? Was that all she was looking for?

He'd never been jealous about a woman, not like this. He'd never felt so flustered and overwhelmed and obsessed. It was fucking terrible.

"What's wrong with you?" Alma asked, watching him.

Yep, there it was. She'd figured him out already, but he wouldn't go down without a fight. "What do you mean?" he tried to keep his voice even.

"You look like you swallowed a seashell."

Grace looked up. Finally, her eyes met his. Finally, she inspected him, and even though he was trying so damn hard to look normal, he was obviously failing, and whatever she saw on his face made her expression darken.

"I'm fine. Just trying to understand why you two are drunk in my kitchen talking about hooking up with guys this early in the morning."

"We're not hooking up with any guys," Grace said, keeping her eyes on his.

"But you said we could do anything I want today," Alma whined.

Grace snorted. "Within reason."

"You're a beautiful single woman, and I want to live vicariously through you. That seems reasonable to me."

"Come on, Alma. Give her a break," Rafael said. Alma narrowed her eyes, and he realized his mistake. He shouldn't have an opinion about this.

"What do you care?" she asked.

Grace's eyes went wide, but she didn't move.

"I don't," he said. "You're just asking a lot of your friend, and you know she would do anything for you."

Alma scowled. "I don't know if I like you two living together if you're going to team up against me, preventing me from watching Grace make out with a stranger on the street."

"God, Alma," Grace grumbled, her face completely red.

Rafael tried to think of a delicate way to change the subject. But also,

Grace was so cute when she was embarrassed. And when she was sleeping. And when she had her mouth around his—

"I'm starving," Alma announced. "I didn't think I'd be able to eat anything, but I had nothing at all last night, and it's catching up to me."

"Especially now that you're hammered," Grace chimed in.

"I'm not hammered. Some of us can handle our alcohol, Gracie. I just feel a little bouncy." She bobbed in her seat to demonstrate.

"Well, that's an improvement," Rafael said.

"Yes, and now I need the toilet." Alma jumped off her stool and marched toward the bathroom. "Keep thinking about that stranger hook up, Grace. Just consider it." She slammed the door behind her, and then, suddenly, Grace and Rafael were alone.

Even though there was still a good bit of space between them, Rafael thought he could hear her breathing. He was attuned to her—every sound she made, every blink.

"Hey," he said.

She bit her lip. "Hi."

"How are you this morning?"

He swore he could see her swallow, too, from across the room. "Good."

He took a few steps in her direction, slowly. And then he took a few more, rounding the counter and getting close enough to reach out for her.

"Raf—" she huffed.

"What?" He ran his thumb along her jawline, his fingers at the back of her neck.

"Alma will be right back."

"I don't care," he said. She'd lit some kind of fuse inside of him, and it was burning, burning, so ready to explode.

"I do. Today is supposed to be about her. I need to make her happy. She's done everything for me, and if she finds out about us—"

"You don't think she'll be happy?" He knew it might be awkward for Alma, maybe a little uncomfortable at first as she adjusted to this new development. It had been enough to deter him from making a move earlier and complicating everything, but now that the move had been made, surely Alma wouldn't be too bothered by his interest in Grace.

Grace shook her head, lines wrinkling across her forehead. "Um, no. I don't think so. Anyway, it will distract from my mission as her best friend."

"What about my mission?" he asked, dipping his head toward her, eyes on her mouth.

"Wh-what's your mission?" At the distant sound of the toilet flushing, Grace jumped up and moved away from him, grabbing her glass and looking around for the champagne bottle. He snatched it up and dangled it in front of her, but she took it out of his hands and scooted away from him quickly.

Rafael really wished they'd had that conversation about what all of this meant, because he was getting more uncertain by the minute. Did she not want to tell Alma because she didn't have feelings for him? Because he was just a fun lay, and he meant nothing to her? Was she just waiting for the right time? He'd never had this many questions about a woman in his life.

"Have we figured out a plan?" Alma asked as she charged back into the room.

He hadn't figured out a plan. In fact, it seemed all his plans had been knocked entirely off course, because the only thing he wanted to do this weekend was get Graciela naked in his bed again, her leg draped over his thighs as he traced circles on her skin. They could talk about everything then—about art and monasteries, cooking shows and Spanish history, about what all of this meant. Obviously, it didn't look like that would be happening anytime soon, but it was quite clear that it would be damn near impossible to think about anything else.

"No plan yet," Grace said before taking a long gulp of champagne.

They'd had a surprisingly pleasant day. Rafael had joined Grace and Alma in their morning festivities, and they drank more champagne than anyone ever should on a Sunday morning. They took a walk around the neighborhood, stumbling occasionally, and then they napped until late afternoon. Rafael would have preferred to nap with Grace snuggled up next to him, but he still woke up refreshed and happy, excited that he would get to see her again so soon.

And he did. She had already been awake and reading on the couch when he had emerged, and he couldn't help but notice she was also finally, *mercifully*, alone.

"Did you sleep?" he asked, sitting beside her.

"I basically passed out."

He laughed, inching closer. "Where's Alma?"

Grace paused, looking at him, biting her lip. "Still sleeping."

"Good," he said, leaning toward her, giving her plenty of time to protest if she wanted to avoid him. Instead, she closed the distance between them in an instant, surprising him with the voracity of her lips on his. He exhaled as she melted against him.

It felt…right.

But then Grace pulled away too soon, smiling. "It's going to be hard to stay away from you when Alma's here."

"About that, where did we land on inviting Obinna over and forcing them to make up immediately?"

"I think they both need a little more time to figure it out."

Rafael pressed his lips to Grace's neck. "Well, for my sake, let's hope that happens soon."

Grace shook her head. "For your sake?"

"I don't know how long you think I'll be able to stay away from you, Graciela, but I feel like I'm already at my limit."

Grace leaned into his touch, her breath heavy. "I know what you mean, but Alma..."

"I know," Rafael nodded against Grace's shoulder. "I know. I *am* worried about her. I've never seen her like this in our entire lives. I'm not sure how to help her, but she needs us. This morning was a good start. You got her laughing at least."

Grace put her hands in her lap. "The champagne got her laughing, but it's something."

"I know it will all work out for her," he said, his voice full of conviction. "But she needs us to help her through it. After she would have a fight with our mother, we would always hide in the linen closet and eat popsicles together, complaining about everything and throwing the hand towels on the floor with our sticky fingers. She just needed someone there with her, someone to be on her side no matter what."

Grace leaned back and searched his face, as if assessing him with fresh eyes.

"What?" he asked.

She smiled. "I'm just imagining you as a child wreaking havoc on the laundry."

Rafael grinned back at her. "Then I have quite a number of stories you will enjoy."

It was a short moment, but Rafael felt it sustained him. Everything was so easy and comfortable between them, if only for a moment. Alma awoke from her nap soon after, and Raf was forced to keep his distance once again, but that teasing look Grace had given him, that kiss, it had been enough

Hours later, Alma was sprawled across the sofa, her long legs hanging over Grace's lap. Rafael never imagined he'd be so jealous of his own sister, who'd been casually touching and cuddling Grace all evening—grabbing her hand, leaning her head on her shoulder—while he'd kept his distance, sitting across the room and trying to breathe, even though he wanted nothing more than to throw Grace over his shoulder and carry her away to his bedroom.

"So how are things going with your little museum?" Alma asked. "It seems like you've managed not to murder each other in the process of creating this whole exhibit."

"It's going well, I think," Grace answered, likely realizing that Rafael was lost in thought. She probably just didn't imagine how much he was thinking about her.

"Yes," he jumped in. "Grace had some fantastic ideas. She was a great help, and now it's really coming along. Christian's going to have an opening party to see how it goes. And I hope you'll both be there, of course."

"We're invited?" Grace asked, raising an eyebrow. "I assumed Christian would want that to be an exclusive billionaire party, too."

Rafael smiled. "Grace, you are the reason this exhibit doesn't completely suck. Seriously, I would have been fired from this job in a heartbeat. Of course you're invited. And Christian loves you, anyway. He insisted you be there."

"I would like to take credit for the whole idea of having Grace work with you in the first place," Alma said, wiggling her toes over the armrest.

"The pieces are beautiful, Alma. You'll be amazed." She pinched one of Alma's feet.

"Beautiful might not be the word I would use." Rafael grinned, and Grace shot him a look.

"For a man of such sophistication, you know very little about art," Grace said, annoyance flaring in her voice.

"You know Pablo's just not my cup of tea."

"But you know it's not just Picasso, Raf. There's a Matisse and several Blanchards and a Gilot. There's a Braque, too."

"I think you're just making up names," Alma said.

"And I'm supposed to appreciate weird faces and giant—" Rafael started.

Grace shook her head. "I know you're just trying to play it cool for your sister right now, but you're a newly minted art connoisseur. Don't deny it."

"I still can't decide if I actually like any of that abstract stuff, though," he said.

"Come on," Alma broke in before Grace could berate him. "I wasn't trying to start a war. I was just marveling that you hadn't killed each other, remember?"

Rafael smiled. He loved when Grace was all riled up about art. It got him riled up, too…in a completely different way.

"Did Grace tell you about the party for her class?" He could tell that Grace was flustered, but he couldn't stop himself from bringing it up, not when he was so pleased about how happy it made her.

"A party? At the museum?" Alma asked.

"Raf got Christian to agree to host my students there to see what we've been working on. Though I swear I hardly did anything." She stared at Rafael with a shy smile.

He tried not to let the full force of his grin take over his face. "The place would be a mess without you. And Christian knows that."

Grace turned back to Alma, the blush creeping up her face. "My students are thrilled. Raf and I are making up fancy little invitations and everything."

"Sounds lovely," Alma said. Then she glanced away wistfully, her eyes losing focus as she stared at the front door. In the matter of a moment, she'd drifted away again, and Rafael was sure she was thinking of Obinna. He always seemed to be at the forefront of Alma's thoughts, one second from taking over and darkening her mood.

Rafael noticed that she kept checking her phone. Kept…waiting. The operation to get his sister back with her boyfriend wasn't going very well, though they hadn't done much so far. Once the unhappy couple had a chance to cool off and think it over, then, surely, he could get them to make up, and Alma would be back to her old self—the woman she'd been for as long as he could remember. Carefree and calm, so sure of herself in every way, ready to take on their mother and take on the world. Admittedly, Rafael had been annoyed at first when his sister had suddenly become obsessed with Obinna, when she started talking about him constantly. But now Rafael thought he might be starting to understand it, and he wanted Alma to be able to hold onto that feeling. He wanted her to get it all back—that joy—and once she was happy again, Rafael could return to the person that had been consuming his thoughts lately, the person that had started to keep him up at night.

He was lucky Alma was too distracted to notice when he caught himself staring at Grace again. She looked up, and their eyes met, and that was all it took for the corners of his mouth to tug upward. Grace shook her head slightly, scolding him for being so obvious, even though she was smiling.

Guau! That smile. It did things to him. One of them was highly inappropriate, and the other was incredibly wholesome. He wanted her so badly, in so many ways.

Alma let out a sigh, and Rafael tried to maneuver his face into a blank expression. "I can't believe I have to work tomorrow," she said. "How do people work at a time like this? You're just supposed to wake up and go about your day like you aren't completely cracking into pieces?"

"I think everyone has days like that," Grace said, squeezing Alma's leg, "where it's hard to pretend."

"Raf doesn't," Alma accused. "He's always perfectly level-headed and under control."

He shook his head and stole another glance at Grace. Alma was right in a lot of ways, actually. He always had been able to separate business and personal, to keep things professional. But he was starting to understand what she was talking about. And he was starting to have days, like everyone else apparently, where it was hard to pretend.

CHAPTER NINETEEN

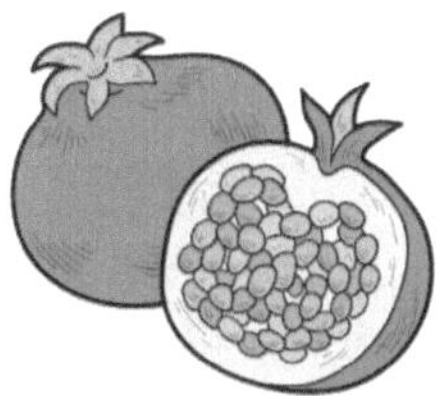

"REMEMBER WHAT I SAID, GRACIE, OKAY?" Alma dusted blush on her cheeks in front of the little mirror in Rafael's bathroom. Her skin was already glowing, her dark eyes lidded with shadow in a way Grace had never been able to master. Alma had managed to go to work that week, to brush her hair and put on shoes and do all of the things people were required to do, even when they were hurting so badly.

"What you said about what?" Grace asked.

"About Raf. Maybe he hasn't done much yet, but I'm getting the feeling you're in trouble. He watches you sometimes. You probably haven't noticed, but I have. And I don't think he would do it on purpose, but I don't want him to take advantage of you right now, after everything you've been through. He'd probably think it was just a bit of fun, but you..."

Grace pursed her lips, debating whether she should come clean. She was dying to tell Alma the truth—to admit she couldn't stop thinking about Rafael even if she didn't know what that meant. She was on the cusp of understanding she was head over heels for him, too stupidly enamored to be objective or cautious, but she refused to peek behind that curtain. She couldn't bring it to light. If this thing between them could just be casual sex and nothing more, it would really be a relief. She'd been slogging through so many difficult emotions lately, carrying all her *feelings* like a weight she couldn't drop. For once, ignoring her emotions sounded all too appealing.

But Alma was her person, the one who saw her, who truly knew her. Actually, Alma was probably the only person left in the world who understood her, and Grace hated keeping this secret. The words clawed at her throat, desperate to crawl into the open, but Grace clamped her mouth shut. She would tell Alma soon, but she wanted her to be in a good place, happy with Obinna, secure in her own life. Grace spent too much time talking about herself lately, sucking up all of Alma's sympathy like a vacuum and leaving nothing in its wake. This was an opportunity to stay focused on Alma's needs. So for the time being, she just cleared her throat. "I…what?"

Alma set down the blush and picked up her comb. "You feel everything."

Grace coughed, not wanting to accept how true this might be.

"I'm serious, Gracie, and I know you're brilliant, and you've never liked him much, anyway, but you still have to be careful. He's incredibly charming. And I guess people think he's good looking, too." Alma tossed her hair to the side, as if conscious that she shared these good looks as well. They had great DNA, there was no denying it. "Look, I love him, and I hope someday he'll work out all his shit and learn to let people in, but you're vulnerable right now. I just don't want you to get hurt," Alma said, turning back to the sink and swiping the comb through her curtain bangs.

Grace understood Alma's concern about how vulnerable she was right now, but a simple seduction didn't seem to accurately define the thing percolating between them. The way he supported her, the way he made her feel when they were together—well, Grace couldn't imagine those were just simple methods for trying to get into a girl's pants. But maybe she was just naïve. She didn't know him that well. She hadn't been around for all of the womanizing and heartbreaking Alma had supposedly witnessed. "Why do you think he would even bother with me?" she asked.

Alma shrugged, unaware of how eagerly Grace awaited her response. "Because that's what he does. He has his fun, and then he moves on. He's just not a relationship guy. You on the other hand… Well." Alma took a breath, and Grace couldn't help but notice the wet sheen of her eyes and the way her posture deflated. "I know how it feels when your heart is broken."

Something twisted in Grace's stomach. It might have been because of how much she hated seeing her best friend this way. It was so out of character, it was almost extraordinary. Alma gave her a sad smile, and Grace felt her own heart breaking. If Obinna didn't fix this soon, she would be marching over to his studio apartment and having a few choice words with him.

But there was something else gnawing at the back of Grace's mind, something about Almas's casual assurances that Rafael was just another pretty playboy looking for a good time. She was supposed to have mentally prepared for this—that this magnetic attraction was just a bit of fun, that, yes, Raf was hot, and sex with him was worth any emotional turmoil. She was aware of the risks and the consequences, and she was supposed to have hardened herself to the fact that he could disappear from her life at any moment, but the way Alma's words dug under her skin still made her feel queasy.

Because Alma was right. No matter how hard she tried not to, Grace *did* feel everything. And as much as she'd been wanting to ignore it, she couldn't seem to stifle the part of her was starting to hope Raf felt it too, that this thing between them could actually be something real. Even if Alma's assessment didn't seem to even allow for that possibility.

"Grace?" Alma was staring at her reflection in the mirror.

"I—" Grace tried to organize her thoughts around the most important thing, around helping Alma through her own heartbreak. "Look, I just want to talk about you right now. Stop worrying about me so I can be worried about you instead. I know you've had to deal with me being a wreck for months, but it's time to put all of our energy into your problems. What have you been thinking about? Have you imagined your future with Obinna?"

Alma frowned at her best friend for a moment before letting out a long sigh. "I—" Alma started. Then she pressed her lips together, and Grace thought she could see Alma trying to hold in her pain, as if it all might spill out of her mouth if she let it. "It's all I've been imagining. I don't understand how he could think I don't feel the same way about him. Maybe I haven't dealt in specifics about where we'll get married or how many dogs or children we'll have, but that doesn't mean I'm not—" Her voice broke on the last word, and Grace wrapped an arm around her waist, leaning her chin onto Alma's shoulder.

"Are you going to tell him that?" Grace asked.

"I tried, Gracie." Alma fanned her face, working hard not to mess up her fresh makeup.

"I know, but emotions were running high. Maybe he wasn't really hearing you."

Alma nodded. Grace could tell Alma was uncomfortable, that she wasn't used to talking about this kind of stuff. She'd never had to before, and Grace knew that if she could have swept it all under the rug and forgotten it, she would have done just that.

They had a lot in common at the moment.

"Can I ask you one other thing?" Alma said, applying lipstick to finish off the "get ready" routine Grace had watched her perfect over the years. Even heartbroken and miserable, Alma would moisturize and contour.

"Are you changing the subject?"

Alma smirked, mischief in her eyes.

Suddenly, Grace was wary. It seemed clear that she wasn't the best person to be doling out love advice. Everything with Derek had crumbled right under her nose. "Yes?"

"I borrowed your laptop to look at something really quick—didn't think you'd mind—but when I opened it, it was on a page about how to eat a pomegranate."

Grace laughed, entirely embarrassed but also a little relieved. This was a conversation she could handle. "It's not a big deal. I've just never eaten one before. I don't know how to do it."

Alma's mouth fell open as she capped the lipstick. "You've never eaten a pomegranate?"

"No. I've had pomegranate juice, but I just haven't eaten the fruit on its own. And I cut one open once, but I didn't know how I was supposed to do it or what parts to eat, so I had to do some research."

Alma laughed more than she had since she'd shown up at Raf's apartment, somehow even more than when she'd been drunk off mimosas. "You're ridiculous."

"I'm aware."

Alma's eyes gleamed. "Have you tried it yet? After what you learned on the internet?"

Grace clicked her tongue, stalling. She knew there was no way Alma was going to let this go. "I haven't had the chance."

A sly grin spread across her best friend's face. "Well, if something good can come from moping around my brother's apartment, at least I can coach you to eat a pomegranate for the first time."

Grace rolled her eyes. "That's seriously not necessary. I think I can try it on my own. I don't need assistance."

"This isn't a hero's quest, Gracie. I'm here to support you in this time of need, as always. And I can't wait to witness it."

Grace let out a long sigh. "Really?"

"You underestimate how badly I need a distraction." Alma brushed past her friend toward the kitchen, almost shouting. "Do we have pomegranates in the house right now? Let's get this party started!"

Grace trailed behind her, shaking her head. She was trying to be there for her in every possible way, even if it meant eating a pomegranate for the first time like it was a form of entertainment.

Of course, there were pomegranates in the house. They were always there on the counter, waiting, taunting Grace on a daily basis because she didn't know what in the world to do with them, even though Rafael always had them there in that pretty little bowl on the counter.

Rafael was working on his laptop in the living room when Alma made a mad dash for said pretty little bowl, taking a pomegranate in her hand and holding it out to Grace. "Do you know that story of Persephone?" she asked.

"Yes, Hades tricked her into eating the pomegranate seeds, and then she was stuck with him."

"Half of the year in the underworld," Alma added.

"Why do you two always seem like you're up to something?" Rafael asked with a raised brow.

"Because we are," Alma admitted.

"There are paintings about the myth," Grace said quietly. "*Woman with Pomegranate*. That's a good one."

Rafael stood up and approached them. "What on earth are you doing?"

"Did you know that Grace has never eaten a pomegranate?"

Raf's eyes locked on hers in that particular way they had. There was something so intense about his stare. She felt it travel through her body, like his eyes were all over her, like his look had made its way into her bloodstream. "I did know that," he drawled.

"Well, she's been doing her research, and we've decided—"

"You've decided." Grace groaned.

Alma clapped her hands together. "Come on, you know you want to, Gracie. It's time to have a taste."

It was a strange way to spend an afternoon, but there was no escaping it. Grace was about to eat a pomegranate in front of her best friend and her lover as if this were some kind of exhibition. Alma sliced the thing open on the top—which was a small mercy because cutting into it was quite a chore. The pomegranate looked like it had on YouTube, at least. No major surprises about the insides. So far, so good.

"Are we using the underwater method?" Grace asked, showing off what she'd gleaned from her deep dive on the internet.

"You really have done your research," Raf laughed. "Haven't you seen me do this before?"

She thought for a moment. She remembered him spooning seeds into his mouth, but everything that came before that was a blur. "I wasn't paying enough attention, I guess."

"I like to spank the pomegranate," he said with a smirk.

Alma pointed the knife in his direction. "Ew, come on, Rafa, this is scientific, okay? Grace is trying to learn something new."

Raf took one half of the pomegranate into his palm. "Yes, you *would* turn it into a science experiment."

"Honestly, neither of you need to be present right now. I was hoping to just experiment with my pomegranate-eating in private." Grace had never been so mortified about eating a piece of fruit, but both of the Ferrer-Martíns were staring at her expectantly.

"Fine," she said, resigned. "At least let me scoop out the insides myself to practice."

She took the first half from Raf and spanked the pomegranate—much to Rafael's delight—before resorting to scraping the seeds into a bowl of water. Then she dumped the seeds into a strainer and gave them a rinse. Honestly, it was a lot of work for a fruit. A banana she could get behind. Oranges were reasonable. You could bite into an apple on the go, no problem, but the pomegranate made you work for it.

"Careful of the juice," Alma warned. "It will stain your clothes to hell."

"YouTube said that, too."

"YouTube is very thorough on this topic, apparently." Raf laughed.

Grace squeezed one pomegranate seed between her fingers, just to see the juice inside. It was quite a lot for one little seed, actually. She licked her fingers, enjoying the taste. Alma grabbed a spoon from a drawer and handed it over to her, so she could scoop up more from the bowl.

Grace glanced at the siblings, who were still eyeing her with anticipation. "You guys are so weird." She should have known to be more careful about her internet history when Alma was around. They shared everything, and of course Alma would delight in Grace's foray to new fruit, clinging for any chance of distraction. Grace sighed and took a bite.

It was good, though rather anticlimactic, honestly. She felt like she needed to put on some kind of show, though, so she nodded with a smile and an "mmm" vibrating from her lips. She supposed this gave Raf a good excuse to stare at her mouth at least, and that's what he was doing, watching her lick her lips with a hunger in his eyes that sent goosebumps up her arms. No wonder Alma thought she was in trouble.

"Can I eat the rest of this in peace, or are the two of you going to stare at me the whole time?"

Rafael looked sheepish.

Alma waved a hand. "What other foods have you never had? I like this game! What about a cherimoya?"

Grace frowned. "I don't know what that is."

"Oh good," Alma said, clearly delighted. "That's next on the list. We can tell you how to eat it, Gracie. You won't even need to do internet research beforehand."

"There's a good reason I looked up how to eat this on the internet, rather than asking you about it."

Alma shook her head. "I'm proud to be a part of your cultural education."

Grace wiped her hands on a towel. "Well, I'm glad you enjoyed yourself, but I think that's enough for today."

Alma let out a low "booooo" before turning to Rafael. "You're awfully quiet."

He rubbed a hand through his hair. "I'm just taking it all in, just like I always do when the two of you start up your shenanigans."

Grace bit back a smile. He'd witnessed plenty of their shenanigans and had never wanted to go along with them. Until now.

"I don't think this can be called a shenanigan," Alma said. "This is tamer than tame. We are literally watching Grace eat fruit."

"This is our wild weekend now." Grace shrugged. She remembered singing at the top of her lungs in late-night taxis, dancing with strangers on tables, cartwheels in the park, trays full of tequila shots. She remembered shoving Raf's arm and telling him to lighten up, forever hoping he would smile at her just once like he did when she'd spanked the pomegranate.

"And I can hardly keep up," Raf said. "Cherimoyas next? You're out of control."

Grace grinned up at him. "I knew you wouldn't be able to handle it, old man."

Rafael gasped playfully. "You take that back."

Back in Barcelona, she'd teased him about being older than them. Not just because he was actually a few years older, but because he always had his arms crossed and a frown on his face in an attempt to discourage them from whatever they were about to do.

"Is that a gray hair?" Grace asked, tugging at one of his perfect dark locks.

Rafael snatched her hand in his in an instant, holding it tight. "You'll pay for that."

Alma cleared her throat, and Grace noticed the way her eyes were darting between them. *Shit.* Raf dropped her hand. Grace took a step back. She waited for accusations or for Alma to pull her aside to claim the situation was dire, and Grace needed to leave the apartment immediately. Instead, Alma just shook her head, her demeanor suddenly changed.

"You okay, Alma?" Grace asked. Alma appeared to have drifted off again, as if the spell of eating the pomegranate had been easily broken, and she was being forced to reckon with the constant cycle of thoughts that had been plaguing her all week.

"I think I'm going to try calling Obinna," she said, as if it had just occurred to her for the first time that this was a thing she could do. Maybe it had just occurred to her that she was brave enough to pick up the phone and try.

Grace breathed a sigh of relief. "Good."

"Yeah," Alma said, turning away, her voice suddenly so quiet. "I think it's time to see where we stand. I'll let you know how it goes."

Grace's eyes followed her best friend across the room, and she remembered late nights at their favorite restaurant with a mountain of nachos between them, cheese painting the corners of their mouths. She remembered lying in one of their beds on a Sunday afternoon talking about the future—careers in biotech and grad programs in art history and then all the painful details of their family histories. Throughout all of it, so many years of getting to know this amazing person, she'd never seen Alma so sad. Alma was always the strong one; she always had a plan and never suffered fools. Alma had never come close to a broken heart, and Grace felt helpless in the face of it. She knew exactly how it was to have that sadness hovering over you, lingering through every interaction. She just hoped that for Alma, it would be short-lived.

CHAPTER TWENTY

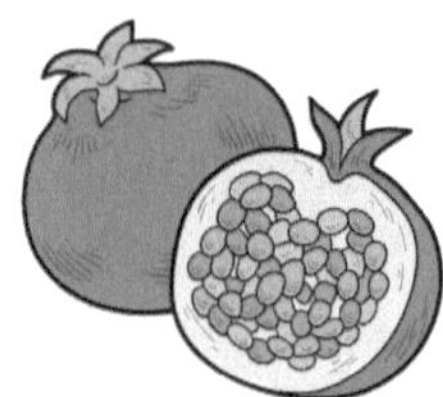

POMEGRANATES WERE SUPPOSED to be safe. They were one of Rafael's acceptable topics of conversation with Grace, something to keep him in check, to keep him from wanting her all the time. Look how well that had worked out. Not only had he slept with his sister's best friend, but now he was drooling over her as he watched her lick pomegranate juice from her fingers. There was a spot on her lip where a tiny bead of juice had avoided her tongue, and he wanted to rub his thumb over it. Not just his thumb. He wanted to suck it into his mouth, to taste her pomegranate lips, and he knew he was doing a terrible job of hiding it.

When Alma left the room with her phone pressed to her ear, Rafael let out a long breath.

"Sorry," he said, rubbing a hand against the back of his head.

"For what?" Grace asked, genuinely confused.

"For—um—not being able to resist you?"

Grace rolled her eyes, but she was smiling. Then she gestured to where Alma had just exited. "I hope this is a good sign. Calling Obinna."

"I hope so, too." He touched a lock of hair that had fallen against her neck.

"I really think they'll get back together. Even in his tiny apartment, they were having so much fun. But…" She lowered her eyes. "I guess either way you'll have your place all to yourself again."

Rafael felt his entire body tense. "All to myself? What about you?"

Grace shifted on her feet. "Oh, Alma didn't mention it? She heard from the landlord yesterday. He said the apartment is almost ready. Finally."

Rafael dropped the piece of her hair he'd been tugging, suddenly feeling like he'd just fallen from a great height. "Oh. How soon would you be able to move back in?"

"Just another week or so, he thinks." She glanced away from him again, suddenly very interested in the remaining pomegranates on the counter.

Rafael nodded. Obviously, this was what was meant to happen. Grace had been staying with him longer than anticipated already, so of course she would be leaving soon. Still, the thought made it hard to swallow. It felt so natural to have her there all the time. He hadn't been back in Spain for very long, and she'd quickly become part of his life there, part of his home.

He cleared his throat. He could hear the hum of Alma's voice through Grace's bedroom door. He could only think of it as Grace's bedroom now. What would it be when she was gone? It would still belong to her. He would still remember the way she stared out the little window, studying the city through a pane of glass. He didn't know what to say. What was he going to do, beg her to stay because they'd slept together twice even though they weren't really dating? It was too soon, especially for someone who had never had a real relationship before…and for another someone who had just gotten out of a long one. It didn't make any sense.

That didn't stop him from imagining it though, what it would be like if she were to stay, if they could belong to each other.

He stared into her eyes for a long time without speaking, trying to read the look on her face, to make sense of her feelings about moving out of his apartment.

"What are you thinking?" he asked.

"I'm wondering why you're looking at me like that."

Rafael shook his head, uncertain how to navigate the tension between them, how to cross the line between flirtation and something deeper. "You know why."

Grace glanced up at him with some measure of surprise and released a shuddering breath. "Maybe." She brushed some hair from her face and tilted her head at him as if something had just occurred to her. "You know what else I'm wondering?" she asked.

He rubbed a knuckle against the back of her wrist, waiting.

"In Barcelona... I know you didn't even like me." Rafael immediately tried to protest, but she stopped him with a held up hand. "I know you didn't. It's okay. I was immature, and you were...too mature."

"I was an idiot." He let out a soft laugh, unsure of where this was going.

"But I've always wanted to know," she continued. "If you didn't like me, then why did you try to kiss me that night at the club? Were you just drunk?"

Rafael froze, but Grace laughed. "You don't have to be nervous. It was forever ago. I'm just curious."

"It's not that I disliked you." Rafael pulled back from her, putting a hand on the counter.

Grace snorted, clearly skeptical of his explanation.

"I mean, maybe, yes, it came off like that. And maybe I did dislike you, but it wasn't *because* of you. I think I was just jealous."

She frowned, scrunching up her nose. "Jealous of what?"

Rafael sorted his thoughts, trying to figure out what to say. "You were so young and easy-going and carefree, just as you should have been. Alma, too. I'd never been like that. I didn't know how. My father would have thought I was ridiculous."

Grace rubbed the tips of her fingers along the back of his hand, reaching for him. He turned up his palm, welcoming her touch.

Rafael pushed on, unsure if any of this was coming out right. "Somehow, though, I always felt like you saw me, or saw through me, maybe. You knew it was all an act, and I was drawn to that. I hoped some of your joy might rub off on me. I guess maybe I thought you seemed like someone who could really know me, not just the person I was pretending to be."

Grace stared at him. "So, it wasn't just that you'd had one too many glasses of sangria?"

Rafael pulled a face.

"I'm kidding," she said, and then she tightened her grip on his hand. "I do want to really know you," she said, almost in a whisper.

He started to pull her toward him, his other hand sliding up the back of her arm, but then they heard the sound of the doorknob rattling, and Alma emerged from the bedroom.

Grace turned away from him quickly, stepping backward. "Everything okay?" she asked her best friend. A flush crept up Grace's neck and onto her cheeks. Rafael wanted to search every inch of her to see where else she'd turned that shade of pink.

Alma was pulling her hair back into a high bun. "Yes. Well, maybe. Obinna said he's been doing a lot of thinking about where to go from here, and he realizes he might have put too much pressure on me, but he wants to talk it out some more. I'm going to head over to his place so we can hash it out for a while."

"Good," Grace said. "Very good, Alma. I really hope it goes well. I mean, I think it will."

Alma shrugged but she was almost fluttering around the apartment as she collected her keys and her purse.

"Do you think you'll be returning tonight?" Rafael asked, trying to sound completely nonchalant. He was truly hoping that his sister was going to work things out, that she might spend the night with Obinna and find that thread of happiness she'd been following ever since she'd met him. Admittedly, though, Rafael was also trying to assess whether or not he'd be able to spend the night with Alma's best friend.

Alma thought for a moment. "Yes. Maybe. I don't know what's going to happen, but even if we're back together, I want to manage my expectations. Maybe we shouldn't go right back to living together again, you know? And my apartment will be ready soon."

"That makes sense," Grace agreed.

Alma glanced back at them before she started toward the from door. *"Hasta luego."*

"Wait," Grace said suddenly, rushing over and pulling her into a hug. "Good luck." She whispered something else, and Alma looked at her with eyes full of tenderness.

Rafael gave a little wave. "*Buena suerta, Alma.* If he gives you any trouble, go straight for the towels."

Alma smiled and gave him a little acknowledgment of their shared history, of the difficult home where they'd relied on each other so long ago.

Just like that, she was out the door, and Rafael and Grace were alone again. Every day since Alma had been there, it had been rare that they were alone together in the apartment, and even when they were, they'd hardly touched, anticipating Alma's return at any moment.

Silence fell over the room in her absence. Grace and Rafael were as still as statues until he managed to growl, "Get over here."

Grace moved toward him slowly, as if being reeled in on a tether. As soon as she was within his reach, he wrapped his arms around her, pulling her into a tight hug.

"I need to tell Alma tonight," Grace said into his chest. "Or tomorrow, whenever she's back. I know I'm a terrible friend for not telling her sooner, but I didn't want to distract from this thing with Obinna or add more to her plate. I almost blurted it out fifteen times today, though, and I can't keep it from her any longer. I have to..." She swallowed. "I need to tell her we slept together."

Rafael eased back so he could see her face. "That we slept together?" he asked, enunciating each word. "Or that we're sleeping together?"

She pursed her lips, almost as if she would refuse to answer.

"Grace," he said, the serious tone of his own voice surprising him. She didn't let him continue, though. In an instant she was back in his arms, and he molded against her on instinct, arching his hips to meet hers, tangling his fingers in the hair at the back of her neck. It felt like he'd used every ounce of his self-control, and finally, he could give in. He could stop holding himself back. He traced his nose along her jawline before sliding his lips up to meet hers.

She let out a low hum of satisfaction, and he wondered if she was experiencing the same relief he was. She slid her tongue into his mouth, and he welcomed it eagerly. He cupped her ass, lifting her off the ground before she squeezed her legs around him with a delicious pressure that had him feeling feral. Even if Alma was coming back tonight, she'd surely be gone for hours, and Rafael could finally have Grace all to himself again.

Neither of them must have heard the front door opening or the clacking of footsteps in the entryway. Neither of them must have noticed the loud gasp or the sound of keys hitting the floor. He was so focused on Grace; someone might have waltzed right in and robbed the whole place without him realizing it. The only thing that finally managed to pull his attention away from the woman in his arms was the sound of his sister's voice echoing through the room.

"What the fuck?"

He and Grace both froze, their lips still pressed together. As if in slow motion, they turned their heads toward Alma. "*Mierda,*" Rafael huffed.

Slowly, Grace unwrapped her legs from around his body and slid her feet to the floor as he gently released her from his grasp.

Alma's voice grew louder. "Can someone please explain what is happening right now? Gracie, we literally just talked about this. I don't understand."

"I—um," Grace stuttered. "We've been planning to tell you, but you don't need to worry, I swear. It's not a big deal."

Rafael stiffened beside her, but he didn't contradict her. He supposed he should allow her to handle this however she wanted.

"But you said..." Alma stared at Grace in disbelief. "You told me there was nothing happening. How long has this been going on?" Alma asked, glancing between them. "Did you just start having sex as soon as you moved in?" Alma walked toward them, her boots so hard on the wood Rafael didn't know how he'd missed the sound earlier. She turned to look at him, her face etched with disappointment. "You knew she was vulnerable, Rafa. You knew what she'd been through."

"Don't put that on him," Grace said. "I promise he didn't take advantage of me. I'm okay."

Rafael swallowed and interjected to respond to Alma's initial question. "It started the night before you came here, the night before you and Obinna started fighting. It started before that for me, but that was..." He glanced at Grace, trying to catch her eye, but she was focused on Alma. "It was the first time..." He couldn't seem to force out another word.

"Seriously?" Alma exhaled.

"We were going to tell you," Grace said again, still not looking in Raf's direction. "We *wanted* to tell you, but it was happening right at the same time as everything else, and you were going through so much." She took a few rushed steps toward Alma, her voice full of remorse. "I didn't want to spring this on you. And it's nothing to worry about, seriously. We were just having fun."

Rafael frowned. Once again, he really wished they would have had that conversation about what all of this meant. Was Grace telling the truth? Earlier she'd said she wanted to really know him, and he'd been sure she didn't just mean sex. He'd held her when she cried. They'd *talked* about things—not just Picasso. Her grandmother, his father. He'd made her laugh. It had to be more than just having fun, but it wasn't exactly something they could analyze while Alma was standing there waiting for a thorough explanation that he didn't seem to have.

"Grace..." Alma looked at her friend with such care and sympathy, Rafael wondered what he could have done to elicit this level of concern. "After everything you've been through this year, I just want you to be happy. I don't want you to get hurt again, and I'm just afraid that's exactly what will happen. I know Rafael is fun and charming." She glanced over at him with a sad smile. "But I know you, Gracie. I know how you can't help caring." She put a hand on Grace's arm. "And he's my brother. That's why I tried to prevent this when we talked before. I don't want it to complicate things between us. Between any of us."

They had talked about this? Rafael looked toward Grace, just starting to understand there was an element of this conversation that had never included him.

"Look," Grace said, surprisingly calm. "I know you're worried about me. I know you have good reasons to be concerned. You've had to witness every moment of my breakdown this year. But Raf and I are adults, and this just happened. We should have told you, and I was planning to. Really, Alma, I wanted to talk to you about it right away, but I knew how much you were hurting, and I didn't want to add this to everything you were going through. For once, I don't want you to focus all of your energy on taking care of me, especially when you're trying to work things out with

Obinna. I'm fine. I promise. And I promise nothing will happen that will mess up your relationship with me or Raf."

"Do you not remember what it was like, Gracie?" Alma asked, her voice so quiet and sad. "How much you were hurting? You *can't* handle it." Alma shook her head, her grip tightening on her friend.

Rafael could see the sheen of tears in Grace's eyes, and he wanted to reach for her, to hold her again, even if Alma might not have appreciated such a gesture. He refrained, though. He didn't move. He didn't even know if that's what Grace wanted, anyway, if they were just having fun.

"I know how bad it was," Grace said, deflated. "You think I don't? I know how much you cared for me, how much you've done for me. But this is the first thing in a long time that's made me feel normal."

"With my brother, though? Did you have to have a secret fling with him?"

Rafael felt the sting of the comment, but he didn't react. He knew who he'd been in the past—nonchalant in his relationships, sometimes even cold. He knew Alma had no reason to suspect how much he cared for Grace, that this was something entirely different, but her lack of trust cut him, all the same.

Grace looked as if Alma had slapped her across the face. She retreated slightly, backing

against the wall.

"Alma," Rafael said sharply.

"Sorry, I didn't mean that. I just meant…"

"I'm sorry," Grace said. "I didn't mean for it to happen, and it wasn't supposed to be a secret. We barely even—"

"Stop." Rafael finally broke in. He didn't want to hear that. He didn't want her to be sorry. He didn't want her to think it was a mistake. It wasn't a fucking mistake. "I didn't mean for it to happen either. I tried so hard not to do it. I tried to stop thinking about her every second, but I couldn't. I couldn't get enough of her. And it's not just fun for me. I—" He turned to Grace and met her eyes. "I know we haven't talked about all of this yet, but I want to be with you, Graciela."

Alma and Grace both turned and stared at him, both wide-eyed.

"Rafael—" his sister started.

"I'm serious. I'm sorry to say it like this, but if we're going to be honest about everything, then I guess I should be honest about that."

"You've never been with anyone like that." Alma's mouth turned down in a pout. "Maybe you do have feelings for her, but are you really ready for a relationship? She's been wracked with grief, Rafa. Are you willing to take that on and promise you won't cause her more pain?"

Rafael balled his hands into fists. To some degree, Alma was giving voice to his fears. He hadn't ever cared for anyone like this before, and he wasn't sure if he knew how to do it, but his defensive response hijacked all other trains of thought. "You're not her babysitter, Alma. She's not a child."

"Would you both stop talking about me like I don't have a say in this?" Grace said, her eyes gleaming with tears. "I know what you've done for me, Alma. I'd be completely lost without you. I honestly don't know how I would have survived this year if I didn't have you. But I can make my own choices, even if you don't agree with them. Maybe you had to pick up the pieces last time, but I think I'm a little stronger now, and I meant it when I told you not to worry. I'll be okay."

Rafael watched Grace, trying to interpret what she was saying. Did this mean she was choosing him? That she was all in? Did she mean this thing between them was real, and she was willing to go for it?

"I need to go talk to Obinna," Alma resolved. "So maybe you guys should work some shit out between you, and we can discuss this when I get back."

"I don't think we need to ask your permission," Rafael said.

"Stop," Grace said, clearly exasperated. "I do want her permission. Or her blessing at least."

"My blessing for what exactly?" Alma asked, searching her friend's face. "What is this to you, Gracie? You're the one who said it wasn't a big deal."

Grace's eyes went from Alma to Rafael, settling on him for a long moment. He didn't think he took a breath the whole time.

"I guess that's something we'll have to talk about while you're gone," she admitted. "I'm sorry again, Alma. I—I didn't want it to happen like this."

Rafael unclenched his fists. His palms were sweating as he took in Grace's words. It wasn't exactly a resounding declaration. Just something to figure out.

Alma nodded. "Look, I had to come back for my toothbrush," she said, moving toward the bathroom. "Just in case. I might not be back until tomorrow, and then we can talk again."

Rafael watched Grace swallow. "I hope it goes well with Obinna," she called out. "I think he really loves you."

Alma looked back at her friend before sparing Rafael one last glance as well. He felt something in his insides twist. Alma teased him often enough, but rarely was she actually mad at him. He knew how deeply she cared about Grace. She would do anything to make her friend happy, and Rafael didn't want to be in the middle of that. Perhaps he hadn't given as much thought as he should have to their friendship. He didn't want to come between them, but he also didn't think he could. Whatever happened, he knew the two of them would work out anything. "I'm sorry, Alma," he said. "I know you just want to protect her."

She nodded, acknowledging his attempt to understand her point of view. "We'll talk more later, *si*?" She sighed before she left the apartment again.

Rafael blew out a breath and turned toward Grace. "Is that how you saw that going?" he attempted to ask playfully, trying to lighten the mood.

Grace's face was pale and unsmiling. She shook her head. "Not exactly what I was imagining."

"What did you imagine, Grace?" Rafael asked.

"I need a glass of water," she replied, brushing past him. "Or maybe a glass of wine."

CHAPTER TWENTY-ONE

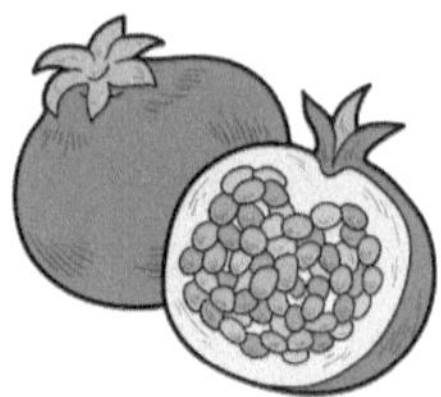

GRACE SAT beside Rafael on the couch with a cushion between them. It was better that they weren't touching, then maybe she could keep a clear head. God, he'd said he wanted to be with her, and she'd just stood there like an idiot, unable to translate the sentence in her brain even though he was speaking English.

She didn't know whether to feel elated or terrified.

Okay, she couldn't help being elated, actually, because just look at him. He was beautiful and caring. He'd let her live with him. He'd conjured up a whole event for her students at a secret art exhibit. He'd trotted her around the city and held her in the night. He'd made her body absolutely quake with pleasure. If this man wanted more than just a good time, then it was a cause for celebration. Like, a marching band and a giant sheet cake kind of celebration.

But also, Alma was right. Grace knew Alma was right, because Alma knew her better than anyone in the universe. Grace had been a total mess of a human being, and she still was. She was completely vulnerable. Rafael could absolutely destroy her. All of those things were also true.

Maybe it *was* too soon. Maybe even entertaining the idea of dating her best friend's brother should be entirely out of the question. She was already in over her head. How could she have a relationship with such a perfect human specimen? It didn't seem real. She let out a little laugh at the thought.

"What?" Rafael asked.

She opened her mouth, searching for words. "It's just—you're *you.*"

Rafael frowned. "I am, I suppose. What does that mean?"

Grace almost snorted. "You're this hot womanizer who could have anyone on the planet, and you're telling me you want to be with me?"

He squinted at her. "Are you serious right now?"

"What?" She scanned his face, sure he must understand what she meant.

"Graciela, you..." He cleared his throat. "I could never deserve you. I would understand if you don't even want to give me a chance, but not if it's because you can't imagine I would want to be with you. It's true that I've never exactly done this before. A relationship, I mean. I don't entirely know how. But if it means we get to be together? That's the simple part. That's all I want."

Grace chewed the tip of her thumb nail trying not to turn to complete mush at his words. She had no clue how to respond. Obviously, she wanted him, but she didn't want to cling to him to escape the realities of her grief and pain. She didn't want him to be a rebound, not anymore. Not if he was offering her something real. She just didn't know if she was ready for something real.

She should have listened to Alma in the first place. She should have stayed away. If she'd never kissed him, never slept with him, then all of this would be so much easier. She'd still want him, sure, but she could go on like that forever if she didn't know how he tasted.

"Do you care about me?" Rafael asked so earnestly that she wanted to reach out and stroke his hair. She wanted to make him laugh.

"Yes, dummy, of course I care about you."

He smiled. "So? Maybe we could give it a shot?"

Grace stood up and started pacing in front of him. "But Alma is right, Raf. She's right about everything. I'm a mess, and you're—"

"A guy who's never had a real relationship." He finished her sentence like it was a foregone conclusion.

Grace swiped a hand across her face. This fucking hurt, just like she knew it would. But it would be worse later. It would be so much worse if she loved him. It had already happened once. She'd completely melded her life to someone else's, so sure that they had a secure future in front of them, only for all of it to be ripped away. Derek had barely offered an explanation—just that things had changed. They were complacent and distant by the end of it, and what was to stop the exact same thing from happening with Rafael? How many months or years would it take until he was bored of her, too? It wouldn't matter how much she wanted him then. It wouldn't matter how tightly she held on. "I do have feelings for you, obviously, but it is a lot of pressure, and I don't want to be so broken again. It's too risky." She hung her head, letting her hair fall in front of her face like a curtain, unable to look at him.

Rafael jumped up from the couch, taking her hand in his. "It's worth the risk."

Grace stared at a tiny hole in the sleeve of her sweater. "You don't know that. We have to be able to be in the same room. For Alma." She felt like throwing something but settled for pulling away and continuing to stride back and forth without looking toward the devastating man standing in the middle of the room trying to change her mind.

"But it could work between us, Graciela. Why are you so sure it wouldn't?"

She finally let her eyes drift back over to him. "Well, most relationships don't work out, do they? There's a good chance this is a terrible idea. And what's the alternative? We're just happy together forever?"

Rafael shrugged, giving her a smug look, like maybe that was possible.

"We barely know each other."

"We live together," Raf countered.

"For a matter of weeks, Raf. I lived with Derek for years." There it was. She'd finally said her ex-boyfriend's name aloud, and it cut through their conversation like a knife. Here was her proof that things never worked out even when you were so sure they would, even when you thought you had forever. She was finally offering it up for Rafael to study, her most solid evidence, finally letting him in on the truth of the matter.

Rafael's expression darkened. "I'm not Derek," he said.

"I know." She let out a breath.

"I won't hurt you."

"You can't promise that."

"I can, and I will, if you don't hurt me."

"I can't promise that either."

"Grace," Rafael said sternly. "Do you want to be with me or not? Is it worth it to try? Because for me, it is. I've never felt like this before. I'm not just going to go out and find someone else that makes me feel like you do, because it's never happened in my lifetime. And I promise to be an adult if it blows up. I promise to make things as easy for Alma as possible. But Alma will be fine. Don't base your decision on her. Base your decision on you and me. Is this what you want?"

Grace stopped pacing and breathed deeply, taking in his words. She didn't want to lose everything again. That had already happened once, and even if she was sure she'd be stronger this time around, she didn't want to have to rebuild her entire life again. Especially not without Alma.

"I can't, Raf." She put a hand to her chest, surprised at the physical pain there. "Alma is my family. She's basically all I have." Her voice almost broke on the last word.

"You have me," he argued. "I'll be here for you, Grace, and Alma will get used to it."

She stared at him. She didn't know what else to say. He seemed to be seeing all of this through rose-colored glasses, as if everything would be so easy between them, as if she only had to say yes and the rest would fall into place. But he didn't know what he was talking about; he didn't know how it felt to have nothing. She could still remember Alma's voice on the phone, every syllable filled with concern, after Derek broke things off. She could still remember crying to her best friend, the aching absence that had only gotten worse when she lost Gram. Grace didn't want to go through it all again, and she didn't want to have to pretend everything was okay just to spare Alma from the consequences she should have seen coming.

"Grace," Raf said, his voice colder than before. "You can't tell me you don't want to be with me. You can't take it all away the one time I've ever..."

She shook her head, wishing he wouldn't say anymore. She pressed her lips together for a moment before she was able to speak again. "Maybe I should get out of here for a while? I don't know what to do. I wish I could make everything go back to normal."

He threw a hand in the air. "What's normal in this situation? I secretly want you without telling you? Because that's what my normal was before."

God, his eyes were so beautiful even when they looked all sad; they made her feel like her throat was closing up. She didn't want to hurt him. She didn't want to hurt herself. But how could this possibly go? They could sleep together for a while and delay the inevitable, only to destroy each other later? It was the only thing Grace could foresee, the only prophecy that seemed possible.

"I'm sorry," she said, grasping for the last bits of strength she could find inside herself. "It's just better if we put a stop to it now."

His nostrils flared. "Better for who? Better for you? Better for Alma?"

"Raf—" She wanted to console him. She wanted to press her head against his chest and console herself, but it would only make things worse.

"No, it's fine. Clearly, you know what you want, and it's not me. I can't argue with that."

She did want him, and he knew it too. He had to know it in every desperate glance she'd given him the past week, in every reckless kiss they'd shared. He had to have felt the rush of her pulse under his fingers, and he must have realized how hard this was for her, to walk away from all of it. But it was too dangerous. It was too difficult. And it was way too much to lose.

"My apartment should be ready in a week. I can find somewhere else to stay until then."

"No," he said, his voice rough. "You said you wanted things back to normal, and that's not normal. I would never kick you out."

"You're not kicking me out."

"Well then you're staying until your place is livable."

Grace sucked in a breath. She didn't know how she would manage it, being so close to him and not being able to do anything about it. But she'd survived while Alma was there. She'd just have to avoid him at all costs, just for a while. And then they would both get over it and move on with their lives. Time would sprawl out before them until enough of it had passed for the pain to subside. They'd go back to being acquaintances, occasionally falling into each other's orbit because of Alma, letting everything settle back to how it had been. And then maybe after that, with enough distance, they could be friends again. She didn't imagine it would take Raf too long to move on, even if he couldn't believe it now. "I don't have to stay," she said.

"Don't you want to show Alma how mature we are about this whole thing? How nothing has changed?"

Grace felt the tears welling her eyes, but she wouldn't let them fall. She gave the tiniest nod. "Alma said there was someone else before." She hesitated. Why was she even bringing this up? There was no point talking about it, but her mouth moved without permission. "Another one of her friends?"

Rafael's face hardened in an instant. "That was completely different. She knew it was just for a night, and I wasn't interested in anything more."

"And it was never just supposed to be a one-night thing with me?"

He exhaled. "I didn't know, Grace. I was confused and needed time to figure out this thing with us, and I'm telling you now, it's different. If I had thought there was nothing more between us, I would have told you upfront. I'm not trying to string anyone along."

Grace bit her lip and turned away. She realized she believed him, even if it didn't matter either way. Just because he felt this way now didn't mean it would last. Grace wanted some peace for a while, some stability. She didn't want to live in fear of another disaster just around the corner.

"I see." Rafael's hands twitched at his sides, and he nodded with resignation. "Well, I guess I'll see you tomorrow then," he said, walking toward the coat rack and grabbing a jacket.

The lump in her throat seemed to grow. "Where are you going?"

"What does it matter?"

He headed for the door, and she didn't stop him, because she had no idea what she would do if he stayed. She'd lived through everything else the past year. She'd had the shittiest time of her life, and she'd survived, and Grace promised herself she would survive this, too, no matter how much pain crawled under her bones, making her ache everywhere.

She finally let herself cry when he was gone. She crawled into her bed in her tiny, perfect room, and she cried until her eyes were almost swollen shut. She was used to the tears, salty and familiar on her cheeks. She was used to grief. But the gaping hole in her heart was only calling for one thing in that particular moment. It was yearning for him.

"Well look who's in her own bed," Alma said the following morning.

Grace groaned and rolled toward the wall, shielding her eyes. "Everything okay?' she mumbled.

"I'll tell you all about it when you're up," Alma replied. "Where's Raf?"

A chill ran over Grace's skin. "He's not here?"

"Doesn't seem to be," Alma said, her voice harder than usual.

"Don't be mad at him, Alma," Grace whispered. "I kissed him first." Grace wished she could have seen her best friend's expression, but she couldn't bring herself to roll toward her, and she also didn't know what her miserable face might look like after all the tears.

"Well, I didn't mean to wake you," Alma said flatly, even though it was clear that was exactly what she'd intended to do. "I'm going to go make coffee."

"Okay," Grace croaked. "I'll be out in a minute."

Alma left the room without another word, and Grace moved toward the nightstand to check her phone. Nothing from Rafael, not that she'd expected it. She turned on the selfie camera and checked her face. It could have been worse. It could have just been exhaustion if you didn't know she'd been crying. She took another breath and got out of bed.

Alma's back was toward her in the kitchen when Grace trudged in to get the kettle going. "How did it go with Obinna?" Grace asked.

"I'm very happy with the outcome," Alma said in a monotone voice.

"You don't sound very happy." She measured some tea leaves into a strainer and couldn't help but notice she didn't sound all that happy herself.

Alma let out a long sigh. "Things with Obinna are better, Gracie. At least, I think they will be. It's you that I'm worried about."

"That's the problem. It's been about me for too long." She ran a hand over her face. "You two made up?"

Finally, Alma turned toward her, a ghost of a smile on her lips. "We talked for hours. And maybe we both still have some reservations, but we love each other so much. I'm going to take my stuff back over tonight if that's okay with you."

In spite of everything else she was feeling, a wide grin spread across Grace's face. She'd been sure things would work out between them and was thrilled to be right "Of course that's okay with me. Why wouldn't it be?"

"Because you might need me here to stop you from jumping on top of my idiot brother."

Grace froze, unsure how to react.

"You kissed him first?" Alma squinted her eyes at Grace, as if she'd been puzzling over this singular fact for a long while.

Grace nodded. "I kissed him, though I guess he did make it clear that something similar had been on his mind lately. But I was the one who did it."

"Did he tell you he wasn't interested in anything more than that?" Alma asked, like she was truly curious and wanted to understand.

"No..." Grace trailed off. If nothing else, she believed that Rafael really did feel something for her, even if it didn't align with Alma's view of the whole situation. She just didn't know how to convince Alma of it or if there was a point in trying.

Alma rested her back against the counter. "Listen, it's not like I think he was trying to hurt you on purpose or anything. He's usually upfront about his emotional distance, at least, but he's just not—"

"It doesn't matter anymore," Grace said, staring down into the bottom of her mug.

"What does that mean?"

Alma's voice had lost some of its edge, and Grace released a breath. She knew Alma wouldn't stay upset now that things between Grace and Raf were over. She and Alma had been friends long enough to forgive anything. Their love was lifelong and unconditional. They were stuck together like family, even though Grace was decidedly unstuck from most of her blood relatives. Alma had become her blood instead, the person she'd call about anything, the person who'd always be there.

"It means that we've called it off," Grace said evenly, trying not to let the pain creep into her tone. "It's not worth hurting you."

"You mean it's not worth hurting yourself," Alma corrected. "That's the really important part."

"Yeah," Grace grabbed some sugar from the cabinet, taking in Alma's words. "Of course."

Alma took a gulp of coffee and then continued her line of questioning. "Who called it off? I'm sure Raf wouldn't have come up with that idea."

Grace paused.

Alma nodded to herself, as if all of her opinions were validated by Grace's lack of protest. "Well, good for you, Gracie. I tried to warn you, but at least I can protect you now."

"Why are you so sure he couldn't have feelings for me?" Grace asked, her voice small.

Alma shook her head. "It's not *you.* It's not even *him,* not really. Maybe he really believes the two of you could have something, but it seems irresponsible to experiment with you in light of everything you've been through. I just worry he's not ready, and you aren't either."

"I know what you mean. That's why I told him..." Grace thought back to the night before, to telling Rafael a relationship between them was too risky. Still, she couldn't help defending the idea of it, even if she hadn't been willing to take that chance. "But you haven't really been in anything serious either, until now. And maybe it won't be with me, but someday he might want a relationship."

Alma pressed her lips together, considering Grace's argument. "Maybe that's true. I hope he will figure things out someday. He's had it rough with our father, trying to emulate him and then trying to distance himself from him. I don't think he's had enough of a chance to figure out who he is and what he wants without Papá's influence. Starting his company was a first step, but I'm not sure if he's had enough time to understand himself yet."

Grace hadn't considered Rafael's father's influence before, even though she could recall the pain and defiance that seemed to affect his entire demeanor whenever his father came up in conversation. "You're right that the timing is terrible. And you're right that I don't want to lose anything else. And you're right that he's your brother, and I don't want to put you in an awful situation."

Alma's mouth quirked up. "I'm not used to you telling me I'm right about so much stuff."

"Just—" Grace started. "Take it easy on him, please."

Alma made a motion to zip her lips. "I won't say another word about it. We can all just pretend this never happened. Though I might not be able to help my gag reflex when I see the two of you in the same room."

Alma said it like it was all a big joke. A silly story for the future. A little misstep on their ultimate journey. But Grace couldn't see it like that. She didn't know if she ever could, not when it felt like her heart had been broken all over again.

Alma studied her face. "I'm telling you, it's for the best."

"Yeah." The kettle whistled, and Grace was thankful for the opportunity to turn away, to try to hide all her anguish and lock it deep inside. When she turned back to her best friend, she'd regained her composure.

Alma poured another mug of coffee and blew across the top.

"Tell me about Obinna," Grace said, looking forward to the change in topic, one with a happy ending.

Alma smiled, and it really was like nothing had happened. They'd resolved the Rafael issue, nipped it in the bud, and now they could go on with their friendship.

Alma told her all of the details—the long conversation about where their relationship was going, how she'd admitted to Obinna how terrified she'd been to think of their future, and how she'd been even more terrified to think they might not have one. She gave Grace a breakdown of the whole thing, point by point until the moment when Obinna had finally kissed her. "I love him so much," Alma gushed. "I don't know how he could have thought otherwise."

Grace smiled, happy for her friend even if her own pain was still tattooed under her skin. She knew Alma had never felt like this before, that she'd never wanted this kind of commitment. And if Alma was able to commit to Obinna, to consider marriage and children and all the things she'd never given a second thought, then surely, Rafael could have a girlfriend. He wanted it. He was ready to try.

But it wouldn't be with Grace. Alma was right—Grace certainly wasn't in a position to be Raf's relationship guinea pig. And she'd made that clear to him the night before...right before he'd disappeared. As happy as Grace was that everything had worked out for Alma, she also just wanted to go back to bed and force the day to come to an end as quickly as possible. One day and then another and another. That was the only way to move forward. And she knew from experience, from long days and treacherous nights, it was the only way to move on.

CHAPTER TWENTY-TWO

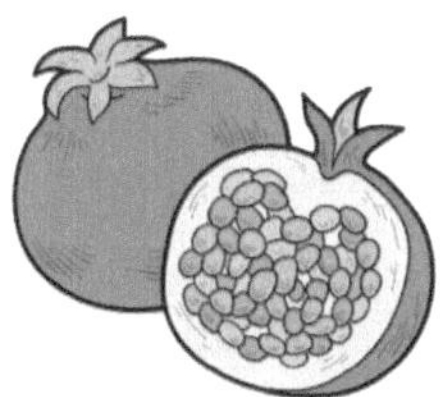

RAF THREW himself into his work. There were deadlines for everything—for the catering and the bartenders and the insurance policies and the framing of the paintings. The inaugural event at the underground museum was in two weeks, and everything had to be perfect. He was glad, in fact, that he had so much to do. He could stay busy at every moment, do everything he could to fight the burning in his chest that liked to remind him that he could never have Grace Cameron and he was supposed to be fine with it.

There were deadlines for dealing with that, too. Grace was moving out in a matter of days, her apartment almost back to perfect condition, and then they would go back to being strangers. They'd hardly seen each other lately since he'd been avoiding his home like the plague despite promising to act like nothing was wrong, but he still liked to imagine her there in her little bedroom, staring out the window over the tops of nearby buildings, concentrating so hard on something he could never see. He couldn't imagine how lonely the place would feel without her, so he mostly tried to never let himself think of it, to pretend it wasn't real.

They offered each other polite nods when passing through the kitchen. He rushed out of whatever room she was in, even when she opened her mouth to speak, even when she managed to say his whole name, he was gone before she could finish a sentence.

It was rude, certainly, but also, he'd never hurt so much in his life, so he thought he deserved to be a little rude to the person who'd done this to him, the person who'd made him feel like he was gliding through the night sky with liquid skin, only to splash him all over the pavement.

He wasn't speaking to Alma, either, not that she minded. She was off with her boyfriend, because for some reason she deserved a chance at love even if Rafael did not. He'd pursued the wrong woman, and he'd known it all along. It was stupid to develop feelings for your sister's best friend, even stupider to act on them. But it wasn't exactly like he'd *picked* Grace. She'd shown up with her blue eyes and her pink lips and her perfect laugh and her long, rambling descriptions of Picasso paintings, and she'd wriggled her way in before he'd even noticed, before he'd even had a chance to fight her off.

"It's looking good, *mijo*," Christian said, striding into the biggest room of the gallery.

Rafael shook himself, trying to remember what he was doing. He was standing in front of one of the paintings of Dora Maar, one Grace had described in great detail. She'd loved this portrait and how it captured Maar's passion, the way you could see that Picasso's lover challenged him and lit a fire inside of him. Rafael always felt trapped by it whenever he walked by, like it was reaching out and holding him still.

"I'm glad you approve," he replied. "Any complaints?"

"That one over there that looks like an octopus? Odd placement next to the naked lady with the book, don't you think?"

Rafael cleared his throat. "Grace said the octopus one is also a naked lady, I think."

Christian let out a barking laugh. "I'm teasing you, Rafa," he said. "Lighten up. The place is beautiful, and it's about time to have a little fun."

"It's not quite ready yet," Rafael admitted. "One of the frames—"

"Relax," Christian said. "It will be ready in time for the first event. We're almost there. Anyway, where is Grace? I was hoping she might have another look before opening to make sure everything was hung in the right place. She mapped it all out so well."

"Oh, right. Well, she...did this as a favor, so I can't really ask her to come back again."

Christian frowned. "That's a shame. Why am I paying you so much money instead of her?" He wiggled his fingers at Rafael. "I guess you're the one with the connections. You certainly got the job done, but I think maybe I should be offering a position to Senorita Cameron. She will be at the first party, though, right? To see how it all turned out?"

"I—uh. I don't know." Rafael scratched the back of his head as Christian eyed him warily.

"What'd you do?" Christian asked, his voice teasing.

Rafael started, giving himself away. "Me? I didn't do anything."

Christian's tone turned somber as he studied Rafael more intensely. "You break her heart?"

Rafael sighed. This wasn't a very professional conversation, and it certainly wasn't something he ever would have discussed with any other client. But Christian wanted to know, and Rafael thought it might be nice for at least one person to be aware of his utter agony. "The other way around, really," he admitted.

Christian nodded knowingly. "Any chance to win her back? Grand gesture? Anything like that?"

Rafael rubbed a hand against the back of his neck, pretending to think this over as if he hadn't thought all of it over a million times. "It's complicated."

Christian slapped a hand on his back. "It always is," he said. "But let me know if I can be of use to you."

Rafael shook his head. "What would you do?"

"Well, I don't know, really. But I'm one of those men who likes to think they can solve any problem. Love is a little more difficult than most things, though, no doubt about that."

Love. Rafael had been unwilling to even think the word. Even as Christian stood there considering him, he wouldn't let it enter his thoughts, wouldn't give it the opportunity to spark a flame in his brain. That wouldn't lead to anything good. Only more pain. There was no use even thinking about the possibility of loving Grace. There was no use wondering if he already did.

"Thanks for the offer," Rafael said, scrambling to think of a way to change the subject. "Didn't you say you wanted some kind of signature cocktail for the evening? What were you thinking it should be?"

They stepped away from Dora Maar's almost lifelike eyes, but Rafael could still feel them on him, like she was seeing right through him.

He'd meant it when he said he didn't know if Grace would attend the first party. She'd been invited and had planned to come before everything had happened, but since they hadn't spoken, he had no idea if she would attend.

He hoped she would.

He wouldn't ask, though, or try to convince her. He knew there was no use if she'd made up her mind. And soon he wouldn't even have the opportunity to avoid her. She would be gone from his apartment, leaving the largest void he'd ever known, and he couldn't help feeling impossibly dramatic about the whole thing. If only Alma could have witnessed it, she would have been shocked. Her cool, collected, hard-as-stone brother brought to his knees by his own wretched emotions.

There was a light under Grace's door when Rafael returned from work. Well, from work and the hours-long dinner alone he'd indulged in just to get home as late as he could. He'd hoped she would already be sleeping, which helped to curb the temptation of bursting into her bedroom and trying to convince her to reconsider.

He was quiet in the kitchen as he fixed himself a drink, quiet as he eased onto the sofa, book in hand. Usually, he retreated to his room as quickly as possible, just to limit the chance that their paths might cross, but he let himself linger there, hoping she might emerge and try to talk to him and simultaneously dreading it as well.

He was almost drifting off on the couch when the sound of her door creaking open startled him, and he turned his head to find her there in her hamster pajamas, her hair swirling around her shoulders, her eyes immediately searching for his.

"Sorry," she almost whispered. "Just getting some water."

"By all means," he said.

She padded across the room in her bare feet, and he didn't bother to take his eyes from her, didn't even try to pretend he wasn't looking.

She glanced back at him, and their eyes met again. "How are things going with the gallery?" she asked.

He couldn't help the glare that slipped onto his face, the sarcasm that crept into his tone. "Is this us being normal?"

Even from his position on the sofa, he could see her frown. His words had hit their mark.

"Sorry," she said. "Should I just get my water and go? I thought you might want to talk."

He tried and failed to keep his tone even. "What's there to talk about?"

"I don't know," she said. "Whatever we used to talk about? Life?"

He let out a little hmmm. "The gallery is good. Thanks for asking. Still coming to the event?" *Damn, he was asking her after all.*

"I'm not sure." She fidgeted with a button on her pajamas without looking at him.

"Don't let me stop you. It will be crowded. You can just pretend I'm not there. And you put a lot of work into making it look right."

She looked up again and met his gaze. "I didn't do much."

He hated when she tried to belittle her contributions. "It would be a mess without your input."

"It was you, Raf. You did great work."

He gave her a wry smile. "Have to appease the billionaires, right? I'm good at that."

She watched him, and he wished he could know what was going through her head. What did she think of him? Did she hurt half as much as she did? Probably not. She'd been through worse. He was just another bump in the road.

"You ready to get back to your apartment?" he asked. He could make small talk. No problem at all.

Her face didn't change, and she still just stared at him, her fingers wrapped around a water glass. "I guess so."

"And your classes? It's about the end of the term, right?"

"They're good. Some of my students promised they'll come see me and keep in touch."

"That's not surprising." Rafael felt stupidly jealous of her students then, that they got to keep in touch. They got to be near her, to openly adore her. They got to make the decision to be in her life while he fell by the wayside.

"I'm sorry, Rafael," she said softly.

He took a small amount of satisfaction at the sadness in her eyes, but it also made him remember that she'd given him up, too. She'd given him up when she could have fought for him. She could have believed it when he told her how he felt. She could have at least *tried.*

He swallowed and buried every painful thought that flashed through his mind. He didn't want her to read any of it on his face or hear any of the ache in his voice. "Don't apologize, Grace. You did what you had to do."

She nodded and walked back toward her bedroom door. "Goodnight," she said, so quietly he almost could have missed it. Then she slipped into her bedroom without another glance at him.

"Goodnight," he whispered to the closed door.

He couldn't stop himself from helping her move her belongings. He'd convinced her to live with him and helped her move in, the least he could do was help her get her stuff out.

"You don't have to," she said, of course. She was always saying "thank you" or "sorry," always trying to avoid taking up too much space or inconveniencing anyone. He wanted to scream at her, to tell her she deserved everything, that she should take up loads of space and expect all the help in the world, that she could ask anything of him and he'd do it.

"I don't have to," he said, "but here I am."

He carried her suitcases up the three flights of stairs, just as he had the night she'd arrived in Granada. The apartment looked completely normal. You couldn't even tell it had just been through a flood and weeks of construction. It didn't even smell bad, which was one of Alma's great concerns.

"Hi Rafa," Alma said, kissing him on both cheeks in the entryway. This was how she'd acted the few times he'd seen her since she discovered his relationship with Grace—as if it had never happened at all. As if she hadn't been so concerned that he would fall for her best friend that she'd completely dissolved his relationship with said best friend and any chance they had together. He supposed he should have been relieved Alma wasn't angry with him, but he also couldn't help being angry with her. Sure, Grace was one of the most important people in her life, but what if Grace had also become one of the most important people in his life as well? Didn't that count for anything?

Grace walked in behind him, carrying a backpack and a lamp. "How did I already collect so much stuff here? It's only been a few months."

"It must be because you feel so at home." Alma smiled. "You've settled right in."

She'd settled right in with *him*, in his apartment. That's where she'd felt so at home, Rafael thought, but he kept his mouth shut. There was no use fighting that battle. He'd already lost.

"I'll just take these to the bedroom," he said, gesturing toward the suitcases. He heaved them across the brand-new floor while Grace and Alma adjusted plants and lamps in the living room. Once he was alone, he stared at Grace's bed. It was the first thing they'd moved back into her room. He couldn't help feeling like it didn't belong there, like it didn't look quite right. He stared and stared, unmoving, forgetting what he was supposed to be doing.

"Raf?" Grace said, walking up behind him. "Everything okay?"

He blinked, clearing his head. "Yeah. Is there something else I can help with?"

She stopped right beside him, both of them scanning the room. Then he could feel her eyes on him. "It seems like forever since I've been here," she said. "I forgot what it looked like."

He turned to meet her gaze, and then they stayed like that for a moment, staring. Wanting. At least, he knew that's what he was doing—wishing everything was different, wishing he wasn't about to walk out of her apartment with no reason to see her again.

He moved his arm, almost imperceptibly, and his hand just barely brushed against hers. She didn't pull away though. She didn't look away from him either.

"I'm really struggling with this rug!" Alma called.

Grace jerked her hand out of reach. "On it," she called. She gave Rafael a sad smile. "It is a really big rug. Alma picked it out."

"I guess we should help her."

They unrolled the massive thing in the living room without making eye contact. They weren't alone the rest of the day, but sometimes he noticed her glancing in his direction. She still looked at him, and maybe that was a good sign. Or maybe it was just another form of torture. He needed to accept that he couldn't have her. He needed to let it go.

Alma continued to act as if nothing had ever happened, which he supposed is what Grace wanted all along. If Alma was happy, they could get on with their lives, never mind the fact that he was brokenhearted for the first time in his entire life. That didn't matter as long as they could pretend. They just had to act like it was normal, and maybe someday it would be true.

Rafael couldn't imagine that though, especially not when they finished organizing the furniture, and it was time for him to go. He should have been kissing Grace goodbye, should have been making plans to see her again as soon as possible. Instead, he didn't know what tomorrow would bring. He didn't know if he'd ever have a reason to be alone with her again, and the thought cut through him like a dagger.

"Thanks for the help, Rafa," Alma chirped.

He nodded. "See you at the Picasso party?" he asked. He glanced toward Grace as well, since he was really asking her, and he noticed her flinching before she turned back to the bookshelf she was organizing.

"Wouldn't miss it," Alma said.

"Don't call it a Picasso party," Grace said, and maybe he was fooling himself, but there seemed to be a tinge of humor to her voice. She just couldn't stop herself from correcting him. "That was kind of my whole point, remember?"

Rafael tried to match her nonchalance, but his response was flat. "Ah, yes, we are not celebrating the man. I know that. And there are a lot of other artists there to admire."

Alma looked confused. "I'll be interested to see it."

"Right…yeah. I'll see you there then." Rafael rubbed the back of his head, and without another word from Grace, without another look, he left to return to his very empty apartment.

CHAPTER TWENTY-THREE

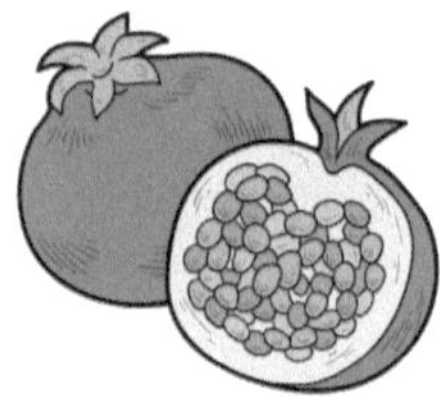

THE END of the term arrived out of nowhere. Grace had been teaching students from across the world, students who spoke different languages, had vastly different lifestyles and cultures, and yet, she'd felt so relaxed in that room, having hours-long discussions about how institutions evaluate art and Marcel Duchamp's Fountain. She belonged there somehow. And so did her students. They all fit together so well.

As she sat in the auditorium while her last section of students scribbled diligently on their final exams, Grace's mind wandered. On paper, things were good. Classes had gone well, and she was hopeful about her contract being renewed the following year. She even had a new course to teach, Feminism in Art, and Marco had already enrolled, despite the fact that he didn't need it for his program of study and was only taking it for fun. It was a relief, though. She was going to miss a lot of the brilliant students she'd had in her classes, but at least she'd have Marco and the connection to his mother. Lucia had agreed to take up the brush again, and Grace couldn't wait to see her new work.

Additionally, she was back in her apartment with Alma, and things were going well there, too. Alma seemed to be making it a point to stay in the apartment with Grace more often, instead of sleeping at Obinna's place every night. She and Alma stayed up late gossiping like teenagers, just like they had in college—joking about their colleagues, planning out Alma's future with Obinna, reading juicy details from celebrity news sites even though neither of them cared all that much. They ate too much cheese and drank too much wine and sprawled across their newly installed floor trying to do different yoga poses, even though they mostly just ended up lying there.

"Corpse pose," Alma would say, "my favorite."

Grace felt settled in a way she'd never expected after uprooting her entire life. She felt like she was rebuilding everything from the bottom up, but it was actually working, and maybe...maybe she could be happy in Spain, long term.

The problem was that despite all the things that were finally looking up, she wasn't exactly there yet. *Happy.* Actually, she was miserable most of the time, lost again in the dark hole without Rafael to offer a hand, but this time it was because of him. Or it was because of her, really. She was the one who ended it, even if it had been for perfectly logical and valid reasons.

Still, her brain kept returning to him—images of his dark eyes searching for hers across the room, the way he'd said he wanted to be with her for real, that it wasn't just sex to him. She missed him. And no matter how well everything else was going, she couldn't seem to get him out of her head.

"No need to bother grading that one," Marco said, handing over his exam paper. "That's an A+ for sure."

"Is that right?" Grace smiled. "I seem to remember you mixing up Tzara and Janco on your last quiz."

"No, no," Marco chided. "Don't worry, *Profe,* you haven't stumped me with the Dadaists again. I've figured it out."

"We'll see," Grace said. Then she whispered, "how's your mother?"

Marco beamed. His pride in his mother's artwork was unparalleled, and Grace was honored to be a part of it. She only wanted to encourage Lucia to keep painting, because the way Lucia saw the world—the way she captured the beauty in the smallest, most mundane details—it was something that gave Grace hope.

"She's good," he replied. "I haven't seen her this excited about something in a long time.

"She's coming to the student night, right?"

"Of course. She doesn't shut up about it," Marco joked with a twinkle in his eye. "Thanks for inviting us."

Grace nodded absently. Just thinking of the museum was another thing that brought Raf to the forefront of her mind. Hours of sorting through paintings and planning and talking to each other. And then there was the time she'd kissed him right there in the middle of the cave. God, she could still feel his lips on hers.

She hadn't decided whether or not to attend the opening night. She'd be there soon for the event for her students, after all, and maybe one trip to the exhibit was more than enough. But Alma and Obinna were going, and Grace was supposed to be fine. She also couldn't seem to help herself from taking every opportunity to get a glimpse of Rafael, even if she kept her distance and didn't speak to him.

"I'll see you there, then," she said to Marco. "And I'll see you next term."

He gave her a little wave. "Just wait until you see how well I did on that exam. I'm telling you."

Grace grinned at him again. "Get out of here before you distract the whole class, Marco."

"What are you wearing to this thing?" Grace asked Alma, holding up the hangers of two different dresses, one floral and one with too many buttons, both admittedly terrible options.

Alma shrugged. "Gracie, you're the one who should know what to wear to an exhibit."

Grace pursed her lips. "This isn't just an exhibit, though, this is a party. This is *your* area of expertise."

Alma sighed. "Okay, then, don't be offended when I say you can't wear either of those."

"I'm not offended, but I really need help."

Of course, Grace also wanted to look *good,* not that she would admit that to Alma. Rafael had seen her sweaty from moving furniture, he'd seen her sobbing in her bed, he'd seen her brushing her teeth in the bathroom sink, but for once, she just wanted to look put together, even if there was nothing between them anymore. Just one time, she could look like she wasn't a total mess.

"I think we're going to need to raid my closet," Alma said.

Grace followed Alma to her bedroom. Raiding Alma's closet would certainly mean she would look different than usual. Alma was glamorous, sexy, and adventurous, while Grace's usual attire didn't come close to any of those things.

"This is what I'm wearing," Alma said, holding up a low-cut red dress with a slit up the side. Grace could tell it would be form-fitting, too, which meant Alma would look hot as hell, as always. "And Obinna's wearing a suit with a little red pocket square to match."

"It's like you're going to prom," Grace said.

Alma ignored her. "You look good in blue because of your eyes," she said. "I bet there are going to be a lot of handsome, rich guys there tonight." She gave Grace a wink.

Grace wasn't sure what facial expression she made in response to that, but she could tell it wasn't the right one when Alma frowned. "You're okay, right Gracie?"

Grace tried to put on a smile but kept her eyes trained on the dress. They hadn't talked about Rafael. They'd barely talked about anything that had happened at all, which Grace hated. She was used to sharing everything with Alma, but she couldn't bring herself to admit how much she missed Raf. She was supposed to be strong. "I could try this one on."

Alma eyed her suspiciously for a moment longer. "Try this one, too," she said, pulling another blue dress from the closet. "I've never even worn it, but I feel like it will look great on you."

Grace hadn't really considered the parking situation in Sacromonte near the museum, and when she arrived with Alma and Obinna, she realized that this was another challenge Rafael must have been concerned about in this setting. It was simple enough to park one or two cars on the little curve outside the cave, but enough for a whole party?

It turned out that the road curved around to a dead end, however, one they managed to set up like a parking lot. There was even a valet who was taking cars and parking them on the hill wherever he could manage, and by the time the three of them arrived in Obinna's car, there was still a good amount of room where they would be able to accommodate even more guests.

"This is so beautiful!" Alma exclaimed as they headed toward the front entrance, her hand reaching out for Obinna.

It *was* beautiful. Grace remembered the first time she'd driven up here with Raf, the way she hadn't been able to take her eyes off the whitewashed dwellings on the side of the road, the view of the city and the Alhambra like a castle in the sky on the horizon. It was like nothing she'd ever seen.

When they stepped inside the exhibit, Grace didn't even recognize it. It was so bright it was almost sparkling. A framed print on an easel welcomed guests to the gallery and offered a brief description of the collection. Gone were the dismantled frames and scattered boxes. Everything was in its place, ready to show off. Alma gave their names to the attendant while Grace was busy staring in disbelief, amazed by how everything had been transformed since her last visit. The first room was glowing with a light that shined from new fixtures that hadn't been there before. They'd worried about the lighting, how to make it easy to see the paintings without everything having a clinical feel, but somehow Rafael had found a balance between brightness and comfort.

There was a new plaque on the wall, too, shiny and bronze and far larger than she would have anticipated. Alma and Obinna joined her as she read through the text that dedicated the exhibit to the Roma people who called these caves home in the past and in the present. That was something, at least. Raf and Christian had come through on that promise and the one to have days where the local community who'd heard of it could visit for free. They also planned to invest in the area as well, though Grace wasn't clear on the details.

"Ready for some Picassos, Gracie?" Alma asked.

She was ready, even if she'd seen them all before. It would be another thing entirely to view them when they were properly hung and displayed in their full glory. A number of people milled about the first room of the exhibit, but not enough to make it feel too crowded. Rafael had been careful with that, she knew, emphasizing to Christian just how few people they could fit in here without the place feeling too tight. A waiter offered them champagne from a tray and they all accepted. Grace was perhaps a little too eager to get her hands on the glass, to have at least one serving of liquid courage before an inevitable encounter with Rafael, even if it wouldn't help all that much.

After she'd had a few gulps, Grace slowly scanned the room. It was beautiful, honestly, not that she was surprised. Rafael had gotten the job done. The paintings stole the show, but it didn't feel too busy. They were well-organized, and there was enough space to move through the room and admire them. The setting still retained all the beauty and character of the original cave, but Rafael had managed to seamlessly blend the artwork into the scene, to make it a part of the cave as if it belonged. She hadn't even gotten the largest room with the new wall, yet, but she already knew he'd managed to pull this whole thing off, and Christian must be elated.

"You helped with all of this, right Grace?" Obinna asked by her side as they stopped at a painting, one of Picasso's earlier self-portraits from the Blue period.

"Yeah," she confirmed. "I was lucky enough to get the behind-the-scenes view of all of this coming together." She swallowed another mouthful of champagne. There were smaller plaques on the wall about the artists and the different rooms as well, and Grace skimmed over them and remembered when she and Raf sat together over his notes, trying to determine what to say. They referred to Picasso as a complicated figure and made sure to mention criticisms of his treatment of women and cultural appropriation. They categorized the treatment of his lovers and explained how influenced he'd been by African art. They quoted descriptions of his life and work from those who knew him best. They also gave overviews of Braque and Matisse and all the other artists in the gallery. Even though she and Rafael had discussed all of this to some extent, she couldn't believe how he'd listened to her and used this information. It was clear he'd even done more research on some of the things she mentioned, and he'd managed to bring it all together seamlessly —story and art, legend and artist.

Her eyes skimmed over the plaque about Francoise Gilot's work. Not only did it discuss some of her paintings, but it also mentioned how the contract with her art dealer was terminated after she broke off her ten-year relationship with Picasso. For years, dealers would say they were interested in her paintings but couldn't dare risk buying them and pissing off Pablo. Grace was glad Rafael had included the detail.

"I've never been to a party quite like this before," Obinna said.

"Neither have I," Alma chimed in. "And I've been to a lot of parties."

Grace gave her a small smile as they moved to the next painting. She wished she could be celebrating this with Rafael. Instead, she felt nervous and out of place, scared that he'd come around the corner at any moment and her heart would leap into her throat, but also scared that she might not get to see him at all. It didn't matter much either way, she supposed, since he would barely speak to her. No matter what happened, it would hurt.

The large gallery with the new wall held some of the most abstract pieces, but the first thing Grace noticed was how bright and colorful everything looked where it was hung. They made it that way purposefully, so even if you weren't focusing on a specific painting, you'd still be drawn in by the shape and color. Everything bold, everything eye-catching. And the wall with some of the later work seemed to work perfectly in the middle of the room.

That's where she saw him, near his favorite painting of Dora Maar, drink in hand, chatting in Spanish with a small group of well-dressed people. He looked so good in his dark gray suit, his hair swept to the side, a fancy watch gleaming on his wrist. She couldn't take her eyes off him. And she couldn't believe she'd slept with this man. He'd kissed her everywhere. He'd cradled her face in his hands with such tenderness, and she'd walked away from it all for what? To save her most important friendship? To save herself?

Grace sucked in a breath and traded her empty champagne glass for a fresh one. She could smell the hor d'ouerves, and her stomach growled. The delicious scents wafting through the air, the champagne bubbles tickling her nose, the exhibit, the amazing man standing across the room. It would have been the perfect evening in other circumstances. Maybe it was the perfect evening for everyone else.

"*Sumamente hermosa,*" a voice said, approaching her from the side.

She turned to find Christian smiling next to hear.

"*Si.* Yes, it turned out very well," Grace stuttered.

"I wasn't talking about the paintings, senorita, but they do look quite spectacular. I want you to meet my wife," he said, gesturing toward the woman beside him. "She's been looking forward to talking with you."

"Oh." Grace studied the sophisticated woman who wore a black cocktail dress and a bright red jacket. Her hair fell past her shoulders in luxurious curls that shined with silver strands. "Nice to meet you."

"I'm Miri," she said with a thick accent. "I've heard that I have you to thank for sorting through this whole collection."

"No, I didn't—" Grace deflected.

"Take some credit, Grace," Christian boomed. "Rafael won't stop telling me how great a help you were to him, even if he wouldn't allow me to drag you back here for a final inspection."

Grace glanced across the room, where Raf was still charming some of the guests. Christian had wanted her to return, and Raf had never even asked? She would have done it, of course, not that he needed her. But she would have taken any excuse…

"We were just saying it's unlike anything we've ever experienced," Miri said. "And I'm so glad you were able to convince my husband to bring in some local artists. It's a terrific idea."

"Oh," Grace said, blushing "I'm so excited to see their work." Then she gestured toward Alma and Obinna before making introductions, wishing she could blend into the wall behind them and disappear.

"I hope you'll all enjoy yourselves," Christian said. "I'm so delighted to share this with you."

"Yes," Miri said. "I still have to congratulate Rafael. What a job well done!" She squeezed Grace's shoulder as she followed her husband to greet another group of guests.

Grace felt the swell of pride in her chest. Not for her own work, but for his. He'd been so cocky about his expertise before they'd started working together, but in the days they'd spent going over the artwork, she'd seen just how meticulous and brilliant he was. And that didn't even cover everything else he'd accomplished in order to make Christian's fanciful dream a reality.

"So that's Christian, huh?" Alma asked. "Seems nicer than some of the other pretentious snobs Rafael has worked for. I'm sorry to tell you, Gracie, but some of his American bosses were real dicks."

"That doesn't surprise me." Grace laughed, taking another step toward the next painting, another step toward Rafael. She knew what she was doing, even if she was using all of her willpower not to look in his direction. Instead, she allowed herself to be absorbed by Dora Maar all over again, by the color and shapes that Picasso had used to capture his mistress. She lost herself in the curves and angles, and the glare of Dora's knowing eyes. For a moment, she forgot that there was anyone else in the room. It reminded her of going to the Chicago Institute with Gram as a child, of watching her grandmother become absolutely enthralled in a work of art until it was like she'd been swept away to somewhere else entirely. And as Grace got older, she knew what her grandma had been feeling. She'd discovered exactly what it was to get lost in the perfect brushstrokes, and she'd managed to make a career out of it.

Gram would have loved this, Grace thought, her breath catching. She would have wanted to stay for hours on end, asking Grace questions about every single painting on the wall.

"Thanks for coming."

Grace had been so caught up in her thoughts, she hadn't noticed that Raf had made his way across the room, and she didn't know if he was talking to her or Alma. She glanced over at him and felt her cheeks warm.

"Hola, Rafa," Alma said, and then she started talking excitedly in Spanish. Grace could only make out a few words like "incredible" and "marvelous," so she stood unmoving while Rafael responded and embraced Alma and Obinna. Then he turned to her and leaned closer, kissing the air beside her cheek. Grace's breath caught for a moment.

This was ridiculous. She was an adult woman. Her heart shouldn't be pounding like she'd just sprinted up three flights of stairs and her legs shouldn't be shaking with nerves because of a stupid air kiss.

"I'll admit I've been eager to hear what you think, Grace. How did we do?"

"*We?* Everyone keeps giving me way too much credit."

He shook his head, ever so slightly. "That's not true." Then, quietly, he added, "I couldn't even picture it without you."

Grace felt the heat rushing between her legs. God, his lips. His whole… everything. He was too gorgeous for his own good. For *her* own good certainly. She could barely stand it. If only she didn't know how much he'd changed since the first time they'd met. If only she could keep pretending he was just some stuck-up douche with no sense of humor. But it wasn't true. He was so dedicated and caring, and he *did* have a sense of humor. She was so desperate to make him laugh.

"It's amazing, Raf," she said. "And as much as you try to say I helped you, you're really the one who made this happen. You put all the pieces together, and it's absolutely beautiful."

And I want to kiss you until my lips implode.

Rafael kept his eyes on her, and she couldn't manage to look away. She could hear her breath quickening as he licked his lips. The foot of air between them seemed to rise in temperature, and then Alma cleared her throat, stepping closer.

Grace backed away a step and pretended to look at the nearest painting, trying to look at the entire exhibit with a more critical eye, as if she didn't have feelings for the man who'd organized it, as if she'd hadn't been part of it herself. Maybe the exhibit wasn't perfect. Maybe there were still problems that concerned her—the way it would be received, if the guests would really pay attention to the whole story, to the words Raf had put on plaques in Spanish and in English. And maybe it was still too exclusive and snobbish, too much of a commodity, like great art so often was. Still, she was proud of how it had turned out, of all the work Raf had done. She was in awe of him.

"So what's the best part, Rafael?" Alma asked. "Is there a space you're particularly fond of?"

"There is," he said, gesturing toward another room. Grace swallowed, becoming more aware of where Rafael was leading them with every step. Her body tensed as they approached the little alcove where they had kissed, where one of the largest paintings of the collection loomed over them.

"Ah," Obinna commented. "That's—uh—interesting."

It was a painting of another of Picasso's mistresses, and it was somehow incredibly sensual and peaceful at the same time. The woman looked completely comfortable as she sat in repose with one of her breasts exposed, of course. But Rafael wasn't looking at the painting. He was staring at a blank space on the wall, a spot that held nothing except for a searing memory. Then he turned to Grace and locked eyes with her again.

"This is your favorite piece?" Alma asked.

"Not necessarily," Raf replied. "I just love this alcove. It's a great little hideaway where you can sneak off and admire the work. You feel like you're all alone with it for a moment."

Alma looked around, examining the alcove. "That's true. I suppose I—"

Grace looked up, trying to ascertain why Alma had stopped speaking. She peered out of the alcove and soon discovered they weren't alone after all. One of the most intense and intimidating men Grace had ever known was heading straight for them with long powerful strides.

"Hola, Papá," Alma said.

CHAPTER TWENTY-FOUR

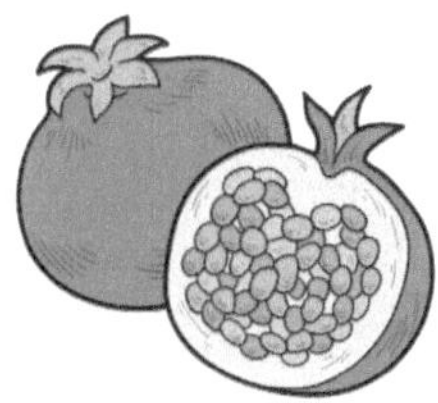

RAFAEL KNIT his brow in confusion. He certainly hadn't invited his father to the event, so what in the hell was he doing there?

Simón Ferrer-Martín wrapped Alma in a hug before glancing around at the rest of their little group, assessing each of them in turn.

"You remember Grace, right Papá?" Alma asked, using English for Grace's benefit.

His father reached out and took Grace's hand, kissing it. "Of course," he said. "How nice to see you again."

"You as well," Grace said, but Rafael noticed she stole a glance at him. She was checking on him, making sure he was okay with this new development. He didn't know if it made him hurt more or less that she still cared.

"And Rafael, am I to understand that you've had something to do with this little project?"

Rafael tried to school his face so as not to reveal his irritation. *Little project*. Of course his father would belittle it in any way he could. And maybe he was right. What was designing cultural experiences and events compared to running a multi-million dollar company? Rafael knew his father thought he was wasting his potential, that he was just messing around until it was time to move on to a more lucrative and powerful career option.

"I did," Rafael said, his entire body rigid.

His father arched a brow. "Hmmm."

"And to what do we owe the pleasure of your attendance this evening?" Rafael asked. He liked sticking to English. At least he had a little edge on his father there, even if it wasn't much.

"Christian is a friend of a friend, I suppose. How intriguing that the invitation didn't come from you."

Rafael raised a shoulder. "Didn't know you'd be interested."

He wouldn't have been interested if the whole thing wasn't a rich dude schmooze fest. Simón only interacted with the people he deemed worthy, and it just so happened that this event was one that included quite a number of those "worthy" people. And even if he'd created most of it, Rafael wasn't a guest. In his father's eyes, he was more like the help. It was beneath him. It didn't matter if Rafael loved what he did, if making his vision come to life and curating the perfect setting, made him happy. It would never be enough.

"I always love to see how you're spending your time. Interesting location though. Don't you think it's a bit cramped? And the cave walls? That's quite an interesting way to display priceless works of art."

"That's funny," Grace chimed in. Rafael had forgotten she was standing right there, witnessing this humiliation. "Rafael said the same thing to Christian when they first came here. He didn't think it would be possible. But I guess he's the kind of person who can accomplish anything. He made it happen against all the odds, and now everyone's raving about it."

Simón turned, studying Grace again as if perhaps he'd missed something before. Rafael couldn't help his lips curving slightly. Whatever else was broken between them, she was proud of him. Even if she thought a secret art party for billionaires was stupid to begin with, she was proud of *him*.

"Ah," Simón said at last. "So you must think that hanging paintings and throwing parties is all very worthwhile then?"

Grace's smile faltered, but she kept her tone cool and didn't hesitate. "I think sharing historic artwork in a way that brings people joy is worthwhile, yes. But I am biased. I'm an art professor, and my students will get to come here as well. It will be an amazing experience for them, thanks to Rafael."

"How nice for your students." Simón's smile didn't reach his eyes.

Alma tried to diffuse the tension, as she always did when Rafael and his father were in the same room. She took Simón's arm. "Papá', have you seen this painting that looks like an octopus?" she asked, leading him out of the alcove.

Normally Rafael might have been seething, or at least annoyed. But he couldn't find it in himself to get worked up about his father being an ass again. So what if his father thought he was wasting his potential, never living up to the man that had reared him? For once, he couldn't manage to care all that much.

Rafael stared at Grace as she gave him a sheepish smile. It took everything in him not to reach out and pull her into his arms. Clearly, she still felt something for him, but he had to respect her wishes. She'd made her decision. She'd pushed him away again. And as much as he wanted to press her to the wall of that alcove and put his mouth all over her, he wouldn't let himself move a muscle.

"Thanks for that," he said.

She shrugged. "For what?"

"For defending me when my dad was being a dick."

Her eyes glimmered. "I was defending modern art, Raf." Rafael grinned, well aware that it wasn't Picasso who she'd claimed was the kind of person who could accomplish anything. "Some people just can't appreciate the significance of a good cultural event. We get that kind of thing a lot in the arts and humanities."

I love you, Rafael thought accidentally. His eyes went wide with alarm. He'd managed to startle himself, and he hoped Grace didn't see the tension on his face as he held his tongue, waiting for the moment to pass. He locked the words in a reinforced mind vault and casually put a hand in his pocket. "Such a shame, isn't it?" he said.

The way she smiled at him made his heart stutter, but he wouldn't show it. He could understand that she needed to rebuild her life. He could understand that she would choose Alma over him. But he was still bitter that she wouldn't believe him—wouldn't believe his feelings for her and the fact that this could be something real, as if it was all a game to him. She'd never even given him a chance to show her how much this meant to him. She'd run at the first sign of trouble, and maybe he shouldn't blame her. The way she'd spoken to his father had given him a glimmer of hope, but she was still so calm and controlled, already inching away from him, ready to flee to another room and never look back. Ready to let it all go.

He supposed he needed to do the same thing. That was the only way to go on with his life. He had to find a way to let her go as well.

Days later, Alma popped her head in at La Finca, where Rafael was waiting at a table and writing an email to a potential client on his phone. Rafael had been surprised to hear from her, especially since things had seemed a bit distant between them since everything had fallen apart with Grace. And Alma asking Rafael to grab coffee on a random Tuesday was not exactly commonplace. He didn't know if she felt guilty about her part in wrecking his love life or if the niceness was a gesture of forgiveness for his seduction of her best friend, but either way, it was good for them to spend some time together.

He wanted to try to move past the fact that Alma was a large part of the reason Grace had called things off between them. But, still, it was hard to get it out of his head. Alma thought he was a fuckboy, and maybe she was right. Maybe he'd given her no reason to believe that he could care about Grace, and maybe that was his own fault.

"Hey, are you the guy who designed that whole underground art museum in the cool cave?" she asked playfully in Spanish.

"I have no idea what you're talking about. Must be some other handsome, talented businessman."

She scoffed. "Could have sworn it was you," she said, leaning back in her chair and inspecting him. Rafael noticed her watching him more closely lately, as if she was sizing him up. For what, he didn't know. "How are you?"

"I'm well," he said warily, unfolding a napkin and fiddling with its edges. "How are you? Things back on course with Obinna?"

Her smile stretched wide across her face. “On the best course. It’s quite exciting.”

“Well, I’m happy to hear that,” he said. “I’ve never seen you so obsessed.” He was happy for her, truly. He wanted his sister to be in a loving, healthy relationship. He was also just sad for himself.

She eyed him again curiously. “What did Christian have to say about all of your success? He seemed pleased.”

“He was pleased. He’s already got a ton of interested parties who want to hold events there.”

“And what happens to you? Do you keep running those events?”

“It seems likely. It won’t take as much of my time, and I’ll be focusing on other clients, but he wants to retain me to plan that other stuff.”

“And the event for Grace’s classes? When does that happen?”

Rafael started, surprised that Alma had just said Grace’s name so casually, though he supposed she didn’t know that just the thought of Grace sent his entire body into shock. They hadn’t spoken of Grace since the night everything had changed.

“It’s coming up,” he said. “It was one of the first things we put on the calendar.” Rafael shifted in his seat. He wondered, occasionally, if he should try to plead his case to Alma, if that would make any difference. But Rafael knew it was more than Alma standing in his way. Maybe she’d been influential, but ending things had been Grace’s decision, and she had her reasons. He didn’t want to go behind her back to try to get Alma on his side, and as loyal as Alma might be to him, he knew where her true loyalty lay. He’d probably be a fool to try to sway her, to beg her to convince Grace to give him a chance.

He tried to change the subject. “How’s it going with that study you were working on with the—um—big and little reproductive cells?”

“You have no idea what you’re talking about.” Alma smiled and shook her head.

“But I’m close, right?”

“Close enough for me to have an inkling about what you’re referring to, I guess. But you sound like an imbecile.”

“Well, I’m not a scientist.”

“Clearly.”

"You know I'm always trying to take an interest in your career."

Alma stifled a laugh. "I guess I can appreciate your effort, but don't say that kind of shit in front of other people. It's embarrassing my own brother understands so little about biology."

"Well, tell me about it, and maybe—" Rafael's phone started vibrating on the table, and he glanced down.

Alma followed his gaze. "Mr. Billionaire seems to be calling."

"You mind if I take it?" Rafael asked.

Alma waved a hand, gesturing for him to answer Christian's call. He turned in his chair and answered the phone, hoping it was something he could deal with quickly, without leaving the table.

"Just a quick question for you, Rafael," Christian said casually, as if this was barely even a conversation.

Rafael let out a breath. "What can I do for you?"

Then Christian started talking, explaining what he wanted, and Rafael forgot about privacy.

He forgot that Alma was sitting there watching him as his brow furrowed. He forgot she could see how quickly his lips pressed into a hard line. He forgot she was absorbing every word as Rafael responded to Christian, as his voice heated, his tone sharper with every sentence. All of his energy was focused on the phone call, on the fury that speared through him in an instant, on the idiocy of Christian's request.

He couldn't even remember everything he said to Christian. It was unusual for him to lose his temper like that, to abandon his careful professionalism. But there was one moment that stood out to him. He could hear his own words echoing in his ears.

"No," he said, the word a dagger dealing the final blow. "That's not happening."

When Rafael hung up the phone, throwing it on the table, he glanced up to find Alma watching him again.

"Sorry," he said, suddenly aware she probably thought he was nuts.

But a calm grin spread across her face and her eyes sparkled as if she'd just won a prize. Rafael wasn't familiar with the look, but he felt like maybe he should be afraid.

CHAPTER TWENTY-FIVE

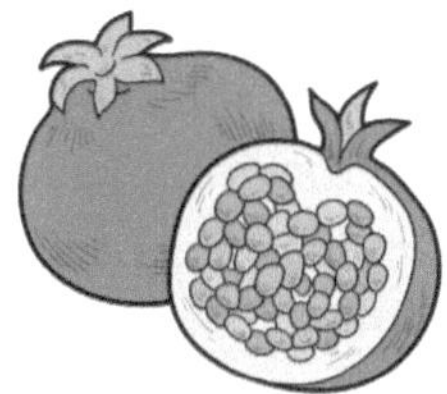

GRACE WAS JOTTING down notes for a class lecture in her bedroom even though the new term was yet to begin. It felt so natural, really, almost like she was her old self, even if she was simultaneously an entirely different person. The past six months since she'd lost Gram had changed her in a way she'd never imagined. It had been true agony, the worst time of her life, but she'd found something inside herself as well. Some kind of strength or resiliency. It was possible to rebuild a life, even if that life would never look the same. It was possible to keep going, even if some days felt insurmountable. Because there were also days that felt...okay.

There were also days that she missed Rafael. Yes, fine, she could admit it to herself. She missed him every day. She missed her tiny bedroom and just knowing he was sleeping right next door. She missed pomegranates on the counter and heated looks and the lines around his mouth when he smiled. Perhaps she'd made the right decision, and it was all for the best. Perhaps they could be friends one day without the sexual tension. In fact, Rafael was probably already over the whole incident. But not Grace, not yet. She needed a bit more time.

There was a light knock on her door, and Grace looked up to find Alma peeking through the crack.

"Hey." Grace grinned up at her best friend.

"Hey," Alma said, joining Grace on the bed. "You're going to Sacromonte tonight?"

Grace nodded. "Yes. My students feel so special. I guess Raf and Christian were right about that. Keeping the exhibit as a hidden gem did make it exciting and extra desirable."

"No kidding."

"I won't lie. I don't know if anyone would care if it was just a museum. But it's a *private* museum, so almost everyone is coming."

"And there's free food," Alma added. "That's always a big draw."

"Good point. And now that they've finished up the rest of their exams, they're ready to celebrate," Grace said. Alma smiled, but Grace felt like she was being analyzed. "What is it?"

Alma cocked her head to the side. "I was just wondering if you knew that Christian tried to cancel the event."

Grace frowned, confused. The event had been planned for a month. Christian had been on board from the beginning. She didn't know why he would want to cancel. "What do you mean? How do you know this?"

"I had lunch with Rafael, and I'll admit I had some ulterior motives. I saw how the two of you were at the exhibit opening, and I thought maybe I should just see..."

Grace froze, unsure of where this was headed. "What?"

"If he really has changed. I thought maybe I could dance around it a little, try to get a sense of what's going on in his head, if he really had feelings for you, but I didn't even have to try, Gracie."

Grace shifted uncomfortably. "I'm still confused."

"Christian called Rafael while I was there. Apparently, he has a friend who wants to host an auction as soon as possible, and Christian wanted to push your student night to accommodate their schedule."

Grace swallowed. She was surprised, but not shocked exactly. Who wouldn't want to cancel a free night for students when there was money to be made? "Then what happened?" she asked, her heartbeat fluttering.

Alma's lips twisted into a smirk. "Rafael said no."

"What do you mean Rafael said no? To Christian?"

"He said a lot of things—that it was a bad precedent, that clients wouldn't be able to trust their schedule, that it was unethical, and that he'd already put all the work into the event, and changing it was an impossibility."

Grace let out a breath. "Well that's…"

"Unheard of," Alma finished. "I've never seen him stand up to a client like that. He always does whatever he can to please them. Honestly, it wouldn't have surprised me in the least if he went right along with what Christian wanted and cancelled the event, even if it was double the work for him. But he was livid, Gracie. He outright refused."

Grace put a hand to her chest, where something was cracking open inside her.

"I think," Alma continued, "that I might have been wrong about him. Maybe he is different now. I mean, he's never even talked that way to our father, let alone someone he's working for. But he stood up for himself." Her eyes narrowed. "He stood up for you."

Grace jerked her head up. What was Alma saying? Yes, Rafael had told his client it was ridiculous and unprofessional to cancel a previously scheduled event, which might have been a little out of character, but surely Alma wasn't reading more into it than that?

"Maybe you didn't end things with him because of me. Maybe you had a million other reasons. But if it was because of me…"

"You told me he wasn't a relationship person, that he didn't know himself enough to be ready for a serious commitment."

"I thought he wasn't. And maybe he's not. I don't know. But this—talking to a client like that, caring so much about doing something for someone else—is different for him. And the way you talked to Papá at the exhibit? It sounded like maybe you haven't quite given up on Rafael yet."

Grace tried to compose herself. "What are you saying, Alma?"

"I'm trying to say that you have every reason not to give my brother a chance. But if *I'm* the biggest reason, then…I don't want to be anymore. You were right when you said you could make your own decisions. And you were right when you said you're stronger now. And if everything goes to shit with you and Rafa, then we'll manage."

Grace brushed a hand through her hair, trying to process this. Maybe Alma had been wrong about whether or not Rafael had feelings for her, but everything else she'd said—all the reasons Grace had called it off—

were still true. She was still vulnerable and trying to put herself back together. He could still just change his mind tomorrow when things got hard. He could leave her in an instant. "Where is this coming from? One lunch with Rafael, and he's changed your mind completely?"

Alma shook her head as if she couldn't believe it either. "If he would have just told me he wanted you, I still wouldn't have believed him, but I saw it, Gracie. I saw how different he was. And if you want to be with him, then you should be, regardless of what I say. It should be your choice. And whether or not it works out or whatever happens, you're my sister. Nothing changes that."

Grace took a breath. And then another. She wasn't sure whether she was about to burst out laughing or break into tears. "That's sweet," she said, "but please don't say I'm your sister, because that would make dating your brother very weird."

Alma laughed. "That's a good note." She raised an eyebrow and nudged Grace's shoulder. "So, you want to date him?"

Grace's stupid heart leapt into her chest. She could barely think straight. Did she want to date him? Yes, obviously. That still didn't mean she should. "You're right that there are a million reasons not to be with him."

"And it's okay if you don't want to. I'm done pressuring you either way, though. You know I'd do anything to protect you, but it's a decision you have to make for yourself."

It was a decision Grace didn't know how to make. She was rebuilding her life after all, brick by excruciating brick. And Rafael had the power to bring so much of it crumbling down.

But she would still have Alma, no matter what. She would still have her students and art. She would still have Spain. Maybe she could have Raf, too, if she was willing to try.

"He's probably over this whole thing by now. He probably doesn't even care. Just because he saved one little event. I mean, it's a savvy business decision."

Alma snorted. "Yeah, maybe, but I don't think cancelling a free student event would hurt the little museum too much with the kind of company Christian keeps. I doubt Christian really needs to hold any events at the museum. He just gets an ego boost from its existence. I think there was no way in hell that Rafael would let something happen that would hurt you. And that's the kind of motivation I can understand." She took Grace's hand in hers and squeezed. "But I don't know. I guess he's the person you have to talk to. Or don't. Do whatever you think is best, and I'll love you no matter what."

"Thank you," Grace almost whispered.

Alma sighed with mock exasperation. "Why are you thanking me this time? I thought we'd moved past this."

Grace leaned forward and rested her head on Alma's shoulder. "I don't know. This is just a big blanket thank you, I guess. Thank you for being you. Thank you for telling me about what happened. Thank you for being my friend."

Alma wrapped an arm around Grace and squeezed. "Thank you for being *my friend*. You literally let me sleep in your tiny bed for a week when I was fighting with Obinna, and you never even complained when I stole all the blankets."

"I was cold, too," Grace teased.

Alma flicked her arm. "So, what now? What are you going to do?"

"I have no idea."

"Is Rafa going to be at the event tonight?"

"I don't know." Could she really be in the same room with him now that she had Alma's permission to care about him? What would that even look like?

"But you have feelings for him, right? I've been watching the two of you, and even if you were pretending to be normal for my sake, there was something there."

Grace pressed her lips together. "I need to think for a while."

"Right," Alma said, getting up. "Very smart. You ponder it for a while and let me know if there's anything I can help with."

Grace sunk back into her pillows, still unmoored by Alma's revelations. "What would you help with, Alma?"

Alma shrugged. "I don't know. If you had any questions about him? He's my brother, though, this is very new territory."

Grace smiled. This was the most they'd discussed Rafael since Grace had broken things off with him. It felt like old times in their friendship, teasing each other about the men they were dating. "I mean, I did always think he was hot."

Alma gagged dramatically. "This is going to be so gross for me to witness."

Lucia and Marco gave Grace a ride to the caves. She sat in the back seat of their little car twisting the hem of her dress in her hands. She truly didn't know if Raf would be there, and she hadn't come to any decisions about what she would do if he was. Probably just say hello and try not to think about the possibility of going home with him, of letting him touch her everywhere again. She had to keep reminding herself that Alma could be wrong. The fact that Rafael had apparently saved this event could mean nothing. He was just doing the right thing. And even if he had really meant it that he wanted to be with her before, he'd probably already moved on.

She wasn't even sure she wanted to admit how she felt for him anyway. It was probably easier to keep forging ahead without getting bogged down by any more emotions.

"You are very quiet," Lucia said, glancing in the rear-view mirror.

Marco turned in his seat and looked her over as well. "Everything okay back there?" he asked.

"Oh, yeah. Just lost in my head, I guess."

"Thinking about Expressionism? That's basically what I imagine is always going on in your head, if I'm honest."

Grace smiled. If only. "It does occupy my thoughts on a regular basis."

Lucia glanced at Marco, and he translated for her. They went back and forth in Spanish for a bit. "Mama thinks you have the mind of an artist," Marco said.

"I don't know what you mean by that, Lucia, but *gracias*."

"You look for the beauty," Lucia said.

Grace tilted her head. "That's what you do, Lucia. That's why I love your paintings so much."

"You love them because you know," Lucia replied slowly, thinking about each word. "You can see."

Marco and his mother went back and forth in Spanish again, and Marco nodded enthusiastically. After a while, Lucia said, "You understand it, Grace, what I put into my work."

Grace was quiet for a moment. "I think I do," she said.

Rafael wasn't at the exhibit, and Grace didn't know how to feel about that. She supposed she was disappointed since just the sight of him filled her with joy, but she could also do without the distraction. Keeping an eye out for him the whole night would have been exhausting. Spending the evening trying to figure out if she should change her mind all over again and what to say to him would have been even worse. Instead, she was able to enjoy the time with her students—or former students, really—to offer mini lectures on some of the different paintings because she just couldn't help herself, to mingle and laugh and forget about everything except art and teaching and Picasso.

Lucia ran her keen eyes over every painting in the place, and Grace loved to watch her taking it all in. This was the kind of place where Lucia belonged with her talent. Maybe Christian would want to start collecting Lucia's work and develop a secret museum dedicated to that. Probably not, but Grace certainly hoped to have some of Lucia's work on her own walls.

For a while, she and Lucia stood side by side in the small corner with the local art from Sacromonte, both of them perhaps imagining what it would be like for Lucia's paintings to be hanging among them.

"I like this one," Lucia said. It was the skyline of Granada from one of the hills, a view Grace was sure she'd seen several times before, and it looked just as good as her memories. "I'm glad they included these pieces from the area. They're very good."

"Thank you for saying that," said a deep voice from behind them.

Grace and Lucia both turned to find a man she recognized from the opening night. She'd been introduced to him briefly, but they hadn't been able to talk much. "You painted this?" she asked.

"I did. I've painted that view a thousand times actually. I grew up looking at it, but I can never quite seem to get it right."

"It's lovely," Grace said. "I'm sorry. I don't remember your name. I'm Grace and this is Lucia."

"Alejandro," the man said. He had streaks of silver in his hair, and Grace would have called him a silver fox if anyone would have asked for a description.

"You're from Sacromonte?" Lucia asked.

"I was born here," he said. "I've traveled a lot, but this is still my home. They invited me to meet the students tonight, and I thought it sounded like fun."

"That was a great idea," Grace remarked as she wondered who had come up with it. Probably the person who'd put this whole thing together, the person who made sure it happened.

Just as Grace was about to ask, Alejandro continued. "You know Rafael? He has been meeting with our group of local artists and asking to see more of our work. He's asked us for our thoughts and ideas about the exhibit as well."

Grace stared in wonder, trying to take it all in. Not only had Rafael invited Alejandro tonight, but he'd also been meeting with a group of local artists and asking for their input? She was too stunned to speak.

Luckily, Lucia jumped in. "Do you all have a similar style?" she asked, gesturing toward Alejandro's painting. "You and the other artists?"

"Oh, no," Alejandro said, gesturing to a painting. "We're actually all very different in our style and technique."

Grace finally found her voice and couldn't help but to sing Lucia's praises. "Lucia is a painter as well. Her work is incredible."

Alejandro's eyes lit from within. "Is that so?"

They talked for a while about his work and some of the other local paintings, but as Grace excused herself, he and Lucia switched to Spanish and continued chatting. A smile passed over her face. It seemed Lucia and Alejandro were kindred spirits, both so passionate about their craft. An interesting development.

Grace ate too many appetizers and talked far too much about Salvador

Dali and Frida Kahlo. Her students almost seemed to be buzzing around her, all of them excited and chatting about the art as if they were the experts, and in a lot of ways they were. They knew enough to know what they liked and why; they knew enough to articulate the merits of each piece and Grace was so proud as she stood there listening to them, so happy she was a part of it.

"This place is seriously cool," Marco said, sidling up next to her. "I can't believe you made this."

"Oh," Grace said. "Did I give that impression? I didn't create this. I just consulted."

"That's not true," a voice said from behind them. "You rambled on about all of these paintings for quite a long time."

Grace's breath caught in her throat. He was there. Had he been there the whole time? It seemed impossible that she could have missed him in this familiar little series of caves, but it didn't matter. He was there, and Grace was speechless.

"Is everything going well?" Rafael asked.

Grace nodded until she finally found her voice. "It's great, yes. Marco, this is Rafael, he's the one who—well, he's the one who really did all of this."

"A pleasure to meet you," Raf said with a charming smile. He was as calm and debonair as always, the perfect picture of a high society gentleman who knew how to throw a party.

Marco's eyes widened just a bit, and Grace just knew he was assessing Rafael's beautiful face, because it's what she was doing, too. "Uh—nice to meet you, too. Did you also make these little *croquetas*, because they are wildly delicious."

Rafael laughed. "No, I didn't cook the food, but I was the one who chose the menu, so I'll still take that as a compliment."

Marco nodded. "You should, honestly. Between the paintings and the food, I think you've got to have good taste."

"Marco," Lucia called, beckoning her son toward one of Picasso's early self-portraits where she stood with Alejandro. She gave Grace a knowing little glance as if she could see exactly what had been on Grace's mind all evening.

"Nice museum," Marco commented to Rafael before sliding off toward his mother.

Grace and Rafael stood silently for a long moment. She cleared her throat as if she was about to say something, but no words came out. She didn't know how to act normal around him, not anymore, not since Alma had given her permission to want him.

She really, really wanted him. She just didn't know exactly what that meant. She didn't know if she was ready to give *herself* permission to want him. How sustainable could this thing between them be?

"Well, Marco seems to be a good judge of character," Rafael said at last, a small smile tugging at his lips. "Did you have a good time tonight?"

"Yes." Grace was almost breathless. "I could tell my students loved it."

"Good. They're lucky to get to see the work and hear about it straight from your mouth."

She couldn't help noticing how much interest he was taking in her mouth as he said those words.

They stared at each other again. "How long have you been here?"

Rafael ran a hand through his hair. "I was here before the event to make sure everything was set up, but then I went to run errands."

"Is it true that Christian wanted to cancel?" Grace asked in a rush.

Rafael frowned. "Where did you hear that?"

Grace swept some hair behind her ear and glanced away from him.

"Alma," he said, and Grace nodded. "Well, I told him we couldn't cancel, and here we are. It worked out."

Grace's eyes met his again. "Because of you," she said.

Rafael coughed. "How'd you get up here? Can I drive you home?"

"Yes," Grace replied without hesitation.

"Find me whenever you're ready to go." His hand just barely slid past the side of her arm as he walked by. She was going to be alone with him again, and it was impossible to think about anything else.

They were silent for much of the drive. Grace stared out the window trying to gather her thoughts even though it was useless. Her thoughts resisted gathering. Instead, they scrambled over everything—her grandmother and pomegranates and the feel of Rafael's skin. She thought about how content Lucia had been at the exhibit. She thought about Alma. She was full of gratitude and grief and longing.

She glanced over at Rafael. *Yes, lots and lots of longing.*

They were almost to her apartment, but Grace didn't want to go to her apartment. She wanted to go home with him, even if she didn't know how to broach the subject. She supposed she could have used their time in the car trying to get a sense of how he felt about her or maybe talking about her feelings for him, but she was still tangled up in her own thoughts, unsure of exactly what she wanted or how to express it. Still terrified.

He turned down Alma's street. *Her* street.

"What if—" she started. If she wanted any chance of more time with him, she had to say it, but the words lodged in her throat.

He glanced over at her and raised an eyebrow. "I'd kill to know just what's going on in your head," he said.

"Maybe we could go to your place and talk."

He scrunched up his forehead and glanced at her again. "We've barely spoken this entire trip, and you think we need to go and talk?"

She swallowed hard. "Yes, I mean, I just think it would be easier if you weren't driving?" She didn't know how to explain it to him, and she didn't even know where she would begin. She just knew she didn't want him to drop her off.

He didn't respond to that, and her heart lurched. God, she was sweating. She should just take it back and go home and bury herself in bed and forget she ever spoke those words.

But Rafael drove past Alma's apartment. Grace glanced over at him in surprise.

"I don't know what's going on," he said, staring forward at the road.

Grace's hands fidgeted in her lap. "Neither do I, honestly."

Raf blew out a breath, and she knew he must be confused and angry and sick of her indecisiveness. "You're not going to give me any clue about what's happening here? What are you thinking?"

Grace's cheeks were hot. "Right now, I'm thinking I want you to take me home. To *your* home. I—I don't know about after that."

CHAPTER TWENTY-SIX

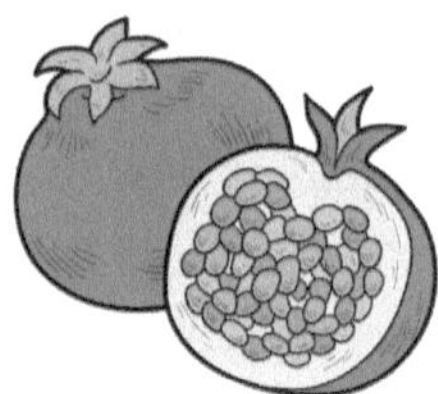

HE WASN'T GOING to argue with that. Who knew where this night would lead him, but if Grace wanted to go back to his place, then he would oblige. It was probably stupid. It would probably blow up in his face all over again. It was probably a mistake. And he was going to do it anyway.

He had no self-control when it came to her, and it wasn't something he'd ever experienced. He was used to being in control of himself and his feelings. He was used to knowing what the hell the woman he was with wanted. With Grace, he had no idea.

She was going to tear him right open, and he was going to let her.

He parked the car. They walked to his place. He unlocked the door, and they slipped inside. They removed their coats. He asked if she wanted a drink. She shook her head, and then they stood there, about two meters apart, staring at each other.

"What do you want, Graciela?" he asked at last. "What is this?"

She moved toward him slowly and then put her hands on his chest as she pressed herself up on her toes. He watched her mouth move toward him—closer and closer—until finally she pressed her lips against his.

He was stiff at first, trying not to lose himself, trying to keep his head for a second so he could puzzle out what the hell was happening. What had changed? Why was she kissing him now after weeks of avoiding him?

But he couldn't hold back very long before sinking into her, sliding his hands to her hips and around her back, opening his mouth and deepening the kiss, pressing his tongue to meet hers before letting out a little groan. He rubbed his thumb against her neck and angled her head back to kiss her even harder, and he felt her fingers digging into his skin.

Then, he pulled away for a moment, pushing a strand of hair from her eyes and searching her face. "I'm very confused," he said.

"So am I," Grace replied.

"Why are you here?" His own voice sounded pathetic in his ears, too desperate, too eager.

Grace's hands slid along his back. "Because Alma told me what you did for me. How you fought for the event."

He wrinkled up his forehead, unsure of how that made much of a difference. "That wasn't a big deal."

She pressed closer to him, eyes searching his face. "It was to me, Raf."

He let out a long breath.

"Why did you do it? Alma said you yelled at Christian."

"I didn't yell. Or maybe I did. I kind of blacked out." He took a moment to appreciate the fact that she was still in his arms. She wasn't going anywhere, at least not yet.

"Why?"

Rafael kept his voice low, trying to keep it from breaking. "Because I knew how much it meant to you, Graciela. I wasn't going to let him take that away. And it would have been irresponsible and rude no matter what the occasion was. I didn't think Alma would tell you. I didn't know she was paying that much attention."

Grace stared at him. "She was."

She tried to kiss him again, but Rafael held back. He wasn't done with this conversation. He needed more answers. He never knew what anything meant with her. Was this just an attraction? A way to get out of her own head? Or did she feel every second of it in her bones like he did?

"You really want this, Graciela?" he asked. "You really want me?"

She looked down, away from his face, and took a shuddering breath. It didn't inspire a ton of confidence, but he had to know what he was getting here. Was this just a night? Or was it all of her?

He wanted everything, but he knew he would settle for less. He just needed to have an idea of where he stood.

CHAPTER TWENTY-SEVEN

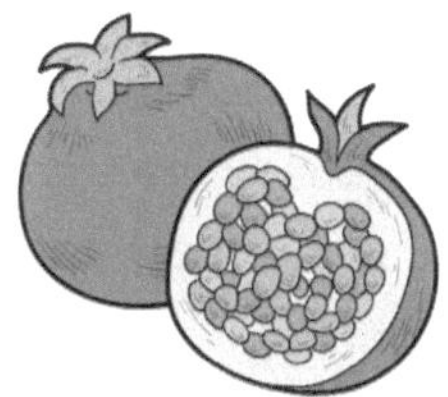

GRACE CLOSED her eyes for a moment. Fear seemed to rush through her veins. She wanted to tell him the truth, but what was the truth? She'd stayed away for Alma's sake, but also for her own. She didn't want to hurt again. She didn't want to have to rebuild a whole new life if all of this went to pieces. She didn't want to be vulnerable anymore. She didn't want more pain. But now that Alma had rescinded her objections to Grace's relationship with Rafael, it seemed like every other concern was falling by the wayside. If she had Alma's support, she knew she could get through anything. She'd done it before. And maybe it was still risky, but Grace felt a strength she hadn't in the past. She knew Gram would have wanted her to take a risk, because it was what she'd encouraged Grace to do her entire life—to move downtown, to study art, to find what she loved and hold onto it. Even if Rafael's feelings for her were something abstract, something she was never able to pin down and hold in her hands, that didn't make them any less real, and it didn't mean they would disappear.

Rafael had asked her a straightforward question, and in that moment, she knew the answer. No matter what else was holding her back, all her worries and fears and brokenness from before, she knew. "Yes," she breathed.

He moved closer to her in an instant, as if that was all he needed to hear. He brought his hands to the sides of her face, inching his lips closer to hers. "This is what I want," he said. "*You* are what I want."

One of his hands slid to the back of her neck, and he kissed her again. God, she'd been waiting for that for ages, but it felt even better than she'd imagined—to have him kiss her again, desire radiating from him in waves.

Rafael broke the kiss and exhaled sharply as he pressed his forehead against hers. "Come to bed," he said, his voice deep with want.

Grace nodded, which was hard with her forehead pressed to his, but not impossible. She found herself smiling.

There were times over the past several months when she'd thought she would never be happy again, when she was sure she had lost herself, and there was no way to get that person back. She didn't think she'd be able to find a moment of peace from the constant grief that rolled through her, the knowledge that her true family was gone, and nothing would ever be the same.

But Rafael had shown her it was possible. Even though the sadness would live inside her forever, a hard little kernel of pain deep in her chest, she could still find a way back to herself. She could still find happiness, too, on occasion. She knew that because of him, because as he took her hand and led her to his bed, his fingers interlaced with hers, she was happy.

When they got to his bedroom, he kissed her slowly, like they had all the time in the world. There was no Alma to walk in on them this time. There seemed to be no one else in the world. Rafael left the door to his bedroom wide open as he pushed Grace toward the bed. He kissed and sucked the side of Grace's neck. He took his time trailing his fingers up the skin of her back, pressing her close against him.

They stayed that way for a long time, lying on the bed making out, slowly exploring each other. Grace ran her palm along his abs, delighting in how firm he was. This beautiful, incomparable human specimen wanted her. She bit at his bottom lip with her teeth, letting that knowledge sink in and fuel her desire even further. She'd never even dared to imagine it before—that he might want her as much as she wanted him.

Slowly, Rafael stripped her bare and splayed her across the white sheets. Grace watched as he kneeled over her, tugging off his shirt. She could see his arousal pressed against his slacks, and it only made her heart pound harder. She would never get enough of him. She hungered for him in a way she never had anyone else before. The *want* spread through her so easily, so constantly. She pulled him toward her and hitched a leg around his. He brought his mouth to her breast, teasing her with his tongue. Her fingers wove through his hair. "Rafael," she whispered, overwhelming need pulsing between her legs. He slid a hand down her soft belly and then lower, until he was almost to the place she wanted him most. She wriggled beneath him, trying to get his hand to move down farther.

"What do you want Graciela?" he whispered.

"Touch me," she said.

"Where?"

She arched toward him, and finally his fingertips pressed against her in just the right position. "There," she said. "Everywhere."

He did just as she had asked, and Grace gasped with pleasure.

It felt so good, but Grace still wasn't satisfied. It still wasn't enough of him. She reached out, sliding a hand up his thigh before she ripped open the button on his pants and reached for his length, letting out a breath as he continued to touch her.

"You don't have to be quiet this time," he said. "This time I want to hear every sound you make." He kissed her again, and she hummed against his mouth. He wriggled to work his pants lower, until finally he reached down and yanked them over his feet. Then he spread her legs wider.

Grace pushed against him, hauling her weight up and rolling them until she was on top of him. She bit her lip as she felt his erection press right between her legs. She leaned against him and kissed him harder as his hands roamed her back, then tangled up in her hair.

"I want you so badly," he said.

"You can have me," she said, grabbing him.

"You're sure about that? I don't just want tonight. I want all of you, Graciela."

She nodded but had no words. Instead, she leaned back and guided him inside of her. Rafael pressed his fingertips into her hips, and Grace shuddered, enjoying the feel of him all over.

They moved together in the dark, both of them moaning and letting out shallow breaths, both of them desperate and reckless.

If Grace would have been able to think, she might have been awestruck by how comfortable she felt with him, even though everything was wild and exciting and new, it still felt like they were intimate friends, like they knew and trusted each other. As it was, however, Grace could barely put two words together, and when she managed that, all she was able to say was, "holy shit."

Grace rolled her hips, taking Raf even deeper, and every time she pulled back, their bodies snapped back together in the middle like magnets. Raf's grunts became more fevered as he lost himself in her, and Grace relished every moment of it. She felt so sexy and powerful. She felt desired like never before.

It was enough to send her over the edge with a breathless laugh. Her entire body seemed to spasm before she bent forward over Rafael, touching her breasts to his chest and kissing him fiercely as he followed her into oblivion, groaning her name and continuing to thrust into her while he rode out his own orgasm. Then he laughed, too, and he sounded so *happy*, it made Grace's heart turn to mush. How was it possible that she'd been with Derek for three years and never felt like this a day in her life? She'd been entirely comfortable with him but also too complacent. They'd often felt more like roommates than lovers, boring and bland and distant. And yet, she and Rafael had started out that way—as roommates—but the word had never seemed to fit. There'd always been something more, something so far from boring and complacent, something comfortable and untamed all at the same time. How was it possible that this snobbish playboy, a man she'd completely written off ten years ago, could envelop her in this completely sexy, delicious emotional tornado?

They lay in the dark together, their sticky skin still touching wherever possible—Grace's leg hooked around his middle, his hand on her thigh, her cheek against his chest. He let out a contented sigh, and it was the cutest fucking sound.

Damn it. She was in love with him. Grace pressed her nose against his nipple and nuzzled playfully. She hadn't wanted that to be true. She wanted to keep as much emotional distance as possible for a little longer, at least until they actually started dating, if that's what they were going to do next. It would have been nice to go out to dinner a few more times, sleep together once or twice more, before admitting to herself that she was absolutely head over heels in love with this man. Being in love with him meant that there was no way to tread lightly anymore, and if this all went to shit, it was really going to suck for Grace, of course, but it was really going to suck for Alma as well, which is why she'd tried to prevent it from happening from the start. The problem hadn't exactly gone away just because she had Alma's blessing.

But they could be adults about this whole thing, even if it ended badly. They could manage not to put Alma in an unpleasant position if they tried hard enough.

"You're quiet over there," Raf said. "Everything good?"

"Yes. I just need to stop thinking."

"Hmmm. Why don't you just replay everything that just happened in your head again? That's what I'm doing. Starting with the part where you said you wanted me." Grace couldn't see his face, but she could hear his smile. "Actually, starting with the part where you were eating that pomegranate."

Grace nuzzled into his chest again. "Oh yeah? That's what does it for you? Spanking some fruit?"

"I never realized it, but the way you slapped the skin on that thing? It gave me chills." He shivered against her dramatically.

She poked him in the ribs. "Oh how the mighty have fallen. Losing your head over a little light pom dom."

Rafael snorted. "Pom dom?"

"Pomegranate dominance. Was that a stretch?"

Grace could feel Raf's chest shaking as he laughed. "The mighty have fallen indeed," he whispered. Then he kissed the top of her head again, and Grace's brain started screaming. She loved him, and the words were crawling up her throat, begging to be set free.

What a terrible move that would be. Seriously. It was too soon. It was too much to handle, and she didn't want Rafael to feel responsible for protecting her feelings just because she'd had a shitty year. She didn't want to put that on his shoulders.

She pressed her mouth closed. Actually, there were better things to do with her mouth. She leaned up on her arm until she could reach his neck, and licked the soft skin below his ear until he turned his head and started kissing her lips. She just had to keep kissing him. That was the best plan of action. No more talking. And then maybe she could keep her explosive feelings to herself.

They made love again in the dark. At least, it was making love to Grace even if she didn't know what it was to Rafael. The way he moved his hands all over her was insanely addictive, like he couldn't get enough of her hair, her breasts, her thighs, her ass. He was everywhere, and she was so on board, offering herself up to him in every way, because she couldn't get enough of him either.

They showered together in the little bathroom where she'd only dreamed of showering with him before. Of course, she'd fantasized about him when she was in there alone, naked, and he was on the other side of the wall brewing coffee or working on his laptop or scrolling on his phone, and she was just wishing he would walk right in and press her against the shower stall. The fact that this whole scenario could be a real possibility was thrilling, even if she was already completely spent.

She dressed in his clothes, and they held each other again, his soft breath like a lullaby, more comforting than she ever would have imagined.

"What about Alma?" Raf asked.

Grace glanced up at him. "She gives us her blessing."

"What? She already knows?"

"When she told me about the event and what happened with Christian, she said she thought you really might have changed. She said I could do whatever I wanted, but if I wanted *you,* then she'd be okay with that."

"Alma said that? My stubborn, over-protective sister?"

"I think those are family traits," Grace said, and Raf pinched her.

"It is unusual for the Ferrer-Martíns to admit they were wrong about something," Rafael said with a laugh.

Grace shifted slightly. Her only worry was that Alma wasn't wrong. Maybe she was wrong about the fact that Rafael hadn't cared, and he wasn't just trying to get Grace in bed, but what if she was right about all of this being a terrible mistake?

Especially now that Grace loved him. Rafael obviously wanted her. He obviously had feelings for her, but the man had still never been in love. He'd never been in a real relationship, and just a few short months after Grace's entire world had fallen apart, after her heart had been squashed on the side of the street like roadkill, she'd already lost it again.

Clearly, she was ridiculous, but also, as she looked over at the gorgeous man lying next to her, she wondered what else she possibly could have done. She should have known she would fall in love with him the second she agreed to move into his apartment. And if she would have known, well… She would have done the same thing all over again a hundred times.

CHAPTER TWENTY-EIGHT

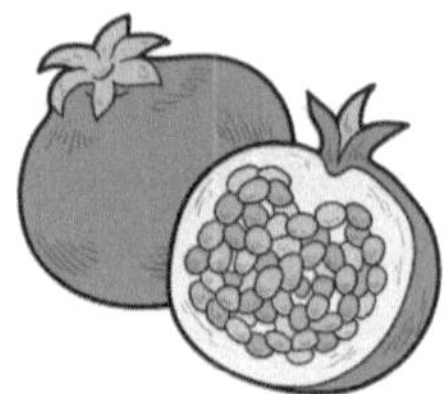

RAFAEL WAS happy to wake up for the first time in weeks. He absolutely was not the kind of person to wallow, but that's what he'd been doing since Grace had walked away from him. Wallowing. It couldn't even be called something as cool as brooding, because it wasn't even all angry and moody and sexy. It was just sad.

He should probably be scared that Grace had such an impact on his emotions, but it was hard to care when she'd come home with him, when he'd gotten to hear those sounds she made in the dark again without any fear of his sister overhearing, when she'd slept flush against his body like it was right where she wanted to be.

When Rafael finally stopped lingering in the memories of the night before and opened his eyes, however, he realized that Grace was gone. His door was closed, but there was noise coming from somewhere beyond, and he slid out of bed, eager to pick up where he'd left off with Grace. There would be no awkwardness or sight-seeing or monasteries this time. This time, he wanted to spend every minute alone with her.

She was standing in the kitchen, making every attempt to hack into the side of a pomegranate. He couldn't help the grin that spread across his face at the sight. There she was in *his* clothes in *his* apartment doing God-knows-what to that poor pomegranate.

"Having some trouble?" he asked.

"I swear I've done this before. This one's just a tough little sucker."

He walked around behind her and took the knife from her hand, slicing right along one of the ridges of the pomegranate with ease.

"Show off," she said.

"You're welcome."

"Do you want to do the spanking or should I?"

He raised a brow. "You know I'd like to watch you take a whack at it."

Her lips twitched like she was holding back a smile, and she proceeded to slap the seeds from the fruit and into a large bowl.

"Here's my plan," Rafael said.

Grace continued to struggle with the fruit but didn't ask for help. "Oh, you have plans, do you?"

Rafael shrugged. "I do."

"I'm not sure why you think you're the one in charge," she teased.

He leaned against the counter and folded his arms across his chest. "Used to getting my way, I suppose. Except there seems to be one particular person who completely throws me off my game and brings me to my knees. I'm hoping she might humor me this time."

"It's not necessary to talk about me in the third person." Grace shook her head. The way she looked at him with that fake little scowl made him want to lift her right up onto the countertop and have his way with her. Actually, that wasn't a bad idea. He would add that to the plan.

"Well?" Grace asked.

"Eggs," he said. "And carbohydrates. And lots of water."

"So...breakfast? That's the big plan?"

"A breakfast of champions, Graciela, so that afterward, I can take you back to my bedroom with enough stamina to have my way with you for hours. Or we might not make it to the bedroom." He winked at her. He was truly enjoying himself this morning. He felt lighter than air. "We can play it by ear."

"So, no trips to various cathedrals today?" Grace quipped.

He narrowed his eyes. "Very funny. I was nervous. I wanted to sweep you off your feet."

Grace smiled, drinking him in with her gaze.

"If you'd put that knife down again, I'd really like to kiss you."

Grace had been cutting a second pomegranate—with better success this time—but slowly she placed the knife on the counter.

"There we go," Rafael said, moving in. He kissed her hard, like a promise of all the things that were going to follow. She let out a little gasp, and Rafael was instantly hard. Maybe they should start with the new plan *before* breakfast.

"I really should go home at some point," Grace said. She was fully clothed, despite his best efforts, but after several rounds of sex and another shower, he couldn't be too sad that they were relaxing on the couch for a while. At least she was still next to him giving him the cutest play by play of the latest season of *The Great British Bake Off*.

After a while, she mentioned returning to her apartment, and Rafael jumped in. "What do you need from home? We can go pick it up and come back here."

"Well, I should probably talk to Alma. I haven't told her the latest developments, and I think I need to be totally open with her this time."

Rafael gave her a quizzical look.

"Well, okay, not totally open. That would be weird."

"Why don't you just call her?" he asked, taking Grace's hand in his.

"You know Alma, right? I think you've met her once or twice before? She is not going to be satisfied with a phone call. And I just need to get my head in order."

Grace was right about Alma. A phone call was not going to satisfy her in this instance, but he didn't know what Grace could possibly mean about her head. What part of her head was not in order? Everything in Rafael's head felt perfectly ordered. In fact, he'd never felt so sure about anything in his life.

"What's wrong with your head?"

Grace bit her lip, which he knew meant there was something she didn't want to say. A flash of panic struck him in the chest.

She leaned back from him and twisted a strand of hair between her fingers. "I was just thinking maybe we should take this slow," she said. "I don't want to rush into anything."

His mouth formed a hard line. "We haven't rushed, Graciela. We lived together for over a month. We spent every single day together, and now one day is too much?"

She took his hand, rubbing her thumb again his knuckles. "It's not too much. I just thought maybe we should go out and have dinner a few times and ease into it…like regular dating for a while."

Rafael nodded slowly. He could handle that. It seemed completely unnecessary, but if Grace wanted to be courted, that was definitely something he could excel at. What he really wanted was to spend every second with her and tell her he was already in love with her anyway, but that probably didn't count as taking things slow, so he would go along with whatever she needed.

"Okay," he said.

"Yeah?" She leaned toward him, pressing her shoulder to his.

Rafael kept his tone casual. "If that's what you think will work best for us, then that's what we'll do."

"Really?"

He took a moment to inhale her scent—it was his soap and shampoo, but there was something more underneath, something sweet and delicious and completely *her.* "Yes, really. See? I'm not so stubborn after all."

Grace's mouth tilted in a half-smile. "Debatable."

Rafael pressed a kiss to her temple and decided to take his chances. "Could we have dinner this evening, then? If that's what we're doing now?"

Grace eyed him for a moment, and he held his breath. "Yes," she said.

"Good." He exhaled. He could handle one step at a time, as long as the next step was in sight.

Grace's eyes crinkled with delight. "Good. Then I guess I should go home."

"I'll admit I'm still used to the days when you thought this was home." *Shit.* He didn't mean to say that. Did it sound like he was suggesting she should live with him again? So much for having no problem taking things slow.

Grace faltered for a moment like she wasn't quite sure how to take his statement either. "It's nice to know my room is still available pending any unnatural disasters," she said calmly.

He tried to relax and make a joke. "Oh, you still think of that as *your* room, do you?"

She elbowed him in the side. "You know what I mean."

He did know what she meant, because it still felt that way to him too, like she belonged there. And that meant taking things slow was going to be a struggle.

Grace wanted a proper date, and that's what she was going to get. He knocked on the door of her apartment that evening and didn't even flinch when Alma answered the door. He'd brought flowers, and Alma gave him a thorough once over before shaking her head and opening the door wider to let him inside.

"He's here," Alma called. She crossed her arms. "Where are you taking her?" she asked Rafael in Spanish.

"Ummm, La Tomasas," he said.

"Fancy."

He shrugged.

"Should I expect her to come home this evening?" Alma asked, all prim and proper like she was Grace's chaperone.

Rafael didn't know what to say to that. This was just as weird as Grace's had always feared, but Alma would get used to it. She had to. "You'll have to ask her that," he said. "Thank you for saying whatever you said to her. I know this must be strange for you."

Alma grinned, softening slightly. "It is, but I know it must be strange for you, too. Don't you dare hurt her, though, Rafa. I mean it."

Rafael rubbed his hand against his jaw. "I know you do. But maybe you could tell her not to hurt me, too?"

"What are you guys talking about?" Grace asked as she glided into the room. She was wearing a tight black dress and her hair fell across her shoulders in a way that made Rafael want to reach for it on instinct, but he forced himself to refrain. At least for a little while.

"You, of course," Alma said, switching to English.

Grace scrunched up her face. "What about me? You better be nice to my date, Alma."

Alma spun on her heel toward him. "He has nothing to fear from me if he behaves himself."

"I'll be on my best behavior," Rafael said. "Don't worry."

In an instant, Alma was in his arms, pulling him into a hug. They weren't exactly a hug-giving, sentimental kind of family with the kind of patriarch they had to deal with, so Rafael almost stumbled backward with surprise.

"I want you to be happy," Alma whispered in his ear.

"I am," he replied.

When Alma pulled away he looked over to Grace to find her watching them with wary eyes.

"She didn't even make any death threats," Rafael assured her.

"I didn't," Alma confirmed. "I'm being very supportive."

"Okay," Grace said skeptically before pulling Alma into a hug of her own and heading toward the door. She didn't touch Rafael at all, not yet, but something glimmered in her eyes that managed to put air in his lungs, filling them until his chest puffed up.

"These are for you," he said, handing her the flowers. Grace's expression could only be described as suspicious. "What? You don't like flowers?"

She tilted her head at him. "I do."

"Then what's the problem?" *Flowers were a typical gesture of affection, right?*

Grace glanced at Alma. "I don't know. I just wasn't expecting this. It's... romantic."

Rafael's words expelled from his lips in a rush. "You don't sound like it's romantic. You sound nervous. You wanted me to take you out on dates and take things slow, so here we go. First date."

Grace pushed her hair behind her ear. "I know, but you don't need to go out of your way. I mean, just be you..."

Rafael rolled his eyes. He'd thought he was doing exactly what she wanted. "I am being me. I can be romantic, Graciela."

"I know that."

Alma was watching them from a stool near the kitchen. "You guys are bickering like this is your one hundredth date."

Rafael narrowed his eyes at her for a quick moment before turning toward the door. "Ready?" he asked Grace.

She handed the flowers off to Alma and followed his lead. "Ready."

It was everything it was supposed to be. The restaurant was gorgeous with a *romantic* ambiance and delicious food. Grace held his hand when they wove past the bar and over to their table. She smiled at him from across the table. But despite everything going according to plan, something felt off, like she wasn't entirely herself. This was supposed to be their first date, but he knew her, and he knew that something was wrong.

"Good wine," she said.

He nodded.

"Why are you looking at me like that?"

"Like what?" he asked.

"Like something very serious is going on in your brain?"

Rafael sighed. "Because you look uncomfortable. I can tell."

Grace bristled. "What do you mean?"

Rafael sat back in his chair and stared at her. "You're all stiff and you keep glancing around like you're looking for an escape route if something goes wrong."

Slowly, she shook her head. "I'm fine. I'm happy to be here."

"I'm happy to be here," Rafael countered, like a challenge.

"Well, then let's enjoy ourselves," she commanded, but there was a light of mischief in her eyes. That was more like it. More like *Grace.*

He took another sip of his wine. "Tell me about something. What's on the syllabus for your new class next term?"

She did tell him. About every female artist she was planning to put in her lesson plans. She told him about her latest faculty meeting and the assurances that her contract would be renewed for the following year. That was a relief, honestly. She told him how Alma had burned a fish on the stove the other day, and the whole place started smoking so much she was afraid they were in for another disaster, and she would have to move out of their apartment all over again.

"You turned up the temperature, didn't you?" Rafael asked. "You're just looking for an excuse to come back to my place."

He watched the blush creeping over her face. It was almost normal then, but not quite. Rafael could tell that something was still bothering her, but he didn't know what it was. He didn't want to push her, but he was also a little desperate. She had a lot of power here—power to send him right back to his state of wallowing—so he wanted to know what was messing with her brain. If there was a way to fix it, whatever it was, then he needed to figure out how.

"Will you come home with me?" he whispered in her ear after the meal, as they started to walk out of the restaurant.

"On a first date?" she teased.

"Yes." He kissed the top of her head and waited for a response. The seconds that passed felt like millions of years.

"Yes," she said.

CHAPTER TWENTY-NINE

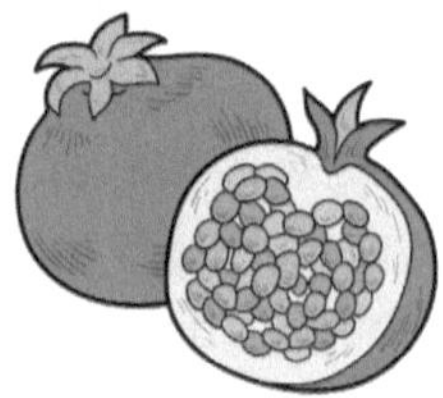

DON'T SAY IT. *Don't say it. Don't say it.*

Rafael looked over at Grace again like he was trying to read her mind, and thank goodness he couldn't or he would just hear her brain screaming that she was in love with him, and that was the information she was trying to keep to herself at all costs. This was his first fucking relationship, and she wasn't going to ruin it by telling him she loved him on day one and freaking him out so much that he immediately started to push her away. She had to keep herself in check so this whole thing didn't fall apart before it had even started.

So she sat on her stool in his kitchen keeping her lips firmly pressed together except for the brief moments when she allowed herself to sip from a glass of water.

Rafael refilled her glass, but instead of sliding it back across the counter toward her, he walked around and stood beside her as if waiting for something. She turned toward him slightly and reached out her hand, but he put the glass firmly on the counter before spinning her stool and slowly easing her legs apart with his thigh. The black fabric of her dress slid up bunched against her belly, leaving her almost bare underneath except for the silk of her underwear.

Then, Rafael positioned his entire body right in front of her and slid his thumb against her neck. She eased her head back until her eyes met his and she swallowed.

"You haven't even kissed me yet," he said.

She didn't reply but held her position, waiting as his head tilted down toward hers, his lips inching closer and closer with every breath. "Is that something you might be interested in?" he asked.

She smiled and strained toward him, straightening as much as possible until finally, his mouth was against hers. It felt very possible that she might just topple off the stool altogether, but maybe he could sense that, because his arm wrapped around her back, pulling her even closer toward him and holding her firmly in place. She felt him smile against her lips, and her heart seemed to bounce in her chest like her lungs were a trampoline. She loved that smile. She loved that it was meant for her. She loved him. *Shit.*

Rafael raised his head so they were making eye contact again. Her body had tensed without meaning to, and of course, he'd noticed. He seemed to be so aware of her, which wasn't exactly helpful when she was trying to go on with their date and pretend like she wasn't totally obsessed with him in a way that might send him running for the hills.

"What's wrong, Graciela? Just tell me."

"It's—" What could she possibly say? She decided to try as much truth as possible without giving him everything. "You make me nervous. I know this is new for you, and I want it to go perfectly, but that feels like a lot of pressure."

He eased back from her, giving her more space. "You feel pressured by me?"

She grabbed his hand, keeping him from going too far away. "No. Of course not. I feel pressured by *me.* I don't want to mess this up."

He scoffed. "That's not possible."

Grace bit her lip. She wanted him to understand, to know everything she was thinking. It all just felt too precarious, like they were standing on the edge of a cliff and one gust of wind in the wrong direction could topple this whole thing. "Maybe you don't think so now..."

"Grace. I know you said you wanted to take things slow, and I can respect that, but don't forget that I know you. I know the little sounds you make when you're about to come. I know you can ramble on about Picasso for hours and somehow make it the most interesting thing I've ever heard. I know you stand up for people when it matters, and you're the most loyal friend I've ever seen. You keep saying this is our first date, and maybe it is, but I'm already yours."

Oh, wowza. Something was happening in her stomach. Not butterflies, exactly. More like a plague of locusts beating their wild wings. "Well, that's—" she faltered. "That does make me feel better. I'm just trying to navigate how we do this whole thing when we have lived together, and your Alma's brother, and I already..."

She clamped her stupid mouth shut. She should just go back to kissing him to keep from spilling her secret, but before she could even pull his face toward her again, he was already leaning in to kiss her—a fierce, hungry kiss that made her clench her thighs around him.

"It might take some getting used to," he said, breaking away and pressing his forehead to hers. "Maybe we don't have it all figured out yet, but the thing is, Grace..."

He paused for so long that she pulled away to get another good look at him. Now she was the one trying to figure out what the hell he was thinking. He brought his hands to the sides of her face and cradled her cheeks in his hands, and she relished every moment of it.

"You've been through a lot recently," he continued. "And like I said, I don't want to put any more pressure on you or make you think you need to feel a certain way. This is all new to me."

"I know," she said. "That's why I thought it would be good to take things slow."

His brow furrowed. "You mean that was for my sake?"

She chewed her lip. "It was for both of us. It just seemed like the practical way to go about this, and I know you haven't really had this kind of relationship before."

Rafael hung his head. "You're killing me, Graciela."

"What?" Her eyes scanned his face, searching for clues as to what she'd done wrong.

"Sure, this is my first serious thing, but that doesn't mean I don't know when I'm in love. I'm not a total *gillipollas,* despite what my sister might have you believe."

Grace cocked her head to the side, considering him closely again. She could feel her heartbeat. She could hear it ringing in her ears. "When you're in love?"

"I didn't mean to say that," he grumbled in a low voice.

Grace tried to keep her voice steady, but she felt like she could scream. "So you didn't mean it?"

He frowned at her like he was disappointed. "Of course I meant it. I just didn't mean to say it yet. I guess it's too late now, though, so I might as well tell you properly. Should I?"

Grace sucked in a breath and nodded. Fireworks seemed to be going off inside of her, in her head, in her belly, sparking through her blood like it was the Fourth of July in her veins.

Rafael tilted her chin up to him. "I love you, Grace. I'll do whatever you want to do in this relationship. If you want to just go on dates, if you want to stop sleeping together, if you want to move in tomorrow. I don't care what it looks like or if you want to go slow or fast or whatever you need. None of it will change the fact that I'm in love with you. None of it will change that I want to spend every moment with you, making you laugh. No matter how you want this to look, I'll do anything. I've never felt this way about anyone else, I guess I can't help wanting you to know that, even if it's too soon to say it."

Grace opened her mouth and then closed it again. An overwhelming wave of warmth seemed to flood her entire body.

"Sorry." Rafael ran a hand through his hair, his fingers twitching.

Grace shook her head as a disbelieving smile spread across her face. There was no holding it back now. She tried not to shout at him. "Rafael, I love you," she said, her voice scratchy, the words almost catching in her throat.

"You do?" He already looked so smug about it, and it might have been the hottest look she'd ever seen.

Grace almost laughed, the relief of saying the words aloud coursing through her. "Yes, that's why I've been acting like a weirdo, because I've been trying so hard to keep my mouth shut."

Raf's eyes went wide. "Why would you want to do that?"

"Because it's so soon. And I didn't want to freak you out. I thought maybe if we could just date for a while, then in a month or so it wouldn't be totally crazy that I'm completely in love with you."

The grin that flashed across his face almost made her heart stop. "Well, that makes everything a hell of a lot easier," he teased. "I'm glad it's out in the open. Then he lowered his voice and his tone became more serious. "I'm really, truly glad, actually,"

He pulled her against him again, and Grace let the revelation of it all sink into her skin. He loved her. It seemed almost unfathomable, but also, it felt incredibly natural and right.

"Does Alma know?" he asked.

"No, I didn't want her to think I was completely crazy either."

"We're both crazy, then," he said. "How long? When did you know you loved me?"

She pulled at the fabric of his shirt. "Don't go getting all cocky—"

"It's been a long time for me, Grace, just so you know. I've been a lovesick little fool, even though you were barely even speaking to me."

"I guess I've been a fool, too, since you were all I wanted. It didn't matter that I promised Alma I wouldn't go falling for you. I couldn't stop it." Grace nuzzled into his chest, aching to have him closer to her.

Apparently, he felt the same way because in an instant Rafael slid his hands down her back to her ass and lifted her right off the stool. Grace wrapped her arms around his neck and clung to him with a little squeal of delight, and he carried her through the apartment.

"Can we agree that you'll be staying here tonight?" he whispered in her ear as he walked. "And any night, as many as you want."

"Yes," she said. "Can we agree that we won't leave this bedroom for several hours until I've thoroughly had my way with you?"

Rafael pressed his lips to her neck. "I absolutely agree. Can we agree never to speak of the embarrassing time I tried to kiss you ten years ago, and you completely rejected me?"

Grace laughed. "Oh no, I think I'd like to talk about that quite often."

He bit at her earlobe. "I was an asshole."

"That's why I didn't kiss you," she said, turning to kiss his cheek.

He grinned. "You're kissing me now. You love me."

"And what a surprise this would be for young Grace," she said, before Raf threw her onto the bed and dove to join her. "Honestly even old Grace is kind of surprised."

"You're surprised at how you feel about me?"

Grace considered that for a moment. "I'm surprised this is real," she said. And she meant it. After everything she'd lost, all the pieces of herself she was so sure would never fit together again. She'd found some semblance of peace and hope—because of her job, because of her friendships, because of the art exhibit, because of *him*.

"This is the realest thing I've ever felt in my life," Raf said.

Grace started to unbutton his shirt, drinking in the sight of his bare chest, her fingers nimbly working their way down and down. She almost laughed when something her grandmother said jumped into her mind. *A man with a firm torso is a special kind of gift.* They'd been looking through one of Gram's coffee table books, probably staring at a picture of a Michelangelo sculpture. Gram had a thing for abs, and she wasn't shy about it. If she could see Rafael, then she would be absolutely giddy with delight on Grace's behalf.

"What is it?" Rafael asked.

Grace ran a hand over his stomach. "You're a work of art," she said.

He laughed and shook his head. "You might be a little biased."

"Maybe," she said. "But I'm still an expert."

EPILOGUE

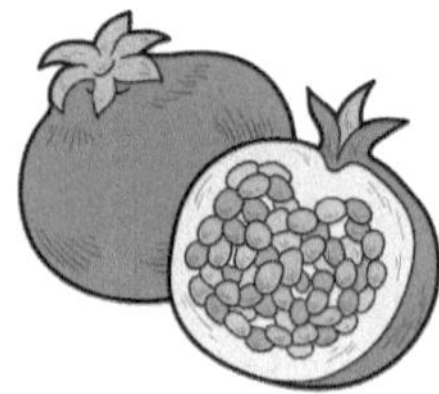

GRACE RACED up the stairs to her apartment, her satchel banging into the side of her leg with every step. She had to pause and catch her breath outside the door for a moment, because despite walking all over the entire city of Granada, a flight of steps still did her in. She regained her composure after a moment and then opened the door.

Rafael was on the phone, but his face broke into a bright smile when he saw her. He gave a little wave, which was frankly adorable. Grace moved to the office to drop off her bag, and by the time she was out again, she could tell Rafael was wrapping up. Her Spanish was still a work in progress, but very much improved. She could recognize that Raf was saying he had to go, and he would talk to the person on the other end of the line later. Based on the tone in Raf's voice, it was probably a client.

Sometimes, Rafael would only speak in Spanish to help Grace learn the language, but she also just loved listening to him speak in his native tongue. She was finally able to understand more of the dirty things he whispered to her in the dark, though he kept coming up with new filthy vocabulary, and she could never quite keep up. It was still hot as hell.

He rose and walked toward her. "*Feliz Cumpleanos, mi amora.*"

She'd been living in Spain for over a year but only living with Rafael—

this time—for a little over a month. It had been a mutual decision between Grace and Rafael, Grace and Alma, Alma and Obinna. Obinna was living in Alma's apartment now, and Grace was surprised at how easy it was to feel at home at Rafael's place again—bowl of pomegranates on the counter, the little window from what was now their shared office looking out over the rooftops along the slanted street, the stool where she'd been sitting the moment he told her he loved her.

Rafael kissed her, and Grace let her hand trail down his arm until she reached his hand, their fingers intertwined. "Are you ready to go?" she asked.

They were going out for her birthday with a small gathering. Alma and Obinna, of course. Lucia and Marco and Marco's boyfriend, Felipe. Marco had graduated and wasn't her student any longer, but he was still her friend. Grace was also Lucia's biggest fan, but they'd become friends over the past several months as well. Alejandro from Sacromonte was there, and Nora, the travel writer, and her fiancée were in town, and they'd been happy to join for the festivities. Nora still didn't know about the secret art exhibit, or rather, Grace had a feeling that she *did* know, and chose not to mention it or print anything about the place. The little museum was still a well-kept secret, but sometimes Grace joined the crowds of locals that gathered for free entry on one Saturday of the month. Word had spread amongst a group of nearby art-lovers, and they liked to take advantage when it was open to the public. Sometimes they all went out for coffee afterward.

"Not quite ready yet," Rafael said. "I wanted to give you one of your presents before we go."

"One of my presents?" Grace asked. "Meaning there are several?"

"One of them will have to wait until later…in the bedroom," he said in a seductive purr before nipping at her ear.

"Interesting," she said, leaning into his touch again.

"Here." Rafael took her hands and led her to the couch. "Sit down and close your eyes."

"Really?" Grace hovered for a moment before taking a seat.

Raf squeezed her hands. "Yes, just do it, Graciela."

Grace did as she was told, placing her hands over her eyelids for dramatic effect. She heard Rafael moving through the apartment, until finally she felt the familiar warmth of him beside her.

"Okay," he said. "You can open them."

She removed her hands from her face and searched for the surprise. It didn't take long to spot it settled on one of the stools leaning back against the counter. A painting.

Grace couldn't help standing up and moving toward it to get a closer look. She recognized the image instantly; it was the view through the window of her little bedroom the first time she'd lived in Rafael's apartment. The rooftops stretched out down the hill, and a few cars passed each other on the street. The sun was bright, like early afternoons when Grace would stare and stare out that window just thinking, mulling over anything that was on her mind—usually Rafael.

You could see the windowsill as well, where a whole pomegranate rested on the ledge, as well as a little book that had belonged to Grace's grandmother. It was breathtaking and perfect and it seemed to transport her to such a specific time, months earlier, when she'd been falling in love with Rafael.

"I—How did you?" she asked in a breath, and Rafael moved behind her, pressing himself against her back and wrapping his arms around her middle.

"Happy birthday," he said.

Grace stared at the painting a moment longer. She recognized the style, the beautiful brushstrokes. She knew one artist who would see that view from the window and be able to capture it like that, to find the beauty in every tiny detail.

"Lucia?" she whispered.

"Of course."

"When did she even find the time? How did you get her to do this?"

Rafael laughed. "Believe it or not, Grace, she was thrilled. She loved having the opportunity to create something for you. She started before you ever moved in."

"It's so beautiful," she said. There were tears in her eyes. An ache rose in her chest. She wished Gram could see it.

"You like it then?"

"Are you kidding?" Grace let out a little snort and let the swell of emotions fill her up. The grief, the love, the happiness. It was all there, and it swirled together, mixing into something new, some new existence, some version of herself that had fallen apart and gotten put back together. And maybe the pieces were arranged in a new order. Maybe she didn't look quite like she had before all the destruction. But she'd still managed to find the very best things in life and hold onto them.

Rafael leaned in and kissed the side of her neck, and Grace rested her head back against his shoulder, offering more of her skin for him to taste.

"We better get going," he said. "Alma's got a few surprises up her sleeve as well, and she'll give me a hard time if I make you late."

Grace let out an impatient groan. "But I never want you to stop kissing me," she said.

Rafael laughed against her neck. "Don't worry. After dinner, we'll have all night. Just you and me."

Grace smiled and looked back at the painting. It seemed to say something to her, conjuring a memory she couldn't quite place. Or maybe it was just a strange nostalgia. Lucia's work always had a way of giving her that feeling, but this was different. It was stronger, and it seemed to rush up from somewhere deep inside of her.

Rafael nuzzled against her cheek and then went to grab his jacket before holding Grace's out to her. Just as Grace started to turn toward him, slipping an arm into the coat, she stepped back again, one more time, eyes on the painting. The blend of colors. The way the light shined over the street. The gleam of the pomegranate in the window. Grace finally put her finger on it, on the specific way it spoke to her. Maybe it was something she never could have understood until she saw it this way, through Lucia's eyes, the beauty of it all captured forever on a small piece of canvas.

It felt like home.

Thank you for reading! Did you enjoy? Please add your review because nothing helps an author more and encourages readers to take a chance on a book than a review.

And don't miss more from Hannah Ledford with ELEPHANT AND CASTLE available now. Turn the page for a sneak peek!

You can also sign up for the City Owl Press newsletter to receive notice of all book releases!

SNEAK PEEK OF ELEPHANT AND CASTLE

Nora Shrapsan spun in a slow circle on a street just south of the Thames. Not that she knew which direction was north or south or which way was to the river or to Buckingham Palace. Seven years ago, Nora had zipped through the streets of London like a local, hopping on red double-decker buses and hailing midnight cabs, emerging from the labyrinth of underground stations with the ease and confidence of someone who'd lived there for years, though it had only been one summer. Nora had found her way around the city without any problems when she was a teenager with few responsibilities and nowhere in particular to go, so she had foolishly assumed that she could just pick up right where she left off in her relationship with ye olde London Town. She had assumed that she—an expert traveler and experienced tour-book copy editor—could jump on the Tube with ease and get to where she was going.

She was wrong.

When she'd gotten off the Underground and pulled up the address on her phone, the little blue arrow kept spinning in circles, changing its mind about which way she should turn. If Nora didn't figure it out soon, she was going to be late for the first meeting with her new editor, and she was going to have moved all the way across the Atlantic just to get fired, which would really be a shame, honestly. She'd been preparing for months—paperwork and visas, packing and parting words to friends. She had even broken up with her super-hot boyfriend, abandoning the comfort of upstate New York and regularly scheduled above-average sex. The breakup was a thrill for her mother, who always said that she shouldn't bother with Brandon anyway. Too pretty, too shallow. According to her mother, above-average sex wasn't worth the hassle of dating someone who made you watch Monday Night Football, but Nora was quick to point out that this was coming from a woman who wasn't getting laid at all.

"We're very comfortable together," Nora had explained to her mother again and again.

Kathleen Shrapsan, cancer survivor and member of the Binghamton City Council, did not take "comfortable" for an answer. They had the same conversation in perpetuity: "Brandon is very easy to look at," her mother would say. Even she couldn't deny it. "And he's nice to you. Heck, I feel comfortable with him too, but that doesn't mean he has any interest in marrying and impregnating you."

"Mom—"

"And you're too smart for him," her mother complained. Nora stopped arguing that a lot of men didn't care as much about *smart.*

"I want you to get married and have lots of babies and be happy, happy, happy, but I don't want you to do any of that with a man whose favorite book is *Sports Illustrated*. Also, not getting laid is a choice."

As usual, Nora knew her mother was right. Kathleen had been overjoyed when she heard the news about the London job, and she immediately waved off all the guilt Nora felt about abandoning her in-recovery matriarch. That was just a minuscule con in a long list of pros: no more football, no more dinners with finance bros, no more Brandon. With little regard for any of Nora's fears or concerns, her mother was praising the Lord that she wasn't going to just be *comfortable* anymore.

Even though her breakup was so fresh, and Nora kind-of-rudely told him two weeks before leaving the country, she was only partly concerned about the end of her relationship with Brandon and only slightly more concerned about the fact that she couldn't read a map. There was also the matter of the diary. A diary that had turned up while she was searching for her passport. A diary that was still sitting at the bottom of the overstuffed backpack slung over her shoulder, practically throbbing like it was a freaking tell-tale heart.

Nora decided she better just pick a direction and take her chances. She had done this before, after all; she'd trekked all over that city by herself or with her British boyfriend and his friends. She'd walked in the footsteps of The Beatles and Anne Boleyn and Idris Elba, probably. She shouldn't have a problem finding a company office in Southwark. She lifted her chin and marched down the sidewalk.

"Make a U-turn," her phone said. Nora wanted to fling it into oncoming traffic.

The diary had only started taunting her recently, and in fact she didn't even remember it existed until a few weeks ago when she'd opened an old shoe box, praying it wasn't going to be a smelly pair of Keds. Inside, there were old photographs, ticket stubs, a crinkled map, and a loose bunch of old tampons (not used, obviously). There was no passport, but underneath it all she found a diary with a pink, faux-leather cover that she recognized immediately. With her fingers touching the fake leather, Nora couldn't help abandoning the search for items that may have actually had some use to her as she prepared to move to a different country, and she took the little book over to the couch where she could sink into the cushions, crack it open, and remember for a second what it felt like to be nineteen. It was impossible not to memorize the words while studying the pages like an anthropologist who had uncovered a discovery that could unlock the secrets of a lost world.

London, June 5

Hugh keeps saying such romantic things, things that I don't know if I believe, but it's nice to hear them anyway. "I was perfectly content before I met you," he says, "but now I can't imagine what I'll ever do without you." He tells me he's sure I will ruin him. I know in my head that it's cheesy and he probably says stuff like this to every girl he dates, but I can't help feeling like it might be possible that he's falling in love with me too.

London, June 29

Here's the honest truth. There is nothing like getting kissed by a British man in an elevator at three o'clock in the morning...

London, July 7

I have never slept with anyone before...well until now. I have roommates, and Hugh has roommates, so it's not like we get a lot of privacy, and even when I would stay over at his place just to cuddle, I still felt a little embarrassed at what Dev might be thinking. One morning I walked out, and Julian was over, and I think we both turned bright red. Dev eavesdropping on my love life is one thing, but Julian...he's so sophisticated and shy. So Hugh got a hotel room, and that's where we went. "I think maybe I'm a bad influence on you," he said. Maybe he's right. He's five years older, and he's a man, and I know very little about men. But I wanted it to happen all along. I wanted him to take me somewhere private. I wanted to kiss him all over, even if I was worried about looking like an idiot and not knowing what I was doing. When I was there with him, I didn't really worry about that at all.

Nora could admit that discovering this significant artifact may have had something to do with her breakup as well. Sure, she'd been preparing to leave the country, but long distance was a thing. She and Brandon could have tried that. She wasn't sure exactly how long she would be in London; they could get back together when she returned. But after reading those pages and remembering how she felt that summer, Nora thought maybe she had known Hugh Jeffries better than Brandon from just three wonderful British summer months. She knew she was probably being stupid and idealizing their whole relationship. For one, she had been so young and had never been abroad before, and she was already inclined to indulge in romantic notions. Then there was the man himself. Hugh was a musician. With an accent. And he wrote songs about her.

How could you not be head over heels for someone who wrote songs about you? It really wasn't a fair fight.

If she had stayed, she would have grown up, and the rose-colored glasses would have come off. They would fight, and she would get bored, and he would get lazy and messy and forget her birthday after spending more time in the pub with his friends than making her happy. They had just never gotten to that part. A long time ago, she stopped fantasizing that Hugh Jeffries would show up on her doorstep and sweep her off her feet.

Still, Nora realized as she shuffled down the street—slightly frazzled and increasingly panicked—one part of her brain was looking for her office, but another part was disobediently searching for Hugh, as if she could imagine him into existence just by standing on a street in the city where he lived. You would think that someone who had finally gotten the chance at her dream job—or at least a lot closer to her dream job than sitting in a tiny office copy editing articles about beautiful places she would never get to visit—would have more important things to think about than men they'd been in love with when they were teenagers. She should be worrying about money, or how to actually do well in her new position, or the fact that she would only be freelance and the company could drop her contract and abandon her in the UK at the drop of a hat.

So no more NSFW British ex-boyfriend fantasies. She should probably wall the diary up behind a big stack of bricks and never look at it again. *Oh, wait. That was "The Cask of Amontillado."*

Nora was relieved to find that she had finally picked the right direction when her phone didn't command her to turn around again. With her eyes focused on the screen, she almost walked into a couple of well-dressed Londoners before she discovered the small office space with a big window and little yellow sign with purple lettering that read "99 Flamingo Publishing." Perhaps for the first time since exiting the Tube, Nora exhaled.

It was cozy inside—little desks blocked out at different angles, an office and a conference room in the back, and the sound of constant clacking as each person in the main room banged away on their keyboard. It wasn't exactly what she had imagined when she packed up her life and left America. She'd been picturing a big corporate office with elevators and a first floor Starbucks. This was kind of a rinky-dink operation, a one floor, very cramped, and very brown workplace situation. She knew publishing didn't have the budget it used to, and 99 Flamingo was only a very small imprint of a larger press, but this was still a surprise.

"Nora?" A woman at the front desk stood up and removed her glasses.

Nora did a double take, wondering if she should already be acquainted with this person. Surely the arrival of one American writer was of little significance to this place. "How did you know?"

The woman smiled warmly. "Well, we don't get a lot of people wandering in here, and we're expecting you." She reached out a hand for Nora to shake.

"I found the place," Nora said. It was an obvious statement, but she meant it more as an affirmation for herself than a conversation starter, as if she weren't a travel journalist with a terrible sense of direction.

"Give me a minute, and I'll take you back to Darcy," the woman said. "Also, I'm Jasmine. Did I mention that?"

Nora had forgotten how much she loved being surrounded by British accents, the way it made her feel as if she had stepped into a Jane Austen novel or a George Bernard Shaw play. It made her want to shout "hear, hear!" in raucous agreement whenever anyone said something exciting. She smiled to herself while she waited for Jasmine to introduce her to Darcy—of course her editor would be named Darcy. She wondered if it was a man or a woman. Perhaps it was a Mr. Darcy and her wildest *Pride and Prejudice* fantasies would play out in the little publishing office.

"Come on back, Shrapsan!" a smoky voice called from the back office, and Nora jumped. The other people in the main room kept their heads down with their eyes on their computer screens as she passed by them. *Friendly,* Nora thought sarcastically.

She popped her head around the corner and peeked inside the back office to see a mess of books and papers, maps and notes, ashtrays and takeout containers. Behind the desk was a beautiful woman in her mid-thirties with giant dark eyes and round cheeks. Her black hair was pulled back from her face, and her lips formed a displeased pout.

"Have a seat," Darcy said, and Nora quickly did as she was told.

Jasmine slipped back out of the office, leaving Nora alone in a sea of publishing debris with her new boss. Actually, Darcy was just her editor, but Nora couldn't stop thinking the word "boss." She'd thought it so much that it didn't totally seem like a real word anymore until she saw Darcy. She appeared to embody the term, and despite the fact that she looked the opposite of Mr. Darcy in every way, she did exude his same sternness and derision. Nora had been practicing this moment in her mind, planning her first impression, but she didn't even get a chance to say hello before Darcy started going on in her raspy voice.

"Well, here you are then," she said, not looking up from the note she was writing on her desk. "They insisted on having an American do some research and writing for the project, though I find it unnecessary. We can easily write the book on our own city and every other place they throw at us."

"Right," Nora said. "Well, I suppose they just want multiple perspectives for the app."

Darcy scoffed. "Our perspectives are good enough, I think. But we do have a bit of ground to cover in a relatively short amount of time, so I'll want you writing and editing blurbs as quickly as possible. Am I correct that this will be your first time writing this kind of content?"

"Yes," Nora said quietly. She didn't know how to elaborate. She was pretty sure that she would be great at this. She'd been waiting for the chance for so long, but this woman was already making her doubt herself.

She tried to give herself a mini pep talk in her mind. *You can do this.* She could focus on her writing and publish incredible travel guides and forget that she was once again in the same city as the most beautiful man who had ever touched her. A man with stormy eyes and incredible fingers, the first man to ever give her an org—*Nope, get it together, Nora.*

"We'll check out the first place on the list together, go over what kind of details we're looking for," Darcy was saying. "That will be your training. It may be unusual, but I think it's important that you get a feel for the tone of the book." Nora nodded. "This isn't just a run-of-the-mill guide. It has personality and a special appeal for young, chic travelers. There's a restaurant in Kensington they want to include. A couple of new clubs in Piccadilly. A hotel in Marylebone. Those are going to get bigger write-ups in the book, but there will be even more content on the app. God knows I'm too old to go to the clubs, but you can do that with Timothy. Did you meet everyone?"

"No, not yet," Nora stuttered.

"Timothy!" Darcy called, and a pencil-thin, dark-haired man appeared in the doorway almost immediately. He would have looked like a steampunk villain if only he'd been sporting an oddly manicured mustache. "This is Timothy. He does some writing, some IT, and whatever else," Darcy announced, as if that gave Nora all the information she would ever need to know about him.

"Hello, lovely, it's a great pleasure to make your acquaintance," Timothy said, running his hands through his hair. His accent wasn't as charming as she would have expected.

"That's enough," Darcy snapped, and Timothy was gone again. Nora felt terrified but also like she should be laughing her head off at the same time. It was not at all the nurturing mentorship she had been expecting with her new editor in her dream job. "Anyway," Darcy said, "about the museums…" She proceeded to talk about the project as if in bullet points, not pausing even when Nora tried to ask a question. Nora jostled the things in her backpack, searching for a pen as quickly as possible so she could take notes on everything Darcy was firing at her. Darcy wasn't even looking in her direction while she was talking—she was simultaneously typing an email on the computer. Nora tried to say something, but Darcy cut her off again. "You'll need to get to know some locals, as it helps to get some context about the different neighborhoods from their view. You want to get input from the kind of people that pass by these places every day as well. We're not just writing reviews or telling people about the latest events. We're telling a story. Though, you know, there will also be a lot of brochures to collect and facts to check."

"Ok, what do you think about—" Nora tried, but Darcy cut in again.

"I guess now is as good a time as any. Let's go."

"Go?"

"To the new restaurant. Training. Have you been paying attention?"

She mostly had been paying attention; there was just that one little part in the middle where she really zoned out. Maybe if she burned the diary, she could somehow stop her weird memory/fantasy life from taking over.

Darcy stood. "Come on then, let's get started."

When Nora was starting college, she wasn't quite sure what she wanted to do with her life. She loved studying English, but that wasn't really one of those majors that led to an easy, specific career path. She loved books and stories, but she didn't want to teach, which seemed to be the only thing that anyone expected you to do if you got a BA in Literature. She loved true crime and mysteries, but she didn't have the constitution to be a detective, and even the thought of blood made her queasy. When she found out about the study abroad program in London, it was the closest she had ever come to figuring out what she wanted as a career, because she wanted exactly that, to read Shakespeare and go to plays at the Globe Theatre, and take walking tours around beautiful, historic cities. How did one turn that exact thing into a job that paid you money?

Finally, her chance had come, which was perhaps a testament to the power of perseverance, or even more likely it was proof of the power of begging. The company where she'd been sitting at her cubicle for years had given her a shot in their most low-stakes writing position, and now that the job was hers, she was working hard not to let Darcy's persistent negative attitude depress her. In fact, as they sat in a dim restaurant that was going to get a tiny write-up in the book, Nora was beaming.

"Why are you making that face?" Darcy asked.

"What face?"

"That face like a puppy and a unicorn just had a baby, and it's going to carry you around the Froufrou Forest and grant you three wishes."

"I'm not sure what that means," Nora said.

"Stop smiling so damn much," Darcy barked. "This restaurant isn't even good. It would get one out of five smile emojis in the book."

"My soup isn't bad," Nora said.

"Who orders soup when it's thirty degrees out?"

"Is that hot? I don't know how to convert the temperature to Fahrenheit."

Darcy shook her head, as if embarrassed by Nora's stupidity or perhaps by the stupidity of all of America. "Aren't you dying? My whole body is covered in a layer of sweat. I look like a slimy sea lion."

Nora inspected Darcy for a moment, considering this comparison. "The only thing about you that reminds me of a sea lion," she said, "is your big, dark eyes."

Darcy snorted. "You're forgetting about my whiskers. Anyway, look at this chicken. It looks like my nan made this in 1976, and they've just defrosted it. It's actually wrinkled."

"Is that what you'll write in the review?"

"You're writing the review," Darcy said. "Though I don't really think this place deserves to take up space. This is why you can't trust anything you read on the internet. Now tell me the categories you need to cover in your 150 words."

Nora concentrated. "Year established. Convenience of the location. Atmosphere." Nora didn't mention that she had no idea about the convenience of location for anything, since she didn't know where anything was and would almost certainly get lost on her way anywhere.

"Yes, yes," Darcy said, "but none of that matters when the food is such shite. I'm at least going to try the pie. Excuse me!" Darcy raised a hand to flag down the waiter.

As Darcy bit into a slice of chocolate pie that she absolutely despised, Nora decided to steer the conversation away from the lacking quality of the restaurant. This "training" lunch was the perfect time to get to know Darcy a little better and to see if there was a way to break through to some kind of positive working relationship.

She could almost hear what her mother would say. Kathleen always seemed to understand what was at the heart of people immediately. She would recognize all of Darcy's little insecurities, the way she kept brushing her hair out of her face and gripping the table. She would say it was all a mask, that Darcy was really just scared of something, and she would probably know exactly what that something was, even if Nora hadn't quite put her finger on it. Her mother would know how to handle it too, how to talk to Darcy in a way that put her at ease or put her in her place, whatever was necessary in the moment. Nora just knew how to be nosy.

"So how long have you lived here?" she asked.

"Forever," Darcy said, shutting down any further inquiries. "Have you ever even been here before?"

Nora smiled. "I studied abroad here, and I fell in love with it. I took afternoon strolls through Regent's Park, I browsed record stores near Abbey Road, I went on the Eye at sunset. It's my favorite city in the world."

"The weather's terrible," Darcy said, but Nora could tell that she couldn't complain too much about her hometown. This was where Darcy had grown up, and while she could dislike almost anything, Nora was sure her boss couldn't hate London. "People are idiots too. Brexit? Come on."

Nora laughed. "The people I met here were wonderful."

"Oh gross." Darcy scrunched up her face.

"What?"

"You met a guy here, I can tell."

"What? How can you tell?" Nora looked around the room furtively.

"*The people I met here were wonderful.* Sigh. Wistful look. Memories stirring behind your blue eyes. I can read you like a book, Shrapsan. You batted those long eyelashes all over town, and you fell in love."

Nora stared. She must be so obvious, but she was also relieved. She'd been dying to talk to someone about Hugh, to say everything she'd been thinking for the past seventy-two hours—or maybe the past seven years—out loud, but now that she had the floor, Nora wasn't sure Darcy was the right person to talk to, and she didn't know where to start. It was so much more than a teenage romance to her, but how to explain it so that Darcy wouldn't think she was a dramatic weirdo? Maybe she shouldn't have decided to spill the beans to her boss in the first place. "He was my first love," Nora said. She cleared her throat.

Scenes from the life of nineteen-year-old, losing-her-virginity Nora kept playing in her mind. Make out sessions on Tower Bridge in the rain. White teeth glowing in black lights while they danced at Ministry of

Sound. Steam wafting from hotel bathrooms, droplets of wine dotting the side of the bathtub.

"Well, that is serious," Darcy said, and Nora blinked hard, forcing herself back into the present.

"We met at the pub where he worked, and he was in a band. It sounds silly now, doesn't it?" She tried to shrug nonchalantly. "The first time he ever spoke to me, I could tell immediately there was just this *something* about him. He told me I couldn't handle my liquor and I'd be 'Oliver Twist' in no time. I didn't know what that meant, even though I love the musical.

"You Americans always fall for that Cockney bullocks," Darcy said. "A couple of rhymes, 'Oliver Twist' instead of 'pissed,' and you're completely charmed."

Nora laughed. "I totally was. I fell for it immediately. Even when I thought logically this guy is just charismatic and I shouldn't be so smitten, I couldn't help it. I was done for. And he was right that I couldn't hold my liquor."

"Wow, you're gullible." Darcy shook her head. "Seriously. How do you survive in this world?"

Nora was on a roll, and she ignored Darcy's comment. "I liked him, but I didn't take him that seriously. We always had an expiration date. I knew it would just be a summer fling. But then I got to know him… The band was actually amazing. I think it clouded my judgment." Nora looked off into the distance wistfully.

"So he gave you the struggling musician bit, and you ate it right up. You were probably throwing your panties on stage in no time." Darcy laughed at her own joke. "What was the band?"

Nora was still in another world, remembering all the things that Hugh had said to her, how much she'd wanted to believe him. When he'd told her he loved her. That had been real, right? That wasn't just some line to get in her pants. "Oh, it's not like you would have heard of them. They were just—the Pet Rockers," she said finally, and Darcy actually did a spit take. She had cider dribbling down her chin.

"You're fucking with me," Darcy said, suddenly alert and completely invested in the conversation.

"What?"

"You did not date a guy from the Pet Rockers. You're good, Shrapsan. I didn't think you had it in you to make up such a load."

Nora stared at her, eyebrows wrinkled. "What are you talking about? You know about a band called the Pet Rockers?"

Darcy was shaking her head. "I don't know whether to believe you or not. They are a relatively well-known local band, at least if you're into the music scene at all. They do shows all over the city. In fact, I have tickets to a special event they're doing just north of here."

"That's crazy," Nora said. "There's no way it's the same band, right? I mean, literally no one knew who they were when they used to play at the Goose and Cobbler."

Darcy stared at her as if trying to solve a puzzle. "No, that's it. You're not fooling me anymore. What's this bit you're doing? I don't get it," Darcy grumbled.

"What are you talking about?" Nora suddenly felt sick, and she wasn't sure if it was from the soup or some other kind of nausea.

"The show this weekend—*this* fucking weekend—is a special show at the Goose and Cobbler." Darcy tossed down her fork as if the sheer ridiculousness of this situation wouldn't allow her to hold it a second longer. Nora sat in stunned silence, but everything felt too loud. Her head was cloudy, as if she was just waking from a strange dream. Darcy was still saying something, but she couldn't quite make out the words. The diary in the bottom of her bag still seemed to be beating, and Nora couldn't hear anything else.

"You really aren't making this up, are you?" Darcy said, her voice finally breaking through. "I was going to have my roommate go with me, but she doesn't care about it anyway. I would much rather take you and see you reunite with your boyfriend."

Nora's mouth was hanging open. She'd been having the stupid debate in her head, ever since she found the diary, about whether or not to pop into the Goose and Cobbler for old-time's sake. She never thought Hugh would still be there, behind the bar, waiting for her. And she really never thought that his now semi-famous band would be playing a show in the very place where she had first laid eyes on him. She was trying to convince herself that there was no way any of this was possible—there was no actual way that she could set foot in the pub and fall in love with Hugh Jeffries all over again after seven years. But as Darcy sat there snapping her fingers in front of Nora's face to try to break her from her total state of shock, Nora realized the truth. There was no way in hell she was missing that show.

AUTHOR'S NOTE

To my knowledge, there is no secret, exclusive exhibit in the caves of Sacromonte in Granada, Spain, but there are some fascinating museums there. The Sacromonte Cave Museum that focuses on the history of the Roma people in the caves is real, as well as the Museo de la Zambra Cueva de Curro, which covers the history of the Flamenco and includes live performances in the cave.

While I love traveling and representing different international cities in my work, I strongly encourage anyone traveling to Granada or nearby areas (or anywhere in the entire world) to do their own research in advance and to be respectful and considerate of those who call the destination home.

I would be remiss not to mention the impact of Françoise Gilot's memoir, *My Life With Picasso* in the development of this novel. Picasso attempted to prevent the publication of Gilot's book in 1964, but instead it managed to cause quite a stir at that time. However, it wasn't until more recently that scholars and critics started to reconsider Picasso's legacy and how to present his work in light of the revelations about his personal life.

Finally, all paintings mentioned by name or referred to by description in the book are real, except for the fictional works attributed to Lucia and Alejandro. However, in some instances, the paintings have been relocated or placed in the underground exhibit in the interest of the story, and since Christian is a fictional billionaire, he doesn't actually own the Picassos and other paintings mentioned. In reality, they are housed in various museums and private collections all over the world. Many of the pieces Grace remembers viewing as a child with her grandmother can be found at the Art Institute of Chicago.

Don't miss more from Hannah Ledford with ELEPHANT AND CASTLE available now, and keep up-to-date at www.hannahledford.com

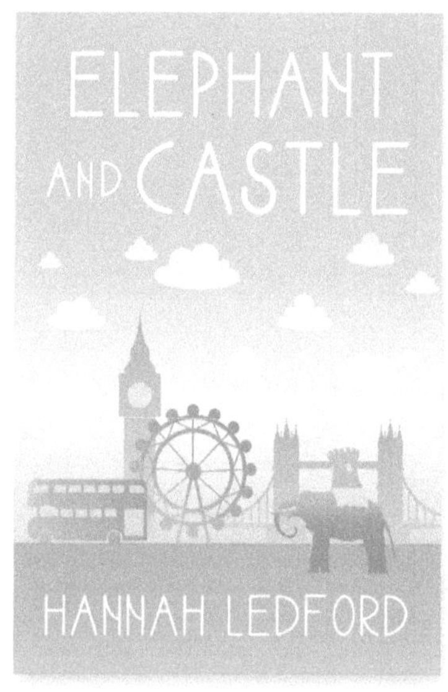

If only there was a guidebook on how to land the London boy of your dreams...

Nora Shrapsan is literally writing the book on London, and she's not going to let fantasies about her sexy British ex-boyfriend break her stride. So what if she has been reunited with semi-famous rock star Hugh Jeffries, and their chemistry is still palpable? He's engaged, and Nora needs to focus on...anything besides Hugh's lips.

Julian Rhodes is Hugh's best mate, and his secret feelings for Nora are one thing that won't stay in the past. When a desperate Nora begs him to help her navigate London, Julian has to say yes—strictly to keep her from getting fired, of course. Surely, they can go to murder tours, magic shows, and museums without any feelings getting in the way. No problem.

But the more time Nora and Julian spend together, the less Nora finds herself thinking of Hugh. Maybe her second-chance romance didn't go according to plan, but that doesn't mean Nora could ever fall for her ex's best friend, right?

Please sign up for the City Owl Press newsletter for chances to win special subscriber-only contests and giveaways as well as receiving information on upcoming releases and special excerpts.

All reviews are **welcome** and **appreciated**. Please consider leaving one on your favorite social media and book buying sites.

Escape Your World. Get Lost in Ours! City Owl Press at www.cityowlpress.com.

ACKNOWLEDGMENTS

I'm so grateful to so many people for helping me bring this book to life. To everyone at City Owl Press, especially my editor, Jessica. Thanks for bearing with me when the book just didn't feel complete yet. And for going along on this journey with me.

Thank you to my early readers and everyone who offered such great insights about the novel. Sarah, I can never tell you how much I appreciated all of your comments, especially the ones that just said "oooo spicy," but also all of those that were extremely helpful for making this a better story. Josh, thank you for making writing so fun. There's nothing like idol chit chat with the Plaza Writing Team.

A big thanks to everyone in office book club for your support. I don't know what I'm doing half the time, but Lauren, you are amazing at all the book stuff. And Abby, thanks for talking art and Picasso with me. And to all the ARC readers and bookstores and so many awesome friends who built up excitement for the novel and took the time to share it with other people. I am so grateful. Olga, thank you so much for being on-call for all of my Spanish language questions (any mistakes are my own).

To the Cincy authors coven, thank you for letting me lurk and soak up your knowledge. Being part of such a savvy and supportive group is a serious gift.

A big thank you to the people I met in Granada who helped me to learn about its history and fall in love with it immediately. And to Lisa, for being my fellow trip planner and one of my favorite people. Thank you for helping me get the bird poop out of my hair.

To my whole family for being so wonderful and supportive, especially my fantastic parents. And to John, the best guy I know. Someday I will write the book you want, but in the meantime, thanks for reading this one and supporting me in everything I do. To my boys, you can't read this, but I love when you ask about my book and tell everyone to read it and give it 5 stars.

To you! Thank you for being here and reading this book! It means the world to me.

ABOUT THE AUTHOR

HANNAH LEDFORD is a romance novelist with a PhD in English. She loves travel, giant sweaters, and making up bedtime stories about Bigfoot in space. She's lived many different places, including a tiny flat on Tower Bridge Road. *Elephant and Castle* is her first novel.

Follow her across social media and find out more on her website at www.hannahledford.com

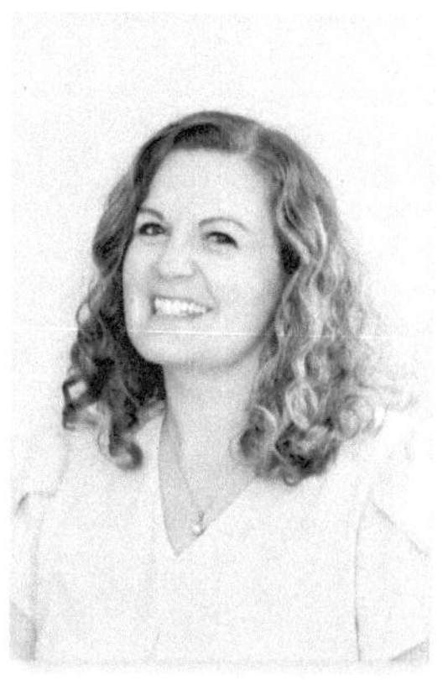

Photo by Dyane Foltz

instagram.com/hannahledfordwrites
tiktok.com/@hannahledfordwrites
facebook.com/hannahledfordwrites

ABOUT THE PUBLISHER

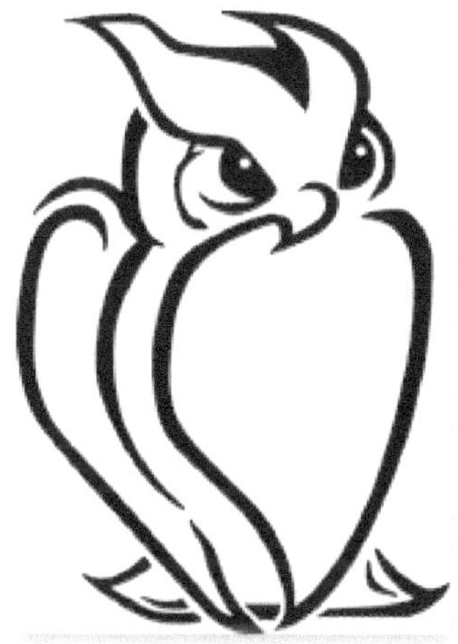

City Owl Press is a cutting edge indie publishing company, bringing the world of romance and speculative fiction to discerning readers.

Escape Your World. Get Lost in Ours!

www.cityowlpress.com

facebook.com/CityOwlPress
x.com/cityowlpress
instagram.com/cityowlbooks
pinterest.com/cityowlpress
tiktok.com/@cityowlpress

www.ingramcontent.com/pod-product-compliance
Lightning Source LLC
LaVergne TN
LVHW041115080826
845145LV00007B/1821

* 9 7 8 1 6 4 8 9 8 5 8 1 2 *